THE LOEB CLASSICAL LIBRARY

FOUNDED BY JAMES LOEB

EDITED BY

G. P. GOOLD

SEXTUS EMPIRICUS

III

LCL 311

SEXTUS EMPIRICUS

AGAINST THE PHYSICISTS
AGAINST THE ETHICISTS

WITH AN ENGLISH TRANSLATION BY

R. G. BURY

HARVARD UNIVERSITY PRESS
CAMBRIDGE, MASSACHUSETTS
LONDON, ENGLAND

First published 1936
Reprinted 1953, 1960, 1968, 1987, 1997

LOEB CLASSICAL LIBRARY® is a registered trademark
of the President and Fellows of Harvard College

ISBN 0-674-99344-6

Printed in Great Britain by St Edmundsbury Press Ltd,
Bury St Edmunds, Suffolk, on acid-free paper.
Bound by Hunter & Foulis Ltd, Edinburgh, Scotland.

CONTENTS

ΠΡΟΣ ΦΥΣΙΚΟΥΣ

A

1 Τὴν μὲν αἰτίαν δι᾽ ἣν μετὰ τὸ λογικὸν τῆς φιλοσοφίας μέρος εἰς ἐπίσκεψιν ἡμῖν ἄγεται τὸ φυσικόν, καίπερ χρόνῳ τῶν ἄλλων προήκειν δοκοῦν, ἀνώτερον ὑπεμνήσαμεν· τὸν αὐτὸν δὲ τρόπον τῆς ζητήσεως πάλιν ἐνταῦθα συστησόμεθα, οὐκ ἐμβραδύνοντες τοῖς κατὰ μέρος, ὁποῖόν τι πεποιήκασιν οἱ περὶ τὸν Κλειτόμαχον καὶ ὁ λοιπὸς τῶν Ἀκαδημαϊκῶν χορός (εἰς ἀλλοτρίαν γὰρ ὕλην ἐμβάντες καὶ ἐπὶ συγχωρήσει τῶν ἑτεροίως δογματιζομένων ποιούμενοι τοὺς λόγους ἀμέτρως ἐμήκυναν τὴν ἀντίρρησιν), ἀλλὰ τὰ κυριώτατα καὶ συνεκτικώτατα κινοῦντες, ἐν οἷς ἠπορημένα ἕξομεν καὶ τὰ λοιπά.

2 καθάπερ γὰρ ἐν ταῖς πολιορκίαις οἱ τὸν θεμέλιον τοῦ τείχους ὑπορύξαντες τούτῳ συγκαταφερομένους ἔχουσι τοὺς πύργους, οὕτως οἱ ἐν ταῖς φιλοσόφοις σκέψεσι τὰς πρώτας τῶν πραγμάτων ὑποθέσεις χειρωσάμενοι δυνάμει τὴν παντὸς πράγ-

3 ματος κατάληψιν ἠθετήκασιν. οὐκ ἀπιθάνως γοῦν τινὲς ἀπεικάζουσι τοὺς μὲν εἰς τὰς κατὰ μέρος ζητήσεις συγκαταβαίνοντας τοῖς ἐκ ποδὸς τὸ

* See *Adv. Log.* i. 20 ff.

AGAINST THE PHYSICISTS

BOOK I

WE have explained above [a] the reason why the 1
physical division of philosophy is being examined by
us after the logical, although in point of time it seems
to precede all the other divisions ; and with regard
to it we shall pursue again the same method of
inquiry, and not delay long on particular points as
Cleitomachus [b] has done and the rest of the Academic
troupe (for by plunging into alien subject matter and
framing their arguments on the basis of assent to
dogmatic assumptions not their own they have unduly prolonged their counter-statement); instead of
this, we shall attack the most important and most
comprehensive dogmas, as in the doubts cast on these
we shall find the rest also included. For just as, in 2
a siege, those who have undermined the foundation
of a wall find that the towers tumble down along
with it,[c] so too in philosophical investigations those
who have routed the primary assumptions on which
the theories are based have potentially abolished the
apprehension of every particular theory. Thus it is 3
not without plausibility that some people compare
those who join in plunging into inquiries into par-

---

[b] The disciple of Carneades, *cf*. Vol. I. Introd. p. xxxiii.
[c] *Cf. P.H.* ii. 84.

θηρίον διώκουσι κυνηγοῖς ἢ ἀπὸ ὁρμιᾶς ἁλιεύουσιν
ἢ ἰξῷ καὶ καλάμῳ τοὺς ὄρνις θηρεύουσιν, τοὺς
δὲ ἀπὸ τῶν συνεκτικωτάτων πάντα τὰ ἐπὶ μέρους
σαλεύοντας τοῖς λίνα καὶ στάλικας καὶ σαγήνας
περιβαλλομένοις. ὅθεν ὡς πολλῷ τεχνικώτερόν
ἐστι τοῦ καθ' ἕκαστον θήραμα πονεῖσθαι τὸ διὰ
μιᾶς ἐφόδου πολλὰ δύνασθαι ἀγρεύειν, οὕτω πολλῷ
χαριέστερον τὸ κοινῇ κατὰ πάντων κομίζειν ἀντίρρησιν τοῦ προσειλεῖσθαι τοῖς κατὰ μέρος.

4 Ἐπεὶ οὖν οἱ δοκοῦντες ἀκριβέστερον κατὰ τὸν
φυσικὸν τόπον περὶ τῶν τοῦ παντὸς ἀρχῶν δια-
τετάχθαι τὰς μέν τινας αὐτῶν δραστηρίους εἶναι
λέγουσι τὰς δὲ ὑλικάς (ὧν τῆς δόξης ἀρχηγὸς
ἀξιοῦται τυγχάνειν ὁ ποιητὴς Ὅμηρος καὶ μετὰ
τοῦτόν γε Ἀναξαγόρας ὁ Κλαζομένιος καὶ Ἐμπεδοκλῆς ὁ Ἀκραγαντῖνος καὶ ἄλλοι παμπληθεῖς,—
5 ὁ μὲν γὰρ ποιητὴς περὶ τούτων ἀποδιδοὺς φησιν
ἐν οἷς περὶ Πρωτέως καὶ Εἰδοθέας ἀλληγορεῖ, τὸ
μὲν πρῶτον καὶ ἀρχικώτατον αἴτιον Πρωτέα κα-
λῶν, τὴν δὲ εἰς εἴδη τρεπομένην οὐσίαν Εἰδοθέαν.
6 ὁ δὲ Ἀναξαγόρας φησὶν " ἦν πάντα ὁμοῦ χρή-
ματα, νοῦς δὲ ἐλθὼν αὐτὰ διεκόσμησεν," τὸν μὲν
νοῦν, ὅς ἐστι κατ' αὐτὸν θεός, δραστήριον ὑποτιθέμενος ἀρχήν, τὴν δὲ τῶν ὁμοιομερειῶν πολυμιγίαν
7 ὑλικήν. ὁ δὲ Ἀριστοτέλης καὶ Ἑρμότιμόν φησι
τὸν Κλαζομένιον καὶ Παρμενίδην τὸν Ἐλεάτην καὶ
πολὺ πρότερον τὸν Ἡσίοδον ταῦτα φρονεῖν· κατα-
σκευάζοντες γὰρ τὴν τῶν ὅλων γένεσιν ἔρωτα

---

[a] Cf. P.H. iii. 1.
[b] See Homer, Odyss. iv. 365 ff. The allegorizing (absurdly
ascribed to Homer) is based on etymology (Πρωτεύς from
πρῶτος, and εἰδοθέα from εἴδη, " particulars ").

ticulars to hunters who pursue the quarry on foot or men who fish with a line or catch birds with bird-lime on a cane ; whereas those who call in question all the particulars by starting with the most comprehensive postulates, they compare to men who surround ⟨their prey⟩ with lines and stakes and drag-nets. Hence, as it shows much more art to be able to catch a great number with a single onset than to hunt after the game laboriously one by one, so too it is much more artistic to bring one's counter-argument against all in common rather than to develop it against the particular tenets.

Seeing, then, that those who, in the department of 4 Physics, seem to have classified most precisely the principles of the Universe declare that some of these are efficient, others material,[a]—and it is claimed that the originators of their opinion was the poet Homer, who was followed by Anaxagoras of Clazomenae and Empedocles of Acragas and a vast number of others. For the poet makes a statement about these prin- 5 ciples where he speaks allegorically about Proteus and Eidothea,[b] calling the first and most original cause " Proteus," and the substance which turns into particulars " Eidothea." And Anaxagoras says— 6 " All things were together, and Mind came and set them in order," assuming that Mind, which according to him is God, is the efficient principle, and the multi-mixture of homoeomeries [c] the material principle. And Aristotle [d] says that Hermotimus of Clazomenae 7 and Parmenides of Elea and, much earlier, Hesiod held this view ; for in picturing the birth of all things

    [c] *i.e.* " things with like parts "—Aristotle's name for the material " elements " of Anaxagoras. *Cf. P.H.* iii. 32.
    [d] See Aristot. *Metaph.* i. 3, 984 b 18 ff. Hermotimus was an early Ionian physicist (date uncertain).

συμπαρέλαβον, τουτέστι τὴν κινητικὴν καὶ συν-
8 αγωγὸν τῶν ὄντων αἰτίαν, ὁ μὲν Ἡσίοδος λέγων

ἤτοι μὲν πρώτιστα χάος γένετ᾽, αὐτὰρ ἔπειτα
γαῖ᾽ εὐρύστερνος, πάντων ἕδος ἀσφαλὲς αἰεί,
ἠδ᾽ ἔρος, ὃς κάλλιστος ἐν ἀθανάτοισι θεοῖσιν,

9 ὁ δὲ Παρμενίδης ῥητῶς ἀποφηνάμενος

πρώτιστον μὲν ἔρωτα θεῶν μητίσατο πάντων.

10 δόξαι δ᾽ ἄν, ὡς προεῖπον, καὶ Ἐμπεδοκλῆς τοιοῦτος
εἶναι· σὺν γὰρ τοῖς τέσσαρσι στοιχείοις τὸ νεῖκος
καὶ τὴν φιλίαν καταριθμεῖται, τὴν μὲν φιλίαν ὡς
συναγωγὸν αἰτίαν, τὸ δὲ νεῖκος ὡς διαλυτικήν·

" πῦρ " γάρ φησι " καὶ ὕδωρ καὶ γαῖα καὶ ἠέρος
ἤπιον ὕψος,
νεῖκός τ᾽ οὐλόμενον δίχα τῶν, ἀτάλαντον ἁπάντῃ,
καὶ φιλότης μετὰ τοῖσιν, ἴση μῆκός τε πλάτος τε.

11 οὐ μὴν ἀλλὰ καὶ οἱ ἀπὸ τῆς στοᾶς δύο λέγοντες
ἀρχάς, θεὸν καὶ ἄποιον ὕλην, τὸν μὲν θεὸν ποιεῖν
ὑπειλήφασι, τὴν δὲ ὕλην πάσχειν τε καὶ τρέπεσθαι).
12 ἐπεὶ οὖν τοιαύτη τις ἔστι παρὰ τοῖς ἀρίστοις τῶν
φυσικῶν διάταξις, φέρε περὶ τῶν ποιητικῶν ἀρχῶν διαπορῶμεν πρῶτον, σκεπτόμενοι ὁτὲ μὲν οἷον
δογματικῶς περὶ θεοῦ, ὁτὲ δὲ ἀπορητικώτερον
περὶ τοῦ μηδὲν εἶναι τὸ ποιοῦν ἢ πάσχον. ἀλλ᾽
ἐπεὶ κατὰ πᾶσαν ζήτησιν προτάττεται ἡ τοῦ ζητου-
μένου πράγματος νόησις, ἴδωμεν πῶς εὐθὺς ἔννοιαν
ἐλάβομεν θεοῦ.

6

they joined in introducing Love (that is to say, the moving and unifying cause of existents) ; as when 8 Hesiod says [a]—

> Verily first created of all was Chaos, thereafter
> Earth broad-bosom'd, unshakable seat of all things for ever,
> Aye and Love, who of all the immortal gods is the fairest—

and Parmenides, when he expressly declares that   9

> Love was the first of the gods whom she in her wisdom created.

And, as I said before, Empedocles would seem to hold 10 a like view ; for he enumerates Strife and Love along with his four elements (Love as a unifying, Strife as a disintegrating cause), saying—

> Fire and water and earth, and soft air reaching to heaven,
> Strife pernicious, divided from these, and evenly balanc'd,[b]
> Love, together with these, in length and in breadth ever equal.

Moreover, the Stoics also, when they declare that 11 there are two principles, God and unqualified matter, suppose that God acts and that matter is passive and altered :—seeing then that some such classification is 12 made by the best of the Physicists, come and let us first express our doubts about the efficient principles, arguing on the one hand dogmatically concerning God, and on the other hand more sceptically concerning the non-existence of anything active or passive. But since, in regard to every inquiry, the conception of the subject of inquiry must come first, let us consider how exactly we acquired the notion of God.

[a] See Hesiod, *Theog.* 116 ff.
[b] Lit. "equal in weight every way," "in perfect equipoise," *i.e.* symmetrical (like "Love" in the next line).

ΠΕΡΙ ΘΕΩΝ

13 Ὁ περὶ θεῶν λόγος πάνυ ἀναγκαιότατος εἶναι
δοκεῖ τοῖς δογματικῶς φιλοσοφοῦσιν. ἐντεῦθεν
τὴν φιλοσοφίαν φασὶν ἐπιτήδευσιν εἶναι σοφίας,
τὴν δὲ σοφίαν ἐπιστήμην θείων τε καὶ ἀνθρωπίνων
πραγμάτων. ὅθεν ἐὰν παραστήσωμεν ἡμεῖς ἠπορη-
μένην τὴν περὶ τῶν θεῶν ζήτησιν, δυνάμει ἐσόμεθα
κατεσκευακότες τὸ μήτε τὴν σοφίαν ἐπιστήμην
εἶναι θείων καὶ ἀνθρωπίνων πραγμάτων μήτε τὴν
φιλοσοφίαν ἐπιτήδευσιν σοφίας.

14 Ἔνιοι τοίνυν ἔφασαν τοὺς πρώτους τῶν ἀνθρώπων προστάντας καὶ τὸ συμφέρον τῷ βίῳ
σκεψαμένους, πάνυ συνετοὺς ὄντας, ἀναπλάσαι τὴν
περί τε τῶν θεῶν ὑπόνοιαν καὶ τὴν περὶ τῶν
15 ἐν ᾅδου μυθευομένων δόξαν. θηριώδους γὰρ καὶ
ἀτάκτου γεγονότος τοῦ πάλαι βίου (ἦν γὰρ χρόνος,
ὡς φησὶν ὁ Ὀρφεύς,

> ἡνίκα φῶτες ἀπ᾽ ἀλλήλων βίον εἶχον
> σαρκοδακῆ, κρείττων δὲ τὸν ἥττονα φῶτ᾽ ἐδάιζεν)

ἐπισχεῖν βουλόμενοι τοὺς ἀδικοῦντας πρῶτον μὲ
νόμους ἔθεντο πρὸς τὸ τοὺς φανερῶς ἀδικοῦντας
16 κολάζεσθαι, μετὰ δὲ τοῦτο καὶ θεοὺς ἀνέπλασαν
ἐπόπτας πάντων τῶν ἀνθρωπίνων ἁμαρτημάτων
τε καὶ κατορθωμάτων, ἵνα μηδὲ κρύφα τολμῶσί
τινες ἀδικεῖν, πεπεισμένοι ὅτι οἱ θεοὶ

> ἠέρα ἑσσάμενοι πάντῃ φοιτῶσιν ἐπ᾽ αἶαν,
> ἀνθρώπων ὕβρεις τε καὶ εὐνομίας ἐφορῶντες.

17 Εὐήμερος δὲ ὁ ἐπικληθεὶς ἄθεος φησὶν "ὅτ᾽ ἦν

8

Concerning Gods

The doctrine concerning Gods certainly seems to 13
the Dogmatic philosophers to be most necessary.
Hence they assert that " philosophy is the practice
of wisdom, and wisdom is the knowledge of things
divine and human." Accordingly, if we shall establish the doubtfulness of the inquiry concerning Gods,
we shall virtually have demonstrated that neither is
wisdom the knowledge of divine and human things,
nor philosophy the practice of wisdom.

Some, then, have asserted that those who first led 14
mankind and considered what is of profit for life, being
men of great intelligence, invented both the fancy
about the Gods and the belief in the mythical events
in Hades. For, since life in old times was brutish and 15
disorderly (for, as Orpheus says,—

There was a time when ev'ry man liv'd by devouring his
      fellow
Cannibal-wise, and the stronger man did feast on the weaker),—

purposing to check the wrongdoers they laid down
laws, in the first place, for the punishing of such as
were manifestly doing wrong, and after this they also 16
invented Gods as watchers of all the sinful and
righteous acts of men, so that none should dare to
do wrong even in secret, believing that the Gods

Cloaked in garments of mist all over the earth go roaming,
Watching the violent doings of men and their lawful be-
      haviour.[a]

And Euhemerus, nick-named " the Atheist," [b] says— 17

[a] *Cf.* for the 1st verse Hesiod, *Works and Days*, 255; for
the 2nd, Homer, *Odyss.* xvii. 487.
[b] Euhemerus was probably a Sicilian, and lived at the
court of Cassander, king of Macedonia (*circa* 315 B.C.).
He was chiefly noted as the rationalizer of myths.

SEXTUS EMPIRICUS

ἄτακτος ἀνθρώπων βίος, οἱ περιγενόμενοι τῶν
ἄλλων ἰσχύι τε καὶ συνέσει ὥστε πρὸς τὰ ὑπ'
αὐτῶν κελευόμενα πάντας βιοῦν, σπουδάζοντες
μείζονος θαυμασμοῦ καὶ σεμνότητος τυχεῖν, ἀνέπλασαν περὶ αὑτοὺς ὑπερβάλλουσάν τινα καὶ θείαν
δύναμιν, ἔνθεν καὶ τοῖς πολλοῖς ἐνομίσθησαν
18 θεοί." Πρόδικος δὲ ὁ Κεῖος " ἥλιον," φησί, " καὶ
σελήνην καὶ ποταμοὺς καὶ κρήνας καὶ καθόλου
πάντα τὰ ὠφελοῦντα τὸν βίον ἡμῶν οἱ παλαιοὶ
θεοὺς ἐνόμισαν διὰ τὴν ἀπ' αὐτῶν ὠφέλειαν,
καθάπερ Αἰγύπτιοι τὸν Νεῖλον"· καὶ διὰ τοῦτο τὸν
μὲν ἄρτον Δήμητραν νομισθῆναι, τὸν δὲ οἶνον
Διόνυσον, τὸ δὲ ὕδωρ Ποσειδῶνα, τὸ δὲ πῦρ
Ἥφαιστον καὶ ἤδη τῶν εὐχρηστούντων ἕκαστον.
19 Δημόκριτος δὲ εἴδωλά τινά φησιν ἐμπελάζειν
τοῖς ἀνθρώποις, καὶ τούτων τὰ μὲν εἶναι ἀγαθοποιὰ
τὰ δὲ κακοποιά (ἔνθεν καὶ εὔχετο[1] εὐλόγχων[2]
τυχεῖν εἰδώλων), εἶναι δὲ ταῦτα μεγάλα τε καὶ
ὑπερφυῆ, καὶ δύσφθαρτα μέν, οὐκ ἄφθαρτα δέ,
προσημαίνειν τε τὰ μέλλοντα τοῖς ἀνθρώποις,
θεωρούμενα καὶ φωνὰς ἀφιέντα. ὅθεν τούτων
αὐτῶν φαντασίαν λαβόντες οἱ παλαιοὶ ὑπενόησαν
εἶναι θεόν, μηδενὸς ἄλλου παρὰ ταῦτα ὄντος θεοῦ
20 [τοῦ][3] ἄφθαρτον φύσιν ἔχοντος. Ἀριστοτέλης δὲ
ἀπὸ δυοῖν ἀρχῶν ἔννοιαν θεῶν ἔλεγε γεγονέναι ἐν
τοῖς ἀνθρώποις, ἀπό τε τῶν περὶ ψυχὴν συμβαινόντων καὶ ἀπὸ τῶν μετεώρων. ἀλλ' ἀπὸ μὲν τῶν
περὶ τὴν ψυχὴν συμβαινόντων διὰ τοὺς ἐν τοῖς
ὕπνοις γινομένους ταύτης ἐνθουσιασμοὺς καὶ τὰς

----
[1] εὔχετο NLE: εὔχεται Bekk.
[2] εὐλόγχων NLE: εὐλόγων Bekk.
[3] [τοῦ] secl. Kayser.

10

" When the life of mankind was without order, those who so far excelled the rest in strength and intelligence that all men lived subservient to their commands, being intent to gain for themselves more admiration and veneration, invented for themselves a kind of superhuman and divine authority, and in consequence were by the populace accounted Gods." And Prodicus of Ceos [a] says—" The ancients ac- 18 counted as Gods the sun and moon and rivers and springs and in general all the things that are of benefit for our life, because of the benefit derived from them, even as the Egyptians deify the Nile." And he says that it was for this reason that bread was worshipped as Demeter, and wine as Dionysus, and water as Poseidon, and fire as Hephaestus, and so on with each of the things that are good for use. And 19 Democritus says that certain images impinge on men, and of these some are beneficent, others maleficent (whence also he prayed that he might have " propitious images "), and these images are great and gigantic, and are hard to destroy although not indestructible, and they signify the future to men beforehand, as they are visible and utter sounds. Hence the ancients, on receiving a presentation of these images, supposed that God exists, God being none other than these images, and possessed of an indestructible nature. And Aristotle [b] said that the 20 conception of Gods arose amongst mankind from two originating causes, namely from events which concern the soul and from celestial phenomena. It arose from events which concern the soul because of the inspired states of the soul which occur in sleep and

---

[a] Cf. Vol. I. Introd. p. xv ; § 52 infra.
[b] Aristot. Frag. 10 (Rose).

SEXTUS EMPIRICUS

21 μαντείας. ὅταν γάρ, φησίν, ἐν τῷ ὑπνοῦν καθ᾽
ἑαυτὴν γένηται ἡ ψυχή, τότε τὴν ἴδιον ἀπολαβοῦσα
φύσιν προμαντεύεταί τε καὶ προαγορεύει τὰ μέλλοντα. τοιαύτη δέ ἐστι καὶ ἐν τῷ κατὰ τὸν
θάνατον χωρίζεσθαι τῶν σωμάτων. ἀποδέχεται
γοῦν καὶ τὸν ποιητὴν Ὅμηρον ὡς τοῦτο παρατηρή-
σαντα· πεποίηκε γὰρ τὸν μὲν Πάτροκλον ἐν τῷ
ἀναιρεῖσθαι προαγορεύοντα περὶ τῆς Ἕκτορος
ἀναιρέσεως, τὸν δ᾽ Ἕκτορα περὶ τῆς Ἀχιλλέως
τελευτῆς. ἐκ τούτων οὖν, φησίν, ὑπενόησαν οἱ
ἄνθρωποι εἶναί τι θεῖον,[1] τὸ καθ᾽ ἑαυτὸ ἐοικὸς τῇ
22 ψυχῇ καὶ πάντων ἐπιστημονικώτατον. ἀλλὰ δὴ
καὶ ἀπὸ τῶν μετεώρων· θεασάμενοι γὰρ μεθ᾽
ἡμέραν μὲν ἥλιον περιπολοῦντα, νύκτωρ δὲ τὴν
εὔτακτον τῶν ἄλλων ἀστέρων κίνησιν, ἐνόμισαν
εἶναί τινα θεὸν τὸν τῆς τοιαύτης κινήσεως καὶ
εὐταξίας αἴτιον.

23   Τοιοῦτος μὲν καὶ ὁ Ἀριστοτέλης· ἄλλοι δέ εἰσιν
οἱ φάσκοντες ὅτι ὁ νοῦς ὀξὺς ὢν καὶ εὐκίνητος
ἐν τῷ ἐπιβάλλειν τῇ αὐτοῦ φύσει ἦλθε καὶ εἰς
ἔμφασιν τοῦ παντός, καὶ ὑπενόησέ τινα ὑπερ-
βαλλόντως δύναμιν νοητικήν, καὶ ἀναλογοῦσαν μὲν
24 αὐτῷ θείαν δὲ τὴν φύσιν. εἰσὶ δὲ οἱ ἀπὸ τῶν γιγνομένων κατὰ τὸν κόσμον παραδόξων ὑπονοήσαντες
εἰς ἔννοιαν ἡμᾶς ἐληλυθέναι θεῶν, ἀφ᾽ ἧς φαίνεται
εἶναι δόξης καὶ ὁ Δημόκριτος· ὁρῶντες γάρ, φησί,
τὰ ἐν τοῖς μετεώροις παθήματα οἱ παλαιοὶ τῶν
ἀνθρώπων, καθάπερ βροντὰς καὶ ἀστραπὰς κεραυ-
νούς τε καὶ ἄστρων συνόδους ἡλίου τε καὶ σελήνης
ἐκλείψεις, ἐδειματοῦντο, θεοὺς οἰόμενοι τούτων
25 αἰτίους εἶναι. Ἐπίκουρος δὲ ἐκ τῶν κατὰ τοὺς

[1] θεῖον N : θεόν cet., Bekk.

12

because of prophecies. For, says he, when the soul 21
is by itself in sleep, then it takes on its own proper
nature and prophesies and predicts the future. And
it is in this state also when it is being separated from
bodies at death. He certainly agrees that the poet
Homer observed this fact; for Homer told of how
Patroclus at the time of his death predicted the
slaying of Hector, and Hector the end of Achilles.[a]
Owing, then, to these reasons (he says) men conceived the existence of some divinity, in itself like
unto the soul and of all things the most intelligent.
Moreover ⟨they derived this conception⟩ from celestial 22
phenomena also; for when they beheld the sun
circling round in the day-time, and by night the
orderly motion of the other stars, they supposed
some God to be the cause of such motion and order-
liness.[b]

Such, then, was the view of Aristotle; but there 23
are others who assert that the mind, which is keen
and mobile, while inspecting its own nature pro-
ceeded also to reflection on the Universe and conceived a Power superlatively cognitive, and analogous
to itself but of a divine nature. And there are some 24
who have supposed that we have arrived at the conception of Gods from those events in the world which
are marvellous; which opinion seems to have been
held by Democritus, who says—" For when the men
of old time beheld the disasters in the heavens, such
as thunderings and lightnings, and thunderbolts and
collisions between stars, and eclipses of sun and moon,
they were affrighted, imagining the Gods to be the
causes of these things." But Epicurus thinks that 25

[a] See Homer, *Il.* xvi. 850 ff., xxii. 358 ff.
[b] *Cf.* Lucret. v. 1183 ff.

ὕπνους φαντασιῶν οἴεται τοὺς ἀνθρώπους ἔννοιαν
ἐσπακέναι θεοῦ· μεγάλων γὰρ εἰδώλων, φησί, καὶ
ἀνθρωπομόρφων κατὰ τοὺς ὕπνους προσπιπτόντων
ὑπέλαβον καὶ ταῖς ἀληθείαις ὑπάρχειν τινὰς τοιού-
26 τους θεοὺς ἀνθρωπομόρφους. ἔνιοι δὲ ἐπὶ τὴν
ἀπαράβατον καὶ εὔτακτον τῶν οὐρανίων κίνησιν
παραγινόμενοι φασὶ τὴν ἀρχὴν ταῖς τῶν θεῶν
ἐπινοίαις ἀπὸ ταύτης γεγονέναι πρῶτον· ὥσπερ
γὰρ εἴ τις ἐπὶ τῆς Τρωικῆς καθεζόμενος Ἴδης
ἑώρα τὴν τῶν Ἑλλήνων στρατείαν μετὰ πολλοῦ
κόσμου καὶ τάξεως τοῖς πεδίοις προσιοῦσαν,

ἱππῆας μὲν πρῶτα σὺν ἵπποισιν καὶ ὄχεσφιν,
πεζοὺς δ᾽ ἐξόπιθεν,

πάντως ἂν ὁ τοιοῦτος εἰς ἔννοιαν ἦλθε τοῦ ὅτι ἔστι
τις ὁ διατάσσων τὴν τοιαύτην τάξιν καὶ ἐγκελευό-
μενος τοῖς ὑπ᾽ αὐτὸν [ἐγ]κοσμουμένοις στρατιώταις,
οἷον Νέστωρ ἢ ἄλλος τις τῶν ἡρώων, ὃς ᾔδει

κοσμῆσαι ἵππους τε καὶ ἀνέρας ἀσπιδιώτας,

27 καὶ ὃν τρόπον ὁ ἔμπειρος νεώς, ἅμα τῷ θεάσασθαι
πόρρωθεν ναῦν οὐρίῳ διωκομένην πνεύματι καὶ
πᾶσι τοῖς ἱστίοις εὐτρεπιζομένην, συνίησιν ὅτι
ἔστι τις ὁ κατευθύνων ταύτην καὶ εἰς τοὺς προ-
κειμένους λιμένας κατάγων,[1] οὕτως οἱ πρῶτον εἰς
οὐρανὸν ἀναβλέψαντες καὶ θεασάμενοι ἥλιον μὲν
τοὺς ἀπὸ ἀνατολῆς μέχρι δύσεως δρόμους στα-
διεύοντα, ἀστέρων δὲ εὐτάκτους τινὰς χορείας,
ἐπεζήτουν τὸν δημιουργὸν τῆς περικαλλοῦς ταύτης
διακοσμήσεως, οὐκ ἐκ ταὐτομάτου στοχαζόμενοι

---

[1] κατάγων N (cj. Bekk.): καταντῶν cet., Bekk.

men derived the conception of God from the presentations received in sleep ; " for," says he, " when great images of human shape impressed them during sleep, they supposed that some such Gods of human shape really existed." [a] And some have recourse to the 26 unalterable and orderly motion of the heavenly bodies, and say that the first beginning of conceptions about the Gods arose from this ; for just as, if a man seated on Trojan Ida had been gazing at the host of the Greeks marching along the plain in splendid order and array—

> Riding first, in the van, were the knights with their chariots and horses
> Next came the men on foot : [b]—

such a man would certainly have arrived at the idea that there exists someone who orders this array and gives commands to the soldiers marshalled under him, such as Nestor (or some other hero) who understood how

> Rightly to marshal the steeds and the warriors armèd with bucklers.[c]

And just as the man who is familiar with ships, as 27 soon as he sees in the distance a ship with a favouring wind behind it and with all its sails well set, concludes that there is somebody who directs its course and brings it into its appointed havens,—so too those who first looked up to heaven and beheld the sun running its courses from east to west and the orderly processions of the stars sought for the Artificer of this most beautiful array, conjecturing that it had not come

---

[a] *Cf.* Lucret. v. 1168 ff.
[b] See Homer, *Il.* iv. 297.
[c] Homer, *Il.* ii. 554.

συμβαίνειν αὐτὴν ἀλλ᾽ ὑπό τινος κρείττονος καὶ
28 ἀφθάρτου φύσεως, ἥτις ἦν θεός. τῶν δὲ νεωτέρων
στωικῶν φασί τινες τοὺς πρώτους καὶ γηγενεῖς
τῶν ἀνθρώπων κατὰ πολὺ τῶν νῦν συνέσει διαφέροντας γεγονέναι, ὡς πάρεστι μαθεῖν ἐκ τῆς ἡμῶν
πρὸς τοὺς ἀρχαιοτέρους ⟨συμβλήσεως⟩,[1] καὶ ἥρωας
ἐκείνους ὥσπερ τι περιττὸν αἰσθητήριον σχόντας
τὴν ὀξύτητα τῆς διανοίας ἐπιβεβληκέναι τῇ θείᾳ
φύσει καὶ νοῆσαί τινας δυνάμεις θεῶν.

29   Τὰ μὲν οὖν λεγόμενα παρὰ τοῖς δογματικοῖς
φιλοσόφοις περὶ τῆς τῶν θεῶν ἐννοίας ἐστὶ τοιαῦτα,
οὐκ οἰόμεθα δὲ αὐτὰ χρείαν ἔχειν ἀντιρρήσεως·
τὸ γὰρ πολύτροπον τῆς ἀποφάσεως τὴν ἀγνωσίαν
τοῦ [παντὸς][2] ἀληθοῦς ἐπισφραγίζεται, πολλῶν μὲν
δυναμένων εἶναι τρόπων τῆς τοῦ θεοῦ νοήσεως,
τοῦ δὲ ἐν αὐτοῖς ἀληθοῦς μὴ καταλαμβανομένου.
ὅμως δὲ κἂν ἐπὶ τὰς κατὰ μέρος ὑπομνήσεις
χωρῶμεν, οὐδὲν εὑρεθήσεται τῶν εἰρημένων βέ-
30 βαιον.   αὐτίκα γὰρ οἱ μὲν νομοθέτας τινὰς οἰόμενοι
καὶ συνετοὺς ἀνθρώπους ἐμπεποιηκέναι τοῖς ἄλλοις
τὴν περὶ θεῶν δόξαν οὐ πάνυ τι φαίνονται τῷ
ζητουμένῳ προσβάλλειν. ἐζητεῖτο γὰρ ἀπὸ τίνος
ἀρχῆς ὁρμηθέντες ἄνθρωποι ἦλθον ἐπὶ τὸ θεοὺς
31 νομίζειν· οἱ δὲ διαφοδοῦντές φασιν ὅτι νομοθέται
τινὲς ἐνεποίησαν τοῖς ἀνθρώποις τὴν περὶ θεῶν
δόξαν, μὴ εἰδότες ὅτι τὸ ἀρχῆθεν ἄπορον[3] αὐτοὺς
περιμένει, ζητήσαντος ἄν τινος, πόθεν δὲ οἱ νομο-

---

[1] ⟨συμβλήσεως⟩ add. Hervetus ("sed plura exciderunt,"
Bekk.).
[2] [παντὸς] seclusi : πάντως cj. Rüstow.
[3] ἄπορον Heintz : ἄτοπον mss.. Bekk.

about spontaneously but by the agency of some superior and imperishable nature, which is God. And some of the later Stoics [a] declare that the first 28 men, the sons of Earth, greatly surpassed the men of to-day in intelligence (as one may learn from a comparison of ourselves with the men of the past), and that those ancient heroes possessed, as it were, in the keenness of their intellect, an extra organ of sense and apprehended the divine nature and discerned certain powers of the Gods.

Such, then, are the statements of the Dogmatic 29 philosophers regarding the conception of the Gods ; but we do not suppose that they call for refutation ; for the variety of the modes of conception which they assume stamps them with ignorance of the truth ; for while there can be many modes of conceiving God, that one of them which is true is not apprehended. Yet even were we to deal with the particular suggestions, none of the statements will be found to be well-grounded. Thus, for instance, those 30 who think that certain lawgivers and clever men implanted in the rest the belief in Gods do not appear at all to attack the problem. For the problem was— "from what starting-point did men set out when they arrived at a belief in Gods ? " ; whereas those 31 men make the irrelevant statement that certain lawgivers implanted in men this opinion about Gods, not seeing that they have the original difficulty still remaining, when someone may inquire " But how did

[a] e.g. Seneca, Epist. 90 " sed primi mortalium quique ex his geniti naturam incorrupti sequebantur . . . non tamen negaverim fuisse alti spiritus viros et, ut ita dicam, a dis recentes "; cf. Juvenal, Sat. xv. 69—

> nam genus hoc vivo iam decrescebat Homero,
> terra malos homines nunc educat atque pusillos.

θέται, μηδενὸς πρότερον παραδόντος αὐτοῖς θεούς,
32 ἦλθον εἰς ἐπίνοιαν θεῶν;   εἶτα πάντες μὲν
ἄνθρωποι τούτων ἔχουσιν ἔννοιαν, οὐχ ὡσαύτως
δέ, ἀλλὰ Πέρσαι μὲν, εἰ οὕτω τύχοι, τὸ πῦρ θεο-
φοροῦσιν, Αἰγύπτιοι δὲ τὸ ὕδωρ, ἄλλοι δὲ ἄλλο
τι τῶν τοιούτων. ἀπίθανόν τε ἦν πάντας ἀνθρώπους ὑπὸ τῶν νομοθετῶν εἰς τὸ αὐτὸ συναχθέντας
ἀκοῦσαί τι περὶ θεῶν· ἀνεπίμικτα γὰρ ἦν τὰ τῶν
ἀνθρώπων φῦλα καὶ ἄγνωστά γε, κατὰ τὴν ναυ-
τιλίαν δὲ τὴν Ἀργὼ πρωτόπλουν τι σκάφος διὰ
33 τῆς ἱστορίας παρειλήφαμεν. ναί, ἀλλ᾽ ἴσως τις
πρὸ τούτων πάντων φήσει ὅτι οἱ παρ᾽ ἑκάστοις
νομοθέται καὶ ἡγεμόνες ἀνέπλασαν τὴν τοιαύτην
νόησιν, καὶ διὰ τοῦτο ἄλλοι ἄλλους θεοὺς ὑπάρχειν
ὑπέλαβον. ὅπερ ἐστὶν εὔηθες· κοινὴν γὰρ πάλιν
πρόληψιν ἔχουσι πάντες ἄνθρωποι περὶ θεοῦ, καθ᾽
ἣν μακάριόν τί ἐστι ζῷον καὶ ἄφθαρτον καὶ τέλειον
ἐν εὐδαιμονίᾳ καὶ παντὸς κακοῦ ἀνεπίδεκτον,
τελέως δέ ἐστιν ἄλογον τὸ κατὰ τύχην πάντας τοῖς
αὐτοῖς ἐπιβάλλειν ἰδιώμασιν, ἀλλὰ μὴ φυσικῶς
οὕτως ἐκκινεῖσθαι. οὐ τοίνυν θέσει οὐδὲ κατά τινα
νομοθεσίαν παρεδέξαντο οἱ παλαιοὶ τῶν ἄνθρωπων
εἶναι θεούς.
34 Οἱ δὲ λέγοντες τοὺς πρώτους τῶν ἀνθρώπων
ἡγεμονεύσαντας καὶ διοικητὰς τῶν κοινῶν πραγμάτων γενομένους, πλείονα δύναμιν αὐτοῖς περι-
θέντας καὶ τιμὴν πρὸς τὸ ὑπακούειν τὰ πλήθη,
τούτους χρόνῳ τελευτήσαντας θεοὺς ὑποληφθῆναι,
πάλιν οὐ συνιᾶσι τὸ ζητούμενον. αὐτοὶ γὰρ οἱ εἰς
θεοὺς ἀνάγοντες αὐτοὺς πῶς ἔννοιαν ἔλαβον θεῶν
εἰς ἣν αὐτοὺς ἐνέταξαν; τοῦτο γὰρ δεόμενον ἀπο-

the lawgivers arrive at the conception of Gods, when nobody before had given them any tradition about Gods ? "—Further, all men possess a conception of 32 Gods, but not in the same way ; thus the Persians, for example, deify fire, the Egyptians water, and others other things of that sort. It is improbable, too, that all men should have been assembled together by the lawgivers to hear something about the Gods ; for the tribes of mankind were not mixed together but un- known to one another, and it has been handed down to us by history that, as regards voyaging, the Argo was the first bark to sail the seas. Yes, but before 33 all this, someone perhaps will say, the lawgivers and leaders of each tribe invented this conception, and on this account different peoples conceived the existence of different Gods. But this is silly ; for, on the con- trary, all men have one common preconception about God, according to which he is a blessed creature and imperishable and perfect in happiness and recep- tive of nothing evil, and it is quite contrary to reason that all men should apprehend the same character- istics by chance instead of gaining these impressions naturally. Hence, the men of old times did not accept the existence of Gods by convention or owing to legislation.

And those who say that the men who first led man- 34 kind and were the controllers of their public affairs, decked themselves with greater power and honour in order to secure the obedience of the multitude, and afterwards, when they died, were regarded as Gods,— they again fail to understand the problem. For how did the men who raised themselves to the position of Gods obtain that conception of the gods under which they ranked themselves ? For this point,

19

35 δείξεως παρεῖται. ἄλλως τε καὶ ἀπίθανόν ἐστι τὸ
ἀξιούμενον. τὰ γὰρ ὑπὸ τῶν ἡγεμόνων γινόμενα,
καὶ μάλιστά γε τὰ ψευδῆ, ζῶσι μόνον συμπαρα-
μένει τοῖς ἡγουμένοις, τελευτησάντων δὲ ἀναιρεῖται,
καὶ πάρεστι πολλοὺς ἐπελθεῖν τοὺς παρὰ μὲν τὸν
τῆς ζωῆς χρόνον ἐκθειασθέντας μετὰ δὲ τὴν
τελευτὴν καταφρονηθέντας, εἰ μή τινας προσηγορίας θεῶν ὑποστέλλοιεν, ὥσπερ ὁ Ἡρακλῆς ὁ
36 ἐξ Ἀλκμήνης καὶ Διός. ἦν μὲν γὰρ ἐξ ἀρχῆς, ὡς
φασίν, Ἀλκαῖος τοὔνομα, ὑπέδραμε δὲ τὴν Ἡρακλέους προσηγορίαν νομιζομένου παρὰ τοῖς τότε
θεοῦ. ὅθεν καὶ ἐν ταῖς Θήβαις λόγος ἔχει πάλαι
ποτὲ ἀνδριάντα ἴδιον Ἡρακλέους εὑρῆσθαι ἐπι-
γραφὴν ἔχοντα '' Ἀλκαῖος Ἀμφιτρύωνος Ἡρακλεῖ
37 χαριστήριον.'' καὶ τοὺς Τυνδαρίδας δέ φασι τὴν
τῶν Διοσκούρων δόξαν ὑπελθεῖν πάλιν νομιζομένων
εἶναι θεῶν· τὰ γὰρ δύο ἡμισφαίρια, τό τε ὑπὲρ γῆν
καὶ τὸ ὑπὸ γῆν, Διοσκούρους οἱ σοφοὶ τῶν τότε
ἀνθρώπων ἔλεγον. διὸ καὶ ὁ ποιητὴς τοῦτο
αἰνιττόμενός φησιν ἐπ' αὐτῶν

ἄλλοτε μὲν ζώουσ' ἑτερήμεροι, ἄλλοτε δ' αὖτε
τεθνᾶσιν, τιμὴν δὲ λελόγχασιν ἶσα θεοῖσιν.

πίλους τ' ἐπιτιθέασιν αὐτοῖς, καὶ ἐπὶ τούτοις
ἀστέρας, αἰνισσόμενοι τὴν τῶν ἡμισφαιρίων κατα-
38 σκευήν. οἱ μὲν δὴ οὕτως ὑποδραμόντες τὴν τῶν
θεῶν τιμὴν ἐκράτησάν πως τῆς προθέσεως, οἱ δὲ
αὐτόθεν αὑτοὺς ἀναγορεύσαντες θεοὺς κατεφρο-
νήθησαν μᾶλλον.

ᵃ *i.e.* Castor and Pollux, sons of Tyndareus by Leda. Note
that the Greek words here rendered by "assume" imply
sheltering oneself or hiding one's identity (under a divine

which needs explanation, is passed over. More- 35
over, the view thus maintained is improbable. For
the things done by leaders,—and especially such
things as are false,—remain unaltered only during
the life-time of the leaders, and at their death are
done away, and one may meet with many who
were counted as Gods during their life-time but
were despised after their death, unless they had
assumed some divine appellation, like Heracles the
son of Zeus and Alcmena. For originally, as they say, 36
his name was Alcaeus, but he assumed the appellation of Heracles, who was regarded as a God by the
men of that age. Hence, too, there is a story that at
Thebes long ago a private statue of Heracles was
discovered bearing the inscription " Alcaeus, son of
Amphitryon, as a thank-offering to Heracles." And 37
they say that the sons of Tyndareus *a* assumed the
title of " Dioscuri," who likewise were reputed to be
Gods ; for the wise men of that time called the two
hemispheres, that above the earth and that below the
earth, " Dioscuri." Wherefore also the poet, in
riddling allusion to this, says about them *b*—

Living on one day, dying the next, in alternate succession—
So they exist, and honour is theirs no less than the Godhead's.

And they set caps of felt *c* upon them, and upon these
stars, symbolizing the construction of the hemispheres. Those, then, who thus assumed the rank of 38
these Gods somehow secured that pre-eminence, but
those who openly proclaimed themselves Gods in
their own right were, instead, despised.

title already recognized, as contrasted with claiming divinity
in one's own name, see § 38).
  b See Homer, *Odyss.* xi. 303 f.
  ɔ *Cf.* Catullus xxxvii. 2, where C. and P. are called " pil-
leati fratres."

39 Καὶ μὴν οἱ λέγοντες ὅτι πάντα τὰ τὸν βίον ὠφελοῦντα ὑπενόησαν οἱ παλαιοὶ τῶν ἀνθρώπων θεοὺς
ὑπάρχειν, ὡς ἥλιον καὶ σελήνην ποταμούς τε καὶ
λίμνας καὶ τὰ ὅμοια, σὺν τῷ ἀπιθάνου προΐστασθαι
δόξης ἔτι καὶ τὴν ἀνωτάτω εὐήθειαν καταψηφί-
ζονται τῶν ἀρχαίων. οὐ γὰρ οὕτως εἰκὸς ἐκείνους
ἄφρονας εἶναι ὥστε τὰ ὀφθαλμοφανῶς φθειρόμενα
ὑπολαβεῖν εἶναι θεοὺς ἢ τοῖς πρὸς αὐτῶν κατεσθιο-
μένοις καὶ διαλυομένοις θείαν προσμαρτυρεῖν δύ-
40 ναμιν. τινὰ μὲν γὰρ λόγου ἴσως ἔχεται, καθάπερ
τὸ τὴν γῆν θεὸν νομίζειν, οὐ τὴν αὐλακοτομουμένην
ἢ ἀνασκαπτομένην οὐσίαν, ἀλλὰ τὴν διήκουσαν ἐν
αὐτῇ δύναμιν καὶ καρποφόρον φύσιν καὶ ὄντως
δαιμονιωτάτην. τὸ δὲ λίμνας καὶ ποταμούς, καὶ
εἴ τινα ἄλλα συνωφελεῖν ἡμᾶς πέφυκεν, ἡγεῖσθαι θεοὺς οὐδεμίαν ὑπερβολὴν ἐμβροντησίας ἀπο-
41 λέλοιπεν. οὕτω γὰρ ἐχρῆν καὶ τοὺς ἀνθρώπους
καὶ μάλιστα τοὺς φιλοσοφοῦντας ἡγεῖσθαι θεούς,
συνωφελοῦσι γὰρ ἡμῶν τὸν βίον, τῶν τε ἀλόγων
ζῴων τὰ πολλά, συνεργοπονεῖ γὰρ ἡμῖν, τά τε κατ᾽
οἰκίας [ζῷα] σκεύη τε καὶ πᾶν εἴ τι τούτων ἐστὶ
ταπεινότερον. ἀλλὰ ταῦτά γε σφόδρα ἐστὶ γελοῖα·
τοίνυν οὐδὲ τὴν ἐκκειμένην δόξαν ῥητέον ὑγιῆ
τυγχάνειν.
42 Ὁ δὲ Δημόκριτος τὸ ἧττον ἄπορον διὰ τοῦ
μείζονος ἀπόρου διδάσκων ἄπιστος ἐστίν. εἰς μὲν
γὰρ τὸ πῶς νόησιν θεῶν ἔσχον ἄνθρωποι πολλὰς
καὶ ποικίλας ἡ φύσις δίδωσιν ἀφορμάς· τὸ δὲ
εἴδωλα εἶναι ἐν τῷ περιέχοντι ὑπερφυῆ καὶ ἀν-
θρωποειδεῖς ἔχοντα μορφὰς καὶ καθόλου τοιαῦτα

Again, those who say [a] that the ancients supposed 39
that all the things which benefit life are Gods,—such
as the sun and moon, rivers and lakes, and the like,—
are not only defending an improbable view but also
convicting the ancients of the utmost stupidity. For
it is not likely that they were so foolish as to imagine
that things they saw perishing before their eyes are
Gods, or that they attributed divine power to things
which were being devoured by themselves and dis-
solved. For some things, perhaps, are reasonable, 40
such as believing the Earth to be divine,—not that
substance which is plowed into furrows or dug up, but
the power which pervades it and its fruitful, and
really most divine, nature. But to suppose that lakes
and rivers, and whatsoever else is of a nature to be
useful to us, are Gods surpasses the height of lunacy.
For, on this showing, one ought also to believe that 41
men, and especially philosophers, are Gods (for
they help to benefit our life), and most of the irrational animals (for they co-operate with us), and our
domestic furniture and whatsoever else there is of a
still more humble kind. But all this is extremely
ludicrous ; so that one must declare that the view set
forth is not sound.

Nor is Democritus [b] to be credited in that he 42
explains the less doubtful by the more doubtful. For
nature supplies a great number and variety of facts
which go to explain how men acquired the conception
of Gods ; but the notion that " there exist in the
circumambient gigantic images of human shape,"

[a] *e.g.* Prodicus, see § 18 *supra*.
[b] *Cf.* § 19 *supra*; Vol. I. Introd. p. xii. " The circumambient " is the air around us.

ὁποῖα βούλεται αὑτῷ ἀναπλάττειν Δημόκριτος,
παντελῶς ἐστι δυσπαράδεκτον.

43 Τὰ δὲ αὐτὰ καὶ πρὸς τὸν Ἐπίκουρον ἔνεστι
λέγειν, οἰόμενον ὅτι κατὰ τὰς ἐνυπνιδίους φαντασίας τῶν ἀνθρωπομόρφων εἰδώλων ἐνοήθησαν
θεοί· τί γὰρ μᾶλλον ἀπὸ τούτων νόησις ἐγίγνετο
44 θεῶν ἢ ὑπερφυῶν ἀνθρώπων; καὶ καθόλου καὶ
πρὸς πάσας τὰς ἐκκειμένας δόξας ἐνέσται λέγειν
ὅτι οὐ κατὰ ψιλὸν μέγεθος ἀνθρωποειδοῦς ζῴου
νόησιν θεοῦ λαμβάνουσιν ἄνθρωποι, ἀλλὰ σὺν τῷ
μακάριον εἶναι καὶ ἄφθαρτον καὶ πλείστην δύναμιν
ἐν τῷ κόσμῳ προφερόμενον. ἅπερ οὐ διδάσκουσιν,
ἀπὸ τίνος ἀρχῆς ἢ πῶς ἐπενοήθη παρὰ τοῖς πρῶτον ἔννοιαν σπάσασι θεοῦ, οἱ τὰς ἐνυπνιδίους αἰτιώ-
μενοι φαντασίας καὶ τὴν τῶν οὐρανίων εὐταξίαν.

45 Οἱ δὲ καὶ πρὸς τοῦτό φασιν ὅτι ἡ μὲν ἀρχὴ τῆς
νοήσεως τοῦ εἶναι θεὸν γέγονεν ἀπὸ τῶν κατὰ τοὺς
ὕπνους ἰνδαλλομένων ἢ ἀπὸ τῶν κατὰ τὸν κόσμον
θεωρουμένων, τὸ δὲ ἀΐδιον εἶναι τὸν θεὸν καὶ
ἄφθαρτον καὶ τέλειον ἐν εὐδαιμονίᾳ παρῆλθε κατὰ
τὴν ἀπὸ τῶν ἀνθρώπων μετάβασιν. ὡς γὰρ τὸν
κοινὸν ἄνθρωπον αὐξήσαντες τῇ φαντασίᾳ νόησιν
ἔσχομεν Κύκλωπος, ὃς οὐκ ἐῴκει

  ἀνδρί γε σιτοφάγῳ ἀλλὰ ῥίῳ ὑλήεντι

  ὑψηλῶν ὀρέων, ὅτε φαίνεται οἷον ἀπ' ἄλλων,

οὕτως ἄνθρωπον εὐδαίμονα νοήσαντες καὶ μακάριον
καὶ συμπεπληρωμένον πᾶσι τοῖς ἀγαθοῖς, εἶτα
ταῦτα ἐπιτείναντες τὸν ἐν αὐτοῖς ἐκείνοις ἄκρον
46 ἐνοήσαμεν θεόν. καὶ πάλιν πολυχρόνιόν τινα
φαντασιωθέντες ἄνθρωπον οἱ παλαιοὶ ἐπηύξησαν

---

[a] Cf. § 25 supra.
[b] Cf. § 21 supra. [c] Homer, Odyss. ix. 191 f.

and, in general, all such fictions as Democritus is
pleased to invent for himself, is wholly inadmissible.

Against Epicurus,[a] too, one may make the same 43
objections ; as he imagines that Gods were conceived
" in accordance with the presentations during sleep
of images of human shape " ; for why did there spring
from these the conception of Gods rather than of
gigantic men ? And one may object generally, 44
against all the views set forth, that men do not form
a notion of God by means of merely magnifying a
creature of human shape, but by including also the
fact that he is blessed and imperishable and exhibiting
very great power in the Universe. But how, or from
what starting-point, these qualities came to be conceived by those who first derived the conception of
God, is not explained by those who attribute it to
presentations during sleep or to the orderly array of
the heavenly bodies.

But to this they reply that, while the notion of God 45
originated in the images presented during sleep [b] or
in the phenomena of the Universe, the idea that God
is eternal and imperishable and perfect in happiness
was introduced by way of transference from mankind.
For just as by magnifying in fantasy the ordinary
man we have obtained the conception of Cyclops,
who was not—

Like to a corn-eating man, but rather a peak well-wooded
High on the mountain-tops, when it loometh apart from its
    fellows,[c]

so when we have formed a notion of a man who is
happy and blessed and fulfilled with all things good,
then by intensifying these qualities we form a notion
of God as he who excels in them all. And again, 46
when the ancients had imagined a long-lived man

τὸν χρόνον εἰς ἄπειρον, προσσυνάψαντες τῷ ἐνεστῶτι καὶ τὸν παρῳχημένον καὶ τὸν μέλλοντα·
εἶτα ἐντεῦθεν εἰς ἔννοιαν ἀιδίου[1] παραγενόμενοι
47 ἔφασαν καὶ ἀίδιον εἶναι τὸν θεόν. οἱ δὴ τοιαῦτα
λέγοντες πιθανῆς μὲν προΐστανται δόξης, ἠρέμα
δὲ εἰς τὸν δι’ ἀλλήλων ἐμπίπτουσι τρόπον, ὅς ἐστιν
ἀπορώτατος. ἵνα γὰρ πρῶτον εὐδαίμονα νοήσωμεν
ἄνθρωπον καὶ ἀπὸ τούτου κατὰ μετάβασιν τὸν
θεόν, ὀφείλομεν νοῆσαι τί ποτέ ἐστιν εὐδαιμονία,
ἧς κατὰ μετοχὴν νοεῖται ὁ εὐδαίμων. ἀλλ’ ἦν γε
εὐδαιμονία κατ’ αὐτοὺς δαιμονία τις καὶ θεία φύσις,
καὶ εὐδαίμων ἐκαλεῖτο ὁ εὖ τὸν δαίμονα διακείμενον
ἔχων. ὥσθ’ ἵνα μὲν λάβωμεν τὴν περὶ ἄνθρωπον
εὐδαιμονίαν, πρότερον ἔχειν ὀφείλομεν νόησιν θεοῦ
καὶ δαίμονος, ἵνα δὲ τὸν θεὸν νοήσωμεν, πρότερον
ἔχειν ὀφείλομεν ἔννοιαν εὐδαίμονος ἀνθρώπου.
τοίνυν ἑκάτερον περιμένον τὴν ἐκ θατέρου νόησιν
ἀνεπινόητον γίνεται ἡμῖν.
48 Καὶ δὴ ταῦτα μὲν εἰρήσθω πρὸς τοὺς ζητοῦντας
πῶς οἱ πρότερον νόησιν θεῶν ἔσχον ἄνθρωποι·
ἀκολούθως δὲ ζητῶμεν καὶ περὶ τοῦ εἰ εἰσὶ θεοί.

ΕΙ ΕΙΣΙ ΘΕΟΙ

49 Ἐπεὶ οὐ πᾶν τὸ ἐπινοούμενον καὶ ὑπάρξεως μετείληφεν, ἀλλὰ δύναταί τι ἐπινοεῖσθαι μέν, μὴ ὑπάρχειν δέ, καθάπερ Ἱπποκένταυρος καὶ Σκύλλα,
δεήσει μετὰ τὴν περὶ τῆς ἐπινοίας τῶν θεῶν ζήτησιν καὶ περὶ τῆς ὑπάρξεως τούτων σκέπτεσθαι.
τάχα γὰρ ἀσφαλέστερος παρὰ τοὺς ὡς ἑτέρως φιλο-

---

[1] ἀιδίου Mutsch. (sec. Hervetum): ἀίδιον mss., Bekk.

they extended his life-time to infinity, by linking
together with the present both the past and the
future ; and having thus arrived at the conception of
eternity they went on to say that God is eternal.
Those that argue thus maintain, indeed, a plausible 47
view, but they slide gently into circular reasoning,
which is the most hopeless kind. For in order to
conceive first the happy man, and from him to pass
on to a conception of God, we ought to have conceived
what happiness is, through participation in which the
happy man is conceived. But, according to them,
" happiness is a certain daemonic and divine nature,"
and " he who has his daemon well disposed " is said
to be " happy." [a] So that, in order to grasp human
happiness we must previously have a notion of " God "
and " daemon," and in order that we may conceive
God we must have a previous conception of the happy
man. So then, as each of these waits for its conception to be derived from the other, it becomes for us
inconceivable.

Let this, then, serve as our criticism of those who 48
inquire how the men of a past age acquired the notion
of Gods ; and let us inquire in the next place if there
are Gods.

Do Gods Exist ?

Since not everything which is conceived partakes 49
also in existence, but it is possible for a thing to be
conceived and not exist—like a Hippocentaur and
Scylla,—after our inquiry about the conception of
Gods we shall have to examine also the question of
their existence. For perchance the Sceptic, as compared with philosophers of other views, will be found

[a] The point of this is lost in the English, as it lies in the
etymology (εὐδαίμων = εὖ δαίμων).

σοφοῦντας εὑρεθήσεται ὁ σκεπτικός, κατὰ μὲν τὰ
πάτρια ἔθη καὶ τοὺς νόμους λέγων εἶναι θεοὺς καὶ
πᾶν τὸ εἰς τὴν τούτων θρησκείαν καὶ εὐσέβειαν
συντεῖνον ποιῶν, τὸ δ' ὅσον ἐπὶ τῇ φιλοσόφῳ
ζητήσει μηδὲν προπετευόμενος.

50   Τῶν οὖν περὶ ὑπάρξεως θεοῦ σκεψαμένων οἱ μὲν
εἶναί φασι θεόν, οἱ δὲ μὴ εἶναι, οἱ δὲ μὴ μᾶλλον
εἶναι ἢ μὴ εἶναι. καὶ εἶναι μὲν οἱ πλείους τῶν
51 δογματικῶν καὶ ἡ κοινὴ τοῦ βίου πρόληψις, μὴ
εἶναι δὲ οἱ ἐπικληθέντες ἄθεοι, καθάπερ Εὐήμερος,

γέρων ἀλαζών, ἄδικα βιβλία ψήχων,

καὶ Διαγόρας ὁ Μήλιος καὶ Πρόδικος ὁ Κεῖος καὶ
Θεόδωρος καὶ ἄλλοι παμπληθεῖς· ὧν Εὐήμερος μὲν
ἔλεγε τοὺς νομιζομένους θεοὺς δυνατούς τινας
γεγονέναι ἀνθρώπους καὶ διὰ τοῦτο ὑπὸ τῶν ἄλλων
52 θεοποιηθέντας δόξαι θεούς, Πρόδικος δὲ τὸ
ὠφελοῦν τὸν βίον ὑπειλῆφθαι θεόν, ὡς ἥλιον καὶ
σελήνην καὶ ποταμοὺς ⟨καὶ λίμνας⟩[1] καὶ λειμῶνας
53 καὶ καρποὺς καὶ πᾶν τὸ τοιουτῶδες. Διαγόρας
δὲ ὁ Μήλιος, διθυραμβοποιός, ὡς φασί, τὸ πρῶτον
γενόμενος ὡς εἴ τις καὶ ἄλλος δεισιδαίμων· ὅς γε
καὶ τῆς ποιήσεως ἑαυτοῦ κατήρξατο τὸν τρόπον
τοῦτον " κατὰ δαίμονα καὶ τύχην πάντα τελεῖται "·
ἀδικηθεὶς δὲ ὑπό τινος ἐπιορκήσαντος καὶ μηδὲν
ἕνεκα τούτου παθόντος μεθηρμόσατο εἰς τὸ λέγειν
54 μὴ εἶναι θεόν. καὶ Κριτίας δὲ εἷς τῶν ἐν Ἀθήναις

---

[1] ⟨καὶ λίμνας⟩ add. N, Mutsch.

[a] Cf. P.H. iii. 2.

in a safer position, since in conformity with his
ancestral customs and the laws, he declares that the
Gods exist,[a] and performs everything which contributes to their worship and veneration, but, so
far as regards philosophic investigation, declines to
commit himself rashly.

Of those, then, who have inquired as to the 50
existence of God some say that God exists, some that
he does not exist, some that he has existence " no
more " than non-existence. That he exists is the
view of most of the Dogmatists and the general preconception of ordinary folk ; that he does not exist 51
is the view of those who are designated " atheists,"
such as Euhemerus [b]—

> A hoary braggart, penning wicked books,

and Diagoras of Melos,[c] and Prodicus of Ceos, and
Theodorus, and a host of others. Of these, Euhemerus
declared that those counted as Gods were certain
men of power, because of which they were deified by
the rest and reputed to be Gods ; but Prodicus said 52
that what benefits life is God, such as the sun and
moon and rivers and lakes and meadows and crops
and everything of that kind. And Diagoras of Melos, 53
the dithyrambic poet, was at first, they say, god-
fearing above all others ; for he began his poem in
this fashion—" By Heaven's will and Fortune all
things are accomplished " ; but when he had been
wronged by a man who had sworn falsely and suffered
no punishment for it, he changed round and asserted
that God does not exist. And Critias, one of the 54

---

[b] Cf. § 17 *supra* ; the quotation is from Callimachus
(*Frag.* 86).
[c] D. was a disciple of Democritus (*circa* 420 B.C.). Theodorus was a Cyrenaic (*circa* 310 B.C.), *cf.* Vol. I. Introd. p. xvii.

τυραννησάντων δοκεῖ ἐκ τοῦ τάγματος τῶν ἀθέων
ὑπάρχειν, φάμενος ὅτι οἱ παλαιοὶ νομοθέται ἐπί-
σκοπόν τινα τῶν ἀνθρωπίνων κατορθωμάτων καὶ
ἁμαρτημάτων ἔπλασαν τὸν θεὸν ὑπὲρ τοῦ μηδένα
λάθρᾳ τὸν πλησίον ἀδικεῖν, εὐλαβούμενον τὴν ὑπὸ
τῶν θεῶν τιμωρίαν. ἔχει δὲ παρ' αὐτῷ τὸ ῥητὸν
οὕτως.

 ἦν χρόνος ὅτ' ἦν ἄτακτος ἀνθρώπων βίος
 καὶ θηριώδης ἰσχύος θ' ὑπηρέτης,
 ὅτ' οὐδὲν ἆθλον οὔτε τοῖς ἐσθλοῖσιν ἦν
 οὔτ' αὖ κόλασμα τοῖς κακοῖς ἐγίγνετο.
 κἄπειτά μοι δοκοῦσιν ἄνθρωποι νόμους
 θέσθαι κολαστάς, ἵνα δίκη τύραννος ᾖ
 ⟨γένους βροτείου⟩[1] τήν θ' ὕβριν δούλην ἔχῃ·
 ἐζημιοῦτο δ' εἴ τις ἐξαμαρτάνοι.
 ἔπειτ' ἐπειδὴ τἀμφανῆ μὲν οἱ νόμοι
 ἀπεῖργον αὐτοὺς ἔργα μὴ πράσσειν βίᾳ,
 λάθρᾳ δ' ἔπρασσον, τηνικαῦτά μοι δοκεῖ
 ⟨πρῶτον⟩ πυκνός τις καὶ σοφὸς γνώμην ἀνὴρ
 θεῶν δέος θνητοῖσιν ἐξευρεῖν ὅπως
 εἴη τι δεῖμα τοῖς κακοῖσι κἂν λάθρᾳ
 πράσσωσιν ἢ λέγωσιν ἢ φρονῶσί τι.
 ἐντεῦθεν οὖν τὸ θεῖον εἰσηγήσατο,
 ὡς ἔστι δαίμων ἀφθίτῳ θάλλων βίῳ,
 νόῳ τ' ἀκούων καὶ βλέπων, φρονῶν τε καὶ
 προσέχων τε ταῦτα, καὶ φύσιν θείαν φορῶν,
 ὃς πᾶν τὸ λεχθὲν ἐν βροτοῖς ἀκούσεται,
 τὸ δρώμενον δὲ πᾶν ἰδεῖν δυνήσεται.
 ἐὰν δὲ σὺν σιγῇ τι βουλεύῃς κακόν,
 τοῦτ' οὐχὶ λήσει τοὺς θεούς· τὸ γὰρ φρονοῦν
 ⟨αὐτοῖς⟩[2] ἔνεστι. τούσδε τοὺς λόγους λέγων

Tyrants at Athens,[a] seems to belong to the company
of the atheists when he says that the ancient lawgivers invented God as a kind of overseer of the right
and wrong actions of men, in order to make sure that
nobody injured his neighbours privily through fear of
vengeance at the hands of the Gods ; and his statement runs thus [b] :—

> A time there was when anarchy did rule
> The lives of men, which then were like the beasts',
> Enslaved to force ; nor was there then reward
> For good men, nor for wicked punishment.
> Next, as I deem, did men establish laws
> For punishment, that Justice might be lord
> Of all mankind, and Insolence enchain'd ;
> And whosoe'er did sin was penalized.
> Next, as the laws did hold men back from deeds
> Of open violence, but still such deeds
> Were done in secret,—then, as I maintain,
> Some shrewd man first, a man in counsel wise,
> Discovered unto men the fear of Gods,
> Thereby to frighten sinners should they sin
> E'en secretly in deed, or word, or thought.
> Hence was it that he brought in Deity,
> Telling how God enjoys an endless life,
> Hears with his mind and sees, and taketh thought
> And heeds things, and his nature is divine,
> So that he hearkens to men's every word
> And has the power to see men's every act.
> E'en if you plan in silence some ill deed,
> The Gods will surely mark it ; for in them
> Wisdom resides.   So, speaking words like these,

[a] *i.e.* one of " the Thirty " Tyrants of 404 B.C.
[b] For this poem Sextus is our only authority and in several
places the text is dubious.   I follow for the most part that of
Diels (*Frag. d. Vorsokr.* p. 571).

---

[1] ⟨γένους βροτείου⟩ add. Grotius : ⟨ὁμῶς ἀπάντων⟩ Diels.
[2] ⟨αὐτοῖς⟩ add. Mutsch. : ⟨ἄγαν⟩ Diels.

διδαγμάτων κέρδιστον[1] εἰσηγήσατο,
ψευδεῖ καλύψας τὴν ἀλήθειαν λόγῳ.
ναίειν δ' ἔφασκε τοὺς θεοὺς ἐνταῦθ' ἵνα
μάλιστ' ἂν ἐξέπληξεν ἀνθρώπους λέγων,
ὅθεν περ ἔγνω τοὺς φόβους ὄντας βροτοῖς
καὶ τὰς ὀνήσεις τῷ ταλαιπώρῳ βίῳ,
ἐκ τῆς ὕπερθε περιφορᾶς, ἵν' ἀστραπὰς
κατεῖδεν οὔσας, δεινὰ δὲ κτυπήματα
βροντῆς, τό τ' ἀστερωπὸν οὐρανοῦ δέμας,
χρόνου καλὸν ποίκιλμα, τέκτονος σοφοῦ,
ὅθεν τε λαμπρὸς ἀστέρος στείχει μύδρος,
ὅ θ' ὑγρὸς εἰς γῆν ὄμβρος ἐκπορεύεται.
τοίους πέριξ ἔστησεν ἀνθρώποις φόβου
στοίχους, καλῶς τε τῷ λόγῳ κατῴκισεν
τὸν δαίμον' οἰκεῖν ἐν πρέποντι χωρίῳ,
τὴν ἀνομίαν τε τοῖς νόμοις κατέσβεσεν.

καὶ ὀλίγα προσδιελθὼν ἐπιφέρει

οὕτω δὲ πρῶτον οἴομαι πεῖσαί τινα
θνητοὺς νομίζειν δαιμόνων εἶναι γένος.

55 Συμφέρεται δὲ τούτοις τοῖς ἀνδράσι καὶ Θεόδωρος ὁ ἄθεος καὶ κατά τινας Πρωταγόρας ὁ
Ἀβδηρίτης, ὁ μὲν διὰ τοῦ περὶ θεῶν συντάγματος
τὰ παρὰ τοῖς Ἕλλησι θεολογούμενα ποικίλως
56 ἀνασκευάσας, ὁ δὲ Πρωταγόρας ῥητῶς που
γράψας " περὶ δὲ θεῶν οὔτε εἰ εἰσὶν οὔθ' ὁποῖοί
τινές εἰσι δύναμαι λέγειν· πολλὰ γάρ ἐστι τὰ
κωλύοντά με." παρ' ἣν αἰτίαν θάνατον αὐτοῦ
καταψηφισαμένων τῶν Ἀθηναίων διαφυγὼν καὶ
57 κατὰ θάλατταν πταίσας ἀπέθανεν. μέμνηται δὲ

---

[1] κέρδιστον Nauck : ἥδιστον mss., Diels.

Most cunning doctrine did he introduce,
The truth concealing under speech untrue.
The place he spoke of as the God's abode
Was that whereby he could affright men most,—
The place from which, he knew, both terrors came
And easements unto men of toilsome life—
To wit the vault above, wherein do dwell
The lightnings, he beheld, and awesome claps
Of thunder, and the starry face of heaven,
Fair-spangled by that cunning craftsman Time,—
Whence, too, the meteor's glowing mass doth speed
And liquid rain descends upon the earth.
Such were the fears wherewith he hedged men round,
And so to God he gave a fitting home,
By this his speech, and in a fitting place,
And thus extinguished lawlessness by laws.

And, after proceeding a little farther, he adds—

Thus first did some man, as I deem, persuade
Men to suppose a race of Gods exists.

Theodorus " the Atheist," too, is of the same mind 55
as these men, and (according to some) Protagoras of
Abdera ; the former, seeing that he demolished the
theological beliefs of the Greeks by a variety of
arguments in his treatise *Concerning Gods* ; and 56
Protagoras, where in one place he wrote expressly—
"Concerning Gods I am not able to say either whether
they exist or of what sort they are ; for the things
which prevent me are many." And when, because
of this, the Athenians had condemned him to death
he escaped, and died by shipwreck at sea. Mention 57

33

ταύτης τῆς ἱστορίας καὶ Τίμων ὁ Φλιάσιος ἐν τῷ
δευτέρῳ τῶν σίλλων ταῦτα διεξερχόμενος,

⟨πάντων πρωτίστῳ τό⟩ τε[1] καὶ μετέπειτα σο-
  φιστῶν
οὔτ' ἀλιγυγλώσσῳ οὔτ' ἀσκόπῳ οὔτ' ἀκυλίστῳ
Πρωταγόρῃ· ἔθελον δὲ τέφρην συγγράμματα
  θεῖναι,
ὅττι θεοὺς κατέγραψ' οὔτ' εἰδέναι οὔτε δύνασθαι
ὁπποῖοί τινές εἰσι καὶ οἵ τινες ἀθρήσασθαι,
πᾶσαν ἔχων φυλακὴν ἐπιεικείης. τὰ μὲν οὖ οἱ
χραίσμησ', ἀλλὰ φυγῆς ἐπεμαίετο, ὄφρα μὴ οὔτως
Σωκρατικὸν πίνων ψυχρὸν πότον ἄϊδα δύῃ.

58 καὶ Ἐπίκουρος δὲ κατ' ἐνίους ὡς μὲν πρὸς τοὺς
πολλοὺς ἀπολείπει θεόν, ὡς δὲ πρὸς τὴν φύσιν τῶν
59 πραγμάτων οὐδαμῶς. οὐ μᾶλλον δὲ εἶναι ἢ μὴ
εἶναι θεοὺς διὰ τὴν τῶν ἀντικειμένων λόγων ἰσοσθένειαν ἔλεξαν οἱ ἀπὸ τῆς σκέψεως. καὶ τοῦτο
εἰσόμεθα ἑκατέρωθεν τὰ ἐπιχειρούμενα συντόμως
ἐπιδραμόντες.

60 Οἱ τοίνυν θεοὺς ἀξιοῦντες εἶναι πειρῶνται τὸ
προκείμενον κατασκευάζειν ἐκ τεσσάρων τρόπων,
ἑνὸς μὲν τῆς παρὰ πᾶσιν ἀνθρώποις συμφωνίας,
δευτέρου δὲ τῆς κοσμικῆς διατάξεως, τρίτου δὲ
τῶν ἀκολουθούντων ἀτόπων τοῖς ἀναιροῦσι τὸ
θεῖον, τετάρτου δὲ καὶ τελευταίου τῆς τῶν ἀντι-
61 πιπτόντων λόγων ὑπεξαιρέσεως. ἀλλ' ἀπὸ μὲν
τῆς κοινῆς ἐννοίας λέγοντες ὡς ἅπαντες ἄνθρωποι
σχεδὸν Ἕλληνές τε καὶ βάρβαροι νομίζουσιν εἶναι

---

[1] ⟨πάντων ... τό⟩ τε Diels: ὡς Bekk.: ἔσητε N: ὥστε cet.

34

is made of this story by Timon of Phlius, in the second
book of his *Silli*,—

First of the Sophists existing then or that shall be hereafter,
Neither in speech unclear nor dull of sight or of action,
Protagoras ; and they wished to reduce his writings to ashes,
For that he wrote of the Gods that he knew not and could not
    discover
Who, if any, they truly are, and what is their nature,
Giving all heed to candour. But that did profit him nothing ;
Wherefore he hastened to flee, that he might not descend into
    Hades,
Doomed to drink of that potion cold which Socrates swal-
    lowed.[a]

And, according to some, Epicurus in his popular 58
exposition allows the existence of God, but in ex-
pounding the real nature of things he does not allow
it. And the Sceptics have declared that, owing to 59
the equipollence of the opposed arguments, the Gods
are existent " no more " than non-existent. This
we shall learn when we have briefly run through the
arguments urged on either side.

Those, then, who maintain that Gods exist try to 60
establish their thesis by four modes, arguing, firstly,
from the universal agreement of mankind ; secondly,
from the orderly arrangement of the Universe ;
thirdly, from the absurd consequences of the denial
of the existence of deity ; fourthly and lastly, by under-
mining the opposing arguments.[b] Arguing from the 61
universal conception, they say that practically all men,
both Greeks and barbarians,[c] believe in the existence

---

[a] P. was condemned to death (by hemlock) at Athens on
a charge of impiety (§ 56 *supra*). For Timon and his writings
see Vol. I. Introd. p. xxxi.
[b] S. deals with these four arguments as follows—(1) in
§§ 61-74 ; (2) in §§ 75-122 ; (3) in §§ 123-126 ; (4) in §§ 127-136.
[c] *Cf. Adv. Log.* ii. 187.

τὸ θεῖον, καὶ διὰ τοῦτο συμφώνως μὲν θύουσί τε
καὶ εὔχονται καὶ τεμένη θεῶν ἀνιστῶσιν, ἄλλοι δὲ
ἄλλως ταῦτα ποιοῦσιν, ὡς ἂν κατὰ μὲν τὸ κοινὸν
πεπιστευκότες τὸ εἶναί τι θεῖον, μὴ τὴν αὐτὴν δὲ
ἔχοντες περὶ τῆς φύσεως αὐτοῦ πρόληψιν. εἰ δέ
γε ψευδὴς ὑπῆρχεν ἡ τοιαύτη πρόληψις, οὐκ ἂν
62 οὕτω πάντες συνεφώνουν. εἰσὶν ἄρα θεοί. καὶ
γὰρ ἄλλως αἱ ψευδεῖς δόξαι καὶ πρόσκαιροι φάσεις
οὐκ ἐπὶ πλεῖον παρεκτείνουσιν, ἀλλὰ συντελευτῶσιν
ἐκείνοις ὧν χάριν ἐφυλάττοντο. οἷον τιμῶσι
βασιλεῖς ἄνθρωποι θυσίαις τε καὶ ταῖς ἄλλαις
θρησκείαις, αἷς [ὡς]¹ θεοὺς προστρέπονται· ἀλλὰ
ταῦτα μέχρις ἐκείνων αὐτῶν διατηροῦσιν, τελευτησάντων δὲ ὡς ἄθεσμά τινα καὶ ἀσεβῆ κατα-
λείπουσιν. ἡ δέ γε τῶν θεῶν ἔννοια καὶ ἐξ αἰῶνος
ἦν καὶ εἰς αἰῶνα διαμένει, ἐξ αὐτῶν, ὡς εἰκός, τῶν
63 γιγνομένων μαρτυρουμένη. οὐ μὴν ἀλλὰ καὶ
εἰ τὴν ἰδιωτικὴν ὑπόνοιαν δεῖ παραλείπειν, τοῖς
δὲ συνετοῖς καὶ μεγαλοφυεστάτοις τῶν ἀνδρῶν
πείθεσθαι, πάρεστι μὲν τὴν ποιητικὴν ὁρᾶν μηδὲν
μέγα μηδὲ λαμπρὸν ἐκφέρουσαν ἐν ᾧ μὴ θεός
ἐστιν ὁ τὴν ἐξουσίαν καὶ τὸ κράτος τῶν γινομένων
πραγμάτων ἐνημμένος, ὥσπερ καὶ τῷ ποιητῇ
Ὁμήρῳ κατὰ τὸν ἀναγραφέντα τῶν Ἑλλήνων
64 καὶ βαρβάρων πόλεμον. πάρεστι δὲ καὶ τὴν τῶν
φυσικῶν πληθὺν ἰδεῖν σύμφωνον τῇ ποιητικῇ· καὶ
γὰρ Πυθαγόρας καὶ Ἐμπεδοκλῆς καὶ οἱ ἀπὸ τῆς
Ἰωνίας Σωκράτης τε καὶ Πλάτων καὶ Ἀριστοτέλης καὶ οἱ ἀπὸ τῆς στοᾶς, τάχα δὲ οἱ ἀπὸ τῶν
κήπων, ὡς αἱ ῥηταὶ τοῦ Ἐπικούρου λέξεις μαρ-

¹ [ὡς] om. Hervetus (καὶ cj. Bekk.).

of the Divine, and because of this they agree in sacrificing and in praying and in setting up shrines for the Gods ; and some do this in one way, some in another, as though all of them in common believed in the existence of some Divinity, but did not possess the same preconception regarding its nature. But if this preconception had been false, they would not all have agreed in this way ; therefore Gods exist. And 62 besides, false opinions and temporary appearances do not survive longer but come to an end together with the persons for whose sakes they were retained. For example, men honour kings with sacrifices and with all the other religious rites with which they worship the Gods ; but they observe these practices only so long as the kings themselves are there, and when they are dead they give them up as being illegal and impious. But the conception of the Gods has existed from eternity and persists unto eternity, as it probably derives its evidence from the very facts of existence. —Moreover, even if one ought to pass over the belief 63 of the ordinary man and put one's trust in men who are clever and most highly gifted, one may see how poetry produces no great or brilliant work in which God is not the person invested with authority and power over the events which take place,—even as he was by the poet Homer in the war he described between the Greeks and barbarians. And one may 64 also see the host of the Physicists in accord with poetry ; for Pythagoras and Empedocles and the Ionians and Socrates and Plato and Aristotle and the Stoics, and perhaps " the Garden philosophers " [a] too (as the express statements of Epicurus testify), allow

---

[a] *i.e.* the Epicureans, so called from the garden at Athens in which Epicurus established his school of philosophy.

SEXTUS EMPIRICUS

65 τυροῦσι, θεὸν ἀπολείπουσιν. ὥσπερ οὖν εἰ περί
τινος τῶν ὑπὸ τὴν ὅρασιν πιπτόντων ἐζητοῦμεν,
εὐλόγως ἂν τοῖς ὀξυωπεστάτοις ἐπιστεύομεν, καὶ
εἰ περί τινος τῶν ἀκουστῶν, τοῖς ὀξυηκουστάτοις,
οὕτω σκεπτόμενοι περί τινος τῶν λόγῳ θεωρουμένων οὐκ ἄλλοις τισὶ πιστεύειν ὀφείλομεν ἢ τοῖς
τὸν νοῦν καὶ τὸν λόγον ὀξυωποῦσιν, ὁποῖοί τινες
ἦσαν οἱ φιλόσοφοι.

66 Ἀλλ' εἰώθασιν ἀνθυποφέροντες πρὸς τοῦτο
λέγειν οἱ ἐξ ἐναντίας ὅτι καὶ περὶ τῶν ἐν ᾅδου
μυθευομένων κοινὴν ἔννοιαν ἔχουσιν ἅπαντες ἄνθρωποι καὶ συμφώνους ἔχουσι τοὺς ποιητάς, καὶ
μᾶλλόν γε περὶ τούτων ἢ περὶ[1] τῶν θεῶν, ἀλλ'
οὐκ ἂν εἴποιμεν ταῖς ἀληθείαις ὑπάρχειν τὰ καθ'
67 ᾅδου μυθευόμενα, μὴ συνιέντες πρῶτον μὲν ὅτι
οὐ μόνον τὰ καθ' ᾅδου πλαττόμενα ἀλλὰ καὶ
κοινῶς πάντα μῦθον μάχην περιεσχηκέναι συμβέβηκε καὶ ἀδύνατον εἶναι. οἷον ἦν

καὶ Τιτυὸν εἶδον, Γαίης ἐρικυδέος υἱόν,
κείμενον ἐν δαπέδῳ· ὁ δ' ἐπ' ἐννέα κεῖτο πέλεθρα,
γῦπε δέ μιν ἑκάτερθε παρημένω ἧπαρ ἔκειρον,
δέρτρον ἔσω δύνοντες· ὁ δ' οὐκ ἀπαμύνετο χερσίν·
Λητὼ γὰρ ἤσχυνε Διὸς κυδρὴν παράκοιτιν.

68 εἰ μὲν γὰρ ἄψυχος ἦν ὁ Τιτυός, πῶς οὐδεμίαν
συναίσθησιν ἔχων ὑπὸ τιμωρίαν ἔπιπτεν; εἰ δὲ
69 εἶχε ψυχήν, πῶς τετελευτήκει; καὶ πάλιν ὅταν
λέγηται

καὶ μὴν Τάνταλον εἰσεῖδον κρατέρ' ἄλγε' ἔχοντα,
ἑσταότ' ἐν λίμνῃ· ἡ δὲ προσέκλυζε γενείῳ.

[1] περὶ N, Mutsch.: ὅτι Bekk.

God's existence. Therefore, just as, if we had been 65
inquiring about something which is perceived by
sight, it would have been reasonable for us to have
trusted those who have the sharpest sight, and if it
had been about something audible, those of the
sharpest hearing,—so also, when we are examining
one of the things observed by reason we ought to
trust none except those who are sharp of sight in
mind and reason, such as were the philosophers.

But in reply to this those of the opposite side are 66
accustomed to argue that all men have a common
conception about the legendary doings in Hades as
well, and have the poets in agreement with them ;
and even more so about these things than about the
Gods ; yet we would not assert that the legendary
doings in Hades are real facts, through failing to 67
understand, in the first place, that not only the
fictions about Hades but, in general, every legend is
such as to contain conflicting elements and to be
impossible ; as, for instance—

Tityus, too, I beheld, the glorious Earth-mother's offspring,
Lying flat on the ground ; nine roods did he cover extended ;
Vultures twain sat on either side and tore at his liver,
Plunged in his inward parts ; with his hands he could not
    repel them :
Seeing he shamed the consort of Zeus, illustrious Leto.[a]

For if Tityus was lifeless, how was he under punish- 68
ment when he possessed no consciousness ? And if
he possessed life, how was he dead ? And again, 69
when it is related [b]—

Tantalus, too, I beheld with mine eyes in agonies grievous
Standing within a lake ; and up to his chin came the water ;

    [a] Homer, *Odyss.* xi. 576 ff. ; *cf.* Lucret. iii. 996 ff.
    [b] Homer, *Odyss.* xi. 582 ff.

στεῦτό τε διψάων, πιέειν δ' οὐκ εἶχεν ἑλέσθαι·
ὁσσάκι γὰρ κύψει' ὁ γέρων πιέειν μενεαίνων,
τοσσάχ' ὕδωρ ἀπολέσκετ' ἀναβροχέν, ἀμφὶ δὲ
ποσσὶν
γαῖα μέλαινα φάνεσκε, καταζήνασκε δὲ δαίμων.

70 εἰ γὰρ μήποτε ὑγροῦ καὶ τροφῆς ἐγεύετο, πῶς
διέμενεν ἀλλ' οὐ σπάνει τῶν ἀναγκαίων διεφθείρετο;
εἰ δὲ ἀθάνατος ἦν, πῶς τοιοῦτος ἐστίν; μάχεται
γὰρ ἀθάνατος φύσις ἀλγηδόσι καὶ βασάνοις,
71 ἐπείπερ πᾶν τὸ ἀλγοῦν θνητόν ἐστιν. ἀλλὰ γὰρ
ὁ μὲν μῦθος οὕτως ἐν αὑτῷ τὸν ἔλεγχον περιεῖχεν,
ἡ δὲ περὶ θεῶν ὑπόληψις οὐ τοιαύτη τις ἐστίν,
οὐδὲ μάχην ὑπέβαλλεν, ἀλλὰ σύμφωνος τοῖς γιγνο-
μένοις ἐφαίνετο. καὶ γὰρ οὐδὲ τὰς ψυχὰς ἔνεστιν
ὑπονοῆσαι κάτω φερομένας· λεπτομερεῖς γὰρ
οὖσαι καὶ οὐχ ἧττον πυρώδεις ἢ πνευματώδεις εἰς
72 τοὺς ἄνω μᾶλλον τόπους κουφοφοροῦσιν. καὶ καθ'
αὑτὰς δὲ διαμένουσι καὶ οὐχ, ὡς ἔλεγεν ὁ Ἐπίκουρος, ἀπολυθεῖσαι τῶν σωμάτων καπνοῦ δίκην
σκίδνανται. οὐδὲ γὰρ πρότερον τὸ σῶμα διακρατη-
τικὸν ἦν αὐτῶν, ἀλλ' αὐταὶ τῷ σώματι συμμονῆς
73 ἦσαν αἴτιαι, πολὺ δὲ πρότερον καὶ ἑαυταῖς. ἔκ-
σκηνοι γοῦν ἡλίου γενόμεναι τὸν ὑπὸ σελήνην
οἰκοῦσι τόπον, ἐνθάδε τε διὰ τὴν εἰλικρίνειαν τοῦ
ἀέρος πλείονα πρὸς διαμονὴν λαμβάνουσι χρόνον,
τροφῇ τε χρῶνται οἰκείᾳ τῇ ἀπὸ γῆς ἀναθυμιάσει
ὡς καὶ τὰ λοιπὰ ἄστρα, τὸ διαλῦσόν τε αὐτὰς ἐν
74 ἐκείνοις τοῖς τόποις οὐκ ἔχουσιν. εἰ οὖν δια-
μένουσιν αἱ ψυχαί, δαίμοσιν αἱ αὐταὶ γίνονται· εἰ

Thirsty he stood, nor could he attain to reach it and drink it;
Nay, for as oft as the old man stoop'd desirous of drinking
Just so oft did the wave surge back; and close to his foot-
    prints
Black did the earth appear, so parch'd was it made by the
    Daemon.

For if he never tasted drink or food how did he 70
survive and not perish through lack of necessary
sustenance?   And if he was immortal, how is he
in the state described?   For an immortal nature
is inconsistent with pains and torments, since everything that suffers pain is mortal.   But, ⟨retort the 71
Stoics,⟩ whereas the myth does thus contain within
itself its own refutation, the conception of Gods
is not of this kind, nor does it introduce inconsistency, but is evidently in accord with facts.   Nor,
indeed, is it possible to suppose that souls move
downwards; for since they are of fine particles, and
no less of a fiery than of a vaporous nature, they
rather soar lightly to the upper regions.   Also, they 72
persist as they are in themselves, and are not (as
Epicurus said) "dispersed like smoke when released
from their bodies." [a]   For before that it was not the
body that was in control of them, but it was they that
were the causes of the body's conjoined existence
and, much more, of their own.   For having quitted 73
the sphere of the sun [b] they inhabit the region below
the moon, and there because of the pureness of the
air they continue to remain for a long time, and for
their sustenance they use the steam which rises from
the earth, as do the rest of the stars,[b] and in those
regions they have nothing to dissolve them.   If, 74
then, souls persist, they are the same as daemons;

[a] Cf. Lucret. iii. 437 f., 457 f.
[b] This was a Stoic theory, cf. Cicero, Nat. D. ii. 15.

δὲ δαίμονές εἰσι, ῥητέον καὶ θεοὺς ὑπάρχειν, μηδὲν
αὐτῶν τὴν ὕπαρξιν βλαπτούσης τῆς περὶ τῶν ἐν
ᾅδου μυθευομένων προλήψεως.

75 Ὁ μὲν οὖν ἀπὸ τῆς κοινῆς καὶ συμφώνου οἰήσεως
τοῦ θεοῦ λόγος ἐστὶ τοιοῦτος· σκοπῶμεν δὲ καὶ
τὸν ἀπὸ τῆς τοῦ περιέχοντος διακοσμήσεως. ἡ
τοίνυν τῶν ὄντων οὐσία, φασίν, ἀκίνητος οὖσα
ἐξ αὑτῆς καὶ ἀσχημάτιστος ὑπό τινος αἰτίας ὀφείλει
κινεῖσθαί τε καὶ σχηματίζεσθαι· καὶ διὰ τοῦτο, ὡς
χαλκούργημα περικαλλὲς θεασάμενοι ποθοῦμεν
μαθεῖν τὸν τεχνίτην ἅτε καθ' αὑτὴν τῆς ὕλης
ἀκινήτου καθεστώσης, οὕτω καὶ τὴν τῶν ὅλων
ὕλην θεωροῦντες κινουμένην καὶ ἐν μορφῇ τε καὶ
διακοσμήσει τυγχάνουσαν εὐλόγως ἂν σκεπτοίμεθα
τὸ κινοῦν αὐτὴν καὶ πολυειδῶς μορφοῦν αἴτιον.

76 τοῦτο δὲ οὐκ ἄλλο τι πιθανόν ἐστιν εἶναι ἢ δύναμίν
τινα δι' αὐτῆς πεφοιτηκυῖαν, καθάπερ ἡμῖν ψυχὴ
πεφοίτηκεν. αὕτη οὖν ἡ δύναμις ἤτοι αὐτοκίνητός
ἐστιν ἢ ὑπὸ ἄλλης κινεῖται δυνάμεως. καὶ εἰ μὲν
ὑφ' ἑτέρας κινεῖται, τὴν ἑτέραν ἀδύνατον ἔσται[1]
κινεῖσθαι μὴ ὑπ' ἄλλης κινουμένην, ὅπερ ἄτοπον.
ἔστι τις ἄρα καθ' ἑαυτὴν αὐτοκίνητος δύναμις, ἥτις
ἂν εἴη θεία καὶ ἀίδιος. ἢ γὰρ ἐξ αἰῶνος κινήσεται
ἢ ἀπό τινος χρόνου. ἀλλ' ἀπό τινος χρόνου μὲν
οὐ κινήσεται· οὐ γὰρ ἔσται τις αἰτία τοῦ ἀπό
τινος αὐτὴν χρόνου κινεῖσθαι. ἀίδιος τοίνυν ἐστὶν
ἡ κινοῦσα τὴν ὕλην δύναμις καὶ τεταγμένως αὐτὴν
εἰς γενέσεις καὶ μεταβολὰς ἄγουσα. ὥστε θεὸς ἂν

77 εἴη αὕτη.　　καὶ ἔτι τὸ γεννητικὸν λογικοῦ καὶ
φρονίμου πάντως καὶ αὐτὸ λογικόν ἐστι καὶ

---

[1] ἔσται N, Mutsch.: εἶναι Bekk.

and if daemons exist, one must declare also that Gods exist, their existence being in no wise hindered by the preconception about the legendary doings in Hades.

Such, then, is the argument from the general and unanimous opinion about God ; and let us also con- 75 sider that which is based on the orderly arrangement of the Universe. The substance of existing things being of itself, they say, motionless and shapeless must be put in motion and shape by some cause ; and on account of this just as, when we behold some very beautiful piece of bronze-work, we are anxious to know who the craftsman is, since the material is of itself motionless, so also when we behold the matter of the Universe moving and existing in definite shape and orderly arrangement we shall naturally look for the cause which moves it and shapes it into various forms. And it is probable that this is nothing else 76 than some power which pervades it, even as our soul pervades ourselves. This power, then, is either self-moving or moved by some other power. And if it is moved by another power, it will not be possible for that other to be moved unless it is moved by a further power ; which is absurd. There exists, therefore, a power which is of itself self-moving, and this will be divine and eternal. For either it will be in motion from eternity or from some definite point of time. But it will not be in motion from a point of time ; for there will exist no cause of its motion from a given point of time. So then, the power which moves matter and subjects it to ordered forms of generation and change is eternal. Consequently this power will be God.—Moreover, that which generates what is rational 77 and wise is certainly itself both rational and wise ;

SEXTUS EMPIRICUS

φρόνιμον· ἡ δέ γε προειρημένη δύναμις ἀνθρώπους
πέφυκε κατασκευάζειν· λογικὴ τοίνυν καὶ φρονίμη
γενήσεται, ὅπερ ἦν θείας φύσεως. εἰσὶν ἄρα θεοί.

78 τῶν τε σωμάτων τὰ μέν ἐστιν ἡνωμένα τὰ δὲ
ἐκ συναπτομένων τὰ δὲ ἐκ διεστώτων. ἡνωμένα
μὲν οὖν ἐστὶ τὰ ὑπὸ μιᾶς ἕξεως κρατούμενα
καθάπερ φυτὰ καὶ ζῶα, ἐκ συναπτομένων δὲ τὰ
ἔκ τε παρακειμένων καὶ πρὸς ἕν τι κεφάλαιον
νευόντων συνεστῶτα ὡς ἁλύσεις καὶ πυργίσκοι καὶ
νῆες, ἐκ διεστώτων δὲ τὰ ἐκ διεζευγμένων καὶ [ἐκ]
κεχωρισμένων καὶ καθ' αὑτὰ ὑποκειμένων συγ-
79 κείμενα ὡς στρατιαὶ καὶ ποῖμναι καὶ χοροί. ἐπεὶ
οὖν καὶ ὁ κόσμος σῶμά ἐστιν, ἤτοι ἡνωμένον ἐστὶ
σῶμα ἢ ἐκ συναπτομένων ἢ ἐκ διεστώτων. οὔτε
δὲ ἐκ συναπτομένων οὔτε ἐκ διεστώτων, ὡς
δείκνυμεν ἐκ τῶν περὶ αὐτὸν συμπαθειῶν. κατὰ
γὰρ τὰς τῆς σελήνης αὐξήσεις καὶ φθίσεις πολλὰ
τῶν τε ἐπιγείων ζώων καὶ θαλασσίων φθίνει τε
καὶ αὔξεται, ἀμπώτεις τε καὶ πλημμυρίδες περί
τινα μέρη τῆς θαλάσσης γίνονται. ὡσαύτως δὲ
καὶ κατά τινας τῶν ἀστέρων ἐπιτολὰς καὶ δύσεις
μεταβολαὶ τοῦ περιέχοντος καὶ παμποίκιλοι περὶ
τὸν ἀέρα τροπαὶ συμβαίνουσιν, ὁτὲ μὲν ἐπὶ τὸ
κρεῖττον ὁτὲ δὲ λοιμικῶς. ἐξ ὧν συμφανὲς ὅτι
80 ἡνωμένον τι σῶμα καθέστηκεν ὁ κόσμος. ἐπὶ μὲν
γὰρ τῶν ἐκ συναπτομένων ἢ διεστώτων οὐ συμ-
πάσχει τὰ μέρη ἀλλήλοις, εἴγε ἐν στρατιᾷ πάντων,
εἰ τύχοι, διαφθαρέντων τῶν στρατιωτῶν οὐδὲν
κατὰ διάδοσιν πάσχειν φαίνεται ὁ περισωθείς· ἐπὶ

ᵃ Cf. Adv. Log. i. 102.
ᵇ For the Stoic use of ἕξις, "attraction" (lit. "holding"),

44

but the aforementioned power is of such a nature as to construct men ; therefore it will be rational and wise, and this is the mark of a divine nature.   Gods, therefore, exist.—Of bodies, too, some are unified, some 78 formed of things conjoined, some of separate things. Unified [a] bodies are such as are controlled by a single " attraction," [b] such as plants and animals ; those formed of conjoined parts are such as are composed of adjacent elements which tend to combine into one main structure, like cables and turrets and ships ; those formed of separate things are such as are compounded of things which are disjoined and isolated and existing by themselves, like armies and flocks and choruses. Seeing, then, that the Universe also is a body, it is 79 either unified or of conjoined or separate parts.   But it is neither of conjoined nor of separate parts, as we prove from the " sympathies " it exhibits.   For in accordance with the waxings and wanings of the moon many sea and land animals wane and wax, and ebb-tides and flood-tides occur in some parts of the sea.   And in the same way, too, in accordance with certain risings and settings of the stars alterations in the surrounding atmosphere and all varieties of change in the air take place, sometimes for the better, but sometimes fraught with pestilence.   And from these facts it is obvious that the Universe is a unified body.   For in the case of bodies formed from 80 conjoined or separate elements the parts do not " sympathize " with one another, since if all the soldiers, say, in an army have perished ⟨save one⟩ the one who survives is not seen to suffer at all through transmission ; but in the case of unified

to denote the principle of cohesion and unity in things inorganic see §§ 81 ff. *infra* ; *cf.* Vol. I. Introd. p. xxv.

SEXTUS EMPIRICUS

δὲ τῶν ἡνωμένων συμπάθειά τις ἔστιν, εἴγε δακτύλου τεμνομένου τὸ ὅλον συνδιατίθεται σῶμα.
ἡνωμένον τοίνυν ἐστὶ σῶμα καὶ ὁ κόσμος.
81 ἀλλ' ἐπεὶ τῶν ἡνωμένων σωμάτων τὰ μὲν ὑπὸ
ψιλῆς ἕξεως συνέχεται τὰ δὲ ὑπὸ φύσεως τὰ δὲ ὑπὸ
ψυχῆς, καὶ ἕξεως μὲν ὡς λίθοι καὶ ξύλα, φύσεως
δὲ καθάπερ τὰ φυτά, ψυχῆς δὲ τὰ ζῷα, πάντως δὴ
82 καὶ ὁ κόσμος ὑπό τινος τούτων διακρατεῖται. καὶ
ὑπὸ μὲν ψιλῆς ἕξεως οὐκ ἂν συνέχοιτο. τὰ γὰρ
ὑπὸ ἕξεως κρατούμενα οὐδεμίαν ἀξιόλογον μεταβολήν τε καὶ τροπὴν ἀναδέχεται, καθάπερ ξύλα
καὶ λίθοι, ἀλλὰ μόνον ἐξ αὐτῶν πάσχει τὴν κατὰ
83 ἄνεσιν καὶ τὴν κατὰ συμπιεσμὸν διάθεσιν. ὁ δὲ
κόσμος ἀξιολόγους ἀναδέχεται μεταβολάς, ὀτὲ μὲν
κρυμαλέου τοῦ περιέχοντος γιγνομένου ὀτὲ δὲ
ἀλεεινοῦ, καὶ ὀτὲ μὲν αὐχμώδους ὀτὲ δὲ νοτεροῦ,
ὀτὲ δὲ ἄλλως πως κατὰ τὰς τῶν οὐρανίων κινήσεις
ἑτεροιουμένου. οὐ τοίνυν ὑπὸ ψιλῆς ἕξεως ὁ
84 κόσμος συνέχεται. εἰ δὲ μὴ ὑπὸ ταύτης, πάντως
ὑπὸ φύσεως· καὶ γὰρ τὰ ὑπὸ ψυχῆς διακρατούμενα
πολὺ πρότερον ὑπὸ φύσεως συνείχετο. ἀνάγκη
ἄρα ὑπὸ τῆς ἀρίστης αὐτὸν φύσεως συνέχεσθαι,
ἐπεὶ καὶ περιέχει τὰς πάντων φύσεις. ἡ δέ γε τὰς
πάντων περιέχουσα φύσεις καὶ τὰς λογικὰς περι-
85 έσχηκεν. ἀλλὰ καὶ ἡ τὰς λογικὰς περιέχουσα
φύσεις πάντως ἐστὶ λογική· οὐ γὰρ οἷόν τε τὸ ὅλον
τοῦ μέρους χεῖρον εἶναι. ἀλλ' εἰ ἀρίστη ἐστὶ
φύσις ἡ τὸν κόσμον διοικοῦσα, νοερά τε ἔσται
καὶ σπουδαία καὶ ἀθάνατος. τοιαύτη δὲ τυγ-
86 χάνουσα θεός ἐστιν. εἰσὶν ἄρα θεοί. εἴπερ
τε ἐν γῇ καὶ θαλάσσῃ πολλῆς οὔσης παχυμερείας
ποικίλα συνίσταται ζῷα ψυχικῆς τε καὶ αἰσθητικῆς
46

bodies there exists a certain " sympathy," since, when the finger is cut, the whole body shares in its condition. So then, the Universe also is a unified body.—But since of unified bodies some 81 are held together by mere " attraction," others by organic structure, others by soul,—by attraction, like stones and sticks ; by organic structure, like plants ; and animals by soul,—the Universe also is certainly controlled by one of these. Now it will not 82 be held together by mere attraction. For the things controlled by attraction (such as sticks and stones) do not admit of any considerable alteration or change, but merely suffer the conditions produced by expansion or compression. But the Universe admits of con- 83 siderable alterations, as the atmosphere becomes at one time frosty, at another torrid, and at one time dry, at another damp, and at other times modified in other ways according to the motions of the heavenly bodies. So then, the Universe is not held together by mere attraction. But if not by this, then certainly 84 by organic structure ; for even the bodies which are controlled by soul were first of all held together by organic structure. Necessarily, then, it must be held together by the best structure, since it contains the structures of all things. But that which contains the 85 structures of all things contains also such as are rational ; and, moreover, that which contains the rational organic structures is certainly rational ; for it is not possible for the whole to be inferior to the part. But if that structure which governs the Universe is the best, it will be intelligent and virtuous and immortal. And being such, it is God. Therefore Gods exist.—Also, if there exist on the earth and 86 in the sea, which have very dense parts, a variety of

μετέχοντα δυνάμεως, πολλῷ πιθανώτερόν ἐστιν
ἐν τῷ ἀέρι, πολὺ τὸ καθαρὸν καὶ εἰλικρινὲς ἔχοντι
παρὰ τὴν γῆν καὶ τὸ ὕδωρ, ἔμψυχά τινα καὶ νοερὰ
συνίστασθαι ζῶα. καὶ τούτῳ συμφωνεῖ τὸ τοὺς
Διοσκούρους ἀγαθούς τινας εἶναι δαίμονας, σωτῆρας
εὐσέλμων νεῶν, καὶ τὸ

τρὶς γὰρ μύριοί εἰσιν ἐπὶ χθονὶ πουλυβοτείρῃ
ἀθάνατοι Ζηνὸς φύλακες μερόπων ἀνθρώπων.

87 ἀλλ' εἰ ἐν τῷ ἀέρι πιθανὸν ὑπάρχειν ζῷα, πάντως
εὔλογον καὶ ἐν τῷ αἰθέρι ζῴων εἶναι φύσιν, ὅθεν
καὶ ἄνθρωποι νοερᾶς μετέχουσι δυνάμεως, κἀκεῖθεν
αὐτὴν σπάσαντες. ὄντων δὲ αἰθερίων ζῴων, καὶ
κατὰ πολὺ τῶν ἐπιγείων ὑπερφέρειν δοκούντων τῷ
ἄφθαρτα εἶναι καὶ ἀγέννητα, δοθήσεται καὶ θεοὺς
ὑπάρχειν, τούτων μὴ διαφέροντας.

88 Ὁ δὲ Κλεάνθης οὕτως συνηρώτα. εἰ φύσις
φύσεώς ἐστι κρείττων, εἴη ἄν τις ἀρίστη φύσις· εἰ
ψυχὴ ψυχῆς ἐστι κρείττων, εἴη ἄν τις ἀρίστη ψυχή·
καὶ εἰ ζῷον τοίνυν κρεῖττόν ἐστι ζῴου, εἴη ἄν τι
κράτιστον ζῷον· οὐ γὰρ εἰς ἄπειρον ἐκπίπτειν
πέφυκε τὰ τοιαῦτα. ὡσπεροῦν οὔτε ἡ φύσις ἐδύνατο
ἐπ' ἄπειρον αὔξεσθαι κατὰ τὸ κρεῖττον οὔθ' ἡ ψυχὴ
89 ⟨οὕτως⟩ οὐδὲ[1] τὸ ζῷον. ἀλλὰ μὴν ζῷον ζῴου κρεῖττον
ἐστίν, ὡς ἵππος χελώνης, εἰ τύχοι, καὶ ταῦρος ὄνου
καὶ λέων ταύρου. πάντων δὲ σχεδὸν τῶν ἐπιγείων
ζῴων καὶ σωματικῇ καὶ ψυχικῇ διαθέσει προέχει
τε καὶ κρατιστεύει ὁ ἄνθρωπος· τοίνυν κράτιστον
90 ἂν εἴη ζῷον καὶ ἄριστον. καὶ οὐ πάνυ τι ὁ ἄν-

---

[1] ⟨οὕτως⟩ οὐδὲ Heintz: οὔτε mss., Bekk.

ᵃ Hesiod, *Works and Days*, 252 f.

animals which share in the faculties of soul and of sense, it is much more probable that there exist in the air (which, as compared with earth and water, is very clear and pure) some animals endowed with soul and intelligence. And in accord with this is the saying that the Dioscuri are good daemons, " saviours of well-benched ships," and that

> Zeus over mortal men, upon Earth the sustainer of many,
> Thrice ten thousand guardians has set, ⟨divine and⟩ immortal.[a]

But if it is probable that animals exist in the air, it is 87 certainly reasonable that animal organisms should also exist in the aether, from which men too derive their share of intellectual power, having drawn it from thence. And as ethereal animals exist, and are deemed to be far superior to terrestrial animals through being imperishable and unbegotten, it will be granted that Gods, which are no wise different from these, exist as well.

And Cleanthes argued thus : " If one nature is 88 better than another, there will be some best nature ; if one soul is better than another, there will be some best soul : if, then, one animal is better than another, there will be some best animal ; for such things are not of a kind to proceed *ad infinitum.* So then, as nature is not capable of increasing to infinity in goodness, nor soul, neither is the animal capable. One animal, however, is better than another, as (say) 89 the horse than the tortoise, and the bull than the ass, and the lion than the bull. And of all the terrestrial animals Man is the highest and best in respect of the disposition of both body and soul ; therefore a certain best and most excellent animal will exist. Yet Man cannot be absolutely the best 90

49

θρωπος κράτιστον εἶναι δύναται ζῶον, οἷον εὐθέως
ὅτι διὰ κακίας πορεύεται τὸν πάντα χρόνον, εἰ δὲ
μή γε, τὸν πλεῖστον (καὶ γὰρ εἴ ποτε περιγένοιτο
ἀρετῆς, ὀψὲ καὶ πρὸς ταῖς τοῦ βίου δυσμαῖς περιγίνεται), ἐπίκηρόν τ᾽ ἐστὶ καὶ ἀσθενὲς καὶ μυρίων
δεόμενον βοηθημάτων, καθάπερ τροφῆς καὶ σκεπα-
σμάτων καὶ τῆς ἄλλης τοῦ σώματος ἐπιμελείας,
πικροῦ τινὸς τυράννου τρόπον ἐφεστῶτος ἡμῖν καὶ
τὸν πρὸς ἡμέραν δασμὸν ἀπαιτοῦντος, καὶ εἰ μὴ
παρέχοιμεν ὥστε λούειν αὐτὸ καὶ ἀλείφειν καὶ
περιβάλλειν καὶ τρέφειν, νόσους καὶ θάνατον
ἀπειλοῦντος. ὥστε οὐ τέλειον ζῶον ὁ ἄνθρωπος,
91 ἀτελὲς δὲ καὶ πολὺ κεχωρισμένον τοῦ τελείου. τὸ
δὲ τέλειον καὶ ἄριστον κρεῖττον μὲν ἂν ὑπάρχοι
ἀνθρώπου καὶ πάσαις ταῖς ἀρεταῖς συμπεπληρωμένον καὶ παντὸς κακοῦ ἀνεπίδεκτον, τοῦτο δὲ
οὐ διοίσει θεοῦ. ἔστιν ἄρα θεός.

92 Ἀλλ᾽ ὁ μὲν Κλεάνθης ἐστὶ τοιοῦτος· ἠρώτησε δὲ
καὶ Ξενοφῶν ὁ Σωκρατικὸς λόγον εἰς τὸ εἶναι θεούς,
Σωκράτει περιθεὶς τὴν ἀπόδειξιν πρὸς τὸν Ἀριστό-
δημον ζητοῦντι, δι᾽ ὧν κατὰ λέξιν φησίν '' εἰπέ
μοι ὦ Ἀριστόδημε, εἰσὶν οὕς τινας ἐπὶ σοφίᾳ
τεθαύμακας; ἔγωγε, ἔφη. τίνες οὖν εἰσὶν οὗτοι;
ἐπὶ μὲν οὖν ποιητικῇ ἔγωγε Ὅμηρον τεθαύμακα,
ἐπὶ δὲ ἀνδριαντοποιίᾳ Πολύκλειτον, ζωγραφίας γε
93 μὴν χάριν Ζεῦξιν. τούτους οὖν ἀποδέχῃ οὐ διὰ
τὸ τὰ ὑπ᾽ αὐτῶν κατεσκευασμένα περισσῶς δεδημιουργῆσθαι; ἔγωγε, ἔφη. εἰ οὖν ὁ Πολυ-
κλείτου ἀνδριὰς καὶ ἐμψυχίαν προσλάβῃ, οὐ πολὺ
μᾶλλον ἀποδέξῃ τὸν τεχνίτην; καὶ μάλα. ἆρ᾽
οὖν ἀνδριάντα μὲν ὁρῶν ἔφης ὑπό τινος τεχνίτου
δεδημιουργῆσθαι, ἄνθρωπον δὲ ὁρῶν κατά τε

animal, because, for instance, he walks in wickedness all his life, or, if not, at least for the greater part of it (for if ever he attains virtue, he attains it late and at the setting of life's sun), and he is the victim of fate and feeble and in need of countless aids—such as food and coverings, and all the other requirements of the body, which stands over us like a rigorous tyrant and demands its daily tribute, and threatens us with disease and death unless we provide for its washing and anointing and clothing and feeding. So that Man is not a perfect animal, but imperfect and far removed from the perfect. But that which is 91 perfect and best will be better than Man and fulfilled with all the virtues and not receptive of any evil ; and this animal will not differ from God. God, therefore, exists."

Such, then, is the view of Cleanthes. Xenophon, 92 too, the Socratic, propounded an argument for the existence of Gods, ascribing the proof to Socrates, when in his interrogation of Aristodemus, he expresses himself in the following terms [a] : " Tell me, Aristodemus, are there any persons whom you have admired for their wisdom ? Yes, said he. Who then are they ? I have admired Homer for his poetry, Polycleitus for his statuary, Zeuxis of course for his painting.[b] Then is it not because of the superlative 93 craftsmanship of their productions that you approve of them ? Yes, said he. If, then, the statue of Polycleitus should also become alive, would you not approve of the artist far more ? Most certainly. Now, if when you saw a statue you said that it had been wrought by some artist, when you see a man

[a] See Xen. *Mem.* i. 4. 2.
[b] P. and Z. were famous Greek artists (*circa* 440–400 B.C.).

ψυχὴν εὖ κινούμενον καὶ κατὰ τὸ σῶμα εὖ κεκοσμη-
μένον οὐκ οἴει ὑπό τινος νοῦ περιττοῦ δεδημιουρ-
94 γῆσθαι; εἶτα δὲ ὁρῶν θέσιν τε καὶ χρῆσιν μερῶν,
πρῶτον μὲν ὅτι διανέστησε τὸν ἄνθρωπον, ὄμματά
γε μὴν ἔδωκεν ὥστε ὁρᾶν τὰ ὁρατά, ἀκοὴν δὲ ὥστε
ἀκούειν τὰ ἀκουστά. ὀσμῆς γε μὴν τί ἂν ἦν
ὄφελος, εἰ μὴ ῥῖνας προσέθηκεν, χυμῶν τε μὴν
ὁμοίως, εἰ μὴ γλῶσσα ἡ τούτων ἐπιγνώμων ἐν-
ειργάσθη; καὶ ταῦτα ” φησὶν “ εἰδὼς ὅτι γῆς τε
μέρος μικρὸν ἔχεις ἐν τῷ σώματι πολλῆς οὔσης,
ὑγροῦ τε μὴν βραχὺ πολλοῦ ὄντος, πυρὸς ἀέρος τε
ὁμοίως· νοῦν δὲ ἄρα μόνον οὐδαμοῦ ὄντα εὐτυχῶς
πόθεν δοκεῖς συναρπάσαι; ”

95 Τοιοῦτος μὲν οὖν ὁ τοῦ Ξενοφῶντός ἐστι λόγος,
δύναμίν γε ἐπαγωγικὴν ἔχων καὶ τοιαύτην. γῆς
πολλῆς οὔσης ἐν τῷ κόσμῳ μικρὸν μέρος ἔχεις, καὶ
ὑγροῦ πολλοῦ ὄντος ἐν τῷ κόσμῳ μικρὸν μέρος
ἔχεις· καὶ νοῦ ἄρα πολλοῦ ὄντος ἐν τῷ κόσμῳ
μικρὸν μέρος ἔχεις. νοερὸς ἄρα ὁ κόσμος ἐστίν,
96 καὶ διὰ τοῦτο θεός. παραβάλλουσι δέ τινες τῷ
λόγῳ τὰ λήμματα μεταποιοῦντες αὐτοῦ, καὶ φασί
“ γῆς πολλῆς οὔσης ἐν τῷ κόσμῳ μικρὸν μέρος
ἔχεις· ἀλλὰ καὶ ὑγροῦ πολλοῦ ὄντος ἐν τῷ κόσμῳ
μικρὸν μέρος ἔχεις, καὶ ἤδη ἀέρος καὶ πυρός· καὶ
πολλῆς ἄρα χολῆς οὔσης ἐν τῷ κόσμῳ μικρόν τι
μέρος ἔχεις, καὶ φλέγματος καὶ αἵματος.” ἀκο-

well disposed in soul and well equipped in body, do you not think that he has been wrought by some superexcellent mind? And when you observe 94 further the arrangement and function of his parts; and, in the first place, that he has made man upright, and has given him eyes that he may see what is visible and ears that he may hear what is audible. And of what use would smell have been if he had not also supplied him with nostrils, or flavours either if he had not had a tongue constructed within him which discerns them? And when you know also that you have in your body a small portion of the earth, of which so much exists, and a little of the water of which so much exists, and so likewise of fire and of air; from what source do you think that you have by good luck derived your mind, if it alone is nowhere existent?"

Such, then, is the argument of Xenophon; and the 95 inductive value which it has is this:—" Of the great quantity of earth which exists in the Universe you possess a small portion, and of the great quantity of water which exists in the Universe you possess a small portion; therefore, you also possess a small portion of the mind which exists in the Universe in large quantity. Therefore the Universe is intelligent, and consequently is God." But some meet this with a 96 parallel argument, by altering its premisses, and say —" Of the great quantity of earth which exists in the Universe you possess a small portion; but also of the great quantity of water existing in the Universe you possess a small portion, and also of air and fire; therefore you possess also a small portion of the great quantity of gall existing in the Universe, and phlegm and blood. It will follow, therefore, that the Universe

λουθήσει καὶ χολοποιὸν καὶ αἵματος γεννητικὸν
97 εἶναι τὸν κόσμον· ὅπερ ἐστὶν ἄτοπον. οἱ δὲ ἀπο-
λογούμενοί φασιν ἀνόμοιον εἶναι τὴν παραβολὴν τῷ
Ξενοφῶντος λόγῳ. ἐκεῖνος μὲν γὰρ ἐπὶ τῶν ἁπλῶν
καὶ πρώτων σωμάτων ποιεῖται τὴν ζήτησιν, ὥσπερ
γῆς καὶ ὕδατος ἀέρος τε καὶ πυρός, οἱ δὲ τῇ παρα-
βολῇ χρώμενοι μετεπήδησαν ὡς ἐπὶ τὰ συγκρίματα·
χολὴ γὰρ καὶ αἷμα καὶ πᾶν τὸ ἐν τοῖς σώμασιν
ὑγρὸν οὐκ ἔστι πρῶτον καὶ ἁπλοῦν ἀλλ᾽ ἐκ τῶν
πρώτων καὶ στοιχειωδῶν σωμάτων συγκείμενον.
98 Ἔνεστι δὲ καὶ οὕτως τὸν αὐτὸν συνερωτᾶν λόγον.
εἰ μὴ ἦν τι γεῶδες ἐν τῷ κόσμῳ, οὐδὲ ἐν σοί τι ἂν
ἦν γεῶδες, καὶ εἰ μὴ ἦν τι ὑγρὸν ἐν κόσμῳ, οὐδ᾽
ἂν ἐν σοὶ ἦν τι ὑγρόν, καὶ ὁμοίως ἐπὶ ἀέρος καὶ
πυρός. τοίνυν καὶ εἰ μὴ ἦν τις ἐν κόσμῳ νοῦς,
οὐδ᾽ ἂν ἐν σοί τις ἦν νοῦς· ἔστι δέ γε ἐν σοί τις
νοῦς· ἔστιν ἄρα καὶ ἐν κόσμῳ. καὶ διὰ τοῦτο
νοερός ἐστιν ὁ κόσμος. νοερὸς δὲ ὢν καὶ θεὸς
99 καθέστηκεν.   τῆς δὲ αὐτῆς δυνάμεώς ἐστι καὶ
ὁ τοῦτον τὸν τρόπον ἔχων λόγος. ἆρά γε ἄγαλμα
εὖ δεδημιουργημένον θεασάμενος διστάσειας ἂν εἰ
τεχνίτης νοῦς τοῦτο ἐποίησεν; ἢ οὐ τοσοῦτον[1] ἂν
ἀπόσχοις τοῦ ὑπονοεῖν τι τοιοῦτον ὡς καὶ θαυμάζειν
τὴν περιττότητα τῆς δημιουργίας καὶ τὴν τέχνην;
100 ἆρ᾽ οὖν ἐπὶ μὲν τούτων τὸν ἔξωθεν θεωρῶν τύπον
προσμαρτυρεῖς τῷ κατεσκευακότι καὶ φὴς εἶναί
τινα τὸν δημιουργόν· τὸν δὲ ἐν σοὶ ὁρῶν νοῦν,
τοσαύτῃ ποικιλίᾳ διαφέροντα παντὸς ἀγάλματος
καὶ πάσης γραφῆς, γεννητὸν ὄντα νομίζεις ἀπὸ
τύχης γεγονέναι, οὐχὶ δὲ ὑπό τινος δημιουργοῦ

_____
[1] οὐ τοσοῦτον] οὔτ᾽ Bekk.: οὕτως N, Mutsch.: τοσοῦτον
cj. Bekk.

is gall-making and productive of blood ; which is absurd." But others allege in defence that this 97 parallel argument is not similar to the argument of Xenophon. For whereas he bases his inquiry on the simple and primary bodies,—such as earth and water and air and fire,—those who employ the parallel argument jump aside to compounds ; for neither gall nor blood nor any bodily fluid is primary and simple, but a compound of the primary and elemental bodies.

It is also possible to propound the same argument 98 in this form : " If there had not been something earthy in the Universe, there would not have been anything earthy in you ; and if there had not been something fluid in the Universe, there would not have been anything fluid in you ; and so likewise with air and fire. Hence, too, if there had not been some mind in the Universe, there would not have been any mind in you ; but there is mind in you. And because of this the Universe is rational ; and being rational, it is also God."—To the same effect is the argument which is 99 put in this form :—" If you saw a statue which was well wrought would you be in doubt as to whether an artistic intelligence had made it ? Or would you not be so far from having any such suspicions that you would actually admire the excellence of its workmanship and its artistic quality ? If then, in such cases, 100 when you behold the external form you take it as evidence of a constructor and assert that there exists a craftsman who made it,—when you see the mind within yourself, which is so far superior in its intricacy to any statue or any painting, do you suppose that it came into being as the creation of chance and not by

SEXTUS EMPIRICUS

δύναμιν καὶ σύνεσιν ὑπερβάλλουσαν ἔχοντος;
ὅσπερ οὐκ ἂν ἄλλοθί που διατρίβοι ἢ ἐν τῷ κόσμῳ,
διοικῶν αὐτὸν καὶ τὰ ἐν αὐτῷ γεννῶν τε καὶ αὔξων.
οὗτος δέ ἐστι θεός· εἰσὶν ἄρα θεοί.

101 Ζήνων δὲ ὁ Κιτιεὺς ἀπὸ Ξενοφῶντος τὴν ἀφ-
ορμὴν λαβὼν οὑτωσὶ συνερωτᾷ. τὸ προϊέμενον
σπέρμα λογικοῦ καὶ αὐτὸ λογικόν ἐστιν· ὁ δὲ
κόσμος προΐεται σπέρμα λογικοῦ· λογικὸν ἄρα
ἐστὶν ὁ κόσμος. ᾧ συνεισάγεται καὶ ἡ τούτου
102 ὕπαρξις. καὶ ἔστιν ἡ τῆς συνερωτήσεως πιθανότης
προὖπτος. πάσης γὰρ φύσεως καὶ ψυχῆς ἡ
καταρχὴ τῆς κινήσεως γίνεσθαι δοκεῖ ἀπὸ ἡγεμονικοῦ, καὶ πᾶσαι αἱ ἐπὶ τὰ μέρη τοῦ ὅλου
ἐξαποστελλόμεναι δυνάμεις ὡς ἀπό τινος πηγῆς
τοῦ ἡγεμονικοῦ ἐξαποστέλλονται, ὥστε πᾶσαν
δύναμιν τὴν περὶ τὸ μέρος οὖσαν καὶ περὶ τὸ ὅλον
εἶναι διὰ τὸ ἀπὸ τοῦ ἐν αὐτῷ ἡγεμονικοῦ δια-
δίδοσθαι. ὅθεν οἷόν ἐστι τὸ μέρος τῇ δυνάμει,
103 τοιοῦτον πολὺ πρότερόν ἐστι τὸ ὅλον. καὶ διὰ
τοῦτο εἰ προΐεται λογικοῦ ζῴου σπέρμα ὁ κόσμος,
οὐχ ὡς τὸν ἄνθρωπον κατὰ ἀποβρασμόν, ἀλλὰ καθὸ
περιέχει σπέρματα λογικῶν ζῴων· περιέχει ⟨δὲ⟩[1]
[τὸ πᾶν], οὐχ ὡς ἂν εἴποιμεν τὴν ἄμπελον γιγάρ-
των εἶναι περιεκτικήν, τουτέστι κατὰ περιγραφήν,
ἀλλ᾿ ὅτι λόγοι σπερματικοὶ λογικῶν ζῴων ἐν αὐτῷ
περιέχονται. ὥστε εἶναι τοιοῦτο τὸ λεγόμενον '' ὁ
δέ γε κόσμος περιέχει σπερματικοὺς[2] λόγους λογικῶν
ζῴων· λογικὸς ἄρα ἐστὶν ὁ κόσμος.''

[1] ⟨δὲ⟩ add. cj. Bekk., [τὸ πᾶν] secl. cj. Heintz.
[2] σπερματικοὺς cj. Bekk.: σπέρματος mss., Bekk.

[a] For this Stoic term see Vol. I. Introd. p. xxv.

some craftsman possessed of power and intelligence to a superlative degree ? And he can dwell nowhere else save in the Universe, governing it and generating and increasing the things that are therein. And this person is a God ; therefore Gods exist."

And Zeno of Citium, taking Xenophon as his start-101 ing-point, argues thus :—" That which projects the seed of the rational is itself rational : but the Universe projects the seed of the rational ; therefore the Universe is rational. And thereby the existence thereof is also concluded." The plausibility of this 102 argument is obvious. For the origin of motion in every nature and soul seems to come from " the regent part," [a] and all the powers that are sent forth into the parts of the whole are sent forth from the regent part as from a fount, so that every power which exists in the part exists also in the whole owing to its being distributed from its regent part. Hence, what the part is in point of power, that the whole must certainly be first. Consequently, if the Uni-103 verse projects the seed of a rational animal, it does not do so, like man, by frothy emission, but as containing the seeds of rational animals ; but it does not contain them in the same way as we might speak of the vine " containing " its grapes,—that is, by way of inclusion,—but because the " seminal reasons "[b] of rational animals are contained in it. So that the argument is this—" The Universe contains the seminal reasons of rational animals ; therefore the Universe is rational."

[b] According to Stoic doctrine the Universal Reason (Logos) is present in particular things as their vital formative principle, and these pluralizations of Reason are termed " seminal reasons "; cf. Vol. I. Introd. p. xxiv.

SEXTUS EMPIRICUS

104 Καὶ πάλιν ὁ Ζήνων φησίν, " [εἰ] τὸ λογικὸν τοῦ
μὴ λογικοῦ κρεῖττον ἐστίν· οὐδὲν δέ γε κόσμου
κρεῖττον ἐστίν· λογικὸν ἄρα ὁ κόσμος. καὶ
ὡσαύτως ἐπὶ τοῦ νοεροῦ καὶ ἐμψυχίας μετέχοντος.
τὸ γὰρ νοερὸν τοῦ μὴ νοεροῦ καὶ τὸ ἔμψυχον τοῦ
μὴ ἐμψύχου κρεῖττον ἐστίν· οὐδὲν δέ γε κόσμου
κρεῖττον· νοερὸς ἄρα καὶ ἔμψυχός ἐστιν ὁ κόσμος."
105 Κεῖται δὲ καὶ παρὰ τῷ Πλάτωνι τῇ δυνάμει
τοιοῦτος λόγος, κατὰ λέξιν αὐτοῦ γράφοντος
" λέγωμεν δὴ δι᾽ ἣν αἰτίαν γένεσιν καὶ πᾶν τόδε
ὁ συνιστὰς συνέστησεν. ἀγαθὸς ἦν, ἀγαθῷ δὲ
οὐδὲ εἷς περὶ οὐδενὸς ἐγγίνεται φθόνος. τούτου
δὴ ἐκτὸς ὢν πάντα ὅσα μάλιστα ἐβουλήθη γίγνεσθαι παραπλήσια ἑαυτῷ. ταύτην δὲ γενέσεως καὶ
κόσμου μάλιστα ἄν τις ἀρχὴν κυριωτάτην παρὰ
ἀνδρῶν φρονίμων ἀποδεχόμενος ὀρθότατα ἀπο-
106 δέχοιτο ἄν." εἶτ᾽ ὀλίγα διελθὼν ἐπιφέρει λέγων
" διὰ δὴ τὸν λογισμὸν τόνδε νοῦν μὲν ἐν ψυχῇ ψυχὴν
δὲ ἐν τῷ σώματι συνιστὰς τὸ πᾶν συνετεκταίνετο,
⟨ὅπως⟩¹ ὅ τι κάλλιστον ἂν εἴη κατὰ φύσιν ἄριστον
τε² ἔργον ἀπειργασμένος. οὕτως οὖν δὴ κατὰ
λόγον τὸν εἰκότα δεῖ λέγειν τόνδε τὸν κόσμον ζῷον
ἔμψυχον ἔννουν τε τῇ ἀληθείᾳ διὰ τὸ τῇ θεοῦ
107 γενέσθαι προνοίᾳ." δυνάμει δὲ τὸν αὐτὸν τῷ
Ζήνωνι λόγον ἐξέθετο· καὶ γὰρ οὗτος τὸ πᾶν κάλλιστον εἶναί φησι, κατὰ φύσιν ἀπειργασμένον ἔργον
καὶ κατὰ τὸν εἰκότα λόγον ζῷον ἔμψυχον νοερόν
τε καὶ λογικόν.

¹ ⟨ὅπως⟩ add. e Plat. Mutsch.
² τε sec. Plat., Heintz: τὸ mss., Bekk.

ᵃ Plato, Timaeus 29 D ff.

And Zeno says again : " The rational is better than 104
the non-rational ; but nothing is better than the Universe ; therefore the Universe is rational. And so
likewise with the intelligent and that which partakes
of animation ; for the intelligent is better than the
non-intelligent and the animate than the non-animate ; but nothing is better than the Universe ;
therefore the Universe is intelligent and animate."

A similar argument is stated by Plato, where he 105
writes in these terms [a] :—" Let us declare the cause
wherefor he that constructed constructed Becoming
and this All. He was good and in him that is good
there is no envy concerning anything. And being
devoid of envy, he desired that all things should be,
so far as possible, like unto himself. This principle,
then, we shall be wholly right in accepting from men
of wisdom as being above all the supreme originating
principle of Becoming and the Cosmos." Then, after 106
a few further remarks, he goes on to say—" So because of this reflection he constructed reason within
soul and soul within body as he fashioned the All, that
so the work he was executing might be of its nature
most fair and most good. Thus, then, in accordance
with the likely account, we must declare that this
Cosmos is verily a living creature endowed with soul
and reason because it has come into existence through
the providence of God." Thus Plato has set out 107
virtually the same argument as Zeno ; for the former
also asserts that " the All is most fair, being a work
executed according to nature and according to the
likely account a living creature endowed with soul,
both intelligent and rational."

108 Ἀλλ' ὅ γε Ἀλεξῖνος τῷ Ζήνωνι παρέβαλε τρόπῳ
τῷδε. τὸ ποιητικὸν τοῦ μὴ ποιητικοῦ καὶ τὸ
γραμματικὸν τοῦ μὴ γραμματικοῦ κρεῖττον ἐστί,
καὶ τὸ κατὰ τὰς ἄλλας τέχνας θεωρούμενον κρεῖττόν ἐστι τοῦ μὴ τοιούτου· οὐδὲ ἓν δὲ κόσμου
κρεῖττον ἐστίν· ποιητικὸν ἄρα καὶ γραμματικόν
109 ἐστιν ὁ κόσμος. πρὸς ἣν ἀπαντῶντες παραβολὴν
οἱ στωικοί φασιν ὅτι Ζήνων τὸ καθάπαξ κρεῖττον
εἴληφεν, τουτέστι τὸ λογικὸν τοῦ μὴ λογικοῦ καὶ
τὸ νοερὸν τοῦ μὴ νοεροῦ καὶ τὸ ἔμψυχον τοῦ μὴ
110 ἐμψύχου, ὁ δὲ Ἀλεξῖνος οὐκέτι· οὐ γὰρ ἐν τῷ
καθάπαξ τὸ ποιητικὸν τοῦ μὴ ποιητικοῦ καὶ τὸ
γραμματικὸν τοῦ μὴ γραμματικοῦ κρεῖττον. ὥστε
μεγάλην ἐν τοῖς λόγοις θεωρεῖσθαι διαφοράν· ἰδοὺ
γὰρ Ἀρχίλοχος ποιητικὸς ὢν οὐκ ἔστι Σωκράτους
τοῦ μὴ ποιητικοῦ κρείττων, καὶ Ἀρίσταρχος
γραμματικὸς ὢν οὐκ ἔστι Πλάτωνος τοῦ μὴ
γραμματικοῦ κρείττων.

111 Πρὸς τούτοις καὶ ἀπὸ τῆς τοῦ κόσμου κινήσεως
ἐπιχειροῦσι κατασκευάζειν τὴν τῶν θεῶν ὕπαρξιν
οἵ τε ἀπὸ τῆς στοᾶς καὶ οἱ τούτοις συμπνέοντες.
ὅτι γὰρ κινεῖται ὁ κόσμος πᾶς ἄν τις ὁμολογήσειεν
112 ὑπὸ πολλῶν εἰς τοῦτο ἐναγόμενος. ἤτοι οὖν ὑπὸ
φύσεως κινεῖται ἢ ὑπὸ προαιρέσεως ἢ ὑπὸ δίνης
καὶ κατ' ἀνάγκην. ἀλλ' ὑπὸ μὲν δίνης καὶ κατ'
ἀνάγκην οὐκ εὔλογον. ἤτοι γὰρ ἄτακτός ἐστιν ἢ
διατεταγμένη ἡ δίνη. καὶ εἰ μὲν ἄτακτος, οὐκ ἂν
δυνηθείη τεταγμένως τι κινεῖν· εἰ δὲ μετὰ τάξεώς

ᵃ A. was a disciple of Eubulides, the Megaric philosopher,
and a contemporary of Zeno the Stoic (*circa* 300 B.C.); *cf.*
Vol. I. Introd. p. xvi.

But Alexinus [a] opposed Zeno with a parallel argu- 108 ment in this form :—" The poetic is better than the non-poetical and the grammatical than the non-grammatical, and the artistic product of the other arts than the inartistic ; but nothing is better than the Universe ; therefore the Universe is poetical and grammatical." But in answer to this counter-argu- 109 ment the Stoics say that, whereas Zeno has chosen what is absolutely better—that is, the rational than the non-rational, and the intelligent than the non-intelligent and the animate than the non-animate,— Alexinus has not done so ; for the poetic is not 110 absolutely better than the non-poetic or the grammatical than the non-grammatical. So that we observe a great difference between the two arguments ; for notice how Archilochus who is poetical is not better than the non-poetical Socrates, and Aristarchus [b] who is grammatical is not better than the non-grammatical Plato.

Furthermore, the Stoics and their supporters try to 111 demonstrate the existence of the Gods from the motion of the Universe. For that the Universe is in motion everyone will admit, being driven thereto by many things. It is moved, then, either by nature or 112 by will or by vortex [c] and of necessity. But that ⟨it is moved⟩ by vortex and of necessity is not probable. For the vortex is either disorderly or orderly. And if it is disorderly, it will not be able to move anything in an orderly way ; but if it moves anything in a way

[b] Archilochus of Paros was an iambic poet *circa* 700 B.C. Aristarchus was a famous grammarian and literary critic at Alexandria, *circa* 150 B.C. In these §§ 108-110 " grammatical " means " possessed of the grammarian's art."

[c] In the doctrine of Democritus " vortex " (δίνη) was the name for the whirling force giving spiral motion to the atoms.

SEXTUS EMPIRICUS

τι κινεῖ καὶ συμφωνίας, θεία τις ἔσται καὶ δαιμόνιος·
113 οὐ γὰρ ἄν ποτε τεταγμένως καὶ σωτηρίως τὸ ὅλον
ἐκίνει μὴ νοερὰ καὶ θεία καθεστῶσα. τοιαύτη δὲ
οὖσα οὐκέτι ἂν εἴη δίνη· ἄτακτον γάρ ἐστιν αὕτη
καὶ ὀλιγοχρόνιον. ὥστε κατ' ἀνάγκην μὲν καὶ
ὑπὸ δίνης, ὡς ἔλεγον οἱ περὶ τὸν Δημόκριτον, οὐκ
114 ἂν κινοῖτο ὁ κόσμος. καὶ μὴν οὐδὲ φύσει ἀφαν-
τάστῳ, παρόσον ἡ νοερὰ φύσις ἀμείνων ἐστὶ ταύτης.
ὁρῶνται δὲ τοιαῦται φύσεις ἐν κόσμῳ περιεχόμεναι·
ἀνάγκη ἄρα καὶ αὐτὸν νοερὰν ἔχειν φύσιν ὑφ' ἧς
τεταγμένως κινεῖται, ἥτις εὐθέως ἐστὶ θεός.
115 Τά γε μὴν αὐτομάτως κινούμενα τῶν κατα-
σκευασμάτων θαυμαστότερά ἐστι τῶν μὴ τοιούτων.
τὴν γοῦν Ἀρχιμήδειον σφαῖραν σφόδρα θεωροῦντες
ἐκπληττόμεθα, ἐν ᾗ ἥλιός τε καὶ σελήνη κινεῖται
καὶ τὰ λοιπὰ τῶν ἀστέρων, οὐ μὰ Δία ἐπὶ τοῖς
ξύλοις οὐδ' ἐπὶ τῇ κινήσει τούτων τεθηπότες, ἀλλ'
ἐπὶ τῷ τεχνίτῃ καὶ ταῖς κινούσαις αἰτίαις. ὅθεν
ὅσῳ θαυμασιώτερά ἐστι τὰ αἰσθανόμενα τῶν
αἰσθητῶν, τοσούτῳ θαυμασιώτεραί εἰσιν αἱ ταῦτα
116 κινοῦσαι αἰτίαι. ἐπεὶ γὰρ ὁ ἵππος θαυμασιώτερος
τοῦ φυτοῦ, καὶ ἡ κινητικὴ τοῦ ἵππου αἰτία θαυμασιωτέρα τῆς τοῦ φυτοῦ αἰτίας· καὶ ἐπεὶ ὁ ἐλέφας
θαυμασιώτερος ἵππου, καὶ ἡ κινητικὴ τοῦ ἐλέφαντος
αἰτία, τηλικοῦτόν γε ὄγκον διαβαστάζουσα, θαυμα-
117 σιωτέρα τῆς τοῦ ἵππου. τούτων δέ γε πασῶν κατὰ
τὸν ἀνωτάτω λόγον καὶ ἡ τοῦ ἡλίου καὶ σελήνης
καὶ ἀστέρων, καὶ πρὸ τούτων ἡ τοῦ κόσμου φύσις,
ἥτις καὶ τούτων ἐστὶν αἰτία. ἡ μὲν γὰρ τοῦ μέρους

---

that is orderly and harmonious, it will be divine and supernatural ; for it would never have moved the 113 whole in an orderly and conserving way had it not been intelligent and divine. And if it is such, it will no longer be vortex ; for this is disorderly and of short duration. So that the Universe will not be moved of necessity and by vortex, as Democritus said. Nor yet 114 by a non-perceptive nature, inasmuch as the intelligent nature is superior to this ; and such natures are seen to be contained in the Universe ; of necessity, therefore, it must itself possess an intelligent nature by which it is moved in an orderly way, and this indubitably is God.

Moreover, constructions which move of their own 115 accord are more marvellous than other kinds. Thus when we behold an Archimedean sphere [a] in which the sun and moon and all the other stars are in motion, we are immensely struck by it—not, to be sure, because we are amazed at the woodwork or at the motion of these bodies, but at the artificer and the causes of the motion. Hence in the degree that percipients are more marvellous than things perceived, in the same degree the causes which move the former are the more marvellous. For since the horse is more 116 marvellous than the plant, the moving cause of the horse is more marvellous than that of the plant ; and since the elephant is more marvellous than the horse, the moving cause of the elephant, which transports so huge a bulk, is more marvellous than that of the horse ; and—to rise to the highest kinds—⟨more 117 marvellous⟩ than all the foregoing are the moving causes of the sun and moon and stars, and still more than these that which is their cause, the nature of the Universe. For the cause of the part does not extend

63

αἰτία οὐ διατείνει ἐπὶ τὸ ὅλον, οὐδ' ἔστι τούτου
αἰτία, ἡ δὲ τοῦ ὅλου διατέτακεν εἰς τὰ μέρη· διὸ
καὶ θαυμασιωτέρα ἐστὶ τῆς τοῦ μέρους αἰτίας.
118 ὥστε ἐπεὶ ἡ τοῦ κόσμου φύσις ἐστὶν αἰτία τῆς
τοῦ ὅλου κόσμου διακοσμήσεως, εἴη ἂν αἰτία καὶ
τῶν μερῶν. εἰ δὲ τοῦτο, κρατίστη ἐστίν. εἰ δὲ
κρατίστη ἐστί, λογική τέ ἐστι καὶ νοερά, προσέτι
δὲ ἀΐδιος ἂν εἴη. ἡ δὲ τοιαύτη φύσις ἡ αὐτή ἐστι
θεῷ. ἔστι τοίνυν τι θεός.

119   Καὶ μὴν ἐν παντὶ πολυμερεῖ σώματι καὶ κατὰ
φύσιν διοικουμένῳ ἔστι τι τὸ κυριεῦον, καθὸ καὶ
ἐφ' ἡμῶν μὲν ἢ ἐν καρδίᾳ τοῦτο τυγχάνειν ἀξιοῦται
ἢ ἐν ἐγκεφάλῳ ἢ ἐν ἄλλῳ τινὶ μέρει τοῦ σώματος,
ἐπὶ δὲ τῶν φυτῶν οὐ κατὰ τὸν αὐτὸν τρόπον, ἀλλ'
ἐφ' ὧν μὲν κατὰ τὰς ῥίζας ἐφ' ὧν δὲ κατὰ τὴν
120 κόμην ἐφ' ὧν δὲ κατὰ τὸν ἐγκάρδιον. ὥστε ἐπεὶ
καὶ ὁ κόσμος ὑπὸ φύσεως διοικεῖται πολυμερὴς
καθεστώς, εἴη ἄν τι ἐν αὐτῷ τὸ κυριεῦον καὶ τὸ
προκαταρχόμενον τῶν κινήσεων. οὐδὲν δὲ δυνατὸν
εἶναι τοιοῦτον ἢ τὴν τῶν ὄντων φύσιν, ἥτις θεός
ἐστιν. ἔστιν ἄρα θεός.

121   Ἀλλ' ἴσως τινὲς ἐροῦσιν ὅτι τούτῳ τῷ λόγῳ
ἡγεμονικωτάτην εἶναι συμβέβηκε καὶ κυριωτάτην
ἐν τῷ κόσμῳ τὴν γῆν καὶ ⟨ἔτι⟩[1] ἡγεμονικώτερον
καὶ κυριώτερον τὸν ἀέρα· ἄνευ γὰρ τούτων οὐχ
οἷόν τέ ἐστι συστῆναι κόσμον. ὥστε καὶ τὴν γῆν
122 καὶ τὸν ἀέρα φήσομεν εἶναι θεόν. ὅπερ ἐστὶν
εὔηθες, καὶ ὅμοιον τῷ λέγειν κυριώτατον ἐν τῇ
οἰκίᾳ καὶ ἡγεμονικώτατον εἶναι τὸν τοῖχον· ἄνευ

---

[1] ⟨ἔτι⟩ add. cj. Bekk.

64

to the whole, nor is it the cause thereof, but that of the whole extends to the parts ; wherefore also it is more marvellous than the cause of the part. So that 118 since the nature of the Universe is the cause of the ordering of the whole Universe, it will also be the cause of the parts. And if so, it is most excellent. And if it is most excellent, it is both rational and intelligent, and besides it will be eternal. But such a nature is identical with God. Therefore God is something existent.

Further, in every multipartite body which is 119 regulated by nature[a] there exists some ruling element, even as in our case this is said to exist either in the heart or in the brain or in some other part of the body[b] ; and in the case of plants in a different way,— in some cases in the roots, in others in the leaves, in others again in the central core. Consequently, 120 since the Universe also is multipartite and regulated by nature, there will exist in it an element which rules and originates its motions. And this can be nothing else than the nature of existing things, which is God. God therefore exists.

But perhaps some will say that the result of this 121 argument is that the earth is a most dominant and ruling force in the Universe, and even more dominant and ruling is the air ; for without these it is not possible for the Universe to subsist ; so that we shall assert that both the earth and the air are God. But 122 this is silly, and much like saying that the wall is the most dominant and ruling thing in the house ; for

---

[a] *i.e.* " nature " ($\phi\acute{v}\sigma\iota\varsigma$), or " organic structure," as distinct from " attraction " ($\mathring{\varepsilon}\xi\iota\varsigma$) ; *cf.* § 81 *supra*. The " multipartite body " is an " organism."

[b] *Cf. Adv. Log.* i. 313.

γὰρ τούτου μὴ δύνασθαι τὴν οἰκίαν συστῆναι.
καθάπερ γὰρ ἐνταῦθα ταῖς μὲν ἀληθείαις ἀδύνατόν
ἐστιν ἄνευ τοίχου συστῆναι τὴν οἰκίαν, οὐ μὴν
ὑπερφέρει καὶ κρεῖττόν ἐστι τοῦ οἰκοδεσπότου ὁ
τοῖχος, οὕτω καὶ ἐπὶ τοῦ κόσμου ἀδύνατον μὲν
χωρὶς γῆς καὶ ἀέρος τὴν τοῦ παντὸς σύστασιν
γενέσθαι, οὐ μὴν ταῦτα ὑπερφέρει τῆς διοικούσης
τὸν κόσμον φύσεως, ἥτις οὐ διενήνοχε θεοῦ. ἔστιν
ἄρα θεός.

Τὸ μὲν οὖν γένος τῶν τοιούτων λόγων ἐστὶ
123 τοιοῦτον· σκοπῶμεν δὲ ἑξῆς καὶ τὸν τρόπον τῶν
ἀκολουθούντων ἀτόπων τοῖς ἀναιροῦσι τὸ θεῖον.
εἰ γὰρ μὴ εἰσὶ θεοί, οὐκ ἔστιν εὐσέβεια [μόνον τῶν
αἱρετῶν]¹ ὑπάρχουσα. ἔστι γὰρ εὐσέβεια ἐπιστήμη
θεῶν θεραπείας, τῶν δ' ἀνυπάρκτων οὐ δύναταί τις
εἶναι θεραπεία, ὅθεν οὐδὲ ἐπιστήμη τις περὶ ταύτην γενήσεται· καὶ ὡς οὐχ οἷόν τε περὶ τὴν τῶν
ἱπποκενταύρων θεραπείαν ἐπιστήμην εἶναι ἀνυπάρκτων ὄντων, οὕτως οὐδὲ περὶ τὴν τῶν θεῶν θεραπείαν, εἴπερ εἰσὶν ἀνύπαρκτοι, ἔσται τις ἐπιστήμη.
ὥστε εἰ μὴ εἰσὶ θεοί, ἀνύπαρκτός ἐστιν ἡ εὐσέβεια.
ὑπάρχει δὲ εὐσέβεια· τοίνυν ῥητέον εἶναι θεούς.
124   καὶ πάλιν, εἰ μὴ εἰσὶ θεοί, ἀνύπαρκτός ἐστιν
ἡ ὁσιότης, δικαιοσύνη τις οὖσα πρὸς θεούς· ἔστι δέ
γε κατὰ τὰς κοινὰς ἐννοίας καὶ προλήψεις πάντων
ἀνθρώπων ὁσιότης, καθό τι καὶ ὅσιόν ἐστιν· καὶ τὸ
125 θεῖον ἄρα ἔστιν.   εἴγε μὴν μὴ εἰσὶ θεοί, ἀναιρεῖται
σοφία, ἐπιστήμη οὖσα θείων τε καὶ ἀνθρωπείων
πραγμάτων· καὶ ὃν τρόπον οὐδεμία ἔστιν ἐπιστήμη
ἀνθρωπείων τε καὶ ἱπποκενταυρείων πραγμάτων
διὰ τὸ ἀνθρώπους μὲν ὑπάρχειν ἱπποκενταύρους δὲ
μὴ ὑπάρχειν, οὕτως οὐδὲ ἐπιστήμη τις ἔσται θείων

without it the house cannot subsist. For just as, in this case, although the house cannot in fact subsist without the wall, yet the wall does not overrule and is not better than the master of the house,—so also in the case of the Universe, although it is impossible for the structure of the Whole to exist without earth and air, yet these do not overrule the nature which regulates the Universe ; and this does not differ from God. God, therefore, exists.

Such, then, is the general character of these arguments. Next let us consider the nature of the absurd 123 consequences of abolishing Divinity. If Gods do not exist, piety is not existent. For piety is " the science of service to the Gods," and there cannot be any service of things non-existent, nor, consequently, will any science thereof exist ; and just as there cannot be any science of service to Hippocentaurs, they being non-existent, so there will not be any science of service to the Gods if they are non-existent. So that, if Gods do not exist, piety is non-existent. But piety exists ; so we must declare that Gods exist.— Again, if Gods do not exist, holiness is non-existent, 124 it being " a kind of God-ward justice " ; but according to the common notions and preconceptions of all men holiness exists, and because of this a holy thing also exists ; and therefore the Divine exists.—If, 125 however, Gods do not exist, wisdom is abolished, it being " the science of things both divine and human " ; and just as there is no science of things both human and Hippocentaurean owing to the fact that men exist but Hippocentaurs do not exist, so too there will

---

¹ [μόνον τῶν αἱρ.] secl. ego: μία τῶν ἀρετῶν cj. Bekk.: [μόνον . . . ὑπάρχ.] secl. Kayser.

καὶ ἀνθρωπείων πραγμάτων, ἀνθρώπων μὲν ὑπαρχόντων θεῶν δὲ μὴ ὑφεστώτων. ἄτοπον δέ γε
λέγειν μὴ εἶναι σοφίαν· ἄτοπον ἄρα καὶ τὸ τοὺς
θεοὺς ἀξιοῦν ἀνυπάρκτους.

126 Καὶ μὴν εἴπερ καὶ ἡ δικαιοσύνη κατὰ τὴν ἐπιπλοκὴν τῶν ἀνθρώπων πρός τε ἀλλήλους καὶ πρὸς
θεοὺς εἰσῆκται, εἰ μὴ εἰσὶ θεοί, οὐδὲ δικαιοσύνη
127 συστήσεται· ὅπερ ἄτοπον. οἱ μὲν οὖν περὶ τὸν
Πυθαγόραν καὶ τὸν Ἐμπεδοκλέα καὶ τῶν Ἰταλῶν
πλῆθος φασὶ μὴ μόνον ἡμῖν πρὸς ἀλλήλους καὶ πρὸς
τοὺς θεοὺς εἶναί τινα κοινωνίαν, ἀλλὰ καὶ πρὸς τὰ
ἄλογα τῶν ζῴων. ἓν γὰρ ὑπάρχειν πνεῦμα τὸ διὰ
παντὸς τοῦ κόσμου διῆκον ψυχῆς τρόπον, τὸ καὶ
128 ἑνοῦν ἡμᾶς πρὸς ἐκεῖνα. διόπερ καὶ κτείνοντες
αὐτὰ καὶ ταῖς σαρξὶν αὐτῶν τρεφόμενοι ἀδικήσομέν
τε καὶ ἀσεβήσομεν ὡς συγγενεῖς ἀναιροῦντες. ἔνθεν
καὶ παρήνουν οὗτοι οἱ φιλόσοφοι ἀπέχεσθαι τῶν
ἐμψύχων, καὶ ἀσεβεῖν ἔφασκον τοὺς ἀνθρώπους

βωμὸν ἐρεύθοντας μακάρων θερμοῖσι φόνοισιν.

129 καὶ Ἐμπεδοκλῆς πού φησιν

οὐ παύσεσθε φόνοιο δυσηχέος; οὐκ ἐσορᾶτε
ἀλλήλους δάπτοντες ἀκηδείῃσι νόοιο;

καὶ

μορφὴν δ’ ἀλλάξαντα πατὴρ φίλον υἱὸν ἀείρας
σφάζει ἐπευχόμενος μέγα νήπιος· οἱ δ’
ἀπορεῦνται[1]
λισσόμενοι θύοντος. ὁ δ’ αὖ[2] νήκουστος ὁμο-
κλέων

---

[1] ἀπορεῦνται Diels: ἐπορεῦνται Bekk.: οἱ δὲ (οἶδα N) πο-
ρεῦνται MSS.   [2] δ’ αὖ Diels: δὲ Bekk.

be no science of things divine and human if men exist
but Gods subsist not. But it is absurd to assert that
wisdom does not exist ; therefore it is also absurd to
maintain that the Gods are non-existent.

Furthermore, if justice too has been introduced 126
because of the connexion of men with one another and
with the Gods, if Gods exist not, neither will justice
subsist ; which is absurd. Now Pythagoras and Em- 127
pedocles and the rest of the Italian company declare
that we have some fellowship not only with one another and with the Gods but also with the irrational
animals. For there is one spirit which pervades, like
a soul, the whole Universe, and which also makes
us one with them. Wherefore if we slay them and 128
feed on their flesh we shall be doing what is unjust
and impious, as destroying our kindred. Hence, too,
these philosophers advised abstinence from animal
food, and declared that those men were impious who

Redden'd the Blessed Ones' altars with warm blood pouring
from victims.

And Empedocles somewhere says—   129

Will ye not cease from the harrowing sound of slaughter ?
Nor see ye
How in your reckless frenzy of mind ye devour one another ?

And—

Raising his dear one on high—his son with visage how
alter'd !—
Witless the sire doth slay him, with prayer : and the rest are
astonied
Begging him e'en as he slays ; but he, ever deaf to their
outcries,

69

σφάξας ἐν μεγάροισι κακὴν ἀλεγύνατο δαῖτα.
ὣς δ' αὔτως πατέρ' υἱὸς ἑλὼν καὶ μητέρα παῖδες
θυμὸν ἀπορραίσαντε φίλας κατὰ σάρκας ἔδουσιν.

130 ταῦτα δὴ παρήνουν οἱ περὶ τὸν Πυθαγόραν πταί-
οντες. οὐ γὰρ εἰ ἔστι τι διῆκον δι' ἡμῶν τε καὶ
ἐκείνων πνεῦμα, εὐθὺς ἔστι τις ἡμῖν δικαιοσύνη
πρὸς τὰ ἄλογα τῶν ζῴων. ἰδοὺ γὰρ καὶ διὰ τῶν
λίθων καὶ διὰ τῶν φυτῶν πεφοίτηκέ τι πνεῦμα,
ὥστε ἡμᾶς αὐτοῖς συνενοῦσθαι, ἀλλ' οὐδέν ἐστιν
ἡμῖν δίκαιον πρὸς τὰ φυτὰ καὶ λίθους, οὐδὲ μὴν
τέμνοντες καὶ πρίζοντες τὰ τοιαῦτα τῶν σωμάτων
131 ἀδικοῦμεν.   τί οὖν φασὶν οἱ στωικοὶ δικαιοσύνην
τινὰ καὶ ἐπιπλοκὴν ἔχειν τοὺς ἀνθρώπους πρὸς
ἀλλήλους καὶ τοὺς θεούς; οὐ καθόσον ἔστι τὸ
ἐληλακὸς διὰ πάντων πνεῦμα, ἐπεὶ ἂν καὶ πρὸς τὰ
ἄλογα τῶν ζῴων ἐσῴζετό τι δίκαιον ἡμῖν, ἀλλ' ἐπεὶ
λόγον ἔχομεν τὸν ἐπ' ἀλλήλους τε καὶ θεοὺς δια-
τείνοντα, οὗ τὰ ἄλογα τῶν ζῴων μὴ μετέχοντα οὐκ
ἂν ἔχοι τι πρὸς ἡμᾶς δίκαιον. ὥστε εἰ ἡ δικαιοσύνη
κατά τινα κοινωνίαν ἀνθρώπων πρὸς ἀλλήλους καὶ
ἀνθρώπων πρὸς θεοὺς νενόηται, δεήσει μὴ ὄντων
θεῶν μηδὲ δικαιοσύνην ὑπαρκτὴν εἶναι. ὑπαρκτὴ
δέ ἐστιν ἡ δικαιοσύνη· ῥητέον ἄρα καὶ θεοὺς
ὑπάρχειν.

132   Πρὸς τούτοις εἰ μὴ εἰσὶ θεοί, οὐδὲ μαντικὴ
ὑπάρχει, ἐπιστήμη οὖσα θεωρητικὴ καὶ ἐξηγητικὴ
τῶν ὑπὸ θεῶν ἀνθρώποις διδομένων σημείων, οὐδὲ
μὴν θεοληπτικὴ καὶ ἀστρομαντική, οὐ θυτική,[1] οὐχ
ἡ δι' ὀνείρων πρόρρησις. ἄτοπον δέ γε τοσοῦτο

---

[1] θυτική Fabr.: λογική mss., Bekk.

Still in his halls doth slay and his horrible banquet prepareth.
Likewise the son doth capture the sire, the children the
    mother,
Reave them of life, and greedily feed on the flesh of their
    kinsfolk.

This, then, was the advice of Pythagoras, but mis- 130
taken ; for it does not at once follow that, if there
exists a spirit which pervades both us and them, there
exists some form of justice as between us and the
irrational animals. For, look you, the spirit also
ranges through stones and through plants, so that we
are united with them, but we have no relation of
justice with plants and stones, nor to be sure do we
act unjustly in cutting and sawing bodies of that
kind.—Why then do the Stoics assert that men have a 131
certain just relation and connexion with one another
and with the Gods ? Not on account of the existence
of the spirit which runs through all things,—since
then there would also remain for us a duty towards
the irrational animals,—but because we possess that
reason which reaches out to one another and the
Gods, whereas the irrational animals, having no share
in this, will have no relation of justice towards us.
So that, if justice is conceived because of a certain
fellowship between men and men and between
men and Gods, if Gods do not exist, it must follow
that justice also is non-existent. But justice is
existent ; we must declare, therefore, that Gods also
exist.

In addition,—if Gods exist not, neither does 132
prophecy exist, it being " the science which observes
and interprets the signs given by Gods to men " ; nor
yet inspiration and astrology, nor divination, nor
prediction by means of dreams. But it is absurd

SEXTUS EMPIRICUS

πλῆθος πραγμάτων ἀναιρεῖν πεπιστευμένων ἤδη παρὰ πᾶσιν ἀνθρώποις. εἰσὶν ἄρα θεοί.

133 Ζήνων δὲ καὶ τοιοῦτον ἠρώτα λόγον. τοὺς θεοὺς εὐλόγως ἄν τις τιμώη· τοὺς δὲ μὴ ὄντας οὐκ ἄν τις εὐλόγως τιμώη· εἰσὶν ἄρα θεοί. ᾧ λόγῳ τινὲς παραβάλλοντές φασι " τοὺς σοφοὺς ἄν τις εὐλόγως τιμώη· τοὺς δὲ μὴ ὄντας οὐκ ἄν τις εὐλόγως τιμώη· εἰσὶν ἄρα σοφοί." ὅπερ οὐκ ἤρεσκε τοῖς ἀπὸ τῆς στοᾶς, μέχρι τοῦ νῦν ἀνευρέτου ὄντος τοῦ κατ'
134 αὐτοὺς σοφοῦ. ἀπαντῶν δὲ πρὸς τὴν παραβολὴν Διογένης ὁ Βαβυλώνιος τὸ δεύτερόν φησι λῆμμα τοῦ Ζήνωνος λόγου τοιοῦτον εἶναι τῇ δυνάμει " τοὺς δὲ μὴ πεφυκότας εἶναι οὐκ ἄν τις εὐλόγως τιμώη." τοιούτου γὰρ λαμβανομένου δῆλον ὡς
135 πεφύκασιν εἶναι θεοί. εἰ δὲ τοῦτο, καὶ εἰσὶν ἤδη. εἰ γὰρ ἅπαξ ποτὲ ἦσαν, καὶ νῦν εἰσίν, ὥσπερ εἰ ἄτομοι ἦσαν, καὶ νῦν εἰσίν· ἄφθαρτα γὰρ καὶ ἀγένητα τὰ τοιαῦτά ἐστι κατὰ τὴν ἔννοιαν τῶν σωμάτων. διὸ καὶ κατὰ ἀκόλουθον ἐπιφορὰν συνάξει ὁ λόγος. οἱ δέ γε σοφοὶ οὐκ ἐπεὶ πεφύ-
136 κασιν εἶναι, ἤδη καὶ εἰσίν. ἄλλοι δέ φασι τὸ πρῶτον λῆμμα τοῦ Ζήνωνος, τὸ " τοὺς θεοὺς εὐλόγως ἄν τις τιμώη," ἀμφίβολον εἶναι· ἓν μὲν γὰρ σημαίνειν " τοὺς θεοὺς εὐλόγως ἄν τις τιμώη," ἕτερον δὲ " τιμητικῶς ἔχοι." λαμβάνεσθαι δὲ τὸ πρῶτον, ὅπερ ψεῦδος ἔσται ἐπὶ τῶν σοφῶν.
137 Οἱ μὲν οὖν κομιζόμενοι λόγοι παρά τε τοῖς στωικοῖς καὶ παρὰ τοῖς ἀπὸ τῶν ἄλλων αἱρέσεων

---

[a] A Stoic philosopher, disciple of Chrysippus (*circa* 160 B.C.)
[b] By "pay honour to" is meant "worship" (with offerings, etc.), whereas "hold in honour" implies merely the respect paid to any "honourable man."

to abolish such a multitude of things which are
already believed in by all men.   Therefore, Gods
exist.

Zeno propounded this argument also :—" One may 133
reasonably honour the Gods ; but those who are non-
existent one may not reasonably honour ; therefore
Gods exist."   But some oppose to this argument a
parallel one—" The wise one may reasonably honour ;
but one may not reasonably honour the non-existent ;
therefore wise men exist."   Which conclusion was
unpleasing to the Stoics, as their " Wise man " has
remained indiscoverable up till now.   In reply to the 134
counter-argument Diogenes the Babylonian [a] asserts
that the second premiss in Zeno's argument is virtually
this—" But those who are not of such a nature as to
exist one may not reasonably honour " ; for when
this premiss is accepted it is evident that the Gods
are of such a nature as to exist.   But if so, they do 135
actually exist.   For if they had once existed at any
time, they also exist now, just as, if atoms had existed,
they also exist now ; for according to the conception
of such bodies, they are imperishable and uncreate.
Hence the argument will deduce a consequent conclusion.   But it is not true of the wise that they
actually exist because they are of such a nature as to
exist.   But others say that Zeno's first premiss— 136
" One may reasonably honour the Gods "—is am-
biguous ; for one of its significations is " one may
reasonably pay honour to the Gods," the other " one
may hold them in honour." [b]   But the first is taken as
the premiss, and in the case of the wise this will be
false.

Such, then, in their character are the arguments 137
brought forward by the Stoics, and by those of the

εἰς τὸ ὑπάρχειν θεοὺς τοιοῦτοί τινές εἰσι κατὰ τὸν
χαρακτῆρα· ὅτι δὲ οὐ λείπονται τούτων ἕνεκα τῆς
περὶ τὸ πείθειν ἰσοσθενείας καὶ οἱ τὸ μὴ εἶναι θεοὺς
138 διδάσκοντες παρακειμένως ὑποδεικτέον. εἴπερ τοίνυν εἰσὶ θεοί, ζῷα εἰσίν· καὶ ᾧ λόγῳ οἱ ἀπὸ τῆς
στοᾶς ἐδίδασκον ὅτι ζῷόν ἐστιν ὁ κόσμος, τῷ αὐτῷ
χρησάμενος ἄν τις κατασκευάζοι ὅτι καὶ ὁ θεός
ἐστι ζῷον. τὸ γὰρ ζῷον τοῦ μὴ ζῴου κρεῖττον
ἐστίν, οὐδὲν δὲ κρεῖττόν ἐστι θεοῦ· ζῷον ἄρα ἐστὶν
ὁ θεός, συμπαραλαμβανομένης τούτῳ τῷ λόγῳ καὶ
τῆς κοινῆς τῶν ἀνθρώπων ἐννοίας, εἴγε καὶ ὁ βίος
καὶ οἱ ποιηταὶ καὶ ἡ τῶν ἀρίστων φιλοσόφων
πληθὺς μαρτυρεῖ τῷ ζῷον εἶναι τὸν θεόν. ὥστε
139 σῴζεσθαι τὰ τῆς ἀκολουθίας. εἰ γὰρ εἰσὶ θεοί,
ζῷα εἰσίν. εἰ δὲ ζῷα εἰσίν, αἰσθάνονται· πᾶν
γὰρ ζῷον αἰσθήσεως μετοχῇ νοεῖται ζῷον. εἰ δὲ
αἰσθάνονται, καὶ πικράζονται καὶ γλυκάζονται· οὐ
γὰρ δι' ἄλλης μέν τινος αἰσθήσεως ἀντιλαμβάνονται
τῶν αἰσθητῶν, οὐχὶ δὲ καὶ διὰ τῆς γεύσεως. ὅθεν
καὶ τὸ περικόπτειν ταύτην ἤ τινα αἴσθησιν ἄλλην
140 ἁπλῶς τοῦ θεοῦ παντελῶς ἐστιν ἀπίθανον· περιτ-
τοτέρας γὰρ αἰσθήσεις ἔχων [ὁ ἄνθρωπος] ἀμείνων
αὐτοῦ γενήσεται, δέον μᾶλλον, ὡς ἔλεγεν ὁ
Καρνεάδης, σὺν ταῖς πᾶσιν ὑπαρχούσαις πέντε
ταύταις αἰσθήσεσι καὶ ἄλλας αὐτῷ περισσοτέρας
προσμαρτυρεῖν, ἵν' ἔχῃ πλειόνων ἀντιλαμβάνεσθαι
πραγμάτων, ἀλλὰ μὴ τῶν πέντε ἀφαιρεῖν. ῥητέον
οὖν τινὰ γεῦσιν ἔχειν τὸν θεόν, καὶ διὰ ταύτης

ᵃ Cf. P.H. iii. 2 ff.

other Schools, in favour of the existence of Gods ; and
in similar fashion we must show that those which
maintain the non-existence of Gods do not fall short
of the former in respect of their equipollence as
regards persuasion.[a] If, then, Gods exist, they are 138
animals[b]; and, employing the same argument as that
by which the Stoics maintained [c] that the Universe is
an animal, one may demonstrate that God, too, is an
animal. For " the animal is better than the non-
animal ; but nothing is better than God ; therefore
God is an animal " ; and in support of this argument
is adduced also the common conception of mankind,
since ordinary folk and the poets, too, and the majority
of the best philosophers testify to the fact that God is
an animal. So that the steps of the logical sequence
are secured. For if Gods exist, they are animals. 139
But if they are animals, they have sensation ; for
every animal is conceived as an animal by its participation in sensation. And if they have sensation,
they also feel bitterness and sweetness ; for they do
not perceive sense-objects through some other sense,
and not through taste as well ; hence it is wholly
improbable that God should be entirely deprived of
this or of any other sense ; for the more numerous 140
the senses he has, the better he will be, since it is
preferable—as Carneades said—that, in addition to
the five senses which belong to all men, yet others
should supply him with evidence, in order that he
may be able to apprehend a greater number of things,
rather than that he should be robbed of the five. We
must assert, then, that God possesses taste, and by it

[b] *i.e.* " animals " in the sense of " living creatures " (*cf.*
§ 107)—not as opposed to " men."
[c] *Cf.* § 107 *supra.*

SEXTUS EMPIRICUS

141 ἀντιλαμβάνεσθαι τῶν γευστῶν. ἀλλ' εἰ διὰ γεύσεως
ἀντιλαμβάνεται, γλυκάζεται καὶ πικράζεται. γλυ-
καζόμενος δὲ καὶ πικραζόμενος εὐαρεστήσει τισὶ καὶ
δυσαρεστήσει. δυσαρεστῶν δέ τισι καὶ ὀχλήσεως
ἔσται δεκτικὸς καὶ τῆς ἐπὶ τὸ χεῖρον μεταβολῆς. εἰ
δὲ τοῦτο, φθαρτός ἐστιν. ὥστε εἴπερ εἰσὶ θεοί,
φθαρτοί εἰσιν. οὐκ ἄρα θεοὶ εἰσίν.

142 Εἴγε μὴν ἔστι θεός, ζῷον ἐστίν. εἰ ζῷον ἐστί,
καὶ αἰσθάνεται· τὸ γὰρ ζῷον τοῦ μὴ ζῴου οὐκ ἄλλῳ
τινὶ διαφέρει ἢ τῷ αἰσθάνεσθαι. εἰ δὲ αἰσθάνεται,
καὶ ἀκούει καὶ ὁρᾷ καὶ ὀσφραίνεται καὶ ἅπτεται.

143 εἰ δὲ τοῦτο, ἔστι τινὰ τὰ καθ' ἑκάστην αἴσθησιν
οἰκειοῦντα αὐτὸν καὶ ἀλλοτριοῦντα, οἷον κατὰ μὲν
ὅρασιν τὰ συμμέτρως ἔχοντα καὶ οὐχ ἑτέρως, κατὰ
δὲ ἀκοὴν αἱ ἐμμελεῖς φωναὶ καὶ οὐχ αἱ μὴ οὕτως
ἔχουσαι, κατὰ τὰ αὐτὰ δὲ καὶ ἐπὶ τῶν ἄλλων
αἰσθήσεων. εἰ δὲ τοῦτο, ἔστι τινὰ τῷ θεῷ ὀχληρά·
καὶ εἰ ἔστι τινὰ θεῷ ὀχληρά, γίνεται ἐν τῇ ἐπὶ τὸ
χεῖρον μεταβολῇ θεός, ὥστε καὶ ἐν φθορᾷ. φθαρτὸς
ἄρα ὁ θεός. τοῦτο δὲ παρὰ τὴν κοινὴν ἔννοιαν
ὑπῆρχεν αὐτοῦ· τοίνυν οὐκ ἔστι τὸ θεῖον.

144 Ἔστι δὲ καὶ ἐπὶ μιᾶς αἰσθήσεως ἐπεξεργαστικώ-
τερον τιθέναι τὸν λόγον, οἷον τῆς ὁράσεως. εἰ γὰρ
ἔστι τὸ θεῖον, ζῷον ἐστίν. εἰ ζῷον ἐστίν, ὁρᾷ
[ὅλος]¹·

οὖλος γὰρ ὁρᾷ, οὖλος δὲ νοεῖ, οὖλος δέ τ' ἀκούει.

145 εἰ δὲ ὁρᾷ, καὶ λευκὰ ὁρᾷ καὶ μέλανα. ἀλλ' ἐπεὶ
λευκὸν μέν ἐστι τὸ διακριτικὸν ὄψεως μέλαν δὲ τὸ

---

¹ [ὅλος] secl. Heintz.

76

perceives things gustable. But if he perceives by 141
means of taste, he feels sweetness and bitterness; and
feeling sweetness and bitterness, he will be pleased
by some things and displeased by others; and being
displeased by some things, he will be receptive of
vexation and of change for the worse. But if so, he
is perishable. So that if Gods exist, they are perishable. Therefore Gods do not exist.

If, however, God exists, he is an animal. If he is 142
an animal, he has sensation; for the animal differs
from the not-animal by nothing else than by sensation. But if he has sensation, he hears and sees and
smells and touches. And if so, there are certain 143
things in connexion with each sense which are congenial or repellent to him,—for instance, in respect
of sight, things which are symmetrical and not the
reverse; and in respect of hearing, sounds which are
musical and not those of a different kind; and
similarly with the rest of the senses. But if so, there
are certain things which are vexatious to God; and
if there are certain things vexatious to God, God is
subject to change for the worse, and thus also to
decay. Therefore God is perishable. But this is
contrary to the general conception of him. Therefore
the Divine does not exist.

And it is also possible to base the argument still 144
more effectively on a single sense,—for instance,
vision. For if the Divine exists, it is an animal. And
if it is an animal, it sees, for—

> He with the whole of his being beholdeth and marketh
> and heareth.[a]

And if he sees, he sees both white things and black.
But since white is what is divisive of sight, and black 145

* Xenophanes, *Frag. 2.*

77

συγχυτικὸν ὄψεως, διακρίνεται τὴν ὄψιν καὶ συγχεῖται ὁ θεός. εἰ δὲ διακρίσεως καὶ συγχύσεώς ἐστι δεκτικός, καὶ φθορᾶς ἐστι δεκτικός. τοίνυν εἰ ἔστι τὸ θεῖον, φθαρτόν ἐστιν. οὐχὶ δέ γε φθαρτόν ἐστιν· οὐκ ἄρα ἔστιν.

146 Καὶ μὴν ἡ αἴσθησις ἑτεροίωσίς τις ἐστίν· ἀμήχανον γὰρ τὸ δι᾽ αἰσθήσεώς τινος ἀντιλαμβανόμενον μὴ ἑτεροιοῦσθαι ἀλλὰ οὕτω διακεῖσθαι ὡς πρὸ τῆς ἀντιλήψεως διέκειτο. εἰ οὖν αἰσθάνεται ὁ θεός, καὶ ἑτεροιοῦται· εἰ δὲ ἑτεροιοῦται, ἑτεροιώσεως

147 δεκτικός ἐστι καὶ μεταβολῆς· δεκτικὸς δὲ ὢν μεταβολῆς πάντως καὶ τῆς ἐπὶ τὸ χεῖρον μεταβολῆς ἔσται δεκτικός. εἰ δὲ τοῦτο, καὶ φθαρτός ἐστιν. ἄτοπον δέ γε τὸ λέγειν τὸν θεὸν φθαρτὸν ὑπάρχειν· ἄτοπον ἄρα καὶ τὸ ἀξιοῦν εἶναι τοῦτον.

148 Πρὸς τούτοις, εἰ ἔστι τι θεῖον, ἤτοι πεπερασμένον ἐστὶν ἢ ἄπειρον. καὶ ἄπειρον μὲν οὐκ ἂν εἴη, ἐπεὶ καὶ ἀκίνητον ἂν εἴη καὶ ἄψυχον. εἰ γὰρ κινεῖται τὸ ἄπειρον, τόπον ἐκ τόπου μετέρχεται· τόπον δὲ ἐκ τόπου μετερχόμενον ἐν τόπῳ ἐστίν, ἐν τόπῳ δὲ ὂν πεπέρασται. εἰ ἄρα ἐστί τι ἄπειρον, ἀκίνητόν ἐστιν· ἢ εἴπερ κινεῖται, οὐκ ἔστιν ἄπειρον.

149 ὡσαύτως δὲ καὶ ἄψυχόν ἐστιν. εἰ γὰρ ὑπὸ ψυχῆς συνέχεται, πάντως ἀπὸ τῶν μέσων ἐπὶ τὰ πέρατα καὶ ἀπὸ τῶν περάτων ἐπὶ τὰ μέσα φερόμενον συνέχεται. ἐν δὲ ἀπείρῳ οὐδέν ἐστι μέσον οὐδὲ πέρας· ὥστε οὐδὲ ἔμψυχόν ἐστι τὸ ἄπειρον. καὶ διὰ τοῦτο εἰ ἄπειρόν ἐστι τὸ θεῖον, οὔτε κινεῖται οὔτε ἔμψυχον

---

^a Alluding to the theory of Plato, *Timaeus* 67 E, that the stream of particles which issues from a white object " divides " the visual current which proceeds from the eyes, while that from a black object " compresses " it.

78

what is compressive of sight,[a] God has his sight divided and compressed. And if he is receptive of division and compression, he is receptive also of decay. So then, if the Divine exists, it is perishable. But it is not perishable ; therefore it does not exist.

Again, sensation is a kind of alteration ; for it is 146 impossible for that which apprehends by means of a sense not to be altered, but to remain in the same condition in which it was before the act of apprehension. If God, then, has sensation, he is altered ; and if he is altered, he is receptive of alteration and change ; and being receptive of change, he will cer- 147 tainly be receptive of change for the worse. And if so, he is also perishable. But it is absurd to say that God is perishable ; therefore it is absurd also to claim that he exists.

Furthermore, if any Divinity exists, it is either 148 limited or unlimited. And it will not be unlimited, since then it would be both motionless and inanimate. For if the unlimited moves, it passes from place to place ; and if it passes from place to place, it is in space, and being in space it is limited. Therefore, if any unlimited exists, it is motionless ; or if it moves, it is not unlimited. So likewise it is inanimate ; for 149 if it is held together by soul, it is certainly held together by movement from the centres to the limits and from the limits to the centres.[b] But in the unlimited there is no centre nor limit ; so that the unlimited is not animate either. And on account of this, if the Divine is unlimited it neither moves nor is

[b] Alluding to the Stoic view that sensation is effected by means of breath-currents passing between the central sense-organ (the heart) and the peripheral sense-organs (eye, ear, etc.).

ἐστιν. κινεῖται δὲ τὸ θεῖον καὶ ἐμψυχίας ἀξιοῦται
150 μετέχειν· οὐκ ἄρα ἄπειρόν ἐστι τὸ θεῖον.   καὶ
μὴν οὐδὲ πεπερασμένον. ἐπεὶ γὰρ τὸ πεπερασμένον τοῦ ἀπείρου μέρος ἐστί, τὸ δὲ ὅλον τοῦ
μέρους κρεῖττον ἐστί, δῆλον ὡς τὸ ἄπειρον τοῦ
θείου κρεῖττον ἔσται καὶ κρατήσει τῆς θείας
φύσεως. ἄτοπον δὲ τὸ λέγειν θεοῦ τι κρεῖττον, καὶ
κρατεῖν τῆς τοῦ θεοῦ φύσεως· τοίνυν οὐδὲ πεπερασμένον ἐστὶ τὸ θεῖον.   ἀλλ' εἰ μήτε ἄπειρόν ἐστι
μήτε πεπερασμένον, παρὰ δὲ ταῦτα οὐδὲν ἔστι
τρίτον νοεῖν, οὐδὲν ἔσται τὸ θεῖον.

151   Καὶ μὴν εἰ ἔστι τι τὸ θεῖον, ἤτοι σῶμά ἐστιν ἢ
ἀσώματον· οὔτε δὲ ἀσώματόν ἐστιν, ἐπεὶ ἄψυχόν
ἐστι καὶ ἀναίσθητον καὶ οὐδὲν δυνάμενον ἐνεργεῖν
τὸ ἀσώματον, οὔτε σῶμα, ἐπεὶ πᾶν σῶμα μετα-
βλητόν τέ ἐστι καὶ φθαρτόν, ἄφθαρτον δὲ τὸ θεῖον·
οὐ τοίνυν ὑπάρχει τὸ θεῖον.

152   Εἴγε μὴν ἔστι τὸ θεῖον, πάντως καὶ ζῷόν ἐστίν.
εἰ δὲ ζῷόν ἐστίν, πάντως καὶ πανάρετόν ἐστι καὶ
εὐδαῖμον· εὐδαιμονία δὲ χωρὶς ἀρετῆς οὐ δύναται
ὑποστῆναι· εἰ δὲ πανάρετός ἐστι, καὶ πάσας ἔχει
τὰς ἀρετάς. ἀλλ' οὐ πάσας μὲν ἔχει τὰς ἀρετάς,
οὐχὶ δέ γε καὶ ἐγκράτειαν ἔχει καὶ καρτερίαν. οὐχὶ
δέ γε ταύτας μὲν ἔχει τὰς ἀρετάς, οὐχὶ δέ γε ἔστι
τινὰ δυσαπόσχετα καὶ δυσεγκαρτέρητα τῷ θεῷ.

153 ἐγκράτεια γάρ ἐστι διάθεσις ἀνυπέρβατος τῶν κατ'
ὀρθὸν λόγον γιγνομένων, ἢ ἀρετὴ ὑπεράνω ποιοῦσα
ἡμᾶς τῶν δοκούντων εἶναι δυσαποσχέτων· ἐγ-
κρατεύεται γάρ, φασίν, οὐχ ὁ θανατιώσης γραὸς
80

animate. But the Divine moves and participates, as is claimed, in animation ; therefore the Divine is not unlimited.—Nor yet is it limited. For since the 150 limited is a part of the unlimited, and the whole is superior to the part, it is plain that the unlimited will be superior to the Divine and will master the Divine nature. But it is absurd to say that anything is superior to God and master over the nature of God ; so then, the Divine is not limited either. <u>But if it is neither unlimited nor limited, and besides these one can conceive no third possibility, the Divine will be nothing</u>.

Again, if the Divine is anything, it is either a body 151 or incorporeal ; but it is not incorporeal, since the incorporeal is inanimate and insensitive and incapable of any action ; nor is it a body, since every body is both subject to change and perishable, whereas the Divine is imperishable ; so then, the Divine does not exist.

If, however, the Divine exists, it is certainly 152 an animal. And if it is an animal, it is certainly both all-virtuous and happy (and without virtue happiness cannot subsist). And if it is all-virtuous, it possesses all the virtues. But it does not possess all the virtues unless it possesses both continence and fortitude. And it does not possess these virtues unless there are certain things which are hard for God to abstain from and hard to endure. For continence is " a state of mind in- 153 capable of transgressing the rules of right reason, or a virtue which makes us superior to the things which seem hard to abstain from." For a man, they say, is continent not when he abstains from an old woman with one foot in the grave, but when he

ἀπεχόμενος, ἀλλ' ὁ Λαΐδος καὶ Φρύνης ἤ τινος
τοιαύτης δυνάμενος ἀπολαῦσαι, εἶτα ἀπεχόμενος.
154 καρτερία δέ ἐστιν ἐπιστήμη ὑπομενετέων καὶ οὐχ
ὑπομενετέων, ἢ ἀρετὴ ὑπεράνω ποιοῦσα ἡμᾶς τῶν
δοκούντων εἶναι δυσυπομενήτων· χρῆται γὰρ καρ-
τερίᾳ ὁ τεμνόμενος καὶ καιόμενος, εἶτα [δὲ] δια-
155 καρτερῶν, ἀλλ' οὐχ ὁ οἰνόμελι πίνων. ἔσται οὖν
τινὰ τῷ θεῷ δυσυπομένητα καὶ δυσαπόσχετα. εἰ
γὰρ μὴ ἔσται, οὐχὶ ταύτας ἕξει τὰς ἀρετάς, τοῦτ-
156 έστι τὴν ἐγκράτειαν καὶ τὴν καρτερίαν. εἰ δὲ
ταύτας οὐκ ἔχει τὰς ἀρετάς, ἐπεὶ μεταξὺ ἀρετῆς
καὶ κακίας οὐδὲν ἔστι, τὰς ἀντιθέτους ταῖσδε ταῖς
ἀρεταῖς ἕξει κακίας ὥσπερ τὴν μαλακίαν καὶ τὴν
ἀκρασίαν· καθάπερ γὰρ ὁ μὴ ἔχων τὴν ὑγείαν
νόσον ἔχει, οὕτως ὁ μὴ ἔχων ἐγκράτειαν καὶ
καρτερίαν ἐν ταῖς ἀντικειμέναις ἐστὶ κακίαις, ὅπερ
157 ἄτοπον ἐπὶ θεοῦ λέγεσθαι. εἰ δὲ ἔστι τινὰ δυσαπόσχετα καὶ δυσυπομένητα τῷ θεῷ, ἔστι τινὰ καὶ τὰ
ἐπὶ τὸ χεῖρον αὐτοῦ μεταβλητικὰ καὶ ὀχλήσεως
ποιητικά. ἀλλ' εἰ τοῦτο, δεκτικός ἐστιν ὀχλήσεως
ὁ θεὸς καὶ τῆς ἐπὶ τὸ χεῖρον μεταβολῆς, διὸ καὶ
φθορᾶς. ὥστε εἴπερ ἔστιν ὁ θεός, φθαρτός ἐστιν·
οὐχὶ δὲ τὸ δεύτερον, οὐκ ἄρα τὸ πρῶτον.

158 Ἔτι δὲ σὺν τοῖς προκειμένοις, εἰ πανάρετόν ἐστι
τὸ θεῖον, καὶ ἀνδρίαν ἔχει· εἰ δὲ ἀνδρίαν ἔχει, ἐπιστήμην ἔχει δεινῶν καὶ οὐ δεινῶν καὶ τῶν μεταξύ,
159 καὶ εἰ τοῦτο, ἔστι τι θεῷ δεινόν. οὐ γὰρ δή γε ὁ
ἀνδρεῖος διὰ ταῦτά ἐστιν ἀνδρεῖος ὅτι ἐπιστήμην ἔχει

has the power of enjoying Laïs *a* or Phryne *a* or some
such charmer and then abstains. And fortitude is 154
" the science of things endurable and not endurable,
or a virtue which makes us superior to the things
which seem hard to endure." For it is the man who
holds firm when he is being cut and burned that shows
fortitude, and not the man who is drinking sweet
wine. There will, then, exist certain things which 155
are hard for God to endure and hard to abstain from.
For if these do not exist, he will not possess these
virtues,—namely, continence and fortitude. And if 156
he does not possess these virtues, since there is no
mean state between virtue and vice, he will possess
the vices which are contrary to these virtues, such as
effeminacy and incontinence ; for just as he who has
not health has disease, so he who has not continence
and fortitude is subject to the opposite vices, which
is an absurd thing to say about God. And if there are 157
some things which are hard for God to abstain from
and hard to endure, there are some things which are
able to change him for the worse and to cause him
vexation. But if so, God is receptive of vexation and
of change for the worse, and hence of decay also. So
that if God exists, he is perishable ; but the second
is not ⟨true⟩ ; therefore the first is not ⟨true⟩.

Further, in addition to the foregoing arguments,— 158
if God is all-virtuous he possesses courage ; and if he
possesses courage he possesses " knowledge of things
fearful and not fearful and of things intermediate " ;
and if so, there is something which is fearful to God.
For, to be sure, the courageous man is not courageous 159
because he possesses knowledge of the sort of things

a Two Greek courtesans famed for their beauty ; P. sat
as a " model " to Praxiteles and Apelles (*circa* 330 B.C.).

τοῦ ποῖά ἐστι τὰ δεινὰ τῷ γείτονι, ἀλλὰ τὰ αὐτῷ
ἅπερ οὐκ¹ ἀπαράλλακτά ἐστι τοῖς τοῦ πλησίον
δεινοῖς. ὥστε ἐπεὶ ἀνδρεῖός ἐστιν ὁ θεός, ἔστι
160 τι αὐτῷ δεινόν. εἰ ἔστι τι θεῷ δεινόν, ἔστι τι
τῷ θεῷ ὀχλήσεως ποιητικόν. εἰ δὲ τοῦτο, ἐπι-
δεκτικός ἐστιν ὀχλήσεως, διὰ δὲ τοῦτο καὶ φθορᾶς.
ὅθεν εἰ ἔστι τὸ θεῖον, φθαρτόν ἐστιν. οὐχὶ δὲ
φθαρτόν ἐστιν· οὐκ ἄρα ἔστιν.

161 Καὶ μὴν εἰ πανάρετόν ἐστι τὸ θεῖον, καὶ τὴν
μεγαλοψυχίαν ἔχει. εἰ δὲ μεγαλοψυχίαν ἔχει,
ἐπιστήμην ἔχει ποιοῦσαν ὑπεραίρειν τῶν συμβαινόντων. εἰ τοῦτο, ἔστι τινὰ τὰ συμβαίνοντα αὐτῷ
ὧν ὑπεράνω γίνεται. εἰ δὲ τοῦτο, ἔστι τινὰ καὶ
ὀχληρὰ τὰ συμβαίνοντα αὐτῷ, καὶ οὕτω φθαρτὸς
ἔσται. οὐχὶ δέ γε τοῦτο· τοίνυν οὐδὲ τὸ ἐξ ἀρχῆς.

162 Πρὸς τούτοις, εἴπερ πάσας ἔχει τὰς ἀρετὰς ὁ
θεός, καὶ φρόνησιν ἔχει. εἰ φρόνησιν ἔχει, ἔχει καὶ
ἐπιστήμην ἀγαθῶν τε καὶ κακῶν καὶ ἀδιαφόρων.
εἰ δὲ ἐπιστήμην ἔχει τούτων, οἶδε ποῖά ἐστι τὰ
163 ἀγαθὰ καὶ κακὰ καὶ ἀδιάφορα. ἐπεὶ οὖν καὶ ὁ
πόνος τῶν ἀδιαφόρων ἐστίν, οἶδε καὶ τὸν πόνον
[καὶ] ποῖός τις ὑπάρχει τὴν φύσιν. εἰ δὲ τοῦτο, καὶ
περιπέπτωκεν αὐτῷ· μὴ περιπεσὼν γὰρ οὐκ ἂν
ἔσχε νόησιν αὐτοῦ, ἀλλ' ὃν τρόπον ὁ μὴ περιπεπτωκὼς λευκῷ χρώματι καὶ μέλανι διὰ τὸ ἐκ
γενετῆς εἶναι πηρὸς οὐ δύναται νόησιν ἔχειν χρώματος, οὕτως οὐδὲ θεὸς μὴ περιπεπτωκὼς πόνῳ
164 δύναται νόησιν ἔχειν τούτου. ὁπότε γὰρ ἡμεῖς οἱ
περιπεσόντες πολλάκις τούτῳ τὴν ἰδιότητα τῆς

---

¹ οὐκ NLE: om. cet., Bekk.

which are fearful to his neighbour, but of those which are fearful to himself; and these are not to be identified with those which are fearful to his neighbour. Consequently, since God is courageous, there is something which is fearful to him. If there is some- 160 thing fearful to God, there is something which causes vexation to God. And if so, he is receptive of vexation, and therefore of decay. Hence, if the Divine exists, it is perishable. But it is not perishable; therefore, it does not exist.

Moreover, if the Divine is all-virtuous, it also 161 possesses greatness of soul. And if it possesses greatness of soul, it possesses " knowledge which makes it rise superior to circumstances." If so, there exist certain circumstances above which it rises superior. And if so, there exist certain circumstances which are vexatious to it, and thus it will be perishable. But this is not ⟨true⟩; neither, then, is the original supposition.

Furthermore: if God possesses all the virtues, 162 he possesses wisdom. If he possesses wisdom, he possesses " knowledge of things good and evil and indifferent." And if he possesses knowledge of these, he knows what the good things are and the evil and the indifferent. Since, then, suffering is one of the 163 indifferent things, he knows both suffering and what its real nature is. And if so, he has experienced it; for without experience he would not have formed a notion of it, but, just as the man who has not experienced white colour and black, owing to his being blind from birth, cannot possess a notion of colour, so too God cannot have a notion of suffering if he has not experienced it. For when we, who have often 164 experienced it, are unable to discern distinctly the

85

περὶ τοὺς ποδαλγικοὺς ἀλγηδόνος οὐ δυνάμεθα
τρανῶς γνωρίζειν, οὐδὲ διηγουμένων ἡμῖν τινων
συμβαλεῖν, οὐδὲ παρ᾽ αὐτῶν τῶν πεπονθότων
συμφώνως ἀκοῦσαι διὰ τὸ ἄλλους ἄλλως ταύτην
ἑρμηνεύειν καὶ τοὺς μὲν στροφῇ τοὺς δὲ κλάσει
τοὺς δὲ νύξει λέγειν ὅμοιον αὐτοῖς παρακολουθεῖν,
ἢ πού γε θεὸς μηδ᾽ ὅλως πόνῳ περιπεπτωκὼς
165 ⟨οὐ⟩[1] δύναται πόνου νόησιν ἔχειν. νὴ Δί᾽, ἀλλὰ
πόνῳ μέν, φασίν, οὐ περιπέπτωκεν, ἡδονῇ δέ, κἀκ
ταύτης ἐκεῖνον νενόηκεν. ὅπερ ἦν εὔηθες. πρῶτον
μὲν γάρ ἐστιν ἀμήχανον μὴ πειραθέντα πόνου νόησιν ἡδονῆς λαβεῖν· κατὰ γὰρ τὴν παντὸς τοῦ ἀλγύ-
166 νοντος ὑπεξαίρεσιν συνίστασθαι πέφυκεν. εἶτα καὶ
τούτου συγχωρηθέντος πάλιν ἀκολουθεῖ τὸ φθαρτὸν
εἶναι τὸν θεόν. εἰ γὰρ τῆς τοιαύτης διαχύσεως
δεκτικός ἐστι, καὶ τῆς ἐπὶ τὸ χεῖρον μεταβολῆς
ἔσται δεκτικὸς ὁ θεὸς καὶ φθαρτός ἐστιν. οὐχὶ δέ
γε τοῦτο, ὥστε οὐδὲ τὸ ἐξ ἀρχῆς.

167 Εἴπερ τε πανάρετόν ἐστι τὸ θεῖον καὶ τὴν φρόνησιν ἔχει, ἔχει καὶ τὴν εὐβουλίαν, παρόσον ἡ εὐ-
βουλία φρόνησίς ἐστι πρὸς τὰ βουλευτά. εἰ δὲ τὴν
168 εὐβουλίαν ἔχει, καὶ βουλεύεται. εἰ δὲ βουλεύεται,
ἔστι τι ἄδηλον αὐτῷ· εἰ γὰρ μηδέν ἐστιν ἄδηλον
αὐτῷ, οὐ βουλεύεται οὐδὲ τὴν εὐβουλίαν ἔχει τῷ
τὴν βουλὴν ἀδήλου τινὸς ἔχεσθαι, ζήτησιν οὖσαν
περὶ τοῦ πῶς ἐν τοῖς παροῦσιν ὀρθῶς διεξάγομεν.
ἄτοπον δέ γέ ἐστι τὸ μὴ βουλεύεσθαι μηδὲ εὐβουλίαν ἔχειν τὸν θεόν. τοίνυν ἔχει ταύτην, καὶ
169 ἔστι τι ἄδηλον αὐτῷ. εἰ δὲ ἔστι τι ἄδηλον θεῷ, οὐκ

[1] ⟨οὐ⟩ N, Mutsch.

special quality of the pain suffered by gouty patients, or to guess it from descriptions, or to get consistent accounts from the actual sufferers, since they explain it in different ways, and some say that they find it to resemble twisting, others bending, others stabbing,— surely, if God has had no experience at all of suffering, he cannot possess a notion of suffering. Truly, they 165 reply, he has not experienced suffering, but pleasure, and from this he has formed a notion of the other. But this is silly. For, in the first place, it is impossible to acquire a notion of pleasure without having experienced suffering; for it is owing to the withdrawal of everything that gives pain that pleasure really subsists. And, in the next place, if this be 166 granted, it follows once more that God is perishable. For if he is receptive of such a collapse, God will be receptive of change for the worse, and is perishable. But this is not ⟨true⟩, nor, in consequence, is the original supposition ⟨true⟩.

Also, if the Divine is all-virtuous and possesses 167 wisdom, it possesses sound-deliberation, inasmuch as sound-deliberation is " wisdom regarding things requiring deliberation." And if it possesses sound-deliberation, it deliberates. And if it deliberates, 168 there is something which is non-evident to it; for if there is nothing non-evident to it, it does not deliberate nor does it possess sound-deliberation, since deliberation is attached to what is non-evident, being " a search for the way of conducting ourselves rightly under present circumstances." But it is absurd that God should not deliberate nor possess sound-deliberation. So then, he does possess this, and there is something which is non-evident to him. And if there is something non-evident to God, it is 169

ἄλλο μέν τι ἔστιν ἄδηλον θεῷ, οὐχὶ δέ γε καὶ τὸ
τοιοῦτον οἷον εἰ ἔστι τινὰ αὐτοῦ ἐν τῇ ἀπειρίᾳ
φθαρτικά. ἀλλ' εἰ τοῦτό ἐστιν ἄδηλον αὐτῷ,
πάντως κατὰ τὴν προσδοκίαν τῶν φθαρτικῶν αὐτοῦ
τούτων, ἐξ ὧν ἐν συνθροήσει τινὶ καὶ κινήματι
170 γενήσεται, κἂν φοβοῖτο. εἰ δὲ ἐν [συγ]κινήματι
τοιούτῳ γίνεται, καὶ τῆς ἐπὶ τὸ χεῖρον μεταβολῆς
ἔσται δεκτικός, διὰ δὲ τοῦτο καὶ φθαρτός. ᾧ
ἀκολουθεῖ τὸ μηδ' ὅλως αὐτὸν ὑπάρχειν.

171 Καὶ ἄλλως, εἰ μηδὲν ἄδηλόν ἐστι θεῷ ἀλλ'
αὐτόθεν ἐκ φύσεως πάντων καταληπτικὸς καθέστηκεν, οὐκ ἔχει τέχνην, ἀλλ' ὃν τρόπον οὐκ ἂν
εἴπαιμεν περὶ τὸν βάτραχον ἢ τὸν δελφῖνα, φύσει
νηκτικοὺς ὄντας, τέχνην εἶναι νηκτικήν, τὸν αὐτὸν
τρόπον οὐδὲ περὶ τὸν θεὸν ἐκ φύσεως πάντα κατα-
λαμβανόμενον εἴπαιμεν ἂν εἶναι τέχνην τῷ ἀδήλου
τινὸς καὶ [τοῦ]¹ αὐτόθεν μὴ καταλαμβανομένου
172 ἐφάπτεσθαι τὴν τέχνην. ἀλλ' εἰ μὴ ἔστι περὶ τὸν
θεὸν τέχνη, οὐδ' ἡ περὶ τὸν βίον τέχνη ἔσται περὶ
αὐτόν, εἰ δὲ τοῦτο, οὐδὲ ἡ ἀρετή. μὴ ἔχων δὲ θεὸς
ἀρετὴν ἀνύπαρκτός ἐστιν.   καὶ ἄλλως, λογικὸς
ὢν ὁ θεός, εἰ μὴ ἔχει τὴν ἀρετήν, πάντως τὴν
173 ἀντίθετον ἔχει κακίαν· οὐχὶ δέ γε τὴν ἀντίθετον ἔχει
κακίαν· ἔχει ἄρα τέχνην ὁ θεός, καὶ ἔστι τι ἄδηλον
τῷ θεῷ. ᾧ ἔπεται τὸ φθαρτὸν αὐτὸν εἶναι, καθὼς
πρότερον ἐπελογισάμεθα. οὐδέ γε φθαρτός ἐστιν·
οὐκ ἄρα ἔστιν.

174 Εἴπερ τε μὴ ἔχει φρόνησιν, ὡς ὑπεμνήσαμεν,
οὐδὲ σωφροσύνην ἔχει· ἔστι γὰρ ἡ σωφροσύνη ἕξις
ἐν αἱρέσεσι καὶ φυγαῖς σῴζουσα τὰ τῆς φρονήσεως

---

¹ [τοῦ] secl. Heintz.

88

impossible that this—if anything else—should not be
non-evident to God, namely, whether there exist in
the infinite any things destructive of himself.   But if
this is non-evident to him, he will certainly be afraid,
owing to the expectation of these destructive things
which will put him in a state of alarm and commotion.
And if he comes to be in a commotion of this sort, 170
he will be receptive also of change for the worse,
and therefore he will be perishable.   From which it
follows that he does not exist at all.

Here, too, is another argument : If nothing is non- 171
evident to God, but he of his own nature is capable of
apprehending all things, he does not possess art, but
just as we should not say that there exists in the frog
or the dolphin, which swim by nature, an art of
swimming, in the same way we should not say of God,
who of his own nature apprehends all things, that he
has art, since art has to do with a thing that is non-
evident and not apprehended of itself.   But if God 172
has not art, he will not have the art of living ; and if
so, neither will he have virtue.   But if God has not
virtue, he is non-existent.—And again : God being
rational, if he does not possess virtue, he certainly 173
possesses its opposite, vice ; but he does not possess
its opposite, vice ; therefore God possesses art, and
there is something non-evident to God.   From which
it follows that he is perishable, as we argued before.[a]
But he is not perishable ; therefore, he does not
exist.

Also, if (as we have shown [b]) he does not possess 174
wisdom, neither does he possess temperance ; for
temperance is "a state which preserves, in pre-
ferences and aversions, the decisions of wisdom."

[a] *Cf.* § 169.   [b] *Cf.* §§ 162, 167 ff.

175 κρίματα. καὶ ἄλλως δέ, εἰ μηδὲν ἔστιν ὃ τὰς τοῦ
θεοῦ ὀρέξεις κινήσει, μηδὲ ἔστι τι ὃ ἐπισπάσεται
τὸν θεόν, πῶς ἐροῦμεν αὐτὸν εἶναι σώφρονα, τῆς
σωφροσύνης κατὰ τοιοῦτόν τινα λόγον ἡμῖν νενοη-
μένης; καθὰ γὰρ οὐκ ἂν εἴποιμεν τὸν κίονα
σωφρονεῖν, κατὰ τὸν αὐτὸν τρόπον οὐδὲ τὸν θεὸν
δεόντως φήσομεν σώφρονα τυγχάνειν. περιαιρου-
μένων δὲ αὐτοῦ τούτων τῶν ἀρετῶν περιαιρεῖται
καὶ ἡ δικαιοσύνη καὶ αἱ λοιπαί. ἀλλ' εἰ μηδεμίαν
ἀρετὴν ἔχει ὁ θεός, ἀνύπαρκτός ἐστι. τὸ δὲ
ἡγούμενον· τὸ ἄρα λῆγον.

176 Πάλιν εἰ ἔστι τὸ θεῖον, ἤτοι ἔχει ἀρετὴν ἢ οὐκ
ἔχει. καὶ εἰ μὲν οὐκ ἔχει, φαῦλόν ἐστι τὸ θεῖον καὶ
κακοδαιμονικόν, ὅπερ ἄτοπον. εἰ δὲ ἔχει, ἔσται
τι τοῦ θεοῦ κρεῖττον· ὃν γὰρ τρόπον ἡ τοῦ ἵππου
ἀρετὴ αὐτοῦ τοῦ ἵππου ἐστὶ κρείττων καὶ ἡ τοῦ
ἀνθρώπου ἀρετὴ τοῦ ἔχοντος ἐστὶ κρείττων, τὸν
αὐτὸν τρόπον ἡ τοῦ θεοῦ ἀρετὴ καὶ αὐτοῦ τοῦ θεοῦ

177 ἔσται κρεῖττων. εἰ δέ ἐστι κρεῖττων τοῦ θεοῦ,
δῆλον ὡς ἐλλιπῶς ἔχων φαύλως ἕξει καὶ φθαρτὸς
γενήσεται. ἀλλ' εἰ μεταξὺ μὲν τῶν ἀντικειμένων
οὐδὲν ἔστιν, εἰς οὐδέτερον δὲ ὁρᾶται τῶν ἀντικειμένων ἐμπίπτων ὁ θεός, ῥητέον μὴ εἶναι θεόν.

178 Καὶ ἔτι, εἰ ἔστιν, ἤτοι φωνᾶέν ἐστιν ἢ ἄφωνον.
τὸ μὲν οὖν λέγειν ἄφωνον τὸν θεὸν τελέως ἄτοπον
καὶ ταῖς κοιναῖς ἐννοίαις μαχόμενον. εἰ δὲ φωνᾶέν
ἐστί, φωνῇ χρῆται καὶ ἔχει φωνητικὰ ὄργανα,
καθάπερ πνεύμονα καὶ τραχεῖαν ἀρτηρίαν γλῶσσάν
τε καὶ στόμα. τοῦτο δὲ ἄτοπον καὶ ἐγγὺς τῆς
Ἐπικούρου μυθολογίας. τοίνυν ῥητέον μὴ ὑπάρχειν

179 τὸν θεόν. καὶ γὰρ δὴ εἰ φωνῇ χρῆται, ὁμιλεῖ. εἰ
δὲ ὁμιλεῖ, πάντως κατά τινα διάλεκτον ὁμιλεῖ. εἰ

And besides, if there is nothing which will excite the 175
desires of God, and nothing which will attract God,
how shall we say that he is temperate, when temperance is conceived by us in accordance with this
kind of definition ? For just as we should not say
that the pillar is temperate, so also we are bound to
deny that God is temperate. And if he is stripped
of these virtues, he is stripped of justice also and
the rest. But if God possesses no virtue, he is non-
existent ; and the antecedent ⟨is true⟩, therefore the
consequent ⟨is true⟩.

Again, if the Divine exists, it either has or has not 176
virtue. And if it has it not, the Divine is base and
unhappy, which is absurd. But if it has it, there will
exist something which is better than God ; for just as
the virtue of the horse is better than the horse itself
and the virtue of the man better than he who has it,
so also the virtue of God will be better than God himself. But if it is better than God, plainly he, as 177
deficient, will be in a bad state and will be perishable.
But if there is nothing intermediate between the
opposites, and it is seen that God falls under neither
of the opposites, one must declare that God does not
exist.

Further, if he exists, he is either gifted with speech 178
or speechless. But to say that God is speechless is
perfectly absurd and in conflict with our general conceptions. But if he is gifted with speech, he employs
speech and has organs of speech, such as lungs and
windpipe, tongue and mouth. But this is absurd and
borders on the fairy-tales of Epicurus. So then, one
must assert that God does not exist. Moreover, if he 179
employs speech, he converses. And if he converses,
he certainly converses in some dialect. But if so,

91

δὲ τοῦτο, τί μᾶλλον τῇ Ἑλληνίδι ἢ τῇ βαρβάρῳ
χρῆται γλώσσῃ; καὶ εἰ τῇ Ἑλληνίδι, τί μᾶλλον
τῇ Ἰάδι ἢ τῇ Αἰολίδι ἤ τινι τῶν ἄλλων; καὶ μὴν
οὐδὲ πάσαις· οὐδεμιᾷ τοίνυν. καὶ γὰρ εἰ τῇ Ἑλληνίδι χρῆται, πῶς τῇ βαρβάρῳ χρήσεται, εἰ μὴ
ἐδίδαξέ τις αὐτόν; ⟨πῶς δὲ διδάξει τις αὐτόν⟩,[1]
εἰ μὴ ἑρμηνεῖς ἔχει παραπλησίους τοῖς παρ᾽ ἡμῖν
δυναμένοις ἑρμηνεύειν; ῥητέον τοίνυν μὴ χρῆσθαι
φωνῇ τὸ θεῖον, διὰ δὲ τοῦτο καὶ ἀνύπαρκτον
εἶναι.

180   Πάλιν εἰ ἔστι τὸ θεῖον, ἤτοι σῶμά ἐστιν ἢ ἀ-
σώματον. ἀλλ᾽ ἀσώματον μὲν οὐκ ἂν εἴη διὰ
τὰς ἔμπροσθεν ἡμῖν εἰρημένας αἰτίας. εἰ δὲ σῶμα
ἐστίν, ἤτοι σύγκριμά ἐστιν ἐκ τῶν ἁπλῶν στοιχείων
ἢ ἁπλοῦν ἐστι καὶ στοιχειῶδες σῶμα. καὶ εἰ μὲν
σύγκριμά ἐστι, φθαρτόν ἐστιν· πᾶν γὰρ τὸ κατὰ
σύνοδόν τινων ἀποτελεσθὲν ἀνάγκη διαλυόμενον
181 φθείρεσθαι. εἰ δὲ ἁπλοῦν ἐστι σῶμα, ἤτοι πῦρ
ἐστὶν ἢ ἀὴρ ἢ ὕδωρ ἢ γῆ. ὁποῖον δ᾽ ἂν ᾖ τούτων,
ἄψυχόν ἐστι καὶ ἄλογον· ὅπερ ἄτοπον. εἰ οὖν
μήτε σύγκριμά ἐστιν ὁ θεὸς μήτε ἁπλοῦν σῶμα,
παρὰ δὲ ταῦτα οὐδὲν ἔστι, ῥητέον μηδὲν εἶναι
τὸν θεόν.

182   Τοιοῦτον μὲν δὴ καὶ τὸ τῶν λόγων τούτων εἶδός
ἐστιν· ἠρώτηνται δὲ ὑπὸ τοῦ Καρνεάδου καὶ
σωριτικῶς τινές, οὓς ὁ γνώριμος αὐτοῦ Κλειτό-
μαχος ὡς σπουδαιοτάτους καὶ ἀνυτικωτάτους
ἀνέγραψεν, ἔχοντας τὸν τρόπον τοῦτον. εἰ Ζεὺς
θεός ἐστι, καὶ ὁ Ποσειδῶν θεός ἐστιν·

---

[1] ⟨πῶς . . . αὐτόν⟩ add. cj. Bekk.

why does he employ the Greek tongue rather than the barbarian ? And if the Greek, why the Ionian rather than the Aeolic or any of the others ? And, of course, he does not employ them all ; and so he employs none. For if he employs the Greek, how will he employ the barbarian, unless someone has taught him ? ⟨But how will anyone teach him,⟩ unless he has interpreters similar to those amongst us who are able to interpret ? We must say, then, that the Divine does not employ speech, and on this account it is non-existent.

Again, if the Divine exists, it is either a body or 180 incorporeal. But it will not be incorporeal for the reasons we have already stated.[a] And if it is a body, it is either a compound of the simple elements or a simple and elemental body. And if it is a compound, it is perishable ; for everything which is constructed by the union of things must necessarily dissolve and perish. And if it is a simple body, it is either fire 181 or air or water or earth. But whichever of these it is, it is without soul or reason, which is absurd. If, then, God is neither a compound nor a simple body, and besides these there is no other alternative, one must declare that God is nothing.

Such, then, is the character of these arguments. 182 And some have been propounded, in the form of a " sorites," [b] by Carneades, which his friend Cleito-machus recorded as being most excellent and convincing ; and this is the form they take :—If Zeus is a God, Poseidon also is a God :—

---

[a] *Cf.* § 151.
[b] For the " sorites " or chain-argument *cf. P.H.* ii. 253 n.

τρεῖς γάρ τ' ἐκ Κρόνου ἦμεν ἀδελφεοί, οὓς τέκετο
Ῥέα,
Ζεὺς καὶ ἐγώ, τρίτατος δ' Ἀΐδης ἐνέροισιν
ἀνάσσων.
τριχθὰ δὲ πάντα δέδασται, ἕκαστος δ' ἔμμορε
τιμῆς.

ὥστε εἰ ὁ Ζεὺς θεός ἐστι, καὶ ὁ Ποσειδῶν ἀδελφὸς
183 ὢν τούτου θεὸς γενήσεται. εἰ δὲ ὁ Ποσειδῶν θεός
ἐστι, καὶ ὁ Ἀχελῷος ἔσται θεός· εἰ δὲ ὁ Ἀχελῷος,
καὶ ὁ Νεῖλος· εἰ ὁ Νεῖλος, καὶ πᾶς ποταμός· εἰ πᾶς
ποταμός, καὶ οἱ ῥύακες ἂν εἶεν θεοί, καὶ εἰ οἱ
ῥύακες, καὶ αἱ χαράδραι. οὐχὶ δὲ οἱ ῥύακες· οὐδὲ
ὁ Ζεὺς ἄρα θεός ἐστιν. εἰ δέ γε ἦσαν θεοί, καὶ ὁ
184 Ζεὺς ἦν ἂν θεός. οὐκ ἄρα θεοὶ εἰσίν. καὶ μὴν
εἰ ὁ ἥλιος θεός ἐστιν, καὶ ἡ ἡμέρα ἂν εἴη θεός· οὐ
γὰρ ἄλλο τι ἦν ἢ ἡμέρα ἢ ἥλιος ὑπὲρ γῆς. εἰ δ'
ἡ ἡμέρα ἐστὶ θεός, καὶ ὁ μὴν ἔσται θεός· σύστημα
γάρ ἐστιν ἐξ ἡμερῶν. εἰ δὲ ὁ μὴν θεός ἐστι, καὶ
ὁ ἐνιαυτὸς ἂν εἴη θεός· σύστημα γάρ ἐστιν ἐκ
μηνῶν ὁ ἐνιαυτός. οὐχὶ δέ γε τοῦτο· τοίνυν οὐδὲ
τὸ ἐξ ἀρχῆς. σὺν τῷ ἄτοπον εἶναι, φασί, τὴν
μὲν ἡμέραν θεὸν εἶναι λέγειν, τὴν δὲ ἕω καὶ τὴν
185 μεσημβρίαν καὶ τὴν δείλην μηκέτι. εἴγε μὴν ἡ
Ἄρτεμις θεός ἐστιν, καὶ ἡ Ἐνοδία τις ἂν εἴη θεός·
ἐπ' ἴσης γὰρ ἐκείνη καὶ αὕτη δεδόξασται εἶναι θεὰ
⟨· εἰ δὲ θεὰ⟩[1] ἡ Ἐνοδία, καὶ ἡ Προθυριδία καὶ
Ἐπιμύλιος καὶ Ἐπικλιβάνιος. οὐχὶ δέ γε τοῦτο·
186 οὐκ ἄρα τὸ ἐξ ἀρχῆς. εἴγε μὴν τὴν Ἀφροδίτην
θεὰν λέγομεν εἶναι, ἔσται καὶ ὁ Ἔρως υἱὸς ὢν
187 Ἀφροδίτης θεός. ἀλλ' εἰ ὁ Ἔρως θεός ἐστι, καὶ ὁ

---

[1] ⟨· εἰ δὲ θεὰ⟩ add. Heintz.

Brethren three were we, all children of Cronos and Rhea,
Zeus and myself and Hades, the third, with the Shades for
his kingdom.
All things were parted in three, and each hath his share of
the glory.[a]

So that if Zeus is a God, Poseidon also, being his
brother, will be a God. And if Poseidon is a God, 183
Achelous,[b] too, will be a God ; and if Achelous,
Neilos ; and if Neilos, every river as well ; and if
every river, the streams also will be Gods ; and if the
streams, the torrents ; but the streams are not Gods ;
neither, then, is Zeus a God. But if there had been
Gods, Zeus would have been a God. Therefore, there
are no Gods.—Further, if the sun is a God, day will 184
also be a God ; for day is nothing else than sun above
the earth. And if day is God, the month too will be
God ; for it is a composite made up of days. And if the
month is God, the year too will be God ; for the year is
a composite made up of months. But this is not ⟨true⟩ ;
neither then is the original supposition. And besides,
they say, it is absurd to declare that the day is God,
but not the dawn and midday and the evening.—
Again, if Artemis is a Goddess, Enodia [c] too will be 185
a Goddess ; for the latter has been accounted a
Goddess equally with the former ; ⟨and if⟩ Enodia
⟨is a Deity⟩, so also is Prothyridia and Epimylius
and Epiclibanius.[d] But this is not ⟨true⟩ ; neither is
the original supposition.—Again, if we declare that 186
Aphrodite is a Goddess, Eros, being the son of
Aphrodite, will be a God ; but if Eros is a God, Eleos 187

[a] Homer, *Il.* xv. 187 ff. (Poseidon being the speaker).
[b] A river of Aetolia, as Neilos (the Nile) of Egypt.
[c] *i.e.* " Our Lady of the Wayside " (Lat. *Trivia*).
[d] These epithets (treated as proper names) signify respectively " Our Lady of the Porch,"—" of the Mill," and
—" of the Oven."

SEXTUS EMPIRICUS

Ἔλεος ἔσται θεός· ἀμφότερα γάρ ἐστι ψυχι ὰ
πάθη, καὶ ὁμοίως ἀφωσίωται τῷ Ἔρωτι καὶ ὁ
Ἔλεος· παρὰ Ἀθηναίοις γοῦν Ἐλέου βωμοί τινες
188 εἰσίν. εἰ δὲ ὁ Ἔλεος θεός ἐστι, καὶ ὁ Φόβος·

ἀμορφότατος [γὰρ] τὴν ὄψιν, εἰμὶ γὰρ φόβος,
πάντων ἐλάχιστον τοῦ καλοῦ μετέχων θεός.

εἰ δὲ ὁ φόβος, καὶ τὰ λοιπὰ τῆς ψυχῆς πάθη. οὐχὶ
δέ γε ταῦτα· οὐδὲ ἡ Ἀφροδίτη ἄρα θεός ἐστιν. εἰ
δέ γε ἦσαν θεοί, κἂν Ἀφροδίτη θεὸς ὑπῆρχεν· οὐκ
189 ἄρα εἰσὶ θεοί.   καὶ μὴν εἰ ἡ Δημήτηρ θεός
ἐστι, καὶ ἡ Γῆ θεός ἐστιν· ἡ γὰρ Δημήτηρ, φασίν,
οὐκ ἄλλο τί ἐστιν ἢ Γῆ μήτηρ.   εἰ ἡ Γῆ θεός ἐστι,
καὶ τὰ ὄρη καὶ αἱ ἀκρωτηρίαι καὶ πᾶς λίθος ἔσται
θεός.   οὐχὶ δέ γε τοῦτο· τοίνυν οὐδὲ τὸ ἐξ ἀρχῆς.
190   καὶ ἄλλους δὴ τοιούτους σωρίτας ἐρωτῶσιν
οἱ περὶ τὸν Καρνεάδην εἰς τὸ μὴ εἶναι θεούς· ὧν τὸ
γένος ἀπὸ τῶν προεκκειμένων αὐτάρκως γέγονε
πρόδηλον.
191   Ἀλλὰ τὰ μὲν ἀντεπιχειρούμενα παρὰ τοῖς δογματικοῖς φιλοσόφοις εἰς τὸ εἶναι θεοὺς καὶ εἰς τὸ
μὴ εἶναι τοιαῦτά τινα καθέστηκεν. ἐφ' οἷς ἡ τῶν
σκεπτικῶν ἐποχὴ συνεισάγεται, καὶ μάλιστα προσ-
γενομένης αὐτοῖς καὶ τῆς ἀπὸ τοῦ κοινοῦ βίου
192 περὶ θεῶν ἀνωμαλίας.   ἄλλοι γὰρ ἄλλας καὶὰ
συμφώνους ἔχουσι περὶ τούτων ὑπολήψεις, ὥστε
μήτε πάσας εἶναι πιστὰς διὰ τὴν μάχην μήτε τινὰς
διὰ τὴν ἰσοσθένειαν, προσεπισφραγιζομένης τὸ
τοιοῦτο καὶ τῆς παρὰ τοῖς θεολόγοις καὶ ποιηταῖς

---

[a] i.e. " Pity " ; and " Phobos," in the next sentence, is
" Fear."

too will be a God ; for both are psychic affections, and
Eleos [a] has been worshipped like Eros ; at any rate,
amongst the Athenians there are some altars to Eleos.
And if Eleos is a God, so also is Phobos—   188

> Fear am I, most unshapely to behold,
> The god who shares in beauty least of all.[b]

And if Phobos, then all the rest of the soul's affections.
But these are not Gods ; neither, then, is Aphrodite
a Goddess. But if they had been Gods, Aphrodite
too would have been a Goddess. Therefore Gods do
not exist.—Again, if Demeter is a Goddess, Gê too is 189
a Goddess ; for Demeter, they say, is nothing else
than Gê-meter.[c] If Gê is a Goddess, the mountains
and the cliffs and every stone will be a God. But this
is not ⟨true⟩ ; neither, then, is the original supposition.—And Carneades propounds other sorites-argu- 190
ments of this kind to show that Gods do not exist, the
general character of which is sufficiently plain from
the examples already set forth.

Well then, such are the opposing arguments alleged 191
by the Dogmatic philosophers in favour of the existence and of the non-existence of Gods. As a result
of these the Sceptics' suspension of judgement is introduced, especially since they are supplemented by the
divergency of the views of ordinary folk about the
Gods. For different people have different and dis- 192
cordant notions about them, so that neither are all
of these notions to be trusted because of their inconsistency, nor some of them because of their equipollence ; and this is further confirmed by the
mythologizing of the theologians and the poets ; for

---

[b] *Frag. Com. adesp.* 154 (Kock).
[c] *i.e.* " Earth-Mother."

SEXTUS EMPIRICUS

μυθοποιήσεως· πάσης γὰρ ἀσεβείας ἐστὶ πλήρης.
193 ἔνθεν καὶ ὁ Ξενοφάνης διελέγχων τοὺς περὶ Ὅμηρον
καὶ Ἡσίοδον φησὶ

πάντα θεοῖς ἀνέθηκαν Ὅμηρός θ᾽ Ἡσίοδός τε
ὅσσα παρ᾽ ἀνθρώποισιν ὀνείδεα καὶ ψόγος ἐστίν,
κλέπτειν μοιχεύειν τε καὶ ἀλλήλους ἀπατεύειν.

194 Πλὴν ἐκ τούτων παραστήσαντες ὅτι ἀκολουθεῖ
τοῖς περὶ τῶν δραστηρίων ἀρχῶν δογματικῶς
εἰρημένοις ἡ ἐποχή, μετὰ τοῦτ᾽ ἤδη καὶ σκεπτικώ-
τερον διδάσκωμεν ὅτι κοινῶς ἄπορός ἐστι τῷ[1] περὶ
τοῦ ποιοῦντος αἰτίου καὶ ὁ περὶ τῆς πασχούσης
ὕλης λόγος.

ΠΕΡΙ ΑΙΤΙΟΥ ΚΑΙ ΠΑΣΧΟΝΤΟΣ

195 Περὶ μὲν τῆς τοῦ αἰτίου νοήσεως ἐν ἄλλοις
ἀκριβέστερον διελέχθημεν· νῦν δὲ ἀρκούμενοι τῇ
ὁλοσχερεῖ τούτου ἐπινοήσει, λέγομεν ὅτι τῶν σκεψαμένων περὶ αὐτοῦ οἱ μὲν ἔφασαν εἶναί τί τινος
αἴτιον, οἱ δὲ μὴ εἶναι, οἱ δὲ μὴ μᾶλλον εἶναι ἢ μὴ
εἶναι. καὶ εἶναι μὲν οἱ πλεῖστοι τῶν δογματικῶν
ἢ πάντες σχεδόν, μὴ εἶναι δὲ οἱ τὴν μεταβλητικὴν
καὶ μεταβατικὴν κίνησιν ἀνελόντες σοφισταί· οὐ
χωρὶς γὰρ ταύτης ὑφίσταται τὸ ποιοῦν. μὴ μᾶλλον δὲ εἶναι ἢ μὴ εἶναι τὸ αἴτιόν φασιν οἱ ἀπὸ
τῆς σκέψεως. καὶ ὅτι οὐκ ἀσκόπως, ἐκ τῶν εἰς
196 ἑκάτερον ἐπιχειρουμένων πάρεστι μαθεῖν. ἀρχὴ δὲ
γινέσθω πρῶτον ἀπὸ τῶν ἀξιούντων εἶναί τί τινος
αἴτιον.

Εἴπερ τοίνυν, φασίν, ἔστι σπέρμα, ἔστι καὶ αἴτιον,

---

[1] ἄπορός . . . τῷ N, Mutsch.: ἄπορόν . . . τὸ cet., Bekk.

98

it is full of all kinds of impiety. Hence, too, Xeno- 193
phanes, in his criticism of Homer and Hesiod, says—

Unto the gods are ascrib'd by Hesiod, like as by Homer,
All of the acts which are counted by men disgraceful and
  shameful,
Thieving and wenching and dealing deceitfully one with
  another.

Now, however, that we have established on these 194
grounds that suspension follows from the dogmatic
arguments concerning the efficient principles, let us
next show, by a more sceptical discussion, that the
account given of passive matter is no less open to
doubt than that of the active cause.

Concerning Cause and the Passive

We have elsewhere [a] discussed more exactly the 195
notion of Cause ; and now, contenting ourselves with
the general conception of it, we affirm that, of those
who have examined it, some have asserted that a
cause of things exists, others that it does not exist,
others that it is " no more " existent than non-
existent. Most, or almost all, of the Dogmatists
assert its existence ; the Sophists who deny change
and transient motion assert its non-existence, as
without such motion the agent does not subsist.
And the Sceptics assert that cause is " no more "
existent than non-existent. And that they do not do
this inconsiderately one may learn from the arguments adduced on either side. Let us begin first 196
with those who maintain that a cause of things
exists.

If, say they, seed exists, cause also exists since the

[a] Cf. §§ 4-12 supra, P.H. iii. 13 ff. ; also Adv. Phys. ii.
70 ff.

ἐπείπερ τὸ σπέρμα αἴτιόν ἐστι τῶν ἐξ αὐτοῦ φυομένων τε καὶ γεννωμένων· ἔστι δέ γε σπέρμα, ὡς
ἐκ τῶν σπειρομένων καὶ ζωογονουμένων δείκνυται·
197 ἔστιν ἄρα αἴτιον.   καὶ πάλιν, εἰ ἔστι τι φύσις,
ἔστι τι αἴτιον· τῶν γὰρ φυομένων ἢ ἐκπεφυκότων
αἴτιόν ἐστιν ἡ φύσις. ὑπάρχει δὲ αὕτη, ὡς ἀπὸ τῶν
ἀποτελεσμάτων συμφανές· καὶ γὰρ ἄτοπον, φασίν,
εἰς ἀνδριαντοποιοῦ μὲν ἡμᾶς ἐργαστήριον παρ-
ελθόντας καὶ θεασαμένους τῶν ἀνδριάντων τοὺς
μὲν τελείους καὶ ἀπηρτισμένους τοὺς δὲ ἡμιτελεῖς,
ἄλλους δὲ ἀρχὴν ἔχοντας τυπώσεως, πιστεύειν ὅτι
ἔστι τις τούτων τεχνίτης καὶ δημιουργός, εἰς δὲ
τοῦτον τὸν κόσμον εἰσελθόντας καὶ γῆν μὲν ἐν
μέσῳ θεωροῦντας ὕδωρ δὲ μετὰ ταύτη, καὶ τρίτην
ἀνάτασιν ἀέρος, οὐρανόν τε καὶ ἀστέρας λίμνας τε
καὶ ποταμοὺς καὶ ζώων παντοδαπῶν γένη καὶ
φυτῶν ποικιλίας, μὴ ὑπολαμβάνειν εἶναί τινα καὶ
τῆς τούτων δημιουργίας αἴτιον. τοίνυν εἰ ἔστι
φύσις, ἔστι τι αἴτιον. ἀλλὰ μὴν τὸ πρῶτον· ἄρα τὸ
198 δεύτερον.   καὶ ἄλλως, εἰ ἔστι τι ψυχή, ἔστιν
αἴτιον· αὕτη γὰρ καὶ τοῦ ζῆν καὶ τοῦ θνήσκειν αἰτία
γίνεται, τοῦ μὲν ζῆν παροῦσα, τοῦ δὲ θνήσκειν
χωριζομένη τῶν σωμάτων. ἔστι δέ γε ψυχή,
φασίν, εἴγε καὶ ὁ λέγων μὴ εἶναι ψυχὴν αὐτῇ προσ-
χρώμενος τοῦτο ἀποφαίνεται· ἔστιν ἄρα αἴτιον.
199   πρὸς τούτοις, εἰ ἔστι θεός, ἔστιν αἴτιον· οὗτος
γὰρ ἦν ὁ τὰ ὅλα διοικῶν. ἔστι δέ γε κατὰ τὰς
κοινὰς ἐννοίας τῶν ἀνθρώπων θεός· ἔστιν ἄρα
αἴτιον. καίτοι κἂν μὴ θεὸς ὑπάρχῃ, ἔστιν αἴτιον·
τὸ γὰρ μὴ εἶναι θεοὺς διά τινα αἰτίαν γίνεται. καὶ

---

^a Cf. §§ 99 f. supra.

seed is the cause of the things which grow and are generated ; but seed exists, as is proved by the plants sown and the animals generated ; cause, therefore, exists.—And again : If nature exists at all, a 197 cause exists ; for nature is the cause of the things which grow or have grown up naturally. But nature exists, as is plain from its effects. For it is in fact absurd, they say, that when we have visited a sculptor's workshop and have seen some of his statues complete and finished off, and some half-completed, and others in the first stage of their shaping, we should believe that there exists some craftsman and artificer of these things,[a] but when we enter into this Universe and behold the earth in its centre, and next to this water, and thirdly the extent of air above, and the heaven and its stars, and the lakes and rivers, and the tribes of animals of every kind, and the varieties of plants, we should not suppose that there exists someone who is the cause of the construction of these things. So then, if nature exists, a cause exists. But in fact the first ⟨is true⟩ ; therefore the second ⟨is true⟩.—Further : If a soul exists at all, it is a 198 cause ; for it is the cause of both living and dying, —of living when it is present, and of dying when it is being separated from its bodies. But the soul, they assert, exists, seeing that even he who says that the soul does not exist makes this statement by employing it. Therefore cause exists. —Moreover, if God exists, cause exists ; for he is 199 the governor of all things. But according to the general notions of mankind God exists ; cause, therefore, exists. Yet even if God does not exist, cause exists ; for the non-existence of Gods is due to some cause. And thus both from the existence

τῷ οὖν ὑπάρχειν θεὸν καὶ τῷ μὴ ὑπάρχειν ἐπ'
200 ἴσης ἀκολουθεῖ τὸ εἶναί τι αἴτιον.   πολλῶν γε
μὴν γεννωμένων καὶ φθειρομένων αὐξομένων τε καὶ
μειουμένων κινουμένων τε καὶ ἀκινητιζόντων, ἐξ
ἀνάγκης ὁμολογεῖν δεῖ τὸ εἶναί τινα τούτων αἴτια,
τὰ μὲν γενέσεως τὰ δὲ φθορᾶς, καὶ τὰ μὲν αὐξήσεως
τὰ δὲ μειώσεως καὶ ἤδη κινήσεως ἢ ἀκινησίας.
201 σὺν τῷ κἂν μὴ ὑπάρχῃ ταῦτα τὰ ἀποτελέσματα,
φαίνηται δὲ μόνον, πάλιν εἰσάγεσθαι τὴν ὕπαρξιν
τῶν αἰτίων· τοῦ γὰρ φαίνεσθαι μὲν ἡμῖν αὐτὰ ὡς
ὑποκείμενα, μὴ ὑποκεῖσθαι δέ, αἴτιόν τι καθέστηκεν.
202   καὶ μὴν εἰ μηδέν ἐστιν αἴτιον, πάντα
ἐκ παντὸς δεήσει γίνεσθαι καὶ ἐν παντὶ τόπῳ,
ἔτι καὶ κατὰ πάντα καιρόν. ὅπερ ἄτοπον· εὐθέως
γὰρ εἰ μηδέν ἐστιν αἴτιον, οὐδὲν τὸ κωλῦον ἐξ ἀν-
203 θρώπου ἵππον συνίστασθαι. [αἴτιον ἄρα τι ἔσται.]
μηδενὸς δὲ ὄντος τοῦ κωλύοντος συστήσεταί ποτε
ἐξ ἀνθρώπου ἵππος, καὶ οὕτως, εἰ τύχοι, ἐξ ἵππου
φυτόν. κατὰ ταῦτα δὲ οὐκ ἀδύνατον ἔσται χιόνα
μὲν ἐν Αἰγύπτῳ πήγνυσθαι, ἀβροχίαν δὲ ἐν Πόντῳ
συμβαίνειν, καὶ τὰ μὲν τοῦ θέρους ἐν χειμῶνι
γίγνεσθαι, τὰ δὲ τοῦ χειμῶνος ἐν θέρει συνίστασθαι. ὅθεν εἴπερ ᾧ ἕπεταί τι ἀδύνατον,[1] καὶ αὐτὸ
ἔσται ἀδύνατον,[1] τῷ δὲ μὴ εἶναι αἴτιον ἕπεται πολλὰ
τῶν ἀδυνάτων, ῥητέον καὶ τὸ μὴ εἶναι αἴτιον τῶν
204 ἀδυνάτων ὑπάρχειν.   ὅ τε λέγων μὴ εἶναι
αἴτιον ἤτοι χωρὶς αἰτίας τοῦτο λέγει ἢ μετά τινος
αἰτίας. καὶ εἰ μὲν χωρίς τινος αἰτίας, ἄπιστός
ἐστιν, μετὰ τοῦ ἀκολουθεῖν αὐτῷ τὸ μὴ μᾶλλον
τοῦτο ἀξιοῦν ἢ τὸ ἀντικείμενον τούτῳ, αἰτίας

[1] ἀδύνατον (bis) Arnim: δυνατόν mss., Bekk.

of God and from his non-existence there follows equally the existence of a cause.—And further, 200 since many things become and perish, increase and decrease, move and cease from movement, one must necessarily allow that there exist some causes of these things—some of becoming, others of perishing ; some of increase, others of decrease ; and also of motion or want of motion.[a] Moreover, even if these effects 201 do not really exist but merely appear, the existence of their causes is introduced once more ; for there exists some cause of their appearing to us as really existing things and not being such.—Again, if there is no 202 cause all things will have to come from everything and in every place, and also at every time. But this is absurd ; for indisputably, if nothing is a cause, there is nothing to prevent a horse being formed from a man. And if there is nothing to prevent this, a 203 horse will some time be formed from a man, and likewise, perchance, a plant from a horse. And for the same reason it will not be impossible for snow to congeal in Egypt and drought to occur in Pontus, and things proper to summer to happen in winter and things proper to winter to take place in summer. Hence, if what has for its consequence something impossible is itself also impossible, and many impossible consequences follow from the non-existence of cause, one must declare that the non-existence of cause also is a thing impossible.—Also, he who says 204 that cause does not exist says so either without a cause or with some cause. And if he does so without any cause, he is untrustworthy, besides the consequence he incurs of not maintaining this position any more than its opposite, as there pre-exists no

[a] With §§ 200-204 cf. P.H. iii. 17-19.

εὐλόγου μὴ προϋποκειμένης, δι' ἣν φησιν ἀνύπαρκτον εἶναι τὸ αἴτιον. εἰ δὲ μετά τινος αἰτίας,
περιτρέπεται, κἂν τῷ λέγειν μὴ εἶναί τι αἴτιον
205 τίθησι τὸ εἶναί τι αἴτιον. ὅθεν καὶ ἀπὸ τῆς αὐτῆς
δυνάμεως ἐρωτᾶν ἔξεστι καὶ τὸν ἐπὶ τοῦ σημείου
καὶ τῆς ἀποδείξεως διὰ τῶν ἔμπροσθεν ἀποδοθέντα
λόγον, ὃς ἕξει τὴν σύνταξιν τοιαύτην· " εἰ ἔστι τι
αἴτιον, ἔστιν αἴτιον· ἀλλὰ καὶ εἰ μὴ ἔστι τι αἴτιον,
ἔστιν αἴτιον· ἤτοι δὲ ἔστιν ἢ οὐκ ἔστιν· ἔστιν ἄρα."
τῷ τε γὰρ εἶναι αἴτιον ἀκολουθεῖ τὸ εἶναί τι αἴτιον,
μὴ διαφέροντος παρὰ τὸ ἡγούμενον τοῦ λήγοντος,
206 τῷ τε μηδὲν εἶναι αἴτιον ἀκολουθεῖ πάλιν τὸ εἶναί
τι αἴτιον, ἐπείπερ ὁ λέγων μηδὲν εἶναι αἴτιον ὑπό
τινος αἰτίας κινηθεὶς λέγει μηδὲν εἶναι αἴτιον. ὥστε
καὶ τὸ διεζευγμένον πρὸς τοῖς δυσὶ συνημμένοις
ἀληθὲς γίνεσθαι ἐξ ἀντικειμένων διεζευγμένον, καὶ
τὴν ἐπιφορὰν τοῖς τοιούτοις λήμμασι συνεισάγεσθαι,
καθὼς ἀνώτερον παρεμυθησάμεθα.

Καὶ δὴ ταῦτα μέν, ὡς κεφαλαιωδέστερον εἰπεῖν,
εἰς τοῦτο τὸ μέρος εἴωθε λέγεσθαι παρὰ τοῖς
207 δογματικοῖς· σκοπῶμεν δὲ ἀκολούθως καὶ τοὺς τῶν
ἀπορητικῶν λόγους· φανήσονται γὰρ καὶ οὗτοι τοῖς
ἐκκειμένοις ἰσοσθενεῖς καὶ ἕνεκα πειθοῦς μὴ διαφέροντες αὐτῶν. τὸ αἴτιον τοίνυν, φασί, τῶν πρός
τι ἐστίν· τινὸς γάρ ἐστιν αἴτιον καὶ τινί, οἷον τὸ
σμιλίον τινὸς μέν ἐστιν αἴτιον καθάπερ τῆς τομῆς,
208 τινὶ δὲ καθάπερ τῇ σαρκί. τὰ δέ γε πρός τι
ἐπινοεῖται μόνον ἀλλ' οὐχ ὑπάρχει, καθὼς ἐν τοῖς
περὶ ἀποδείξεως παρεστήσαμεν· καὶ τὸ αἴτιον ἄρα

___

ᵃ This is an argument " by two hypotheses," consisting of
a double hypothetical major premiss (" If A is, B is ; and if
A is not, B is ") and a disjunctive minor (" A either is or is

104

reasonable cause which makes him say that cause is non-existent. But if he says so with some cause, he is self-refuted, and in the act of saying that no cause exists he is affirming the existence of some cause. Hence also it is possible to propound to the same effect 205 the argument stated above, relating to the sign and proof, which will take the following shape [a] :—" If a cause exists, cause exists ; but also if a cause does not exist, cause exists ; but either it does or does not exist ; therefore it exists." For the existence of a cause follows from the existence of cause, as the antecedent does not differ from the consequent ; and 206 the existence of a cause follows again from the existence of no cause, since he who says that no cause exists is moved by some cause when he says that no cause exists. So that the disjunctive in addition to the two hypothetical premisses is true, being composed of contradictories, and the conclusion is inferred from these premisses, as we have shown above.[b]

Such then, summarily stated, are the arguments customarily adduced on this side by the Dogmatists. Let us consider next the arguments of the Doubters ; 207 for these will give expression to arguments just as forcible as those set forth and nowise different from them in point of persuasiveness. Cause then, they say, is a relative thing ; for it is a cause of something and to something, as, for instance, the lancet is a cause of something, namely cutting, and to something, namely flesh. But relatives are only conceived 208 and do not exist, as we have established in our chapter " Concerning proof "[c] ; therefore cause, too, will

not "), with the conclusion " therefore B is " ; cf. P.H. ii. 3 n. and § 199 supra.   [b] Cf. Adv. Log. ii. 281 f., 466 f.
   [c] See Adv. Log. ii. 453-461.

209 ἐπινοηθήσεται μόνον, οὐχ ὑπάρξει δέ.   εἴπερ τε
αἴτιόν ἐστιν, ὀφείλει ἔχειν τὸ οὗ λέγεται αἴτιον,
ἐπεὶ ⟨εἰ μὴ ἔχει⟩¹ οὐκ ἔσται αἴτιον, ἀλλ᾽ ὃν τρόπον
τὸ δεξιὸν μὴ παρόντος τοῦ πρὸς ὃ λέγεται δεξιὸν
οὐκ ἔστιν, οὕτω καὶ τὸ αἴτιον μὴ παρόντος τοῦ πρὸς
ὃ νοεῖται οὐκ ἔσται αἴτιον. ἀλλὰ μὴν οὐκ ἔχει τὸ
αἴτιον οὗ ἔστιν αἴτιον, διὰ τὸ μήτε γένεσιν μήτε
φθορὰν μήτε πεῖσιν μήτε κοινῶς κίνησιν ὑπάρχειν,
ὡς ἐπὶ τῶν οἰκείων γινόμενοι τόπων διδάξομεν.
οὐκ ἄρα ἔστιν αἴτιον.

210 Καὶ μὴν εἰ ἔστιν αἴτιον, ἤτοι σῶμα σώματός
ἐστιν αἴτιον ἢ ἀσώματον ἀσωμάτου ἢ σῶμα
ἀσωμάτου ἢ ἀσώματον σώματος· οὔτε δὲ σῶμα
σώματος, ὡς παραστήσομεν, οὔτε ἀσώματον ἀ-
σωμάτου οὔτε σῶμα ἀσωμάτου οὔτε ἐναλλὰξ ἀ-
211 σώματον σώματος· οὐκ ἄρα ἔστιν αἴτιον. ἀμέλει καὶ
αἱ γιγνόμεναι τῶν δογματικῶν στάσεις συμφωνοῦσι
τῇ ἐκκειμένῃ διαιρέσει, εἴγε στωικοὶ μὲν πᾶν αἴτιον
σῶμά φασι σώματι ἀσωμάτου τινὸς αἴτιον γίνεσθαι, οἷον σῶμα μὲν τὸ σμιλίον, σώματι δὲ τῇ
σαρκί, ἀσωμάτου δὲ τοῦ τέμνεσθαι κατηγορήματος,
καὶ πάλιν σῶμα μὲν τὸ πῦρ, σώματι δὲ τῷ ξύλῳ,
212 ἀσωμάτου δὲ τοῦ καίεσθαι κατηγορήματος.   οἱ δὲ
ἀσώματον ὑποθέμενοι τὸν κοσμοποιὸν² καὶ τὸν
πάντα διοικοῦντα θεὸν τοὐναντίον ἀσώματον σώματος λέγουσιν ὑπάρχειν τὸ αἴτιον. ὁ δ᾽ Ἐπίκουρος
καὶ σώματα σωμάτων καὶ ἀσώματα ἀσωμάτων

¹ ⟨εἰ μὴ ἔχει⟩ addo : ⟨μὴ ἔχον⟩ add. cj. Bekk.
² κοσμοποιὸν] κόσμον, οἷον mss., Bekk. (τὸν κόσμον del. cj.
Heintz). (? secl. τὸν post καί.)

ᵃ See §§ 218-231, 267 ff. ; *Adv. Phys.* ii. 45 ff., 310 ff.
ᵇ For " expression " (λεκτόν) as incorporeal *cf. Adv. Log.*

only be conceived and will not exist.—Also, if cause 209
exists, it must have the thing whereof it is said to be
the cause, as ⟨without this⟩ it will not be a cause, but
just as right is not right in the absence of that to
which it is said to be relative, so also cause will not be
cause in the absence of that to which it is conceived
as relative.   But, in fact, cause has not that whereof
it is cause, owing to the non-existence of becoming
and perishing and affection and motion in general, as
we shall show in their proper places when we come to
them.ᵃ   Therefore cause does not exist.

Further, if cause exists, either body is cause of 210
body, or the incorporeal of the incorporeal, or body
of the incorporeal, or the incorporeal of body ; but, as
we shall establish, body is not cause of body, nor the
incorporeal of the incorporeal, nor body of the incorporeal, nor conversely the incorporeal of body ;
therefore cause does not exist.   Moreover, the exist- 211
ing sects of the Dogmatists agree about the distinctions set forth, since the Stoics declare that "every
cause is a body which is the cause to a body of something incorporeal " ; for example, the lancet is a
body, and " the flesh " is a body, and the expression " being cut " is incorporeal ᵇ ; and again, fire
is a body, and " the wood " is a body, and the
expression " being burnt " is incorporeal.   But 212
those who assume that the God who is the World-
maker and governs all things is incorporeal assert,
on the contrary, that the incorporeal is the cause of
body.   And Epicurus says that both bodies are the
causes of bodies and incorporeals of incorporeals,—

ii. 12.   Notice that the cases (dat. and gen.) in the Greek
are due to the grammatical form of the full sentences—" the
lancet is the cause *to* the flesh *of* being cut "—" the fire is the
cause *to* the wood *of* being burnt."

φησὶν αἴτια τυγχάνειν, καὶ σώματα μὲν σωμάτων
ὡς τὰ στοιχεῖα τῶν συγκριμάτων, ἀσώματα δὲ
ἀσωμάτων ὡς τὰ τοῖς πρώτοις σώμασι συμβεβηκότα ἀσώματα τῶν τοῖς συγκρίμασι συμβεβηκότων
213 ἀσωμάτων. ὥστε ἐὰν δείξωμεν ὅτι οὔτε τὸ σῶμα
τοῦ σώματος οὔτε τὸ ἀσώματον τοῦ ἀσωμάτου
οὔτε τὸ ἀσώματον τοῦ σώματος οὔτ᾽ ἐναλλὰξ
δύναται τυγχάνειν αἴτιον, αὐτόθεν ἐσόμεθα κατεσκευακότες καὶ τὸ μηδεμίαν τῶν ἐκκειμένων στά-
214 σεων κατωρθῶσθαι.   σῶμα μὲν οὖν σώματος
οὐκ ἂν εἴη ποτὲ αἴτιον, ἐπείπερ ἀμφότερα τὴν
αὐτὴν ἔχει φύσιν· καὶ εἰ τὸ ἕτερον αἴτιον λέγεται
παρόσον ἐστὶ σῶμα, πάντως καὶ τὸ λοιπὸν
σῶμα καθεστὼς αἴτιον γενήσεται. κοινῶς δὲ ἀμφοτέρων αἰτίων ὄντων οὐδέν ἐστι τὸ πάσχον, μηδενὸς
δὲ πάσχοντος οὐδὲ τὸ ποιοῦν γενήσεται. εἰ ἄρα
σῶμα σώματός ἐστιν αἴτιον, οὐδέν ἐστιν αἴτιον.
215   καὶ μὴν οὐδὲ ἀσώματον ἀσωμάτου λέγοιτ᾽ ἂν
εἶναι ποιητικὸν διὰ τὴν αὐτὴν αἰτίαν· εἰ γὰρ ἀμφότερα τῆς αὐτῆς μετέσχε φύσεως, τί μᾶλλον τόδε
216 τοῦδε ῥητέον αἴτιον ἢ τόδε τοῦδε;   λείπεται
οὖν ἢ σῶμα ἀσωμάτου λέγειν αἴτιον ἢ ἀνάπαλιν
ἀσώματον σώματος. ὅπερ πάλιν τῶν ἀδυνάτων·
τό τε γὰρ ποιοῦν θιγεῖν ὀφείλει τῆς πασχούσης
ὕλης, ἵνα ποιήσῃ, ἥ τε πάσχουσα ὕλη θιχθῆναι
ὀφείλει, ἵνα πάθῃ, τὸ δὲ ἀσώματον οὔτε θιγεῖν οὔτε
217 θιχθῆναι πέφυκεν. τοίνυν οὐδὲ σῶμα ἀσωμάτου ἢ
ἀσώματον σώματός ἐστιν αἴτιον. ᾧ ἕπεται τὸ
μηδὲν ὑπάρχειν αἴτιον· εἰ γὰρ μήτε σῶμα σώματός
ἐστιν αἴτιον μήτε ἀσώματον ἀσωμάτου μήτε σῶμα

bodies of bodies as the elements are of the compounds, and incorporeals of incorporeals as the incorporeal attributes of the primary bodies are of the incorporeal attributes of the compounds. So that if 213 we shall show that body cannot be a cause of body, nor the incorporeal of the incorporeal, nor the incorporeal of body, nor the converse, we shall thereby have established that none of the views mentioned is correct.—Now body will never be the cause of body 214 since both have the same nature ; and if the one is said to be a cause inasmuch as it is body, the other also, as being a body, will certainly be a cause. And as both equally are causes, there is no passive effect, and when nothing is passive there will be no efficient agency. Therefore, if body is the cause of body, there is no cause.—Moreover, the incorporeal cannot 215 be said to be productive of the incorporeal, for the same reason ; for if both partook of the same nature, why should this one be called the cause of that one rather than that one of this one ? It remains for us, then, to say either that body 216 is the cause of the incorporeal, or conversely that the incorporeal is the cause of body. But this again is imposssible ; for that which acts must touch the passive matter in order to act, and the passive matter must be touched, in order to be acted on, but the incorporeal is not of such a nature as either to touch or be touched.[a] So then 217 neither is body the cause of the incorporeal nor the incorporeal of body. From which it follows that no cause exists ; for if body is not a cause of body, nor the incorporeal of the incorporeal, nor body of the

---

[a] Cf. §§ 223, 281 ; Lucr. i. 304 " tangere et tangi nisi corpus nulla potest res."

SEXTUS EMPIRICUS

ἀσωμάτου μήτε ἐναλλάξ, παρὰ δὲ ταῦτα οὐδὲν ἔστι,
κατ᾽ ἀνάγκην οὐδέν ἐστιν αἴτιον.

218 Ἀφελέστερον μὲν οὖν οὕτω τινὲς παραμυθοῦνται
τὰ τοῦ ἐκκειμένου λόγου λήμματα· ὁ δὲ Αἰνησίδημος διαφορώτερον ἐπ᾽ αὐτῶν ἐχρῆτο ταῖς περὶ
219 τῆς γενέσεως ἀπορίαις. τὸ γὰρ σῶμα τοῦ σώματος
οὐκ ἂν εἴη αἴτιον, ἐπείπερ ἢ ἀγένητόν ἐστι τὸ
τοιοῦτον σῶμα καθάπερ ἡ κατ᾽ Ἐπίκουρον ἄτομος,
ἢ γενητὸν ὡς ἄνθρωπος,[1] καὶ ἢ φανερὸν ὡς σίδηρος
καὶ πῦρ, ἢ ἀφανὲς ὡς ἄτομος. ὅ τι δ᾽ ἂν ᾖ τούτων,
220 οὐδὲν δύναται ποιεῖν. ἤτοι γὰρ καθ᾽ ἑαυτὸ μένον
ἕτερόν τι ποιεῖ ἢ ἑτέρῳ συνελθόν. ἀλλὰ μένον μὲν
καθ᾽ ἑαυτὸ πλεῖον αὑτοῦ καὶ τῆς οἰκείας φύσεως
οὐκ ἂν δύναιτό τι ποιεῖν· συνελθὸν δὲ ἑτέρῳ τρίτον
οὐκ ἂν δύναιτο ἀποτελεῖν, ὃ μὴ πρότερον ἐν τῷ
εἶναι ὑπῆρχεν. οὔτε γὰρ τὸ ἓν γενέσθαι δύο δυνα-
221 τόν ἐστιν, οὔτε τὰ δύο τρίτον ἀποτελεῖ. εἰ γὰρ
τὸ ἓν δύο γενέσθαι δυνατὸν ἦν, καὶ ἑκάτερον τῶν
γενομένων ἓν ὂν δύο ἀποτελέσει, καὶ τῶν τεσσάρων
ἕκαστον ἓν ὂν δύο ποιήσει, καὶ ὁμοίως τῶν ὀκτὼ
ἕκαστον, καὶ οὕτως εἰς ἄπειρον. παντελῶς δέ γε
ἄτοπόν ἐστι τὸ ἐξ ἑνὸς ἄπειρα λέγειν γίνεσθαι·
ἄτοπον ἄρα καὶ ἐκ τοῦ ἑνὸς λέγειν τι πλεῖον
222 γεννᾶσθαι. τὰ δ᾽ αὐτὰ κἂν ἀξιῶ τις ἐκ τῶν
ἡσσόνων κατὰ σύνοδον πλείονα ἀποτελεῖσθαι· εἰ
γὰρ τὸ ἓν τῷ ἑνὶ συνελθὸν τρίτον ποιεῖ, καὶ τὸ
τρίτον προσγενόμενον τοῖς δυσὶ τέταρτον ἀποτελέσει, καὶ τὸ τέταρτον προσγενόμενον τοῖς τρισὶ
πέμπτον ἀποτελέσει, καὶ οὕτω πάλιν εἰς ἄπειρον.
οὐκοῦν σῶμα μὲν σώματος οὐκ ἔστιν αἴτιον.

[1] ἄνθρωπος Hirzel: ἔθος mss., Bekk. (ἔρνος Fabr.: ? ἔρος).

110

incorporeal, nor the converse, and besides these there is no other possibility, of necessity nothing is a cause.

It is thus, then, that some state in more simple form 218 the premisses in the arguments now set forth ; but Aenesidemus[a] has, in his treatment of them, made a more elaborate use of the difficulties concerning becoming. Body will not be the cause of body, since 219 such a body is either ungenerated, like the atom of Epicurus, or generated, as is man, and either visible like iron and fire, or invisible like the atom. And whichever of these it is, it cannot effect anything. For it acts on another thing either while continuing 220 by itself or after uniting with the other. But while it remains by itself it would not be able to effect anything more than itself and its own nature ; and when united with another it would not be able to produce a third thing which was not previously in existence. For neither is the one thing able to become two, nor do the two produce a third thing. For if one 221 is able to become two, each of the units which have so become, being one, will produce two, and each of the four, being one, will make two, and similarly each unit of the eight, and so on *ad infinitum* ; but it is wholly absurd to say that an infinite number proceeds from one ; therefore it is also absurd to say that anything more is generated from the one.—The same ⟨objection holds good⟩ 222 should anyone maintain that more is produced from less by addition ; for if the one added to the one makes a third, the third added to the two will produce a fourth, and the fourth added to the three will produce a fifth, and so on, again, *ad infinitum*. Body, then is not the cause of body.—Moreover, for the 223

[a] For Aenesidemus, see Vol. I. Introd. p. xxxvii.

SEXTUS EMPIRICUS

223 καὶ μὴν οὐδὲ ἀσώματον ἀσωμάτου διὰ τὰς αὐτὰς
αἰτίας· οὔτε γὰρ ἐξ ἑνὸς οὔτε ἐκ πλειόνων ἢ ἑνὸς
γένοιτ᾽ ἄν τι πλεῖον. καὶ ἄλλως ἀναφὴς φύσις
καθεστὼς τὸ ἀσώματον οὔτε ποιεῖν οὔτε πάσχειν
224 δύναται. ὥστε οὐδὲ ἀσώματον ἀσωμάτου ποιητικόν ἐστιν· οὕτως δὲ οὐδὲ τὸ ἐναλλάξ, τουτέστι
σῶμα ἀσωμάτου ἢ ἀσώματον σώματος. τό τε γὰρ
σῶμα οὐκ ἔχει ἐν αὑτῷ τὴν τοῦ ἀσωμάτου φύσιν,
τό τε ἀσώματον οὐκ ἐμπεριεῖχε τὴν τοῦ σώματος
φύσιν. διόπερ οὐδέτερον ἐξ οὐδετέρου συστῆναι
225 δυνατόν ἐστιν, ἀλλ᾽ ὡς ἐκ πλατάνου οὐ γίνεται
ἵππος διὰ τὸ μὴ εἶναι ἐν τῇ πλατάνῳ τὴν τοῦ ἵππου
φύσιν, οὐδὲ ἐξ ἵππου συνίσταται ἄνθρωπος διὰ τὸ
μὴ εἶναι ἐν ἵππῳ τὴν τοῦ ἀνθρώπου φύσιν, οὕτως
οὐδὲ ἐκ σώματος ἔσται ποτ᾽ ἂν τὸ ἀσώματον διὰ
τὸ μὴ εἶναι ἐν τῷ σώματι τὴν τοῦ ἀσωμάτου φύσιν,
226 οὐδὲ ἀνάπαλιν ἐκ τοῦ ἀσωμάτου τὸ σῶμα. καίτοι
κἂν ᾖ τὸ ἕτερον ἐν τῷ ἑτέρῳ, πάλιν οὐ γενήσεται
τὸ ἕτερον ἐκ τοῦ ἑτέρου. εἰ γὰρ ὄν ἐστιν ἑκάτερον,
ἐκ τοῦ ἑτέρου οὐ γίνεται, ἀλλ᾽ ἤδη ἔστιν ἐν τῷ
εἶναι, ἤδη δὲ ὂν ἐν τῷ εἶναι οὐ γίνεται διὰ τὸ τὴν
γένεσιν ὁδὸν ὑπάρχειν εἰς τὸ εἶναι. οὐδὲ σῶμα οὖν
ἀσωμάτου ἢ ἀσώματον σώματός ἐστιν αἴτιον· ᾧ
ἀκολουθεῖ τὸ μηδὲν εἶναι αἴτιον.

227 Καὶ πάλιν, εἰ ἔστι τί τινος αἴτιον, ἤτοι τὸ μένον
τοῦ μένοντος αἴτιόν ἐστιν ἢ τὸ κινούμενον τοῦ
κινουμένου ἢ τὸ κινούμενον τοῦ μένοντος ἢ τὸ
μένον τοῦ κινουμένου· οὔτε δὲ τὸ μένον τῷ μένοντι
γένοιτ᾽ ἂν μονῆς αἴτιον, οὔτε τὸ κινούμενον τῷ
κινουμένῳ κινήσεως, οὔτε τὸ μένον τῷ κινουμένῳ

112

same reasons, the incorporeal is not the cause of the incorporeal ; for nothing more can become either from one or from more than one. And besides, the incorporeal being an intangible nature cannot be either active or passive. So that neither is the in- 224 corporeal capable of creating the incorporeal. And thus the converse is not possible either,—-that is to say, body creating the incorporeal or the incorporeal, body. For body does not contain within itself the nature of the incorporeal, and the incorporeal does not include the nature of body. Hence neither of them can be produced from the other, but just as a 225 horse does not spring from a plane-tree because the nature of the horse does not exist in the plane-tree, nor is a man produced from a horse because the nature of the man does not exist in the horse, so the incorporeal will never come into existence from body because the nature of the incorporeal does not exist in body ; nor, conversely, will body come from the incorporeal. Yet 226 if the one does exist in the other, even so the one will not spring from the other. For if either of them is existent, it does not come into existence from the other, but it is already in existence and being already in existence it does not become, since becoming is the process towards existence. Neither, then, is body the cause of the incorporeal nor the incorporeal of body ; from which it follows that nothing is a cause.

And again : If there exists any cause of anything, 227 either the unmoved is the cause of the unmoved, or the moved of the moved, or the moved of the un-moved, or the unmoved of the moved : but the motionless will not be the cause to the motionless of its want of motion, nor the moved to the moved of its motion, nor the motionless to the moved of want of

μονῆς, οὔτε ἐναλλάξ, ὡς παραστήσομεν· οὐκ ἄρα
228 ἔστι τι αἴτιον. τὸ μὲν οὖν μένον τῷ μένοντι μονῆς
καὶ τὸ κινούμενον τῷ κινουμένῳ κινήσεως οὐκ ἂν
ὑπάρχοι αἴτιον δι᾽ ἀπαραλλαξίαν. ἀμφοτέρων γὰρ
ἐπ᾽ ἴσης μενόντων ἢ ἀμφοτέρων κατ᾽ ἴσον κινουμένων οὐ μᾶλλον τόδε τῷδε ἐροῦμεν εἶναι αἴτιον
μονῆς καὶ κινήσεως ἢ τόδε τῷδε. εἰ γὰρ τὸ ἕτερον,
ὅτι κινεῖται, τῷ ἑτέρῳ τῆς κινήσεως αἴτιον ὑπ-
άρχε, ἐπεὶ καὶ τὸ ἕτερον ὡσαύτως κινεῖται, λεχθήσεται τῷ λοιπῷ κινήσεως εἶναι παρεκτικόν. οἷον
κινεῖται μὲν ὁ τροχός, κινεῖται δὲ καὶ ὁ τροχηλάτης·
τί οὖν μᾶλλον διὰ τὸν τροχὸν [καὶ] ὁ τροχηλάτης
κινεῖται ἢ ἀνάπαλιν διὰ τὸν τροχηλάτην ὁ τροχός;
εἴ γέ τοι τὸ ἕτερον μὴ κινοῖτο, οὐδὲ τὸ λειπόμενον κινήσεται. ὅθεν εἰ αἴτιόν ἐστιν οὗ παρόντος
γίνεται τὸ ἀποτέλεσμα, ἐπεὶ ἀμφοτέρων παρόντων
γίνεται τὸ ἀποτέλεσμα καὶ οὔτε τοῦ τροχοῦ ἀπόντος
τελειοῦται οὔτε τοῦ τροχηλάτου, ῥητέον μὴ μᾶλλον
τὸν τροχηλάτην αἴτιον εἶναι τῆς κινήσεως τῷ τροχῷ
229 ἢ τὸν τροχὸν τῷ τροχηλάτῃ. καὶ πάλιν μένει μὲν
ὁ στῦλος, μένει δὲ καὶ τὸ ἐπιστύλιον. ἀλλ᾽ οὐ
μᾶλλον διὰ τὸν στῦλον ῥητέον μένειν τὸ ἐπιστύλιον
ἢ διὰ τὸ ἐπιστύλιον τὸν στῦλον· τοῦ ἑτέρου γοῦν
ἀρθέντος καὶ τὸ ἕτερον καταφέρεται. ὥστε τὸ μὲν
μένον τῷ μένοντι μονῆς καὶ τὸ κινούμενον τῷ
κινουμένῳ κινήσεως διὰ τοῦτο οὐκ ἂν εἴποιμεν
230 αἴτιον. ὡσαύτως δὲ οὐδὲ τὸ μένον τῷ κινουμένῳ κινήσεως ἢ τὸ κινούμενον τῷ μένοντι μονῆς
δι᾽ ἐναντιότητα φύσεως· καθὰ γὰρ τὸ ψυχρὸν οὐκ
ἔχον τὸν τοῦ θερμοῦ λόγον οὐδέποτε δύναται θερ-

114

motion, nor the converse, as we shall establish.
Therefore, no cause exists. Now the motionless will 228
not be the cause to the motionless of its want of
motion, nor the moved to the moved of its motion,
because of their being indistinguishable. For when
both are equally motionless, or both equally in
motion, we shall no more say that this is the cause to
that of its want of motion or its motion than that to
this. For if the one, because it moves, is the cause
of motion to the other, since the other also moves in
like manner it will be said to be supplying motion to
the first. For example, the hoop moves and the
hoop-trundler also moves ; why, then, should the
hoop-trundler move because of the hoop rather than,
conversely, the hoop because of the hoop-trundler ?
Certainly if the one does not move, neither will the
other move. Hence if cause is " that by the presence
of which the effect takes place," since the effect takes
place with both present, and it is effected when
neither the hoop is absent nor the hoop-trundler, one
must declare that the hoop-trundler is no more the
cause of motion to the hoop than the hoop to the
hoop-trundler. And again, the pillar is motionless, 229
and the lintel also is motionless. But one should not
say that the lintel is motionless because of the pillar
any more than the pillar because of the lintel ; for
when the one is removed the other tumbles down.
So that for this reason we will not say that the motionless is the cause to the motionless of its want of
motion or the moving to the moving of its motion.—
So likewise the motionless is not the cause of motion 230
to the moving, nor the moving to the motionless of
its want of motion, because of their opposite natures ;
for just as the cold can never heat, since it does not

μαίνειν, καὶ ὡς τὸ θερμὸν μὴ ἔχον τὸν τοῦ ψυχροῦ
λόγον οὐδέποτε δύναται ψύχειν, οὕτως οὐδὲ τὸ
κινούμενον, μὴ ἔχον τὸν τοῦ μένοντος λόγον, οὐδέποτε δύναται μονῆς εἶναι ποιητικόν, ἢ τὸ ἀνά-
231 παλιν.   ἀλλ᾽ εἴπερ οὔτε τὸ μένον τῷ μένοντι
μονῆς ἐστιν αἴτιον οὔτε τὸ κινούμενον τῷ κινουμένῳ
κινήσεως οὔτε τὸ μένον τῷ κινουμένῳ τοῦ κινεῖσθαι
οὔτε τὸ κινούμενον τῷ μένοντι τοῦ μένειν, παρὰ δὲ
ταῦτα οὐδὲν ἔστιν ἄλλο τι προσεπινοεῖν, λεκτέον
μηδὲν ὑπάρχειν αἴτιον.
232 Πρὸς τούτοις, εἰ ἔστι τί τινος αἴτιον, ἤτοι τὸ
ἅμα ὂν τοῦ ἅμα ὄντος ἐστὶν αἴτιον ἢ τὸ πρότερον
τοῦ ὑστέρου ἢ τὸ ὕστερον τοῦ πρότερον· οὔτε δὲ τὸ
ἅμα ὂν τοῦ ἅμα ὄντος αἴτιόν ἐστιν οὔτε τὸ πρότερον
τοῦ ὑστέρου οὔτε τὸ ὕστερον τοῦ πρότερον, ὡς
233 παραστήσομεν· οὐκ ἄρα ἔστι τι αἴτιον. τὸ μὲν οὖν
ἅμα ὂν τοῦ ἅμα ὄντος οὐ δύναται τυγχάνειν αἴτιον
διὰ τὸ συνυπάρχειν ἀμφότερα καὶ μὴ μᾶλλον τόδε
τοῦδε γεννητικὸν ὑπάρχειν ἢ τόδε τοῦδε, ἑκατέρου
234 τὴν ἴσην ὕπαρξιν ἔχοντος. οὐδὲ τὸ πρότερον δὲ
ἔσται τοῦ ὑστέρου γενομένου ποιητικόν. εἰ γὰρ ὅτε
ἔστι τὸ αἴτιον, οὔπω ἔστι τὸ οὗ ἐστὶν αἴτιον, οὔτε
ἐκεῖνο ἔτι αἴτιόν ἐστι, μὴ ἔχον τὸ οὗ αἴτιόν ἐστιν,
οὔτε τοῦτο ἔτι ἀποτέλεσμα, μὴ συμπαρόντος αὐτῷ
τοῦ οὗ ἀποτέλεσμά ἐστι· τῶν γὰρ πρός τι ἑκάτερόν
ἐστι τούτων, καὶ τὰ πρός τι κατ᾽ ἀνάγκην δεῖ
συνυπάρχειν ἀλλήλοις καὶ οὐ τὸ μὲν προηγεῖσθαι τὸ
235 δὲ ὑστερεῖν. λείπεται οὖν τὸ ὕστερον λέγειν τοῦ

possess the quality of the hot, and as the hot can
never chill, since it does not possess the quality of
the cold, so too the moving can never be productive
of want of motion, since it does not possess the quality
of the motionless, nor can the converse take place.—
But if neither the motionless is the cause to the 231
motionless of its want of motion, nor the moving to
the moving of its motion, nor the motionless to the
moving of its motion, nor the moving to the motionless
of its want of motion, and besides these there is no
other possibility conceivable, we must assert that
nothing is a cause.

Furthermore, if anything is the cause of anything, 232
either the simultaneous is the cause of the simultaneous, or the prior of the posterior, or the posterior
of the prior [a]; but the simultaneous is not the cause
of the simultaneous, nor the prior of the posterior, nor
the posterior of the prior, as we shall establish. Therefore there does not exist any cause. Now the simul- 233
taneous cannot be the cause of the simultaneous
owing to the co-existence of both and the fact that
this one is no more capable of generating that one
than is that one of this one, since both are equal in
point of existence. Nor will the prior be capable of 234
producing that which comes into being later ; for if,
when the cause exists, that whereof it is cause is not
yet existent, neither is the former any longer a cause,
as it has not that whereof it is the cause, nor is the
latter any longer an effect, since that whereof it is the
effect does not co-exist with it. For each of these is
a relative thing, and relatives must necessarily co-
exist with each other, instead of one preceding and
the other following. It only remains for us, then, to 235

[a] *Cf. P.H.* iii. 25 ff.

προτέρου αἴτιον γίνεσθαι. ὅπερ ἐστὶν ἀτοπώτατον
καὶ ἀνδρῶν τὰ πράγματα ἀναστρεφόντων· δεήσει
γὰρ τὸ ἀποτέλεσμα πρεσβύτερον λέγειν τοῦ ποιοῦντος αὐτό, διὰ δὲ τοῦτο μηδ᾽ ὅλως ἀποτέλεσμα
τυγχάνειν ὡς ἂν μὴ ἔχον τὸ οὗ ἐστιν ἀποτέλεσμα.
ὅνπερ οὖν τρόπον ἠλίθιόν ἐστι τὸ λέγειν υἱὸν μὲν
πατρὸς εἶναι πρεσβύτερον, ἄμητον δὲ σπόρου προήκειν τοῖς χρόνοις, οὕτως εὔηθες τὸ ἀξιοῦν [τι]¹
236 αἴτιον εἶναι τοῦ ἤδη ὄντος τὸ μήπω ὄν.   ἀλλ᾽ εἰ
μήτε τὸ ἅμα ὂν τοῦ ἅμα ὄντος μήτε τὸ πρότερον τοῦ
ὑστέρου μήτε τὸ ὕστερον τοῦ προτέρου ἐστὶν αἴτιον,
παρὰ δὲ ταῦτα οὐδὲν ἔστιν, οὐκ ἂν εἴη τι αἴτιον.

Καὶ μὴν εἰ ἔστι τι αἴτιον, ἤτοι αὐτοτελῶς καὶ
237 ἰδίᾳ μόνον προσχρώμενον δυνάμει τινός ἐστιν αἴτιον,
ἢ συνεργοῦ πρὸς τοῦτο δεῖται τῆς πασχούσης ὕλης,
ὥστε τὸ ἀποτέλεσμα κατὰ κοινὴν ἀμφοτέρων νοεῖσθαι σύνοδον.   καὶ εἰ μὲν αὐτοτελῶς καὶ ἰδίᾳ
238 προσχρώμενον δυνάμει ποιεῖν τι πέφυκεν, ὤφειλε
διὰ παντὸς ἑαυτὸ ἔχον καὶ τὴν ἰδίαν δύναμιν πάντοτε ποιεῖν τὸ ἀποτέλεσμα καὶ μὴ ἐφ᾽ ὧν μὲν
ποιεῖν ἐφ᾽ ὧν δὲ ἀπρακτεῖν. εἰ δέ, ὡς φασί τινες
239 τῶν δογματικῶν, οὐ τῶν ἀπολελυμένων καὶ ἀφ-
εστηκότων ἐστὶν ἀλλὰ τῶν πρός τι διὰ τὸ καὶ αὐτὸ
πρὸς τῷ πάσχοντι θεωρεῖσθαι καὶ τὸ πάσχον πρὸς
αὐτῷ, χεῖρόν τι ἀνακύψει. εἰ γὰρ τὸ ἕτερον πρὸς
240 τῷ ἑτέρῳ νοεῖται, ὧν² τὸ μὲν ποιοῦν τὸ δὲ πάσχον,
ἔσται μία μὲν ἔννοια, δυοῖν δ᾽ ὀνομάτων τεύξεται,
τοῦ τε ποιοῦντος καὶ τοῦ πάσχοντος· καὶ διὰ τοῦτο
οὐ μᾶλλον ἐν αὐτῷ ἢ ἐν τῷ λεγομένῳ πάσχειν
ἐγκείσεται ἡ δραστήριος δύναμις. ὡς γὰρ αὐτὸ

¹ [τι] secl. Mutsch.
² ὧν Herv., Mutsch.: οὗ mss., Bekk.

say that the posterior is the cause of the prior ; but this is a most absurd notion, worthy of men who turn things topsy-turvy ; for we shall have to say that the effect is older than what produced it, and consequently is not an effect at all since it is without that whereof it is the effect. So just as it is foolish to say that the son is older than his father, or that the harvest is earlier in date than the sowing, so it is silly to maintain that what is as yet non-existent is the cause of what already exists.—But if the simultaneous is not 236 the cause of the simultaneous, nor the prior of the posterior, nor the posterior of the prior, and besides these there is no other possibility, no cause will exist.

Moreover, if a cause exists it is the cause of some- 237 thing either wholly of itself and using only its own power, or else it needs for the purpose the assistance of the passive matter, so that the effect is conceived as due to the combination of both jointly. And if it 238 is its nature to effect something of itself and by using its own power, since it is constantly in possession of itself and its own power it ought always to be producing its effect, and not be at one time active and at another inactive. But if, as some of the Dogmatists 239 say, cause is not an absolute and independent thing but a relative thing, since it is viewed in relation to the thing affected and the thing affected also in relation to it, a worse consequence will emerge. For 240 if the one is conceived as relative to the other, and of these the one is active, the other passive, they will be one in conception but will be called by two names, the active and the passive ; and because of this the efficient power will not reside in the cause any more than in that which is said to be passive. For just as

119

SEXTUS EMPIRICUS

οὐδὲν δύναται ποιεῖν χωρὶς τοῦ λεγομένου πάσχειν,
οὕτως οὐδὲ τὸ λεγόμενον πάσχειν δύναται χωρὶς
241 τῆς ἐκείνου παρουσίας πάσχειν. ὥσθ' ἕπεται τὸ
μὴ μᾶλλον ἐν αὐτῷ ἢ ἐν τῷ πάσχοντι ὑποκεῖσθαι
τὴν δραστήριον τοῦ ἀποτελέσματος δύναμιν. οἷον
(ἔσται γὰρ σαφὲς τὸ λεγόμενον ἐπὶ ὑποδείγματος)
εἴπερ τὸ πῦρ καύσεώς ἐστιν αἴτιον, ἤτοι αὐτοτελῶς
καὶ τῇ ἰδίᾳ μόνον προσχρώμενον δυνάμει καύσεώς
ἐστι ποιητικόν, ἢ συνεργοῦ δεῖται πρὸς τοῦτο τῆς
242 καιομένης ὕλης. καὶ εἰ μὲν αὐτοτελῶς καὶ τῇ ἰδίᾳ
φύσει ἀρκούμενον ποιεῖ τὴν καῦσιν, ἐχρῆν καὶ
πάντοτε ἔχον αὐτὸ¹ τὴν ἰδίαν φύσιν διὰ παντὸς
καίειν. οὐχὶ δὲ πάντοτε καίει, ἀλλὰ τινὰ μὲν καίει
τινὰ δὲ οὐ καίει· οὐκ ἄρα αὐτοτελῶς καὶ τῇ ἰδίᾳ
243 φύσει προσχρώμενον καίει. εἰ δὲ σὺν τῇ ἐπιτηδειότητι τῶν καιομένων ξύλων, πόθεν ἔχομεν
λέγειν ὅτι αὐτό ἐστι τῆς καύσεως αἴτιον, ἀλλ' οὐχ
ἡ ἐπιτηδειότης τῶν ξύλων; ὃν γὰρ τρόπον μὴ
ὄντος αὐτοῦ οὐ γίνεται καῦσις, οὕτω καὶ τῆς ἐπι-
τηδειότητος τῶν ξύλων ἀπούσης οὐ γίνεται καῦσις.
ταύτῃ τε, εἰ αὐτό ἐστιν αἴτιον ὅτι παρόντος αὐτοῦ
γίνεται τὸ ἀποτέλεσμα καὶ ἀπόντος οὐ γίνεται,
ἔσται καὶ ἡ ἐπιτηδειότης δι' ἑκάτερον τούτων
244 αἴτιον. ὥσπερ οὖν τῆς δι συλλαβῆς ἔκ τε τοῦ δ καὶ
ι συνεστώσης ἄτοπός ἐστιν ὁ λέγων αἴτιον μὲν τοῦ
ἀποτελεῖσθαι τὴν τοιαύτην συλλαβὴν τὸ δ, οὐκ αἴτιον
δὲ τὸ ι, οὕτω συλλαβῇ μὲν ἐοικότος τοῦ καίεσθαι,
στοιχείῳ δὲ τοῦ πυρὸς καὶ τῶν ξύλων, ἀτοπώτατός
ἐστιν ὁ τὸ μὲν πῦρ αἴτιον λέγων τοῦ καίεσθαι, τὰ
δὲ ξύλα μηδαμῶς. οὔτε γὰρ δίχα τοῦ πυρὸς οὔτε
χωρὶς τῶν ξύλων γίνεται τὸ καίεσθαι, καθάπερ οὐδὲ

¹ ἑαυτὸ ⟨καὶ⟩ cj Mutsch.: ? κατὰ.

120

the cause cannot act without what is called the passive thing, so also the so-called passive thing cannot be passive without the presence of the cause. So it 241 follows that the power productive of the effect does not reside in the cause any more than in the passive thing. Thus (for our meaning will be made clear by an example) if fire is the cause of burning, either it is productive of burning by itself and using only its own power, or it needs for this purpose the co-operation of the burning material. And if it produces the 242 burning by itself, being sufficient of its own nature, then, since it always possesses its own nature, it ought to have been continually burning. But it does not burn always, but burns some things and does not burn others ; therefore it does not burn by itself and by using its own nature. But if it does so in con- 243 junction with the suitability of the burning wood, how can we assert that it, rather than the suitability of the wood, is the cause of the burning ? For just as no burning takes place if the fire is non-existent, so also no burning takes place if the suitability of the wood is absent. Thus also, if it is the cause because the effect occurs when it is present and does not occur when it is absent, the suitability too will be the cause for both these reasons. So just as, in the case of the 244 syllable " *di*," which consists of the letters *d* and *i*, it is absurd of a man to say that the cause of the construction of this syllable is the *d*, and that the *i* is not the cause, so if we compare the act of burning to a syllable and the fire and the wood to letters, it is most absurd of a man to say that the fire is the cause of the burning and the wood not the cause. For the burning neither takes place without the fire nor without the wood, just as the syllable does not exist

SEXTUS EMPIRICUS

245 ἡ συλλαβὴ χωρὶς τοῦ δ ἢ τοῦ ι. ὅθεν πάλιν εἰ
μήτε αὐτοτελῶς ποιητικόν τινός ἐστι τὸ αἴτιον μήτε
σὺν ἐπιτηδειότητι τοῦ πάσχοντος, οὐδενὸς ποιητικόν
ἐστι τὸ αἴτιον.

246 Ἔτι εἰ ἔστι τὸ αἴτιον, ἤτοι μίαν ἔχει τὴν δραστήριον δύναμιν ἢ πολλάς· οὔτε δὲ μίαν ἔχειν δύναται,
ὡς παραστήσομεν, οὔτε πολλάς, ὡς διδάξομεν· οὐκ

247 ἄρα τι ἔστιν αἴτιον. μίαν μὲν γὰρ οὐκ ἔχει δύναμιν,
ἐπείπερ εἰ μίαν εἶχεν, ὤφειλε πάντα ὁμοίως δια-
τιθέναι καὶ μὴ διαφερόντως. οἷον ὁ ἥλιος καίει
μὲν τὰ περὶ τὴν Αἰθιοπίαν μέρη, θάλπει δὲ τὰ πρὸς
ἡμᾶς, καταυγάζει δὲ μόνον τοὺς Ὑπερβορέους, καὶ
πήττει μὲν τὸν πηλόν, τήκει δὲ τὸν κηρόν, καὶ
λευκαίνει μὲν τὰ ἐσθήματα, μελαίνει δὲ τὴν ἡμετέ-
ραν ἐπιφάνειαν, ἐρυθαίνει δὲ καρπούς τινας, καὶ
ἡμῖν μὲν τοῦ ὁρᾶν αἴτιος γίνεται, τοῖς νυκτινόμοις
δὲ τῶν ὀρνίθων, οἷον γλαυξὶ καὶ νυκτερίσι, τοῦ μὴ
ὁρᾶν. ὥστε εἰ μίαν εἶχε δύναμιν, ὤφειλε ταὐτὸν
ἐπὶ πάντων ποιεῖν· οὐχὶ δὲ ταὐτὸν ἐπὶ πάντων

248 ποιεῖ· οὐκ ἄρα μίαν ἔχει δύναμιν. καὶ μὴν οὐδὲ
πολλάς, ἐπεὶ ἐχρῆν πάσας ἐπὶ πάντων ἐνεργεῖν, οἷον
πάντα φλέγειν ἢ πάντα χεῖν ἢ πάντα πηγνύναι. εἰ
δὲ μήτε μίαν ἔχει δύναμιν μήτε πολλάς, οὐκ ἂν εἴη
τινὸς αἴτιον.

249 Ναί, ἀλλ᾽ εἰώθασι πρὸς τοῦτο ὑποτυγχάνειν οἱ
δογματικοί, λέγοντες ὅτι παρὰ τὰ πάσχοντα καὶ τὰ
διαστήματα πέφυκεν ἐξαλλάσσεσθαι τὰ γινόμενα
ὑπὸ τοῦ αὐτοῦ αἰτίου ἀποτελέσματα, καθάπερ τοῦ
ἡλίου. σύνεγγυς μὲν γὰρ ὢν τοῖς Αἰθίοψιν ἔοικε
καίειν, μετρίως δὲ ἡμῶν ἀφεστηκὼς θάλπειν, πολὺ
δὲ τῶν Ὑπερβορέων κεχωρισμένος θάλπει μὲν οὐ-

250 δαμῶς, καταυγάζει δὲ μόνον· καὶ πήττει μὲν τὸν

without the *d* or without the *i*.   Hence, once more, 245
if the cause is not productive of anything either by
itself or in conjunction with the suitability of the
passive subject, the cause is productive of nothing.

Further, if the cause exists, it either has one 246
efficient power or many ; but it cannot have one, as
we shall establish, nor yet many, as we shall explain ;
therefore no cause exists.   It has not one power, 247
since if it had one power it ought to affect all things
alike and not in different ways.   The sun, for instance,
burns the regions about Ethiopia, but warms our
regions, and only illumines the Hyperboreans [a] ; and
it dries mud,[b] but melts wax ; and it whitens clothes,
but blackens our complexion, and reddens certain
fruits ; and it is the cause of seeing to us, but of not
seeing to the birds which feed by night, such as owls
and bats.   So that, if it had one power, it ought to
produce the same effect in all cases ; but it does not
produce the same effect in all cases ; therefore it has
not one power.   Nor yet has it many, since then it 248
ought to operate with them all in every case—burn
everything, for example, or fuse everything, or congeal everything.   But if it neither has one power nor
many, it will not be the cause of anything.

Yes, but the Dogmatists usually reply to this by 249
saying that the effects produced by the same cause
naturally vary owing to the materials affected and
the distances, as in the case of the sun.   For being
close to the Ethiopians it naturally burns them, and
being at a moderate distance from us it warms us,
and being far removed from the Hyperboreans it does
not warm them at all but merely illumines them ; and 250

[a] Dwellers in the extreme North, " Laplanders."
[b] *Cf. Adv. Log.* ii. 194.

πηλὸν τὸ ὑδατῶδες τοῦ γεώδους ἐξατμίζων, τήκει
δὲ τὸν κηρὸν διὰ τὸ μὴ ἔχειν τὴν τοῦ πηλοῦ
251 ἰδιότητα. οἱ δὴ χρώμενοι τῇ τοιαύτῃ ὑποτεύξει
σχεδὸν ἀμάχως ἡμῖν συγχωροῦσι τὸ μὴ ἕτερον
εἶναι τοῦ πάσχοντος τὸ ποιοῦν. εἰ γὰρ οὐ διὰ
τὸν ἥλιον γίνεται ἡ τῆξις τοῦ κηροῦ ἀλλὰ διὰ τὴν
ἰδιότητα τῆς περὶ τὸν κηρὸν φύσεως, φανερὸν ὡς
οὐδὲ τὸ ἕτερον αἴτιόν ἐστι τῆς τήξεως τῷ κηρῷ, ἡ
δὲ ἀμφοτέρων συνέλευσις, τοῦ τε ἡλίου καὶ τοῦ
κηροῦ. τῆς δὲ ἀμφοτέρων συνόδου ποιούσης τὸ
ἀποτέλεσμα, τουτέστι τὴν τῆξιν, οὐ μᾶλλον διὰ τὸν
ἥλιον ὁ κηρὸς τήκεται ἢ διὰ τὸν κηρὸν ὁ ἥλιος
τήκει. οὕτω τε ἄτοπον τὸ ἐκ συνόδου δυοῖν γινόμενον ἀποτέλεσμα μὴ τοῖς δυσὶν ἀνατιθέναι, τῷ δὲ
ἑτέρῳ μόνῳ προσμαρτυρεῖν.

252 Καὶ μὴν εἰ ἔστι τί τινος αἴτιον, ἤτοι κεχώρισται
τῆς πασχούσης ὕλης ἢ σύνεστιν αὐτῇ· οὔτε δὲ
κεχωρισμένον αὐτῆς δύναται τυγχάνειν αἴτιον τοῦ
πάσχειν αὐτὴν οὔτε συνὸν αὐτῇ, καθὼς παρα-
253 στήσομεν· οὐκ ἄρα ἔστι τί τινος αἴτιον. καὶ δὴ
κεχωρισμένον μὲν αὐτῆς αὐτόθεν οὔτε αὐτὸ αἴτιόν
ἐστι, μὴ παρούσης τῆς πρὸς ἣν λέγεται αἴτιον, οὔτε
254 ἐκείνη πάσχει, μὴ συμπαρόντος τοῦ ποιοῦντος. εἰ
δὲ συνδυάζοι τὸ ἕτερον τῷ ἑτέρῳ, ἤτοι αὐτὸ μόνον
ποιεῖ τὸ λεγόμενον αἴτιον ὑπάρχειν, οὐχὶ δὲ πάσχει,
ἢ ποιεῖ ἅμα καὶ πάσχει. καὶ εἰ μὲν ἅμα ποιεῖ καὶ
πάσχει, ἑκάτερον ἔσται ποιοῦν τε καὶ πάσχον· ἢ
μὲν γὰρ αὐτὸ ποιεῖ, ἔσται πάσχουσα ἡ ὕλη, ἢ δὲ ἡ
ὕλη ποιεῖ, ἔσται ἐκεῖνο τὸ πάσχον. καὶ οὕτως οὐ
μᾶλλον τὸ ποιοῦν γενήσεται ποιοῦν ἢ πάσχον, καὶ

124

it dries mud by making the watery part steam out of the earthy part, but melts wax because it has not the peculiar quality of mud. Now those who make 251 this reply grant us, almost without dispute, that what acts is not different from what is acted upon. For if the melting of the wax occurs not because of the sun but because of the property of the substance of the wax, it is plain that neither of them is the cause of the melting of the wax but the combination of both of them, the sun and the wax. And as it is the conjunction of both which produces the effect,— namely, the melting,—the wax is not melted because of the sun any more than the sun melts because of the wax. And thus it is absurd not to ascribe the effect produced by the conjunction of two things to those two, but to attribute it to one of them only.

Moreover, if there exists any cause of anything, 252 either it is separate from the matter affected or it co-exists with it ; but neither when separate from it nor when co-existing with it can it be the cause of its being affected, as we shall establish ; therefore no cause of anything exists. Now when separated from 253 its matter, obviously it is not a cause, since the matter with respect to which it is termed a cause is not present, nor is the matter affected, since that which affects it is not present with it. But if the one is 254 coupled with the other, that one which is said to be the cause either acts only and is not acted upon, or both acts and is acted upon at once. And if it both acts and is acted upon, each of them will be both active and passive ; for in so far as the cause acts the matter will be passive, but in so far as the matter acts the cause will be the passive thing. And thus that which acts will be no more active than passive, and

τὸ πάσχον οὐ μᾶλλον ἔσται πάσχον ἢ ποιοῦν· ὅπερ
255 ἄτοπον.   εἰ δὲ ποιεῖ μέν, οὐκ ἀντιπάσχει δέ,
ἤτοι κατὰ ψιλὴν ψαῦσιν, τουτέστι τὴν κατ᾽ ἐπιφάνειαν, ποιεῖ, ἢ κατὰ διάδοσιν. καὶ ἔξωθεν μὲν
προσπῖπτον καὶ κατὰ ψιλὴν τὴν ἐπιφάνειαν παραβαλλόμενον τῇ πασχούσῃ ὕλῃ οὐ δυνήσεταί τι
ποιεῖν· ἡ γὰρ ἐπιφάνεια ἀσώματός ἐστιν, τὸ δ᾽
256 ἀσώματον οὔτε ποιεῖν οὔτε πάσχειν πέφυκεν. οὐκ
ἄρα κατὰ ψιλὴν παραβαλλόμενον τὴν ἐπιφάνειαν τὸ
αἴτιον τῇ ὕλῃ τι ποιεῖν δύναται. καὶ μὴν οὐδὲ
κατὰ διάδοσιν οἷόν τέ ἐστιν αὐτὸ δρᾶν. ἤτοι γὰρ
διὰ στερεῶν σωμάτων διίξεται ἢ διὰ νοητῶν τινων
καὶ ἀναισθήτων πόρων. ἀλλὰ διὰ μὲν στερεῶν
σωμάτων οὐκ ἂν φέροιτο· σῶμα γὰρ διὰ σώματος
257 οὐ δύναται χωρεῖν. εἰ δὲ διὰ πόρων τινῶν, ὀφείλει
ταῖς περιγραφούσαις τοὺς πόρους ἐπιφανείαις
προσπῖπτον ποιεῖν. ἀλλ᾽ αἵ γε ἐπιφάνειαί εἰσιν ἀ-
σώματοι, καὶ τὸ ἀσώματον οὔτε ποιεῖν οὔτε πάσχειν
εὔλογόν ἐστιν. τοίνυν οὐδὲ κατὰ διάδοσιν ποιεῖ τὸ
αἴτιον. ᾧ ἕπεται τὸ μηδ᾽ ὅλως αἴτιον αὐτὸ τυγχάνειν.
258 Ἔνεστι δὲ καὶ ἀπὸ τῆς ἁφῆς κοινότερον τῷ τε
ποιοῦντι καὶ τῷ πάσχοντι ἐπαπορεῖν. ἵνα γάρ τι
ποιήσῃ ἢ πάθῃ, ὀφείλει θιγεῖν ἢ θιχθῆναι· οὐδὲν δὲ
οὔτε θιγεῖν οὔτε θιχθῆναι δύναται, καθὼς παρα-
στήσομεν· οὐκ ἄρα ἔστιν ἢ τὸ ποιοῦν ἢ τὸ πάσχον.
259 εἰ γὰρ ἅπτεταί τί τινος καὶ θιγγάνει, ἤτοι ὅλον ὅλου
ἅπτεται ἢ μέρος μέρους ἢ ὅλον μέρους ἢ μέρος

ᵃ Cf. *P.H.* iii. 39.

that which is acted upon will be no more passive than
active ; which is absurd.—But if it acts and is not 255
acted upon, it acts either by mere contact—that is
to say, superficial contact—or by permeation. And
if it imposes itself externally and is applied to the
passive matter on the surface only, it will not be able
to effect anything ; for surface is incorporeal,[a] and
the incorporeal is not of a nature either to act or to
be acted upon. Therefore the cause is not able to 256
act at all upon the matter when applied on the surface
only. Nor yet is it possible for it to act by permeation. For it will penetrate either through solid
bodies or through certain intelligible and imperceptible pores.[b] But it will not move through solid
bodies ; for body cannot pass through body. And if 257
it passes through certain pores, it ought to act while
in contact with the surfaces which enclose the pores.
But the surfaces are incorporeal, and it is contrary to
reason that the incorporeal should either act or be
acted upon. Neither, then, does the cause act by
permeation. And from this it follows that it is not
a cause at all.

Regarding that which acts and that which is 258
acted upon it is also possible to raise difficulties of
a more general kind, based upon contact. For in
order that a thing may act or be acted upon, it
must touch or be touched ; but, as we shall establish,
nothing can either touch or be touched ; therefore
neither that which acts nor that which is acted
upon exists. For if one thing is in contact with 259
another and touches it, it is in contact either as
a whole with the whole, or as a part with a part,
or as a whole with a part or as a part with the

[b] Cf. Adv. Log. ii. 306, 309 ; P.H. ii. 98, 140.

ὅλου· οὔτε δὲ μέρος μέρους οὔτε ὅλον ὅλου οὔτε
ὅλον μέρους οὔτε ἐναλλὰξ ἅπτεται, καθὼς διδά-
ξομεν· οὐκ ἄρα τί τινος ἅπτεται. καὶ εἰ μηδὲν
μηδενὸς ἅπτεται, οὔτε τὸ πάσχον ἔστιν οὔτε τὸ
260 ποιοῦν. ὅλον μὲν οὖν ὅλου οὐχ ἅπτεται κατὰ λόγον·
εἰ γὰρ ὅλον ὅλου ἅπτεται, οὐ θίξις ἔσται ἀλλὰ
ἕνωσις ἀμφοτέρων, καὶ τὰ δύο σώματα ἓν ἔσται
σῶμα, διὰ τὸ καὶ τοῖς κατὰ βάθος ὀφείλειν τὸ
ἕτερον τοῦ ἑτέρου θιγγάνειν διὰ τὸ καὶ ταῦτα τοῦ
261 ὅλου καθεστάναι μέρη. καὶ μὴν οὐδὲ μέρος
μέρους θιγγάνειν δυνατόν ἐστιν. τὸ γὰρ μέρος κατὰ
μὲν τὴν πρὸς τὸ ὅλον σχέσιν νοεῖται μέρος, κατὰ δὲ
τὴν ἰδίαν περιγραφήν ἐστιν ὅλον, πάλιν τε διὰ
ταύτην τὴν αἰτίαν ἤτοι τὸ ὅλον μέρος τοῦ ὅλου
μέρους ἅψεται ἢ μέρος μέρους. καὶ εἰ μὲν
ὅλον ὅλου, ἑνωθήσεται, καὶ ἀμφότερα ἓν γενήσεται
σῶμα· εἰ δὲ μέρει μέρους,[1] ἐκεῖνο πάλιν τὸ μέρος
κατ᾽ ἰδίαν περιγραφὴν ὅλον νοούμενον ἤτοι ὅλον
ὅλου τοῦ μέρους ἅψεται ἢ μέρει τινί τινος μέρους,
καὶ οὕτως εἰς ἄπειρον. οὐ τοίνυν οὐδὲ μέρος
μέρους ἅπτεται. καὶ μὴν οὐδὲ ὅλον μέρους.
262 εἰ γὰρ τὸ ὅλον τοῦ μέρους ἅψεται, ἔσται καὶ τὸ
ὅλον συνυποστελλόμενον τῷ μέρει μέρος καὶ τὸ
μέρος ἀντιπαρεκτεινόμενον τῷ ὅλῳ ὅλον· τὸ γὰρ
ἴσον τῷ μέρει τὴν τοῦ μέρους εἶχεν ἀναλογίαν, καὶ
τὸ ἴσον τῷ ὅλῳ τὴν τοῦ ὅλου. τελέως δὲ ἀπ-
ερρωγός ἐστιν ἢ τὸ ὅλον ποιεῖν μέρος ἢ τὸ μέρος
ἴσον ἀξιοῦν εἶναι τῷ ὅλῳ. τοίνυν οὐδὲ τὸ ὅλον τοῦ
263 μέρους ἅπτεται. καὶ ἄλλως, εἰ τὸ ὅλον τοῦ
μέρους ἅπτεται, ἔσται ἑαυτοῦ μικρότερον καὶ πάλιν

---

[1] μέρους Heintz : μέρος mss., Bekk.

128

whole ; but, as we shall show, it is not in contact either as part with part, or as whole with whole, or as whole with part, or the converse ; therefore nothing touches anything.[a] And if nothing touches anything, neither what is acted upon exists nor what acts. Now it is according to reason that a 260 whole does not touch a whole ; for if whole touches whole, there will not be contact but the union of both, and the two bodies will be one body, because the one must touch the other with its depths, since these too are parts of the whole.—Nor, again, is it possible for 261 part to touch part. For the part is conceived as a part in respect of its relation to the whole, but in respect of its own limited extent it is a whole, and for this reason again either the whole part will touch the whole part, or a part of it a part. And if the whole touches the whole, they will be unified and both will become one body ; while if with a part it touches a part, that part again, being conceived as a whole in respect of its own limited extent, will either touch as a whole the whole part, or touch a part of it with a part—and so on *ad infinitum.* Neither then does a part touch a part.—Nor, again, does a whole touch a part. For if the whole shall touch the part, the 262 whole, being contracted so as to equal the part, will be a part, and the part, being extended so as to match the whole, will be a whole ; for what is equal to the part has the proportion of the part, and what is equal to the whole that of the whole. But it is perfectly absurd either to make the whole into a part or to claim that the part is equal to the whole. Neither then does the whole touch the part.—Moreover, if 263 the whole touches the part it will be smaller than

---

[a] With §§ 259-261 *cf. P.H.* iii. 45 f.

ἑαυτοῦ μεῖζον· ὅπερ ἐστὶ τοῦ προτέρου χεῖρον. τό
τε γὰρ ὅλον εἰ τὸν αὐτὸν ἐπιλαμβάνει τόπον τῷ
μέρει, ἴσον ἔσται τῷ μέρει, ἴσον δὲ τούτῳ γενό-
μενον μικρότερον ἑαυτοῦ ἔσται· καὶ ἀνάπαλιν τὸ
μέρος εἰ ἀντιπαρεκτείνεται τῷ ὅλῳ, τὸν αὐτὸν
ἐφέξει τούτῳ τόπον, τῷ δὲ ὅλῳ τὸν αὐτὸν ἐπ-
264 εσχηκὸς τόπον ἔσται μεῖζον ἑαυτοῦ.   ὁ δὲ αὐτὸς
καὶ ἐπὶ τῆς ἀναστροφῆς ἐστι λόγος· εἰ γὰρ μὴ
δύναται τὸ ὅλον τοῦ μέρους ἅπτεσθαι διὰ τὰς μικρῷ
πρόσθεν ἐπιλογισθείσας αἰτίας, οὐδὲ τὸ μέρος
δυνήσεται τοῦ ὅλου ἅπτεσθαι. ὅθεν εἰ μήτε τὸ ὅλον
τοῦ ὅλου ἅπτεται μήτε τὸ μέρος τοῦ μέρους μήτε
τὸ ὅλον τοῦ μέρους μήτε ἐναλλάξ, οὐδὲν οὐδενὸς
ἅπτεται. διὰ δὲ τοῦτο οὐδὲ αἴτιόν τί τινος ὑπάρξει,
οὐδὲ πάσχον τι ὑπό τινος.

265   Πρὸς τούτοις τε, εἰ ἅπτεταί τί τινος, ἤτοι μεσολαβούμενον ὑπό τινος, οἷον πόρου ἢ γραμμῆς,
ἅψεταί τινος, ἢ ὑπ' οὐδενὸς μεσολαβούμενον. καὶ
εἰ μὲν ὑπό τινος μεσολαβοῖτο, οὐχ ἅψεται οὗ λέγεται ἅπτεσθαι, ἀλλὰ τοῦ μεταξὺ ἀμφοτέρων· εἰ δὲ
μηδενὸς ἀπαξαπλῶς μεταξὺ ἀμφοτέρων ὄντος τὸ
ἕτερον τοῦ ἑτέρου ἅψεται, ἕνωσις ἔσται ἀμφοτέρων
266 ἀλλ' οὐ θίξις. τοίνυν οὐδὲ ταύτῃ τί τινος ἅπτεται.
ὅθεν εἴπερ, ἵνα νοηθῇ τὸ ποιοῦν καὶ τὸ πάσχον, δεῖ
προωμολογῆσθαι τὸ ὅτι ⟨τί⟩[1] τινος ἅπτεται, δέδεικται δὲ μηδὲν μηδενὸς ἁπτόμενον, λεκτέον μήτε
τὸ ποιοῦν μήτε τὸ πάσχον ὑπάρχειν.

        Τὸ μὲν οὖν ποιοῦν αἴτιον οὕτω καὶ κατ' ἰδίαν καὶ
267 κοινῇ μετὰ τοῦ πάσχοντος ἀπορεῖται· ἄπορος δέ
ἐστι κατ' ἰδίαν καὶ ὁ περὶ τοῦ πάσχοντος λόγος. εἰ

[1] ⟨τί⟩ add. Heintz.

itself, and again larger than itself; which is a worse
consequence than the previous one. For if the whole
occupies the same space as the part, it will be equal
to the part, and being equal thereto it will be smaller
than itself; and conversely, if the part is extended
so as to match the whole, it will take up the same
space as it, and as occupying the same space as the
whole it will be larger than itself.—And to the con- 264
verse case the same argument applies; for if the
whole cannot touch the part, for the reasons set forth
a little while ago, neither will the part be able to
touch the whole. Hence, if the whole does not touch
the whole, nor the part the part, nor the whole the
part, nor the converse, nothing touches anything.
And for this reason nothing will be the cause of
anything, nor will anything be affected by anything.

Furthermore, if one thing touches another, it will 265
touch it either when intercepted by something—such
as a pore or a line—or when intercepted by nothing.
And if it is intercepted by something, it will not be
touching what it is said to touch but the thing which
lies between them both; but if the one shall touch
the other with absolutely nothing intervening between them, there will be a union of the two and not
contact. Neither, then, in this way does anything 266
touch anything. Hence, if the conception of activity
and passivity requires the previous agreement that
one thing touches another, and it has been proved
that nothing touches anything, we must declare that
neither the active nor the passive exists.

Thus the active cause is a matter of doubt both
separately in itself and when taken along with the
thing affected by it. And the account given of the 267
thing affected is also doubtful in itself. For if a thing

131

γὰρ πάσχει τι, ἤτοι τὸ ὂν πάσχει τι ἢ τὸ μὴ ὄν·
οὔτε δὲ τὸ ὂν πάσχει τι, ὡς παραστήσομεν, οὔτε τὸ
268 μὴ ὄν, ὡς ὑπομνήσομεν· οὐκ ἄρα πάσχει τι. τὸ
μὲν οὖν ὂν οὐ πάσχει· ἐφ' ὅσον γὰρ ὂν ἐστι καὶ
τὴν ἰδίαν φύσιν ἔχει, οὐ πάσχει· τὸ δὲ μὴ ὂν τῷ
μηδ' ὅλως ὑπάρχειν οὐκ ἂν πάθοι. παρὰ δὲ τὸ
εἶναι καὶ μὴ εἶναι οὐδὲν ἔστιν· οὐκ ἄρα πάσχει τι.
269 οἷον ὁ Σωκράτης ἤτοι ὢν θνήσκει ἢ μὴ ὤν. δύο
γὰρ οὗτοι χρόνοι, εἷς μὲν ὁ καθ' ὂν ἔστι καὶ ζῇ,
ἕτερος δὲ καθ' ὂν οὐκ ἔστιν ἀλλ' ἔφθαρται· διόπερ
ἐξ ἀνάγκης ὀφείλει κατὰ τὸν ἕτερον τούτων θνήσκειν. ὅτε μὲν οὖν ἔστι καὶ ζῇ, οὐ θνήσκει· ζῇ
γὰρ δήπουθεν· θανὼν δὲ πάλιν οὐ θνήσκει, ἐπεὶ
δὶς ἔσται θνήσκων, ὅπερ ἄτοπον. οὐ τοίνυν θνή-
270 σκει Σωκράτης. οἷος δ' ἔστιν ἐπὶ τούτου λόγος,
τοιοῦτος καὶ ἐπὶ τοῦ πάσχοντος. οὔτε γὰρ τὸ ὂν
δύναται πάσχειν ἐφ' ὅσον ὄν ἐστι καὶ κατὰ τὴν
ἀρχῆθεν ὑπόστασιν νοεῖται, οὔτε τὸ μὴ ὄν· ἀρχὴν
271 γὰρ οὐχ ὑφέστηκεν· οὐκ ἄρα πάσχει τι. καὶ ἔτι
τρανότερον, εἴπερ γε τὸ ὄν, ὅτε ὄν ἐστι, πάσχει,
ἔσται τἀναντία ὑφ' ἕν ἐν τῷ αὐτῷ· οὐχὶ δέ γε
τἀναντία ὑφ' ἕν περὶ τῷ αὐτῷ συνίσταται· οὐκ ἄρα
πάσχει τὸ ὄν, ὅτε ὄν ἐστιν. οἷον ἔστω τὸ ὂν τῇ
φύσει σκληρὸν εἶναι καὶ πάσχειν μαλακυνόμενον,
καθάπερ ἐπὶ τοῦ σιδήρου θεωροῦμεν. οὐκοῦν ὅτε
μὲν σκληρόν ἐστι καὶ ὄν, οὐ δύναται μαλακύνεσθαι,
272 ἐπεὶ εἰ μαλακύνεται ὅτε σκληρόν ἐστιν, ἔσται τἀναντία περὶ τῷ αὐτῷ ὑφ' ἕν, καὶ ᾗ μὲν καθέστηκεν

---

^a With §§ 267-268 cf. P.H. iii. 104 f.
^b With § 269 cf. P.H. iii. 111, Adv. Phys. ii. 346.
^c With §§ 271 ff. cf. P.H. iii. 107.

is affected, either what exists is affected or what exists not ; but neither what exists is affected, as we shall establish, nor what exists not, as we shall show ; therefore nothing is affected.[a] Now the existent is 268 not affected, for in so far as it is existent and has its own nature it is not affected ; and the non-existent will not be affected owing to the fact that it does not subsist at all.   But besides existence and non-existence nothing exists ; therefore nothing is affected. For example, Socrates dies either when existing or 269 when not existing.[b] For these are two periods—the one that in which he exists and is alive, the other that in which he exists not but has perished ; wherefore he must necessarily die in one or other of these periods.   Now he does not die when he exists and is alive ; for, to be sure, he is alive ; nor, again, does he die when he has died, since then he will be dying twice over, which is absurd.   So then, Socrates does not die.   And the argument used in this case may 270 similarly be applied to the case of the thing affected. For the existent cannot be affected in so far as it is existent and is conceived according to its original substance ; nor can the non-existent, for it does not subsist at all ; nothing, therefore, is affected.—And 271 still more clearly, if the existent, when it is existent, is affected, opposites will exist in the same thing at the same time ; but opposites do not exist in the same thing at the same time ; therefore the existent, when it is existent, is not affected.[c] For example, let it be granted that the existent is hard in its nature and is affected by softening, as we see in the case of iron. While, then, it is hard and existent it cannot become soft, since, if it becomes soft when it is hard, opposites 272 will exist in the same thing at the same time, and in

ὄν, ἔσται σκληρόν, ᾗ δὲ πάσχει ὂν ὑπάρχον, ἔσται
μαλακόν. οὐ δύναται δὲ τὸ αὐτὸ ὑφ' ἓν καὶ σκληρὸν
καὶ μαλακὸν νοεῖσθαι· οὐ δύναται ἄρα τὸ ὄν, ὅτε
273 ὄν ἐστι, πάσχειν. ὁ δὲ αὐτὸς λόγος καὶ ἐπὶ λευκοῦ
καὶ μέλανος χρώματος. ἔστω γὰρ τὸ ὄν, ᾗ ὄν ἐστι,
καὶ λευκὸν εἶναι, καὶ πάσχειν αὐτὸ μέλαν γινόμενον.
οὐκοῦν εἰ τὸ ὂν [ἔστι] καὶ λευκὸν τότε ἀξιοῦται
πάσχειν ὅτε λευκόν ἐστι μέλαν ⟨γινόμενον⟩[1] ἔσται
συμβεβηκότα ἔχον τὰ ἐναντία· ὅπερ ἄτοπον. οὐ
τοίνυν τὸ ὄν, ἐφ' ὅσον ὄν ἐστι, πάσχειν πέφυκεν.
274 πρὸς τούτοις, εἰ λέγοιμεν τὸ ὄν, ὅτε ὄν ἐστι,
πάσχειν, ἔσται τι πρὶν γεγονέναι γεγονός· ⟨οὐδὲν δέ
ἐστι πρὶν γεγονέναι γεγονός·⟩[2] οὐκ ἄρα τὸ ὄν, ὅτε
275 ὄν ἐστι, πάσχει. εἰ γὰρ σκληρόν ἐστι τὸ ὄν, ἐφ'
ὅσον ὄν ἐστι, σκληρόν ἐστι καὶ οὐ μαλακόν· εἰ δὲ
μαλακόν, πρὸ τοῦ γεγονέναι μαλακὸν ἔσται μαλακόν. ᾗ μὲν γὰρ ὄν ἐστι, σκληρόν ἐστι καὶ οὔπω
μαλακόν· ᾗ δὲ ὅτε ὄν ἐστι τότε ἀξιοῦται πάσχειν,
πρὶν γεγονέναι μαλακὸν γενήσεται μαλακόν. ἄτοπον
δέ γε τὸ τοιοῦτον· οὐκ ἄρα τὸ ὄν, ἐφ' ὅσον ὄν ἐστι,
276 πάσχειν ῥητέον. ὡσαύτως δὲ οὐδὲ τὸ μὴ ὄν,
ὅτε μὴ ὄν ἐστιν. τῷ γὰρ μὴ ὄντι οὐδὲν συμβέβηκεν,
ᾧ δὲ μηδὲν συμβέβηκεν, οὐδὲ τὸ πάσχειν συμ-
βέβηκεν· τοίνυν οὐδὲ τὸ μὴ ὂν πάσχει τι. εἰ δὲ
μήτε τὸ ὂν μήτε τὸ μὴ ὂν πάσχει τι καὶ παρὰ
ταῦτα οὐδὲν ἔστιν, οὐδὲν ἔστι τὸ πάσχον.
277 Καὶ μὴν εἰ ἔστι τι τὸ πάσχον, ἤτοι κατὰ πρόσ-

---

[1] ⟨γινόμενον⟩ addo.
[2] ⟨οὐδὲν . . . γεγονός.⟩ add. N, Mutsch.

so far as it is existent it will be hard, but in so far as it is affected while existent it will be soft. But the same thing cannot be conceived as at once both hard and soft ; therefore, the existent, when it is existent, cannot be affected. And the same argument holds 273 good also in the case of white colour and black. For let it be granted that the existent, in so far as it is existent, is white and that it is affected by becoming black. If then the existent and white is held to be affected by becoming black at the time when it is white, it will have opposite properties ; which is absurd. So then the existent, in so far as it is existent, is not of a nature to be affected.—Further, if we say that 274 the existent, when it is existent, is affected, there will exist something become before it has become ; ⟨but there is nothing become before it has become ;⟩ therefore the existent, when it is existent, is not affected. For if the existent is hard, in so far as it is 275 existent, it is hard and not soft ; and if it ⟨becomes⟩ soft, it will be soft before it has become soft ; for in so far as it is existent it is hard and not yet soft ; but in so far as it is held to be affected at the time when it is existent, it will become soft before it has become soft. But such a result is absurd ; one must, there-fore, declare that the existent, in so far as it is existent, is not affected.—And in the same way, the 276 non-existent is not affected when it is non-existent. For the non-existent has no property, and being affected is not a property of that which has no property ; neither, then, is the non-existent affected at all. But if neither the existent nor the non-existent is affected at all, and besides these there is no other alternative, there is nothing which is affected.

Moreover, if there is something which is affected, it 277

θεσιν πάσχει ἢ κατὰ ἀφαίρεσιν ἢ κατὰ ἑτεροίωσιν
καὶ μεταβολήν· οὔτε δὲ πρόσθεσίς τις ἔστιν οὔτε
ἀφαίρεσις οὔτε μεταβολὴ καὶ ἑτεροίωσις, ὡς ὑπο-
278 δείξομεν· οὐκ ἄρα πάσχει τι.   καθὰ γὰρ ἐπὶ τῶν
ὀνομάτων κατὰ τούτους τοὺς τρεῖς τρόπους γί-
νονταί τινες μεταπτώσεις, καὶ τοῦ μὲν κωβιὸς[a]
ὀνόματος ἀφαιρεθείσης τῆς πρώτης συλλαβῆς γίνεται ἕτερον ὄνομα βίος, καὶ τούτῳ προστεθείσης
τῆς αὐτῆς συλλαβῆς συνίσταται τὸ πρότερον ὄνομα,
καὶ παρὰ ἐναλλαγὴν στοιχείων, ὡς τὸ ἄρχων ὄνομα
γίνεται Χάρων, οὕτω καὶ τὰ σώματα λεχθείη ἂν
πάσχειν τριχῶς, ἤτοι κατὰ ἀφαίρεσιν ἢ κατὰ πρόσ-
279 θεσιν ἢ κατὰ ἑτεροίωσιν, κατὰ ἀφαίρεσιν μὲν οἷον
τὰ φθίνοντα, κατὰ πρόσθεσιν δὲ οἷον τὰ αὐξόμενα,
κατὰ τροπὴν δὲ ὡς τὰ ἐξ ὑγείας εἰς νόσον μετα-
πίπτοντα.   ἐὰν οὖν δειχθῇ ὅτι οὐδὲν οὐδενὸς
ἀφαιρεῖται καὶ ὅτι οὐδὲν οὐδενὶ προστίθεται καὶ
ὅτι οὐδὲν ἀπ' οὐδενὸς μετατίθεται, αὐτόθεν ἔσται
κατεσκευασμένον τὸ μηδὲν εἶναι τὸ πάσχον.
280 λέγωμεν δὲ ἐν πρώτοις περὶ τοῦ κατὰ ἀφαίρεσιν
τρόπου.

Εἰ γὰρ ἀφαιρεῖταί τι ἀπό τινος, ἤτοι σῶμα ἀπὸ
σώματος ἀφαιρεῖται ἢ ἀσώματον ἀπὸ ἀσωμάτου ἢ
σῶμα ἀπὸ ἀσωμάτου ἢ ἀσώματον ἀπὸ σώματος·
οὔτε δὲ σῶμα ἀπὸ σώματος ἀφαιρεῖται, ὡς δείξομεν, οὔτε ἀσώματον ἀπὸ ἀσωμάτου, καθὼς
παραστήσομεν, οὔτε σῶμα ἀπὸ ἀσωμάτου ἢ ἀ-
281 σώματον ἀπὸ σώματος, ὡς καταστησόμεθα· οὐκ
ἄρα ἀφαιρεῖταί τι τινός.   ἀσώματον μὲν οὖν ἀπὸ ἀ-
σωμάτου ἀφαιρεθῆναι τῶν ἀδυνάτων ἐστίν· τὸ γὰρ
ἀφαιρούμενον ἀπό τινος οὐκ ἔστιν ἀθιγές, τὸ δὲ

---

[a] κωβιός, "gudgeon"; βίος, "life."

is affected either through addition or through subtraction or through alteration and change. But no addition nor subtraction nor change and alteration exists, as we shall demonstrate ; nothing therefore is affected. For just as, in the case of nouns, modifi- 278 cations take place in these three ways, and when the first syllable is subtracted from the noun *kōbios* [a] there is formed another noun *bios*, and when the same syllable is added to this the former noun is constructed; and by interchange of letters, as when the noun *archon* becomes *Charon* ;—so, too, bodies may be said to be affected in three ways, either through addition or through subtraction or through altera- tion—through subtraction like decreasing things ; 279 through addition, like increasing things ; through conversion, like things that pass over from health to sickness. If, then, it shall be shown that nothing is subtracted from anything and that nothing is added to anything and that nothing is transposed from anything, it will thereby be established that there is nothing which is affected. And let us discuss in the 280 first place the mode of subtraction. [b]

If one thing is subtracted from another, either body is subtracted from body, or the incorporeal from the incorporeal, or body from the incorporeal, or the incorporeal from body ; but neither body is subtracted from body, as we shall prove, nor the incorporeal from the incorporeal, as we shall demonstrate, nor body from the incorporeal nor the incorporeal from body, as we shall establish ; therefore nothing is sub- 281 tracted from anything. Now, that the incorporeal should be subtracted from the incorporeal is a thing impossible ; for what is subtracted from a thing is not

[b] With this discussion of " subtraction " *cf. P.H.* iii. 85 ff.

ἀσώματον ἀθιγὲς ὂν οὐ παρέχει αὐτὸ πρὸς ἀφ-
282 αίρεσιν καὶ χωρισμόν. ἔνθεν καὶ ματαιάζουσιν
οἱ μαθηματικοί, ὅταν λέγωσι τὴν δοθεῖσαν εὐθεῖαν
δίχα τεμεῖν. ἡ γὰρ ἡμῖν ἐπὶ τοῦ ἄβακος δεικνυμένη
εὐθεῖα αἰσθητὸν ἔχει μῆκος καὶ πλάτος, ἡ δὲ ὑπ᾽
αὐτῶν νοουμένη εὐθεῖα γραμμὴ μῆκός ἐστιν ἀ-
πλατές. καὶ ἡ ἐπὶ τοῦ ἄβακος δεικνυμένη οὐκ ἂν
εἴη γραμμή, καὶ οἱ ἐπιβαλλόμενοι ταύτην τέμνειν οὐ
τὴν οὖσαν γραμμὴν ἀλλὰ τὴν μὴ οὖσαν τέμνουσιν.
283 ἢ καὶ ἄλλως, ἐπεὶ κατ᾽ αὐτοὺς ἡ γραμμὴ
ἐκ στιγμῶν συνεστῶσα νοεῖται, ἔστω τις εὐθεῖα
γραμμή, ἣν λέγουσιν εἰς ἴσα τέμνειν, ἐκ περισσῶν
συνεστῶσα στιγμῶν, οἷον ἐννέα. ἀλλὰ ταύτην γε
τέμνοντες ἢ τὴν πέμπτην διελοῦσι στιγμήν, φημὶ
δὲ τὴν μεταξὺ τῶν τεσσάρων καὶ τῶν τεσσάρων
νοουμένην, ἢ τῶν τμημάτων τὸ μὲν τεττάρων ποιή-
σουσι στιγμῶν τὸ δὲ πέντε. τὴν μὲν οὖν πέμπτην
στιγμὴν οὐκ ἂν φαῖεν τέμνειν· ἀμερὴς γάρ ἐστι κατ᾽
αὐτούς, καὶ τὸ ἀμερὲς ἀδύνατον νοεῖν εἰς μέρη
διαιρούμενον. λείπεται ἄρα τῶν τῆς γραμμῆς
τμημάτων τὸ μὲν τεσσάρων ποιεῖν στιγμῶν τὸ δὲ
πέντε, ὃ πάλιν ἐστὶν ἄτοπον καὶ παρὰ τὴν πρό-
θεσιν αὐτῶν· ὑπισχνοῦνται μὲν γὰρ ἐπιστημονικῶς
τὴν δοθεῖσαν εὐθεῖαν γραμμὴν εἰς ἴσα διαιρεῖν
284 τμήματα, διαιροῦσι δὲ αὐτὴν εἰς ἄνισα. ὁ δὲ
αὐτὸς καὶ ἐπὶ τοῦ κύκλου λόγος νοείσθω. φασὶ γὰρ
κύκλον εἶναι σχῆμα ἐπίπεδον ὑπὸ μιᾶς γραμμῆς
περιεχόμενον, [ἀφ᾽][1] οὗ πᾶσαι αἱ ἀπὸ τοῦ κέντρου
πρὸς τὴν περιφέρειαν ἐκβαλλόμεναι εὐθεῖαι ἴσαι
ἀλλήλαις εἰσίν. εἶτα ἐπὶ τούτοις πρόβλημά ἐστι
τὸν κύκλον δίχα τεμεῖν· ὅπερ ἐστὶν ἀδύνατον. τὸ

---

[1] [ἀφ᾽] secl. Mutsch.: ἐφ᾽ Bekk.

intangible, but the incorporeal, being intangible, does not submit to subtraction and separation. Hence, 282 too, the mathematicians talk idly when they say that they will bisect a given straight line. For the straight line shown to us on the board has length and breadth, whereas the straight line conceived by them is "length without breadth." And the line shown on the board will not be a line, and those who attempt to cut it are cutting not the real line but the unreal.— Or again, since, according to them, the line is con- 283 ceived as composed of points, let us assume a certain straight line, which they say they cut into equal parts, composed of an odd number of points, such as nine. But in cutting this, either they will divide the fifth point (I mean the point conceived as lying between the first four and the last four), or else they will make one of the sections consist of four points and the other of five. Now they will not say that they cut the fifth point ; for, according to them, the point is without parts, and it is impossible to conceive what is without parts as divided into parts. It only remains, therefore, to make the one section of the line consist of four points and the other of five, which again is absurd and at variance with their undertaking ; for they promise to divide the given straight line scientifically into equal sections, but they divide it into unequal ones.—And the same argument may be 284 applied in the case of the circle. For they say that the circle is "a plane form enclosed by one line, of which all the straight lines extending from the centre to the circumference are equal to one another." Then, on these conditions, the problem is to bisect the circle ; and this is impossible. For the centre, which

γὰρ κέντρον, ὅπερ παντὸς τοῦ κύκλου μεσαίτατόν
ἐστιν, ἤτοι δίχα τέμνεται κατὰ τὴν τοῦ κύκλου
διχοτόμησιν ἢ τῷ ἑτέρῳ προσμερίζεται τμήματι.
285 ἀλλὰ δίχα μὲν τμηθῆναι τῶν ἀδυνάτων· πῶς γὰρ
οἷόν τε τὸ ἀμερὲς ἐπινοεῖν μεριζόμενον; εἰ δὲ τῷ
ἑτέρῳ προσμερίζεται τμήματι, ἄνισα γίνεται τὰ
τμήματα καὶ ὁ κύκλος οὐ μέσος διαιρεῖται.
286 τό τε τέμνον τὴν γραμμὴν ἢ τὸν κύκλον ἤτοι σῶμά
ἐστιν ἢ ἀσώματον. ἀλλὰ σῶμα μὲν πῶς ἂν ἐπι-
νοηθείη; ἀθιγὲς γὰρ καὶ ἀσώματον καὶ ἀνυπόπτωτον ἡμῖν τὸ τεμνόμενον, τουτέστιν ἡ γραμμὴ καὶ
ὁ κύκλος. τοιοῦτο δὲ ὂν οὐκ ἂν τμηθείη ὑπὸ
σώματος· τὸ γὰρ ὑπὸ σώματος τεμνόμενον παθεῖν
δεῖ καὶ θιχθῆναι, τὸ δὲ ἀσώματον οὔτε θιγεῖν οὔτε
θιχθῆναι πέφυκεν. ὥστε οὐκ ἔνεστι [νοῆσαι] ὑπὸ
σώματος τεμνομένην τὴν γραμμὴν καὶ διαιρούμενον
287 τὸν κύκλον ἐπινοῆσαι.   καὶ μὴν οὐδὲ ὑπὸ
ἀσωμάτου τινός. εἰ γὰρ ἀσώματόν ἐστι τὸ διαιροῦν
τὴν γραμμὴν ἢ τὸν κύκλον, ἤτοι στιγμὴ στιγμὴν
τέμνει ἢ γραμμὴ γραμμήν. οὔτε δὲ στιγμὴ τὴν
στιγμὴν οὔτε γραμμὴ τὴν γραμμὴν οἷά τέ ἐστι
288 τέμνειν, ἀλλὰ στιγμὴ μὲν τὴν στιγμὴν οὐκ ἂν τέμοι,
ἐπεὶ ἑκατέρα ἐστὶν ἀμερής, καὶ οὔτε ἡ τέμνουσα
ἔχει οἷς τεμεῖ οὔτε ἡ τεμνομένη τὰ εἰς ἃ τμη-
289 θήσεται. γραμμὴ δὲ τὴν γραμμὴν πάλιν οὐκ ἂν
διαιροίη. ἐάν τε γὰρ πλαγίως ἐπιζευχθῇ ἐάν τε
ὀρθίως ἡ τέμνουσα τῇ τεμνομένῃ, κατ' ἀνάγκην
ὀφείλει στιγμῇ ἑαυτῆς ἐπιζεύγνυσθαι τῇ κατὰ τὴν
διαιρουμένην γραμμὴν στιγμῇ. ἀμεροῦς μὲν οὖν
οὔσης καὶ τῆς ἐπιζευγνυμένης, ἀμεροῦς δὲ καὶ τῆς
ἐν τῇ τεμνομένῃ, οὐ γενήσεταί τις διαίρεσις διὰ τὸ
μήτε τὴν τέμνουσαν εὐθυῶς ἔχειν πρὸς τὸ τέμνειν,

is in the very middle of the whole circle, either is bisected in the bisection of the circle, or is added on to one or other of the sections. But it is impossible 285 for it to be bisected ; for how is it possible to conceive what is without parts as partitioned ? And if it is added on to either of the sections, the sections become unequal and the circle is not divided in the middle.— Also, that which cuts the line or the circle is either a 286 body or incorporeal. But how can it be conceived as a body ? For the thing cut—namely, the line or the circle—is intangible and incorporeal and imperceptible by us. And being such, it will not be cut by a body ; for what is cut by a body must be acted upon and be touched, but the incorporeal is not of a nature either to touch or be touched. So that it is not possible to conceive of the line being cut or the circle divided by a body.—Nor yet by anything incorporeal. 287 For if what divides the line or the circle is incorporeal, it is either a point that cuts a point or a line a line. But neither can a point cut the point nor a line the line. For a point will not cut the point since each of 288 them is without parts, and the one which cuts has no parts wherewith to cut, nor has the one which is being cut any parts into which it may be cut. Nor, again, 289 will the line divide the line. For whether the cutting line is joined to the line that is being cut at an acute or at a right angle, it must necessarily be joined at a point in itself to a point in the divided line. As, however, the point of the joined line is without parts, and the point in the cut line is also without parts, no division will take place, since neither the cutting line is suited by nature for cutting, being without parts,

οὖσαν ἀμερῆ, μήτε τὴν τεμνομένην πρὸς τὸ τέμνε-
290 σθαι τῷ παντὸς ἐστερῆσθαι μέρους.   καὶ μὴν
οὐδ᾽ ἔνεστι λέγειν ὅτι τὸ τέμνον τὴν γραμμὴν
μεταξὺ δυοῖν στιγμῶν τῶν ἐν τῇ τεμνομένῃ γραμμῇ
πῖπτον τέμνει τὴν γραμμήν.   τοῦτο γὰρ τῶν προειρημένων ἐστὶν ἀτοπώτερον. πρῶτον μὲν γὰρ
ἐν συνεχείᾳ γραμμῆς ἀδύνατόν ἐστι μέσον πεσεῖν
πέρας, ἀλλ᾽ ἀνάγκη κατὰ στιγμῆς φερόμενον νοεῖν
291 τὸ τέμνον. εἶτα κἂν συγχωρηθῇ μεταξὺ δυοῖν
στιγμῶν τῶν ἐν τῇ τεμνομένῃ γραμμῇ φερόμενον
τὸ τέμνον τέμνειν τὴν γραμμήν, χεῖρόν τι ἀνα-
δύσεται τοῖς γεωμέτραις. αἱ γὰρ συνθετικαὶ τῆς
γραμμῆς στιγμαὶ ἤτοι οὕτως εἰσὶ συνεχεῖς ὡς μὴ
παραδέχεσθαι μεταξὺ ἀλλήλων ἔξωθέν τινα στιγμήν, ἢ οὐκ ἔσται ἡ ἐξ αὐτῶν σύνθετος συνεχὴς καὶ
292 μία γραμμή. εἰ δ᾽ οὕτως εἰσὶ συνεχεῖς ὡς ἀνεπινόητον ἔχειν μεταξὺ ἀλλήλων τόπον στιγμῆς, ἵνα
τὸ τέμνον διχάζῃ τὴν γραμμήν, δυοῖν θάτερον, ἢ τὴν
στιγμὴν δεῖ τὴν καθ᾽ ἧς φέρεται νοεῖν διχαζομένην,
ἢ τούτου ἀδυνάτου καθεστῶτος τὰς ὑποκειμένας
στιγμὰς τῆς γραμμῆς νοεῖν ὑπαναχωρούσας καὶ
τόπον καὶ διάστασιν παρεχομένας, τοτὲ μὲν ἐπὶ
τόδε τὸ μέρος συστελλομένων τοτὲ δὲ ἐπὶ τόδε, ὧν
293 ἑκάτερόν ἐστιν ἄτοπον· οὔτε γὰρ στιγμή, καθὼς
προπαρεμυθησάμεθα, τέμνεσθαι δύναται τῷ ἀμερὴς
ὑπάρχειν, οὔτε αἱ ἐν τῇ τεμνομένῃ γραμμῇ στιγμαὶ
ὑπαναχωρεῖν πεφύκασιν· ἀκίνητοι γάρ εἰσιν. τοίνυν
καὶ τὸ ἀσώματον οὔτε ἀφαιρεῖται ἀπό τινος ἀ-
294 σωμάτου οὔτε ἐπιδέχεται τὴν ἀφαίρεσιν.   κἂν ἐπὶ
τῶν αἰσθητῶν δὲ γραμμῶν καὶ κύκλων, τουτέστι

142

nor the cut line for being cut, owing to its wholly lacking parts.—Moreover, it is not possible to say 290 that what cuts the line cuts the line by falling between two points in the line that is being cut. For this is still more absurd than the foregoing. For, in the first place, it is impossible that an intermediate limit [a] should be set within the continuity of a line, and one must necessarily conceive the thing which cuts as striking at a point. And, secondly, even if it be con- 291 ceded that the sector cuts the line between two of the points in the line which is being cut, a worse result for the geometers will emerge. For the points which compose the line either are so continuous as not to admit of any point from outside coming between them, or else the line composed of them will not be a single and continuous line. But if they are so continuous 292 that there is no conceivable space between them for a point, so as to enable the sector to bisect the line, then one or other of two results must follow—either we must conceive the point on which it strikes as being divided, or, if this is impossible, we must con- ceive the existing points of the line as receding and affording it space and an interval, by crowding to- gether now towards this side, and now towards that ; and each of these suppositions is absurd ; for, as we 293 have pointed out above, the point cannot be cut, owing to its being without parts, nor are the points in the line that is being cut of such a nature as to recede, for they are immobile. So then, the incorporeal neither is subtracted from an incorporeal nor admits of subtraction.—And even if the geometers propose 294

[a] *i.e.* a point (of the sector) which acts as a " limit " (or ends the line) in the middle of the line by breaking its continuity.

SEXTUS EMPIRICUS

τῶν ἐπὶ τοῦ ἄβακος βλεπομένων, θέλωσι στήσαντες
τὸν λόγον οἱ γεωμέτραι διδάσκειν τί τινος ἀφαιρούμενον, οὐ δυνήσονται· οὔτε γὰρ ἀφ᾽ ὅλης
τῆς γραμμῆς ἢ ἀφ᾽ ὅλου τοῦ κύκλου δύναταί τις ἀφαίρεσις γενομένη νοεῖσθαι οὔτε ἀπὸ μέρους, ὡς
μικρὸν ὕστερον προβάντος τοῦ λόγου διδάξομεν,
ὅταν εἰς τὴν περὶ τῶν τεμνομένων σωμάτων ζήτησιν
συγκαταβαίνωμεν.

295   Νῦν δὲ συντόμως δειχθέντος ὅτι οὐδὲν ἀσώματον
οὐδενὸς ἀσωμάτου ἀφαιρεῖσθαι δύναται, λείπεται
λέγειν ἢ σῶμα ἀπὸ σώματος χωρίζεσθαι ἢ ἀ-
σώματον ἀπὸ σώματος ἢ σῶμα ἀπὸ ἀσωμάτου.
ἀλλὰ σῶμα μὲν ἀπὸ ἀσωμάτου ἀφαιρεῖσθαι αὐτό-
296 θεν ἐστὶν ἀδιανόητον, ἀσώματον δὲ ἀπὸ σώματος
χωρίζεσθαι τῶν ἀδυνάτων· θιγεῖν γὰρ δεῖ τοῦ
ἀφαιρουμένου τὸ ἀφαιροῦν, ἀθιγὲς δέ ἐστι τὸ
ἀσώματον καὶ ἀδύνατος δέδεικται ἡ θίξις· ὥστε
οὐδὲ ἀσώματον σώματος χωρισθείη ποτ᾽ ἄν. καὶ
ἄλλως τὸ χωριζόμενόν τινος οἱονεὶ μέρος ἐστὶ τοῦ
ἀφ᾽ οὗ χωρίζεται, τὸ δὲ ἀσώματον τοῦ σώματος
297 οὐκ ἂν εἴη μέρος.   καὶ μὴν οὐδὲ σῶμα σώματος
δύναται ἀφαιρεῖσθαι. εἰ γὰρ σῶμα ἀπὸ σώματος
ἀφαιρεῖται, ἤτοι τὸ ἴσον ἀπὸ ἴσου ἀφαιρεῖται ἢ τὸ
ἄνισον ἀπὸ τοῦ ἀνίσου· ἀλλ᾽ οὔτε τὸ ἴσον ἀπὸ τοῦ
ἴσου ἀφαιρεῖσθαι δύναται, ὡς διδάξομεν, οὔτε τὸ
ἄνισον ἀπὸ τοῦ ἀνίσου, ὡς ὑπομνήσομεν· οὐκ ἄρα
298 σῶμα ἀπὸ σώματος ἀφαιρεῖται. ἴσον μὲν οὖν ἀπὸ
ἴσου οὐκ ἂν ἀφαιρεθείη, καθάπερ ἀπὸ πήχεως
πῆχυς, ἐπεὶ οὐκ ἔσται τὸ τοιοῦτον ἀφαίρεσις
299 ἀλλὰ παντελὴς τοῦ ὑποκειμένου ἀναίρεσις. καὶ

ᵃ Cf. § 282.
ᵇ Cf. §§ 297 ff., 331 ff.

to show how one thing is subtracted from another by basing their argument on sensible lines and circles—that is, on those seen on the board,[a]—they will not be able ; for no subtraction can be conceived as taking place from the whole line or the whole circle, or from a part of them, as we shall show a little farther on in our exposition,[b] when we come to deal with the investigation of bodies which are divided.

And now that it has been shown concisely that no 295 incorporeal can be subtracted from any incorporeal, it remains for us to say either that body is separated from body, or the incorporeal from body, or body from the incorporeal. But the subtraction of body 296 from the incorporeal is of itself inconceivable, and the separation of the incorporeal from body is a thing impossible ; for what subtracts must touch what is subtracted, but the incorporeal is intangible and touch has been proved to be impossible [c] ; so that neither will the incorporeal ever be separated from body. And besides : what is separated from anything is, as it were, a part of that from which it is separated, but the incorporeal will not be a part of the body.—Nor, 297 again, can body be subtracted from body.[d] For if body is subtracted from body, either the equal is subtracted from the equal, or the unequal from the unequal ; but the equal cannot be subtracted from the equal, as we shall show, nor the unequal from the unequal, as we shall explain ; therefore body is not subtracted from body. Now the equal will not be 298 subtracted from the equal,—the cubit, for instance, from the cubit,—since such a thing is not subtraction but the complete removal of the object. And besides 299

[c] *Cf.* §§ 258 ff.
[d] With §§ 297-307 *cf. P.H.* iii. 85-88.

ἔτι ἤτοι ἀπὸ μένοντος τοῦ πήχεως ποιησόμεθα τὴν
ἀφαίρεσιν ἢ ἀπὸ μὴ μένοντος. καὶ εἰ μὲν ἀπὸ
μένοντος, διπλασιάσομεν τὸν πῆχυν ἀλλ' οὐκ
ἐλαττώσομεν· πῶς γὰρ ἔτι πῆχυς ὑπόκειται ὁ
πῆχυς πήχεως ἐξ αὐτοῦ ἀφαιρεθέντος; εἰ δὲ ἀπὸ
μὴ μένοντος, οὐδὲν ἀπολείπομεν τὸ τὴν ἀφαίρεσιν
ἐπιδεξόμενον· ἀπὸ γὰρ τῶν μὴ ὄντων ἀμήχανόν τι
ἀφαιρεθῆναι. ὥστε ⟨τὸ⟩[1] ἴσον μὲν ἀπὸ τοῦ ἴσου οὐκ
300 ἀφαιρεῖται. καὶ μὴν οὐδὲ τὸ ἄνισον ἀπὸ τοῦ
ἀνίσου. εἰ γὰρ τοῦτο, ἤτοι τὸ μεῖζον ἀπὸ τοῦ
ἥττονος ἀφαιρεῖται, ὥσπερ ἀπὸ παλαιστοῦ πῆχυς,
ἢ ἀπὸ μείζονος τὸ ἧττον, ὡς τὸ παλαιστιαῖον ἀπὸ
301 τοῦ πηχυαίου. ἀλλὰ τὸ μὲν μεῖζον ἀπὸ τοῦ
ἥττονος οὐκ ἂν ἀφαιρεθείη· δεῖ γὰρ τὸ ἀπό τινος
ἀφαιρούμενον περιέχεσθαι ἐν ἐκείνῳ τῷ ἐξ οὗ ἡ
ἀφαίρεσις, ἐν δὲ τῷ ἥττονι οὐ περιέχεται τὸ μεῖζον.
καὶ διὰ τοῦτο, ὡς οὐκ ἔστιν ἀπὸ τῶν πέντε
ἀφαιρεῖν τὰ ἕξ (οὐ γὰρ ἐμπεριέχεται τοῖς πέντε τὰ
ἕξ), οὕτως οὐδὲ ἀπὸ τοῦ ἥττονος δυνατόν ἐστιν
ἀφαιρεῖν τὸ μεῖζον· οὐ γὰρ ἐμπεριέχεται τῷ ἥττονι
τὸ μεῖζον. τοίνυν οὐκ ἀφαιρεῖται ἀπὸ τοῦ ἥττονος
302 τὸ μεῖζον. καὶ μὴν οὐδὲ ἀπὸ τοῦ μείζονος
τὸ ἧττον. ὡς γὰρ ἐλέγομεν, δεῖ τὸ ἀπό τινος
ἀφαιρούμενον ἐμπεριέχεσθαι τῷ ἐξ οὗ ἡ ἀφαίρεσις.
οὐχὶ δέ γε τὸ ἔλαττον ἐμπεριέχεται τῷ πλείονι·
ἀκολουθήσει γὰρ καὶ τὸ μεῖζον καὶ τὸ πλεῖον ἐμπεριέχεσθαι τῷ ἥττονι, ἀδύνατον δὲ τοῦτο ἐδείκνυτο.
ὥστε οὐδὲ τὸ ἧττον ἐμπερισχεθήσεται τῷ μείζονι,
303 οὑτωσὶ δ' οὐδ' ἀφαιρεθήσεται. καὶ ὅτι τῷ ὄντι
σώζεται τὰ τῆς ἀκολουθίας, σκοπῶμεν ἐπὶ τῶν

---

[1] ⟨τὸ⟩ addo.

we will make the subtraction from the cubit either while it remains or while it does not remain. And if we do so while it remains, we shall be doubling the cubit instead of diminishing it ; for how will the cubit still be really a cubit after a cubit has been subtracted from it ? And if ⟨the subtraction be made⟩ while it does not remain, we are leaving nothing behind to submit to the subtraction ; for it is impossible for anything to be subtracted from non-existents. So that the equal is not subtracted from the equal.— Nor, again, is the unequal subtracted from the un- 300 equal. For if so, either the greater is subtracted from the less, as a cubit from a palm ; or the less from the greater, as that which is a palm in length from that which is a cubit in length. But the greater will 301 not be subtracted from the less ; for that which is subtracted from anything must be included in the thing from which the subtraction takes place, but the greater is not included in the less. And because of this, just as it is not possible to subtract six from five (for five does not include six), so too it is not possible to subtract the greater from the less ; for the greater is not included in the less. So then, the greater is not subtracted from the less.—Nor, again, is the less 302 subtracted from the greater. For, as we have said, that which is subtracted from anything must be included in that from which the subtraction takes place. But the less is not included in the more ; for if so, it will follow that both the greater and the more are included in the less, and this was shown to be impossible. So that the less will not be included in the greater, and thus it will not be subtracted either. And that the rules of logical consistency are 303 observed we may see from the examples given by

τιθεμένων τοῖς ἀπορητικοῖς ὑποδειγμάτων. εἰ γὰρ
ἐν τοῖς ἓξ ἐμπεριέχεται τὰ πέντε ὡς ἐν πλείονι
ἐλάττονα, ἀνάγκη κἂν τοῖς πέντε περιέχεσθαι τὰ
τέσσαρα ὡς ἐν πλείονι ἐλάττονα, κἂν τοῖς τέσσαρσι
τὰ τρία, κἂν τοῖς τρισὶ τὰ δύο, κἂν τοῖς δυσὶ τὸ
ἕν, καὶ διὰ τοῦτο ἐν τῷ ἓξ ἀριθμῷ περιέχεσθαι τὰ
πέντε καὶ τὰ τέσσαρα καὶ τρία καὶ δύο καὶ ἕν,
304 ἅπερ ἐστὶ πεντεκαίδεκα. ἀλλ' εἰ ἐν τῷ ἓξ κατὰ
τὸν ἴδιον αὐτοῦ λόγον ἐμπεριέχεται τὰ πεντεκαίδεκα
κατ' ἀνάγκην τῷ πέντε περισχεθήσεται τὰ τέσσαρα
καὶ τρία καὶ δύο καὶ ἕν, ἅπερ ἐστὶ δέκα. καὶ ὃν
τρόπον ἐν τοῖς πέντε περιέσχηται τὰ δέκα, οὕτω
κἂν τοῖς τέσσαρσιν ἔσται τὰ τρία καὶ δύο καὶ ἕν,
τουτέστι τὰ ἕξ, καὶ κατὰ τὸ ἀνάλογον ἐν τοῖς τρισὶ
τὰ δύο καὶ τὸ ἕν, ἅπερ ἐστὶν ἄλλα τρία, κἂν τοῖς
305 λειπομένοις δυσὶ τὸ ἕν. ταύτῃ συντιθεμένων τῶν
ἐν τοῖς ἓξ ἀριθμῶν, φημὶ δὲ τοῦ πεντεκαίδεκα καὶ
τοῦ δέκα καὶ τοῦ ἓξ καὶ τοῦ τρία, ἔτι καὶ τοῦ ἑνός,
ἔσται ὁ ἓξ ἀριθμὸς περιεσχηκὼς τὸν τριάκοντα
306 πέντε ἀριθμόν. τούτου τ' ἔτι συγχωρηθέντος
ἀπειράκις ἀπείρων ἀριθμῶν περιληπτικὸς ἔσται ὁ
ἕξ· πάλιν γὰρ ὁ τριάκοντα πέντε τῶν ὑποβεβηκό-
των ἀριθμῶν ἔσται περιληπτικός, οἷον τοῦ τριάκοντα τέσσαρα, καὶ οὗτος τοῦ τριάκοντα τρία, καὶ
οὗτος τοῦ τριάκοντα δύο, καὶ οὕτω καθ' ὑπόβασιν
307 μέχρις ἀπείρου. ἀλλ' εἴπερ ἵνα τί τινος
ἀφαιρεθῇ, δεῖ ἐμπεριέχεσθαι τὸ ἀφαιρούμενον τῷ
ἐξ οὗ ἡ ἀφαίρεσις, δέδεικται δὲ οὔτε ἐν τῷ ἥττονι
τὸ μεῖζον περιεχόμενον οὔτε ἐν τῷ μείζονι τὸ
ἔλαττον, καὶ μὴν οὐδὲ ἐν τῷ ἴσῳ τὸ ἴσον (δεῖ
γὰρ τὸ περιέχον μεῖζον εἶναι τοῦ περιεχομένου,
τὸ δέ τινι ἴσον οὔτε ἔλαττόν ἐστιν ἐκείνου οὔτε

the Doubters. Thus, if 5 is included in 6 as the less in the more, 4 also must necessarily be included in 5, as the less in the more, and 3 in 4, and 2 in 3, and 1 in 2; and because of this there are included in the number 6, 5 and 4 and 3 and 2 and 1, which make 15. But if in 6, according to its own proper 304 definition, 15 is included, there will necessarily be contained in 5, 4 and 3 and 2 and 1, which make 10. And just as 10 is included in 5, so also 3 and 2 and 1, which make 6, will inhere in 4; and, by analogy, 2 and 1, which make another 3, in 3; and in the 2 that is still left, 1. Thus when the contents of the 305 6 numbers are added together—I mean the 15 and 10 and 6 and 3, and also the 1, the number 6 will be found to include the number 35. And if this also 306 is granted, the 6 will be capable of including numbers that are infinite times infinite; for the 35, again, will be inclusive of the subordinate numbers, such as 34, and this of 33, and this of 32, and so downwards *ad infinitum*.—But if it is required, in order that 307 one thing may be subtracted from another, that the thing subtracted should be included in that from which the subtraction is made, and it has been proved that neither is the greater included in the less nor the less in the greater, nor yet the equal in the equal (for what includes must be greater than what is included, but what is equal to a thing is neither less nor greater than the thing to which it is equal), then

μεῖζον τοῦ ᾧ ἴσον ἐστί), ῥητέον μηδὲν μηδενὸς ἀφαιρεῖσθαι.

308 Καὶ μὴν εἰ ἀφαιρεῖταί τι τινός, ἤτοι ὅλον ἀπὸ ὅλου ἀφαιρεῖται ἢ μέρος ἀπὸ μέρους ἢ μέρος ἀπὸ ὅλου ἢ ὅλον ἀπὸ μέρους· οὔτε δὲ ὅλον ἀπὸ ὅλου ἀφαιρεῖται οὔτε μέρος ἀπὸ μέρους οὔτε ὅλον ἀπὸ
309 μέρους ἢ μέρος ἀφ' ὅλου, ὡς παραστήσομεν· οὐκ ἄρα ἀφαιρεῖταί τι τινός. τὸ μὲν οὖν ὅλον ἀπὸ τοῦ ὅλου ἀφαιρεῖσθαι τελέως ἐστὶν ἀδύνατον· οὐδεὶς γὰρ ἀπὸ πήχεως ἀφαιρεῖ πῆχυν, οὐδὲ ἀπὸ κοτύλης κοτύλην, ἐπεὶ τὸ τοιοῦτον οὐκ ἔσται τινὸς ἀφαίρεσις ἀλλὰ ὁλοσχερὴς τοῦ ὑποκειμένου ἀναίρεσις.
310 ἀδιανόητον δέ ἐστι καὶ τὸ ὅλον λέγειν ἀπὸ τοῦ μέρους ἀφαιρεῖσθαι. τὸ γὰρ μέρος ἧττόν ἐστι τοῦ ὅλου, καὶ τὸ ὅλον πλεῖόν ἐστι τοῦ μέρους· ἀπὸ δὲ τοῦ ἥττονος λέγειν τὸ πλέον ἀφαιρεῖσθαι σφόδρα ἐστὶν ἀπίθανον. οὐδὲ γὰρ ὑπέκειτο ἐν τῷ μέρει τὸ ὅλον, ἵνα ἀπ' αὐτοῦ λάβῃ τὴν ἀφαίρεσιν, ἀλλ'
311 ἐν τῷ ὅλῳ τὸ μέρος.   λείπεται οὖν τὸ πιθανώτερον εἶναι δοκοῦν, ἢ τὸ μέρος ἀπὸ τοῦ ὅλου ἀφαιρεῖσθαι ἢ τὸ μέρος ἀπὸ τοῦ μέρους. ἀλλὰ καὶ τοῦτο τῶν ἀπόρων ἐτύγχανεν. σκοπῶμεν δὲ τὸ λεγόμενον, ὡς ἔθος τοῖς ἀπὸ τῆς σκέψεως, ἐπὶ
312 ἀριθμοῦ.   ὑποκείσθω γὰρ δεκάς, καὶ ἀφαιρείσθω ἀπὸ ταύτης μονάς. οὐκοῦν ἡ ἀφαιρουμένη μονὰς ἤτοι ἀπὸ τῆς ὑποκειμένης δεκάδος ἀφαιρεῖται ἢ ἀπὸ τῆς μετὰ τὴν ἆρσιν ὑπολειπομένης ἐννεάδος· οὔτε ἀπὸ τῆς ἐννεάδος δὲ οὔτε ἀπὸ τῆς δεκάδος ἀφαιρεῖται, ὡς δείξομεν· οὐκ ἄρα ἀφαιρεῖται τῆς δεκάδος μονάς, ᾧ ἔπεται τὸ μηδὲν μηδενὸς ἀφ-
313 αιρεῖσθαι. εἰ γὰρ ἀπὸ τῆς δεκάδος ἀφαιρεῖται ἡ

ᵃ With §§ 308-317 cf. P.H. iii. 88-93.

150

one must declare that nothing is subtracted from anything.

Moreover, if one thing is subtracted from another, 308 either it is a whole that is subtracted from a whole, or a part from a part, or a part from a whole, or a whole from a part *a* ; but neither is a whole subtracted from a whole, nor a part from a part, nor a whole from a part, nor a part from a whole, as we shall establish ; 309 therefore one thing is not subtracted from another. Now that a whole should be subtracted from the whole is perfectly impossible ; for no one subtracts a cubit from a cubit, nor a pint from a pint, since such an action will not be subtraction but the complete removal of the existing object. And it is also an 310 inconceivable assertion that the whole is subtracted from the part ; for the part is less than the whole, and the whole is more than the part ; and to say that the more is subtracted from the less is extremely incredible. For the whole did not exist in the part, so as to enable it to undergo subtraction therefrom, but rather the part in the whole.—We are left, then, with 311 what seems the more probable alternative, that either the part is subtracted from the whole or the part from the part. But this, too, is a thing not feasible. Let us consider the statement, as is the practice of the Sceptics, in the case of number. Thus, let a decad 312 be assumed, and from it let a monad be subtracted. Then this subtracted monad is subtracted either from the existing decad or from the nine which remains after the subtraction ; but it is not subtracted either from the nine or from the decad, as we shall show ; therefore the monad is not subtracted from the decad ; and from this follows that nothing is subtracted from anything. For if the monad is sub- 313

μονάς, ἤτοι ἕτερόν τί ἐστιν ἡ δεκὰς παρὰ τὰς κατὰ
μέρος μονάδας, ἢ ἀθροισμὸς τῶν κατὰ μέρος
μονάδων ἐστὶν ἡ δεκάς. ἀλλ᾽ ἑτέραν μὲν τῶν κατὰ
μέρος μονάδων οὐκ εἰκὸς εἶναι τὴν δεκάδα· καὶ
γὰρ ἀναιρεθεισῶν αὐτῶν συναναιρεῖται καὶ ὑποκει-
314 μένων πάρεστιν. εἰ δὲ ἐν αὐταῖς ἐστὶ ταῖς μονάσιν
ἡ δεκάς, πάντως ἐὰν λέγωμεν ἀπὸ τῆς δεκάδος
ἀφαιρεῖσθαι τὴν μονάδα, ἐπεὶ ἡ δεκὰς οὐδέν ἐστι
παρὰ τὰς μονάδας, ὁμολογήσομεν τὴν μονάδα ἀφ᾽
ἑκάστης μονάδος ἀφαιρεῖσθαι· ἀλλὰ καὶ ἀφ᾽ ἑαυτῆς
315 διὰ τὸ σὺν ταύτῃ νοεῖσθαι τὴν δεκάδα. ἀπὸ πάσης
δὲ μονάδος ἀφαιρουμένης καὶ ἀφ᾽ ἑαυτῆς τῆς μιᾶς
μονάδος ἔσται ἡ τῆς μιᾶς μονάδος ἆρσις δεκάδος
ἆρσις. ἄτοπον δέ ἐστι τὴν τῆς μονάδος ἆρσιν
δεκάδος λέγειν ἆρσιν ὑπάρχειν. ἄτοπον ἄρα καὶ
ἀπὸ δεκάδος ἀξιοῦν ἀφαιρεῖσθαι μονάδα.   καὶ
μὴν ἀπὸ τῆς περιλειπομένης ἐννεάδος οὐκ ἂν
εἴποιμεν ταύτην ἀφαιρεῖσθαι. εἰ γὰρ ἀπὸ τῆς
ἐννεάδος ἀφαιρεῖται ἡ μονάς, οὐκ ὤφειλε μετὰ τὴν
ἆρσιν αὐτῆς ὁλόκληρος θεωρεῖσθαι ἡ ἐννεάς· τὸ
γὰρ ἀφ᾽ οὗ τι ἀφαιρεῖται, οὐ μένει ὁλόκληρον μετὰ
τὴν ἀφαίρεσιν, ἐπεὶ οὐκ ἔσται γεγονυῖά τις ἀπ᾽
316 αὐτοῦ ἀφαίρεσις. καὶ ἄλλως, εἰ ἀπὸ τῆς περιλειπομένης ἐννεάδος ἀφαιρεῖται ἡ μονάς, ἤτοι ἀπὸ
ὅλης τῆς ἐννεάδος ἀφαιρεῖται ἢ ἀπὸ τῆς ἐσχάτης
μονάδος. οὔτε δὲ ἀπὸ τῆς ὅλης ἐννεάδος ἀφαιρεῖται,
ἐπεὶ ἔσται, μὴ ἑτέρας οὔσης παρὰ τὰς κατὰ μέρος
μονάδας τῆς ἐννεάδος, ἡ μονάδος ἆρσις ἐννεάδος
317 ἆρσις, ὅπερ ἦν ἄτοπον· οὔτε ἀπὸ τῆς ἐσχάτης
μονάδος, ἐπεὶ πρῶτον μὲν ἀμερὴς καὶ ἀδιαίρετός
ἐστιν ἡ μονάς, ἔπειτα πῶς ὁλόκληρος ἀπολείπεται ἡ

tracted from the decad, either the decad is something
other than the individual monads, or the decad is the
sum total of the individual monads. But it is not
likely that the decad is other than the individual
monads ; for it disappears when they disappear,
and when they exist it too is present. And if 314
the decad consists of the monads themselves, if we
say that the monad is subtracted from the decad,
we shall certainly agree that the monad is subtracted from each monad, since the decad is nothing
else than its monads ; and also that it is subtracted from itself, because the decad is conceived
as including this monad. But if the single monad 315
is subtracted from each monad and from itself, the
removal of the single monad is the removal of the
decad. But it is absurd to say that the removal of
the monad is the removal of the decad. Therefore
it is also absurd to maintain that the monad is subtracted from the decad.—Nor yet shall we say that
the monad is subtracted from the remaining nine.
For if the monad is subtracted from the nine, after
its removal the nine ought not to be found complete ;
for that from which something is subtracted does not
remain complete after the subtraction, since otherwise no subtraction will have been made from it. And 316
besides—if the monad is subtracted from the remaining nine, it is subtracted either from the whole nine
or from its last monad. But it is not subtracted from
the whole nine, since then—as the nine is nothing
else than its individual monads—the removal of the
monad is the removal of the nine, which is absurd ;
nor is it subtracted from the last monad since, firstly, 317
the monad is without parts and indivisible ; and,
further, how is the nine left complete and not

ἐννεάς, ἀλλ᾽ οὐ ⟨μειοῦται⟩[1] παρὰ μονάδα; εἰ δὲ
μήτε ἀπὸ τῆς δεκάδος αἴρεται μονὰς μήτε ἀπὸ τῆς
περιλειπομένης ἐννεάδος, παρὰ δὲ ταῦτα οὐδὲν
ἔστι τρίτον ἐπινοεῖσθαι, λεκτέον μὴ ἀφαιρεῖσθαι
318 τῆς δεκάδος μονάδα.   πρὸς τούτοις, εἰ ἀπὸ
τῆς δεκάδος αἴρεται μονάς, ἤτοι ἀπὸ μενούσης ἔτι
τῆς δεκάδος αἴρεται ἡ μονὰς ἢ ἀπὸ μὴ μενούσης·
οὔτε δὲ ἀπὸ μὴ μενούσης αἴρεταί ποτε μονὰς οὔτε
ἀπὸ μενούσης· παρὰ δὲ τὸ εἶναι καὶ μὴ εἶναι οὐδὲν
ἔστιν· οὐκ ἄρα ἀφαιρεῖται ἀπὸ τῆς δεκάδος μονάς.
319 ἀπὸ μὲν οὖν μενούσης τῆς δεκάδος αὐτόθεν φαίνεται
μὴ ἀφαιρεῖσθαι ἡ μονάς· ἐφ᾽ ὅσον γὰρ μένει δεκάς,
οὐδὲν ἀφαιρεῖται ἀπ᾽ αὐτῆς. ἀπὸ δὲ μὴ μενούσης
πάλιν ἀφαιρεῖσθαι ἄτοπον· ἀπὸ γὰρ τοῦ μὴ ὄντος
οὐδὲ ἀφαιρεθῆναί τι δύναται. οὐκ ἄρα ἀφαιρεῖταί
320 τι τινός.   ὁ δὲ αὐτὸς λόγος καὶ περὶ τῆς ἐπὶ[2]
τῶν μετρητῶν ἀφαιρέσεως, οἷον τῆς ἀπὸ χοέως
ἀφαιρουμένης κοτύλης ἢ τοῦ ἀπὸ πήχεως ἀφαιρουμένου παλαιστοῦ. ἢ γὰρ ἀπὸ ὅλου τοῦ χοέως
ῥητέον γίνεσθαι τὴν ἀφαίρεσιν ἢ ἀπὸ μέρους, καὶ
ἤτοι ἀπὸ μένοντος ἢ μὴ μένοντος· ἀπ᾽ οὐδενὸς δὲ
τούτων, ὡς παρεστήσαμεν· τοίνυν οὐδὲ ταύτῃ
ἀφαιρεῖταί τι τινός.
321 Ἀλλ᾽ ὅτι μὲν οὐδέν ἐστιν ἀφαίρεσις, ἐκ τούτων
συμφανές· ὅτι δὲ οὐδὲ προστίθεταί τι τινί, παρακειμένως διδάσκωμεν.   ὑποκειμένου τοίνυν πηχυαίου σώματος καὶ προστιθεμένου τούτῳ παλαι-

---

[1] ⟨μειοῦται⟩ add. Rüstow.
[2] ἐπί Heintz : ἀπό mss., Bekk.

---

[a] The κοτύλη (" cup ") was a liquid measure, about ½ pint ;

154

⟨diminished⟩ by one ? But if the one is taken neither from the ten nor from the remaining nine, and besides these no third possibility can be conceived, one must declare that the one is not subtracted from the ten.—Furthermore, if the one is taken from the ten, the one **318** is taken away either while the ten is still remaining or while it is not remaining ; but the one is never taken away from it either while it remains or while it does not remain ; but there is no other alternative besides existence or non-existence ; therefore the one is not subtracted from the ten. Now that the one is not **319** subtracted from the ten whilst it remains is at once apparent ; for in so far as the ten remains, nothing is subtracted from it. And that it should be subtracted from it whilst it does not remain is also absurd. For nothing can be subtracted from the nonexistent. Therefore, one thing is not subtracted from another.—And the same argument applies also **320** to subtraction in the case of things measured,—for example, the subtraction of a cup from a gallon,[a] or the subtraction of a palm from a cubit. For we must say that the subtraction is made either from the whole pint or from a part of it, and either whilst it remains or whilst it does not remain ; but it is made from none of these, as we have shown ; neither, then, in this way is one thing taken from another.

So then, it is quite evident from these arguments **321** that subtraction is nothing ; and in the next place let us demonstrate that neither is one thing added to another.[b] Let us suppose, then, a body of a cubit's length, and added to this one of a palm's length, so

---

the χοῦς (" gallon ") was 12 κοτύλαι, about ¾ gallon. A
" cubit " contained 6 " palms " of about 3 inches each.
[b] With §§ 321-327 cf. P.H. iii. 94-96.

στιαίου ὥστε ἑπταπάλαιστον γίνεσθαι τὸ ἐκ τοῦ
ὑποκειμένου καὶ τῆς προσθέσεως ἀποτελεσθέν,
ζητῶ [ἐν]¹ τίνι ποτὲ γέγονεν ἡ τοῦ παλαιστοῦ
322 πρόσθεσις; ἤτοι γὰρ αὐτῷ προστέθειται ὁ παλαιστὴς ἢ τῷ προϋποκειμένῳ πήχει ἢ τῷ ἐξ ἀμφοτέρων ἀποτελεσθέντι ἑπταπαλαίστῳ μεγέθει· οὔτε
δὲ αὐτῷ προστίθεται ὁ παλαιστὴς οὔτε τῷ προϋποκειμένῳ πήχει οὔτε τῷ ἐξ ἀμφοτέρων ἀποτελεσθέντι μεγέθει, φημὶ δὲ ἔκ τε τοῦ προϋποκειμένου
πήχεως καὶ τῆς προσθέσεως· οὐκ ἄρα προστίθεταί
323 τι τινί.   ἑαυτῷ μὲν οὖν οὐκ ἂν προστεθείη ὁ
παλαιστής· μὴ ὢν γὰρ ἕτερος ἑαυτοῦ, καὶ μὴ
διπλασιάζων ἑαυτὸν κατὰ τὴν πρόσθεσιν, οὐκ ἂν
ἑαυτῷ προστεθείη. εἰ δὲ τῷ ὑποκειμένῳ πήχει
προστίθεται, πῶς παντὶ προστιθέμενος οὐ παρ-
ισάζεται αὐτῷ καὶ δύο ποιεῖ πήχεις, ὥστε τὸ μὲν
μεῖζον ἧττον γίγνεσθαι τὸ δὲ ἧττον μεῖζον; εἰ
γὰρ ἐξισοῦται τῇ προσθέσει ὁ παλαιστὴς τῷ
πήχει καὶ ὁ πῆχυς τῷ παλαιστῇ, ὁ μὲν πῆχυς
ἧττονι ἰσαζόμενος μείζων καθεστὼς ἥττων γενήσεται, ὁ δὲ παλαιστὴς μικρὸς ὢν καὶ τῷ πήχει
324 ἰσαζόμενος μείζων καταστήσεται.   ἀλλ᾽ εἰ μήθ᾽
ἑαυτῷ προστίθεται ὁ παλαιστὴς μήτε τῷ προϋποκειμένῳ πήχει, λείπεται λέγειν αὐτὸν τῷ ἐξ
ἀμφοτέρων ἀποτελουμένῳ ἑπταπαλαίστῳ μεγέθει
προστίθεσθαι. ὃ πάλιν ἐστὶν ἀλογώτατον· τὸ γὰρ
πρόσθεσιν ἐπιδεχόμενον προϋποκεῖσθαι δεῖ τῆς
προσθέσεως, οὐχὶ δὲ τὸ γινόμενον ἐξ αὐτῶν προϋπόκειται αὐτῶν. οὐκ ἄρα τῷ γινομένῳ ἔκ τε τῆς
προσθέσεως καὶ ἐκ τοῦ προόντος προστίθεται τὸ
325 προστιθέμενον. διαφέρει γε μὴν ἡ πρόσθεσις τοῦ
γινομένου ἐξ αὐτῆς, καὶ διαφωνεῖ τοῖς χρόνοις

that the body formed of the original body and the addition is of seven palms' length—to what, I ask, is the addition of the palm made ? For the palm is 322 added either to itself or to the originally existing cubit or to the magnitude of seven palms composed of both ; but the palm is not added either to itself or to the original cubit or to the magnitude composed of both,—I mean, of both the pre-existing cubit and the addition. Therefore one thing is not added to another. Now the palm will not be added to itself ; 323 for as it is not other than itself, and does not double itself owing to the addition, it will not be added to itself. And if it is added to the original cubit, how is it that, when it is added to all of it, it does not equal it and make two cubits, so that the greater becomes less and the less greater ? For if by the addition the palm is made equal to the cubit and the cubit to the palm, the cubit, which is the greater, by being made equal to the less will become less, whereas the palm, which is small, by being made equal to the cubit will come to be larger. But if the palm is not added to 324 itself nor to the pre-existing cubit, it is only left to us to say that it is added to the magnitude of seven palms composed of both. But this, again, is most irrational ; for that which receives the addition must be in existence before the addition, but that which comes into existence from them is not in existence before them. Therefore, what is added is not added to what comes into existence from both the addition and what previously existed. Moreover, the addition 325 differs from that which results from it and does not

---

¹ [ἐν] secl. Heintz.

ἐκείνῳ· ὅτε μὲν γὰρ γίνεται ἡ πρόσθεσις, οὔπω
τὸ γινόμενον ἔστιν ἐξ αὐτῶν, ὅτε δὲ ἔστι τὸ
γεγονὸς ἐξ αὐτῶν, οὐκέτι ἔσται πρόσθεσις. ὥστε
οὐδὲ τῷ γινομένῳ ἐκ τῆς προσθέσεως καὶ τοῦ
προϋποκειμένου πήχεως προστίθεται ὁ παλαιστής. ἀλλ᾽ ἐπεὶ τὸ προστιθέμενον πάλιν οὔτε αὐτὸ
ἑαυτῷ προστίθεται οὔτε τῷ προϋποκειμένῳ οὔτε
τῷ ἐξ ἀμφοτέρων, οὐδὲ τὴν ἀρχὴν προστίθεταί
τινι.

326 Ἔνεστι δὲ καὶ περὶ ἀριθμῶν τὴν αὐτὴν κινεῖν
ἀπορίαν. ὑποκειμένης γὰρ τετράδος καὶ προσ-
τιθεμένης ταύτῃ μονάδος σκεπτέον τίνι γίνεται
ἡ πρόσθεσις. ἢ γὰρ ἑαυτῇ προστίθεται ἡ μονὰς
ἢ τῇ τετράδι ἢ τῇ ἐξ ἀμφοτέρων ἀποτελουμένῃ
πεντάδι. οὔτε δὲ ἑαυτῇ προστίθεται διὰ τὸ τὸ
μὲν προστιθέμενόν τινι ἕτερον εἶναι ἐκείνου τοῦ ᾧ
προστίθεται, τὴν δὲ μονάδα μὴ ἑτέραν εἶναι ἑαυτῆς,
καὶ διὰ τὸ μηδὲ ἑαυτὴν διπλασιάζειν, δυάδα γινο-
327 μένην, οὔτε τῇ τετράδι διὰ τὸ μὴ ἰσάζεσθαι αὐτῇ
μηδὲ διπλασιάζειν αὐτήν· τὸ γὰρ ὅλῃ τετράδι
προστιθέμενον, μὴ ἑτέρᾳ οὔσῃ τῶν κατὰ μέρος
τεσσάρων μονάδων, τετράς ἐστιν. καὶ μὴν οὐδὲ
τῇ ἐξ αὐτῆς καὶ τῆς τετράδος ἀποτελουμένῃ πεντάδι διὰ τὸ μὴ προϋποκεῖσθαι τῆς προσθέσεως τὴν
πεντάδα καὶ ἀεί ποτε ὀφείλειν τὸ προστιθέμενον
προϋποκειμένῳ τινὶ προστίθεσθαι. οὐκ ἄρα προστίθεταί τι τινί.

328 Ἀλλ᾽ εἰ μήτε ἀφαιρεῖταί τι τινός, ὡς ὑποδέδει-
κται, μήτε προστίθεταί τι τινί, ὡς παρεμυθησάμεθα,
φανερὸν ὡς οὐδὲ μετατίθεταί τι ἀπό τινος· ἦν γὰρ
329 ἡ μετάθεσις τοῦ μὲν ἄρσις τοῦ δὲ πρόσθεσις. μὴ
ὄντων δὲ τούτων οὐδὲ τὸ πάσχον ὀφείλει εἶναι
158

coincide with it in time ; for when the addition is being made, what results from them is not as yet existent, and when what has resulted from them exists, the addition will exist no longer. So that the palm is not added to what results from the addition and the pre-existing cubit. But since, once more, what is added is not added either to itself or to the pre-existing object or to the sum of them both, it is not added to anything at all.

With regard to numbers also it is possible to raise 326 the same difficulty. For if four be set down and one be added to it, to what, we may inquire, is the addition made ? For the one is added either to itself, or to the four, or to the five which is made up of the sum of both. But it is not added to itself, because what is added to anything is other than the thing whereto it is added, but the one is not other than itself ; and also because it does not double itself by becoming two. Nor is it added to the four, because of its not equalling 327 it or doubling it ; for what is added to the whole four, which does not differ from its four individual ones, is a four. Nor, again, is it added to the five which is made up of itself and the four, because the five is not in existence before the addition, and what is added must always be added to something which pre-exists. Therefore, nothing is added to anything.

But if nothing is subtracted from anything, as has 328 been demonstrated, nor anything added to anything, as we have shown, it is also evident that nothing is transposed from anything [a] ; for transposition consists in the subtraction of one thing and the addition of another. And if these are non-existent, what is 329 affected must also be non-existent, inasmuch as

---

[a] With §§ 328-329 cf. P.H. iii. 97.

159

SEXTUS EMPIRICUS

εἴπερ ἦν κατά τινα τούτων τῶν τρόπων τὸ πάσχειν·
ἄλλως γὰρ οὐκ ἄν τις ἐπινοήσειε δυνάμενόν τι
πάσχειν εἰ μὴ κατὰ τούτους τοὺς τρόπους.

330 Συνῆπται δέ πως τῇ περὶ τούτου ἀπορίᾳ καὶ ἡ
περὶ τοῦ ὅλου ἔτι δὲ τοῦ μέρους ζήτησις, ἐπείπερ
καὶ ἡ ἀφαίρεσις μέρους τινὸς ἀπὸ ὅλου δοκεῖ
ἀφαίρεσις εἶναι καὶ ἡ πρόσθεσις ὅλου πάλιν
ὑπάρχει πρόσθεσις. ὅθεν εἰ δειχθείη ὅτι ἄπορός
ἐστιν ὁ περὶ τοῦ ὅλου καὶ τοῦ μέρους λόγος,
ἐπιδειχθήσεται μᾶλλον τὰ περὶ τῆς προσθέσεως
καὶ ἀφαιρέσεως πάσχοντός τε καὶ δρῶντος προ-
ηπορημένα. τὸ δ' ὅτι οὐκ εὐχερές ἐστι λέγειν τί
τὸ¹ ὅλον ἐστὶ καὶ τί τὸ μέρος, ἀκολούθως διδάσκωμεν.

ΠΕΡΙ ΟΛΟΥ ΚΑΙ ΜΕΡΟΥΣ

331 Ἡ περὶ τοῦ ὅλου σκέψις ἀναγκαία ἐστὶ τοῖς μὲν
φυσικοῖς, ἐπεὶ ἄτοπον καθέστηκε τούτους περὶ τοῦ
ὅλου καὶ τοῦ παντὸς ἐπαγγελλομένους τὸ ἀληθὲς
ἐρεῖν μὴ εἰδέναι τί ποτέ ἐστι τὸ ὅλον καὶ τίνα τὰ
μέρη, τοῖς δὲ σκεπτικοῖς πρὸς ἔλεγχον τῆς τῶν
332 δογματικῶν προπετείας. καὶ δὴ οἱ μὲν ἀπὸ τῆς
στοᾶς φιλόσοφοι διαφέρειν ὑπολαμβάνουσι τὸ ὅλον
καὶ τὸ πᾶν· ὅλον μὲν γὰρ εἶναι λέγουσι τὸν κόσμον,
πᾶν δὲ τὸ σὺν τῷ κόσμῳ ἔξωθεν κενόν, καὶ διὰ
τοῦτο τὸ μὲν ὅλον πεπερασμένον εἶναι, πεπέρασται
γὰρ ὁ κόσμος, τὸ δὲ πᾶν ἄπειρον, τοιοῦτον γὰρ τὸ
333 ἐκτὸς τοῦ κόσμου κενόν. ὁ δὲ Ἐπίκουρος ἀδια-
φόρως τήν τε τῶν σωμάτων καὶ τὴν τοῦ κενοῦ
φύσιν ὅλον τε καὶ πᾶν προσαγορεύειν εἴωθεν· ὁτὲ
μὲν γάρ φησιν ὅτι ἡ τῶν ὅλων φύσις σώματά ἐστι

¹ τὸ Mutsch.: τε mss., Bekk.

affection occurs in some one of these ways.[a] For no one could conceive of any affection possibly taking place otherwise than in one of these ways.

Connected with the difficulty concerning this matter is that concerning the Whole, and also the problem of the Part, since subtraction seems to be the subtraction of a part from a whole, and addition, again, is the addition of a whole. Hence, if it should be proved that the account given of the whole and the part is doubtful, the difficulties previously raised regarding addition and subtraction, and the passive and the active, will be brought out still more clearly. And that it is not easy to define the whole and the part it will be our next task to demonstrate. 330

CONCERNING WHOLE AND PART

The investigation of the Whole is necessary for the Physicists, since it is absurd that they, while professing to tell the truth about the Whole and the All, should not know how to define what the Whole is and what the parts are ; and also for the Sceptics, as a means of convicting the Dogmatists of rashness. 331
Now the philosophers of the Stoic school suppose that " the Whole " differs from " the All " ; for they say that the Whole is the Cosmos, whereas the All is the external void together with the Cosmos, and on this account the Whole is limited (for the Cosmos is limited) but the All unlimited (for the void outside the Cosmos is so). But Epicurus usually gives the name of both Whole and All indifferently both to the nature of bodies and to that of void ; for at one time he says that " the nature of the Whole of things 332

333

---

[a] For further discussion of " affection," or " the passive," see §§ 267 ff., *P.H.* iii. 38.

SEXTUS EMPIRICUS

καὶ κενόν, ὁτὲ δὲ ὅτι τὸ πᾶν κατ᾽ ἀμφότερα
ἄπειρόν ἐστι, κατά τε σώματα καὶ τὸ κενόν, τουτέστι κατά τε τὸ πλῆθος τῶν σωμάτων καὶ κατὰ
τὸ μέγεθος τοῦ κενοῦ, ἀντιπαρηκουσῶν ἀλλήλαις
334 τῶν καθ᾽ ἑκάτερον ἀπειριῶν. οἱ δὲ φάμενοι μηδ᾽
ὅλως εἶναι κενόν, ὡς οἱ ἐκ τοῦ περιπάτου, τὸ ὅλον
καὶ τὸ πᾶν τῶν σωμάτων μόνον, οὐχὶ δὲ καὶ τοῦ
335 κενοῦ ἐπικατηγοροῦσιν.   γέγονε δέ τις διάστασις βραχεῖα καὶ περὶ τοῦ μέρους. Ἐπίκουρος
μὲν γὰρ ἕτερον ἠξίου τυγχάνειν τὸ μέρος τοῦ ὅλου,
καθάπερ τὴν ἄτομον τοῦ συγκρίματος, εἴγε ἐκείνη
μὲν ἄποιός ἐστι, τὸ δὲ σύγκριμα πεποίωται, ἤτοι
λευκὸν ἢ μέλαν ἢ κοινῶς κεχρωσμένον καὶ ἤτοι
336 θερμὸν ἢ ψυχρὸν ἢ ἄλλην τινὰ ἔχον ποιότητα. οἱ
δὲ στωικοὶ οὔτε ἕτερον τοῦ ὅλου τὸ μέρος οὔτε τὸ
αὐτό φασιν ὑπάρχειν· ἡ γὰρ χεὶρ οὔτε ἡ αὐτὴ τῷ
ἀνθρώπῳ ἐστίν, οὐ γάρ ἐστιν ἄνθρωπος, οὔτε
ἑτέρα παρὰ τὸν ἄνθρωπον, σὺν αὐτῇ γὰρ ὁ ἄν-
337 θρωπος νοεῖται ἄνθρωπος. ὁ δὲ Αἰνησίδημος κατὰ
Ἡράκλειτον καὶ ἕτερόν φησι τὸ μέρος τοῦ ὅλου
καὶ ταὐτόν· ἡ γὰρ οὐσία καὶ ὅλη ἐστὶ καὶ μέρος,
ὅλη μὲν κατὰ τὸν κόσμον, μέρος δὲ κατὰ τὴν τοῦδε
τοῦ ζῴου φύσιν. τὸ δὲ μόριον καὶ αὐτὸ λέγεται
διχῶς, καὶ ὁτὲ μὲν ὡς διαφέρον τοῦ ἰδίως νοουμένου μέρους, καθά φασιν αὐτὸ μέρος μέρους εἶναι,
καθάπερ δάκτυλον μὲν τῆς χειρὸς οὓς δὲ τῆς κεφαλῆς, ὁτὲ δ᾽ ὡς μὴ διαφέρον ἀλλὰ μέρος ὂν τοῦ ὅλου,
καθό τινές φασι κοινῶς μόριον εἶναι τὸ συμπληρω-
338 τικὸν τοῦ ὅλου. προδιηρθρωμένων δὲ τούτων [καὶ
τοῦ ὅλου κατὰ τὴν τῶν μερῶν συμπλήρωσιν νοου-
μένου],¹ χωρῶμεν λοιπὸν ἐπὶ τὴν σκέψιν.

¹ [καὶ . . . νοουμένου] secl. Heintz.

162

is bodies and void," and at another time that " the All is unlimited in both respects, in respect of both bodies and void,—that is, both in respect of the number of the bodies and in respect of the extent of the void, the infinity of the one matching that of the other." And those who totally deny the existence 334 of void, such as the Peripatetics, predicate Whole and All only of the bodies and not of the void.—There 335 exists also some small dispute about the Part. For Epicurus maintained that the part is other than the Whole, as the atom is other than the compound, since the former is devoid of quality whereas the compound has qualities, being either white or black or, generally, coloured, and either hot or cold or possessed of some other quality. But the Stoics assert that the part is 336 neither other than the Whole nor the same ; for the hand is neither the same as the man (for it is not a man) nor other than the man (for it is included in the conception of the man as man). And Aenesidemus, 337 " according to Heracleitus,"[a] says that the part is both other than the whole and the same ; for substance is both whole and part, whole in the Universe, but part in the nature of this particular animal. And " particle " itself is used in two senses, at one time as different from the separately conceived part—in which sense they speak of it as a part of a part, as the finger of the hand and the ear of the head—and at another time as not different, but as being a part of the whole, in which sense some say generally that " a particle is that which helps to fill up the whole." And 338 now that these distinctions have been drawn [and the whole conceived as a result of the filling up by the parts], let us next proceed to our investigation.

* Cf. P.H. i. 210 ; Introd. Vol. I. pp. xxxviii f.

Εἴπερ οὖν ἔστι τι ὅλον, οἷον ἄνθρωπος ἵππος
φυτὸν ναῦς (ταῦτα γὰρ ὅλων ὀνόματα), ἤτοι ἕτερόν
ἐστι τῶν μερῶν αὐτοῦ καὶ κατ᾿ ἰδίαν ὑπόστασιν
καὶ οὐσίαν νοεῖται, ἢ τὸ ἄθροισμα τῶν μερῶν
339 λέγεται τυγχάνειν ὅλον. ἀλλ᾿ ἕτερον μὲν τῶν
μερῶν οὐκ ἂν εἴη τὸ ὅλον, οὔτε κατ᾿ ἐνάργειαν
οὔτε κατὰ νόησιν. καὶ κατ᾿ ἐνάργειαν μέν, ἐπεὶ
εἴπερ ἕτερον ἦν καὶ κεχωρισμένον τῶν μερῶν τὸ
ὅλον, ἐχρῆν ἀναιρουμένων τῶν μερῶν ὑπομένον
θεωρεῖσθαι τὸ ὅλον· τοσοῦτον δὲ ἀπέχει τοῦ
πάντων τῶν μερῶν ἀναιρουμένων, οἷον τοῦ ἀνδριάντος, μένειν τὸ ὅλον, ὡς κἂν ἓν μόνον μέρος
ἀναιρεθῇ, μηκέτι θεωρεῖσθαι τὸ ὅλον ὑποκείμενον
340 ὡς ὅλον. κατὰ δὲ νόησιν, ὅτι ὅλον νοεῖται οὗ
οὐδὲν ἄπεστι μέρος. καὶ διὰ τοῦτο, εἰ ἕτερόν ἐστι
τῶν μερῶν τὸ ὅλον, πάντ᾿ ἔσται ἀπόντα τὰ μέρη
τοῦ ὅλου, καὶ οὕτως οὐκέτι ἔσται τὸ ὅλον.
ἄλλως τε τὸ ὅλον τῶν πρός τι ἐστίν· ὡς γὰρ πρὸς
τὰ μέρη νοεῖται ὅλον, καὶ ὃν τρόπον τὸ μέρος τινός
ἐστι μέρος, οὕτω καὶ τὸ ὅλον ἔκ τινων μερῶν
ἐστιν ὅλον. τὰ δὲ πρός τι συνυπάρχειν ἀλλήλοις
δεῖ καὶ ἀχώριστα τυγχάνειν ἀλλήλων. οὐκ ἄρα
ἕτερόν ἐστι τῶν μερῶν τὸ ὅλον, οὐδὲ κεχώρισται
341 αὐτῶν.   λείπεται ἄρα λέγειν τὰ μέρη εἶναι τὸ
ὅλον. ἀλλ᾿ εἰ τὰ μέρη ἐστὶν ὅλον, ἤτοι πάντα τὰ
μέρη ἐστὶν ὅλον ἢ τινὰ τῶν μερῶν ἢ τὶ τούτων.
καὶ τὶ μὲν τῶν μερῶν οὐκ ἂν εἴη ὅλον· οὐ γὰρ δή γε
ἡ κεφαλὴ τἀνθρώπου ὅλος ἐστὶν ἄνθρωπος, οὐδὲ
342 ὁ τράχηλος ἢ ἡ χεὶρ ἢ ἄλλο τι τῶν τοιούτων. καὶ
μὴν οὐδὲ τινὰ τῶν μερῶν ἔσται τὸ ὅλον. πρῶτον
μὲν γὰρ εἴ τινα τῶν μερῶν ὅλον ἐστί, τὰ λειπόμενα

---

^a With §§ 338-349 cf. P.H. iii. 98-101.

If, then, there exists any whole,—such as man, horse, plant, ship (for these are names of wholes),— either it is other than its parts and is conceived according to its own separate reality and substance, or the sum of the parts is said to be the whole.[a] But 339 the whole will not be other than its parts, either in its sensible appearance or in its conception. Not in appearance, since, if the whole were other than its parts and separate, when the parts are removed the whole ought to be found still remaining ; but so far is it from true that when all the parts (say, of a statue) are removed the whole remains that even when but one part only is removed the whole is no longer found to subsist as a whole. Nor yet in its 340 conception, because the whole is conceived as that from which no part is missing. And because of this, if the whole is other than its parts, all the parts will be missing from the whole, and thus the whole will no longer exist.—And again,—the whole is a relative thing, for it is in relation to its parts that it is conceived as a whole, and just as the part is a part of something, so also the whole is a whole made up of certain parts. But relatives must co-exist with each other and be inseparable from each other. The whole, therefore, is not other than its parts nor separate therefrom.—It only remains for us, then, to say that 341 the parts are the whole. But if the parts are the whole, either all the parts are the whole, or a certain number of the parts, or some one of them. Now some one of the parts will not be the whole ; for, assuredly, the head of the man is not the whole man, nor yet his neck or his hand or any other such member. Nor, 342 again, will the whole be a certain number of the parts. For, firstly, if certain of the parts are the

οὐκ ἔσται τοῦ ὅλου μέρη, ὅπερ ἄτοπον. εἶτα καὶ
περιτραπήσεται ἡ νόησις τοῦ ὅλου. εἰ γάρ τινα
τῶν μερῶν ὅλον ἐστί, ψεῦδός ἐστι τὸ ὅτι ὅλον
ἐστὶν οὗ μηδὲν ἄπεστι τῶν μερῶν· τινὰ γὰρ ἄπεστιν.
343 ὥστε οὔτε τὶ μέρος ὅλον ἐστὶν οὔτε τινὰ μέρη. εἰ
δὲ πάντα τὰ μέρη τὸ ὅλον ἐστίν, καὶ οὐδέν ἐστι
τὸ ὅλον εἰ μὴ τὸ ἄθροισμα τῶν μερῶν, οὔτε ἔσται
ὅλον οὔτε τὰ μέρη γενήσεται μέρη. ὡς γὰρ οὐδὲν
ἔστι διάστημα παρὰ τὰ διεστηκότα, οὐδὲ δόκωσις
παρὰ τάς πως διακειμένας δοκούς, οὐδὲ πυγμὴ
παρὰ τήν πως ἐσχηματισμένη χεῖρα, οὕτως ⟨εἰ⟩[1]
οὐδὲν ἔσται ὅλον παρὰ τὸ ἄθροισμα τῶν μερῶν,
344 οὐδὲ[2] τὰ μέρη γενήσεται μέρη. καὶ πάλιν, ὃν τρόπον
δεξιοῦ μὴ ὄντος οὐδὲ ἀριστερὸν ἔστι καὶ τοῦ ἄνω
μὴ νοουμένου οὐδὲ τὸ κάτω νοεῖται, τὸν αὐτὸν
τρόπον εἰ μή ἐστι τὸ ὅλον, οὔτε τὰ μέρη νοεῖται
345 μέρη οὔτε μέρη τινὰ ὑπάρξει.   ἔστω δὲ καὶ
πάντα τὰ μέρη ὅλον εἶναι, ἀλλὰ ζητητέον τε τίνος
ἔσται ταῦτα συμπληρωτικά, ὅλου ⟨ἢ⟩[3] ἀλλήλων ἢ
ἑαυτῶν; οὔτε δὲ τοῦ ὅλου ἐστὶ μέρη οὔτε ἀλλήλων
οὔτε ἑαυτῶν, ὡς παραστήσομεν· οὐκ ἄρα τινός
ἐστι μέρη. ὅλου μὲν οὖν οὐκ ἂν εἴη μέρη· τὸ γὰρ
ὅλον οὐδέν ἐστι παρὰ ταῦτα, ἀλλ' αὐτὰ ταῦτα
346 λέγεται εἶναι ὅλον. οὐδὲ μὴν ἀλλήλων γενήσεται
μέρη. τὰ γάρ τινος μέρη ἐμπεριέχεται τοῖς ὧν
ἐστι μέρη, οἷον ἀνθρώπῳ μὲν ἡ χεὶρ χειρὶ δὲ ὁ
δάκτυλος, τὰ δὲ μέρη τοῦ ἀνθρώπου κατ' ἰδίαν
ὑφέστηκε καὶ οὐκ ἐμπεριέχεται ἀλλήλοις· οὔτε γὰρ
ἡ ἀριστερὰ χεὶρ τὴν δεξιὰν συμπληροῖ οὔτε ἡ δεξιὰ

---

[1] ⟨εἰ⟩ add. N, Mutsch.
[2] οὐδὲ Mutsch.: οὔτε mss. (οὔτε . . . μέρη om. Bekk.).
[3] ⟨ἢ⟩ addo.

whole, the rest will not be parts of the whole, which
is absurd. And, secondly, the conception of the
whole will be overthrown. For if certain of the parts
are the whole, it is false to say that the whole is that
from which none of the parts are missing ; for some
are missing. So that neither some one part nor
certain of the parts are the whole. And if all the 343
parts are the whole, and the whole is nothing else
than the sum of the parts, neither will it be a whole
nor will the parts be parts. For just as separation is
nothing apart from the things separated, or raftering
apart from the rafters arranged in a certain way, or
the fist apart from the hand held in a certain position,
so too if the whole is nothing more than the sum of
the parts, the parts will not be parts. And again, 344
just as, when " right " does not exist, " left " also is
non-existent, and when " above " is not conceived
neither is " below " conceived, in the same way, if
the whole does not exist, the parts are not conceived
nor will any parts exist.—But let it be granted that 345
all the parts are the whole, still we must inquire what
it is that these are to complete—is it the whole, or
one another, or themselves ? But they are not parts
either of the whole or of one another or of themselves,
as we shall establish ; therefore, they are not parts of
anything. Now they will not be parts of the whole ;
for the whole is nothing more than the parts, and they
themselves are said to be the whole. Nor yet will they 346
be parts of one another. For the parts of anything
are included in the things whereof they are parts,—as,
for instance, the hand in the man and the finger in the
hand,—but the parts of the man subsist separately
and are not included in one another; for the left hand
does not complete the right, nor the right the left, nor

167

SEXTUS EMPIRICUS

τὴν ἀριστεράν, οὐχ ὁ ἀντίχειρ τὸν λιχανόν, οὐχ αἱ
χεῖρες τὴν κεφαλήν, ἀλλ᾽ ἴδιον τόπον ἕκαστον τού-
347 των ἀπείληφεν. οὐδὲ ἀλλήλων οὖν μέρη ἐστὶ τὰ
μέρη. καὶ μὴν οὐδὲ ἑαυτῶν· ἀμήχανον γὰρ ἑαυτοῦ
τι μέρος ὑπάρχειν. εἰ οὖν μήτε ἕτερόν ἐστι τῶν
μερῶν τὸ ὅλον μήτε αὐτὰ τὰ μέρη ἐστὶν ὅλον,
348 οὐδέν ἐστι τὸ ὅλον.   καὶ πάλιν τὸ μέρος, οἷον
ἡ κεφαλή, λέγεται τὸν ὅλον ἄνθρωπον συμπληροῦν
καὶ ἀνθρώπου μέρος εἶναι· θεωρεῖται δέ γε ὁ
ἄνθρωπος σὺν τῇ κεφαλῇ ἄνθρωπος· καὶ ἑαυτὴν
ἄρα συμπληροῖ ἡ κεφαλή, καὶ ἑαυτῆς γίνεται
μέρος. διὰ δὲ τοῦτο καὶ μείζων ἐστὶν ἑαυτῆς καὶ
ἐλάσσων· ᾗ μὲν γὰρ συμπεπληρωμένη νοεῖται ὑφ᾽
ἑαυτῆς, μείζων ἐστὶν αὐτῆς, ᾗ δὲ συμπληροῦσα,
349 ἐλάττων. ἡ δὲ αὐτὴ ἀπορία καὶ ἐπὶ φυτοῦ καὶ
ἐπὶ πήχεως καὶ κοινῶς τῶν ἄλλων ἁπάντων ὧν
ἐπικατηγορεῖται τὸ ὅλον· ἐπεὶ γὰρ ὁ παλαιστὴς
μέρος πήχεως νοεῖται (σὺν γὰρ τῷ παλαιστῇ καὶ ὁ
πῆχυς νοεῖται πῆχυς), καὶ ἑαυτοῦ συμπληρωτικός
ἐστιν ὁ παλαιστὴς καὶ μέρος ἑαυτοῦ. ὅπερ ἄτοπον
καὶ σχεδὸν παρὰ τὰς κοινὰς ἐννοίας.
350 Ἅπτεται δὲ ἡ ἀπορία καὶ τῶν τοῦ λόγου μερῶν.
ἐπὶ γὰρ τοῦ τοιούτου στίχου,

μῆνιν ἄειδε θεὰ Πηληιάδεω Ἀχιλῆος,

ζητητέον τὸ μῆνιν καὶ τὸ ἄειδε καὶ τὸ θεά καὶ τὸ
Πηληιάδεω καὶ πρὸς τούτοις τὸ Ἀχιλῆος, τίνος
ἐστὶ μέρη. ἤτοι γὰρ ὅλος ὁ στίχος ἄλλο τί ἐστι
τῶν μερῶν τούτων, ἢ τὸ ἄθροισμα αὐτῶν ὁ στίχος
ἐστίν. καὶ ἐπακτέον τὰς κειμένας ἀπορίας. τὸ
μῆνιν εἰ μὲν τοῦ ὅλου στίχου μέρος ἐστί, καὶ

168

the thumb the forefinger, nor the hands the head, but each of these has its own separate place. So then the 347 parts are not parts of one another. Nor yet of themselves ; for it is impossible for anything to be a part of itself. If, then, the whole is not other than the parts, and the parts themselves are not the whole, the whole is nothing.—And again, the part (such as 348 the head) is said to complete the whole man and be a part of the man : and the man is certainly viewed as a man with head included ; and therefore the head completes itself and is a part of itself. And because of this it is both greater and less than itself ; for in so far as it is conceived as completed by itself it is greater than itself, but in so far as it completes, less. And there is the same difficulty in the case of the 349 plant and the cubit and, in general, of all the other things of which the term " whole " is predicated ; for since the palm [a] is conceived as part of the cubit (for it is with the inclusion of the palm that the cubit is conceived as a cubit), the palm both serves to complete itself and is a part of itself. But this is absurd and contrary, one may say, to our common notions.

This difficulty applies also to the parts of speech. 350 For in a line like this—

Sing, O goddess, the wrath of the son of Peleus, Achilles,[b]—

one must inquire about the words " wrath " and " sing " and " goddess " and " son of Peleus " and also " Achilles," of what are they parts ? For either the whole line is something other than these parts, or the sum of them is the line. But here one must bring up the difficulties already stated. If the word " wrath " is a part of the whole line, it will also be

[a] Cf. § 321. [b] Homer, Il. i. 1.

ἑαυτοῦ γενήσεται μέρος· σὺν αὐτῷ γὰρ ἐνοεῖτο
351 καὶ ὅλος ὁ στίχος· εἰ δὲ τοῦ λοιποῦ τοῦ " ἄειδε
θεὰ Πηληιάδεω Ἀχιλῆος," πῶς οὐ μείζων ἀνακύψει ἀπορία; τὸ γάρ τινος μέρος ἐμπεριέχεται
τῷ οὗ ἐστι μέρος, τὸ δὲ μῆνιν οὐκ ἐμπεριέχεται
τῷ " ἄειδε θεὰ Πηληιάδεω Ἀχιλῆος"· οὐκ ἄρα
μέρος ἐστὶ τὸ μῆνιν τοῦ ὅλου στίχου.
352 Τοιούτων δὲ ἠπορημένων κατὰ τὸν τόπον
εἰώθασιν οἱ δογματικοί, μικρὰν ἀναπνοὴν πορί-
ζοντες αὐτοῖς, λέγειν ὅτι τὸ μὲν ἐκτὸς ὑποκείμενον
καὶ αἰσθητὸν οὔτε ὅλον ἐστὶν οὔτε μέρος, ἡμεῖς δέ
ἐσμεν οἱ ἐκείνου τό τε ὅλον καὶ τὸ μέρος ἐπι-
353 κατηγοροῦντες. ἢν γὰρ τὸ ὅλον τῶν πρός τι· ὡς
γὰρ πρὸς τὰ μέρη ἐνοεῖτο τὸ ὅλον. καὶ πάλιν τὰ
μέρη τῶν πρός τι· ὡς γὰρ πρὸς τὸ ὅλον νοεῖται τὰ
μέρη. τὰ δὲ πρός τι ἐν συμμνημονεύσει ἐστὶν
ἡμετέρα, ἡ δὲ ἡμετέρα συμμνημόνευσίς ἐστιν ἐν
ἡμῖν· τὸ οὖν ὅλον καὶ τὸ μέρος ἐστὶν ἐν ἡμῖν. τὸ
δὲ ἐκτὸς ὑποκείμενον αἰσθητὸν οὔτε ὅλον ἐστὶν
οὔτε μέρος, ἀλλὰ πρᾶγμα οὗ ἡμεῖς ἐπικατηγοροῦμεν
354 τὴν ἡμῶν αὐτῶν συμμνημόνευσιν. ῥητέον δὲ πρὸς
αὐτοὺς πρῶτον μὲν ὅτι ἄτοπόν ἐστι τὸ λέγειν τὸν
τράχηλον ἢ τὴν κεφαλὴν μὴ τοῦ ἐκτὸς ἀνθρώπου
συμπληρωτικὰ εἶναι μέρη ἀλλὰ τῆς ἡμετέρας
συμμνημονεύσεως. εἰ δὲ ἡ κεφαλὴ καὶ ὁ τράχηλος
συμπληρωτικά ἐστι τοῦ ἀνθρώπου καὶ ὁ τράχηλός
ἐστιν ἐν ἡμῖν, δεήσει τὸν ἄνθρωπον εἶναι ἐν ἡμῖν.
ὅπερ ἄτοπον. οὐ τοίνυν ἐν τῇ ἡμετέρᾳ συμμνη-
355 μονεύσει τό τε ὅλον καὶ τὰ μέρη κεῖται.   ναί,
φήσει τις, ἀλλ' ὁ μὲν ὅλος ἄνθρωπός ἐστιν ἐν ἡμῖν
κατὰ συμμνημόνευσιν, συμπληροῦται δὲ οὐχ ὑπὸ
τοῦ ἐκτὸς τραχήλου καὶ τῆς ἐκτὸς κεφαλῆς, ἀλλὰ

a part of itself; for the whole line was conceived as
including it; and if it is a part of the rest of the line 351
(" Sing, O goddess, of the son of Peleus, Achilles "),
surely a greater difficulty will emerge. For the part
of anything is included in that of which it is a part,
but " the wrath " is not included in " Sing, O goddess,
of the son of Peleus, Achilles "; therefore " the
wrath " is not a part of the whole line.

Such being the difficulties raised about this topic, 352
the Dogmatists—by way of providing themselves
with a little breathing-space—are accustomed to
argue that the external real and sensible object is
neither whole nor part, but it is we who apply to it
the terms " whole " and " part." For " whole " is a 353
relative term, since a whole is conceived in relation to
its parts. And again, " parts " are relative, for the
parts are conceived in relation to the whole. And
relatives are in our consciousness,[a] and our consciousness is in us; so the whole and the part are in us.
And the external real and sensible object is neither a
whole nor a part but a thing of which we predicate
our own consciousness. In reply to them one must 354
say, firstly, that it is absurd to argue that the neck
and the head are not complementary parts of the
external man but of our consciousness. But if the
head and the neck are complements of the man and
the neck is in us, the man will have to be in us. Which
is absurd. So then, the whole and the parts do not
reside in our consciousness.—Yes, someone will say, 355
but the whole man is in us, through consciousness,
and has its complement not in the external neck and

---

[a] Literally, " concurrent recollection."

SEXTUS EMPIRICUS

πάλιν ἐκ τῶν κατὰ ταῦτα τὰ μέρη ἐννοιῶν· καὶ
γὰρ αὐτὸς ὁ ὅλος ἄνθρωπος ἐννόημά ἐστιν ἡμῶν.
356 ὁ δὲ τοῦτο λέγων οὐκ ἐκφεύγει τὴν ἀπορίαν.
πάλιν γὰρ οὗτος ὁ ἐν ἡμῖν ἄνθρωπος, εἴτε ἐννόημά
ἐστιν εἴτε καὶ ἡμετέρα συμμνημόνευσις, ἤτοι
ἕτερος νοεῖται παρὰ τὰ μέρη ἢ τὰ μέρη νοεῖται
ὁ ἄνθρωπος. οὐδέτερον δὲ τούτων δύναται ὑπάρχειν, ὡς παρεστήσαμεν. καὶ αὐτὴ οὖν ἡ νόησις
357 ὑπὸ τὴν αὐτὴν πέπτωκεν ἀπορίαν. εἰ δὲ τοῦτο,
ῥητέον μηδὲν εἶναι ὅλον. ᾧ ἀκολουθεῖ τὸ μηδὲ
μέρος ὑπάρχειν· τῶν γὰρ πρός τι ἑκάτερόν ἐστι, καὶ
τοῦ ἑτέρου τῶν πρός τι ἀναιρεθέντος συναναιρεῖται
καὶ τὸ λοιπόν.
358 Ὧδε μὲν περὶ τούτων ἠπορήσθω· συνεζητηκότες
δὲ αὐτάρκως ἤδη τοῖς δογματικοῖς περὶ τῶν
δραστηρίων τοῦ παντὸς ἀρχῶν, τὸ μετὰ τοῦτο
κοινότερον περί τε τούτων καὶ τῶν ὑλικῶν δια-
ποροῦμεν.

ΠΕΡΙ ΣΩΜΑΤΟΣ

359   Περὶ τῶν ἀνωτάτω καὶ ἀρχικωτάτων στοιχείων
δύο μὲν αἱ πρῶται γεγόνασι στάσεις, πλείους δὲ
κατ' εἶδος. οἱ μὲν γὰρ σώματα ἔλεξαν εἶναι τὰ
360 τῶν ὄντων στοιχεῖα, οἱ δὲ ἀσώματα. καὶ τῶν
σώματα φαμένων Φερεκύδης μὲν ὁ Σύριος γῆν
ἔλεξε πάντων εἶναι ἀρχὴν καὶ στοιχεῖον, Θαλῆς δὲ
ὁ Μιλήσιος ὕδωρ, Ἀναξίμανδρος δὲ ὁ ἀκουστὴς
τούτου τὸ ἄπειρον, Ἀναξιμένης δὲ καὶ Ἰδαῖος ὁ
Ἱμεραῖος καὶ Διογένης ὁ Ἀπολλωνιάτης καὶ
Ἀρχέλαος ὁ Ἀθηναῖος, Σωκράτους δὲ καθηγητής,
καὶ κατ' ἐνίους Ἡράκλειτος ἀέρα, Ἵππασος δὲ ὁ

ᵃ With §§ 359-364 cf. *P.H.* iii. 30-32.

the external head but, once more, in the conceptions which correspond to these parts. For in fact the whole man is itself a concept of ours. But he who 356 argues thus does not escape from the difficulty. For, once again, either this man who is within us, whether he be a concept or our consciousness, is conceived as other than his parts, or else the man is conceived as his parts. But neither of these can be true, as we have established. Thus, too, the very conception itself is overthrown by the same difficulty. And if so, 357 we must declare that no whole exists. From which it follows that no part, either, exists. For each of these is a relative, and when one of a pair of relatives is abolished, the other also is abolished with it.

Let this, then, stand as the statement of our doubts 358 about these matters; and as we have now disputed sufficiently with the Dogmatists regarding the efficient principles of the Universe, let us now state in more general terms the difficulties regarding both these and the material principles.

Concerning Body

Concerning the primary and most fundamental 359 elements there are two leading views, with several sub-divisions; for some have affirmed that the elements of existing things are bodies, others that they are incorporeal.[a] And of those who have de- 360 clared them to be bodies, Pherecydes of Syros said that the principle and element of all things is earth; and Thales of Miletus, water; and his disciple, Anaximander, the unlimited; and Anaximenes and Idaeus of Himera and Diogenes of Apollonia and Archelaus of Athens (Socrates' teacher) and (according to some) Heracleitus, air; and Hippasus of Meta-

173

361 Μεταποντῖνος καὶ κατ' ἐνίους Ἡράκλειτος πῦρ,
Ξενοφάνης δὲ ὕδωρ καὶ γῆν

(πάντες γὰρ γαίης τε καὶ ὕδατος ἐκγενόμεσθα),

Ἵππων δὲ ὁ Ῥηγῖνος πῦρ καὶ ὕδωρ, Οἰνοπίδης δὲ
ὁ Χῖος πῦρ καὶ ἀέρα, Ὀνομάκριτος δὲ ἐν τοῖς
Ὀρφικοῖς πῦρ καὶ ὕδωρ καὶ γῆν, οἱ δὲ περὶ τὸν
362 Ἐμπεδοκλέα καὶ οἱ ἀπὸ τῆς στοᾶς γῆν καὶ ὕδωρ
καὶ ἀέρα καὶ πῦρ

(τέσσαρα γὰρ πάντων ῥιζώματα πρῶτον ἄκουε·
Ζεὺς ἀργὴς Ἥρη τε φερέσβιος ἠδ' Ἀιδωνεὺς
Νῆστίς θ', ἣ δακρύοις τέγγει κρούνωμα βρό-
τειον),

363 Δημόκριτος δὲ καὶ Ἐπίκουρος ἀτόμους, εἰ μή τι
ἀρχαιοτέραν ταύτην θετέον τὴν δόξαν, καὶ ὡς
ἔλεγεν ὁ στωικὸς Ποσειδώνιος, ἀπὸ Μώχου τινὸς
ἀνδρὸς Φοίνικος καταγομένην, Ἀναξαγόρας δὲ ὁ
Κλαζομένιος ὁμοιομερείας, Διόδωρος δὲ ὁ ἐπικληθεὶς Κρόνος ἐλάχιστα καὶ ἀμερῆ σώματα,
Ἀσκληπιάδης δὲ ὁ Βιθυνὸς ἀνάρμους ὄγκους.
364 τῶν δὲ ἀσώματα δογματιζόντων οἱ μὲν περὶ
Πυθαγόραν τοὺς ἀριθμοὺς ἔλεξαν πάντων ἄρχειν,
οἱ δὲ μαθηματικοὶ τὰ πέρατα τῶν σωμάτων, οἱ
365 δὲ περὶ τὸν Πλάτωνα τὰς ἰδέας.   τοιαύτης δὲ
οὔσης τῆς κατὰ γένος καὶ κατ' εἶδος τῶν φυσικῶν
διαστάσεως, ἐνέσται πρὸς πάντας κοινῶς ἀντερεῖν,
ἐν μέρει περί τε τῶν σωμάτων καὶ τῶν ἀσωμάτων
διαπορήσαντας· ὧδε γὰρ ἕκαστος τῶν κατηριθ-

_a_ Zeus probably stands for the element " air," Here for

pontum and (according to some) Heracleitus, fire; 361
and Xenophanes, water and earth—

(Verily all we men are sprung from earth and from water);

and Hippo of Rhegium, fire and water; and Oenopides
of Chios, fire and air; and Onomacritus in his *Orphica*,
fire and water and earth; and Empedocles and the 362
Stoics, earth and water and air and fire—

Four are the roots of all things, and list thou first to their
    titles :
Shining Zeus, and Herê the life-bringer, and Aïdoneus,[a]
Nestis, too, who wetteth with tears the fountain of mortals ;—

and Democritus and Epicurus, atoms, unless one 363
should regard this opinion as more ancient and—
as the Stoic Poseidonius asserted—derived from a
certain Phoenician called Mochus ; and Anaxagoras
of Clazomenae, homoeomeries[b] ; and Diodorus, sur-
named Cronos, minimal and indivisible bodies ; and
Asclepiades the Bithynian, homogeneous molecules.
And of those who have dogmatically asserted that 364
they are incorporeal, the Pythagoreans have said that
the numbers are the principles of all things ; and the
Mathematicians, the limits of bodies ; and Plato, the
ideas.—Such, then, being the divergence of opinion, 365
both in general and in particular, amongst the
Physicists, it will be possible to give one general
answer to them all when we have discussed in turn
the difficulties about bodies and those about incorporeals[c] ; for in this way each of the persons

---

" earth," Aïdoneus for " fire " ; Nestis certainly for " water."
" The fountain " (or physical source) is the semen.
    [b] *i.e.* " things with like parts "—Aristotle's name for the
material " elements " of Anaxagoras.
    [c] " Bodies " are discussed in §§ 366 ff., " incorporeals " in
Adv. Phys. ii.   With § 365 *cf. P.H.* iii. 37.

μημένων σωματικὰς μὲν ἀπολείπων τὰς πάντων
ἀρχὰς ταῖς κατὰ τοῦ σώματος κομιζομέναις
ἀπορίαις ὑποπεσεῖται, ἀσωμάτους δὲ δογματίζων
366 ταῖς κατὰ τῶν ἀσωμάτων. ἡγείσθω δὲ ὁ περὶ
τοῦ σώματος λόγος, τὴν ἀρχὴν τῆς σκέψεως
λαμβάνων ἀπὸ τῆς ἐννοίας.

Εὐθέως τοίνυν κατὰ μὲν τοὺς σῶμα νοοῦντας τὸ
οἷόν τε παθεῖν ἢ διαθεῖναι, ὧν ἀρχηγὸς ἱστορεῖται
Πυθαγόρας, ἤδη σχεδὸν ἀνῃρήκαμεν τὸ σῶμα, καὶ
οὐ δεόμεθα πρὸς τοῦτο καινοτέρων λόγων· εἰ γὰρ
σῶμά ἐστι τὸ οἷόν τε παθεῖν ἢ ποιῆσαι, ἐπεὶ οὐδὲν
ποιοῦν ἢ πάσχον δέδεικται ἡμῖν, οὐδὲν ἂν εἴη τὸ
367 ἐπινοούμενον σῶμα. κατὰ δὲ τὰς τῶν μαθηματικῶν
ἐννοίας νῦν συνακτέον[1] τὸ προκείμενον. φασὶ γὰρ
σῶμα εἶναι τὸ τρεῖς ἔχον διαστάσεις, μῆκος βάθος
πλάτος, ὧν μῆκος μὲν ὑπάρχειν τὸ ἄνωθεν κάτω,
πλάτος δὲ τὸ ἀπὸ ἀριστερῶν ἐπὶ τὰ δεξιά, τρίτην
δὲ διάστασιν ὑπάρχειν, τουτέστι τὸ βάθος, τὸ ἐκ
τῶν ἔμπροσθεν εἰς τοὐπίσω. ὅθεν καὶ παρατάσεις
εἶναι ἕξ, δύο καθ᾽ ἑκάστην διάστασιν, ἄνω κάτω,
368 δεξιὰ ἀριστερά, πρόσω ὀπίσω. ταύτῃ μὲν τῇ
ἐπινοίᾳ πολύ τι πλῆθος ἀποριῶν ἐξακολουθεῖν
φαίνεται. ἤτοι γὰρ χωριστόν ἐστι τούτων τῶν
τριῶν διαστάσεων τὸ σῶμα κατὰ τὴν ἐπίνοιαν,
ὥστε ἄλλο μὲν εἶναι σῶμα ἄλλο δὲ τὸ μῆκος καὶ
βάθος καὶ πλάτος τοῦ σώματος, ἢ ἄθροισμα τούτων
369 τῶν διαστάσεών ἐστι τὸ σῶμα. ἀλλὰ χωριζό-
μενον μὲν τούτων τῶν διαστάσεων τὸ σῶμα οὐκ

[1] συνακτέον cj. Mutsch.: συντακτέον mss., Bekk.

• Cf. P.H. iii. 38.

enumerated who admits that the principles of all
things are corporeal will be brought face to face with
the difficulties raised about body, and every one who
asserts their incorporeality with those raised about
incorporeals. And let our discussion of body come 366
first, commencing with an examination of the conception of " body."

To begin with, then, as against those who conceive body [a] as " what is capable of being acted
upon or of affecting " (and of these it is recorded
that Pythagoras was the leader), we have already
pretty well abolished body and do not need for this
purpose other fresh arguments ; for if body is what
is capable of being acted upon or acting, since we
have proved [b] that there is nothing which acts or is
acted upon, the body as so conceived will be nothing.
But the subject before us must now be treated 367
systematically with reference to the conceptions of
the Mathematicians.[c] They say that body is " that
which has three dimensions, length, depth, breadth " ;
and of these, length is extent from above to below,
breadth from left to right, and the third dimension
(namely, depth) is from front to back. Hence, there
are six modes of extension, two for each dimension,—
up and down, to right and to left, forward and backward. From this conception a vast number of diffi- 368
culties seem to follow. For either body, in respect of
its conception, is separate from these three dimensions, so that the body is one thing and the length
and depth and breadth of the body something
different, or else the body is the sum of these dimensions. But it is not possible to conceive the body as 369

[b] Cf. §§ 195 ff., 266 ff.
[c] With §§ 367-370 cf. P.H. iii. 39-40.

ἔνεστιν ἐπινοεῖν· ὅπου γὰρ μήτε μῆκός ἐστι μήτε
πλάτος μήτε βάθος, ἐκεῖ οὐδὲ σῶμα νοεῖν οἷόν τε
ἐστίν. εἰ δὲ ὁ ἀθροισμὸς τούτων σῶμα καθέστηκεν, ἐπεὶ ἕκαστον αὐτῶν ἀσώματόν ἐστι, τὸ δὲ ἐξ
ἀσωμάτων συγκείμενον πάντως ἐστὶν ἀσώματον,
δεήσει καὶ τὴν κοινὴν αὐτῶν σύνοδον μὴ σῶμα
370 ἀλλ᾽ ἀσώματον ὑπάρχειν· ὡς γὰρ ἡ συνέλευσις τῶν
γραμμῶν ἀσωμάτων οὐσῶν καὶ ὁ ἀθροισμὸς τῶν
στιγμῶν οὐδέποτε πέφυκε στερεὸν ποιεῖν σῶμα
καὶ ἀντίτυπον, οὕτω καὶ ἡ τοῦ μήκους καὶ τοῦ
βάθους καὶ τοῦ πλάτους σύνοδος, ἀσωμάτων οὖσα
σύνοδος, οὐκ ἀποτελεῖ σῶμα. εἰ δὲ μήτε τούτων
χωρίς ἐστί τι σῶμα μήτε ταῦτά ἐστι σῶμα, οὐδέν
371 ἐστι σῶμα.   καὶ ἄλλως, ἐπείπερ ἡ σύνοδος
τοῦ μήκους καὶ πλάτους καὶ βάθους ποιεῖ σῶμα,
ἤτοι πρὶν τῆς συνόδου τούτων ἕκαστον ἰδίᾳ
περιεῖχε τὴν σωματότητα καὶ τοὺς ὥσπερ λόγους
τοῦ σώματος, ἢ μετὰ τὴν συνέλευσιν αὐτῶν ἐπισυνέβη τὸ σῶμα. καὶ εἰ μὲν ἕκαστον πρὶν τῆς
συνόδου περιεῖχε τὴν σωματότητα, ἔσται ἕκαστον
372 σῶμα· εἶτ᾽ ἐπεὶ τὸ σῶμα οὐ μῆκος μόνον ἐστὶν
οὐδὲ πλάτος οὐδὲ βάθος ἀλλὰ καὶ μῆκος καὶ βάθος
καὶ πλάτος, ἕκαστον τούτων ἔχον τὴν σωματότητα τρία γενήσεται, καὶ οὕτω τὸ μῆκος οὐ
μόνον μῆκος ἔσται ἀλλὰ καὶ πλάτος καὶ βάθος,
καὶ τὸ πλάτος οὐχ ἁπλῶς πλάτος ἀλλὰ καὶ μῆκος
καὶ βάθος, ὡσαύτως δὲ καὶ ἡ λειπομένη διάστασις.
373 εἰ δὲ συνελθόντων τούτων τότε ἐπισυνέβη τὸ σῶμα,
ἤτοι συνελθόντων αὐτῶν μένει ἡ ἀρχῆθεν φύσις ἢ
μεταβάλλει εἰς τὴν σωματότητα. καὶ εἰ μὲν μένει
ἡ ἀρχῆθεν φύσις, ἐπεὶ ἀσώματά ἐστι καὶ ἀσώματα

separate from these dimensions ; for where there is neither length nor breadth nor depth, there it is not possible to conceive body. And if the sum of these is body, since each of them is incorporeal and what is compounded of incorporeals is certainly incorporeal, the combination of all these together will have to be, not body but, incorporeal. For just as the conjunc- 370 tion of lines, which are incorporeal, and the sum of points are never of a nature to make a solid and resistant body, so also the combination of length, depth, and breadth, being a combination of incorporeals, will not produce a body. But if there is no body apart from these, and these, too, are not body, nothing is body.—And again, since the combination 371 of length and breadth and depth makes body, either each of these separately, before combining, contained corporeality and the rational germs,[a] as it were, of body, or body supervened after their conjunction. And if each of them, before combining, contained 372 corporeality, each will be a body ; and further, since body is not length only, nor breadth, nor depth, but length and depth and breadth, each of these as possessing corporeality will become three, and thus length will not only be length but also breadth and depth, and depth not simply breadth but also length and breadth, and so likewise with the remaining dimension. And if it is after these are conjoined 373 that body supervenes, either their original nature remains after their conjunction or it changes to corporeality. And if their original nature remains, since they are incorporeal and remain incorporeal,

---

[a] Or " seminal reasons," *i.e.* the creative principles derived from the Cosmic Reason (" Logos ") according to Stoic doctrine; *cf.* Introd. Vol. I. p. xxiv.

374 μένει, οὐ ποιήσει διάφορον σῶμα· εἰ δὲ μεταβάλλει
εἰς τὸ σῶμα, ἐπεὶ τὸ ἐπιδεχόμενον μεταβολήν ἐστι
σῶμα, ἕκαστον τούτων καὶ πρὶν τῆς συνελεύσεως
σῶμα ὄν, πρὶν σώματος ἀποτελέσει σῶμα.

ὥσπερ τε τὸ μεταβάλλον σῶμα ἄλλην μὲν ἀντ'
ἄλλης παραδέχεται ποιότητα, μένει δὲ σῶμα, οἷον
τὸ λευκόν, ἵνα γένηται μέλαν, καὶ τὸ γλυκύ, ἵνα
γένηται πικρόν, ἣν μὲν ἀποβάλλει ποιότητα ἣν δὲ
ἀναδέχεται, μὴ ἐκβαῖνον τοῦ σῶμα εἶναι, οὕτω
καὶ ταῦτα, εἴπερ μεταβάλλει εἰς σῶμα, ἄλλην ἀντ'
375 ἄλλης δέξεται ποιότητα· τοῦτο δὲ πάσχοντα ἔσται
σώματα. εἰ οὖν οὔτε πρὸ τῆς συνελεύσεως τούτων
ἔστι τὸ νοούμενον σῶμα οὔτε μετὰ τὴν συνέλευσιν
αὐτῶν, οὐκ ἔστιν ἐπινοῆσαι τὸ σῶμα.

Πρὸς τούτοις εἰ μηδέν ἐστι μῆκος μηδὲ πλάτος
μηδὲ βάθος, οὐδὲ τὸ κατὰ μετουσίαν τούτων νοούμενον σῶμα γενήσεται· οὐδὲν δέ ἐστι μῆκος καὶ
376 πλάτος καὶ βάθος, ὡς παραστήσομεν· οὐκ ἄρα ἔστι
σῶμα. μῆκος μὲν γὰρ οὐκ ἔστιν, ἐπεὶ τὸ μέγιστον
ἦν τοῦτο τοῦ σώματος διάστημα ὅπερ λέγεται παρὰ
τοῖς μαθηματικοῖς γραμμή, ἡ δὲ γραμμὴ ἦν
στιγμὴ ἐρρυηκυῖα, καὶ ἡ στιγμὴ σημεῖον ἀμερὲς
καὶ ἀδιάστατον. ⟨ὅθεν εἰ μηδὲν ἔστι σημεῖον
ἀμερὲς καὶ ἀδιάστατον⟩,[1] οὐδὲ γραμμὴ γενήσεται,
μὴ οὔσης δὲ γραμμῆς οὐδὲ μῆκος ἔσται, μήκους
δὲ μὴ ὄντος οὐδὲ σῶμα ὑποστήσεται· σὺν μήκει
377 γὰρ σῶμα νοεῖται. ὅτι δὲ οὐδέν ἐστι σημεῖον
ἀμερὲς καὶ ἀδιάστατον, ἐντεῦθεν μάθωμεν. εἰ γὰρ

---

[1] ⟨ὅθεν ... ἀδιάστατον⟩ add. N, Mutsch. (ὥστε ... ἀδ.
add. cj. Bekk.).

---

[a] Or (as compared with "breadth" and "depth") the

they will not produce a different body ; but if it 374
changes to body, then, since what admits of change
is body, each of the dimensions, even before their
conjunction, will be body and will produce body
before there is body.—Also, just as the body which
changes receives one quality instead of another but
remains a body,—the white, for instance, in becoming
black, and the sweet in becoming bitter, casts off
one quality and receives another, while not ceasing
to be a body,—so also these dimensions, if they
change into body, will exchange one quality for
another ; and if they are thus affected they will be 375
bodies. If, then, the body as conceived exists neither
before their conjunction nor after their conjunction,
it is not possible to conceive body.

Furthermore, if there is no length or breadth or
depth, neither will the body which is conceived as
partaking of these exist ; but there is no length and
breadth and depth, as we shall establish ; therefore 376
body does not exist. For length does not exist, since
this, which is termed "line" by the Mathematicians,
is the greatest dimension of body,[a] and the line
is "a point which has flowed," and the point is "a
sign which is without parts and without dimensions."
⟨Hence, if no sign [b] without parts or dimensions exists,⟩
neither will a line exist, and if the line does not exist
neither will length exist, and if length does not exist
neither will body subsist ; for body, as conceived,
includes length. And that there exists no sign with- 377
out parts or dimensions we may learn from what

primary dimension; cf. Nicomachus, *Instit. Arithm.* ii. 6
πρῶτον δὲ διάστημα γραμμὴ λέγεται· γραμμὴ γάρ ἐστι τὸ ἐφ' ἓν
διαστατόν.

[b] "Sign" is used in the sequel in the sense of "point."

ἐστι τοιοῦτόν τι, ἤτοι σῶμά ἐστιν ἢ ἀσώματον.
καὶ σῶμα μὲν οὐκ ἔστιν, ἐπεὶ διαστατὸν ἂν ὑπῆρχε,
τοῦ σώματος τὰς τρεῖς ἔχοντος διαστάσεις. καὶ
378 μὴν οὐδὲ ἀσώματον. εἰ γὰρ ἀσώματόν ἐστιν,
οὐδὲν γενήσεται ἐξ αὐτοῦ· τὸ γὰρ γεννῶν κατὰ
θίξιν γεννᾷ, θίξις δὲ οὐδεμία γενέσθαι δύναται ἐπὶ
ἀσωμάτου φύσεως. τοίνυν οὐδὲ ἀσώματόν ἐστι
τὸ σημεῖον. εἰ δὲ μήτε σῶμα μήτε ἀσώματον,
379 ἀνεπινόητόν ἐστι τὸ σημεῖον. εἰ δὲ οὐκ ἔστι
σημεῖον, οὐδὲ γραμμὴ ἔσται. μὴ οὔσης δὲ τῆς
γραμμῆς οὐδὲ μῆκος ἔσται, ᾧ ἕπεται καὶ ἡ τοῦ
σώματος ἀνυπαρξία.

380 Ἔτι κἂν δοθῇ τὸ σημεῖον εἶναι, οὐκ ἔσται μῆκος.
ἦν γὰρ τὸ μῆκος γραμμή, ἡ δὲ γραμμὴ ῥύσις
σημείου. ἤτοι οὖν ἕν ἐστι σημεῖον ἐκτεταμένον ἡ
γραμμή, ἢ πολλὰ σημεῖα νοεῖται στοιχηδὸν κεί-
381 μενα. ἀλλ᾽ εἰ μὲν ἓν ἐκτεταμένον σημεῖόν ἐστι,
οὐκ ἂν εἴη γραμμή. ἤτοι γὰρ τὸν αὐτὸν ἐπέχει
τόπον τοῦτο τὸ σημεῖον, ἢ τόπον ἐκ τόπου μετατίθεται. καὶ εἰ μὲν τὸν αὐτὸν ἐπέχει τόπον τοῦτο
τὸ σημεῖον, οὐκ ἔσται γραμμὴ ἀλλὰ στιγμή· ῥυὲν
382 γὰρ ἐνοεῖτο γραμμή. εἰ δὲ τόπον ἐκ τόπου μέτεισιν, ἤτοι ὃν μὲν ἀπολεῖπον τόπον οὗ δὲ ἐπιλαμβανόμενον μέτεισιν, ἢ οὗ μὲν ἐχόμενον τόπου εἰς
383 ὃν δὲ ἐκτεινόμενον. οὔτε δὲ ὃν μὲν ἀπολεῖπον
τόπον οὗ δὲ ἐπιλαμβανόμενον ποιήσει γραμμήν·
μενεῖ γὰρ ᾗ¹ ἀρχῆθεν στιγμή, καὶ ᾧ λόγῳ τὸν
πρῶτον ἐπεσχηκὸς τόπον ἐλέγετο στιγμὴ καὶ οὐ
γραμμή, τῷ αὐτῷ καὶ τὸν δεύτερον ἐπειληφὸς καὶ
τὸν τρίτον καὶ τοὺς ἑξῆς οὐκ ἔσται γραμμὴ ἀλλὰ
384 πάλιν στιγμή. εἰ δὲ οὗ μὲν ἐχόμενον τόπου εἰς ὃν

---

¹ ᾗ ego: ἡ mss., Bekk.

follows : if there is any such thing it is either a body
or incorporeal. Now it is not a body, since then it
would have had dimensions, as body has three dimensions. Nor yet is it incorporeal. For if it is incor- 378
poreal, nothing will proceed from it ; for that which
generates generates by contact, but there can be no
contact in the case of an incorporeal nature. So then,
the sign is not incorporeal either. But if the sign is
neither a body nor incorporeal it is inconceivable.
And if the sign does not exist, neither will the line 379
exist. And if the line does not exist, neither will
length exist ; and from this follows also the non-
existence of body.

Moreover, even if it be granted that the sign exists, 380
length will not exist. For length is line, and the line
the flux of a sign. The line then is either one sign
extended, or it is conceived as many signs placed in
a row. But if it is one sign extended, it will not be 381
a line, for this sign either occupies the same place
or changes from place to place. And if this sign
occupies the same place, it will not be a line but a
point ; for the line is conceived as a thing which has
flowed. And if it moves on from place to place it 382
moves either by leaving one place and taking up
another, or by occupying one place and extending
into another. But it will not make a line by leaving 383
one place and taking up another ; for it will remain,
as at first, a point, and just as when it occupied its
first place it was called a point and not a line, so, by
the same reasoning, when it occupies its second place
and its third, and all the rest, it will not be a line but,
as before, a point. And if it makes the line by 384

183

δὲ ἐκτεινόμενον ποιεῖ τὴν γραμμήν, ἤτοι μεριστῷ
ἀντιπαρεκτείνεται τόπῳ ἢ ἀμερίστῳ. καὶ εἰ μὲν
ἀμερίστῳ, μένει στιγμὴ καὶ οὐ γίνεται γραμμή·
385 μεριστὸν γάρ τί ἐστιν ἡ γραμμή· εἰ δὲ μεριστῷ
ἀντιπαρεκτείνεται τόπῳ, ἐπεὶ τὸ μεριστῷ ἀντιπαρεκτεινόμενον τόπῳ μεριστόν ἐστι καὶ ἔχει μέρη,
τὸ δὲ ἔχον μέρη σῶμά ἐστιν, ἔσται τὸ σημεῖον
μεριστόν τε καὶ σῶμα, ὅπερ οὐ βούλονται. τοίνυν
386 οὐχ ἕν ἐστι σημεῖον ἡ γραμμή.   καὶ μὴν οὐδὲ
πολλὰ στοιχηδὸν κείμενα. ταῦτα γὰρ τὰ σημεῖα
ἤτοι ψαύει ἀλλήλων κατὰ τὴν ἐπίνοιαν, ἢ οὐχ
ἅπτεται ἀλλήλων, μεσολαβούμενα δὲ τόποις τισὶ
διορίζεται. εἰ δὲ τόποις μεσολαβεῖται, οὐκέτι μίαν
ποιήσει γραμμήν. εἰ δὲ ἅπτεται ἀλλήλων, ἤτοι ὅλα
387 ὅλων ἅπτεται ἢ μέρεσι μερῶν. καὶ εἰ μὲν μέρεσι
μερῶν, οὐκέτι ἔσται ἀμερῆ· τὸ γὰρ μέσον, εἰ τύχοι,
σημεῖον δυοῖν ἄλλων σημείων πλείονα ἔξει μέρη,
ἓν μὲν ᾧ ἅπτεται τοῦ ἔμπροσθεν σημείου, ἕτερον δὲ
ᾧ θιγγάνει τοῦ ὄπισθεν, τρίτον ᾧ τῆς ἐπιπέδου,
τέταρτον ᾧ τοῦ ὑπερκειμένου μέρους, ὥστε μηκέτι
388 αὐτὸ ἀμερὲς ὑπάρχειν ἀλλὰ πολυμερές. εἰ δὲ ὅλα
ὅλων ἅπτεται, σημεῖα ἐν σημείοις περισχεθήσεται
καὶ τὸν αὐτὸν ἐφέξει τόπον. εἰ δὲ τὸν αὐτὸν ἐφέξει
τόπον, οὐκέτι ἔσται στοῖχος αὐτῶν, ἵνα γένηται
389 γραμμή, ἀλλὰ πάντα μία ἔσται στιγμή. εἴπερ οὖν
ἵνα μὲν ἐπινοηθῇ τὸ σῶμα, δεῖ ἐπινοηθῆναι τὸ
μῆκος, ἵνα δὲ τὸ μῆκος, τὴν γραμμήν, καὶ ἵνα αὕτη,
τὸ σημεῖον, ἐπεὶ δέδεικται ἡ γραμμὴ μήτε σημεῖον

---

[a] *i.e.* that of the board (or paper) on which the point is
marked.   "The part which lies above" is that which is
184

occupying one place and extending into another, it extends over a place that is either divisible or indivisible. And if it is indivisible, it remains a point and does not become a line ; for the line is a divisible thing ; and if it extends over a divisible place, then, 385 since what extends over a divisible place is divisible and has parts, and what has parts is a body, the sign will be both divisible and a body ; and this they do not want to admit. So then the line is not one single sign.—Nor yet is it many signs set in a row. For 386 these signs, as conceived, either are in contact with one another or do not touch one another but are separated by intercepting spaces. But if they are intercepted by spaces they will no longer make one line. And if they touch one another they either touch wholes as wholes or parts with parts. And if 387 they touch parts with parts they will no longer be without parts ; for, to take an example, the sign which stands midway between two other signs will have several parts,—one by which it touches the sign in front of it, another by which it makes contact with that behind it, a third by which it touches the surface,[a] a fourth by which it touches the part which lies above ; so that it is no longer without parts but with many parts. And if they touch wholes as wholes, 388 signs will be contained in signs and will occupy the same place. And if they shall occupy the same place there will no longer be a row of them, so as to form a line, but they will all be one point. If, then, in order 389 to form a conception of body, one must first conceive length, and conceive line, again, before length, and sign before line, then—since the line has been shown

visible to the eye (on a higher level) of the observer, and beneath which is " the part which touches the surface."

ὑπάρχουσα μήτε ἐκ σημείων σύνθετος, οὐδέν ἐστι
γραμμή. εἰ δὲ μή ἐστι γραμμή, οὐδὲ μῆκος· ᾧ
ἀκολουθεῖ τὸ μηδὲ σῶμά τι ὑπάρχειν.

390 Καὶ ἄρτι μὲν ἐπεδείξαμεν ἀνεπινόητον τὴν
γραμμὴν ἐχόμενοι τοῦ σημείου· ἔνεστι δὲ καὶ
προηγουμένως αὐτὴν ἀναιρεῖν ἐχομένους τῆς κατ᾽
αὐτὴν ἐπινοίας. φασὶ γὰρ οἱ γεωμέτραι ὅτι γραμμή
391 ἐστι μῆκος ἀπλατές, ἡμεῖς δὲ σκεπτόμενοι οὔτε ἐν
τοῖς αἰσθητοῖς οὔτε ἐν τοῖς νοητοῖς δυνάμεθα λαβεῖν
μῆκος ἀπλατές· ὅ τι γὰρ ἂν λάβωμεν μῆκος αἰσθητόν, τοῦτο σὺν ποσῷ πλάτει λαμβάνομεν. ὥστ᾽
ἐν μὲν τοῖς αἰσθητοῖς οὐκ ἔστι τι ἀπλατὲς [σῶμα].[1]
392 καὶ μὴν οὐδ᾽ ἐν τοῖς νοητοῖς ἔνεστι ⟨τι⟩[2] τοιοῦτο
φαντασιωθῆναι μῆκος. ἕτερον μὲν γὰρ ἑτέρου
στενώτερον μῆκος δυνάμεθα νοεῖν· ὅταν δὲ τὸ αὐτὸ
φυλάττοντες μῆκος ἐκ τούτου κατ᾽ ὀλίγον σχίζωμεν
ταῖς ἐπινοίαις τὸ πλάτος καὶ τοῦτο ἄχρι τινὸς
ποιῶμεν, ἔλαττον μὲν ἀεὶ καὶ μᾶλλον τὸ πλάτος
γινόμενον νοοῦμεν, ὅταν δὲ φθάσωμεν ἅπαξ στερῆσαι τοῦ πλάτους τὸ μῆκος, οὐκέτι οὐδὲ τὸ μῆκος
νοοῦμεν, ἀλλὰ σὺν τῇ ἄρσει τοῦ πλάτους αἴρεται καὶ
ἡ τοῦ μήκους ἐπίνοια.

393 Καθόλου τε τὸ ἐπινοούμενον πᾶν ἤτοι κατ᾽
ἐμπέλασιν τῶν ἐναργῶν νοεῖται ἢ κατὰ τὴν ἀπὸ τῶν
ἐναργῶν μετάβασιν, καὶ τοῦτο ποικίλως, ὁτὲ μὲν
κατὰ ὁμοιότητα ὁτὲ δὲ κατὰ ἐπισύνθεσιν ὁτὲ δὲ
κατὰ ἀναλογίαν, καὶ ταύτην δὲ ἤτοι αὐξητικὴν ἢ
394 μειωτικήν. κατ᾽ ἐμπέλασιν μὲν οὖν τῶν ἐναργῶν
νοεῖται ὡς λευκὸν καὶ μέλαν καὶ γλυκὺ καὶ πικρόν·

---

[1] [σῶμα] secl. ego: μῆκος cj. Heintz.
[2] ⟨τι⟩ add. LN, Mutsch.

[a] With §§ 393-395 cf. *Adv. Log.* ii. 58-60.

to be neither a sign nor a compound of signs,—the line is nothing. And if the line does not exist, neither does length ; and from this it follows that no body exists either.

We pointed out just now, by examining the sign, 390 that the line is inconceivable ; but it is also possible to abolish it directly by examining its own conception. For the Geometers state that "the line is length without breadth" ; but we in our inquiry are unable to 391 perceive length without breadth either in sensibles or in intelligibles ; for whatever sensible length we perceive we perceive as including a certain breadth. So that there does not exist among sensibles any [body] without breadth. Nor yet is it possible to 392 imagine amongst intelligibles any length of this kind. For although we are able to think of one length as narrower than another, yet when we keep the same length and, in our thoughts, gradually pare off its breadth and keep on doing this up to a certain point, then we conceive the breadth becoming ever less and less, but when we have gone so far as to deprive the length of its breadth altogether, we no longer conceive even the length, but along with the removal of the breadth the conception of the length also is removed.

In general, too, everything which is conceived is 393 conceived either through the presentation of things manifest to the senses or through transition from things manifest,[a] and this again in various ways—at one time through resemblance, at another through composition, at another by analogy, and this again by way either of increase or of decrease. Thus it is 394 through the presentation of things manifest that things like white and black and sweet and bitter are

ταῦτα γὰρ καὶ εἰ αἰσθητά ἐστιν, ἀλλ' οὐδὲν ἧττον
νοεῖται. κατὰ δὲ τὴν ἀπὸ τῶν ἐναργῶν μετάβασιν
ὁμοιωτικῶς μὲν νοεῖται οἷον ἀπὸ [μὲν] τῆς Σω-
395 κράτους εἰκόνος ὁ μὴ παρὼν Σωκράτης, συν-
θετικῶς δὲ οἷον ἀπὸ τοῦ ἀνθρώπου καὶ ἵππου
ὁ μήτε ἄνθρωπος ὢν μήτε ἵππος, σύνθετος δὲ ἐξ
ἀμφοτέρων ἱπποκένταυρος, κατὰ δὲ ἀναλογίαν αὐξητικὴν ἢ μειωτικὴν οἷον ἀπὸ τοῦ ὁρᾶν τὸν κοινὸν
κατὰ μέγεθος ἄνθρωπον καὶ ὑποπίπτοντα αὐξήσαντες μὲν ταῖς φαντασίαις ἐνοήσαμεν τὸν Κύκλωπα, ὃς οὐκ ἐῴκει

   ἀνδρί γε σιτοφάγῳ ἀλλὰ ῥίῳ ὑλήεντι,

μειώσαντες δὲ ἐσπάσαμεν ἔννοιαν τοῦ πυγμαίου
396 ἀνθρώπου. τοσούτων δὴ τρόπων νοήσεως ὄντων,
εἰ ἐπινοεῖταί τι μῆκος ἀπλατές [ἢ γραμμή],[1] κατά
τινα τούτων τῶν τρόπων ὀφείλει νοεῖσθαι· κατ'
οὐδένα δὲ αὐτῶν δύναται νοηθῆναι, ὡς παραστή-
397 σομεν, ὥστε ἀνεπινόητόν ἐστιν. κατὰ μὲν οὖν
ἐμπέλασιν τῶν ἐναργῶν οὐκ ἂν γένοιτο νόησις μήκους τινὸς ἀπλατοῦς· οὐδενὶ γὰρ περιεπέσομεν
μήκει χωρὶς πλάτους ἐν τοῖς φαινομένοις καὶ
398 ἐναργέσι πράγμασιν. κατὰ δὲ τὴν ἀπὸ τῶν
ἐναργῶν μετάβασιν πάλιν τῶν ἀμηχάνων ἐστὶ
φαντασιωθῆναι μῆκος ἀπλατές, οὔτε κατὰ ὁμοιό-
τητα· οὐδὲν[2] γὰρ ἔχομεν ἐν τοῖς ἐναργέσι μῆκος
χωρὶς πλάτους, ἵνα νοήσωμέν τι ὅμοιον τούτῳ
ἀπλατὲς μῆκος. τὸ γάρ τινι ὅμοιον γινωσκομένῳ
καὶ ἑωραμένῳ ὀφείλει ὅμοιον ὑπάρχειν· ἐπεὶ οὖν
οὐδὲν ἔχομεν ἐναργὲς ὑποπίπτον μῆκος χωρὶς

   [1] [ἢ γραμμή] secl. Heintz.
   [2] οὐδὲν Mutsch. : οὐδὲ mss., Bekk.

conceived ; for these things, though they are sensible, are none the less conceived. And things are conceived through transition from things manifest either by way of resemblance (as, for instance, the absent Socrates from a likeness of Socrates) ; or by way of 395 composition (as, for instance, from man and horse the Hippocentaur, which is neither man nor horse but compounded of both) ; or by analogy, which may either magnify or diminish the object,—as when from seeing the man of average size, as presented to our senses, by magnifying him in imagination we conceive the Cyclops who was

> Less like a corn-eating man than a forest-clad peak of the mountains, [a]

and by diminishing him we derive a conception of the pygmy. Seeing, then, that there are so 396 many modes of conception, if a length without breadth is conceived, it must be conceived after one of these modes ; but it cannot be conceived after any of them, as we shall establish, so that it is inconceivable.—Now the conception of a length without 397 breadth will not be formed through the presentation of things manifest ; for we have never met with length without breadth amongst objects that are apparent and manifest to the senses. And it is like- 398 wise impossible for length without breadth to be imagined through transition from things manifest, or through resemblance ; for amongst things manifest we have not got any length without breadth, so as to enable us to conceive a length without breadth resembling it. For what resembles anything ought to bear resemblance to what is known and seen ; since then we have no length without breadth that is

[a] Homer, *Odyss.* ix. 191.

πλάτους, οὐδ' ὅμοιόν τι αὐτοῦ συνεῖναι δυνησόμεθα
399 εἶναι μῆκος ἀπλατές. καὶ μὴν οὐδὲ κατ' ἐπισύνθεσιν ληπτόν ἐστι τοῦτο· εἰπάτωσαν γὰρ ἡμῖν, τίνα
τῶν ἐκ περιπτώσεως ἐναργῶν [καὶ]¹ γιγνομένων
μετὰ τίνων συντιθέντες ἐνόησαν μῆκος ἀπλατές;
400 ὅπερ εἰπεῖν οὐ δυνήσονται. καὶ μὴν οὐδὲ κατὰ
ἀναλογίαν παρῆλθεν ἡ τοῦ ἀπλατοῦς μήκους νόησις.
τὰ γὰρ κατὰ ἀναλογίαν νοούμενα ἔχει τι κοινὸν
πρὸς τὰ ἀφ' ὧν νοεῖται, οἷον ἀπὸ τοῦ κοινοῦ μεγέθους τἀνθρώπου κατὰ παραύξησιν ἐνοήσαμεν τὸν
Κύκλωπα καὶ ἀπὸ τοῦ αὐτοῦ πάλιν κατὰ μείωσιν
401 τὸν πυγμαῖον· ὥστ' εἰ ἔστι τι κοινὸν τοῖς κατὰ
ἀναλογίαν νοουμένοις πρὸς τὰ ἀφ' ὧν νοεῖται,
οὐδὲν δὲ ἔχομεν κοινὸν τοῦ τε ἀπλατοῦς καὶ τοῦ
σὺν πλάτει μήκους, ἵνα ἀπ' ἐκείνου ὁρμηθέντες
νοήσωμεν τὸ ἀπλατὲς μῆκος, οὐδὲ κατὰ ἀναλογίαν
402 οὖν νοεῖται τὸ τοιοῦτον. ὅθεν εἰ ἕκαστον τῶν
νοουμένων κατά τινα τῶν ἐκκειμένων τρόπων
ὀφείλει νοεῖσθαι, ἐδείξαμεν δὲ ἡμεῖς κατὰ μηδένα
τρόπον νοεῖσθαι δυνάμενον τὸ ἀπλατὲς μῆκος,
λεκτέον ἀνεπινόητον εἶναι τὸ ἀπλατὲς μῆκος.
403 Ἀλλ' ἴσως τις ἐρεῖ ὅτι λαβόντες τι μῆκος σὺν
ποσῷ πλάτει κατ' ἐπίτασιν νοοῦμεν τὸ ἀπλατὲς
μῆκος· εἰ γὰρ ἐκ τούτου κατ' ὀλίγον ἐλασσοῦται τὸ
πλάτος, ἐλεύσεταί ποτε καὶ εἰς τὸ ἀπλατές, ὥστε
καταλήγειν τὴν μείωσιν εἰς τὸ χωρὶς πλάτους
404 μῆκος. ἀλλὰ πρῶτον μὲν ἐδείξαμεν ὅτι ἡ παντελὴς
τοῦ πλάτους ἆρσις καὶ τοῦ μήκους ἐστὶν ἀναίρεσις.

¹ [καὶ] om. N (ἐναργῶς γιγνωσκομένων Mutsch.).

ᵃ i.e. of " intensifying," or gradually increasing, the
narrowness of the line (cf. § 405 infra), which is equivalent to
decreasing its breadth.

manifestly perceived, we shall not be able to discern
the existence of any length without breadth which
resembles it. Nor, again, is it perceptible through 399
composition ; for let them tell us what objects
made manifest by sense they compounded with what
in order to form the notion of length without breadth,
—and that they will not be able to tell us. Nor yet 400
was the notion of length without breadth suggested
by analogy. For things conceived by way of analogy
possess something in common with the things from
which their conception is derived ; for example, from
the common feature of man's size, by enlargement,
we conceive the Cyclops, and conversely, by diminution of the same object, the pygmy. Consequently, 401
if things conceived by analogy have some feature in
common with those from which the conception is
derived, but we find nothing that is common both to
length without breadth and to length with breadth,
to enable us by starting from the latter to arrive at
the conception of length without breadth,—then this
conception is not formed by analogy either. Hence, 402
if everything which is conceived must be conceived
in one of the ways mentioned, and we have shown
that length without breadth cannot be conceived in
any way, we must declare that length without breadth
is inconceivable.

But someone, perhaps, will say that we conceive 403
length without breadth by a process of " intension " [a]
when we have taken a certain length with a certain
breadth ; for if, starting with this, the breadth is
gradually diminished, it will come in time to being
without breadth, so that the decrease ends in length
without breadth. But, firstly, we have shown that 404
the complete removal of breadth is also the abolition

191

ἔπειτα τὸ κατ᾿ ἐπίτασιν νοούμενον οὐχ ἕτερόν ἐστι
τοῦ προνοηθέντος, ἀλλ᾿ αὐτὸ ἐκεῖνο ἐπιτεταμένον.
405 ἐπεὶ οὖν ἀπὸ τοῦ ποσὸν ἔχοντος πλάτος κατ᾿ ἐπίτασιν στενότητος νοῆσαί τι θέλομεν, πάντως τὸ μὲν
ἀπλατὲς μῆκος οὐκ ἐπινοήσομεν (ἑτερογενὲς γάρ
406 ἐστιν), ἀεὶ δὲ καὶ μᾶλλον στενώτερον ληψόμεθα
πλάτος, ὥστε τὴν κατάληξιν τῆς νοήσεως ἐν ἐλα-
χιστοτάτῳ γίνεσθαι πλάτει, μετὰ τοῦτο δὲ τὴν εἰς
τὸ ἑτερογενὲς μετάβασιν συμβαίνειν, τουτέστι τοῦ
407 συναναιρουμένου τῷ πλάτει μήκους.   καθόλου
τε, εἰ κατὰ στέρησιν πλάτους νοῆσαι δυνάμεθα
μῆκος ἀπλατές, ἐπεὶ πάντα τὰ στερητικὰ οὐκ ἔστιν
ἐν ὑποκειμένῳ, οὐδὲ τὸ ἀπλατὲς μῆκος· διὸ οὐδὲ
γραμμή. ἵππος μὲν γάρ τι ἔστιν ἐν ὑποκειμένῳ,
οὐχ ἵππος δ᾿ οὐκ ἔστιν, καὶ ἄνθρωπος μὲν ἔστιν,
οὐκ ἄνθρωπος δὲ οὐκ ἔστιν. τοίνυν εἰ ἔχομέν τι
πλάτος ἤ τι μῆκος, ἐν ὑποκειμένῳ ἔσται· ἀπλατὲς
408 δ᾿ οὐχ ὑπάρξει. ὅνπερ οὖν τρόπον οἱ λέγοντες
ὅτι ἕτερον ἑτέρου μέγεθος ὑπερτιθέντες νόησιν
λαμβάνουσι τοῦ ἀπείρου μεγέθους ὡς σώματος
πλανῶνται, καὶ μέγιστον μέν τι καθ᾿ ὑπέρθεσιν
πολλῶν μεγεθῶν λαμβάνουσιν, οὐκ ἄπειρον δὲ τοῦτο
ἀλλὰ πεπερασμένον (ὁ γὰρ ἔσχατον νενοήκασι, τῇ
409 διανοίᾳ περιληπτόν ἐστιν, ὃ δὲ περιληπτόν ἐστι
διανοίᾳ, πεπέρασται, ἐπείπερ τοι τὸ λοιπὸν οὔπω
περιληφθὲν τῇ διανοίᾳ ἐλέγχει τὸ περιληφθὲν ὡς
μὴ ὂν ἄπειρον), οὕτω τοίνυν κἀνθάδε ἡ συναίρεσις
τοῦ πλάτους, εἰς ἐλάχιστον πλάτος καταληγούσης
τῆς διανοίας, πλάτος ἐστὶ καὶ οὐ μῆκος ἀπλατές.

***

[a] "Privation," "privative," are (Aristotelian) terms for
"negation," "negative."

of length. And next, what is conceived through intension is not other than what was previously conceived but that very same thing after undergoing intension. Since, then, we propose to conceive some- 405 thing from that which has a certain breadth, through intension of narrowness, we certainly shall not conceive length without breadth (for this is a heterogeneous thing), but we shall apprehend a breadth that 406 is ever getting more and more narrow, so that our conception ends in the least possible breadth, and after this there follows a transition to what is heterogeneous, that is to say, when the length is abolished along with the breadth.—Also, in general, if we can conceive 407 length without breadth through privation of breadth, since all privatives^a are non-existent in reality, neither does length without breadth exist ; nor, in consequence, the line. Thus, horse is a thing which exists in reality, but " not horse " does not exist ; and man exists, but " not man " does not exist. So then, if we perceive a breadth or a length, it will exist in reality ; but " without breadth " will not exist. As, 408 then, those men who assert that they form a notion of an infinite magnitude as body by superimposing one magnitude on another are in error, and while they grasp a maximum through the superimposition of many magnitudes, yet this is not infinite but limited (for what they conceived last is capable of being contained by the intellect, and what is capable of being con- 409 tained by the intellect is limited, since otherwise, of course, what remains as yet uncontained by the intellect convicts what is contained of not being infinite),—so too in this case, the contraction of the breadth, when the intellect ends with a minimal breadth, is a breadth and not a length without

410   ἄλλως τε, εἰ δυνατόν ἐστι νοήσαντάς τι μῆκος
σὺν ποσῷ πλάτει στερῆσαι αὐτὸ τοῦ πλάτους καὶ
τὸ μῆκος ἀπλατὲς ἐπινοεῖν, ἐνέσται καὶ σάρκα
ἐπινοήσαντας σὺν τρωτῷ ἰδιώματι στερήσει τοῦ
411 τρωτοῦ ἰδιώματος νοῆσαι ἄτρωτον σάρκα, καὶ ἐν-
δέξεται μετὰ ἀντιτύπου ἰδιώματος σῶμα νοήσαντας
στερήσει τοῦ ἀντιτύπου ἰδιώματος λαβεῖν ἀναντίτυπον σῶμα. ὅπερ ἐστὶν ἀδύνατον· τὸ γὰρ ἄτρωτον
νοούμενον οὐκ ἔστι σάρξ, σὺν τρωτῷ γὰρ ἰδιώματι
ἐνοεῖτο ἡ σάρξ, καὶ ἀναντίτυπον οὐκ ἔστι σῶμα,
σὺν γὰρ τῷ ἀντιτύπῳ ἰδιώματι ἐνοεῖτο τὸ σῶμα.
τοίνυν καὶ τὸ νοούμενον χωρὶς πλάτους μῆκος
οὐκ ἔστι μῆκος· σὺν ποσῷ γὰρ πλάτει νοεῖται τὸ
μῆκος.

412   'Αλλ' ὅ γε 'Αριστοτέλης οὐκ ἀδιανόητον ἔλεγεν
εἶναι τὸ παρὰ τοῖς γεωμέτραις ἀπλατὲς μῆκος (τό
γέ τοι τοῦ τοίχου μῆκος λαμβάνομεν χωρὶς τοῦ
ἐπιβάλλειν τῷ πλάτει τοῦ τοίχου) πλανώμενος.
ὅταν γὰρ τὸ τοῦ τοίχου μῆκος λαμβάνωμεν χωρὶς
πλάτους, οὐ χωρὶς παντὸς πλάτους τοῦτο λαμβάνομεν ἀλλὰ χωρὶς τοῦ περὶ τῷ τοίχῳ πλάτους.
ἐνδέχεται γὰρ συγκαταπλέξαντας τὸ τοῦ τοίχου
μῆκός τινι πλάτει καὶ οἱῳδήποτε οὖν νόησιν αὐτοῦ
ποιεῖσθαι, ὥστε μῆκος λαμβάνεσθαι οὐ χωρὶς
413 πλάτους ἀλλὰ χωρὶς τοῦδέ τινος πλάτους. πρού-
κειτο δὲ τῷ 'Αριστοτέλει παραστῆσαι οὐχ ὅτι τὸ
τινὸς πλάτους ἄμοιρον μῆκος ἐνδέχεται νοεῖν, ἀλλ'
ὅτι τὸ παντὸς πλάτους· ὅπερ οὐ παρέστησεν.

414   Πρὸς τούτοις, εἴπερ οἱ γεωμέτραι οὐ μόνον ἀπλατὲς

• Aristot. *Frag.* 29 (Rose).

breadth.—And further : if it is possible for those who 410
have conceived a length with a certain breadth to
deprive it of its breadth and thus to conceive length
without breadth, it will also be possible for them,
when they have conceived flesh which possesses the
property of vulnerability, by privation of the property
of vulnerability to conceive invulnerable flesh ; and 411
after conceiving a body with the property of solidity,
it will be feasible for them, by privation of the property of solidity, to conceive a non-solid body. But
this is impossible ; for what is conceived as invulnerable is not flesh (for flesh was conceived as including
the property of vulnerability), and the non-solid is
not body (for body was conceived as including the
property of solidity). So too the length conceived as
without breadth is not length (for length is conceived
as including a certain breadth).

Aristotle,[a] however, declared that the length with- 412
out breadth of the Geometers is not inconceivable
(" for in fact we apprehend the length of a wall
without having a perception of the wall's breadth ") ;
but he is in error. For when we apprehend the
length of a wall without its breadth, we do not
apprehend it as without any breadth but without the
breadth which belongs to the wall. For it is possible
by connecting the length of the wall with some
breadth (whatever it be) to form a notion of it, so
that its length is not apprehended without breadth
but without this particular breadth. But the task 413
before Aristotle was to establish that it is possible to
conceive, not the length which is devoid of a certain
breadth, but that which is devoid of any breadth
at all ; and this he did not establish.

Furthermore, since the Geometers assert that the 414

SEXTUS EMPIRICUS

μῆκός φασι τὴν γραμμὴν ἀλλὰ καὶ πέρας ἐπιφανείας, [ὃ μῆκός καὶ πλάτος ἐστὶν ἀβαθές,][1]
ἐνέσται κοινότερον περί τε γραμμῆς καὶ ἐπιφανείας
διαπορεῖν. εἰ γὰρ ἡ γραμμὴ πέρας ἐστὶν ἐπιφανείας, [ὅ ἐστι,] μῆκος ἀπλατὲς καθεστηκυῖα,
πάντως ἐπιφανείας ἐπιφανείᾳ παρατεθείσης ἢ
παράλληλοι δύο γίνονται γραμμαὶ ἢ μία ἐξ ἀμφο-
415 τέρων. καὶ εἰ μὲν μία αἱ παράλληλοι δύο γραμμαὶ
γίνονται, ἐπεὶ ἡ γραμμὴ πέρας ἐστὶν ἐπιφανείας, ἡ
δὲ ἐπιφάνεια πέρας σώματος, τῶν δυοῖν γραμμῶν
μιᾶς γινομένων[2] καὶ αἱ δύο ἐπιφάνειαι μία γενήσονται. οὕτωσὶ δὲ καὶ τὰ δύο σώματα ἓν ἔσται
σῶμα, καὶ διὰ τοῦτο ἡ παράθεσις οὐκέτι γενήσεται
παράθεσις ἀλλὰ ἕνωσις. ὅπερ ἐστὶν ἀδύνατον· ἐπὶ
τινῶν μὲν γὰρ παρατιθεμένων ἀλλήλοις σωμάτων
ἕνωσις γίνεσθαι πέφυκεν, ὡς ἐπὶ τῶν ὑγρῶν, ἐπὶ
τινῶν δὲ οὐκέτι· λίθος γὰρ λίθῳ καὶ ἀδάμας ἀδά-
μαντι κατὰ τὴν παράθεσιν οὐχ ἑνοῦται. ὥστε δύο
416 γραμμαὶ οὐκ ἂν γένοιτο μία. καὶ ἄλλως, ἐὰν
δῶμεν μίαν γενέσθαι, καὶ ἕνωσιν διὰ τοῦτο τῶν
σωμάτων, δεήσει τὸν χωρισμὸν αὐτῶν μὴ κατὰ τὰ
αὐτὰ πέρατα γίνεσθαι ἀλλὰ κατ' ἄλλα καὶ ἄλλα
μέρη, βιαίως ἀποσπωμένων αὐτῶν. οὐχὶ δὲ τοῦτο·
τῶν γὰρ περάτων καὶ πρὶν τῆς παραθέσεως καὶ
μετὰ τὸν χωρισμὸν αὐτῶν ἡ αὐτὴ σῴζεται φύσις.
οὐκ ἄρα αἱ δύο παράλληλοι γραμμαὶ μία γίνονται.[3]
    σὺν τούτοις, εἴπερ αἱ δύο γραμμαὶ μία γί-
νονται, τὰ παρατιθέμενα ἀλλήλοις σώματα ἑνὶ ἄκρῳ

[1] [ὃ . . . ἀβαθές] secl. ego: ὃ . . . ἀβαθές N, Mutsch.:
ὃ μ. κ. π. ἐστὶν ἀπλατές cet. (secl. Bekk.).
[2] γινομένων N : γινομένης cet., Bekk.
[3] γίνονται cj. Bekk.: γίνοιντο mss.: γένοιτο edd.

196

line is not only " length without breadth " but also
" the limit of a surface," [this being length and
breadth without depth,] it will be possible for us to
discuss more generally the difficulties involved both
in line and in surface.[a] For if the line is the limit of a
surface, and is length without breadth, then certainly,
when surface is set beside surface either there are two
parallel lines or one compounded of both. And if the 415
two parallel lines become one, since the line is the limit
of the surface and the surface the limit of the body,
when the two lines become one the two surfaces also
will become one. And thus the two bodies also will be
one body, and because of this the juxtaposition will
no longer be juxtaposition but unification. But this
is impossible ; for though in some cases when bodies
are juxtaposed unification is the natural result (as in
the case of liquids), yet in other cases it is not so ;
for stone is not made one with stone, nor adamant
with adamant, by juxtaposition. So that two lines
will not become one.—And again, if we grant that 416
they do become one, and that owing to this there is
unification of the bodies, their separation will have to
take place not at the same limits but in various other
parts, as they are forcibly pulled apart. But this is
not so ; for the nature of the limits remains the same
both before the juxtaposition and after their separation. Therefore the two parallel lines do not become
one.—Moreover, if the two lines become one the
juxtaposed bodies will be smaller by one extreme

[a] For " limits " and " surfaces," in geometry, *cf. P.H.*
iii. 39 ff.

ἔσται ἐλάσσονα· γεγόνασι γὰρ αἱ δύο γραμμαὶ μία,
καὶ ἡ μία κατ᾽ ἀνάγκην ἓν ἔχειν ἄκρον ὀφείλει.
οὐχὶ δέ γε τὰ παρατιθέμενα ἀλλήλοις σώματα ἑνὶ
ἄκρῳ γίνεται ἐλάσσονα, ὥστε οὐκ ἂν εἶεν αἱ δύο
417 γραμμαὶ μία.   εἰ δὲ παράλληλοι δύο μένουσιν
αἱ γραμμαί, τὸ ἐκ τῶν δυοῖν μεῖζον ἔσται τῆς μιᾶς.
εἰ δὲ τὸ ἐκ τῶν δυοῖν γινόμενον μεῖζον ἔσται τῆς
μιᾶς γραμμῆς, ἕξει ἑκατέρα αὐτῶν πλάτος, ὃ μετὰ
τῆς ἑτέρας ταττόμενον μεῖζον ποιεῖ διάστημα. καὶ
οὕτως οὐκ ἔστιν ἀπλατὲς μῆκος ἡ γραμμή· ἢ εἴπερ
ἐστί, σαλεύεσθαι δεήσει τὴν ἐνάργειαν, ὡς παρεστήσαμεν.

418   Προηγουμένως μὲν οὖν ταῦτα ῥητέον πρὸς τὴν
παρὰ τοῖς μαθηματικοῖς περὶ σωμάτων τε καὶ
419 περάτων διάταξιν· μεταβάντες δὲ ἀκολούθως σκοπῶμεν εἰ καὶ κατὰ τὰς αὐτῶν ἐκείνων ὑποθέσεις
δύναται προκόπτειν ὁ λόγος. ἀρέσκει τοίνυν τοῖς
γεωμέτραις τὴν εὐθεῖαν γραμμὴν στρεφομένην πᾶσιν αὐτῆς τοῖς μέρεσι κύκλους γράφειν. τούτῳ δὴ
εὐθὺς αὐτῶν τῷ θεωρήματι μάχεται τὸ μῆκος
420 ἀπλατὲς εἶναι τὴν γραμμήν. ἐπεὶ γὰρ πᾶν μέρος
γραμμῆς, ὥς φασι, σημεῖον ἔχει, τὸ δὲ σημεῖον
στρεφόμενον κύκλον γράφει, ὅταν εὐθεῖα γραμμὴ
στρεφομένη καὶ πᾶσι τοῖς ἑαυτῆς μέρεσι κυκλογραφοῦσα καταμετρῇ τὸ διάστημα τῆς ἐπιπέδου τῆς
ἀπὸ τοῦ κέντρου μέχρι τῆς ἐξωτάτω περιφερείας,
τότε ἤτοι συνεχεῖς εἰσιν οἱ παράλληλοι κύκλοι ἢ
421 διεστᾶσιν ἀπ᾽ ἀλλήλων. ὁπότερον δ᾽ ἂν λέγωσι
τούτων οἱ γεωμέτραι, εἰς ἄλυτον σχεδὸν ἀπορίαν
ἐμπεσοῦνται. εἰ μὲν γὰρ διεστᾶσιν ἀπ᾽ ἀλλήλων,

edge ; for the two lines have become one, and this one must necessarily have one edge. But juxtaposed bodies do not become smaller by one edge, so that the two lines will not be one.—And if the two 417 parallel lines remain two, the sum of the two will be greater than the one. And if the sum of the two shall be greater than the one line, each of them will possess breadth, which when ranged along with the other produces a larger dimension. And thus the line will not be " length without breadth " ; or if it is, the result must be that the evidence of sense is rendered shaky, as we have shown.

Let this, then, serve as our direct reply to the 418 Mathematicians' formal account of bodies and limits ; and let us pass on next to consider whether, even 419 on their own assumptions, their account is admissible. The Geometers, then, are of opinion that the straight line by revolving describes circles with all its parts.[a] But the fact that the line is length without breadth conflicts at once with this theorem of theirs. For since every part of the line, as they 420 assert, contains a sign, and the sign by revolving describes a circle, when the straight line, by revolving and describing a circle with all its parts, has measured out the distance of the surface which extends from the centre to the outermost circumference, then the parallel circles are either continuous or separate from one another. But whichever of 421 these alternatives the Geometers may adopt, they will involve themselves in an almost insuperable difficulty. For if these circles are separate from one

---

[a] *i.e.* if the straight line AB is made to revolve round the (fixed) point A, with this as centre it will describe as many concentric circles as it contains points.

ἔσται τι μέρος τῆς ἐπιπέδου τὸ μὴ κυκλογραφού-
μενον καὶ τῆς γραμμῆς τὸ μὴ κυκλογραφοῦν, ὅπερ
κατὰ τοῦτο τέτακται τὸ διάστημα τῆς ἐπιπέδου.
422 τοῦτο δὲ ἦν ἄτοπον· καὶ γὰρ ἔχει σημεῖον ἡ γραμμὴ
πάντως κατὰ τόδε τὸ μέρος, καὶ τὸ σημεῖον κατὰ
τοῦτο στρεφόμενον κυκλογραφεῖ· τὸ γὰρ ἢ τὴν
γραμμὴν μὴ ἔχειν κατά τι μέρος αὐτῆς σημεῖον, ἢ
τὸ σημεῖον στρεφόμενον μὴ γράφειν κύκλον, παρὰ
423 τὸν γεωμετρικόν ἐστι λόγον. εἰ δὲ συνεχεῖς εἰσιν
οἱ κύκλοι, ἤτοι οὕτω συνεχεῖς εἰσιν ὡς κατὰ τὸν
αὐτὸν τετάχθαι τόπον, ἢ ὥστε ἄλλον παρ᾿ ἄλλον
νοεῖσθαι μεταξὺ μὴ δυναμένου τινὸς παρεμπεσεῖν
σημείου· παρεμπῖπτον γὰρ ὀφείλει κύκλον γράφειν.
καὶ εἰ μὲν τὸν αὐτὸν ἐπέχουσι τόπον, εἰς γενήσονται πάντες, καὶ διὰ τοῦτο ὁ μέγιστος κύκλος οὐ
424 διοίσει τοῦ ἐλαχίστου· εἰ γὰρ ὁ μὲν ἐνδοτάτω
κύκλος καὶ πρὸς τῷ κέντρῳ ἐστὶν ἐλάχιστος, ὁ δὲ
ἐξωτάτω καὶ πρὸς τῇ περιφερείᾳ μέγιστος καθέστηκεν, πάντες δὲ τὸν αὐτὸν κατέχουσι τόπον,
ἔσται ἴσος τῷ μεγίστῳ κύκλῳ ὁ ἐλάχιστος κύκλος·
ὅπερ ἐστὶν ἀπεμφαῖνον. οὐ τοίνυν οὕτως συνεχεῖς
εἰσὶν οἱ κύκλοι ὡς τὸν αὐτὸν ἐπειληφέναι τόπον.
425 εἰ δὲ παράκεινται ἀλλήλοις ὡς μὴ παρεμπίπτειν
μεταξύ τι σημεῖον, συμπληροῦσι τὸ τῆς ἐπιπέδου
πλάτος τὸ ἀπὸ τοῦ κέντρου μέχρι τῆς ἐσχάτης
περιφερείας. ἐπεὶ οὖν τὸ συμπληρωτικὸν πλάτους
ἐξ ἀνάγκης ἔχει πλάτος, οἱ κύκλοι συμπληροῦντες
τὸ τῆς ἐπιπέδου πλάτος ἔξουσι πλάτος. ἦσαν δὲ
γραμμαὶ οἱ κύκλοι· τοίνυν αἱ γραμμαὶ οὐκ εἰσὶν
ἀπλατεῖς.
426 Ἔνεστι δὲ ἀπὸ τῆς αὐτῆς δυνάμεως ὁμοιότροπον
συνθεῖναι ἀπόδειξιν. φασὶ γὰρ οἱ γεωμέτραι τὴν

another there will be a certain part of the surface
which is not formed into a circle, and of the line which
does not form a circle, namely that which is situated
at this interval of the surface. But this is absurd ; 422
for the line certainly contains at this part a sign, and
the sign by revolving at this part describes a circle ;
for that the line at any part of it should not contain
a sign, or that the sign should not by revolving describe a circle, is contrary to the Geometers' doctrine.
And if the circles are continuous, either they are 423
continuous in such a way as to be situated in the same
place or so that they are conceived as lying side by
side in such a way that no sign can be inserted between
them ; for if one is inserted, it is bound to describe a
circle. And if they occupy the same place they will
all become one, and because of this the greatest circle
will not differ from the least ; for if the innermost 424
circle, which is next the centre, is the least, and the
outermost circle, next to the circumference, is the
greatest, and all occupy the same place, the least
circle will be equal to the greatest circle ; which is
contrary to sense. So then, the circles are not continuous in such a way as to occupy the same place.
And if they are so juxtaposed that no sign is inserted 425
between them, they fill up the breadth of the surface
from the centre up to the outermost circumference.
Since, then, what fills up a breadth necessarily
possesses breadth, the circles, as filling up the breadth
of the surface, will possess breadth. But the circles
are lines ; and so the lines are not without breadth.

And it is possible to construct a proof of a similar 426
character to the same effect. The Geometers assert

κυκλογραφοῦσαν εὐθεῖαν δι᾽ αὑτῆς στρεφομένην
κυκλογραφεῖν. διόπερ συνερωτῶντες αὐτοὺς φήσομεν " εἰ ἡ κυκλογραφοῦσα εὐθεῖα δι᾽ αὑτῆς τὸν
κύκλον γράφει, οὐκ ἔστι μῆκος ἀπλατὲς ἡ γραμμή·
ἡ δὲ κυκλογραφοῦσα εὐθεῖα κατ᾽ αὐτοὺς δι᾽ αὑτῆς
τὸν κύκλον γράφει· οὐκ ἄρα μῆκος ἀπλατές ἐστιν
427 ἡ γραμμή." ὅταν γὰρ ἡ ἀπὸ τοῦ κέντρου εὐθεῖα
ἀγομένη στρέφηται καὶ δι᾽ αὑτῆς γράφῃ τὸν κύκλον, ἤτοι κατὰ πάντων τῶν μερῶν τοῦ ἐντὸς τῆς
περιφερείας πλάτους φέρεται ἡ εὐθεῖα γραμμή, ἢ
κατὰ τινῶν μὲν φέρεται κατὰ τινῶν δὲ οὐδαμῶς.
ἀλλ᾽ εἰ κατὰ τινῶν μὲν φέρεται κατὰ τινῶν δὲ μή,
πάντως οὐ γράφει κύκλον, καθ᾽ ὧν μὲν φερομένη
μερῶν τῆς ἐπιπέδου καθ᾽ ὧν δὲ μὴ φερομένη.
εἰ δὲ κατὰ πάντων φέρεται, ὅλον τὸ ἐντὸς τῆς
περιφερείας πλάτος καταμετρήσει, πλάτος δὲ κατα-
μετροῦν ἕξει πλάτος· τὸ γὰρ πλάτους καταμετρη-
428 τικὸν ἔχει πλάτος ᾧ καταμετρεῖ. τοίνυν οὐδὲ διὰ
τοῦτο ῥητέον μῆκος ἀπλατὲς εἶναι τὴν γραμμήν.

Τὸ δὲ αὐτὸ σαφέστερον γίνεται καὶ ὅταν λέγωσιν
οἱ γεωμέτραι τὴν πλάγιον τοῦ τετραγώνου πλευρὰν
καταγομένην δι᾽ αὑτῆς τὸ παραλληλόγραμμον ἐπίπεδον καταμετρεῖν. εἰ γὰρ μῆκος ἀπλατές ἐστιν ἡ
γραμμή, πάντως καὶ ἡ πλευρὰ τοῦ τετραγώνου
ἀπλατὴς οὖσα γραμμὴ οὐ καταμετρήσει τὸ παραλληλόγραμμον ἐπίπεδον πλάτος ἔχον· ἢ καταμε-
τροῦσα τοῦτο ἕξει καὶ αὐτὴ πλάτος ᾧ καταμετρεῖ.
ὥστε ἢ τὸ θεώρημα αὐτοῖς γίνεται ψευδές, ἢ ὅτι ἡ
γραμμὴ μῆκός ἐστιν ἀπλατές.

429 Τόν τε κύλινδρον κατ᾽ εὐθεῖάν φασι γραμμὴν

that the straight line which describes a circle describes it of itself by revolving ; and therefore we will propound to them this syllogism—" If the straight line which describes a circle describes the circle of itself, the line is not a length without breadth ; but the straight line which describes a circle does, according to them, describe the circle of itself ; therefore the line is not a length without breadth." For when the 427 straight line drawn from the centre revolves and of itself describes the circle, either the straight line moves through all the parts of the surface within the circumference, or it moves through some parts and not through others. But if it moves through some parts and not through others, it certainly does not describe a circle, as it moves through some parts of the surface but does not move through others. And if it moves through them all, it will measure out the whole of the breadth within the circumference, and as measuring out the breadth it will possess breadth ; for what is capable of measuring out breadth possesses breadth whereby it measures. So for this reason also 428 one must deny that the line is length without breadth.

The same thing becomes more evident when the Geometers state that the line drawn as side of the square measures of itself the surface bounded by parallel lines. For if the line is length without breadth, certainly the side of the square, being a line without breadth, will not measure out the surface bounded by parallel lines which has breadth ; or, if it measures this, it will itself also have breadth whereby it measures. So that either their theorem proves false, or else the definition of the line as length without breadth.

Also, they say that the cylinder touches the sur- 429

ἄπτεσθαι τῆς ἐπιπέδου, ἐκκυλιόμενόν τε τῇ ἀνὰ
μέρος ἄλλων καὶ ἄλλων εὐθειῶν θέσει καταμετρεῖν
τὴν ἐπίπεδον. εἰ δὴ καὶ κατ᾽ εὐθεῖαν ἅπτεται τῆς
ἐπιπέδου ὁ κύλινδρος καὶ κυλιόμενος τῇ ἀνὰ μέρος
ἄλλων καὶ ἄλλων εὐθειῶν θέσει καταμετρεῖ τὴν
ἐπίπεδον, πάντως καὶ ἡ ἐπίπεδος ἐξ εὐθειῶν συνέστηκε γραμμῶν καὶ ἡ ἐπιφάνεια τοῦ κυλίνδρου
πάλιν ἐξ εὐθειῶν ἐστίν. ἐπεὶ οὖν ἡ ἐπίπεδος
πλάτος ἔχει, ἔχει δὲ καὶ ἡ τοῦ κυλίνδρου ἐπιφάνεια,
τὸ δὲ πλάτους συμπληρωτικὸν οὐκ ἔστιν ἀπλατές,
αἱ γραμμαὶ πλάτος συμπληροῦσαι οὐ γενήσονται
ἀπλατεῖς.

430 Ἔτι κἂν δῶμεν τὴν γραμμὴν μῆκος ἀπλατὲς
ὑπάρχειν, οὐδὲν ἧττον ἄπορος εὑρεθήσεται τοῖς
γεωμέτραις ὁ περὶ τοῦ σώματος λόγος. ὥσπερ γὰρ
τὸ σημεῖον ῥυὲν ποιεῖ γραμμήν, οὕτω καὶ ἡ γραμμὴ
ῥυεῖσα ποιεῖ ἐπιφάνειαν, ἥτις ἐστὶ πέρας σώματος
431 δύο ἔχον διαστάσεις, μῆκός τε καὶ πλάτος. ἐπείπερ
οὖν ἡ ἐπιφάνεια πέρας ἐστὶ σώματος, πάντως
τὸ σῶμα πεπερασμένον ἐστίν. εἰ δὲ τοῦτο, ὅτε
παρατίθεται σῶμα σώματι, τότε ἤτοι τὰ πέρατα
τῶν περάτων ἅπτεται, ἢ τὰ πεπερατωμένα τῶν
πεπερατωμένων, ἢ καὶ τὰ πεπερατωμένα τῶν
πεπερατωμένων καὶ τὰ πέρατα τῶν περάτων, οἷον
(ἔσται γὰρ σαφὲς τὸ λεγόμενον ἐπὶ ὑποδείγματος)
εἰ νοήσαιμεν πέρας μὲν τὸ ἔξωθεν τοῦ ἀμφορέως
ὄστρακον, πεπερατωμένον δὲ τὸν ἐν τῷ ἀμφορεῖ
οἶνον, δυοῖν ἀμφορέων παρατιθεμένων ἀλλήλοις
ἤτοι τὸ ὄστρακον τοῦ ὀστράκου ἅψεται ἢ ὁ οἶνος
τοῦ οἴνου ἢ καὶ τὸ ὄστρακον τοῦ ὀστράκου καὶ ὁ
432 οἶνος τοῦ οἴνου. καὶ εἰ μὲν τὰ πέρατα τῶν περάτων
ἅπτεται, τὰ πεπερατωμένα οὐχ ἅψεται ἀλλήλων,

face along a straight line and when rolling forward,
by the placing of straight lines in turn, one after
another, it measures out the surface. If, then, the
cylinder touches the surface along a straight line and
when rolling measures out the surface by placing its
straight lines in turn, one after another, the surface
certainly consists of straight lines, and the superficies
of the cylinder likewise is made of straight lines.
Since, then, the surface possesses breadth and the
superficies of the cylinder also possesses it, and what
fills up breadth is not without breadth, the lines as
they fill up breadth will not be without breadth.

Moreover, even if we grant that the line is length 430
without breadth, none the less the Geometers will
find that their account of body is hopeless. For just
as the sign when it has flowed makes the line, so also
the line by flowing makes the surface, which is " a
limit of body possessing two dimensions, length and
breadth." Since, then, the surface is a limit of body, 431
body is certainly limited. And if so, when body is
set beside body, then either the limits touch the
limits, or the things limited the things limited, or the
things limited touch the things limited and the limits
also touch the limits. Thus (for our meaning will be
made clear by an example) if we were to conceive the
external earthenware of the jar as the limit and the
wine within the jar as the thing limited, then when
two jars are set side by side either the ware will touch
the ware, or the wine the wine, or both the ware the
ware and the wine the wine. And if the limits touch 432
the limits, the things limited (that is, the bodies) will

τουτέστι τὰ σώματα· ὅπερ ἦν ἄτοπον. εἰ δὲ τὰ
πεπερατωμένα τῶν πεπερατωμένων ἅπτεται, τουτέστι σώματα σωμάτων, δεήσει ταῦτα τῶν οἰκείων
433 περάτων ἐκτὸς γίνεσθαι· ὃ πάλιν ἄτοπον. εἰ δὲ καὶ
τὰ πέρατα τῶν περάτων ἅπτεται καὶ τὰ πεπερατωμένα τῶν πεπερατωμένων, συνδραμοῦνται αἱ ἀπο-
ρίαι· ᾗ μὲν γὰρ τὰ πέρατα ἀλλήλων ἅπτεται, τὰ
πεπερατωμένα ἀλλήλων οὐχ ἅψεται, ᾗ δὲ ταῦτα
ἀλλήλων θιγγάνει, ἐκτὸς ἔσται τῶν οἰκείων πε-
434 ράτων.   καὶ μὴν εἴπερ πέρας ἐστὶν ἡ ἐπιφάνεια,
πεπερατωμένον δὲ τὸ σῶμα, ἤτοι σῶμά ἐστιν ἡ
ἐπιφάνεια ἢ ἀσώματον. καὶ εἰ μὲν σῶμά ἐστι,
ψεῦδος τὸ ἀβαθῆ εἶναι τὴν ἐπιφάνειαν· πᾶν γὰρ
σῶμα βάθους μετεῖχεν. εἶτα οὐδὲ ἅψεταί τινος τὸ
πέρας, ἀλλὰ πᾶν σῶμα γενήσεται ἀπειρομέγεθες·
435 εἰ γὰρ σῶμά ἐστιν ἡ ἐπιφάνεια, ἐπεὶ πᾶν σῶμα
πέρας ἔχει, κἀκεῖνο τὸ πέρας πάλιν σῶμα ὂν ἕξει
πέρας, κἀκεῖνο τρίτον, καὶ τὸ τρίτον τέταρτον, καὶ
οὕτως εἰς ἄπειρον. εἰ δὲ ἀσώματός ἐστιν ἡ ἐπιφάνεια, ἐπεὶ τὸ ἀσώματον οὐδενὸς δύναται θιγεῖν
οὐδὲ ὑπό τινος θιχθῆναι, τὰ πέρατα οὐχ ἅψεται
ἀλλήλων, τούτων δὲ μὴ ἁπτομένων οὐδὲ τὰ πεπε-
436 ρατωμένα ἅψεται. ὥστε κἂν τῆς γραμμῆς ἀπο-
στῶμεν, ὅ γε περὶ τῆς ἐπιφανείας λόγος ἄπορος ὢν
εἰς ἐποχὴν ἡμᾶς καθίστησιν.

Νῦν μὲν οὖν πεποιήμεθα τὰς ζητήσεις ἐχόμενοι
τῶν ἐννοιῶν τῶν τοῦ σώματος καὶ τῶν περάτων, ἔτι
437 δὲ καὶ τῶν γεωμετρικῶν θεωρημάτων· ἔνεστι δὲ
κἀκεῖνον τὸν λόγον ἀναλαμβάνειν,[1] σθεναρῶς συν-
άγοντα τὸ προκείμενον. εἰ γὰρ ἔστι τι σῶμα, ἤτοι

[1] ἀναλαμβάνειν] παραλαμβάνειν NLE: λαμβάνειν cet., Bekk.

not touch each other ; which is absurd. And if the things limited touch the things limited—that is, bodies touch bodies,—they will have to be outside their own limits ; which again is absurd. And if the 433 limits touch the limits and the things limited also the things limited, the difficulties will be combined ; for in so far as the limits touch one another the things limited will not touch one another ; and in so far as the latter are in contact with one another they will be outside their own limits.—Furthermore, if the 434 surface is a limit and the body a thing limited, the surface is either a body or incorporeal.[a] And if it is a body, it is false that the surface is without depth ; for every body partakes of depth. Moreover, the limit will not touch anything, but every body will be of unlimited size ; for if the surface is body, since 435 every body has a limit, that limit again, being a body, will have a limit, and this again a third, and the third a fourth, and so on *ad infinitum*. And if the surface is incorporeal, since the incorporeal cannot touch anything or be touched by anything, the limits will not be in contact with one another, and if these are not in contact neither will the things limited be in contact. So that even if we disregard the line, the hope- 436 lessness of the account given of surface reduces us to a state of suspension.

So, then, we have now carried out our investigations, while confining ourselves to the notions of body and limits, and also to the Geometers' theorems. But it is possible, also, to repeat our former argu- 437 ment which deduces our thesis in a convincing way [b] : If a body exists, it is either sensible or

[a] With § 434 *cf. P.H.* iii. 41-44.
[b] With §§ 437-439 *cf. P.H.* iii. 47-48.

SEXTUS EMPIRICUS

αἰσθητόν ἐστιν ἢ νοητόν. καὶ αἰσθητὸν μὲν οὐκ
ἔστιν. ἀθρόα γὰρ ἦν ποιότης κατ᾽ ἐπισύνθεσιν
σχήματος καὶ μεγέθους καὶ ἀντιτυπίας λαμβανο-
μένη· ποιότης δὲ κατ᾽ ἐπισύνθεσιν τινῶν λαμβανο-
μένη οὐκ ἔστιν αἰσθητή· καὶ τὸ σῶμα ἄρα, ὡς
438 σῶμα νοούμενον, οὐκ ἔστιν αἰσθητόν. καὶ μὴν
οὐδὲ νοητόν. ἵνα γὰρ γένηται νόησις σώματος,
ὀφείλει ἐν τῇ φύσει τῶν πραγμάτων ὑποκεῖσθαί τι
αἰσθητόν, ἀφ᾽ οὗ γενήσεται ἡ τοῦ σώματος νόησις.
οὐδὲν δὲ ἔστιν ἐν τῇ φύσει τῶν πραγμάτων παρὰ
τὸ σῶμα καὶ ἀσώματον, ὧν τὸ μὲν ἀσώματον
αὐτόθεν ἐστὶ νοητὸν τὸ δὲ σῶμα οὐκ αἰσθητόν, ὡς
439 δέδεικται ἡμῖν. μὴ ὄντος οὖν ἐν τῇ φύσει τῶν
πραγμάτων αἰσθητοῦ τινὸς ἀφ᾽ οὗ νόησις ἔσται τοῦ
σώματος, οὐδὲ νοητὸν ἔσται τὸ σῶμα. εἰ δὲ μήτε
αἰσθητόν ἐστι μήτε νοητόν, παρὰ δὲ ταῦτα οὐδὲν
ἔστι, ῥητέον μηδὲν εἶναι τὸ σῶμα.

440 Ἀλλ᾽ ἐπεὶ ἐν τούτοις ὁ περὶ τῶν σωμάτων λόγος
πέφηνεν ἄπορος, ἀπ᾽ ἄλλης ἀρχῆς πειρασόμεθα
διδάσκειν ὅτι καὶ ὁ περὶ τῶν λειπομένων ἀσωμάτων
ὅμοιός ἐστι τούτῳ.

intelligible. And it is not sensible; for it is " a complex quality perceived through the combination of form, size, and solidity " [a]; and a quality perceived through a combination of things is not sensible; therefore the body also, conceived as body, is not sensible. Nor yet is it intelligible. For in order that 438 there may be a conception of body, there must already exist in the nature of things some sensible object from which the conception of body may be formed. But nothing exists in the nature of things besides body and the incorporeal, and of these the incorporeal is of itself intelligible, and body, as we have proved, is not sensible. Since, then, there does not 439 exist in the nature of things any sensible object from which the notion of body may be formed, body will not be intelligible either. But if it is neither sensible nor intelligible, and besides these there is no other alternative, one must declare that body is nothing.

But now that the account given of bodies has been 440 shown by these arguments to be hopeless, we shall start afresh [b] and try to demonstrate that the account given of the other things, the incorporeals, is equally so.

[a] This is an Epicurean definition.
[b] Cf. Adv. Log. i. 446.

B

1 Τοῖς περὶ τοῦ σώματος καὶ τῶν περάτων προ-
ηπορημένοις ἡμῖ νπρός τε τοὺς φυσικοὺς καὶ τοὺς
γεωμέτρας ἀκόλουθος εἶναι δοκεῖ καὶ ἡ περὶ τοῦ
τόπου ζήτησις· ἅπασι γὰρ συμφώνως ἀξιοῦται τὸ
σῶμα ἤτοι ἐν τόπῳ περιέχεσθαι ἢ κατὰ τόπου
2 φέρεσθαι. διὸ προληπτέον ὅτι κατὰ τὸν Ἐπίκουρον τῆς ἀναφοῦς καλουμένης φύσεως τὸ μέν
τι ὀνομάζεται κενὸν τὸ δὲ τόπος τὸ δὲ χώρα,
μεταλαμβανομένων κατὰ διαφόρους ἐπιβολὰς τῶν
ὀνομάτων, ἐπείπερ ἡ αὐτὴ φύσις ἔρημος μὲν καθεστηκυῖα παντὸς σώματος κενὸν προσαγορεύεται,
καταλαμβανομένη δὲ ὑπὸ σώματος τόπος καλεῖται,
χωρούντων δὲ δι᾽ αὐτῆς σωμάτων χώρα γίνεται.
κοινῶς μέντοι φύσις ἀναφὴς εἴρηται παρὰ τῷ
Ἐπικούρῳ διὰ τὸ ἐστερῆσθαι τῆς κατὰ ἀντίβασιν
3 ἀφῆς. καὶ οἱ στωικοὶ δὲ κενὸν μὲν εἶναί φασι τὸ
οἷόν τε ὑπὸ ὄντος κατέχεσθαι, μὴ κατεχόμενον δέ,
ἢ διάστημα ἔρημον σώματος, ἢ διάστημα ἀκαθεκτούμενον ὑπὸ σώματος, τόπον δὲ τὸν ὑπὸ ὄντος
κατεχόμενον καὶ ἐξισαζόμενον τῷ κατέχοντι αὐτόν,
νῦν ὂν καλοῦντες τὸ σῶμα, καθὼς καὶ ἐκ τῆς
μεταλήψεως τῶν ὀνομάτων ἐστὶ συμφανές· χώραν
δέ φασιν εἶναι διάστημα κατὰ μέν τι κατεχόμενον
4 ὑπὸ σώματος κατὰ δέ τι ἀκαθεκτούμενον. ἔνιοι δὲ

210

BOOK II

AFTER the foregoing discussion of body and limits, 1
criticizing both the Physicists and the Geometers, the
investigation of " Place " seems to follow next ; for
it is maintained by them all with one accord that
body either is contained in place or moves in place.
Hence we must notice first that, according to Epi- 2
curus, " of the intangible nature one part is named
' void,' another ' place,' another ' room,' " the names
being varied according to the different applications,
since the same nature is termed " void " when desti-
tute of any body, and is called " place " when occupied
by a body, and becomes " room " when bodies pass
through it. But the general designation " intangible
nature " is given to it by Epicurus owing to its lack
of resistant touch. And the Stoics assert [a] that 3
" void is that which is capable of being occupied by
an existent but is not so occupied, or an interval
empty of body, or an interval unoccupied by body ;
and place is that which is occupied by an existent and
made equal to that which occupies it " (calling body
now " an existent," as is plain from the interchange
of the names) ; and " room," they say, is " an interval
partly occupied by body and partly unoccupied."

---

* With §§ 3-4 cf. P.H. iii. 124.

SEXTUS EMPIRICUS

χώραν ἔλεξαν ὑπάρχειν τὸν τοῦ μείζονος σώματος
τόπον, ὡς ταύτῃ διαφέρειν τοῦ τόπου τὴν χώραν,
τῷ ἐκεῖνον μὲν μὴ ἐμφαίνειν μέγεθος τοῦ ἐμπεριεχομένου σώματος (κἂν γὰρ ἐλάχιστον περιέχῃ
σῶμα, οὐδὲν ἧττον τόπος προσαγορεύεται), τὴν δ᾽
ἀξιόλογον ἐμφαίνειν μέγεθος τοῦ ἐν αὐτῇ σώματος.
5 περὶ μὲν οὖν κενοῦ ποικίλως ἐν τοῖς περὶ στοιχείων
ἐζητήσαμεν, καὶ οὐκ ἀναγκαῖον τὰ νῦν τὸν αὐτὸν
λόγον παλινῳδεῖν· περὶ δὲ τοῦ τόπου καὶ τῆς
συζυγούσης τούτῳ χώρας, ἥτις καὶ αὐτὴ κατὰ τὸ
γένος ἐστὶ τόπος, ἐπὶ τοῦ παρόντος σκεψόμεθα.
προδηλοτέροις γὰρ οὖσι τούτοις καὶ παρὰ πᾶσι
σχεδὸν ὁμολογουμένοις συναπορηθήσεται καὶ ἡ
περὶ τοῦ κενοῦ σκέψις, ὅσῳ καὶ περὶ ἀδηλοτέρου
πράγματος προκόπτει.

A.—ΕΙ ΕΣΤΙ ΤΟΠΟΣ

6 Τῆς τοῦ τόπου νοήσεως δεδηλωμένης καὶ τῶν
συζυγούντων αὐτῷ πραγμάτων ὑποδεδειγμένων
ἀπολείπεται, ὡς ἔστιν ἔθος τοῖς ἀπὸ τῆς σκέψεως,
τοὺς εἰς ἑκάτερον κινῆσαι λόγους καὶ τὴν ἐπ᾽ αὐτοῖς
7 συναγομένην ἐποχὴν κρατύνεσθαι. εἴπερ οὖν ἔστιν
ἄνω καὶ κάτω καὶ εἰς τὰ δεξιὰ καὶ τὰ ἀριστερὰ καὶ
πρόσω καὶ ὀπίσω, ἔστι τις τόπος· μέρη γάρ εἰσιν
αἱ ἐξ αὐταὶ παρατάσεις τοῦ τόπου, καὶ ἀδύνατόν
ἐστί τινος τῶν μερῶν ὑπαρχόντων μὴ οὐχὶ κἀκεῖνο
ὑπάρχειν οὗ ἐστι τὰ μέρη. ἔστι δέ γε ἐν τῇ φύσει
τῶν πραγμάτων ἄνω καὶ κάτω καὶ εἰς δεξιὰ καὶ
ἀριστερὰ καὶ πρόσω καὶ ὀπίσω· ἔστιν ἄρα τόπος.

* Cf. *Adv. Phys.* i. 333 ff.
ᵇ Thus the arguments *for* the existence of " place " (or

212

But some have said that room is " the place of the 4
larger body," so that room differs from place in the
fact that the latter does not imply magnitude of the
contained body (for even if it contains a minimal body
it is none the less termed " place "), whereas the
former implies considerable magnitude in the body it
contains. Now " void " we have already discussed 5
in various ways in our sections " Concerning Elements," [a] and there is no need now to repeat the same
account ; on the present occasion we shall examine
" place " and the allied subject of " room," which
itself also comes under the head of place. For along
with these, which are more evident and subjects of
almost universal agreement, the inquiry about void
also will be shown to involve doubt, in so far as it
deals with a less evident matter.

CHAPTER I.—DOES PLACE EXIST ?

Now that the conception of place has been ex- 6
plained and the things allied therewith indicated, it
remains for us—in accordance with the Sceptics'
custom—to expound the arguments on both sides [b]
and to justify the suspension of judgement deduced
therefrom. If, then, there exist upwards and down- 7
wards, and rightwards and leftwards, and forwards
and backwards, some place exists ; for these six
directions are parts of place, and it is impossible that,
if the parts of a thing exist, the thing of which they
are parts should not exist. But upwards and downwards, and rightwards and leftwards, and forwards
and backwards, do exist in the nature of things ;

" space ") are given in §§ 7-12 (cf. P.H. iii. 120-121)—those
against in §§ 13-19 (cf. P.H. iii. 122-123) ; and further arguments in criticism of "place" are added in §§ 20-36.

SEXTUS EMPIRICUS

8   οὐ μὴν ἀλλ' εἰ ὅπου ἦν Σωκράτης, νῦν ἔστιν ἄλλος, οἷον Πλάτων ἀποθανόντος Σωκράτους, ἔστιν ἄρα τόπος. ὡς γὰρ τοῦ ἐν τῷ ἀμφορεῖ ὑγροῦ ἐκκενωθέντος καὶ ἄλλου ἐπεγχυθέντος λέγομεν ὑπάρχειν τὸν ἀμφορέα τόπον ὄντα καὶ τοῦ προτέρου καὶ τοῦ ὕστερον ἐπεμβληθέντος ὑγροῦ, οὕτως εἰ ὃν τόπον κατεῖχε Σωκράτης ὅτ' ἔζη, τοῦτον ἕτερος νῦν 9 κατέχει, ἔστι τις τόπος.   καὶ ἄλλως, εἰ ἔστι τι σῶμα, καὶ τόπος ἔστιν· ἀλλὰ μὴν τὸ πρῶτον· τὸ ἄρα δεύτερον.   πρὸς τούτοις εἰ ὅπου τὸ κοῦφον φύσει φέρεται, ἐκεῖ τὸ βαρὺ φύσει οὐ φέρεται, ἔστιν ἴδιος τοῦ κούφου καὶ τοῦ βαρέος τόπος· ἀλλὰ μὴν τὸ πρῶτον· τὸ ἄρα δεύτερον. τό γέ τοι πῦρ φύσει κοῦφον καθεστὼς ἀνώφορόν ἐστι, καὶ τὸ ὕδωρ φύσει βαρὺ τυγχάνον κάτω βρίθει, καὶ οὔτε τὸ πῦρ κάτω φέρεται οὔτε τὸ ὕδωρ ἄνω ἄττει. ἔστιν ἄρα ἴδιος καὶ τοῦ φύσει κούφου καὶ τοῦ φύσει 10 βαρέος τόπος.   ὥσπερ τε εἰ τὸ ἐξ οὗ τι γίγνεται ἔστι, καὶ τὸ ὑφ' οὗ τι γίγνεται καὶ τὸ δι' ὅ, οὕτως ὑπάρχοι ἂν καὶ τὸ ἐν ᾧ τι γίγνεται. ἔστι δὲ τὸ ἐξ οὗ τι γίνεται, οἷον ὕλη, καὶ τὸ ὑφ' οὗ, οἷον τὸ αἴτιον, καὶ τὸ δι' ὅ, καθάπερ τὸ τέλος· ἔστιν ἄρα καὶ τὸ ἐν ᾧ τι γίγνεται, τουτέστιν ὁ 11 τόπος.   οἵ τε παλαιοὶ καὶ τὰ ὅλα διακοσμήσαντες ἀρχὴν τῶν πάντων ὑπέθεντο τόπον, κἀντεῦθεν ὁρμηθεὶς ὁ Ἡσίοδος ἀνεφώνησεν

> ἤτοι μὲν πρώτιστα χάος γένετ', αὐτὰρ ἔπειτα
> γαῖ' εὐρύστερνος, πάντων ἕδος ἀσφαλὲς αἰεί,

---

    [a] *Cf.* Aristot. *De caelo* iv. 3.
    [b] Hesiod, *Theog.* 116 f. (*cf. Adv. Phys.* i. 8).

214

therefore place exists.—Moreover, if where Socrates **8** was another man (such as Plato) now is, Socrates being dead, then place exists. For just as, when the liquid in the pitcher has been emptied out and other liquid poured in, we declare that the pitcher, which is the place both of the former liquid and of that poured in later, exists, so likewise, if another man now occupies the place which Socrates occupied when he was alive, some place exists.—Again, if a body **9** exists, place also exists ; but in fact the first ⟨is true⟩ ; therefore the second ⟨is true⟩.—Further, if where what is light naturally moves there what is heavy naturally does not move, there exists a separate place for the light and for the heavy *a* ; but in fact the first ⟨is true⟩ ; therefore the second ⟨is true⟩. For certainly fire, which is naturally light, tends to ascend, and water, which is naturally heavy, presses downwards, and neither does fire move downwards nor water shoot upwards. There exists, therefore, a separate place both for the naturally light and for the naturally heavy.—Also, just as if there exists **10** that from which a thing becomes, and that by which a thing becomes, and that on account of which a thing becomes, so too there will exist that in which a thing becomes. But that from which a thing becomes (namely, its matter) exists, and that by which (namely, its cause), and that on account of which (that is, its end) ; therefore, that in which a thing becomes (that is, its place) exists also.—The **11** ancients also in planning the order of the Universe laid down place as the first principle of all things, and starting out from it Hesiod proclaimed *b* how—

Verily first created of all was Chaos ; thereafter
Earth broad-bosom'd, unshakable seat of all things for ever—

215

χάος λέγων τὸν χωρητικὸν τῶν ὅλων τόπον· μὴ
ὑποκειμένου γὰρ τούτου οὔτε γῆ οὔτε ὕδωρ οὔτε
τὰ λοιπὰ τῶν στοιχείων, οὐχ ὁ σύμπας κόσμος
12 ἐδύνατο συστῆναι. κἂν κατ᾽ ἐπίνοιαν δὲ ἅπαντα
ἀνέλωμεν, ὁ τόπος οὐκ ἀναιρεθήσεται ἐν ᾧ ἦν τὰ
πάντα, ἀλλ᾽ ὑπομένει, τὰς τρεῖς ἔχων διαστάσεις,
μῆκος βάθος πλάτος, χωρὶς ἀντιτυπίας· τοῦτο γὰρ
ἴδιον ἦν σώματος.

Καὶ ἄλλα δὲ εἰώθασι τοιαῦτα οἱ δογματικοὶ τῶν
φιλοσόφων διεξέρχεσθαι πρὸς τὸ καταστῆσαι τὴν
13 ὕπαρξιν τοῦ τόπου. πάντα δὲ μᾶλλον ἢ τοῦτο
δύνανται ποιεῖν. τό τε γὰρ ἀπὸ τῶν μερῶν τοῦ
τόπου θέλειν ἐπιλογίζεσθαι τὸ καὶ τὸν τόπον
ὑπάρχειν τελέως ἐστὶ μειρακιῶδες· ὁ γὰρ μὴ
διδοὺς αὐτοῖς εἶναι τὸ ὅλον, οὗτος οὐδὲ τὰ μέρη συγχωρήσει τοῦ ὅλου. καὶ ἄλλως, ἐπεὶ τὰ τινὸς μέρη
αὐτὸ ἐκεῖνό ἐστιν οὗ τὰ μέρη καθέστηκεν, δυνάμει
ὁ λέγων " εἰ ἔστι τὰ μέρη τοῦ τόπου, ἔστιν ὁ
τόπος " τοῦτό φησιν " εἰ ἔστιν ὁ τόπος, ἔστιν ὁ
τόπος." ὅπερ ἦν ἄτοπον· αὐτὸ γὰρ τὸ ζητούμενον
14 εἰς τὴν αὐτοῦ πίστιν ὡς ἀζήτητον παρείληπται.
τὸ δ᾽ αὐτὸ ῥητέον καὶ ὅταν ἐκ τοῦ ἐν ᾧ ἦν Σωκράτης νῦν εἶναι Πλάτωνα συνάγωσι τὴν ὕπαρξιν
τοῦ τόπου. ἡμῶν γὰρ ζητούντων εἰ ἔστι τι ὁ
τόπος ἐν ᾧ ἔστι τὸ σῶμα, διαφέρων αὐτοῦ τοῦ ἐν
αὐτῷ λεγομένου περιέχεσθαι σώματος, ἐκεῖνοι ὡς
ὁμόλογον ἡμῖν ἀντιφωνοῦσι τὸ ἐν τόπῳ γεγονέναι
Σωκράτην καὶ τὸ ἐν τούτῳ νῦν περιέχεσθαι
15 Πλάτωνα. ὅτι μὲν γὰρ λέγομεν ἀφελῶς ἐν Ἀλεξ-
ανδρείᾳ εἶναί τινα καὶ ἐν γυμνασίῳ καὶ ἐν τῇ

---

^a Cf. P.H. iii. 39.

meaning by "Chaos" the place which serves to contain all things ; for if this had not subsisted neither earth nor water nor the rest of the elements, nor the Universe as a whole, could have been constructed. And even if, in imagination, we abolish all things, 12 the place wherein all things were will not be abolished, but remains possessing its three dimensions—length, depth, breadth,—but without solidity ; for this is an attribute peculiar to body.[a]

There are also other reasons of this kind which the Dogmatic philosophers are wont to enumerate for the purpose of establishing the real existence of place. But they are able to effect anything rather than this. 13 For to try to argue from the parts of place that place itself also exists is perfectly childish ; for he who does not grant them that the whole exists will not concede that the parts of the whole exist. And besides, since the parts of a thing are that very thing whereof they are the parts, he who argues—" If the parts of place exist, place exists "—is virtually saying " If place exists, place exists." But this is absurd ; for the thing in question is brought in for the purpose of confirming itself as though it were not in question. And 14 the same may be said when they deduce the existence of place from the fact that Plato now exists in the place where Socrates existed. For while we are inquiring whether the place in which the body exists, as distinct from the body itself which is said to be contained therein, is an existent thing they reply to us—as though it were agreed—that Socrates was in a place and that Plato is now contained in that place. Now it is agreed that, speaking loosely, we say that a 15 man is in Alexandria [b] or in the gymnasium or in the

[b] Cf. § 95, *P.H.* iii. 221.

σχολῇ, ὁμόλογον· ἀλλ' ἔστιν ἡμῖν ἡ σκέψις οὐ περὶ
τοῦ κατὰ πλάτος ἀλλὰ περὶ τοῦ κατὰ περιγραφὴν
τόπου, πότερον ἔστιν ἢ ἐπινοεῖται μόνον, καὶ εἰ
ἔστι, ποταπὸν τὴν φύσιν, ἆρά γε σωματικὸν ἢ
ἀσώματον καὶ ἐν τόπῳ περιεχόμενον ἢ οὐδαμῶς.
ὧν οὐδὲν ἴσχυσαν παραστῆσαι οἱ ταῖς προειρη-
16 μέναις ὑπομνήσεσι χρώμενοι.   κοῦφόν τε φύσει
οὐ δίδοται εἶναι τὸ σῶμα, ἵνα καὶ εἰς ἴδιον φέρηται
τόπον, ἀλλὰ καὶ τὸ δοκοῦν εἶναι τοιοῦτον ὑπ' ἄλλης
τινὸς αἰτίας καὶ κατηναγκασμένως[1] εἴς τινας
ἀνωθεῖται τόπους. εἶτα κἂν δοθῇ φύσει τυγχάνειν
κοῦφον καὶ φύσει βαρύ, πάλιν οὐδὲν ἧττον ἀπο-
ρήσεται τὸ εἰς τί φέρεται, ἆρα εἴς γε σῶμά τι ἢ
κενὸν ἢ πέρας ἢ ἄλλο τι διαφερούσης μετεσχηκὸς
17 φύσεως. ναί, ἀλλ' εἰ ἔστι τὸ ἐξ οὗ καὶ τὸ ὑφ' οὗ
καὶ τὸ δι' ὅ, εἴη ἂν καὶ τὸ ἐν ᾧ. οὐ πάντως
φήσομεν. εἰ γὰρ ἀπορεῖται τὸ ἐξ οὗ τι γίνεται,
τουτέστι τὸ πάσχον, καὶ τὸ ὑφ' οὗ, καθάπερ τὸ
αἴτιον, καὶ καθόλου τὸ γίνεσθαι καὶ τὸ φθείρεσθαι
ἢ κοινότερον κινεῖσθαι, ἀνάγκη συνηπορῆσθαι καὶ τὸ
ἐν ᾧ. τὸ δ' ὅτι ταῦτ' ἠπόρηται, καὶ πρότερον
ἐδείξαμεν περὶ τοῦ ποιοῦντος καὶ πάσχοντος δι-
εξελθόντες, καὶ ὕστερον διδάξομεν περὶ γενέσεως
καὶ φθορᾶς καὶ πρὸ τούτων ἔτι περὶ κινήσεως
18 σκεπτόμενοι. ὁ μὲν γὰρ εἰπὼν

ἤτοι μὲν πρώτιστα χάος γένετ', αὐτὰρ ἔπειτα
γαῖ' εὐρύστερνος, πάντων ἕδος,

---

[1] κατηναγκασμένως Heintz : κατηναγκασμένης mss., Bekk.

---

[a] For this distinction see § 95 *infra*, and *P.H.* iii. 75.
[b] *Cf. Adv. Phys.* i. 195 ff., 207 ff., 267 ff.
[c] *Cf.* §§ 310 ff. *infra*.

school ; but our investigation is not concerned with place in the broad sense but with that in the circumscribed sense,[a] as to whether this exists or is merely imagined ; and if it exists, of what sort it is in its nature, whether corporeal or incorporeal, and whether contained in place or not. And none of these points have those who employ the foregoing arguments been able to establish.—Nor is it granted that there is any 16 body which is naturally light, so that it moves into a separate place of its own, but even that which seems to be such is driven up into certain places by some cause and through compulsion. And further, even if it be granted that a naturally light and a naturally heavy exist, none the less it will again be a matter of doubt into what it moves, whether into some body or into a void or a limit or something else possessed of a distinct nature. " Yes," (they reply,) " but if the 17 'from which' and the 'by which' and the 'on account of which' exist, the 'in which' will also exist." Not necessarily, we shall say. For if there is doubt about that " from which " a thing becomes (that is, the passive element), and about the " by which "(namely, the cause), and in general about becoming and perishing, or motion generally, then the " in which " also will necessarily be involved in the same doubt. And that these things are matters of doubt we have shown before in our discussion of agent and patient,[b] and we shall point it out again when considering becoming and perishing,[c] and also, at an earlier stage, motion.[d] For he who said [e]—   18

> Verily first created of all was Chaos ; thereafter
> Earth broad-bosom'd, of all things the seat—

---

[d] Cf. §§ 37 ff. infra.   [e] Cf. § 11 supra.

SEXTUS EMPIRICUS

ἐξ αὐτοῦ περιτρέπεται· ἐρομένου γάρ τινος αὐτὸν
ἐκ τίνος γέγονε τὸ χάος, οὐχ ἕξει λέγειν. καὶ
τοῦτό φασιν ἔνιοι αἴτιον γεγονέναι Ἐπικούρῳ τῆς
19 ἐπὶ τὸ φιλοσοφεῖν ὁρμῆς. κομιδῇ γὰρ μειράκισκος
ὢν ἤρετο τὸν ἐπαναγινώσκοντα αὐτῷ γραμματιστὴν
" ἤτοι μὲν πρώτιστα χάος γένετ'," ἐκ τίνος τὸ χάος
ἐγένετο, εἴπερ πρῶτον ἐγένετο. τούτου δὲ εἰπόντος
μὴ αὐτοῦ ἔργον εἶναι τὰ τοιαῦτα διδάσκειν ἀλλὰ
τῶν καλουμένων φιλοσόφων, τοίνυν, ἔφησεν ὁ Ἐπίκουρος, ἐπ' ἐκείνους μοι βαδιστέον ἐστίν, εἴπερ
αὐτοὶ τὴν τῶν ὄντων ἀλήθειαν ἴσασιν.

Ἀλλ' ὅτι μὲν οὐδὲν ἱκνούμενον λέγεται εἰς τὸ
ὑπάρχειν τι τὸν τόπον, ἐκ τούτων ἤδη γνώριμον·
20 ἐπισυναπτέον δὲ αὐτοῖς καὶ τὰ ἀπὸ τῆς σκέψεως.
εἰ γὰρ ἔστι τις ὑποδεκτικὸς τοῦ σώματος τόπος,
ἤτοι σῶμά ἐστιν οὗτος ἢ κενόν. καὶ σῶμα μὲν οὐκ
ἔστιν ὁ ὑποδεκτικὸς τοῦ σώματος τόπος· εἰ γὰρ πᾶν
σῶμα ὀφείλει ἐν τόπῳ εἶναι, ὁ δὲ τόπος ἐστὶ σῶμα,
ἔσται ὁ τόπος ἐν τόπῳ, κἀκεῖνος πάλιν ἐν τρίτῳ,
καὶ ὁ τρίτος ἐν τῷ τετάρτῳ, καὶ οὕτως εἰς ἄπειρον.
21 οὐ τοίνυν σῶμά ἐστιν ὁ ὑποδεκτικὸς τοῦ σώματος
τόπος. εἰ δὲ κενόν ἐστιν ὁ ὑποδεκτικὸς τοῦ σώματος τόπος, ἤτοι μένει τοῦτο τὸ κενὸν ἐπιόντος
αὐτῷ τοῦ σώματος ἢ μεθίσταται ἢ φθείρεται. καὶ
εἰ μὲν μένει ἐπιόντος αὐτῷ τοῦ σώματος, ἔσται
κενὸν ἅμα καὶ πλῆρες, ᾗ μὲν μένει, κενόν, ᾗ δὲ
ἐπιδέχεται τὸ σῶμα, πλῆρες. ἀδιανόητον δέ γε τὸ
αὐτὸ κενόν τε καὶ πλῆρες λέγειν· τοίνυν οὐ μένει τὸ
22 κενὸν ἐπιόντος αὐτῷ τοῦ σώματος. εἰ δὲ μεθίσταται τὸ κενόν, ἔσται σῶμα τὸ κενόν· τὸ γὰρ
μεθιστάμενον τόπον ἐκ τόπου σῶμά ἐστιν. οὐχὶ

is refuted by himself; for if someone asks him " from what did Chaos come into being ?," he will have no answer. And this, as some say, was the reason why Epicurus took to philosophizing. For when still quite 19 a youth [a] he asked his schoolmaster, who was reading out the line " Verily first created of all was Chaos," what Chaos was created from, if it was created first. And when he replied that it was not his business, but that of the men called philosophers, to teach things of that sort, " Well then," said Epicurus, " I must go off to them, if it is they who know the truth of things."

So from this it is already evident that nothing pertinent is said to show that place is a real thing; and to this we must further add the Sceptics' argu- 20 ments :—If there exists any place receptive of body, it is either body or void. But the place receptive of body is not body; for if every body must be in a place, and place is a body, place will be in a place, and this again in a third, and the third in a fourth, and so on *ad infinitum*. So then the place receptive of 21 body is not a body. And if the place receptive of body is a void, this void either remains when the body comes upon it, or moves away, or perishes.[b] And if it remains when the body comes upon it, it will be at once both void and full,—void in so far as it remains, but full in so far as it admits the body. But it is irrational to say that the same thing is both void and full; the void, then, does not remain when the body comes upon it. And if the void moves away, 22 the void will be body, for that which moves away from place to place is a body. But the void is not a

---

[a] At the age of 14, according to Diog. Laert. x. 2.
[b] With §§ 21-23 *cf. P.H.* iii. 129.

δέ γε σῶμά ἐστι τὸ κενόν, ὥστε οὐδὲ μεθίσταται
ἐπιόντος αὐτῷ τοῦ σώματος. καὶ ἄλλως, εἰ μεθίσταται τοῦ σώματος ἐπιόντος, οὐκέτι δέξεται τὸ
23 σῶμα· ὃ καὶ αὐτὸ τῶν ἀτόπων. λείπεται ἄρα
λέγειν φθείρεσθαι τὸ κενόν· ὃ πάλιν ἀδύνατον. εἰ
γὰρ φθείρεται, ἐν μεταβολῇ καὶ κινήσει γίνεται [καὶ
εἰ φθείρεται, γενητόν ἐστι]· τὸ δ' ἐν μεταβολῇ καὶ
κινήσει γινόμενον [γενητόν τε καὶ φθαρτὸν]¹ σῶμα
καθέστηκεν· ὥστε οὐδὲ φθείρεται τὸ κενόν. καὶ
οὕτως, εἰ μήτε σῶμά ἐστιν ὁ τόπος, ὡς παρεστήσαμεν, μήτε κενόν, ὡς ὑπεμνήσαμεν, οὐκ ἂν εἴη τις
τόπος.

24 Πρὸς τούτοις ἔτι, εἰ ὁ τόπος περιεκτικὸς νοεῖται
τοῦ σώματος, τὸ δὲ περιέχον ἐκτός ἐστι τοῦ περιεχομένου, κατ' ἀνάγκην, εἰ ἔστιν ὁ τόπος, ὀφείλει
τι τούτων τυγχάνειν ὧν τὸ μέν ἐστιν ὕλη, τὸ δὲ
εἶδος, τὸ δὲ μεταξὺ διάστημα τῶν ἐσχάτων τοῦ
25 σώματος περάτων, τὸ δὲ πέρατα ἔσχατα. ὕλη μὲν
οὖν οὐκ ἂν εἴη ὁ τόπος κατὰ πολλοὺς τρόπους, οἷον
ἐπεὶ αὕτη μὲν σεσωμάτωται, ὁ δὲ τόπος οὐ σεσωμάτωται, καὶ ἡ μὲν ὕλη μέτεισιν ἀπὸ τόπου εἰς
τόπον, ὁ δὲ τόπος οὐ μετέρχεται ἀπὸ τόπου εἰς
τόπον. καὶ ἐπὶ μὲν τῆς ὕλης λέγομεν ὅτι πρότερον
μὲν ἦν ἀήρ, νῦν δὲ πυκνωθεῖσα γέγονεν ὕδωρ, ἢ
ἀνάπαλιν πρότερον μὲν ὕδωρ ἦν, νῦν δὲ λεπτυνθεῖσα
γέγονεν ἀήρ· ἐπὶ δὲ τοῦ τόπου οὐ λέγομεν τοῦτο,
ἀλλ' ὅτι πάλαι μὲν ἐν αὐτῷ ἦν ἀήρ, νῦν δ' ἔστιν
ἐν αὐτῷ ὕδωρ. οὐ τοίνυν δύναται ὕλη ὁ τόπος
26 νοεῖσθαι. καὶ μὴν οὐδὲ τὸ εἶδος. τὸ γὰρ εἶδος
ἀχώριστόν ἐστι τῆς ὕλης, καθάπερ ἐπὶ τοῦ ἀνδριάντος ἀχώριστόν ἐστι τοῦ ὑποκειμένου χαλκοῦ, ὁ
δὲ τόπος χωρίζεται τοῦ σώματος· μεταβαίνει γὰρ

body, so that it does not move away either when the body comes upon it. And besides, if it moves away when the body comes upon it, it will no longer receive the body ; and this too is itself an absurd notion. It 23 remains, therefore, to declare that the void perishes ; which again is impossible. For if it perishes, it becomes in a state of change and motion [and if it perishes it is generable] ; but that which becomes in a state of change and motion is a body [both generable and perishable]; so that the void does not perish. And so, if place is neither a body, as we have established, nor void, as we have shown, no place will exist.

And furthermore, if place is conceived as containing 24 body, and that which contains is outside of that which is contained, necessarily, if place exists, it must be some one of those things of which one is matter, another form, another the interval between the extreme limits of the body, another the extreme limits. Now place will not be matter for many 25 reasons,—because, for instance, the latter is corporealized but place is not corporealized, and matter passes over from place to place, but place does not pass over from place to place. And as regards matter we say that formerly it was air but now after condensation it has become water, or conversely that formerly it was water but now after rarefaction it has become air ; but we do not speak thus in the case of place, but we say that formerly there was air in it but now there is water in it. So then place cannot be conceived as matter.—Nor, in fact, as form. For 26 form is inseparable from matter,—as in the case of the statue it is inseparable from the underlying bronze,—but place is separate from body ; for the

---

¹ [καὶ . . . ἐστι] et [γενητόν . . . φθαρτὸν] secl. ego.

ἐκεῖνο καὶ εἰς ἕτερον μεθίσταται τόπον μὴ συμ-
μεταβαίνοντος αὐτῷ τοῦ ἐν ᾧ περιείχετο τόπου.
ὥστε εἰ τὸ μὲν εἶδος ἀχώριστόν ἐστι τῆς ὕλης, ὁ
δὲ τόπος χωρίζεται ταύτης, οὐκ ἂν εἴη τὸ εἶδος ὁ
τόπος. καὶ πάλιν τὸ μὲν εἶδος συμμεταβαίνει τῇ
ὕλῃ, ὁ δὲ τόπος, ὡς προεῖπον, οὐ συμμεταβαίνει
τῷ σώματι· τοίνυν οὐδὲ εἶδός ἐστιν ὁ τόπος.

27 ὡσαύτως δὲ οὐδὲ τὸ μεταξὺ τῶν περάτων διάστημα·
τοῦτο γὰρ περιέχεται πρὸς τῶν περάτων, ὁ δὲ
τόπος οὐ βούλεται περιέχεσθαι ὑπό τινος ἀλλ'
ἑτέρων εἶναι περιεκτικός. εἶτα πέρας ἐστὶ τοῦ
σώματος ἡ ἐπιφάνεια, τὸ δὲ μετὰ τὴν ἐπιφάνειαν
διάστημα οὐκ ἄλλο τι ἐστὶν ἢ τὸ πεπερατωμένον
σῶμα. εἰ οὖν φαμὲν τὸ μεταξὺ [τῶν πεπερατωμένων σωμάτων]¹ τόπον εἶναι, ἔσται σῶμα ὁ τόπος·
28 ὅπερ ἐστὶν ἀπεμφαῖνον.   λείπεται οὖν λέγειν
ὅτι τὰ ἔσχατα τοῦ σώματος πέρατά ἐστι τόπος·
ὃ καὶ αὐτὸ τῶν ἀδυνάτων, ἐπείπερ τὰ μὲν ἔσχατα
τοῦ σώματος συνεχῆ ἐστι τῷ σώματι καὶ μέρη
αὐτοῦ καὶ ἀχώριστα, ὁ δὲ τόπος οὔτε συνεχής ἐστι
τῷ σώματι οὔτε μέρος αὐτοῦ οὔτε ἀχώριστος τοῦ
σώματος. οὐκ ἄρα οὐδὲ τὰ ἔσχατα τῶν σωμάτων
29 ἐστὶν ὁ τόπος. εἰ δὲ μήτε ὕλη ὁ τόπος ἐστὶ μήτε
τὸ εἶδος μήτε τὸ μεταξὺ διάστημα τῶν περάτων μήτ'
αὖ τὰ ἔσχατα τοῦ σώματος, παρὰ δὲ ταῦτα οὐδὲν
ἔστιν ἄλλο ἐπινοεῖν, ῥητέον μηδὲν ὑπάρχειν τόπον.

30   Ναί φασιν οἱ ἀπὸ τοῦ περιπάτου φιλόσοφοι,
ἀλλὰ τόπος ἐστὶ τὸ πέρας τοῦ περιέχοντος σώματος. τῆς γὰρ γῆς ὕδατι περιεχομένης καὶ τοῦ
ὕδατος ἀέρι περιεχομένου καὶ τοῦ ἀέρος πυρὶ καὶ

¹ [τῶν . . . σωμάτων] secl. ego: τῶν περάτων τῶν σ. Fabr.
in vers.

latter changes its position and moves on to another place, while the place wherein it was contained does not change position along with it. So that if form is inseparable from matter, whereas place is separate from it, place will not be form. And again,—the form changes its position along with the matter, but place, as I said before, does not change its position along with body ; so then place is not form.—So 27 likewise it is not the interval between the limits ; for this is enclosed by the limits, whereas place refuses to be enclosed by anything, but itself serves to enclose other things. Moreover, surface is a limit of body, and the interval after the surface is nothing else than the limited body. If, then, we assert that what is between [the limited bodies] [a] is place, place will be a body ; which is contrary to sense.—It remains, 28 then, to declare that the extreme limits of the body are place ; but this itself, too, is a thing impossible, since the extremities of the body are continuous with the body and parts thereof and inseparable, whereas place is neither continuous with the body nor a part of it nor inseparable from the body. Neither, then, is place the extremities of the bodies. But if place 29 is neither matter nor form nor the interval between the limits nor the extremities of the body, and besides these one can conceive no other possibility, we must declare that place is nothing.

" Yes," say the Peripatetic philosophers, " but 30 place is the limit of the containing body." [b] For since earth is contained in water, and water contained in air, and air in fire, and fire in Heaven,—just as

---

[a] The words bracketed would imply an interval between different bodies, whereas it seems clear that the reference is to the internal space of a single body.

[b] With § 30 cf. P.H. iii. 131.

τοῦ πυρὸς οὐρανῷ, ὃν τρόπον τὸ τοῦ ἀγγείου πέρας
τόπος ἐστὶ τοῦ ἐν τῷ ἀγγείῳ σώματος, οὕτω καὶ
τὸ τοῦ ὕδατος πέρας ἐστὶ τόπος τῆς γῆς, καὶ τὸ
τοῦ ἀέρος πέρας ἐστὶ τόπος τοῦ ὕδατος, καὶ τὸ τοῦ
πυρὸς πέρας τόπος ἔσται τοῦ ἀέρος, καὶ τὸ τοῦ
31 οὐρανοῦ πέρας τόπος ἔσται τοῦ πυρός. αὐτὸς
μέντοι ὁ οὐρανὸς κατὰ τὸν Ἀριστοτέλη οὐκέτ᾽
ἐστὶν ἐν τόπῳ ἀλλ᾽ αὐτὸς ἐν ἑαυτῷ καὶ τῇ οἰκείᾳ
ἰδιότητι· ἐπεὶ γὰρ τόπος ἐστὶ τὸ ἔσχατον τοῦ περιέχοντος σώματος πέρας, ἐκτὸς δὲ τοῦ οὐρανοῦ
κατὰ τοῦτον τὸν φιλόσοφον οὐδέν ἔστιν, ἵνα καὶ
τὸ τούτου πέρας γένηται τόπος οὐρανοῦ, ἀνάγκη
καὶ τὸν οὐρανὸν ὑπὸ μηδενὸς περιεχόμενον ἐν
ἑαυτῷ εἶναι καὶ τοῖς οἰκείοις περιέχεσθαι πέρασιν,
32 ἀλλὰ μὴ ἐν τόπῳ τυγχάνειν. ὅθεν οὐδέ που ὄν
ἔστιν ὁ οὐρανός· τὸ γάρ που ὂν αὐτό τε ἔστιν
ἐκεῖνο καὶ ἕτερον τὸ ὅπου ἐστίν, ὁ δὲ οὐρανὸς
οὐδὲν ἔχει ἕτερον παρ᾽ αὐτὸν ἔξωθεν, διόπερ αὐτὸς
33 ἐν ἑαυτῷ ὢν οὐδέ που γενήσεται. ὅσον δὲ ἐπὶ
τοῖς οὕτω λεγομένοις ὑπὸ τῶν περιπατητικῶν,
κινδυνεύει ὁ πρῶτος θεὸς τόπος εἶναι πάντων.
κατὰ γὰρ Ἀριστοτέλη ὁ πρῶτος θεὸς ἦν τὸ
πέρας τοῦ οὐρανοῦ. ἤτοι οὖν ὁ θεὸς ἕτερόν ἐστι
παρὰ τὸ οὐράνιον πέρας, ἢ αὐτὸ ἐκεῖνο ὁ θεός
ἐστιν. καὶ εἰ μὲν ἕτερόν ἐστι παρὰ τὸ οὐράνιον
πέρας, ἔσται τι ἕτερον ἐκτὸς τοῦ οὐρανοῦ, καὶ τὸ
τούτου πέρας τόπος γενήσεται οὐρανοῦ, καὶ ταύτῃ
δώσουσιν οἱ περὶ τὸν Ἀριστοτέλη ἐν τόπῳ περιέχεσθαι τὸν οὐρανόν· ὅπερ οὐχ ὑπομενοῦσιν, ἀνθ-
εστῶτες ἑκατέρῳ τούτων, τῷ τε εἶναί τι ἐκτὸς
οὐρανοῦ καὶ τῷ τὸν οὐρανὸν ἐν τόπῳ περιέχεσθαι.

the limit of the vessel is the place of the body in the vessel, so also the limit of water is the place of earth, and the limit of air is the place of water, and the limit of fire will be the place of air, and the limit of Heaven will be the place of fire. When we come to 31 the Heaven itself, however, according to Aristotle,[a] it is not in place but abides within itself and in its own proper selfhood ; for since place is the extreme limit of the containing body, and according to this philosopher nothing exists outside Heaven so that its limit should be the place of Heaven, it is necessary that Heaven, being contained by nothing, should exist in itself and be contained within its own limits, and not exist in place. Hence Heaven is not existent 32 anywhere ; for that which exists anywhere both exists itself and its " where " is other than it, but Heaven has no other thing besides and outside of itself ; and on this account, as existing itself within itself, it will not be anywhere.—And so far as regards 33 these statements of the Peripatetics, it seems likely that the First God is the place of all things. For according to Aristotle [b] the First God is the limit of Heaven. Either, then, God is something other than the Heaven's limit, or God is just that limit. And if He is other than Heaven's limit, something else will exist outside Heaven, and its limit will be the place of Heaven, and thus the Aristotelians will be granting that Heaven is contained in place ; but this they will not tolerate, as they are opposed to both these notions,—both that anything exists outside of Heaven and that Heaven is contained in place. And if God

---

[a] *Cf.* Aristot. *Phys.* iv. 5.
[b] *Cf.* Aristot. *De caelo* i. 3 270 b 6, πάντες τὸν ἀνωτάτω τῷ θείῳ τόπον ἀποδιδόασι . . . (b 22) αἰθέρα προσωνόμασαν τὸν ἀνωτάτω τόπον.

εἰ δὲ ταὐτόν ἐστι τῷ οὐρανίῳ πέρατι ὁ θεός, ἐπεὶ
τὸ τοῦ οὐρανοῦ πέρας τόπος ἐστὶ πάντων τῶν
ἐντὸς οὐρανοῦ, ἔσται κατὰ τὸν Ἀριστοτέλη ὁ θεὸς
πάντων τόπος, ὃ καὶ αὐτὸ τῶν ἀπεμφαινόντων.

34 καθόλου τε, εἴπερ τὸ τοῦ ἐμπεριέχοντος
σώματος πέρας τόπος ἐστὶ τοῦ ἐμπεριεχομένου,
τοῦτο τὸ πέρας ἤτοι σῶμά ἐστιν ἢ ἀσώματον.
καὶ εἰ μὲν σῶμά ἐστιν, ἐπεὶ πᾶν σῶμα ὀφείλει
ἐν τόπῳ εἶναι, ἔσται ὁ τόπος ἐν τόπῳ καὶ οὐκέτι
τόπος· εἰ δὲ ἀσώματόν ἐστι τὸ τοῦ περιέχοντος σώματος πέρας, ἐπεὶ παντὸς σώματος τὸ πέρας ἐστὶν
ἡ ἐπιφάνεια, ἔσται ἑκάστου σώματος τόπος ἐπι-
35 φάνεια, ὅπερ ἄτοπον. καθόλου τε πῶς οὐ κατα-
γέλαστόν ἐστι λέγειν τὸν οὐρανὸν αὐτὸν ἑαυτοῦ
τόπον εἶναι; οὕτω γὰρ ἔσται τὸ αὐτὸ καὶ τὸ ἐν ᾧ
ἐστὶ καὶ τὸ ἐν αὐτῷ, καὶ τὸ αὐτὸ ἕν τε καὶ δύο,
σῶμά τε καὶ ἀσώματον. ᾗ μὲν γὰρ τὸ αὐτό ἐστιν,
ἓν ἔσται, ᾗ δὲ περιέχον καὶ ἐμπεριεχόμενον, δύο
γενήσεται, καὶ ᾗ μὲν περιεχόμενον, σῶμα, ᾗ δὲ
36 περιέχον, ἀσώματον· τόπος γὰρ ἦν. οὐ δύναται δὲ
ἐπινοεῖσθαι τὸ αὐτὸ ἅμα καὶ ἓν καὶ δύο καὶ σῶμα
καὶ ἀσώματον· τοίνυν οὐδὲ κατὰ τὴν τοιαύτην νόησιν
εὐδρομεῖ ἡ τοῦ τόπου κατάληψις.

Ἀλλ᾽ ἐπεὶ καὶ τοῦτον ἀνηρήκαμεν, ἴδωμεν ἑξῆς εἰ
δύναταί τι τῶν ὄντων κατὰ τόπον κινεῖσθαι.

Β΄.—ΕΙ ΕΣΤΙ ΚΙΝΗΣΙΣ

37 Ὁ μὲν Ἀριστοτέλης ἓξ εἴδη τῆς κινήσεως
ἔλεγεν ὑπάρχειν, ὧν τὸ μέν τι εἶναι τοπικὴν μετάβασιν, τὸ δὲ μεταβολήν, τὸ δὲ γένεσιν, τὸ δὲ
38 φθοράν, τὸ δὲ αὔξησιν, τὸ δὲ μείωσιν· οἱ δὲ πλείους,

is identical with Heaven's limit, since Heaven's limit is the place of all things within Heaven, God—according to Aristotle—will be the place of all things ; and this, too, is itself a thing contrary to sense.—Also, in 34 general, if the limit of the enclosing body is the place of the enclosed, this limit is either a body or incorporeal. And if it is a body, since every body must be in a place, place will be in a place and will no longer be place ; but if the limit of the containing body is incorporeal, since the limit of every body is a surface, the place of each body will be a surface, which is absurd.—Also, in general, how is it other 35 than ridiculous to say that Heaven is itself its own place ? For in this case the same thing will be both the container and the contained, and the same thing both one and two, both body and incorporeal. For in so far as it is the same thing it will be one, but in so far as it is both container and contained it will be two ; and in so far as it is contained it will be body, but in so far as it is container, incorporeal ; for it is place. But the same thing cannot be conceived as at 36 once both one and two, both body and incorporeal ; so then, neither with this conception of it does the apprehension of place have an easy course.

And now that we have abolished this also, let us next consider whether any of the existing things can move in space.

Chapter II.—Does Motion Exist ?

Aristotle said [a] that there are six kinds of motion, 37 and of these one is local transition, another change, another becoming, another perishing, another increase, another decrease ; but the majority—amongst 38

---

[a] Cf. Aristot. Categ. 15 a 13. With §§ 37–41 cf. P.H. iii. 64.

ἐν οἷς εἰσὶ καὶ οἱ περὶ τὸν Αἰνησίδημον, διττήν τινα
κατὰ τὸ ἀνωτάτω κίνησιν ἀπολείπουσι, μίαν μὲν
39 τὴν μεταβλητικήν, δευτέραν δὲ τὴν μεταβατικήν,
ὧν μεταβλητικὴ μέν ἐστι κίνησις καθ᾿ ἣν τὸ σῶμα
ἐν τῇ αὐτῇ μένον οὐσίᾳ ἄλλοτ᾿ ἄλλην ἀναδέχεται
ποιότητα καὶ ἣν μὲν ἀπολείπει ἣν δὲ ἐπιλαμβάνει,
ὁποῖόν τι γίνεται ἐπὶ τοῦ εἰς ὄξος μεταβάλλοντος
οἴνου καὶ ἐπὶ τῆς ἐξ ὄμφακος εἰς γλυκὺν χυμὸν
μεταβαλλούσης σταφυλῆς ἢ τοῦ ἄλλοτ᾿ ἄλλως
ποικιλλομένου τὰς χρόας χαμαιλέοντος ἢ πολύ-
40 ποδος. ὅθεν καὶ τὴν γένεσιν καὶ τὴν φθορὰν καὶ
τὴν αὔξησιν ἔτι δὲ μείωσιν εἰδικὰς ῥητέον εἶναι
μεταβολάς· ἃς φασι καὶ τῇ μεταβλητικῇ κινήσει
ὑποστέλλειν, εἰ μή τι τὴν αὔξησιν φήσει τις
ἔχεσθαι τῆς μεταβατικῆς κινήσεως, ὡς πρόβασιν
41 οὖσαν[1] σωμάτων εἴς τε μῆκος καὶ εὖρος. μεταβατικὴ δέ ἐστι κίνησις καθ᾿ ἣν τόπον ἐκ τόπου
μετέρχεται τὸ κινούμενον, ἤτοι ὅλον ἢ κατὰ μέρος,
ὅλον μὲν ὡς ἐπὶ τῶν τροχαζόντων καὶ περιπατούν-
των θεωροῦμεν, κατὰ μέρος δὲ ὡς ἐπὶ τῆς ἐκ-
τεινομένης καὶ συστελλομένης χειρὸς ἢ ἐπὶ τῶν
τῆς περὶ κέντρῳ[2] δινουμένης σφαίρας μερῶν. ὅλης
γὰρ αὐτῆς ἐν τῷ αὐτῷ μενούσης τόπῳ τὰ μέρη
ἀμείβει τοὺς τόπους· τὸ γὰρ κάτω ὂν πρότερον ἄνω
γίνεται καὶ τὸ ἄνω κάτω καὶ τὸ πρόσω ὀπίσω.
42   καίτοι τινὲς τῶν φυσικῶν, ἐξ ὧν ἐστὶ καὶ
ὁ Ἐπίκουρος, τὴν μεταβλητικὴν κίνησιν εἶδος
ἔλεξαν εἶναι τῆς μεταβατικῆς· τὸ γὰρ μεταβάλλον
κατὰ ποιότητα σύγκριμα πάντως κατὰ τὴν τῶν

----

[1] ⟨ὡς⟩ πρόβασιν οὖσαν Heintz: προβαίνουσαν mss., Bekk.
[2] κέντρῳ Mutsch.: κέντροις mss., Bekk.

whom Aenesidemus is included—allow that motion, in its main kinds, is twofold, one sort being that of change, the second that of transition ; and of these 39 the motion of change is that by which the body, while remaining identical in substance, receives different qualities at different times, putting off one quality and putting on another,—the sort of thing which takes place in the case of wine changing into vinegar and in the case of the grape when it changes from a state of acidity to a sweet flavour, or when the chameleon or polypod takes on a variety of different colours at different times. Hence, too, it must be affirmed that 40 becoming and perishing and increase, and decrease as well, are particular forms of change ; and they assert that these come under the head of the motion of change, unless perhaps someone should assert that increase belongs to transitional motion, as it is the progress of bodies towards length and breadth. And 41 transitional motion is that by which the moving object passes from place to place, either wholly or partially, —wholly as we see in the case of runners and walkers, and partially as in the case of a hand which is extended and clenched, or in the case of the parts of a sphere which is spinning round its centre. For while this as a whole remains in the same place, its parts change their places ; for the part which was formerly below becomes above, and the above below, and the before behind.—Some of the physicists, however,— 42 and amongst them Epicurus—have declared that the motion of change is a particular form of transitional motion ; for the composite object which changes in

συγκεκρικότων αὐτὸ λόγῳ θεωρητῶν σωμάτων
τοπικήν τε καὶ μεταβατικὴν κίνησιν μεταβάλλει.
43 οἷον ἵνα τι ἐκ γλυκέος γένηται πικρὸν ἢ ἐκ λευκοῦ
μέλαν, δεῖ τοὺς συνεστακότας αὐτὸ ὄγκους μετα-
κοσμηθῆναι καὶ ἄλλην ἀντὶ ἄλλης τάξιν ἀνα-
δέξασθαι· τοῦτο δ᾽ οὐκ ἂν ἄλλως συμβαίη, ἐὰν μὴ
μεταβατικῶς κινηθῶσιν οἱ ὄγκοι. καὶ πάλιν ἵνα
τι ἐκ σκληροῦ μαλακὸν γένηται ἢ ἐκ μαλακοῦ
σκληρόν, δεῖ τὰ ἐξ ὧν ἔστι μόρια κατὰ τὸν τόπον
44 κινηθῆναι· διατάσει μὲν γὰρ αὐτῶν μαλακύνεται,
συνελεύσει δὲ καὶ πυκνώσει σκληρύνεται. παρ᾽ ὃ
ἡ μεταβλητικὴ κίνησις οὐχ ἑτέρα κατὰ γένος ἐστὶ
τῆς μεταβατικῆς κινήσεως. διόπερ ἡμεῖς πρὸς
ταύτην μάλιστα κομιοῦμεν τὰς ἀπορίας, ἐπείπερ
αἱρομένης αὐτῆς οἰχήσεται καὶ ἡ μεταβλητικὴ
κίνησις.
45 Πρὶν δὲ τῶν ἀποριῶν γνωστέον ὅτι τρεῖς γεγόνασι στάσεις κατὰ τὸ ἀνωτάτω περὶ κινήσεως.
οἱ μὲν γάρ φασι κίνησιν εἶναι, οἱ δὲ μὴ εἶναι, οἱ δὲ
οὐ μᾶλλον εἶναι ἢ μὴ εἶναι. καὶ εἶναι μὲν ὅ τε
βίος,[1] τοῖς φαινομένοις προσέχων, καὶ οἱ πλείους
τῶν φυσικῶν, ὥσπερ οἱ περὶ Πυθαγόραν καὶ
Ἐμπεδοκλέα καὶ Ἀναξαγόραν Δημόκριτόν τε καὶ
Ἐπίκουρον, οἷς καὶ οἱ ἀπὸ τοῦ περιπάτου ἔτι δὲ
καὶ οἱ ἀπὸ τῆς στοᾶς συναπεγράψαντο καὶ ἄλλοι
46 παμπληθεῖς· μὴ εἶναι δὲ οἱ περὶ Παρμενίδην καὶ
Μέλισσον, οὓς ὁ Ἀριστοτέλης στασιώτας τε ⟨τῆς
φύσεως⟩[2] καὶ ἀφυσίκους κέκληκεν, στασιώτας μὲν

---

[1] βίος NL: Βίας cet., Bekk.
[2] ⟨τῆς φύσεως⟩ add. NLE.

---

[a] With §§ 45-49 cf. P.H. iii. 65.
[b] This phrase is derived (by A.) from Plato, Theaet. 181 A,
232

quality changes owing to the local and transitional motion of the rationally perceived bodies which compose it. Thus, in order that a thing may become 43 bitter from sweet, or black from white, the molecules which compose it must be arranged in a new order and take up different positions ; and this could not be brought about otherwise than by the transitional motion of the molecules. And again,—in order that a thing may become soft fróm hard or hard from soft, the parts whereof it is composed must move in place ; for it is made soft by their expansion, but made hard 44 by their coalescence and condensation. And owing to this the motion of change is, generically, nothing else than transitional motion. Consequently, we shall bring our criticisms to bear chiefly on this last, since if it is abolished the motion of change will also disappear.

But before we begin our criticisms we must observe 45 that there have been three main views regarding motion.[a] Some say that motion exists, others that it does not exist, and others that it is " no more " existent than non-existent. That it exists is affirmed both by ordinary folk, who pay attention to appearances, and by the majority of physicists, such as Pythagoras and Empedocles and Anaxagoras and Democritus and Epicurus, to whose view also the Peripatetics have subscribed, and the Stoics as well, and a host of others. But its non-existence is affirmed 46 by Parmenides and Melissus, whom Aristotle has described as " Nature's stationers "[b] and " anti-naturalists "—" stationers " from " standing still,"

where the Eleatics are called τοῦ ὅλου στασιῶται (" partisans of the Whole "), with a play on στασ. (as if from στάσις, " rest ").

ἀπὸ τῆς στάσεως, ἀφυσίκους δὲ ὅτι ἀρχὴ κινήσεώς
ἐστιν ἡ φύσις, ἣν ἀνεῖλον φάμενοι μηδὲν κινεῖσθαι·
47 τὸ γὰρ κινούμενον ὀφείλει ἀνύειν τι διάστημα, πᾶν
δὲ διάστημα διὰ τὸ τὴν εἰς ἄπειρον δέχεσθαι
τομὴν ἀνήνυτόν ἐστιν, ὥστ᾽ οὐδὲ κινούμενόν τι
48 ἔσται. συμφέρεται δὲ τούτοις τοῖς ἀνδράσι καὶ
Διόδωρος ὁ Κρόνος, εἰ μή τι ῥητέον κατὰ τοῦτον
κεκινῆσθαι μέν τι κινεῖσθαι δὲ μηδὲ ἕν, ὡς προ-
βαίνοντος τοῦ λόγου διδάξομεν, ὅταν αὐτοῦ τὴν
στάσιν ἀκριβέστερον ἐπισκεπτώμεθα· τὰ νῦν δὲ
ἀπόχρη τοῦτο γινώσκειν, ὅτι καὶ αὐτὸς ἐπὶ τῆς
αὐτῆς ἐστὶ δόξης τοῖς τὴν κίνησιν ἀνῃρηκόσιν.
49 μὴ μᾶλλον δὲ εἶναι κίνησιν ἢ μὴ εἶναι ἔλεξαν οἱ
ἀπὸ τῆς σκέψεως· ὅσον μὲν γὰρ ἐπὶ τοῖς φαινομένοις εἶναί τι κίνησιν, ὅσον δὲ ἐπὶ τῷ φιλοσόφῳ
λόγῳ μὴ ὑπάρχειν.
50 Τοιαύτη μὲν καὶ ἡ κατὰ τὸν τόπον στάσις· μεθ᾽
ἣν εἰς τὸ μὴ εἶναι κίνησιν ἐπιχειροῦντες πρώτας
κομιοῦμεν ἐνστάσεις, ἐχόμενοι τῆς κατὰ τὴν
κίνησιν ἐννοίας. ἔνιοι τοίνυν ὁριζόμενοι τὴν κίνησίν
φασι "κίνησίς ἐστι μετάβασις ἀπὸ τόπου εἰς
51 τόπον." πρὸς οὓς λέγεται ὅτι τὴν μὲν εὐθικὴν
κίνησιν ἀπέδοσαν, τουτέστι τὴν ἄνω ἢ κάτω ἢ
πρόσω ἢ ὀπίσω ἢ εἰς δεξιὰ ἢ εἰς ἀριστερά, τὴν
δὲ κυκλοφορητικὴν παρέλιπον, οἷον καθ᾽ ἣν ὁ
κεραμεικὸς τροχὸς στρέφεται καὶ ἡ σφαῖρα τοῖς
κνώδαξι περιδινεῖται, ὡσαύτως δὲ καὶ οἱ ἄξονες
καὶ τὰ τύμπανα· ἕκαστον γὰρ τῶν οὕτω κινουμένων σωμάτων οὐ μετέρχεται ἀπὸ τόπου εἰς
τόπον ἀλλ᾽ ἐν τῷ αὐτῷ μένον τόπῳ κινεῖται.
52 ὅθεν τινὲς τὴν τοιαύτην φεύγοντες ἔνστασιν δι-

ᵃ Of the later Megaric School, cf. P.H. ii. 245.

and " anti-naturalists " because Nature is the first
principle of motion, and it they abolished by declaring
that nothing moves.   For what moves must complete 47
a certain interval, but every interval is incapable of
being completed because it admits of division *ad
infinitum*, so that no moving thing will exist.   And 48
with these men Diodorus Cronos [a] also is in agreement, unless it should be said that according to him
something has moved but not a single thing is moving
—as we shall explain later in the course of our argument, when we come to examine his view more
closely.[b]   For the present it is enough to notice this
point, that he too is of the same opinion as those
who have abolished motion.   And that motion is " no 49
more " existent than non-existent has been stated
by the Sceptics ;   for motion is an existent thing if
we are to judge by appearances, but judging by
philosophical argument it is non-existent.

   Such, then, is the dissension with regard to this 50
subject ;   and after this, in our endeavour to show the
non-existence of motion, we shall bring forward our
first objections by concentrating on the conception
of motion.   Some, then, in defining motion assert
that " Motion is transition from place to place."   And 51
to these it is replied that while they have described
straight-line motion—that is, up or down, forwards or
backwards, to right or to left,—they have passed over
circular motion, such as that by which the potter's
wheel revolves and the sphere spins round its pivots,
and likewise axles and drums ;   for each of the bodies
which move in this way does not pass on from place
to place but moves whilst remaining in the same
place.—Hence, by way of escaping this objection, 52

[b] See §§ 85 ff., 120.

ορθοῦνται τὸν ἐκκείμενον ὅρον, καί φασιν ὅτι κίνησίς
ἐστι μετάβασις ἀπὸ τόπου εἰς τόπον ἤτοι ὅλου τοῦ
σώματος ἢ τῶν τοῦ ὅλου μερῶν. ὅ τε γὰρ ἐν τῷ
περιπατεῖν κινούμενος κατὰ ὁλότητα ἀπὸ τόπου
εἰς τόπον μετέρχεται, ἥ τε τοῖς κνώδαξι περιδινου-
μένη σφαῖρα ὅλη μὲν οὐ μεταβαίνει τόπον ἐκ
τόπου, κατὰ μέρη δὲ ἀμείβει τοὺς τόπους, καὶ
στρεφομένης αὐτῆς τὸ μὲν ἄνω μέρος ἐπιλαμβάνει
τὸν κάτω τόπον, τὸ δὲ κάτω μετέρχεται εἰς τὸν
ἄνω· καὶ ἐπὶ τῶν λοιπῶν τὸ ἐναλλάξ. διόπερ τὴν
κίνησιν ῥητέον, φασί, μετάβασιν εἶναι ἀπό τινος
τόπου εἰς τόπον ἤτοι ὅλου τοῦ κινουμένου σώματος
53 ἢ τῶν τοῦ ὅλου μερῶν.   θελήσαντες δὲ οὗτοι
τὴν εἰρημένην φυγεῖν ἀπορίαν εἰς ἑτέραν ἐνέπεσαν.
οὐ γὰρ πᾶν τὸ κινούμενον μεταβατικῶς μέτεισιν
ἀπὸ τόπου εἰς τόπον ἤτοι κατὰ ὁλοσχέρειαν ἢ
κατὰ μέρη, ἀλλ' ἔστι τινὰ τῶν μεταβατικῶς κινουμένων σωμάτων ἅπερ τισὶ μὲν μέρεσιν ἐν τῷ αὐτῷ
μένοντα τόπῳ κινεῖται τισὶ δὲ οὐκ ἐν τῷ αὐτῷ
μένοντα ἀλλ' ἄλλον καὶ ἄλλον ἐπιλαμβάνοντα,
ὁποῖόν τι ἔστιν ἰδεῖν ἐπὶ τοῦ κυκλογραφοῦντος
καρκίνου καὶ τῆς ἀνοιγομένης καὶ κλειομένης
54 θύρας. ἐπὶ μὲν γὰρ τοῦ καρκίνου φαίνεται ἡ τῷ
κέντρῳ ἐνηρεισμένη κεραία κατὰ τὸν αὐτὸν στρεφομένη τόπον καὶ ἡ ἔξωθεν περιαγομένη τε καὶ
κυκλογραφοῦσα ἀπ' ἄλλου εἰς ἄλλον μετιοῦσα
τόπον· ἐπὶ δὲ τῆς κλειομένης ἢ ἀνοιγομένης
θύρας ὁ μὲν κατὰ τοῦ ὀλμίσκου βεβηκὼς στροφεὺς
τῷ αὐτῷ ἐνστρέφεται τόπῳ, τὸ δ' ἀντικείμενον
αὐτῷ τῆς θύρας μέρος διαφερόντως ἐπέρχεται
τόπους καὶ ὃν μὲν ἀπολείπει ὃν δὲ ἐπιλαμβάνει.
55   αὗται μὲν οὖν αἱ κινήσεις ἐκπεπτώκασι τῆς

some rectify the definition put forward and say that
" Motion is transition from place to place either of
the whole body or of the parts of the whole." For he
who moves while walking passes as a whole from place
to place, but the sphere which spins round on its
pivots does not as a whole pass from place to place
but changes its place part by part, and as it turns
round the upper part comes to occupy the lower place
and the lower part passes into the upper place ; and
the remaining parts likewise alternate. Hence, they
say, we must declare that motion is a transition from
place to place either of the whole moving body or of the
parts of the whole.—But these men in trying to escape 53
the difficulty mentioned have fallen into another.
For not everything which moves by way of transition
passes from place to place either in its wholeness or
part by part, but there are some of the bodies moving
by transition which move with some of their parts while
remaining in the same place, but move with others
while not remaining in the same place but occupying
one place after another, as we can see in the case of
compasses when they are describing a circle and of a
door that is being opened or shut. For in the case 54
of the compasses the leg that rests on the centre is
evidently turning in the same place while that which
revolves outside it and describes the circle passes
from one place to another ; and in the case of the
door which is being shut or opened the pivot which is
set in the socket turns there in the same place but
the part of the door opposite thereto passes on to
different places and leaves one and occupies another.
—These motions, then, are omitted from their de- 55

ἀποδόσεως, ἦν δέ τις καὶ ἄλλη παραδοξοτέρα
κίνησις μεταβατική, καθ᾽ ἣν τὸ κινούμενον οὔτε
καθ᾽ ὅλον οὔτε κατὰ μέρος νοεῖται ἐκβαῖνον τοῦ
ἐν ᾧ ἔστι τόπου· ἥτις καὶ αὐτὴ ἐκπέπτωκε τοῦ
ὅρου, καθὼς αὐτόθεν συμφανές. καὶ ἔσται τὸ
ἰδίωμα ταύτης προδηλότερον ἐπὶ ὑποδείγματος
56 ποιησαμένων ἡμῶν τὴν δεῖξιν.[1] εἰ γάρ τις οὐριο-
δρομούσης νηὸς ὑποκέοιτο ἐκ τῆς πρώρας εἰς
πρύμναν ὄρθιον δοκίδα μεταφέρων καὶ ἰσοταχῶς
κινούμενος τῇ νηί, ὥστε καθ᾽ ὃν χρόνον αὕτη εἰς
τοὖμπροσθεν ἀνύει πηχυαῖον διάστημα, κατὰ τὸν
ἴσον καὶ τὸν ἐν αὐτῇ κινούμενον εἰς τοὐπίσω μεταβαίνειν πηχυαῖον διάστημα, πάντως κατὰ ταύτην
τὴν ὑπόθεσιν γενήσεται μὲν μεταβατικὴ κίνησις,
οὔτε δὲ ὅλον τὸ κινούμενον ἐκβήσεται τοῦ ἐν ᾧ
57 ἔστι τόπου οὔτε κατὰ μέρος· ὁ γὰρ ἐν τῇ νηὶ
κινούμενος κατὰ τὴν αὐτὴν κάθετον τοῦ τε ἀέρος
καὶ τοῦ ὕδατος μένει διὰ τό, ὁπόσον ἂν δοκῇ εἰς
τοὐπίσω προκόπτειν, τοσοῦτον σύρεσθαι εἰς τὸ
ἔμπροσθεν. δύναται οὖν τι κινεῖσθαι μεταβατικῶς
ὃ οὔτε καθ᾽ ὁλότητα οὔτε κατὰ μέρος ἐκβαίνει τοῦ
ἐν ᾧ ἔστι τόπου.[2]   ταῦτα μὲν οὖν ἔοικεν εἶναι
58 τοιαῦτα, πάρεστι δὲ καὶ ἑτέρως ἀπορεῖν τοὺς οὕτω
τὴν ἐπίνοιαν τῆς μεταβατικῆς κινήσεως ἀποδιδόν-
τας. ἐὰν γὰρ νοήσωμέν τι ἀμερὲς καὶ ἐλάχιστον
σῶμα ἐν τῷ αὐτῷ στρεφόμενον τόπῳ, τουτέστι
κυκλοφορητικῶς, ἔσται μέν τις μεταβατικὴ κίνησις,
οὔτε δὲ κατὰ ὁλότητα ἐκβήσεται τοῦ ἐν ᾧ ἔστι
τόπου ⟨τὸ⟩[3] κινούμενον οὔτε κατὰ μέρος, καὶ κατὰ

---

[1] δεῖξιν cj. Bekk., Mutsch.: δόξαν mss., Bekk.
[2] τοῦ . . . τόπου Mutsch.: τὸν . . . τόπον mss., Bekk.
[3] ⟨τὸ⟩ add. Heintz.

scription ; but there is also another more surprising kind of transitional motion, in which the moving object is conceived as not going out from the place wherein it is either as a whole or part by part ; and this too is omitted from their definition, as is obvious at once. And the peculiar character of this motion will be more evident when we have explained it by an example. For if we should suppose that, when a 56 ship is running before the wind, a man is carrying an upright rod from the prow to the stern and moving at the same speed as the ship, so that in the time in which the latter completes the distance of a cubit in a forward direction, in an equal time the man who is moving in the ship passes over the distance of a cubit in a backward direction, then, in the case thus supposed there will certainly be transitional motion, but the moving object will not go out from the place wherein it is either wholly or in part ; for the man who is 57 moving in the ship remains in the same perpendicular both of air and of water owing to the fact that he is borne just as far forward as he seems to proceed backward. It is, then, possible for a thing which does not quit the place wherein it is either wholly or in part to move transitionally.—Such then, as it seems, are cases of this sort ; and there are other difficulties 58 which may be encountered by those who thus define the notion of transitional motion. For if we conceive an indivisible and minimal body revolving in the same place,—that is, with a circular motion,—a transitional motion will exist, but the moving body will not quit the place wherein it is either wholly or in part—not

239

ὁλότητα μὲν ἐπεὶ ὑπόκειται ἐν τῷ αὐτῷ τόπῳ
κυκλοφορητικῶς στρεφόμενον, κατὰ μέρος δὲ ἐπεὶ
59 ἀμερές ἐστιν. ὁ δ' αὐτὸς λόγος κἂν συνθῶμέν
τινα εὐθεῖαν γραμμὴν ἐξ ἀμερῶν σωμάτων στοιχηδὸν τεταγμένων, καὶ ταύτην νοήσωμεν στρεφομένην ἐν τῷ αὐτῷ τόπῳ, ὥσπερ τοὺς ἄξονας· πάλιν
γὰρ ἔσται μὲν μεταβατικὴ κίνησις, οὔτε δὲ ὅλη
ἡ[1] εὐθεῖα ἐκβήσεται τοῦ ἐν ᾧ ἔστι τόπου, κυκλοφορητικὴν γὰρ μόνον ἐποιεῖτο τὴν κίνησιν, οὔτε
κατὰ μέρη, τῶν γὰρ ἀμερῶν σωμάτων οὐκ ἔστι μέρη.
60 Ἀλλὰ ταύτας μὲν τὰς ἐνστάσεις διακρούσονται
οἱ μὴ συναρεσκόμενοι τῷ [μὴ] εἶναί τινα ἀμερῆ,
φήσουσί τε μέχρις ἐπινοίας προκόπτειν τὴν τοιαύτην
κίνησιν, δεῖν δὲ αὐτὴν ἐπὶ ὑποστατῶν ἐξετάζεσθαι
61 σωμάτων. ὥσθ' οὗτοι μὲν οὕτως ὑπαντήσονται·
οἱ δ' ἀξιοῦντες ἀμερῆ εἶναι σώματα καὶ τὴν
κατάληξιν τῆς τῶν σωμάτων τομῆς εἰς ἐλάχιστον
γίνεσθαι οὐδὲν ἰσχύσουσι λέγειν πρὸς τὰς τοιουτο-
τρόπους ἀπορίας. οὐ μὴν ἀλλὰ καὶ ἐὰν μετα-
στῶμεν τούτων, εὑρεθήσεται ἰσοσθενὴς ὅ τε κατα-
σκευάζων τὸ μὴ εἶναι κίνησιν λόγος καὶ ὁ δεικνὺς
62 ταύτην ὑπάρχειν.   τῷ μὲν γὰρ εἶναι κίνησιν
συναγορεύει ἡ ἐνάργεια, περὶ δὲ ταύτης ἐστὶ
ζήτησις, παρόσον οἱ μὲν αἰσθήσει λαμβάνεσθαί
φασι τὴν κίνησιν, οἱ δὲ αἰσθήσει μὲν οὐδαμῶς, δι'
63 αἰσθήσεως δὲ τῇ διανοίᾳ. καὶ οἱ μὲν αἰσθητὸν
εἶναι λέγοντες πρᾶγμα τὴν κίνησιν πιστοῦνται τὸ
τοιοῦτο ἐκ τοῦ μὴ τὸ αὐτὸ ἐγγίνεσθαι πάθος τῇ
αἰσθήσει, οἷον τῇ ὄψει, ἀπό τε τοῦ κινουμένου
σώματος, ὅτε κινεῖται, καὶ ἀπὸ τοῦ ἠρεμοῦντος,
ὅτε ἠρεμεῖ, ἀλλὰ διάφορον μὲν ἀπὸ τοῦ ἀκινητί-

---

[1] ὅλη ἡ Heintz : ἡ ὅλη mss., Bekk.

wholly, since it is assumed to be revolving with circular motion in the same spot, nor in part, since it is without parts. And the same argument applies, 59 if we should construct a straight line out of indivisible bodies placed in a row, and conceive this as revolving in the same place, as do axles ; for here again there will be transitional motion but the straight line will not quit the place wherein it is either as a whole (for the motion it has is circular only) or in part (for in indivisible bodies there are no parts).

But those who do not admit the existence of any 60 indivisibles will evade these objections, and they will say that it is only in conception that this sort of motion proceeds, and it must be examined in the case of existing bodies. Consequently, these men will 61 answer thus ; but those who maintain that indivisible bodies exist, and that at the minimal point there is a termination to the division of bodies, will not be able to say anything in reply to criticisms of this kind. Nevertheless, even if we refrain from pursuing these, the argument which establishes the non-existence of motion and that which proves its existence will be found to be equipollent. For the evidence of sense 62 advocates the existence of motion, although about this there is disputation, inasmuch as some assert that motion is perceived by sense, but others that it is not perceived at all by sense but by the intellect through sensation. And those who declare that motion is an 63 object of sense support this view by the fact that the same affection is not produced in the sense—in sight, for example—by a moving object when it moves and by a stationary object when it remains stationary, but the motionless object produces one sort of affec-

ζοντος ἀλλοῖον δὲ ἀπὸ τοῦ κινουμένου, ὥστε κατὰ
64 τοῦτο αἰσθήσει ληπτὴν εἶναι τὴν κίνησιν. οἱ δὲ
ἀξιοῦντες μὴ αἰσθήσει ταύτην λαμβάνεσθαι, ἀλλὰ
δι᾽ αἰσθήσεως μὲν διανοίᾳ δέ, φασὶν ὅτι πᾶσα
κίνησις κατὰ συμμνημόνευσιν γίνεται· ἀναφέροντες
γὰρ ὡς τόδε τὸ σῶμα πάλαι μὲν ἐν τῷδε τῷ τόπῳ
ἐτύγχανε νῦν δὲ ἔστιν ἐν τῷδε, ἔννοιαν λαμβάνομεν
τῆς κινήσεως καὶ τοῦ κεκινῆσθαι. αὐτὸ δὲ τό γε
μνημονεύειν οὐκ ἀλόγου τινὸς αἰσθήσεως, λογικῆς
δὲ δυνάμεώς ἐστιν ἔργον. οὐκ ἄρα τῇ αἰσθήσει,
διανοίᾳ δὲ λαμβάνεσθαι συμβέβηκε τὴν κίνησιν.
65 ἄλλως τε πᾶσα κίνησις κατὰ ἀπόλειψιν καὶ ἐπίληψιν τόπου νοεῖται. ἡ δὲ αἴσθησις οὔτε τόπον
δύναται λαμβάνειν, οὐθεὶς γὰρ τόπος αἰσθητός
ἐστιν, οὔτε ἐπίληψιν καὶ ἀπόλειψιν· μνημονικῶς
γὰρ ταῦτα θεωρεῖται, ἡ δὲ αἴσθησις ἄλογος οὖσα
ἐστὶν ἀμνήμων. οὐκ ἄρα αἰσθητόν τι ἐστὶν ἡ
κίνησις.
66   Πλὴν ἐάν τε αἰσθήσει προηγουμένως λαμβάνηται
ἐάν τε διανοίᾳ, ἀδιάφορον· ἐκεῖνο γὰρ συμφανές
ἐστιν, ὅτι συνᾴδειν δοκεῖ τῷ εἶναι κίνησιν ἡ
ἐνάργεια. παρ᾽ ἣν αἰτίαν καὶ οἱ δογματικοὶ
φιλόσοφοι οὐκ ἄλλοθεν εἰώθασι δυσωπεῖν τοὺς
67 ἀπορητικοὺς ἢ ἀπὸ ταύτης. πῶς γάρ, φασίν,
εἴπερ μὴ ἔστι κίνησις, ἥλιος ἀπὸ ἀνατολῆς μέχρι
δύσεως τοὺς ἰδίους σταδιεύει δρόμους; ἢ πῶς
ὡρῶν γίγνονται μεταβολαί, ἔαρος καὶ θέρους καὶ
μετοπώρου καὶ χειμῶνος; παρὰ γὰρ τὰς τοῦ
ἡλίου κινήσεις συνεγγισμούς τε καὶ ἀποστάσεις
68 αὗται συμβαίνουσιν. πῶς δὲ καὶ νῆες ἀναχθεῖσαι
ἐκ λιμένων εἰς ἑτέρους κατάγονται λιμένας; τίνα
δὲ τρόπον ὁ ἀναιρῶν τὴν κίνησιν ἀπορητικὸς

tion and the moving object a different sort, so that in
this way motion is perceptible by sense. But those 64
who maintain that it is not perceived by sense, but
by the intellect through sensation, assert that every
motion comes about through concurrent recollection ;
for by recalling that this particular body was formerly
in that particular place but now is in this we acquire
the conception of motion and of being moved. But
recollection itself is the work not of any irrational
sense but of the reasoning faculty. It results, therefore, that motion is not perceived by sense but by
intellect. And further, all motion is conceived as 65
involving departure from and occupation of place ;
but sense cannot perceive either place (for no place
is sensible), or occupation and departure (for these
things are observed through memory, but sense being
irrational is without memory). Therefore motion is
not a sensible object.

However, it is a matter of indifference whether 66
motion is apprehended chiefly by sense or by intellect ; for it is plain that the evidence of facts seems
to bear out the view that motion exists. And for
this reason the Dogmatic philosophers are in the
habit of using no other means than this to put the
Doubters to shame. For, say they, if motion does 67
not exist how does the sun run its own special course
from its rising to its setting ? [a] Or how do the
changes of the seasons—spring, summer, autumn and
winter—take place ? For it is owing to the sun's
motions, its advances and recessions, that these occur.
And how do ships, after putting out to sea from har- 68
bours, put in to land in other harbours ? And how is
it that the Doubter who abolishes motion goes forth

* With §§ 67-68 cf. P.H. iii. 66.

ἔωθεν προελθὼν τῆς οἰκίας καί τινα τῶν κατὰ τὸν
βίον πραγματευσάμενος πάλιν ὑποστρέφει; πάντα
γὰρ ταῦτα ἀναντίρρητά ἐστι τῆς κινήσεως τεκμήρια.
ὅθεν καὶ τῶν παλαιῶν τις κυνικῶν τοὺς κατὰ τῆς
κινήσεως ἐρωτώμενος λόγους ἀπεκρίνατο μὲν οὐδὲ
ἕν, ἀναστὰς δὲ περιεπάτει, δι᾽ αὐτῆς τῆς ἐναργείας
69 τὴν ἄνοιαν[1] τοῦ σοφιστοῦ ὀνειδίζων.   καὶ ἄλλα
δὲ παμπληθῆ τοιαῦτ᾽ εἰώθασιν οἱ ἐξ ἐναντίας λέγειν
ὑπὲρ τοῦ κίνησιν εἶναι. οἷς καὶ ἡμεῖς ὡς ἀπο-
χρώσῃ συνηγορίᾳ πρὸς κατασκευὴν τοῦδε τοῦ
μέρους ἀρκεσθέντες εἰς τοὐναντίον ἐπιχειρήσομεν.
ἐὰν γὰρ ἴσον δειχθῇ κατά τε πίστιν καὶ ἀπιστίαν
τῷ εἶναι κίνησιν τὸ μὴ εἶναι κίνησιν, πάντως
ἀκολουθήσει τὸ μηθετέρῳ μὲν συναινεῖν, ἐπέχειν
δὲ περὶ ἀμφοτέρων.

70 Εἴπερ οὖν κινεῖταί τι πρώτως, οἷον στοιχεῖον,
ἤτοι ὑφ᾽ αὐτοῦ κινεῖται ἢ ὑπ᾽ ἄλλου· οὔτε δὲ ὑφ᾽
αὑτοῦ, ὡς δείξομεν, οὔθ᾽ ὑπ᾽ ἄλλου, καθὼς παρα-
μυθησόμεθα· οὐκ ἄρα κινεῖται. αὐτίκα γὰρ εἰ
πᾶν τὸ κινούμενον ὑπὸ ἑτέρου κινεῖται, ἤτοι
συνακολουθοῦντος αὐτῷ τοῦ κινοῦντος κινεῖται ἢ
μὴ συνακολουθοῦντος· οὔτε δὲ συνακολουθοῦντος
οὔτε ἀφισταμένου κινεῖται, ὡς δείξομεν· οὐκ ἄρα
71 τὸ κινούμενον ὑπ᾽ ἄλλου κινεῖται. εἰ γὰρ τὸ κινούμενον συνακολουθοῦντος αὐτῷ τοῦ κινοῦντος
κινεῖται, δεήσει τῷ ὁποιῳδηποτοῦν κινουμένῳ ἑνὶ
πάντα συνακολουθεῖν. εἰ γὰρ λόγου χάριν ἕκαστον
τῶν εἴκοσι τεσσάρων στοιχείων ὑπὸ ἑτέρου κινεῖται,
ἀναγκαῖον τῷ ἄλφα κινουμένῳ ὑπὸ τοῦ βῆτα

----

[1] ἄνοιαν N, Mutsch.: διάνοιαν cet., Bekk.

[a] Diogenes, cf. P.H. ii. 244.
[b] With §§ 70-76 cf. P.H. iii. 67.

from his house in the morning and, after transacting some ordinary business, returns to it again ? For all these are irrefutable signs of motion. Hence also one of the ancient Cynics,[a] when the arguments against motion were propounded to him, made no reply at all but stood up and walked about, thus flouting the folly of the sophist by the evidence of actual fact. And 69 there are hosts of similar arguments which those of the opposite side are wont to adduce in support of the existence of motion. And as we, too, are content with these as affording sufficient support for the establishment of this view, we shall now turn to argue for the opposite view. For if it be shown that the non-existence of motion is equal to the existence of motion in respect of probability and improbability, there will certainly follow assent to neither but suspension of judgement regarding both.

If, then, anything has a primary motion (an ele-70 ment, for instance), it is moved either by itself or by another ; but ⟨it is moved⟩ neither by itself, as we shall show, nor by another, as we shall explain ; therefore it is not moved.[b] Thus, for example, if everything which is moved is moved by another it is moved either while that which moves it accompanies it or while it does not accompany it ; but, as we shall show, it is not moved either while it accompanies or while it recedes from it ; therefore, what is moved is not moved by another. For if what is moved is moved 71 while its mover accompanies it, all things will have to accompany that one thing, whatsoever it be, which is being moved. Thus if, for the sake of argument, each one of the twenty-four letters is moved by another, it is necessary that all the rest should accompany Alpha when it is moved by Beta, since, just as

συνακολουθεῖν τὰ λοιπά, ἐπείπερ ὡς ἕπεται τῷ
ἄλφα τὸ βῆτα, κινοῦν τὸ ἄλφα, οὕτω καὶ τῷ βῆτα
ἀκολουθήσει τὸ γάμμα, κινητικὸν ὂν αὐτοῦ, καὶ τῷ
72 γάμμα τὸ δέλτα, καὶ μέχρι τοῦ ω. τοίνυν καὶ ἐπὶ
τῶν κατὰ τὸν κόσμον πραγμάτων, εἰ ἕκαστον τῶν
κινουμένων ἀκολουθοῦν ἔχειν ὀφείλει τὸ κινοῦν,
ἑνὶ κινουμένῳ πάντα συνακολουθήσει. ἄτοπον
δέ γε ἑνὸς κινουμένου πάντα λέγειν κινεῖσθαι·
οὐκ ἄρα ἕπεται τῷ κινουμένῳ τὸ κινοῦν.
73 εἰ δὲ χωρίζεται αὐτοῦ, καθάπερ ἡ χεὶρ ἀφ-
ίσταται τῆς ἀποπαλλομένης σφαίρας, ἀνάγκη
παθόν πως καὶ διατεθὲν ὑπὸ τοῦ κινοῦντος τὸ
κινούμενον ποιεῖσθαι τὴν ἀπ' αὐτοῦ φοράν. ἐπεὶ
οὖν τὸ πάσχον οὐκ ἄλλως πέφυκε πάσχειν εἰ μὴ
κατὰ πρόσθεσιν ἢ ἀφαίρεσιν ἢ μεταβολήν, δεήσει
καὶ τὸ κινούμενόν τι τούτων παθὸν ὑπὸ τοῦ κινοῦντος κινεῖσθαι, ὡς ἂν μηδὲν αὐτῶν πάθῃ χωρι-
74 σθέντος τοῦ κινοῦντος στήσεται. ἐδείξαμεν δέ γε
ἄπορον τὸν περὶ τῆς ἀφαιρέσεως καὶ προσθέσεως
καὶ μεταβολῆς λόγον, ὥστε οὐδ' ἀφισταμένου τοῦ
75 κινοῦντος κινήσεται τὸ κινούμενον.   καὶ ἄλλως,
εἰ παθὸν κατὰ ἀφαίρεσιν ἢ κατὰ πρόσθεσιν ἢ κατὰ
μεταβολὴν κινεῖται τὸ κινούμενον, αἱ ἄτομοι οὐ
κινηθήσονται διὰ τὸ μήτε πρόσθεσιν μήτε ἀφαίρεσιν
μήτε μεταβολὴν ἐπιδέχεσθαι. τοίνυν οὐδὲ ὑπὸ
ἑτέρου κινεῖται τὸ κινούμενον. εἰ γὰρ ἵνα ὑπὸ
ἑτέρου κινηθῇ, δεῖ συνακολουθοῦντος αὐτῷ ἐκείνου
κινεῖσθαι ἢ μὴ συνακολουθοῦντος, δέδεικται δὲ
ἑκάτερον ἀδύνατον, λεκτέον μὴ ὑπὸ ἑτέρου κινεῖσθαι.
76   καὶ μὴν εἰ πᾶν τὸ κινούμενον ὑπ' ἄλλου τινὸς

Beta in moving Alpha follows Alpha, so also Gamma will accompany Beta as being its mover, and Delta Gamma and so on up to Omega. So, too, with objects 72 in the Universe, if each moving object must have its mover following it, all things will follow after a single moving object. But it is absurd to say that if one thing moves all things move ; therefore the mover does not follow the thing moved.—And if it is 73 separated from it, as the hand is parted from the ball when it is being flung away, the movements away from it must necessarily cause the thing moved to be somehow affected and disposed by that which moves it. Since, then, what is affected cannot be affected otherwise than by way of addition or of subtraction or of change, what is moved will have to undergo one of these modes of affection at the hands of its mover when being moved, since, if it is not affected in any of these ways, it will stand still when its mover is separated from it. But we have shown[a] 74 that the account given of subtraction and addition and change is open to doubt, so that neither when the mover is parted from it will what is moved be in motion.—And besides, if what is moved moves 75 through being affected either by way of subtraction or of addition or of change, the atoms will not move because they do not admit of addition or subtraction or change. Neither, then, is what moves moved by another. For if, in order that it should be moved by another, it must be moved either while that other follows with it or while it does not so follow, and each of these alternatives has been proved to be impossible, we must declare that it is not moved by another.—Moreover, if everything which moves 76

---

[a] *Cf. Adv. Phys.* i. 277 ff.

κινεῖται, ἤτοι τὸ κινοῦν αὐτὸ κινεῖται ἢ ἀκινητεῖ.
καὶ ἀκινητίζειν μὲν ἀδύνατον· τὸ γὰρ κινοῦν ἐν-
εργεῖ τι, τὸ δὲ ἐνεργοῦν κινεῖται, τὸ ἄρα κινοῦν
κινεῖται. εἰ δὲ κινεῖται, ἐπεὶ πᾶν τὸ κινούμενον
ὑπ' ἄλλου τινὸς κινεῖται, δεήσει καὶ αὐτὸ¹ κινούμενον ὑπὸ τρίτου τινὸς κινεῖσθαι, καὶ τὸ τρίτον
ὑπὸ τοῦ τετάρτου, καὶ τὸ τέταρτον ὑπὸ τοῦ πέμ-
πτου, καὶ οὕτως εἰς ἄπειρον, ὥστε ἄναρχον γίνεσθαι τὴν κίνησιν. τοῦτο δὲ ἦν ἄτοπον· οὐκ ἄρα τὸ
κινούμενον ὑπ' ἄλλου κινεῖται.

77 Καὶ μὴν οὐδ' αὐτὸ ὑφ' ἑαυτοῦ κινηθήσεται. εἰ
γὰρ αὐτοκίνητόν ἐστιν, ἤτοι πάντη κινητὴν ἔχει
τὴν φύσιν ἢ εἴς τινα διάστασιν, οἷον ἐπὶ τῶν
πρώτων καὶ στοιχειωδῶν σωμάτων, ἐπεὶ καὶ πρὸς
τοὺς φυσικούς ἐστιν ὁ λόγος. ἀλλ' εἰ μὲν πάντη
78 κινητὴν ἔχει τὴν φύσιν, οὐ κινήσεται· οὔτε γὰρ
ἄνω ἐνεχθήσεται διὰ τὸ καὶ εἰς τὸ κάτω κινητὴν
ἔχειν τὴν φύσιν, οὔτε κάτω διὰ τὸ καὶ εἰς τὸ ἄνω,
οὔτε πρόσω διὰ τὸ καὶ εἰς τὸ ὀπίσω, οὔτ' ὀπίσω
διὰ τὸ καὶ εἰς τοὐμπροσθεν. καὶ ἐπὶ τῶν λειπο-
79 μένων δυοῖν διαστάσεων ὁ αὐτὸς λόγος. εἰ δὲ εἴς
τινα διάστασιν κινητὴν ἔχει τὴν φύσιν, εἰ μὲν εἰς
τὴν ἄνω ὥσπερ τὸ πῦρ καὶ ὁ ἀήρ, πάντ' ἄνω
κινήσεται, εἰ δὲ εἰς τὴν κάτω μόνον ὡς γῆ καὶ
ὕδωρ, πάντα εἰς τὸ κάτω. εἰ δὲ τινὰ μὲν εἰς τὴν
ἄνω διάστασιν κινητὴν ἔχει τὴν φύσιν τινὰ δὲ εἰς
τὴν κάτω, οὐ γενήσεται ἐκ κινουμένων σωμάτων
80 σύγκριμα. εἴτε γὰρ ἀπὸ τοῦ μέσου νοοῖτο κινούμενα τὰ στοιχειώδη σώματα ὡς ἐπὶ τὰ πέρατα,

¹ αὐτὸ Heintz: τὸ mss., Bekk. (τὸ κινοῦν cj. Papp.).
248

is moved by some other thing, that which moves it either is in motion itself or is motionless. But it is impossible for it to be motionless; for what causes motion is active, and what is active is in motion, therefore what causes motion is in motion. And if it is in motion, since everything in motion is moved by something else, it too, being in motion, will have to be moved by some third thing, and the third by a fourth, and the fourth by a fifth, and so on *ad infinitum*; so that motion comes to have no beginning. But this is absurd; therefore what is in motion is not moved by another.

Nor yet will a thing be moved by itself. For if it 77 is self-moved it is of a nature which is movable either in all directions or in some one direction, as in the case of the primary and elemental bodies, since our argument is against the Physicists. But if it has a nature which is movable in all directions, it will not move; for it will not be borne upwards since it is also 78 of a nature which is movable downwards, nor downwards as being movable upwards, nor forwards as movable backwards, nor backwards as movable forwards. And the same argument applies to the two other directions.[a] And if it possesses a nature capable 79 of being moved in some one direction, if this be upwards (like fire and air), all things will move upwards, while if it be downwards only (like earth and water) all things will move downwards. And if it is of a nature which is partly movable in the upward direction and partly in the downward, no combination will take place between the moving bodies; for 80 if the elemental bodies are conceived as moving from the centre towards the limits, the whole will be dis-

---

[a] *i.e.* to the right and to the left.

λυθήσεται τὸ πᾶν· ἑκάτερον γὰρ ἀπὸ θατέρου
χωρισθὲν ὡς ἐπὶ τὴν ἴδιον δραμεῖται κίνησιν, τὸ
μὲν ἀνωφερὲς ἐπὶ τὴν ἄνω, τὸ δὲ κατωφερὲς ἐπὶ
81 τὴν κάτω. εἴτ᾽ ἀπὸ τῶν περάτων ὑποκέοιτο ὡς
ἐπὶ τὸ μέσον συνωθούμενα, πάντως ἢ κατὰ τὴν
αὐτὴν κάθετον ἐνεχθήσεται ἢ οὐ κατὰ τὴν αὐτήν.
καὶ εἰ μὲν κατὰ τὴν αὐτὴν φέροιτο, ἐξ ἀνάγκης
καὶ ἀντιπεσεῖται ἀλλήλοις, καὶ οὕτως ἢ ἰσοκρα-
τοῦντα στήσεται μηθετέρου νικῶντος, μήτε τοῦ κάτω
βιαζομένου μήτε τοῦ ἄνω (ἄτοπον δὲ λέγειν στάσιν
82 γίνεσθαι ἐν τοῖς φύσει κινουμένοις), ἢ τοὐναντίον
ἀνισοκρατοῦντα εἰς ἕνα μόνον ἐνεχθήσεται τόπον,
ἤτοι τὸν ἄνω ἐπικρατησάντων τῶν ἀνωφερῶν, ἢ
εἰς τὸν κάτω ὑπερτερούντων τῶν κατωφερῶν. εἰ
δὲ μὴ κατὰ τὴν αὐτὴν κάθετον φέροιτο, οὐ συμ-
βάλλει ἀλλήλοις, μὴ συμβάλλοντα δὲ οὐδὲ συγκρίματος ἔσται τινὸς ἀποτελεστικά. τοῦτο δὲ ἄτοπον.
τοίνυν οὐδὲ αὐτοκίνητόν ἐστι τὸ κινούμενον.
83 πάλιν εἰ αὐτοκίνητόν ἐστι τὸ κινούμενον, ἐπεὶ πᾶν
τὸ κινοῦν ἤτοι προωθοῦν κινεῖ ἢ ἐπισπώμενον ἢ
ἀνοχλοῦν καὶ θλῖβον, δεήσει καὶ τὸ αὐτοκίνητον
ἑαυτοῦ κινητικὸν ὂν ἤτοι προωστικῶς κινεῖν ἢ ἐπι-
84 σπαστικῶς ἢ ἀνοχλητικῶς καὶ θλιπτικῶς. εἴτε δὲ
προωστικῶς κινοίη, ἔσται ἐξόπισθεν ἑαυτοῦ (τὸ γὰρ
προωθοῦν ἐξόπισθέν ἐστι τοῦ προωθουμένου), εἴτε
ἐπισπαστικῶς, ἔσται ἔμπροσθεν αὐτοῦ, εἴτε ἀνοχλητικῶς καὶ θλιπτικῶς, ὑποκάτωθεν αὐτοῦ. ἀδύνατον
δέ γε νοεῖν τι[1] αὐτὸ ἤτοι ὄπισθεν ἑαυτοῦ ἢ ἔμπροσθεν ἢ ὑποκάτω· οὐκ ἄρα αὐτοκίνητόν ἐστι τὸ

---

[1] τι Heintz : τὸ mss., Bekk.

solved ; for each being separated from each will run
on its own special course, the ascending upwards and
the descending downwards. And if they are sup- 81
posed to be driven together towards the centre from
the limits, they will certainly be transported either
along the same or not along the same vertical line.
And if they are borne along the same line, they will
necessarily collide with one another, and thus they
will either be of equal force and come to rest, neither
side being victorious, and neither the upward nor the
downward body yielding to force (though it is absurd
to say that rest occurs in things which are by nature
in motion), or if, on the contrary, they are of unequal 82
force they will be borne into one place only, either
into that above if the ascending bodies have gained
the mastery, or into that below if the descending
bodies are the more powerful. But if they do not
move along the same vertical line, they do not meet
with one another, and not meeting they will not be
capable of effecting any combination. But this is
absurd. So then, that which is in motion is not self-
moved.—Again, if what is moved is self-moved,[a] since 83
everything which causes motion does so either by
propelling or by dragging or by heaving up and
pressing down, the self-moved too, being the cause
of its own motion will have to cause motion either
by propelling or by dragging or by heaving up and
pressing down. But if it moves by propelling it will 84
be behind itself (for what propels is behind what is
propelled), and if by dragging it will be in front of
itself, and if by heaving and pressing, beneath itself.
But it is impossible to conceive of a thing being
either behind or before or beneath itself ; therefore

* With §§ 83-84 *cf. P.H.* iii. 68-69.

κινούμενον. εἰ δὲ μήτε ὑπ' ἄλλου κινεῖται τὸ κινούμενον μήτε ὑφ' ἑαυτοῦ, παρὰ δὲ ταῦτα οὐδὲν ἔστι,
ῥητέον μὴ κινεῖσθαι τὸ κινούμενον.

85 Κομίζεται δὲ καὶ ἄλλη τις ἐμβριθὴς ὑπόμνησις
εἰς τὸ μὴ εἶναι κίνησιν ὑπὸ Διοδώρου τοῦ Κρόνου,
δι' ἧς παρίστησιν ὅτι κινεῖται μὲν οὐδὲ ἕν, κεκίνηται δέ. καὶ μὴ κινεῖσθαι μέν, τοῦτο ἀκόλουθόν
86 ἐστι ταῖς κατ' αὐτὸν τῶν ἀμερῶν ὑποθέσεσιν. τὸ
γὰρ ἀμερὲς σῶμα ὀφείλει ἐν ἀμερεῖ τόπῳ περιέχεσθαι, καὶ διὰ τοῦτο μήτε ἐν αὐτῷ κινεῖσθαι
(ἐκπεπλήρωκε γὰρ αὐτόν, δεῖ δὲ τόπον ἔχειν
μείζονα τὸ κινησόμενον) μήτε ἐν ᾧ μὴ ἔστιν· οὔπω
γὰρ ἔστιν ἐν ἐκείνῳ, ἵνα καὶ ἐν αὐτῷ κινηθῇ.
ὥστε οὐδὲ κινεῖται. κεκίνηται δὲ κατὰ λόγον· τὸ
γὰρ πρότερον ἐν τῷδε τῷ τόπῳ θεωρούμενον,
τοῦτο ἐν ἑτέρῳ νῦν θεωρεῖται τόπῳ· ὅπερ οὐκ
ἂν ἐγεγόνει μὴ κινηθέντος αὐτοῦ. οὗτος μὲν οὖν
ὁ ἀνὴρ ἐπαρήγειν θελήσας τῷ οἰκείῳ δόγματι
ἄτοπόν τι προσήκατο· πῶς γὰρ οὐκ ἄτοπον τὸ
μηδενὸς κινουμένου λέγειν τι κεκινῆσθαι; οἱ δὲ
ἀπὸ τῆς σκέψεως ἐπ' ἴσης καὶ περὶ τοῦ κινεῖσθαι
καὶ περὶ τοῦ κεκινῆσθαι ἀποροῦντες οὐδὲν ἄτοπον
προσδέξονται, καθάπερ Διόδωρος προσήκατο.

87 πλὴν οὗτός γε τὸν περιφορητικὸν συνερωτᾷ λόγον
εἰς τὸ μὴ κινεῖσθαί τι, λέγων " εἰ κινεῖταί τι, ἤτοι
ἐν ᾧ ἔστι τόπῳ κινεῖται, ἢ ἐν ᾧ μὴ ἔστιν· οὔτε δὲ
ἐν ᾧ ἔστι, μένει γὰρ ἐν αὐτῷ, οὔτε ἐν ᾧ μὴ ἔστιν,
88 οὐ γὰρ ἔστιν ἐν αὐτῷ· οὐκ ἄρα κινεῖταί τι." καὶ
ὁ μὲν λόγος τοιοῦτος, ἡ δὲ παραμυθία τῶν λημ-
μάτων αὐτοῦ προφανής. δυοῖν γὰρ ὄντων τόπων,

---

[a] Cf. § 48.   [b] Cf. P.H. ii. 242, 245; iii. 71.

what is moved is not self-moved. But if what is moved is moved neither by another nor by itself, and besides these there is no other alternative, one must declare that what is moved is not in motion.

And another weighty argument for the non- 85 existence of motion is adduced by Diodorus Cronos,[a] by means of which he establishes that not a single thing *is* in motion, but *has been* in motion. And the fact that nothing is in motion follows from his assumptions of indivisibles. For the indivisible body must 86 be contained in an indivisible place and therefore must not move either in it (for it fills it up, but a thing which is to move must have a larger place) or in the place in which it is not ; for as yet it is not in this place so as to be moved therein ; consequently it *is* not in motion. But, according to reason, it *has been* in motion ; for that which was formerly observed in this place is now observed in another place, which would not have occurred if it had not been moved. Thus this man, in trying to support his own dogma, has admitted what is an absurdity ; for how is it other than absurd to say that while nothing moves something has moved ? But the Sceptics, being equally in doubt about being in motion and having been in motion, will not assent to any absurdity, such as Diodorus has admitted.—This man, however, pro- 87 pounds the familiar argument [b] to show that nothing moves, when he says—" If a thing moves, it moves either in the place where it is or in that where it is not ; but it moves neither in the place where it is (for it remains therein) nor in that where it is not (for it does not exist therein) ; therefore nothing moves." Such then is his argument, and the method of proving 88 its premises is obvious. For as there are two

SEXTUS EMPIRICUS

ἑνὸς μὲν τοῦ ἐν ᾧ τι ἔστιν, δευτέρου δὲ τοῦ ἐν ᾧ μὴ
ἔστιν, καὶ τρίτου παρὰ τούτους μηδ' ἐπινοεῖσθαι
δυναμένου, δεῖ τὸ κινούμενον, εἰ ὄντως κινεῖται,
ἐν τῷ ἑτέρῳ τούτων κινεῖσθαι· ἐν γὰρ τῷ ἀν-
89 επινοήτῳ οὐκ ἂν κινοῖτο. ἐν ᾧ μὲν οὖν ἔστι τόπῳ
οὐ κινεῖται· ἐκπεπλήρωκε γὰρ αὐτόν· καὶ ἐφ'
ὅσον ἔστιν ἐν αὐτῷ, μένει· μένον δὲ ἐν αὐτῷ οὐ
κινεῖται. ἐν ᾧ δὲ μὴ ἔστι, πάλιν ἀδύνατον αὐτὸ
κινεῖσθαι· ὅπου γάρ τι μὴ ἔστιν, ἐκεῖ οὔτε δρᾶσαί
τι οὔτε παθεῖν δύναται, κατὰ ταὐτὰ δὲ οὐδὲ
κινεῖσθαι, καὶ ὡς οὐκ ἄν τις λέγοι τὸν ἐν Ῥόδῳ
ὄντα ἐν Ἀθήναις κινεῖσθαι, οὕτως οὐδὲ κοινῶς
πᾶν σῶμα ἐρεῖ ἐν ἐκείνῳ κινεῖσθαι τῷ τόπῳ ἔνθα
90 μὴ ἔστιν. ὅθεν εἰ δύο εἰσὶ τόποι, ὅ τε ἐν ᾧ ἔστι
καὶ ἐν ᾧ μὴ ἔστι, δέδεικται δ' ἐν μηδετέρῳ τούτων
δυνάμενον κινεῖσθαι τὸ κινούμενον, οὐκ ἂν εἴη τὸ
κινούμενον.

Τοιαύτη μὲν καὶ ἡ τοῦ λόγου παραμυθία,
ποικίλως δὲ καὶ ὑπὸ πολλῶν ἀντείρηται, ὧν τὰς
91 ἐνστάσεις παρακειμένως ἐκθησόμεθα. καὶ δὴ ἔνιοι
μὲν ἀδύνατον εἶναί φασι τῶν συντελεστικῶν
ἀληθῶν ὄντων ψευδῆ εἶναι τὰ παρατατικὰ τούτων,
ἀλλ' ἀληθῆ καθεστάναι, καὶ ψευδῶν ὄντων ἀνα-
λόγως ψευδῆ. οὐ γὰρ ἔστι τι πέρας, ἔστι κἀκεῖνο,
καὶ τοῦ μὴ ὄντος οὐκ ἂν εἴη τι πέρας. εἰ δὲ πέρας
ὑπῆρχε τοῦ παρατατικοῦ τὸ συντελεστικόν, ἀνάγκη
ἄρα τοῦ συντελεστικοῦ ὄντος, ὃ δὴ πέρας ἐστίν,
εἶναι καὶ τὸ παρατατικὸν οὗ τοῦτο πέρας ἐστίν.
92 καὶ ὡς οὐδέν ἐστι τὸ γεγενῆσθαι συντελεστικὸν

---

[a] This (as Heintz points out) must be the meaning, though not clearly expressed in the Greek. (The insertion of τούτων ἐκεῖνα after ψ. ὄντων would help.)

places,—one being that wherein a thing is and the second that wherein it is not, and it being impossible to conceive a third place in addition to these two,—the thing in motion, if it really moves, must move in one or other of these places ; for it will not move in an inconceivable place. Now it does not move in the place wherein it is, for it fills it up ; and, so long as it exists therein, it remains ; and remaining therein it does not move. And it is likewise impossible for it 89 to move in the place wherein it is not ; for where a thing does not exist, there it cannot either effect anything or be affected, and in the same way it cannot move ; and just as no one could say that he who is in Rhodes is moving in Athens, so too in general one will not say of any body that it moves in that place where it does not exist. Hence, if there are two 90 places, that wherein it exists and that wherein it exists not, and it has been proved that the moving object cannot move in either of them, the moving object will not exist.

Such, then, is the method of proving his argument ; but it is opposed by many in various ways, and we shall in the next place expound their objections. Thus some assert that if preterites are true it is 91 impossible that their presents should be false, and they must be true ; and similarly the preterites must be false when the presents are false.[a] For that thing whereof a limit exists, exists also itself, and of a thing non-existent no limit will exist. And if the preterite is a limit of the present, it is therefore necessary that when the preterite, which is a limit, exists the present also, whereof it is the limit, should exist. And just 92 as the preterite " to have become " is nothing if the

μὴ ὄντος ἀληθοῦς τοῦ γίνεσθαι παρατατικοῦ, καὶ
ὃν τρόπον οὐδέν ἐστι τὸ ἐφθάρθαι συντελεστικὸν
μὴ προϋπάρξαντος τοῦ φθείρεσθαι παρατατικοῦ,
ὧδε ἀδύνατόν ἐστι, μὴ ὄντος ἀληθοῦς τοῦ κινεῖσθαι παρατατικοῦ, ἀληθὲς εἶναι τὸ κεκινῆσθαι
συντελεστικόν.

93 Ἄλλοι δέ φασι δύνασθαί τι ἐν ᾧ περιέχεται
τόπῳ κινεῖσθαι· αἱ γὰρ περὶ τοῖς κνώδαξιν
εἰλούμεναι σφαῖραι καὶ οἱ περιδινούμενοι ἄξονες
καὶ ἤδη τὰ τύμπανα καὶ οἱ κεραμευτικοὶ τροχοὶ
καὶ ἄλλα παμπληθῆ τούτοις ἐοικότα σώματα
κινεῖται μέν, ἐν ᾧ δὲ ἔστι τόπῳ κινεῖται, ὥστε
ψεῦδος εἶναι ἕν τι τοῦ λόγου λῆμμα, τὸ μὴ
94 κινεῖσθαί τι ἐν ᾧ ἔστι τόπῳ.   ἄλλοι δὲ παρὰ
τὴν ἔννοιαν τῆς κινήσεως ἠρωτῆσθαί φασι τὸν
λόγον. τὸ γὰρ κινούμενον νοεῖται σὺν τόπῳ τῷ
ἀφ' οὗ κινεῖται καὶ τῷ εἰς ὃν κινεῖται· διόπερ ὅταν
λέγῃ ὁ Διόδωρος " εἰ κινεῖταί τι, ἤτοι ἐν ᾧ ἔστι
τόπῳ κινεῖται ἢ ἐν ᾧ μὴ ἔστιν," μοχθηρόν τι καὶ
παρὰ τὴν τῆς κινήσεως νόησιν λέγει, παρόσον τὸ
κινούμενον οὔτε ἐν ᾧ ἔστι τόπῳ κινεῖται οὔτε ἐν
ᾧ μὴ ἔστιν, ἀλλὰ κατ' ἀμφοτέρων, τοῦ τε ἀφ' οὗ
95 κινεῖται καὶ τοῦ εἰς ὅν.   ἦσαν δὲ οἱ καὶ
ἀμφιβολίαν διεστέλλοντο. τὸ γὰρ ἐν τόπῳ περιέχεσθαι δύο σημαίνειν φασίν, ἓν μὲν ἐν τόπῳ τῷ
κατὰ πλάτος, ὡς ὅταν λέγωμέν τινα ἐν Ἀλεξαν-
δρείᾳ εἶναι, ἕτερον δὲ ἐν τόπῳ τῷ κατ' ἀκρίβειαν,
καθὸ κἀμοῦ λέγοιτ' ἂν εἶναι τόπος ὁ περιτετυπωκὼς
τὴν ἐπιφάνειάν μου τοῦ σώματος ἀήρ, καὶ ἀμφο-
ρεὺς τοῦ ἐν αὐτῷ περιεχομένου προσαγορεύεται
τόπος. διχῶς δὴ καλουμένου νῦν τοῦ τόπου, φασὶ

<hr />

a With §§ 93-95 cf. *P.H.* iii. 72-75.

present " to become " is not true, and just as the preterite " to have perished " is nothing if the present " to perish " has not pre-existed, so too it is impossible that the preterite " to have moved " should be true if the present " to move " is not true.

Others assert [a] that a thing can move in the place 93 wherein it is contained ; for the balls which spin round their pivots, and revolving axles, and drums,[b] too, and potters' wheels, and hosts of other bodies similar to these, move but move in the place wherein they are, so that one premiss of the argument—that nothing moves in the place where it is—is false.—And 94 others assert that the argument is propounded contrary to the conception of motion. For the moving object is conceived in conjunction with the place wherefrom it moves and that whereto it moves ; consequently, when Diodorus says " If a thing moves, it moves either in the place wherein it is or in that wherein it is not " he says what is unsound and contrary to the conception of motion, inasmuch as the moving object does not move either in the place wherein it, or in that wherein it is not, but through both places—both that wherefrom and that whereto it moves.—And there have been some who have dis- 95 cerned an ambiguity. For " being contained in a place," they say, has two meanings,—in the one " in a place " is used in the broad sense, as when we say of a man that he is " in Alexandria," [c] and in the other it is used of place in the exact sense, as the air which is moulded round the surface of my body might be said to be my place, and the jar is called the place of what is contained in it. So as " place " is now applied in two ways, they assert that the

[b] Cf. §§ 51, 103. [c] Cf. § 15.

δύνασθαι τὸ κινούμενον ἐν ᾧ ἔστι τόπῳ κινεῖσθαι,
τῷ κατὰ πλάτος, ἔχοντι διάστημα καθ᾽ ὃ γενήσεται
96 τὰ τῆς κινήσεως.   τινὲς δὲ καὶ ἀπέραντον εἶναι
ᾠήθησαν τὸν τοῦ Διοδώρου λόγον, ἐπείπερ ἄρχεται
μὲν ἀπὸ διεζευγμένου, ψευδοποιεῖ δὲ τοῦτο διὰ τῶν
ἑξῆς, ἑκάτερον τῶν ἐν αὐτῷ δεικνὺς ψεῦδος, τό τε ἐν
ᾧ μὴ ἔστι τι τόπῳ κινεῖσθαι καὶ τὸ ἐν ᾧ ἔστιν.
97   Τοιαῦται μὲν αἱ πρὸς τὸν λόγον ἐνστάσεις,
δοκεῖ δὲ Διόδωρος πρὸς τὴν πρώτην εὐθὺς ὑπ-
ηντηκέναι διδάσκων ὅτι ἐνδέχεται τῶν συντελεστικῶν ἀληθῶν ὄντων τὰ τούτων παρατατικὰ ψευδῆ
τυγχάνειν. ἔστω γάρ τινα πρὸ ἐνιαυτοῦ γεγα-
μηκέναι καὶ ἕτερον μετ᾽ ἐνιαυτόν. οὐκοῦν ἐπὶ
τούτων τὸ μὲν " οὗτοι ἔγημαν " ἀξίωμα συντελεστικὸν ὂν ἀληθές ἐστι, τὸ δ᾽ " οὗτοι γαμοῦσι "
παρατατικὸν καθεστὼς ψεῦδός ἐστιν· ὅτε γὰρ
οὗτος ἐγάμει, οὔπω οὗτος ἐγάμει, καὶ ὅτε οὗτος
ἐγάμει, οὐκέτι οὗτος ἐγάμει. τότε δ᾽ ἂν ἦν
ἀληθὲς ἐπ᾽ αὐτῶν τὸ οὗτοι[1] γαμοῦσιν, εἰ ὁμόσε
ἐγάμουν. δύναται οὖν τοῦ συντελεστικοῦ ἀληθοῦς
98 ὄντος ψεῦδος εἶναι τὸ τούτου παρατατικόν. τοιοῦτο
δέ ἐστι καὶ τὸ " Ἑλένη τρεῖς ἔσχεν ἄνδρας "· οὔτε
γὰρ ὅτε Μενέλαον εἶχεν ἐν Σπάρτῃ ἄνδρα οὔθ᾽
ὅτε Πάριν ἐν Ἰλίῳ, οὔθ᾽ ὅτε θανόντος τούτου
Δηιφόβῳ ἐγαμήθη, ἀληθές ἐστι τὸ παρατατικὸν
τὸ " τρεῖς ἔχει ἄνδρας," ἀληθοῦς ὄντος τοῦ συν-
99 τελεστικοῦ τοῦ " τρεῖς ἔσχεν ἄνδρας." σοφίζεται
δὲ ἐν τούτοις ὁ Διόδωρος, καὶ παρ᾽ ἀμφιβολίαν
βούλεται ἡμᾶς πλανᾶν. τὸ γὰρ " οὗτοι ἔγημαν "

[1] οὗτοι NLE: ὅτι cet., Bekk.

moving object can move in the place wherein it is—
place in the broad sense,—as this possesses extension
through which the processes of motion may take
place.[a]—And some have thought that the argument 96
of Diodorus is inconclusive, since it begins with a
disjunctive premiss, and falsifies this by means of the
succeeding statements, in that it proves that both its
clauses are false,—both that a thing moves in the
place where it is not and ⟨that it does so⟩ where it is.

Such are the objections against the argument ; but 97
Diodorus seems to have answered the first one [b] at
once by explaining that when preterites are true their
presents admit of being false. For suppose that a
certain man married a year before and another a year
after. Then, in the case of these men, the proposition
" these men married," which is a preterite, is true,
but " these men are marrying," which is a present,
is false ; for when this man was marrying that man
was not yet marrying, and when that man was marrying this man was no longer marrying. And in their
case the proposition "these men are marrying" would
have been true of them only if they had been marrying simultaneously. It is possible, then, for the present
to be false when the preterite is true. Of the same 98
sort, too, is the proposition " Helen had three husbands," for neither when she had Menelaus as her
husband in Sparta, nor when she had Paris in Ilium,
nor when, after his death, she married Deïphobus,[c]
is the present—" she has three husbands "—true,
though the preterite—" she had three husbands "—
is true. But here Diodorus is using sophistry and 99
wishes to deceive us by ambiguity. For the proposi-

[b] See §§ 91 ff.
[c] A brother of Paris (son of Priam, king of Troy).

δύο σημαίνει, ἓν μὲν πληθυντικὸν καὶ ἴσον τῷ
" οὗτοι συνέγημαν," ὅπερ ἐστὶ ψεῦδος, ἕτερον δὲ
τὸ κατὰ περίληψιν ἑνικοῦ πράγματος ἐγκεκλιμένου
ἀπὸ τοῦ " οὗτος ἔγημεν " καὶ ἑτέρου ἑνικοῦ τοῦ
" οὗτος ἔγημεν," ὧν πάλιν ἑνικῶν τὰ παρατατικά
ἐστιν ἀληθῆ, τὸ " οὗτος γαμεῖ " καὶ τὸ " οὗτος
γαμεῖ "· ἐπ' ἀμφοτέρων γὰρ ἀληθῆ γέγονε ταῦτα.
100 ἀμήχανον οὖν ἐστι τῶν παρατατικῶν ψευδῶν
ὄντων ἀληθῆ εὑρίσκεσθαι τὰ τούτων συντελεστικά,
ἀλλ' ἀνάγκη συναναιρεῖσθαι ἢ συνυπάρχειν τὰ ἕτερα
τοῖς ἑτέροις.

Νὴ Δί', ἀλλ' εἰς τὴν αὐτὴν ὑπόθεσιν καὶ ἑτέραν
ὁ Διόδωρος κομίζεται παραμυθίαν, σαφεστέρῳ
101 χρώμενος ὑποδείγματι. βαλλέσθω γάρ, φησί,
σφαῖρα εἰς τὸν ὑπερκείμενον ὄροφον. οὐκοῦν ἐν
τῷ μεταξὺ τῆς βολῆς χρόνῳ τὸ μὲν παρατατικὸν
ἀξίωμα " ἅπτεται ἡ σφαῖρα τῆς ὀροφῆς " ψεῦδός
ἐστιν· ἔτι γὰρ ἐπιφέρεται. ὅταν δὲ ἅψηται τῆς
ὀροφῆς, γίνεται ἀληθὲς τὸ συντελεστικόν, τὸ
" ἥψατο ἡ σφαῖρα τῆς ὀροφῆς." ἐνδέχεται ἄρα
ψεύδους ὄντος τοῦ παρατατικοῦ ἀληθὲς ὑπάρχειν
τὸ συντελεστικόν, καὶ διὰ τοῦτο μὴ κινεῖσθαι μέν
τι παρατατικῶς κεκινῆσθαι δὲ συντελεστικῶς.
102 μήποτε δὲ κἀνταῦθα πλανᾶται. τὸ γὰρ παρατατικὸν τὸ " ἅπτεται ἡ σφαῖρα τῆς ὀροφῆς "
γίνεται ἀληθὲς οὐχ ὅτε φέρεται ἐν τῷ μεταξὺ ἀέρι
ἡ σφαῖρα, ἀλλ' ὅτε ἄρχεται ἅπτεσθαι τῆς ὀροφῆς.
ὅταν δὲ τερματίσασα τὴν ψαῦσιν ὑπονοστήσῃ, τότε
καὶ τὸ συντελεστικὸν γίνεται ἀληθές, τὸ " ἥψατο
ἡ σφαῖρα τῆς ὀροφῆς." ἄτοπος οὖν ἐστιν ὁ
Διόδωρος τοῦ μὲν κεκινῆσθαι περιεχόμενος ὡς
ἀληθοῦς, τοῦ δὲ κινεῖσθαι ἀφιστάμενος ὡς ψεύδους,
260

tion " these men married " has two senses, of which the one is plural and equivalent to " these men married together," which is false, but the other is formed by the combination of one singular proposition "this man married," and another singular proposition " that man married," and of these singulars, again, the presents are true, namely, "this man is marrying" and " that man is marrying " ; for these statements are true in both cases. It is, then, impossible, if the 100 presents are false, that their preterites should be found to be true ; and of necessity both of them must either be abolished together or co-exist along with each other.

Nevertheless, Diodorus brings forward another argument against the same assumption, in which he employs a clearer example. Let a ball, he 101 says, be thrown on to an overhanging roof. Then, at the point of time that is midway in the throw, the proposition " the ball touches the roof " is false ; for it is still on its way. But when it has touched the roof, the preterite " the ball has touched the roof " becomes true ; therefore it is possible for the preterite to be true when the present is false, and therefore possible for a thing not " to be moving " in the present but " to have moved " in the preterite. But I suspect 102 that here too he goes astray. For the present—" the ball touches the roof "—is true not when the ball is travelling in mid air but when it begins to touch the roof. But when it comes down again, after ending its contact, then the preterite becomes true—" the ball touched the roof." Therefore it is absurd of Diodorus to accept " to have moved " as true and to reject " to

δέον ἢ ἀμφοτέροις συγκατατίθεσθαι ἢ ἀμφοτέρων
ἀφίστασθαι.

103 Οἱ δὲ φάσκοντες δύνασθαί τι κινεῖσθαι ἐν ᾧ ἔστι
τόπῳ, καὶ τοῦτο μὲν τὰς σφαίρας τοῦτο δὲ τοὺς
ἄξονας καὶ τὰ τύμπανα παρατιθέμενοι, οὐ λύουσι
τὴν ἀπορίαν ἀλλ᾽ ὁμοίως ἐγκυλίονται αὐτῇ. ἕκαστον γὰρ τῶν τοιούτων σωμάτων, καθὼς καὶ ἀνώτερον ὑπεδείκνυμεν, καθ᾽ ὁλότητα μὲν μένει ἐν τῷ
αὐτῷ τόπῳ, κατὰ μέρη δὲ ἀλλάττει τοὺς τόπους,
τοῦ μὲν ἄνω ἀντιλαμβάνοντος τὸν τοῦ κάτω τόπον,
104 τοῦ δὲ κάτω τὸν τοῦ ἄνω. εἰ δὲ τοῦτο, μένει τὰ
τῆς ἀπορίας. ἕκαστον γὰρ τῶν τοιούτων σωμάτων
μέρος ἤτοι ἐν ᾧ ἔστι τόπῳ κινεῖται ἢ ἐν ᾧ μὴ
ἔστιν· οὔτε δὲ ἐν ᾧ ἔστιν, ὡς παρεστήσαμεν, οὔτε
ἐν ᾧ μὴ ἔστιν, ὡς ἐδείξαμεν· οὐκ ἄρα κινεῖται.

105 Ἀλλ᾽ ἀκολούθως[1] ἔφασκόν τινες παρὰ τὴν ἔννοιαν
τοῦ κινουμένου κεκομίσθαι τὸν λόγον· νοεῖσθαι γὰρ
τὸ κινούμενον ὡς δυοῖν ἐχόμενον τόπων, τοῦ τ᾽ ἐξ
οὗ κινεῖται τοῦ τ᾽ εἰς ὃν μετέρχεται. ῥᾴδιον δέ
ἐστι καὶ πρὸς τούτους ὑπαντῶντας λέγειν ὅτι κἂν
τοιαύτην εἶναι συμβεβήκῃ τὴν τοῦ κινουμένου
νόησιν, οὐδὲν πρὸς τὸ προκείμενον διὰ τὸ μὴ περὶ
τῆς νοήσεως τοῦ κινεῖσθαι νῦν εἶναι τὴν ζήτησιν
τοῖς ἀπορητικοῖς προηγουμένως, ἀλλὰ περὶ τῆς
ὑπάρξεως, ὑπὲρ ἧς οὐδὲν εἰρήκασιν οἱ τῇ τοιαύτῃ
106 χρησάμενοι ἐνστάσει. οὐ μὴν ἀλλὰ κἂν τὸν λόγον
ἀνατρέψωμεν, οὐδὲν ἕξουσιν εἰπεῖν πρὸς ἡμᾶς. ὅταν
γὰρ φάσκωσι τὸ κινούμενον δυοῖν ἔχεσθαι τόπων,
τοῦ τε ἐν ᾧ ἔστι καὶ τοῦ εἰς ὃν φέρεται, πευσόμεθ᾽

----
[1] ἀκολούθως most mss.: ἀνακολούθως al., Bekk.

move " as false, when he ought either to assent to both or to reject both.

And those who declare that a thing can move in the 103 place where it is,[a] by alleging the examples now of balls and now of axles and drums, fail to solve the difficulty and are equally entangled in it. For, as we have shown previously,[b] each of these bodies remains in the same place as a whole but in respect of its parts it changes places, the part above occupying instead the place below and the part below the place above. And if so, the difficulty remains. For each 104 part of these bodies moves either in the place where it is or in that where it is not ; but it moves neither in the place where it is, as we have established, nor in that where it is not, as we have proved ; therefore it does not move.

But, in the next place, some have asserted [c] that 105 the argument thus brought forward is contrary to the conception of a moving object ; for a moving object is conceived as occupying two places, both that wherefrom it moves and that into which it passes. But in answer to these, too, it is easy to say that, even if it is the fact that the notion of the moving object is of this kind, it has no bearing on our problem because the question now before the Doubters is chiefly concerned not with the conception of motion but with its real existence, and about this those who make that sort of objection have said nothing. And, moreover, 106 even if we overthrow the argument they will have nothing to say against us. For when they assert that the moving object occupies two places, both that wherein it is and that whereinto it moves, we shall ask

a With §§ 103-110 cf. P.H. iii. 72-75 ; and see § 93 supra.
    b See § 52 supra.   c See § 94 supra.

αὐτῶν πότε μέτεισιν ἀπὸ τοῦ ἐν ᾧ ἔστι τόπου τὸ
κινούμενον εἰς τὸν ἕτερον; ἆρά γε ὅτε ἐν τῷ
πρώτῳ ἔστιν ἢ ὅτε ἐν τῷ δευτέρῳ; ἀλλ' ὅτε μὲν
ἐν τῷ πρώτῳ τόπῳ ἔστιν, οὐ μετέρχεται εἰς ἕτερον·
107 ἔτι γὰρ ἐν τῷ πρώτῳ ἔστιν. ὅτε δὲ οὐκ ἔστιν ἐν
τούτῳ ἀλλ' ἐν τῷ δευτέρῳ, πάλιν οὐ μετέρχεται
ἀλλὰ μετελήλυθεν ἤδη· τῶν γὰρ ἀμηχάνων ἐστὶ καὶ
τῶν ἀνεπινοήτων τὸ μετελθεῖν τι ἐξ ἐκείνου τοῦ
τόπου τοῦ ἐν ᾧ μὴ ἔστιν. ὥστε κἂν τοιαύτην
ἔχωμεν τοῦ κινουμένου νόησιν, μένει οὐδὲν ἧττον ἡ
ἀρχῆθεν ἀπορία.

108 Καὶ μὴν οἱ λέγοντες διχῶς καλεῖσθαι τὸν τόπον,
ἐν πλάτει τε καὶ κατ' ἀκρίβειαν, διὰ δὲ τοῦτο καὶ
τὴν κίνησιν ἐν τῷ κατὰ πλάτος νοουμένῳ τόπῳ
δύνασθαι συμβαίνειν, οὐ πρὸς νοῦν ὑπαντῶσιν.
προηγεῖται γὰρ τοῦ κατὰ πλάτος νοουμένου τόπου
ὁ κατ' ἀκρίβειαν, καὶ ἀδύνατόν ἐστιν ἐν τῷ κατὰ
πλάτος τόπῳ κινηθῆναί τι μὴ προκινηθὲν ἐν τῷ
109 κατ' ἀκρίβειαν· ὡς γὰρ οὗτος περιεκτικός ἐστι τοῦ
κινουμένου σώματος, οὕτως ὁ κατὰ πλάτος τόπος
σὺν τῷ κινουμένῳ σώματι καὶ τὸν κατ' ἀκρίβειαν
τόπον περιέσχηκεν. καθάπερ οὖν οὐδεὶς δύναται
ἐν σταδιαίῳ κινεῖσθαι διαστήματι μὴ προκινηθεὶς
ἐν τῷ πηχυαίῳ διαστήματι, ὧδε τῶν ἀδυνάτων
ἐστὶν ἐν τῷ κατὰ πλάτος τόπῳ κινεῖσθαι μὴ κινού-
110 μενον ἐν τῷ κατ' ἀκρίβειαν. ἠρώτηκε δὲ ὁ Διόδωρος τὸν ἐκκείμενον λόγον κατὰ τῆς κινήσεως τοῦ
κατ' ἀκρίβειαν ἐχόμενος τόπου· τοίνυν ἀναιρου-
μένης ἐπὶ τούτου τῆς κινήσεως οὐθεὶς ἀπολείπεται
λόγος ἐπὶ τοῦ κατὰ πλάτος τόπου.

Τὸ μὲν γὰρ μοχθηρὸν εἶναι τὸν λόγον φάσκειν διὰ

them—" When does the moving object pass over from the place wherein it is to the other place ? Is it when it is in the first place or when it is in the second ? " But when it is in the first place it does not pass over into the other ; for it is still in the first. And when 107 it is not in this but in the second, once again it is not passing over but has already passed over ; for it is a thing impossible and inconceivable that anything should pass over from that place wherein it does not exist. So that, even if we have this sort of conception of the moving object, the original difficulty remains none the less.

Further, those who say that the term " place " has 108 two senses,[a] the " broad " sense and the " exact," and that therefore motion can occur in place when conceived as " broad," are giving an answer that is not to the purpose. For place conceived as exact precedes place conceived as broad, and it is impossible for anything to move in broad place if it has not moved before in exact place ; for as the latter serves 109 to contain the moving body, so the broad place contains, along with the moving body, the exact place as well. As, then, no one can move over a distance of a stade [b] without first having moved over a distance of a cubit, so it is impossible to move over broad place without moving over exact place. And when Dio- 110 dorus propounded the argument against motion which has been set forth he was keeping to the exact sense of place ; so if in its case motion is abolished, there is no argument left in the case of place in the broad sense.

Now it is perfectly foolish to say that the argument

[a] See § 95 *supra.*
[b] About 200 yards, or nearly a furlong. A cubit = $\frac{1}{2}$ yard.

τὸ ἀπὸ διεζευγμένου ἄρχεσθαι καὶ τοῦτο ψευδοποιεῖν
111 τὸ διεζευγμένον τελέως ἐστὶ ληρῶδες. κατ᾽ ἀκολουθίαν γὰρ γέγονε τὰ τῆς ἐρωτήσεως, καὶ δύναμιν
ἔχει τοιαύτην '' εἰ κινεῖταί τι, κατὰ τὸν ἕτερον τῶν
προειρημένων τρόπων ὀφείλει κινεῖσθαι· οὐχὶ δέ γε
τὸ δεύτερον· οὐκ ἄρα τὸ πρῶτον.'' εἰ γὰρ ὄντος
τοῦ πρώτου ἔστι τὸ δεύτερον, τοῦ δευτέρου μὴ
ὄντος οὐδὲ τὸ πρῶτον ἔσται. ὅπερ καὶ κατὰ τὰς
αὐτῶν τῶν διαλεκτικῶν ὑποθέσεις ὑγιές ἐστιν.
112 Ταῦτα μὲν οὖν πρὸς τὰ ἀντιλεγόμενα τῷ ὑπὸ
Διοδώρου κομισθέντι λόγῳ ἀναγκαῖον ἦν εἰπεῖν.
κομίζει δὲ καὶ ἄλλους τινὰς λόγους οὐχ οὕτως
ἐμβριθεῖς ἀλλὰ σοφιστικωτέρους, ὧν τὴν ἔκθεσιν
ποιησόμεθα εἰς τὸ δύνασθαι κατὰ τὰς ζητήσεις
ἕκαστον αὐτῶν ἐκκλίνειν. εὐθέως γάρ φησι τὸ
κινούμενον ἐν τόπῳ ἔστιν, τὸ δὲ ἐν τόπῳ ὂν οὐ
113 κινεῖται· τὸ ἄρα κινούμενον οὐ κινεῖται. διττῆς δὲ
οὔσης κινήσεως, μιᾶς μὲν τῆς κατ᾽ ἐπικράτειαν
δευτέρας δὲ τῆς κατ᾽ εἰλικρίνειαν, καὶ κατ᾽ ἐπικράτειαν μὲν ὑπαρχούσης ἐφ᾽ ἧς τῶν πλειόνων
κινουμένων μερῶν τοῦ σώματος ὀλίγα ἠρεμεῖ, κατ᾽
εἰλικρίνειαν δὲ ἐφ᾽ ἧς πάντα κινεῖται τὰ τοῦ σώματος μέρη, δοκεῖ τούτων τῶν δυοῖν κινήσεων ἡ
κατ᾽ ἐπικράτειαν προηγεῖσθαι τῆς κατ᾽ εἰλικρίνειαν.
114 ἵνα γάρ τι εἰλικρινῶς κινηθῇ, τουτέστιν ὅλον δι᾽
ὅλου, πρότερον ὀφείλει νοεῖσθαι κατ᾽ ἐπικράτειαν
κινούμενον, ὃν τρόπον ἵνα τις κατ᾽ εἰλικρίνειαν γένηται πολιός, ὀφείλει κατ᾽ ἐπικράτειαν προπεπο-
λιῶσθαι, καὶ ἵνα τις κατ᾽ εἰλικρίνειαν ληφθῇ σωρός,
ὀφείλει κατ᾽ ἐπικράτειαν γεγονέναι σωρός· κατὰ

is unsound [a] because of its beginning with a disjunctive premiss and asserting the falsity of this premiss. For the steps in the argument are in logical sequence 111 and the force they have is this,—" If a thing moves, it must move in one or other of the ways stated above ; but the second ⟨clause⟩ is not ⟨true⟩ ; therefore the first is not (true)." For if the second is true when the first is true, when the second is not true the first will not be true either. And this is sound according to the assumptions of the Dialecticians themselves.

These observations, then, it was necessary to make 112 in answer to the objections made against the argument brought forward by Diodorus. And he also brings forward other arguments which are not so weighty but more sophistical, and of these we shall give an exposition so as to be able to avoid each of them in our investigations. For instance, he says, the moving object is in a place, and that which is in a place does not move ; therefore the moving object does not move. And motion being twofold,—the 113 one sort that of the major portion, the second sort absolute,—and that of the major portion being the sort in which while most parts of the body are in motion a few are at rest, and the absolute sort that in which all the parts of the body are in motion,—it seems that of these two motions that of the major portion precedes the absolute kind. For in order 114 that a thing should move absolutely,—that is, as a whole wholly,—it must first be conceived as moving in respect of its major portion ; just as, in order that a man may become completely grey-headed he must first become grey as to the major part, and in order that a complete heap may be obtained, the major part of a heap must first be formed ; in much the

τὸν ὅμοιον τρόπον ἡγεῖσθαι δεῖ τῆς κατ᾽ εἰλικρίνειαν κινήσεως τὴν κατ᾽ ἐπικράτειαν· ἐπίτασις
γὰρ τῆς κατ᾽ ἐπικράτειάν ἐστιν ἡ κατ᾽ εἰλικρίνειαν.
115 οὐχὶ δέ γε ἔστι τις κατ᾽ ἐπικράτειαν κίνησις,
ὡς παραστήσομεν· τοίνυν οὐδ᾽ ἡ κατ᾽ εἰλικρίνειαν
γενήσεται.   ὑποκείσθω γὰρ ἐκ τριῶν ἀμερῶν
συνεστὼς σῶμα, δυοῖν μὲν κινουμένων ἑνὸς δὲ
ἀκινητίζοντος· τοῦτο γὰρ ἡ κατ᾽ ἐπικράτειαν ἀπ-
116 αιτεῖ κίνησις. οὐκοῦν εἰ προσθείημεν τέταρτον
ἀμερὲς ἀκινητίζον τούτῳ τῷ σώματι, πάλιν γενήσεται κίνησις. εἴπερ γὰρ τὸ ἐκ τριῶν ἀμερῶν
συγκείμενον σῶμα, δυοῖν μὲν κινουμένων ἑνὸς δὲ
ἀκινητίζοντος, κινεῖται, καὶ τετάρτου προστεθέντος
ἀμεροῦς κινήσεται· ἰσχυρότερα γὰρ τὰ τρί᾽ ἀμερῆ[1]
μεθ᾽ ὧν πρότερον ἐκινεῖτο, τοῦ προστεθέντος ἑνὸς
ἀμεροῦς. ἀλλ᾽ εἴπερ τὸ ἐκ τεσσάρων ἀμερῶν
συγκείμενον σῶμα κινεῖται, κινήσεται καὶ τὸ ἐκ
πέντε· ἰσχυρότερα γάρ ἐστι τὰ τέσσαρ᾽ ἀμερῆ, μεθ᾽
ὧν πρότερον ἐκινεῖτο, τοῦ προστεθέντος ἀμεροῦς.
117 καὶ εἰ τὸ ἐκ τῶν πέντε συγκείμενον κινεῖται,
πάντως καὶ ἕκτου προσελθόντος ἀμεροῦς κινήσεται,
ἰσχυροτέρων ὄντων τῶν πέντε παρὰ τὸ ἕν. καὶ
οὕτω μέχρι μυρίων ἀμερῶν προέρχεται ὁ Διόδωρος,
δεικνὺς ὅτι ἀνυπόστατός ἐστιν ἡ κατ᾽ ἐπικράτειαν
κίνησις· ἄτοπον γάρ, φησί, τὸ λέγειν κατ᾽ ἐπικράτειαν κινεῖσθαι σῶμα ἐφ᾽ οὗ ἐνακισχίλια ἐνα-
κόσια ἐνενήκοντα ὀκτὼ ἀκινητίζει ἀμερῆ καὶ δύο
μόνον κινεῖται. ὥστε οὐδὲν κατ᾽ ἐπικράτειαν
κινεῖται. εἰ δὲ τοῦτο, οὐδὲ κατ᾽ εἰλικρίνειαν, ᾧ
ἕπεται τὸ μηδὲν κινεῖσθαι.
118   Ἀλλὰ γὰρ ἡ μὲν ἐπιχείρησις τοιαύτη πώς ἐστιν,

―――――
[1] τρί᾽ ἀμερῆ NE: τρία μέρη cet., Bekk.

same way motion as to the major part must precede absolute motion; for absolute motion is an intensification of that of the major part. But there does not 115 exist any motion of the major part, as we shall establish; neither, then, will absolute motion exist.—For let us assume the existence of a body composed of three indivisible parts, two being in motion and one motionless; for this is what motion of the major part demands. If, then, we were to add to this body a 116 fourth indivisible which is motionless, there will again be motion. For if the body composed of three indivisibles, two in motion and one motionless, moves, it will also move when a fourth indivisible is added; for the three indivisibles, with which it was moving before, are stronger than the one indivisible which is added. But if the body composed of four indivisibles moves, that composed of five will also move; for the four indivisibles, with which it was moving before, are stronger than the added indivisible. And if that 117 which is composed of five moves, it will certainly move also when a sixth indivisible is added, the five being stronger than the one. And in this way Diodorus proceeds up to ten thousand indivisibles, by way of proving that motion of the major part is nonexistent; for it is absurd, he says, to assert that a body moves as to its major part when it has 9998 of its indivisibles motionless and two only in motion. So that nothing moves as to its major part. And if so, neither does anything move absolutely; from which it follows that nothing moves.

Well then, such is the argumentation, but it seems 118

φαίνεται δὲ καὶ σοφιστικὴ καὶ παρακείμενον
ἔχουσα τὸν ἔλεγχον· ἅμα γὰρ τῇ τοῦ πρώτου
ἀμεροῦς προσθέσει οἴχεται ἡ κατ᾽ ἐπικράτειαν
κίνησις, δυοῖν κινουμένων ἀμερῶν δυοῖν δὲ ἀκινητιζόντων. ὅθεν τὰς μὲν τοιαύτας ἐπιχειρήσεις
παραιτητέον, ἐκείνοις δὲ μάλιστα χρηστέον τοῖς
119 λόγοις. εἰ κινεῖταί τι, νῦν κινεῖται· εἰ νῦν κινεῖται,
ἐν τῷ ἐνεστῶτι χρόνῳ κινεῖται· εἰ δὲ ἐν τῷ ἐνεστῶτι χρόνῳ κινεῖται, ἐν ἀμερεῖ χρόνῳ ἄρα κινεῖται. εἰ γὰρ μερίζεται ὁ ἐνεστὼς χρόνος, πάντως
εἰς τὸν παρῳχηκότα καὶ μέλλοντα μερισθήσεται,
120 καὶ οὕτως οὐκέτ᾽ ἔσται ἐνεστώς. εἰ δ᾽ ἐν ἀμερεῖ
χρόνῳ τι κινεῖται, ἀμερίστους τόπους διέρχεται. εἰ
δὲ ἀμερίστους τόπους διέρχεται, οὐ κινεῖται. ὅτε
γὰρ ἔστιν ἐν τῷ πρώτῳ ἀμερεῖ τόπῳ, οὐ κινεῖται·
ἔτι γὰρ ἔστιν ἐν τῷ πρώτῳ ἀμερεῖ τόπῳ. ὅτε δὲ
ἔστιν ἐν τῷ δευτέρῳ ἀμερεῖ τόπῳ, πάλιν οὐ κινεῖται
ἀλλὰ κεκίνηται. οὐκ ἄρα κινεῖταί τι.

121 Πρὸς τούτοις πᾶσα κίνησις τριῶν τινων ἔχεται,
καθάπερ σωμάτων τε καὶ τόπων καὶ χρόνων, σωμάτων μὲν τῶν κινουμένων, τόπων δὲ τῶν ἐν οἷς
ἡ κίνησις γίνεται, χρόνων δὲ τῶν καθ᾽ οὓς ἡ
122 κίνησις γίνεται. ἤτοι οὖν πάντων τούτων εἰς
ἀπείρους τεμνομένων τόπους καὶ χρόνους καὶ εἰς
ἄπειρα σώματα γίνεται ἡ κίνησις, ἢ πάντων εἰς
ἀμερὲς καὶ ἐλάχιστον καταληγόντων, ἢ τινῶν μὲν
εἰς ἄπειρον τεμνομένων τινῶν δὲ εἰς ἀμερὲς καὶ
ἐλάχιστον καταληγόντων. ἐάν τε δὲ πάντα εἰς
ἄπειρα τέμνηται ἐάν τε πάντα εἰς ἀμερὲς καταλήγῃ,[1]
ἄπορος ὁ περὶ τῆς κινήσεως εὑρεθήσεται λόγος.

---

[1] καταλήγῃ, ⟨ἐάν τε τινὰ μὲν εἰς ἄπειρον τέμνηται, τινὰ δὲ εἰς
ἀμερὲς καταλήγῃ,⟩ cj. Bekk.

sophistical and its refutation lies ready to hand ; for motion as to the major part disappears simultaneously with the addition of the first indivisible, when there are two indivisibles in motion and two motionless. Hence, one must set aside arguments of that sort, and use chiefly arguments such as these :—" If a thing 119 moves, it moves now ; if it moves now, it moves in the present time ; and if it moves in the present time, it moves, therefore, in an indivisible time. For if the present time is divided, it will certainly be divided into the past and future, and thus it will no longer be present. And if a thing moves in an indivisible time, 120 it passes through indivisible places. And if it passes through indivisible places, it does not move. For when it is in the first indivisible place it does not move ; for it is still in the first indivisible place. And when it is in the second indivisible place, again it does not move but it has moved.[a] Therefore nothing moves.

Furthermore, every motion involves three things,[b] 121 namely bodies and places and times,—bodies which are in motion, places wherein the motion occurs, times during which the motion occurs. Either then 122 the motion occurs while all these are being divided into an infinite number of places and times and into an infinite number of bodies, or while all come to end in what is indivisible and minimal, or while some of them are being divided *ad infinitum* and some coming to end in what is indivisible and minimal. But whether all are divided *ad infinitum* or all end in what is indivisible, the account given of motion will be found doubtful.

[a] *Cf.* §§ 48, 85, 143.
[b] *Cf.* §§ 139, 142, 154, 169.

SEXTUS EMPIRICUS

123 Τάξει δὲ ἀπὸ τῆς πρώτης στάσεως ποιώμεθα
τὴν ἐπιχείρησιν, καθ' ἣν πάντα εἰς ἄπειρον τέμνεται. καὶ δὴ οἱ προεστῶτες αὐτῆς φασὶ τὸ
κινούμενον σῶμα ὑφ' ἕνα καὶ τὸν αὐτὸν χρόνον
ἄθρουν μεριστὸν ἀνύειν διάστημα, καὶ οὐ τὸ πρῶτον
τοῦ διαστήματος ⟨μέρος⟩¹ πρῶτον ἐπιλαμβάνειν τῷ
πρώτῳ αὐτοῦ μέρει καὶ τὸ δεύτερον τῇ τάξει
δεύτερον, ἀλλ' ὑφ' ἓν τὸ ὅλον μεριστὸν διάστημα
καὶ ἀθρόως διέρχεσθαι. ὅπερ ἐστὶν ἄτοπον καὶ
124 ποικίλως τοῖς φαινομένοις μαχόμενον. εἰ γοῦν ἐπὶ
τῶν αἰσθητῶν τούτων σωμάτων νοήσωμέν τινα
κατὰ σταδιαίου τροχάζοντα διαστήματος, πάντως
ὑποπεσεῖται ὅτι ὀφείλει ὁ τοιοῦτος τὸ πρῶτον ἡμιστάδιον ἀνύειν πρῶτον καὶ τὸ δεύτερον τῇ τάξει
δεύτερον· τὸ γὰρ ὑφ' ἓν ἀξιοῦν τὸ ὅλον ἀνύειν τοῦ
125 σταδίου διάστημα τελέως ἄτοπον. καὶ εἰ τέμοιμεν
τὸ ἕτερον ἡμιστάδιον εἰς δύο τεταρτημόρια, πάντως
πρῶτον διελεύσεται τὸ πρῶτον τεταρτημόριον· καὶ
εἰ εἰς πλείονα τέμοιμεν, ὡσαύτως. κἂν κατὰ
πεφωτισμένου δὲ τροχάζῃ τοῦ σταδίου, φαίνεται
ὡς οὐχ ὑφ' ἓν σκιάσει τὸ στάδιον, ἀλλὰ τὸ μέν τι
126 πρῶτον μέρος τὸ δὲ δεύτερον τὸ δὲ τρίτον. καὶ εἰ
παραθέοι δὲ τῷ τοίχῳ μεμιλτωμένῃ τῇ χειρὶ τούτου
ἐφαπτόμενος, οὐχ ὑφ' ἕνα καὶ τὸν αὐτὸν χρόνον τὸν
ὅλον τοῦ σταδίου τοῖχον μιλτώσει ἀλλὰ κατὰ τάξιν,
καὶ κατὰ τὸ πρότερον πρότερον. ὅπερ οὖν ὁ λόγος
ἐπὶ τῶν αἰσθητῶν ἔδειξε πραγμάτων, τουτὶ καὶ
127 ἐπὶ τῶν νοητῶν προσδεκτέον ἐστὶν ἡμῖν. καὶ
ἄλλως δὲ ἔνεστι ταύτην ἀνελεῖν τὴν δόξαν, πολλαῖς
καὶ ποικίλαις εἰς τοῦτο χρωμένους ὑποθέσεσιν. ὑπο-

¹ ⟨μέρος⟩ add. NLE.

Taking them in order, let us commence our argu- 123
ment with the first view, according to which all are
divided *ad infinitum*. Now the champions of this
view[a] assert that the moving body at one and the
same time completes the whole of a divisible interval,
and does not occupy first the first part of the interval
with the first part of itself, and secondly in order the
second part, but passes through the whole divisible
interval all at once and completely. But this is
absurd and conflicts with apparent facts in a variety
of ways. Thus, if, in the case of our sensible bodies, 124
we conceive of a man running over a distance of a
stade, it will certainly be obvious that such a man
must first complete the first half-stade and secondly
in order the second ; for to claim that he completes
all at once the whole distance of a stade is perfectly
absurd. And if we were to divide one of the half- 125
stades into two quarters, he will certainly pass over
the first quarter first, and so likewise if we divide it
into further parts. And if he runs over the stade
when it is lighted up, it is evident that he will not
cast a shadow over the stade all at once, but now over
the first part, now over the second and now over the
third. And if he should run alongside the wall and 126
keep touching it with his hand painted red, he will
not mark the whole of the wall of the race-course
with red paint at one and the same time, but the
successive parts of it successively. What, then, the
argument has proved in the case of things sensible,
this we must also accept in the case of things intelligible.—And besides, it is possible to overthrow this 127
opinion by employing for the purpose a great number
of diverse hypothetical cases. For let us suppose a

---

[a] *i.e.* the Stoics. With §§ 123-126 *cf. P.H.* iii. 76-78.

κείσθω γὰρ πηχυαῖον διάστημα, καὶ διωρίσθω κατὰ
τὴν μεσότητα εἰς δύο ἡμιπήχεα. διωρίσθω δὲ καὶ
τὰ παλαιστιαῖα διαστήματα αὐτοῦ, καὶ ἔστω τὰ
διορίζοντα στερεὰ πρὸς τὸ ἀντικόπτειν καὶ ἱστᾶν
δύνασθαι τὸ κινούμενον. ⟨εἰ οὖν τὸ κινουμένον⟩
ὑφ᾽[1] ἕνα καὶ τὸν αὐτὸν χρόνον ἄθρουν ἀνύει μεριστὸν διάστημα, καὶ οὐ κατὰ τὸ πρότερον πρότερον ἡ κίνησις, καὶ τὸ κατὰ τοῦ προειρημένου
διαστήματος κινούμενον σῶμα ὑφ᾽ ἕνα χρόνον ὑπὸ
τοῦ[2] τὰ δύο ἡμιπηχυαῖα διορίζοντος ἀντικοπήσεται
128 σώματος καὶ ὑπὸ τοῦ τὰ παλαιστιαῖα. ἀλλ᾽ εἰ ἐν
τῷ αὐτῷ χρόνῳ ὑπὸ τούτων ἀντικοπήσεται, ἔσται
τὸ αὐτὸ ἅμα καὶ κεκινημένον καὶ μὴ κεκινημένον· ᾗ
μὲν γὰρ ἀντέκοψεν αὐτῷ τὸ διοριστικὸν τῶν ἡμι-
πηχυαίων διαστημάτων, κεκίνηται τὸ ἡμιπηχυαῖον
διάστημα, ᾗ δὲ καὶ τὸ διοριστικὸν τοῦ παλαιστιαίου
ἀντέκοψεν, πάλιν οὐ κεκίνηται τὸ αὐτὸ διάστημα.
ἄτοπον δέ γε τὸ αὐτὸ λέγειν ἅμα κεκινῆσθαι καὶ μὴ
κεκινῆσθαι. ἄτοπον ἄρα καὶ τὸ ἀξιοῦν τὸ κινούμενον ἄθρουν ὑφ᾽ ἓν μεριστὸν ἀνύειν διάστημα καὶ
μὴ κατὰ τὸ πρότερον πρότερον κινεῖσθαι.
129 πάλιν ὑποκείσθω πηχυαῖον διάστημα, καὶ φερέσθω
τινὰ σώματα ἀφ᾽ ἑκατέρου τῶν ἄκρων ἰσοταχῶς ὡς
αἱ κατ᾽ Ἐπίκουρον ἄτομοι. οὐκοῦν ἐπεὶ ὑπόκειται
ταῦτα τὰ σώματα ἰσοταχῶς κινούμενα, πάντως
κατὰ τὴν μεσότητα τοῦ πηχυαίου διαστήματος
προσκρούσαντα ἀλλήλοις ἢ στήσεται ἢ ἐπὶ τὸν
130 ὅθεν ἦλθε τόπον[3] ἀντικρουσθήσεται. καὶ εἰ μὲν
ἵσταται, πρόδηλόν ἐστιν ὅτι ἑκάτερον αὐτῶν ἐν

---

[1] ⟨εἰ οὖν τὸ κινούμενον⟩ ὑφ᾽ N, cj. Bekk.: ἐφ᾽ cet., Bekk.
[2] ὑπὸ τοῦ N: ὑφ᾽ οὗ cet., Bekk. (ὑπό τε τοῦ cj. Bekk.).
[3] ἐπὶ τὸν . . . τόπον Mutsch.: ἐκ τοῦ . . . τόπου mss., Bekk.

distance of a cubit, and let it be divided at the middle into two half-cubits. And let its distances of a palm's breadth be also divided, and let the divisors be solid so as to be able to resist and bring to rest the moving object. If, then, the moving object completes the whole of a divisible distance in one and the same time, and the motion is not one of orderly succession, the body which moves over the distance mentioned above will be resisted simultaneously both by the body which divides the two half-cubits and by that dividing the palm's breadths. But if it shall be 128 resisted by these at the same time, the same thing will be at once both having moved and not having moved ; for in so far as the divisor of the half-cubit distances has resisted it, it has moved over the half-cubit distance, but in so far as the divisor of the palm's breadth distance has resisted it, it has not, on the contrary, moved over the same distance. But it is absurd to say that the same thing has at once both moved and not moved. Therefore it is also absurd to maintain that the moving object completes a divisible distance at once and as a whole and does not move by gradations.—Again, let us suppose a distance of a 129 cubit, and let certain bodies move at equal speeds, like the atoms of Epicurus, from each of its extremities. Then, since these bodies are assumed to be moving with equal speeds, they will certainly collide with one another in the middle of the distance of the cubit, and will either come to rest or be driven back towards the place from which they came. And if 130 they come to rest, it is quite evident that each of

ἄλλῳ μὲν χρόνῳ ἐκινεῖτο τὸ ἀπὸ τοῦ ἄκρου διάστημα ἄχρι τῆς μεσότητος, ἐν ἄλλῳ δὲ ἔμελλεν
ἀνύειν τὸ ἀπὸ τῆς μεσότητος ὡς ἐπὶ τὸ ἕτερον
ἄκρον. εἰ δὲ ἀνταναβάλλεται ὡς ἐπὶ τὰ τοῦ ὅλου
διαστήματος ἄκρα, πάλιν προῦπτον ὡς ἐν ἄλλῳ μὲν
χρόνῳ διῆλθε τὰ ἀπὸ τῶν ἄκρων διαστήματα¹ ὡς
ἐπὶ τὸ μέσον, ἐν ἄλλῳ δὲ ἀντικρουσθέντα ὑπ-
έστρεψεν ὡς ὑφ᾽ τὰ ἄκρα. καὶ οὕτως οὐδέν ἐστι τὸ
κινούμενον ὑφ᾽ ἓν ἄθρουν μεριστὸν διάστημα.

131 Ἔτι καὶ οὕτως ἐλεγκτέον ἐστὶ τοὺς πάντα μὲν
εἰς ἄπειρον τέμνεσθαι λέγοντας, κινεῖσθαι δὲ τὸ
κινούμενον ὑφ᾽ ἓν ἄθρουν μεριστὸν διάστημα προ-
ειληφότας. δυοῖν γὰρ ἰσοταχῶς κινουμένων σωμάτων ὅσον πηχυαῖον διάστημα, ἀκολουθήσει λέγειν
ἐν τῷ αὐτῷ χρόνῳ μὴ τὸ αὐτὸ διάστημα ἑκάτερον ἀνύειν, ἀλλὰ τὸ μὲν πλεῖον τὸ δὲ ἔλαττον·
132 ὅπερ ἐστὶ παρὰ τὴν ἐνάργειαν. διωρίσθω γὰρ τὸ
πηχυαῖον διάστημα τοῦ ἑτέρου σώματος κατὰ τὴν
μεσότητα, καὶ τὸ διορίζον ἀντικοπτέτω παντὶ προσ-
πίπτοντι. ἐπεὶ οὖν ἐν ἴσῳ χρόνῳ ἀξιοῦσιν ἑκάτερον κινεῖσθαι κἂν τῷ αὐτῷ ἀνύειν τό τε πηχυαῖον
διάστημα καὶ τὰ μέρη τούτου καὶ οὐκ ἐν ἄλλῳ
μὲν τὰ μέρη ἐν ἄλλῳ δὲ τὸ ὅλον, πάντως ἐν ᾧ
χρόνῳ κινεῖται τὸ ἕτερον τούτων τῶν σωμάτων τὸ
ὅλον πηχυαῖον διάστημα, ἐν τῷ ἴσῳ καὶ τὸ λειπόμενον σῶμα κινήσεται τὸ ἡμίπηχυ διάστημα καὶ
133 ἀντικοπὲν στήσεται. ἀλλ᾽ ὑπέκειτο γε ἰσοταχῶς
ἑκάτερον αὐτῶν κινούμενον. τὰ ἄρα ἰσοταχῶς
κινούμενα ἐν τῷ αὐτῷ χρόνῳ ἄνισον κινεῖται διά-

¹ διῆλθε τὰ ἀπὸ τ. ἄκρων διαστήματα Rüstow: διῆλθεν ἀ. τ.
ἄλλων διαστημάτων mss., Bekk. (ἄκρων cj. Bekk.).

them was moving over the distance from the extremity to the centre at one time, and at another time was about to complete the distance from the centre towards the other extremity. But if they are repelled back towards the extremities of the whole distance, it is obvious again that they passed over the distances from the extremities to the centre at one time, and at another were driven back and retreated towards the extremities. And thus there is nothing which moves all at once and as a whole over a divisible distance.

Moreover, in this way one can also refute those who 131 assert that all things are divided *ad infinitum*, and yet assume that a moving object moves at once and as a whole over a divisible distance. If two bodies are moving with equal speeds over the distance of a cubit, it will follow that they must say that they do not both complete the same distance in the same time, but the one a greater the other a less ; which is contrary to evidence. For let the cubit's distance 132 of one of the bodies be divided at the centre, and let the divisor repel everything which collides with it. Since, then, they maintain that both bodies move during an equal time, and during the same time complete both the cubit's distance and the parts thereof, and not the parts in one time and the whole in another, then certainly during the time in which the one of these bodies is moving over the whole distance of the cubit, the remaining body during an equal time will move over the distance of the half-cubit and being repelled will come to rest. But each of them was 133 assumed to be moving at an equal speed. Therefore things which move at equal speeds move over an unequal distance in the same time ; which is contrary

στημα· ὅπερ παρὰ τὴν ἐνάργειάν ἐστιν. τοίνυν οὐ
κινεῖται τὸ κινούμενον ὑφ' ἓν ἄθρουν μεριστὸν διάστημα, ἀλλὰ κατὰ τὸ πρότερον πρότερον ἡ κίνησις
ὀφείλει γίγνεσθαι.

134 Ἔτι πρὸς τοῖς εἰρημένοις τὸ ἐν ἴσῳ χρόνῳ
κινούμενον πλέον διάστημα τοῦ ἐν τῷ αὐτῷ χρόνῳ
ἔλαττον διάστημα κινουμένου ταχύτερόν ἐστιν·
οἷον ἐὰν ἐν ὡριαίῳ διαστήματι καθ' ὑπόθεσιν τῶν
κινουμένων τὸ μὲν εἴκοσι σταδίους ἀνύῃ τὸ δὲ δέκα
μόνον, λεχθήσεται συμφώνως κατὰ πάντας[1] ταχύτερον μὲν εἶναι τὸ τοὺς εἴκοσι σταδίους ἀνύον,
135 βραδύτερον δὲ τὸ τοὺς δέκα. ἀλλὰ τοῦτό γε τὸ
φαινόμενον καὶ ἐναργὲς εἶναι δοκοῦν ἀναιρεῖται
ὅσον ἐπὶ τῇ ἐκκειμένῃ ὑποθέσει καὶ γίνεται ψεῦδος.
ἔσται γὰρ ⟨τὸ⟩[2] ἐν τῷ αὐτῷ χρόνῳ κινούμενον καὶ
ταχύτερον καὶ βραδύτερον· ὅπερ ἦν ἀπεμφαῖνον. εἰ
γὰρ οὐκ ἐν ἄλλῳ μὲν χρόνῳ τὸ ὅλον κινεῖται πηχυαῖον
διάστημα ἐν ἄλλῳ δὲ τὰ τοῦ πηχυαίου διαστήματος
μέρη, ἀλλ' ἐν ἑνὶ καὶ τῷ αὐτῷ τό τε ὅλον διάστημα
διέρχεται καὶ τὰ τοῦ ὅλου μέρη, ἔσται τὸ αὐτὸ ἐν
136 τῷ αὐτῷ χρόνῳ καὶ βραδύτερον καὶ ταχύτερον· ᾗ
μὲν γὰρ πηχυαῖον ἐν τούτῳ διάστημα ἀνύει, ἔσται
ταχύτερον, ᾗ δ' ἐν τῷ αὐτῷ ἡμιπηχυαῖον, ἔσται
βραδύτερον. τελέως δέ ἐστιν ἄτοπον ἐν τῷ αὐτῷ
χρόνῳ λέγειν τι καὶ ταχύτερον εἶναι καὶ βραδύτερον.
τοίνυν οὐκ ἄθρουν μεριστὸν διάστημα κινεῖται τὸ
κινούμενον, ἀλλὰ κατὰ τὸ πρότερον πρότερον.

137 Ἱκανῶς δ' ἂν ἐλέγχοιντο οἱ ταύτης προεστῶτες
τῆς δόξης καὶ διὰ τῆς λεχθησομένης ὑποθέσεως.
ἔστω γάρ τι δακτυλιαῖον διάστημα, διῃρήσθω δὲ

---

[1] πάντας cj. Bekk.: πάντα mss., Bekk.
[2] ⟨τὸ⟩ add. NE.

to evidence. So then the moving object does not move over a divisible distance at once and as a whole, but motion must take place by gradations.

Moreover, in addition to what has been said, the 134 object which moves over a greater distance in an equal time is speedier than that which moves over a less distance in the same time. For example, if of two bodies assumed to be in motion the one completes twenty stades in the space of an hour, the other only ten, it will be asserted unanimously and on all hands that the one which completes the twenty stades is the speedier, and that of the ten stades the slower. But 135 this fact which seems to be apparent and evident is destroyed—if we are to go by the hypothesis put forward—and becomes false. For that which moves in the same time will be both speedier and slower ; which is nonsensical. For if it is not the case that the whole moves over a cubit's distance in one time and over the parts of the cubit's distance in another, but passes through both the whole distance and the parts of that whole in one and the same time, then the same thing will be both slower and speedier in the same time ; for in so far as it completes in this 136 time the cubit's distance it will be speedier, but in so far as it completes that of half-a-cubit in the same time it will be slower. But it is perfectly absurd to say that a thing is, in the same time, both speedier and slower. So, then, the moving object does not move over a divisible interval all at once but by gradations.

But the champions of this opinion [a] may be 137 sufficiently confuted by the hypothetical case now to be stated. Let us suppose the distance of a finger-

---

[a] Cf. § 123.

τοῦτο κατὰ τὴν μεσότητα εἰς δύο ἡμιδακτυλιαῖα
διαστήματα, καὶ ἔστω τὸ διορίζον φύσιν ἔχον
ἀντικοπτικὴν καὶ ἀποβάλλειν δυναμένην τὸ προσπῖπτον, κινείσθω τε σῶμά τι κατὰ τοῦ τοιούτου
διαστήματος· φημὶ δὴ ὅτι κατὰ ταύτην τὴν ὑπόθεσιν, ἐπεὶ τὸ κινούμενον ἐν τῷ αὐτῷ χρόνῳ τό τε
ὅλον ἀνύει διάστημα καὶ τὰ τοῦ ὅλου μέρη, δεήσει
τὸ αὐτὸ ἐν τῷ αὐτῷ χρόνῳ ἐλθεῖν τε καὶ ἀπελθεῖν·
138 ὅ ἐστι τῶν ἀδυνάτων. εἰ γὰρ ἐν ἑνὶ καὶ τῷ αὐτῷ
χρόνῳ ἀνύει τό τε ὅλον δακτυλιαῖον διάστημα καὶ
τὰ μέρη αὐτοῦ, δακτυλιαῖον δ᾿ ἔστι διάστημα τό τε
ἀπὸ τοῦ ἄκρου μέχρι τῆς μεσότητος καὶ τὸ ἀπὸ
ταύτης μέχρι τοῦ ἄκρου, ἐν τῷ αὐτῷ χρόνῳ καὶ
ἀνελεύσεται[1] τὸ κινούμενον καὶ προσκροῦσαν τῷ
διορίζοντι κατελεύσεται. παρὰ τὴν ἐνάργειαν δέ
ἐστι τὸ ἐν τῷ αὐτῷ χρόνῳ ἐλθεῖν τε καὶ ἀπελθεῖν·
παρὰ τὴν ἐνάργειαν ἄρα καὶ τὸ οὕτω γίνεσθαι τὴν
κίνησιν, ὥσπερ καὶ τὸ ἐν τῷ αὐτῷ χρόνῳ λέγειν καὶ
ἐκτείνεσθαι τὴν χεῖρα καὶ συστέλλεσθαι καὶ οὐκ ἐν
ἄλλῳ μὲν ἐκτείνεσθαι ἐν ἄλλῳ δὲ συστέλλεσθαι.
139 Ὥστε τὸ μὲν κατ᾿ ἄθρουν διάστημα γίνεσθαι τὴν
κίνησιν οὕτως ἐστὶν ἄπορον τοῖς προειρημένοις
ἀνδράσιν· πολλῷ δὲ τούτου ἀπορώτερον τὸ μὴ κατ᾿
ἄθρουν γίνεσθαι μεριστὸν διάστημα, ἀλλὰ κατὰ τὸ
πρότερον πρότερον καὶ κατὰ τὸ δεύτερον δεύτερον.
εἰ γὰρ οὕτω γίνεται ἡ κίνησις, πάντων εἰς ἄπειρον
τεμνομένων τῶν τε σωμάτων καὶ τόπων καὶ χρόνων,
140 οὐκ ἔσται τις ἀρχὴ κινήσεως. ἵνα γάρ τι κινηθῇ
πηχυαῖον διάστημα, ὀφείλει τὸ πρῶτον ἡμίπηχυ

---

[1] ἀνελεύσεται ego: ἀπελεύσεται mss., Bekk. (ἐλεύσεται cj.
Bekk.).

length, and let this be divided at the centre into two
distances of half a finger, and let the divisor be of a
nature capable of repelling and able to hurl back the
colliding object, and let there be a body moving over
this distance ; now I assert that, in the case thus
assumed, since the moving object completes in the
same time both the whole distance and the parts of
that whole, the same thing must both approach and
retreat in the same time ; which is a thing impossible.
For if it completes in one and the same time both the 138
whole distance of a finger and the parts thereof, and
the distance of the finger is both that from the
extremity to the centre and that from this to the
extremity, then the moving object will in the same
time both go forward and, after colliding with the
divisor, return backwards. But it is contrary to
evidence that it should both approach and retreat
in the same time ; therefore it is also contrary to
evidence that motion should take place in this way,
just as it is to say that the hand is in the same time
both extended and clenched, and not extended in one
time and clenched in another.

Consequently, the men mentioned above [a] are in 139
a hopeless position in making motion complete a
distance all at once ; and much more hopeless is it
to suppose that it completes a divisible distance not
all at once but gradually—the first stage first, and
secondly the second. For if motion takes place in
this way, when all the bodies and places and times [b]
are divided to infinity, there will be no beginning of
motion. For in order that a thing may have moved 140
over a cubit's distance, it must first pass through the

---

[a] Viz. the Stoics. With §§ 139-141 cf. P.H. iii. 76.
[b] The three requisites for motion, cf. § 121.

διέρχεσθαι πρῶτον καὶ τὸ δεύτερον τῇ τάξει δεύτερον. ἀλλ' ἵνα καὶ τὸ πρῶτον ἀνύσῃ ἡμίπηχυ
διάστημα, ὀφείλει τὸ πρῶτον τεταρτημόριον τοῦ
πηχυαίου διαστήματος διελθεῖν, εἶτα τότε τὸ δεύτερον. ἀλλὰ κἂν εἰς πέντε διαιρεθῇ ⟨τὸ πρῶτον
πεμπτημόριον⟩,[1] κἂν εἰς ἕξ, τὸ πρῶτον ἐκτημόριον.
141 παντὸς οὖν τοῦ πρώτου μέρους ἄλλο πρῶτον ἔχοντος
μέρος διὰ τὴν εἰς ἄπειρον τομήν, ἀνάγκη μηδέποτε
ἀρχὴν γίνεσθαι κινήσεως διὰ τὸ ἀνέκλειπτα εἶναι τὰ
μέρη τοῦ διαστήματος καὶ τὰ τοῦ σώματος, καὶ πᾶν
τὸ ἐκ τούτων λαμβανόμενον ἔχειν ἄλλα μέρη.

142 Πρὸς μὲν οὖν τοὺς εἰς ἄπειρον τέμνεσθαι λέγοντας τά τε σώματα καὶ τοὺς τόπους καὶ τοὺς
χρόνους (οὗτοι δέ εἰσιν οἱ ἀπὸ τῆς στοᾶς) ταῦθ'
ἥρμοζε λέγειν· οἱ δὲ πάντα εἰς ἀμερῆ καταλήγειν
ὑπειληφότες, ὡς οἱ περὶ τὸν Ἐπίκουρον, νεανικω-
τέραις μᾶλλον ἐνέχονται ταῖς ἀπορίαις, καὶ πρῶτον
143 ὅτι οὐκ ἔσται κίνησις, ὡς ὁ Διόδωρος ἐδίδασκε τῶν
ἀμερῶν ἐχόμενος τόπων καὶ σωμάτων. τὸ γὰρ ἐν
τῷ πρώτῳ ἀμερεῖ τόπῳ περιεχόμενον ἀμερὲς σῶμα
οὐ κινεῖται· περιείχετο γὰρ ἐν τῷ ἀμερεῖ τόπῳ καὶ
ἐκπεπληρώκει τοῦτον. καὶ πάλιν, τὸ ἐν τῷ δευτέρῳ
ὑποκείμενον οὐ κινεῖται· κεκίνηται γὰρ ἤδη. εἰ δὲ
μήτε ἐν τῷ πρώτῳ τὸ κινούμενον κινεῖται ἐφ' ὅσον
ἔστιν ἐν τῷ πρώτῳ, μήτ' ἐν τῷ δευτέρῳ, παρὰ δὲ
ταῦτα τρίτος οὐκ ἐπινοεῖται τόπος, οὐ κινεῖται τὸ
144 λεγόμενον κινεῖσθαι.   πάρεστι δὲ καὶ χωρὶς
τῆς τοιαύτης ἀπορίας ἐξ ὑποθέσεως διαβάλλειν τὴν
στάσιν τῶν κατ' Ἐπίκουρον. ἔστω γὰρ διάστημα
ἐξ ἐννέα [τε] συγκείμενον ἀμερῶν τόπων στοιχηδὸν

[1] ⟨τὸ πρῶτον πεμπτημόριον⟩ add. cj. Bekk.

first half-cubit and secondly the second in order. But in order that it may have completed the distance of the first half-cubit, it must first have passed through the first quarter of the cubit's distance, and in the next place the second quarter; so also ⟨the first fifth part⟩, if it be divided into five, and if into six the first sixth part. Since, then, every first part has another 141 first part, because of the division to infinity, of necessity there can never be any beginning of motion, owing to the fact that the parts of the distance and those of the body are endless, and every one of them which is taken contains other parts.

Such, then, are the arguments which it was proper 142 to bring against those who say that bodies and places and times are divided to infinity (and these men are the Stoics); but those who, like Epicurus, have assumed that all things are reducible to indivisibles involve themselves in more formidable difficulties,— such as, firstly, the fact that motion will not exist, as 143 Diodorus [a] showed when treating of indivisible places and bodies. For the indivisible body contained in the first indivisible place does not move; for it is contained in the indivisible place and fills it up. And again: the body situated in the second place does not move, for it has moved already. But if the moving object neither moves in the first place— inasmuch as it exists in the first—nor yet in the second, and besides these no third place is conceived, then that which is said to move does not move.—And 144 even apart from this sort of difficulty, it is possible to attack the position of the Epicureans by means of a hypothetical case. For suppose a distance made up of nine indivisible places arranged in a row, and let

[a] *Cf.* § 86 *supra.*

τεταγμένων, καὶ κινείσθω κατὰ τούτου[1] δὴ τοῦ
διαστήματος δύο ἀμερῆ σώματα ἀφ' ἑκατέρου τῶν
145 ἄκρων, κινείσθω δὲ ἰσοταχῶς. οὐκοῦν ἐπεὶ ἡ
κίνησίς ἐστιν ἰσοταχής, δεήσει ἑκάτερον τῶν
τοιούτων σωμάτων ἀνὰ τέσσαρας ἀμερεῖς διέρχεσθαι τόπους. φθάσαντα δὲ ἐπὶ τὸν πέμπτον τόπον,
ὅς ἐστι μέσος τῶν τεσσάρων καὶ τῶν τεσσάρων, ἢ
στήσεται ἢ τὸ ἕτερον αὐτῶν προκαταταχήσει, ὥστε
τοῦτο μὲν πέντε διελθεῖν ἀμερεῖς τόπους τὸ δὲ
λειπόμενον τέσσαρας μόνον, ἢ οὔτε στήσεται οὔτε
τὸ ἕτερον προκαταταχήσει, συνδραμόντα δὲ ὑφ'
ἓν ἀμφότερα ἐξ ἡμισείας διακαθέξει τὸν πέμπτον
146 ἀμερῆ τόπον. τὸ μὲν οὖν ἀμφότερα στῆναι πάνυ
ἐστὶν ἀπίθανον· τόπου γὰρ [οὐχ][2] ὑποκειμένου καὶ
μηδενὸς πρὸς τὴν κίνησιν ἀντικόπτοντος οὐ στήσεται. τὸ δὲ προκαταταχεῖν τοῦ ἑτέρου τὸ ἕτερον
παρὰ τὴν ὑπόθεσιν· ὑπέκειτο γὰρ ἰσοταχῶς ἑκά-
147 τερον αὐτῶν κινούμενον. λείπεται ἄρα λέγειν ὅτι
εἰς τὸ αὐτὸ συνδραμόντα ἀμφότερα ἐφέξει τὰς
ἡμισείας τοῦ λειπομένου τόπου. εἰ δὲ ἐπέχει
τοῦτο μὲν τὴν καθ' αὑτὸ ἡμίσειαν ἐκεῖνο δὲ τὴν
καθ' αὑτό, οὐκ ἔσται ἀμερὴς ὁ τόπος ἀλλ' εἰς δύο
ἡμισείας μεριστός. οὑτωσὶ δὲ καὶ τὰ σώματα·
μέρει γὰρ αὐτῶν τὸ τοῦ τόπου μέρος ἐπιλαμβά-
148 νοντα οὐκ ἔσται ἀμερῆ. εἰ δὲ καὶ οἱ τόποι
μεριστοὶ καὶ τὰ σώματα οὐκ ἀμερῆ, ἀνάγκη καὶ
τὸν χρόνον μὴ εἶναι ἀμερῆ καὶ ἐλάχιστον. οὐ γὰρ
ἐν ἴσῳ χρόνῳ διέρχεται τὸν ἀμερῆ τόπον τὸ ἀμερὲς
σῶμα καὶ τὸ τοῦ ἀμεροῦς τόπου μέρος, ἀλλ' ἐν
ἄλλῳ μὲν τὸν ὅλον ἀμερῆ τόπον, ἐν ἐλαχίστῳ δὲ τὸ

---

[1] κατὰ τούτου Heintz : κατ' αὐτοῦ mss., Bekk.
[2] [οὐχ] om. N, Heintz.

two indivisible bodies be moving over this distance
from each of its extremities, and let them move at
equal speeds. Then, since their motions are equal in 145
speed, each of these bodies will necessarily pass over
four indivisible places. And on arriving at the fifth
place, which is midway between the one set of four
and the other, they will either come to a halt or one
of them will get there first,—so that this one has
passed through five indivisible places, the other only
four,—or they will not come to a halt nor will one of
them get there first but they will both meet together
in their course and each occupy a half of the fifth
indivisible place. Now that both should come to a 146
halt is extremely improbable ; for when there is a
place existing and nothing repelling their motion
they will not halt. And that the one should get there
before the other is contrary to the assumption ; for
it was assumed that both move at equal speeds. It 147
remains, then, to declare that both will meet together
in their course and occupy the two halves of the
vacant place. But if this one occupies the half on its
side, and that one the half on its side, the place will
not be indivisible but divisible into two halves. And
so too the bodies ; for as occupying a part of the place
with a part of themselves they will not be indivisible.
—But if the places are divisible and the bodies also 148
not indivisible, time too, of necessity, is not indivisible
and minimal. For the indivisible body does not pass
through an indivisible place and a part of that indivisible place in an equal time, but the whole indivisible place in one time and the part of it in a minimal

149 τούτου μέρος.   πάλιν ἔστω τι κανόνιον κέντροις κατὰ τὸ ἕτερον μέρος διειλημμένον, καὶ τοῦτο
περιαγέσθω ἀπὸ τοῦ ἑτέρου τῶν ἄκρων κατά τινος
ἐπιπέδου ἐν ἑνὶ καὶ τῷ αὐτῷ χρόνῳ. καὶ δὴ
τοῦ ἄκρου περιαγομένου κύκλοι καταγραφήσονται
μεγέθει διαφέροντες ἀλλήλων, καὶ ὁ μὲν ἐξωτάτω
καὶ πάντων περιληπτικὸς μέγιστος, ὁ δ᾽ ἐνδοτάτω
βραχύτατος, καὶ οἱ μεταξὺ τούτων ἀνάλογοι, ἤτοι
μείζους καὶ μείζους ἀπὸ τοῦ κέντρου ἐπιόντων
ἡμῶν ἢ ἐλάσσους καὶ ἐλάσσους ἀπὸ τῆς ἐκτὸς
150 περιφερείας ὑποβαινόντων. ἐπεὶ οὖν εἷς ἐστιν ὁ
τῆς περιαγωγῆς χρόνος (ἔστω δὲ ἀμερὴς οὗτος),
ζητῶ πῶς ἑνὸς καὶ τοῦ αὐτοῦ χρόνου καθεστῶτος
καθ᾽ ὃν γέγονε τὰ τῆς καταγραφῆς, μιᾶς δὲ οὔσης
καὶ τῆς κινήσεως, διαφέροντες γεγόνασιν ἀλλήλων
οἱ κύκλοι, καὶ οἱ μὲν μεγάλοι οἱ δὲ μικρὰν ἔχοντες
151 τὴν περίμετρον. οὐδὲ γὰρ ἔνεστι λέγειν ὅτι τῶν
ἀμερῶν χρόνων διαφορά τίς ἐστι παρὰ τὸ μέγεθος
καὶ διὰ τοῦτο τῶν κύκλων οἱ μὲν ἐν μείζοσιν ἀ-
μερέσι καταγραφέντες χρόνοις εἰσὶ μείζους, οἱ δὲ ἐν
ἐλάσσοσι μικρότεροι. εἰ γὰρ ἕτερος ἑτέρου μείζων
ἐστὶν ἀμερὴς χρόνος, οὐκ ἔστιν ἀμερὴς ὁ χρόνος
οὐδὲ ἐλάχιστος, καὶ τὸ κινούμενον οὐ πάντως ἐν
152 ἀμερεῖ χρόνῳ κινεῖται. πρὸς τούτοις οὐδὲ ἐκεῖνο
ἔστι φάναι, ὅτι εἷς μέν ἐστιν ἀμερὴς χρόνος καθ᾽
ὃν ἅπαντες καταγράφονται οἱ κύκλοι, τὰ δὲ μέρη
τοῦ περιαγομένου κανόνος οὐκ ἔστιν ἰσοταχῆ ἀλλὰ
τὰ μὲν ταχύτερον περιάγεται τὰ δὲ βραδύτερον, καὶ
ὑπὸ μὲν τῶν ταχύτερον περιαγομένων οἱ μείζους
συνίστανται κύκλοι ὑπὸ δὲ τῶν βραδύτερον οἱ
153 μικρότεροι. εἰ δὲ τῷ ὄντι τὰ μὲν θᾶττον κινεῖται
μέρη τὰ δὲ βράδιον, ἐχρῆν ἢ διασπᾶσθαι τὸ κα-

time.—Again, suppose there is a certain small ruler 149
which on one side is provided at intervals with points,
and let this be made to revolve, starting from one of
its extremities, over a certain plane surface in one
and the same time. Now as the extremity revolves,
circles will be described which differ from one another
in magnitude, the outermost which surrounds them
all being the greatest and the innermost the smallest,
and the intermediate ones in proportion, becoming
either greater and greater as we advance from the
centre or less and less as we recede from the outer
circumference. Since, then, the time of the revolu- 150
tion is one (and let this be indivisible), I ask how it is
that, when the time in which the process of describing
took place is one and the same and the motion also
is one, the circles have come to be different from one
another, some being great and some having a small
circumference. For it is not possible to say that there is 151
a difference in the indivisible times in respect of magnitude, and because of this those of the circles which were
described in greater indivisible times are greater, and
those in less smaller. For if one indivisible time is
greater than another, the time is not indivisible nor
minimal, and the moving object does not move wholly
in an indivisible time. And furthermore, it is not 152
possible either to assert that, while it is one indivisible
time in which all the circles are described, the parts
of the revolving ruler are not of equal speeds but some
revolve more quickly, others more slowly, and by
those which revolve more quickly the greater circles
are constructed, but by those revolving more slowly
the smaller. But if in reality some parts move more 153
quickly, others more slowly, the ruler ought to have

νόνιον ἐν τῇ περιαγωγῇ ἢ κάμπτεσθαί γε πάντως,
τινῶν μὲν αὐτοῦ μερῶν προκαταχούντων τινῶν δὲ
ὑστερούντων. οὔτε δὲ διασπᾶται οὔτε κάμπτεται·
τοίνυν ἄπορός ἐστιν ἡ κίνησις τοῖς πάντα λέγουσιν
154 εἰς ἀμερῆ καταλήγειν. καθόλου τε, εἰ πάντα
ἀμερῆ ἐστίν, ὅ τε χρόνος ἐν ᾧ γίνεται ἡ κίνησις,
καὶ τὸ σῶμα ὅπερ κινεῖται, ὅ τε τόπος ἐν ᾧ τὰ
τῆς κινήσεως συντελεῖται, πάντα κατ' ἀνάγκην τὰ
κινούμενα ἰσοταχῶς κινήσεται, ὥστε τὸν ἥλιον τῇ
χελώνῃ γίνεσθαι ἰσοταχῆ· καὶ γὰρ αὐτὸς καὶ αὐτὴ
ἐν ἀμερεῖ χρόνῳ ἀμερὲς ἀνύει διάστημα. ἄτοπον
δέ γε πάντα τὰ κινούμενα ἰσοταχῶς λέγειν κινεῖσθαι
ἢ τὴν χελώνην τῷ ἡλίῳ τυγχάνειν ἰσοταχῆ· ἄτοπον
ἄρα τὸ πάντων εἰς ἀμερὲς καταληγόντων ἀξιοῦν
γίνεσθαι τὴν κίνησιν.

155 Λείπεται τοίνυν σκοπεῖν εἰ δύναται κινεῖσθαί τι
τινῶν μὲν εἰς ἄπειρον τεμνομένων τινῶν δὲ εἰς
ἀμερὲς καταληγόντων. καὶ δὴ οὕτως ἠνέχθησαν
οἱ περὶ τὸν Στράτωνα τὸν φυσικόν· τοὺς μὲν γὰρ
χρόνους εἰς ἀμερὲς ὑπέλαβον καταλήγειν, τὰ δὲ
σώματα καὶ τοὺς τόπους εἰς ἄπειρον τέμνεσθαι,
κινεῖσθαί τε τὸ κινούμενον ἐν ἀμερεῖ χρόνῳ ὅλον
ἄθρουν μεριστὸν διάστημα καὶ οὐ κατὰ τὸ πρότερον
156 πρότερον. οὐκοῦν καὶ τὴν τούτων στάσιν ⟨εἶναι⟩
ἀδύνατον¹ ἔσται διδάσκειν πάντως² προδηλοτέρων
ἐχομένους ὑποδειγμάτων. ὑποκείσθω γὰρ τετραδακτυλιαῖον διάστημα, καὶ ἀννέτω τοῦτο τὸ κινούμενον σῶμα ἐν δυσὶν ἀμερέσι χρόνοις, ὥστε τὸ
ἕτερον διδακτυλιαῖον ἐν ἑνὶ ἀμερεῖ χρόνῳ διέρχεσθαι καὶ τὸ λειπόμενον πάλιν ἐν ἑνί. τοιαύτης δὲ

¹ ⟨εἶναι⟩ ἀδύνατον] ἀδύνατον N, cj. Bekk.: δυνατὸν cet.,
Bekk. ² πάντως Fabr.: πάντων mss., Bekk.

been pulled to pieces during its revolution or certainly bent, as some of its parts rush ahead while others lag behind. But it is neither pulled to pieces nor bent ; so then motion is inexplicable for those who assert that all things are reducible to indivisibles.—Also, 154 in general, if they are all indivisible [a]—not only the time in which the motion occurs, but also the body which moves and the place in which the effects of the motion are completed,—then all the moving bodies will of necessity move at equal speeds, so that the sun is equal in speed to the tortoise ; for both the former and the latter complete an indivisible distance in an indivisible time. But it is absurd to say that all moving objects move at equal speeds or that the tortoise is equal in speed to the sun ; therefore it is absurd to maintain that, if all things are reducible to indivisibles, motion exists.

It remains, then, to consider whether anything can 155 move if some things are divided *ad infinitum* and others are reducible to indivisibles. And Strato the physicist,[b] in fact, took this view ; for he supposed that times are reducible to indivisibles, but bodies and places are divided *ad infinitum*, and that the moving object moves over the whole of a divisible distance in an indivisible time all at once and not by gradations. That this view also is impossible one can 156 certainly show by employing quite plain examples. For let us assume a distance of four fingers, and let the moving body complete this in two indivisible times, so that it passes over the one two-fingers' distance in one indivisible time and the other likewise in one. And such being our assumption, from the

[a] With § 154 *cf. P.H.* iii. 77.
[b] Head of the Peripatetic School, 287-269 B.C.

οὔσης ὑποθέσεως ἀφαιρείσθω τοῦ τοσούτου διαστήματος δακτυλιαῖον διάστημα, ὥστε τὸ περιλειπό-
157 μενον διάστημα τριδακτυλιαῖον γίνεσθαι. ἀλλ᾽ εἰ τὸ
ὅλον τετραδακτυλιαῖον διάστημα ἐν δυοῖν ἀμερέσι
χρόνοις τὸ κινούμενον σῶμα διήρχετο, πάντως
τὸ τριδακτυλιαῖον ἀνύσει ἐν ἑνὶ ἀμερεῖ χρόνω καὶ
ἡμίσει, ἐν ἑνὶ μὲν τὸ διδακτυλιαῖον διάστημα, ἐν
ἡμίσει δὲ τὸ λειπόμενον δακτυλιαῖον. καὶ οὕτως
εἰ ἔστι τοῦ ἀμεροῦς χρόνου ἡμίσει λειπόμενος ἀμερὴς χρόνος, οὐκ ἔστι τις ἀμερὴς χρόνος, ἀλλὰ καὶ
158 οὗτος εἰς μέρη τέτμηται. ὁ δ᾽ αὐτὸς λόγος εἰ
πέμπτον δάκτυλον προσθῶμεν τῷ τετραδακτυλιαίῳ
διαστήματι. πῶς γὰρ τοῦτο κινήσεται τὸ κινούμενον; ἆρά γε ἐν ἀμερεῖ χρόνω; ἀλλ᾽ ἐπεὶ καὶ τὸ
διπλοῦν ἐν ἀμερεῖ χρόνω διήνυεν, ἔσται τὸ ἐν τῷ
αὐτῷ χρόνω κινούμενον ταχύ τε ἅμα καὶ βραδύ,
ᾗ μὲν διδακτυλιαῖον ἐν ἀμερεῖ χρόνω ἀνύει, ταχύ,
ᾗ δ᾽ ἐν τῷ ἴσω δακτυλιαῖον διέρχεται, βραδύ. εἰ
δὲ ἐν ἐλάττονι ἀμεροῦς χρόνου ἀνύει τὸν πέμπτον
δάκτυλον, μεριστός ἐστιν ὁ ἀμερὴς χρόνος· ὅπερ οὐ
θέλουσιν.
159 Καὶ μὴν εἰ ἐν ἀμερεῖ χρόνω τὸ κινούμενον ὑφ᾽
ἓν ἄθρουν μεριστὸν ἀνύει διάστημα, στήσεταί τι
ἀναιτίως, ὡς παραστήσομεν· οὐχὶ δέ γε ἵσταταί τι
ἀναιτίως· οὐκ ἄρα κατὰ τοῦτον τὸν τρόπον γίνεται
160 ἡ κίνησις. ἔστω γὰρ ὄρθιόν τι διάστημα, οἷον
δεκάπηχυ, καὶ βαρύ τι σῶμα, οἱονεὶ μολιβῆ σφαῖρα,
ἐν ἑνὶ ἐλαχίστῳ χρόνω ἀννέτω ὅλον τοῦτο τὸ
διάστημα ἄνωθεν κάτω. ἀλλὰ καὶ προστιθέσθω
τούτῳ τῷ διαστήματι ἄλλο πηχυαῖον διάστημα,
ὥστε ὅλον γίνεσθαι ἐνδεκάπηχυ, ἀφιέσθω τε πάλιν
161 ἀπὸ τοῦ ἄκρου ἡ σφαῖρα. οὐκοῦν φθάσασα ἐπὶ τὸ

distance stated let the distance of a finger be subtracted, so that the distance still left is one of three
fingers. But if the moving body passes over the 157
whole distance of four fingers in two indivisible times
it certainly will complete that of three fingers in one
indivisible time and a half,—the distance of two
fingers in one, and the remaining distance of a finger
in a half. And thus, if an indivisible time is less by
half than an indivisible time, no indivisible time exists
but this too is divided into parts. And the same 158
argument applies if we add on a fifth finger to the
distance of four fingers. For how will the moving
object move over this? Will it be in an indivisible
time? But if so, since it also completed double that
distance in an indivisible time, the object which
moves over it in the same time will be both fast and
slow simultaneously,—fast inasmuch as it completes
the distance of two fingers in an indivisible time, but
slow inasmuch as it completes but one finger's distance
in an equal time. But if it completes the fifth finger
in less than an indivisible time, the indivisible time is
divisible ; which they refuse to admit.

Moreover, if the moving object completes all at 159
once a divisible distance in an indivisible time, something will be coming to a halt causelessly, as we shall
establish ; but nothing comes to a halt causelessly ;
therefore motion does not take place in this way. For 160
suppose a certain vertical distance, say of ten cubits,
and let a certain heavy body, such as a leaden ball,
complete the whole of this distance from the top to
the bottom in one minimal time. But to this distance
let there be also added another distance of a cubit, so
that the total becomes eleven cubits, and let the ball
be started again from the top. Then, when it has 161

πέρας μὲν τοῦ δεκάτου πήχεως ἀρχὴν δὲ τοῦ
ἐνδεκάτου ἢ στήσεται ἢ καὶ τοῦτον διελεύσεται,
φημὶ δὲ τὸν ἐνδέκατον πῆχυν. ἀλλὰ τὸ μὲν στῆναι
ἄτοπον· βαρὺ γὰρ οὕτω σῶμα καὶ δι' ἀέρος φερόμενον καὶ μηδενὸς ἀντικόπτοντος, εἰ στήσεται,
162 πάντως ἀναιτίως στήσεται, ὅπερ ἦν ἄτοπον. εἰ δὲ
κινήσεται, ἐπεὶ τὸ ὅλον δεκάπηχυ διάστημα ἐν ἑνὶ
ἀμερεῖ διέρχεται χρόνῳ, τὸ λειπόμενον πηχυαῖον
διάστημα τῆς αὐτῆς οὔσης κινήσεως ἐν δεκάτῳ
μέρει τοῦ ἀμεροῦς χρόνου διελεύσεται, ὥστε τὸν
ἀμερῆ χρόνον πρὸς τῷ μὴ εἶναι ἀμερῆ ἔτι καὶ εἰς
δέκα μέρη τετμῆσθαι.
163 Καὶ μὴν εἰ τὸ κινούμενον ἐν ἑνὶ ἀμερεῖ χρόνῳ
ὅλον ἀνύει μεριστὸν διάστημα, ἐξ ἀνάγκης ἐν ἑνὶ
καὶ τῷ αὐτῷ χρόνῳ ἐν πᾶσι γενήσεται τοῖς τοῦ
διαστήματος μέρεσιν. εἰ δὲ ἐν ἑνὶ καὶ τῷ αὐτῷ
χρόνῳ ἐν πᾶσι γενήσεται τοῖς τοῦ διαστήματος
μέρεσιν, οὐκ ἔσται κεκινημένον τὸ διάστημα ἀλλὰ
164 ἐπεσχηκός· ὅπερ ἄτοπον. οὐ τοίνυν ἐν ἑνὶ καὶ
ἀμερεῖ χρόνῳ κινεῖται τὸ κινούμενον μεριστὸν διάστημα, ἐπεὶ ἔσται τὸ αὐτὸ ἐν τῷ αὐτῷ χρόνῳ
θερμόν τε καὶ ψυχρὸν πεφωτισμένον τε καὶ ἀφώ-
τιστον. ὑποκείσθω γὰρ διπηχυαῖον διάστημα, καὶ
τούτου ὁ μὲν ἕτερος πῆχυς πεπυρακτώσθω ὁ δ'
165 ἕτερος ἐψύχθω. εἰ δὴ τὸ κινούμενον ἐν ἑνὶ καὶ τῷ
αὐτῷ ἀμερεῖ χρόνῳ τὸ ὅλον τοῦτο ἐπιλαμβάνει
διάστημα, ὅτε μὲν κατὰ τοῦ πεπυρακτωμένου πή-
χεώς ἐστιν, ἔσται πεπυρακτωμένον, ὅτε δὲ κατὰ
τοῦ ἐψυγμένου, ἐψυγμένον. γίνεται δὲ κατὰ τὸν
αὐτὸν χρόνον ἔν τε τῷ πεπυρακτωμένῳ καὶ τῷ
ἐψυγμένῳ· τὸ αὐτὸ ἄρα κατὰ τὸν αὐτὸν χρόνον
ἔσται ἅμα θερμόν τε καὶ ψυχρόν· ὃ τῶν ἀδυνάτων
292

reached the end of the tenth cubit and the beginning
of the eleventh, it will either come to a halt or it will
pass over the latter as well—I mean the eleventh
cubit. But that it should come to a halt is absurd ;
for if a body which is so heavy and moving through
the air and having nothing to resist it shall come to a
halt, it will certainly be halting causelessly, which is
absurd. And if it shall keep moving, then, since it 162
passes over the whole distance of ten cubits in one
indivisible time, as the motion is the same it will pass
over the remaining distance of a cubit in the tenth
part of the indivisible time, so that the indivisible
time, in addition to being no longer indivisible, is also
divided into ten parts.

Moreover, if the moving object completes the whole 163
of a divisible distance in one indivisible time, it will
necessarily come to be in all the parts of the distance in
one and the same time. But if it shall be in all the parts
of the distance in one and the same time, it will not
have moved over the distance but will have occupied
it ; which is absurd. So then, the moving object does 164
not move over a divisible distance in one indivisible
time, since ⟨if it does so⟩ the same object at the same
time will be both hot and cold, both illuminated and
not illuminated. For let us suppose a distance of two
cubits, and of this let the one cubit be heated by fire
and the other be chilled. Now if the moving body 165
occupies the whole of this distance in one and the
same indivisible time, when it is in the heated cubit
it will be heated, and when in the chilled one it will
be chilled. But it is both in the heated one and in
the chilled one at the same time ; therefore the same
thing will be at once both hot and cold at the same
time ; and this is a thing impossible. And not only 166

166 ὑπῆρχεν. οὐ μὴν ἀλλὰ καὶ κατὰ τὴν αὐτὴν ἔφοδον
ἔσται διδάσκειν ὅτι ὑφ᾽ ἓν ταὐτὸ ἔσται καὶ πεφωτισμένον καὶ ἀφώτιστον· ὃ καὶ αὐτὸ παρὰ τὴν
ἐνάργειαν.

Πρὸς τούτοις δεήσει ἐν τῷ αὐτῷ χρόνῳ, ὁπη-
λίκον ἄν τις ὑποθῆται διάστημα, κεκινῆσθαι λέγειν
167 τὸ κινούμενον. οἷον ἔστω τετραδακτυλιαῖον διάστημα, καὶ διῃρήσθω εἰς ὀκτὼ μέρη, εὐσήμου τε
χάριν διδασκαλίας τὸ μὲν πρῶτον αὐτοῦ μέρος
καλείσθω Α, τὸ δὲ δεύτερον Β, τὸ δὲ τρίτον Γ, καὶ
κατὰ τὰ ἑξῆς ὁμοίως. εἰ δὴ τὸ κινούμενον ἐν ἑνὶ
καὶ τῷ αὐτῷ χρόνῳ μεριστὸν ἀνύει διάστημα, ἐν ᾧ
χρόνῳ κινεῖται τὸ ΑΒ διάστημα, ἐν τῷ αὐτῷ δυνήσεται κινεῖσθαι τὸ ΒΓ διάστημα. ἀλλ᾽ εἰ ⟨τοῦτο,⟩[1]
ἐν τῷ αὐτῷ κινήσεται καὶ τὸ ΓΔ, καὶ οὕτω μέχρις
ἀπείρου, ὥστε ἐν ἑνὶ καὶ ἀμερεῖ χρόνῳ κινήσεται τὸ
ὅλον τῆς γῆς διάστημα.

168 Εἰ οὖν μήτε εἰς ἄπειρον οὔσης τῆς τομῆς μήτε
εἰς ἀμερὲς τῆς καταλήξεως, μήτε τινῶν μὲν εἰς
ἄπειρον τεμνομένων τινῶν δὲ εἰς ἀμερὲς καταληγόντων, σώζεται ἡ κίνησις, ῥητέον μηδὲν εἶναι
κίνησιν. οἷς ἕπεται ἡ ἐποχὴ διά τε τὴν τῆς ἐναργείας καὶ διὰ τὴν τῶν ἀντικειμένων αὐτῇ λόγων
ἰσοσθένειαν.

Γʹ.—ΕΙ ΕΣΤΙ ΧΡΟΝΟΣ

169 Τῆς κινήσεως τριῶν οὐσιῶν, ὡς προεῖπον, ἐχο-
μένης, σώματός τε τοῦ κινουμένου καὶ τόπου τοῦ
ἐν ᾧ κινεῖται καὶ χρόνου καθ᾽ ὃν ἡ κίνησις συν-

---

[1] ⟨τοῦτο,⟩ add. cj. Bekk.

[a] The first view is that of the Stoics (§§ 123 ff.), the second
that of Epicurus (§§ 142 ff.), the third Strato's (§§ 155 ff.)

so, but by the same method it will be possible to show also that the same thing will be at once both illuminated and not illuminated ; and this too is contrary to the evidence of sense.

Furthermore, one will have to say that the moving object has moved over the distance, whatever the length one assumes this to have, in the same time. For example, suppose a distance of four fingers, and 167 let it be divided into eight parts, and, for the sake of explaining the matter clearly, let the first part of it be called A, the second B, the third C, and so on with the rest. Now if the moving object completes a divisible distance in one and the same time, it will be able to move over the distance BC in the same time in which it moves over the distance AB. But if so, it will also move over CD in the same time, and so on *ad infinitum*, so that in a single and indivisible time it will move over the whole distance of the earth.

If, then, motion is secured neither when there is 168 a division to infinity, nor when there is a reduction to indivisibles, nor when some things are divided to infinity but others reduced to indivisibles,[a] then one must declare that motion is nothing. And from this there follows suspension of judgement because of the equipollence of the sense-evidence and of the arguments which contradict it.[b]

CHAPTER III.—DOES TIME EXIST ?

As motion involves, as I said before,[c] three things— 169 the moving body and the place wherein it moves and the time in which the movement is completed,—now

[b] For " the evidence " of the senses in favour of motion see §§ 66 ff., the counter-arguments being those in §§ 70-168.

[c] See §§ 121, 140, 142, 154.

τελεῖται, ἐπεὶ τό τε σῶμα καὶ τὸν τόπον ἠπορή-
σαμεν, πειρασόμεθα καὶ περὶ χρόνου ζητεῖν· τάχα
γὰρ καὶ περὶ τούτου ὁ λόγος ἄπορος φανεῖται τοῖς
τε αἰώνιον ὑποτιθεμένοις εἶναι τὸν κόσμον φυσικοῖς
καὶ τοῖς ἀπό τινος χρόνου λέγουσιν αὐτὸν συνεστά-
σθαι. καὶ δή τινές φασι χρόνον εἶναι " διάστημα
τῆς τοῦ κόσμου κινήσεως," οἱ δὲ αὐτὴν τὴν τοῦ
κόσμου κίνησιν. οὔτε δὲ κατὰ τοὺς πρώτους οὔτε
κατὰ τοὺς δευτέρους γίνεταί τις χρόνος. εἴπερ γὰρ
τὸ διάστημα τῆς κινήσεως καὶ ἡ κίνησις οὐδέν
ἐστι παρὰ τὸ κινούμενον, ὁ χρόνος τῆς κοσμικῆς
κινήσεος διάστημα καθεστὼς ἢ ἰδιαίτερον κοσμικὴ
κίνησις οὐδὲν ἔσται παρὰ τὸν κινούμενον κόσμον,
ἀλλὰ κόσμος πως ἔχων γενήσεται ὁ χρόνος· ὅπερ
171 ἐστὶν ἄτοπον.   καὶ ἄλλως, τὴν μὲν κίνησιν τοῦ
κόσμου ἐνδέχεται νοεῖν κατά τινα χρόνον μὴ οὖσαν,
ὥστ᾽ οὐκ ἂν εἴη ἡ τοῦ κόσμου κίνησις ⟨ὁ⟩¹ χρόνος.
172   καὶ ἄλλως, πᾶσα κίνησις ἐν χρόνῳ γίνεται,
διὸ καὶ ἡ τοῦ κόσμου κίνησις ἐν χρόνῳ γενήσεται.
ὁ δὲ χρόνος ἐν χρόνῳ οὐ γίνεται· ἤτοι γὰρ ἐν αὐτῷ
γενήσεται ἢ ἐν ἄλλῳ ὡς ἄλλος,² οὔτε δὲ ἐν αὐτῷ
γένοιτ᾽ ἄν (ἔσται γὰρ ὁ αὐτὸς καὶ εἷς καὶ δύο) οὔτε
ἕτερος ἐν ἑτέρῳ διὰ τὸ μήτε τινὰ τῶν ἐνεστώτων
γίνεσθαι ἐν τῷ μὴ ἐνεστῶτι μήτε τινὰ τῶν μὴ
ἐνεστώτων ἐν τῷ ἐνεστῶτι. τοίνυν οὐδὲ διὰ τοῦτο
173 ῥητέον κόσμου κίνησιν εἶναι τὸν χρόνον.   πάλιν
ὥσπερ ἡ κίνησις ἐν χρόνῳ γίνεται, οὕτω καὶ ἡ
μονή· ἀλλ᾽ ὃν τρόπον οὐδεὶς λέγει τὴν μονὴν εἶναι

---

¹ ⟨ὁ⟩ add. Rüstow.
² ὡς ἄλλος] ἢ ἄλλοις mss., Bekk. (del. Kayser).

that we have discussed the difficulties regarding body
and place,ᵃ we shall try also to investigate time ; for
regarding it also the accounts given both by the
Physicists who suppose that the Universe is eternal,
and by those who assert that it was constructed at a
given time, will, perhaps, appear to be hopeless. Now 170
some declare that time is " the interval of the motion
of the Universe," and others that it is " the motion
itself of the Universe." ᵇ But neither according to
the view of the first nor according to that of the second
does any time exist. For if interval of motion and
motion are nothing apart from the moving object,
time, since it is interval of cosmic motion or, more
precisely, cosmic motion, will be nothing else than the
moving Universe, and time will be the Universe in
a certain state ; which is absurd.—And again : it is 171
possible to conceive the motion of the Universe as
non-existent at a certain time, so that time will not
be the motion of the Universe.—And again : all 172
motion takes place in time, therefore the motion of
the Universe also will take place in time. But time
does not take place in time ; for, if so, it will exist either
in itself or as one ⟨time⟩ in another. But it will not
exist in itself (for then the same time will be both
one and two), nor as one time in another, because none
of the things present exists in what is not present and
none of those not present in what is present. So,
then, on this account also one must not assert that
time is the motion of the Universe.—Once more : just 173
as motion takes place in time, so also does rest ; but
just as no one says that rest is time, so neither is one

ᵃ For " body " see *Adv. Phys.* i. 366 ff. ; for " place,"
§§ 37 ff. *supra.*
ᵇ The first of these definitions is Stoic, the second Platonic ;
cf. P.H. iii. 136 f.

χρόνον, οὕτως οὐδὲ τὴν τοῦ κόσμου κίνησιν δεόντως
χρόνον ἀποφαίνεται. ἥ τε τοῦ κόσμου κίνησις
διὰ παντός ἐστιν ἡ αὐτή, ὁ δὲ χρόνος οὐ διὰ παντός
ἐστιν ὁ αὐτός, ἀλλ' ὁτὲ μὲν ὁ αὐτὸς λέγεται ὁτὲ δὲ
ἄνισος, καὶ ὅτε ἄνισος, ὁτὲ μὲν πλείων ὁτὲ δὲ
ἐλάττων. ἕτερον ἄρα ἐστὶν ἡ τοῦ κόσμου κίνησις
174 καὶ ἕτερον ὁ χρόνος. οἵ γε μὴν τὴν τοῦ κόσμου
κίνησιν ἀνελόντες τὴν δὲ γῆν κινεῖσθαι δοξάσαντες,
ὡς οἱ περὶ Ἀρίσταρχον τὸν μαθηματικόν, οὐ
κωλύονται νοεῖν χρόνον. τοίνυν ἕτερον εἶναι λεκτέον τὸν χρόνον καὶ οὐ ταὐτὸν τῇ τοῦ κόσμου
175 κινήσει. οἵ τε ἐν καταγείοις τισὶ καὶ ἀλαμπέσι
σπηλαίοις βιοτεύοντες καὶ οἱ ἐκ γενετῆς πηροὶ τῆς
μὲν τοῦ κόσμου κινήσεως ἔννοιαν οὐκ ἔχουσιν,
καθίσαντες δὲ καὶ ἀναστάντες καὶ περιπατήσαντες,
ἔννοιαν χρόνου λαμβάνουσι τοῦ ἐν ᾧ τὰ τρία ταῦτα
ἐνήργησαν, καὶ πλείονος μὲν τοῦ ἐν ᾧ τὰ τρία,
ἐλάσσονος δὲ τοῦ ἐν ᾧ τὰ δύο, ἐλαχίστου δὲ τοῦ ἐν
ᾧ τὸ ἕν. εἰ δὲ δυνατὸν νοῆσαι χρόνον μὴ νοοῦντας
τὴν οὐράνιον περιφοράν, ἕτερόν ἐστιν αὕτη καὶ
ἕτερον ὁ χρόνος.
176 Ἀριστοτέλης δὲ χρόνον ἔφασκεν εἶναι ἀριθμὸν
τοῦ ἐν κινήσει πρώτου καὶ ὑστέρου. εἰ δὲ τοῦτό
ἐστιν ὁ χρόνος, συμμνημόνευσίς τις τοῦ ἐν κινήσει
πρώτου καὶ ὑστέρου, τὸ ἠρεμοῦν καὶ ἀκινητίζον οὐκ
ἔσται ἐν χρόνῳ. ἢ εἴπερ ἐστὶν ἐν χρόνῳ τὸ ἀκινητίζον, ὁ δὲ χρόνος ἐστὶν ἀριθμὸς τοῦ ἐν κινήσει
πρώτου καὶ ὑστέρου, ἔσται τὸ ἐν χρόνῳ ἠρεμοῦν
177 καὶ κινούμενον· ὅπερ ἀδύνατον. διόπερ Στράτων ὁ

---

[a] Here " the Universe " (κόσμος) means " the Heavens "
(excluding the earth). Aristarchus of Samos was a famous
astronomer at Alexandria (circa 270 B.C.).

right in asserting that the motion of the Universe is time.—Also, the motion of the Universe is perpetually the same but time is not perpetually the same, but is now called the same and again unequal ; and when unequal, now more and now less. Therefore the motion of the Universe is one thing and time another. And in fact those who, like Aristarchus the mathe- 174 matician, have rejected the motion of the Universe,[a] but have held that the earth moves, are not precluded from conceiving time. So, then, we must say that time is another thing and not the same as the motion of the Universe.—Also, those who live in subter- 175 ranean and unlighted caverns and those who are blind from birth have no conception of the motion of the Universe, but after sitting and standing up and walking they get a conception of the time in which they performed these three actions, and of the time of the three as greater, that of two as less, and that of one as least. But if it is possible for them to conceive time without conceiving the revolution of the heavens, this latter is one thing and time another.

Aristotle declared that time is " the number of the 176 prior and posterior in motion." [b] But if time is this— a " joint recollection " of the prior and posterior in motion,—what is at rest and motionless will not exist in time. Or else, if what is motionless is in time, and time is the number of the prior and posterior in motion, then that which is in time will be both at rest and in motion ; which is impossible. On this account 177

[b] *Cf. P.H.* iii. 136 ; Aristot. *Phys.* iv. 11. When the mind distinguishes between past, present, and future, it is using time as the measure (or " number ") of the course of events. For the Stoic term "joint recollection " *cf. Adv. Phys.* i. 353 ff.

φυσικὸς ἀποστὰς τῆσδε τῆς ἐννοίας ἔλεγε χρόνον
ὑπάρχειν μέτρον πάσης κινήσεως καὶ μονῆς· παρήκει γὰρ πᾶσι τοῖς κινουμένοις, ὅτε κινεῖται, καὶ
πᾶσι τοῖς ἀκινήτοις, ὅτε ἀκινητίζει, καὶ διὰ τοῦτο
178 πάντα τὰ γινόμενα ἐν χρόνῳ γίνεται. μήποτε δὲ
πάμπολλά ἐστι καὶ τὰ τούτῳ μαχόμενα· αὔταρκες
δὲ νῦν ἐκεῖνο λέγειν ὅτι τὸ μετροῦν τὴν κίνησιν ἢ
τὴν μονὴν ἐν χρόνῳ γίνεται [καὶ οὐκ ἔστι χρόνος].[1]
εἰ δὲ τοῦτο, οὐκ ἂν εἴη τὸ μετροῦν τὴν κίνησιν καὶ
τὴν μονὴν ⟨ὁ⟩[2] χρόνος· ἐν χρόνῳ γὰρ οὐ γίνεται
179 χρόνος.   ἄλλως τε, εἰ διὰ τοῦτο μέτρον τῆς
κινήσεως καὶ τῆς μονῆς ἐστιν ὁ χρόνος, ἐπεὶ ἀντιπαρήκει τῇ τε κινήσει ἐφ’ ὅσον ἐστὶ κίνησις καὶ
τῇ μονῇ ἐφ’ ὅσον ἐστὶ μονή, ἐπεὶ πάλιν ἡ κίνησις
καὶ ἡ μονὴ ἀντιπαρήκει τῷ χρόνῳ, οὐ μᾶλλον ἔσται
χρόνος μέτρον τῆς κινήσεως καὶ τῆς μονῆς ἢ ἡ
180 κίνησις καὶ ἡ μονὴ μέτρον τοῦ χρόνου.   καὶ τοῦτο
τάχα βέλτιον ἦν εἰπεῖν· ὁ μὲν γὰρ χρόνος δυσθεώ-
ρητόν τι ἐστίν, ἡ δὲ κίνησις καὶ ἡ μονὴ εὐσύνοπτον,
ληφθείη δ’ ἂν οὐκ ἐκ τοῦ δυσθεωρήτου τὸ εὐθεώ-
ρητον ἀλλ’ ἀνάπαλιν.

181   Δοκεῖ δὲ καὶ εἰς τοὺς περὶ Ἐπίκουρον καὶ
Δημόκριτον φυσικοὺς τοιαύτη τις ἀναφέρεσθαι
τοῦ χρόνου νόησις· ''χρόνος ἐστὶν ἡμεροειδὲς καὶ
νυκτοειδὲς φάντασμα,'' καθ’ ἣν πάλιν ἄπορός ἐστιν
ἡ [περὶ] τοῦ χρόνου φύσις. εἰ γὰρ ἀνυπόστατος
δείκνυται ἡ ἡμέρα καὶ ἡ νύξ, ἀκολουθεῖ καὶ τὸ
ἡμεροειδὲς φάντασμα [μὴ εἶναι χρόνον ἢ][3] ἀνυπό-
182 στατον ὑπάρχειν. ἡμέρα γὰρ ἡ καὶ ἰδιαίτερον
νοουμένη καὶ δωδεκάωρος, τουτέστιν ἡ ἀπὸ ἀνα-

---

[1] [καὶ . . . χρόνος] secl. Heintz.
[2] ⟨ὁ⟩ add. N.   [3] [μὴ . . . ἢ] secl. Heintz.

Strato the Physicist [a] rejected this notion and said
that time is " the measure of all motion and rest " ;
for it is co-extensive with all moving objects when they
are moving and with all immobile objects when they are
motionless, and for this reason all things which exist
exist in time. But, very possibly, there is a vast 178
number of things which conflict with his view ; though
it is enough now to mention the fact that what
measures the motion or the rest exists in time [and
is not time] ; and if so, time will not be that which
measures motion and rest ; for time does not exist in
time.—And again : if time is the measure of motion 179
and rest for the reason that it is co-extensive both
with motion in so far as it is motion and with rest in so
far as it is rest, then since, conversely, motion and
rest are co-extensive with time, time will not be the
measure of motion and rest any more than motion and
rest the measure of time. Perhaps, indeed, it would 180
have been better to have said the latter ; for whereas
time is hard to observe, motion and rest are easy to
discern, and what is easy to observe is not to be
perceived through what is hard, but rather the
reverse.

It seems, too, that there is ascribed to the Physi- 181
cists Epicurus and Democritus [b] a conception of time
such as this—" Time is a day-like and night-like
phantasm " [c] ; and according to this, again, the
nature of time is dubious. For if day and night are
shown to be unreal, it follows that the day-like
phantasm also [is not time or] is unreal. For day, in 182
its narrower conception as consisting of twelve hours

[a] Cf. P.H. iii. 137 ; § 228 infra.
[b] Cf. § 219 infra ; P.H. iii. 137.
[c] i.e. image, or mental picture.

τολῆς μέχρι δύσεως, σκεψαμένοις ἡμῖν ἀνυπόστατος
φαίνεται. ὅτε γὰρ ἡ πρώτη ὑφέστηκεν ὥρα, οὔπω
αἱ ἔνδεκα ὑφεστᾶσιν· τῶν δέ γε πλειόνων ὡρῶν μὴ
183 οὐσῶν οὐκ ἂν εἴη ἡμέρα. καὶ πάλιν ὅτε ἡ δευτέρα
ἐνέστηκεν ὥρα, ἡ μὲν πρώτη οὐκέτ' ἔστιν, αἱ δὲ
λειπόμεναι δέκα οὔπω εἰσίν, διὸ τῶν πλειόνων μὴ
οὐσῶν ὡρῶν οὐδ' οὕτως ἔσται ἡ ἡμέρα. πάντοτε
οὖν μιᾶς ὥρας ὑφεστώσης, τῆς δὲ ἡμέρας μιᾶς
184 ὥρας μὴ οὔσης, οὐκ ἂν εἴη τις ἡμέρα. καὶ μὴν
οὐδὲ ἡ μία ὥρα ὑφέστηκεν· κατὰ πλάτος γὰρ
νοεῖται, ἐκ πλειόνων τε καὶ αὐτὴ συνέστηκε μοιρῶν,
ὧν αἱ μὲν οὐδέπω εἰσὶν αἱ δὲ οὐκέτι, ὥστε καὶ τὸ
σύνθετον ἐξ αὐτῶν ἀνυπόστατον γίνεσθαι. εἰ δὲ
μήτε ὥρα τις ἐστὶ μήτε ἡμέρα μήτε κατὰ τὸ ἀνάλογον νύξ, οὐδὲ χρόνος ἔσται ἡμεροειδὲς ἢ νυκτερο-
185 ειδὲς φάντασμα. καὶ μὴν ἡμέρα λέγεται
διχῶς, καθ' ἕνα μὲν τρόπον ἡ ἐκ τῶν δώδεκα
ὡρῶν συνεστῶσα, καθ' ἕτερον δὲ ὁ πεφωτισμένος
ἐξ ἡλίου ἀήρ. ἤτοι οὖν τῆς ἐκ τῶν ὡρῶν συνεστώσης ἡμέρας φάντασμα εἶναι λέγουσιν οἱ περὶ
τὸν Ἐπίκουρον τὸν χρόνον, ἢ τῆς ὡς πεφωτι-
186 σμένου ἀέρος ἐξ ἡλίου. ἀλλὰ τῆς μὲν ἐκ τῶν ὡρῶν
συνεστώσης ἡμέρας οὐκ ἂν εἴπαιεν φάντασμα εἶναι
τὸν χρόνον· αὕτη γὰρ αὐτὴ ἡ ἡμέρα χρόνος ἐστί,
187 φημὶ δὲ τὴν δωδεκάωρον, διόπερ εἰ τὸ φάντασμα
ταύτης χρόνος εἶναι νοεῖται, ἔσται ὁ χρόνος τοῦ
χρόνου φάντασμα· ὅπερ ἦν ἀπεμφαῖνον. τοίνυν οὐ
λεκτέον τὸ τῆς δωδεκαώρου ἡμέρας φάντασμα χρόνον ὑπάρχειν. καὶ μὴν οὐδὲ τὸ τῆς ὡς πεφωτισμένου ἀέρος ἡμέρας φάντασμα· αὕτη γὰρ ἐν χρόνῳ
γίνεται, καὶ διὰ τοῦτο εἰ χρόνος ἐστὶ τὸ ταύτης τῆς
ἡμέρας ἡμέτερον φάντασμα, ἐν τῷ ἡμετέρῳ φαν-

—that is to say, from sunrise to sunset,—appears when we examine it to be unreal. For when the first hour exists, the eleven do not as yet exist ; and when most of the hours are non-existent, day will not exist. And again : when the second hour is present, the 183 first no longer exists and the remaining ten are not yet in existence, so that in this case too, as most of the hours are non-existent, day will not exist. Always, then, if one hour exists but day is not one hour, no day will exist. Nor, in fact, does one hour exist ; for 184 it is conceived by way of extension and is itself also composed of a number of parts of which some are not as yet and others no longer existent, so that what is compounded of them is unreal. But if there exists neither an hour nor a day nor, by analogy, a night, then time will not be a day-like or night-like phantasm.—Moreover, the word " day " has two 185 senses, being in the one sense that which is composed of the twelve hours, and in the other the air which is illuminated by the sun. Epicurus, then, asserts that time is a phantasm either of the day composed of the hours or of that which is air illuminated by the sun. But he would not say that time is a phantasm of the 186 day composed of the hours ; for this day itself—I mean the twelve-hour day—is time, and therefore, if 187 the phantasm of this is conceived to be time, time will be the phantasm of time ; which is nonsensical. So then one must not say that the phantasm of the twelve-hour day is time. Nor yet the phantasm of the day which is illuminated air ; for this exists in time, and therefore, if time is our phantasm of this

τάσματι γενήσεται ἡ τοιαύτη ἡμέρα. ὃ πολλῷ τοῦ
188 πρώτου χεῖρόν ἐστιν.   φθαρέντος τε τοῦ κόσμου
κατὰ Ἐπίκουρον οὔτε ἡμέρα ἔστιν οὔτε νύξ, διὰ δὲ
τοῦτο οὔτε ἡμερήσιον οὔτε νυκτερήσιον φάντασμα.
ἄτοπον δ' ἦν φθαρέντος τοῦ κόσμου λέγειν μὴ εἶναι
χρόνον· καὶ γὰρ τὸ ποτὲ[1] [καὶ τὸ] ἐφθάρθαι καὶ τὸ
φθείρ ꜰθαι χρόνων ἐστὶν ἐμφατικά. εἰ δὲ τοῦτο,
ἕτερον μέν ἐστιν ὁ χρόνος, διάφορον δὲ τὸ ἡμερήσιον
ἢ νυκτερήσιον φάντασμα.

   Ἐκ μὲν οὖν τῆς ἐπινοίας οὕτως ἡ τοῦ χρόνου
189 ὕπαρξις ἠπορήσθω· πάρεστι δὲ καὶ προηγουμένῳ
λόγῳ τὸ προκείμενον κατασκευάζειν. εἴπερ γὰρ
ἔστι χρόνος, ἤτοι πεπέρασται ἢ ἄπειρός ἐστιν· οὔτε
δὲ πεπέρασται, ὡς παραστήσομεν, οὔτε ἄπειρός
ἐστιν, ὡς διδάξομεν· οὐκ ἄρα ἔστι τι χρόνος. εἰ
γὰρ πεπέρασται ὁ χρόνος, ἦν ποτὲ χρόνος ὅτε ὁ
χρόνος οὐκ ἦν, καὶ ἔσται ποτὲ χρόνος ὅτε οὐκ ἔσται
χρόνος. ἄτοπον δέ γε ἢ τὸ γεγονέναι ποτὲ χρόνον
ὅτε ὁ χρόνος οὐκ ἦν, ἢ τὸ ἔσεσθαί ποτε χρόνον ὅτε
χρόνος οὐκ ἔσται· καὶ γὰρ τὸ ποτὲ γεγονέναι καὶ
τὸ ἔσεσθαι, καθὼς προεῖπον, διαφερόντων χρόνων
ἐστὶν ἐμφατικά. οὐ τοίνυν πεπέρασται ὁ χρόνος.
190   καὶ μὴν οὐδὲ ἄπειρός ἐστιν. ἔστι γάρ [τι]
αὐτοῦ τὸ μέν τι παρῳχημένον τὸ δὲ μέλλον. ἤτοι
οὖν ἑκάτερος τούτων τῶν χρόνων ἔστιν ἢ οὐκ ἔστιν.
καὶ εἰ μὲν οὐκ ἔστιν, αὐτόθεν πεπέρασται ὁ χρόνος,
καὶ εἰ πεπέρασται, μένει τὸ ἀρχῆθεν ἄπορον, τὸ
γεγονέναι ποτὲ χρόνον ὅτε χρόνος οὐκ ἦν καὶ τὸ

___
[1] τὸ ποτὲ (om. καὶ τὸ) Mutsch.: ὁπότε mss., Bekk. (τὸ ποτὲ
⟨φθαρῆναι⟩ cj. Bekk.).

304

day, this day will exist in our phantasm. And this is
a result far worse than the first.—Also, when the 188
Universe is destroyed, according to Epicurus,[a] there
exists neither day nor night, and consequently neither
a diurnal nor a nocturnal phantasm. But it is absurd
to say that when the Universe is destroyed time does
not exist ; for the statements that it was destroyed
once and that it is being destroyed are indicative of
times. And if so, time is one thing and the diurnal
or nocturnal phantasm a different thing.

Let this, then, serve as our account of the difficulties regarding the real existence of time which
arise from the conception of it ; but we can also 189
establish our case by means of direct argument. For
if time exists it is either limited or unlimited ; but
neither is it limited, as we shall establish, nor is
it unlimited, as we shall show ; therefore time is
nothing.[b] For if time is limited, there was once a
time when time did not exist, and there will one day
be a time when time will not exist. But it is absurd
to say either that there was once a time when time
did not exist, or that there will one day be a time
when time will not exist, for the statements that
" there once was " and that " there will be " are (as I
said before [c]) indicative of different times. So, then,
time is not limited.—Nor, in fact, is it unlimited. For 190
one part of it is past, the other future. Each of these
times, then, either exists or does not exist. And if
it does not exist, time is at once limited, and if it
is limited the original difficulty remains—that there
was once a time when time did not exist and there

[a] Cf. Lucret. v. 91 ff., 235 ff. for the " exitium caeli terrae-
que futurum."
[b] With §§ 189-193 cf. P.H. iii. 141-142.
[c] In § 188.

191 ἔσεσθαί ποτε χρόνον ὅτε χρόνος οὐκ ἔσται. εἰ δὲ
ἔστιν ἑκάτερος, φημὶ δὲ ὅ τε παρῳχημένος καὶ
ὁ μέλλων χρόνος, ἐν τῷ παρόντι ἔσται. ἐν τῷ
παρόντι δὲ ὑπάρχων, ἐν τῷ ἐνεστῶτι γενήσεται
χρόνῳ ὅ τε παρῳχημένος καὶ ὁ μέλλων. ἄτοπον
δὲ τὸν παρῳχημένον καὶ τὸν μέλλοντα λέγειν κατὰ
τὸν ἐνεστῶτα χρόνον νοεῖσθαι. τοίνυν οὐδ᾽ ἄπειρός
ἐστιν ὁ χρόνος. εἰ δὲ μήτε πεπερασμένος νοεῖται
192 μήτ᾽ ἄπειρος, οὐδ᾽ ὅλως ἔσται.   τό τε μὴν ἐξ
ἀνυπάρκτων συνεστὼς ἀνύπαρκτον ἔσται, ὁ δέ γε
χρόνος ἐξ ἀνυπάρκτων ἀξιοῦται συνεστάναι τοῦ
παρῳχημένου μηκέτ᾽ ὄντος καὶ τοῦ μέλλοντος
μήπω ὄντος· ἀνύπαρκτος ἄρα ἐστὶν ὁ χρόνος.
193   Πρὸς τούτοις, εἰ ἔστι τι χρόνος, ἤτοι ἀμέριστός
ἐστιν ἢ μεριστός· οὔτε δὲ ἀμέριστος εἶναι δύναται,
καθὼς ὑπομνήσομεν, οὔτε μεριστός, ὡς καταστη-
σόμεθα· οὐκ ἄρα ἔστι τις χρόνος. ἀμερὴς μὲν οὖν
οὐ δύναται τυγχάνειν ὁ χρόνος, ἐπεὶ διαιρεῖται εἴς τε
τὸν παρῳχημένον καὶ τὸν ἐνεστῶτα καὶ εἰς τὸν μέλ-
194 λοντα. μεριστὸς δὲ οὐκ ἂν ὑπάρχοι διὰ τὸ πᾶν τὸ
μεριστὸν ὑπό τινος αὐτοῦ μέρους καταμετρεῖσθαι·
οἷον ὁ μὲν πῆχυς ὑπὸ παλαιστοῦ καταμετρεῖται,
καὶ ἔστι τοῦ πήχεως μέρος ὁ παλαιστής, ὑπὸ
δὲ τοῦ δακτύλου ὁ παλαιστής, καὶ ἔστι μέρος τοῦ
παλαιστοῦ ὁ δάκτυλος. τοίνυν εἰ καὶ ὁ χρόνος
μεριστός ἐστιν, ὀφείλει πρός τινος αὐτοῦ μέρους
195 καταμετρεῖσθαι. οὔτε δὲ ὑπὸ τοῦ ἐνεστῶτος ἐνδέχεται τοὺς ἄλλους χρόνους καταμετρεῖσθαι. εἰ γὰρ
ὁ ἐνεστὼς χρόνος καταμετρεῖ τὸν παρῳχημένον,
ἔσται ὁ ἐνεστὼς χρόνος κατὰ τὸν παρῳχημένον,
γινόμενος δὲ κατὰ τὸν παρῳχημένον οὐκέτι ἔσται
ἐνεστὼς ἀλλὰ παρῳχημένος. καὶ εἰ τὸν μέλλοντα

will one day be a time when time will not exist. But 191
if each exists—I mean both past and future time,—
each will be in the present. And as existing in the
present, both past and future time will be in present
time. But it is absurd to say that past and future
are conceived as in present time. So, then, time is
not unlimited either. But if it is neither conceived
as limited nor as unlimited, it will not exist at all.—
Also, what is composed of non-existents will be non- 192
existent, and time is held to be composed of non-
existents—of the past which exists no longer and of
the future which does not as yet exist ; time, therefore, is non-existent.

Furthermore : if time is anything, it is either 193
indivisible or divisible ; but it cannot be either indivisible, as we shall show, or divisible, as we shall
establish ; no time, therefore, exists.[a] Now time
cannot be indivisible, since it is divided into past,
present, and future. And it will not be divisible 194
because everything divisible is measured by a part of
itself ; the cubit, for instance, is measured by the
palm, and the palm is a part of the cubit, and the palm
is measured by the finger, and the finger is a part of
the palm.[b] So, then, if time too is divisible, it ought
to be measured by some part of itself. But it is not 195
possible for the other times to be measured by the
present. For if the present time measures the past,
the present time will be in the past, and being in the
past it will no longer be present but past. And if

[a] With §§ 193-196 cf. P.H. iii. 143.
[b] 4 fingers = 1 palm ; 6 palms = 1 cubit (= 18 inches).

καταμετρεῖ ὁ ἐνεστώς, κατ' αὐτὸν γινόμενος μέλλων ἔσται ἀλλ' οὐχὶ ἐνεστώς. ὅθεν οὐδὲ τοῖς ἄλλοις χρόνοις ἐνδέχεται καταμετρεῖν τὸν ἐνεστῶτα· ἑκάτερος γὰρ αὐτῶν κατὰ τοῦτον γενόμενος ἐνεστὼς ἔσται καὶ οὔτε παρῳχημένος οὔτε μέλλων.

196 ἀλλ' εἰ πάντως μεριστὸν ἢ ἀμέριστον δεῖ νοεῖν τὸν χρόνον, ἐδείξαμεν δὲ ἡμεῖς ὅτι οὔτε μεριστός ἐστιν οὔτε ἀμέριστος, λεκτέον μηδὲν εἶναι τὸν χρόνον.

197 Σὺν τούτοις ὁ χρόνος τριμερής ἐστιν· τὸ μὲν γάρ τι ἦν αὐτοῦ παρῳχημένον, τὸ δ' ἐνεστώς, τὸ δὲ μέλλον. τούτων δὲ τὸ μὲν παρῳχημένον οὐκέτ' ἔστιν, τὸ δὲ μέλλον οὔπω ἔστιν. λείπεται δὲ ἓν εἶναι μέρος ἐνεστηκός. ἤτοι οὖν ὁ ἐνεστηκὼς χρόνος ἀμερής ἐστιν ἢ μεριστός. οὔτε δὲ ἀμερὴς εἶναι δύναται· ἐν ἀμερεῖ γὰρ χρόνῳ οὐδὲν πέφυκε γίνεσθαι μεριστόν, ὡς φησὶ Τίμων, οἷον τὸ γίνεσθαι καὶ τὸ φθείρεσθαι καὶ πᾶν ὃ τούτοις ἔοικεν.

198 εἰ δ' ἀμερής ἐστιν, οὔτε ἀρχὴν ἕξει, ᾗ συνάπτει τῷ παρῳχημένῳ, οὔτε πέρας, ᾧ συνάπτει τῷ μέλλοντι· τὸ γὰρ ἀρχὴν ἔχον καὶ πέρας οὐκ ἀμέριστόν ἐστιν. εἰ δὲ μήτε ἀρχὴν ἔχει μήτε πέρας, οὐδὲ μέσον ἔχει· κατὰ γὰρ τὴν ὡς ⟨πρὸς⟩[1] ταῦτα σύμβλησιν νοεῖται τὸ μέσον. μήτε δὲ ἀρχὴν ἔχων[2] μήτε

199 πέρας μήτε μέσον οὐδ' ὅλως ἔσται. εἰ δὲ μεριστός ἐστιν ὁ ἐνεστὼς χρόνος, ἤτοι εἰς τοὺς ὄντας χρόνους μερίζεται ἢ εἰς τοὺς μὴ ὄντας. καὶ εἰ μὲν εἰς τοὺς μὴ ὄντας χρόνους μερίζοιτο, οὐκέτ' ἔσται χρόνος· τὸ γὰρ εἰς τοὺς μὴ ὄντας χρόνους μεριζόμενον οὐκ ἂν εἴη χρόνος. εἰ δὲ εἰς τοὺς ὄντας χρόνους μερί-

---

[1] ⟨πρὸς⟩ add. Heintz.
[2] ἔχων NLE: ἔχον cet., Bekk.

the present measures the future, being within this it will be future and not present. Hence, too, it is not possible to measure the present by the other times ; for, as being within it, each of them will be present and not either past or future. But if one must 196 certainly conceive time as either divisible or indivisible, and we have shown that it is neither divisible nor indivisible, it must be declared that time is nothing.

Furthermore : time is tripartite ; for one part of 197 it is past, one present, and one future.[a] And of these the past no longer exists and the future does not yet exist. It remains to say that one part exists, the present. The present time, then, is either indivisible or divisible. But it cannot be indivisible, for " nothing divisible is of a nature to exist in indivisible time," as Timon says,—becoming, for example, and perishing, and everything of a similar kind. And if it is in- 198 divisible, it will neither have a beginning whereby it is joined on to the past, nor an end whereby it is joined on to the future ; for that which has a beginning and an end is not indivisible. But if it has neither a beginning nor an end, it will not have a middle either ; for the middle is conceived by way of comparison in its relation to the other two. And as having neither beginning nor middle nor end, it will not exist at all. And if present time is divisible, it is 199 divided either into existent times or into non-existent. And if it should be divided into non-existent times, it will no longer be time ; for that which is divided into non-existent times will not be time. And if it is divided into existent times, it will no longer, as a

• With §§ 197-199 cf. P.H. iii. 144-145.

ζεται, οὐκέτι ἔσται ὅλος ἐνεστώς, ἀλλὰ τὶ μὲν
αὐτοῦ παρῳχημένον τὶ δὲ μέλλον. διὰ δὲ τοῦτο
οὐκέτι ἔσται ὅλος [ἐνεστὼς καὶ]¹ ὑπάρχων, τοῦ μὲν
200 μηκέτι ὄντος αὐτοῦ τοῦ δὲ μήπω ὄντος. ἀλλ' εἰ
τριῶν ὄντων, παρῳχημένου καὶ μέλλοντος καὶ
ἐνεστῶτος, δέδεικται τούτων μηδεὶς ὑπάρχων, οὐκ
ἂν εἴη τις χρόνος.

Οἱ δὲ λέγοντες τὸν ἐνεστῶτα χρόνον πέρας μὲν
εἶναι τοῦ παρῳχημένου ἀρχὴν δὲ τοῦ μέλλοντος, ἐκ
δυοῖν ἀνυπάρκτων χρόνων ἕνα ποιοῦντες, οὐχ ἕνα
μόνον ἀλλὰ καὶ πάντα χρόνον ἀνύπαρκτον ποιοῦσιν.
201 ἄλλως τε, εἰ πέρας ἐστὶ τοῦ παρῳχημένου
ὁ ἐνεστὼς χρόνος, τὸ δὲ πέρας τοῦ παρῳχημένου
συμπαρῴχηκε τῷ οὗ ἐστὶ πέρας, οὐκέτι ἔσται ὁ
ἐνεστὼς χρόνος, εἴπερ πέρας ἐστὶ τοῦ παρῳχη-
202 μένου. καὶ πάλιν, εἰ ἀρχὴ τοῦ μέλλοντός ἐστιν
ὁ ἐνεστὼς χρόνος, ἡ δὲ ἀρχὴ τοῦ μέλλοντος οὔπω
ἔστιν, ὁ ἐνεστὼς χρόνος οὔπω ὑποστήσεται, καὶ
οὕτω τὰ ἐναντιώτατα τούτῳ συμβήσεται· καθὸ μὲν
γὰρ ἐνεστώς ἐστιν, ὑπάρξει, καθὸ δὲ συμπαρῴχηκε
τῷ παρῳχημένῳ, οὐκέτι ἔσται, καθὸ δὲ τῷ μέλ-
λοντι σύνεστιν, οὔπω ἔσται. ἄτοπον δὲ τὸν αὐτὸν
χρόνον νοεῖν καὶ ὄντα καὶ μὴ ὄντα καὶ μηκέτ' ὄντα
καὶ μήπω ὄντα. τοίνυν οὐδὲ ταύτῃ ῥητέον εἶναί
τινα χρόνον.

203 Ἐπακτέον δὲ καὶ οὕτως. εἰ ἔστι τι ὁ χρόνος,
ἤτοι ἄφθαρτός ἐστι καὶ ἀγένητος ἢ φθαρτὸς καὶ
γενητός· οὔτε δὲ ἄφθαρτός ἔστι καὶ ἀγένητος, ὡς
δειχθήσεται, οὔτε φθαρτὸς καὶ γενητός, ὡς καὶ
τοῦτο παρασταθήσεται· οὐκ ἄρα ἔστι τι χρόνος.
ἄφθαρτος μὲν οὖν καὶ ἀγένητος οὐκ ἔστιν εἴ γε
τὸ μέν τι αὐτοῦ παρῴχηκε τὸ δὲ ἐνέστηκε τὸ δὲ

whole, be present but one part of it will be past, another future. And for this reason it will no longer, as a whole, be [present and][1] existent, as part of it no longer exists and part is not as yet existing. But if 200 of the three times—past, future, and present—it has been proved that not one exists, no time will exist.

And those who assert that present time is the limit of the past and the beginning of the future,[a]—thus making one out of two non-existent times,—make not only one but every time non-existent.—And further : 201 if present time is the limit of past, and the limit of the past has passed away together with that whereof it is the limit, present time will no longer exist, if it really is the limit of the past.—And again : if present 202 time is the beginning of the future, and the beginning of the future does not yet exist, present time will not yet exist, and thus it will have most opposite properties ; for inasmuch as it is present it will exist, but inasmuch as it has passed away together with the past it will exist no longer, and inasmuch as it accompanies the future it will not as yet exist. But it is absurd to conceive the same time as both existing and not existing, and no longer existing and not yet existing. So, then, in this way too one must deny that any time exists.

One may also argue thus : if time is anything, it is 203 either imperishable and ingenerable or perishable and generable ; but it is neither imperishable and ingenerable, as shall be proved, nor perishable and generable, as this also shall be established ; time, therefore, is not anything. Now it is not imperishable and ingenerable, seeing that part of it is past, part present,

[a] With §§ 200-205 cf. P.H. iii. 146-148.

---

[1] [ἐνεστὼς καὶ] secl. Heintz.

SEXTUS EMPIRICUS

204 μέλλει. καὶ γὰρ ἡμέρα ἡ μὲν χθὲς οὐκέτι ἔστιν, ἡ
δὲ σήμερον ἔστιν, ἡ δὲ αὔριον οὔπω γέγονεν. ὅθεν
καὶ τοῦ χρόνου τὸ μὲν οὐκέτ' ἔστιν,[1] ὥσπερ τὸ
παρῳχημένον, τὸ δὲ ἔστιν, ὡς τὸ ἐνεστηκός, τὸ δὲ
οὔπω ἔστιν, καθάπερ τὸ μέλλον. διὰ δὲ τοῦτο οὔτε
ἀγένητος οὔτε ἄφθαρτος γενήσεται ὁ χρόνος.
205 εἰ δὲ φθαρτός ἐστι καὶ γενητός, ἄπορον τὸ εἰς τί
φθαρήσεται καὶ ἐκ τίνος ἔσται. οὔτε γὰρ ὁ μέλλων
ἔστιν ἤδη, οὔτε ὁ παρῳχημένος ἔτι ἔστιν. ἐκ δὲ
τῶν μὴ ὄντων πῶς δύναταί τι ⟨γίνεσθαι, ἢ εἰς τὰ μὴ
ὄντα πῶς δύναταί τι⟩[2] φθείρεσθαι; οὐδὲν οὖν ἐστι
χρόνος.
206 Ἐπιχειρητέον δὲ καὶ οὕτως. εἰ ἔστι τι χρόνος,
ἤτοι γενητός ἐστιν ἢ ἀγένητος ἢ τὶς μὲν γενητὸς τὶς
δὲ ἀγένητος· οὔτε δὲ γενητὸς δύναται εἶναι ὁ
χρόνος οὔτε ἀγένητος οὔτε τὶς μὲν γενητὸς τὶς δὲ
207 ἀγένητος· οὐκ ἄρα ἔστι τι[3] χρόνος. εἰ μὲν γὰρ
γενητὸς εἴη, ἐπεὶ πᾶν τὸ γεννώμενον ἐν χρόνῳ γίνεται, καὶ ὁ χρόνος γεννώμενος ἐν χρόνῳ ἔσται
γεννώμενος. ἤτοι οὖν [ὁ][4] αὐτὸς ἔσται ἐν αὐτῷ γεννώμενος ἢ ἕτερος ἐν ἑτέρῳ. καὶ εἰ μὲν [ὁ][4] αὐτὸς
ἐν ἑαυτῷ γεννᾶται, ἔσται τι γεγονὸς πρὶν γεγονέναι·
208 ὅπερ ἄτοπον. ἐπεὶ γὰρ τὸ ἐν ᾧ τι γίνεται ὀφείλει
προϋπάρχειν τοῦ ἐν αὐτῷ γεννωμένου, δεήσει καὶ
τὸν χρόνον ἐν ἑαυτῷ γεννώμενον ἑαυτοῦ προ-
γεγενῆσθαι· οἷον ἐν ἐργαστηρίῳ δημιουργεῖται
ἀνδριάς, ἀλλὰ προϋπόκειται τοῦ ἀνδριάντος τὸ

[1] οὐκέτ' ἔστιν Heintz: οὐκ ἔσται mss., Bekk. (οὐκέτ' cj. Bekk.).
[2] ⟨γίνεσθαι . . . τι⟩ add. Mutsch. (⟨γίν. . . . πῶς⟩ add. cj. Bekk.).
[3] τι NLE: τις cet., Bekk.
[4] [ὁ] secl. Kayser.

312

and part future. For the day of yesterday exists no 204
longer, that of to-day exists, and that of to-morrow
has not yet come into existence. Hence one part
of time (namely, the past) no longer exists, another
(namely, the present) exists, and another (namely,
the future) does not yet exist. And for this reason
time will be neither ingenerable nor imperishable.—
But if it is perishable and generable, it is hard to say 205
what it will perish into and from what it will come
to exist. For neither does the future exist already,
nor the past exist any longer. But how can a thing
⟨come into existence⟩ from non-existents, ⟨or how can
a thing⟩ perish ⟨into non-existents⟩ ? Time, then, is
nothing.

One may attack it also in this way [a] : if time is 206
anything, it is either generable or ingenerable, or
partly generable and partly ingenerable. But time
cannot be either generable or ingenerable or partly
generable and partly ingenerable ; therefore time is
not anything. For if it were generable, since every- 207
thing which is generated becomes in time, time too
being generated will be generated in time. Either,
then, it will be generated as itself in itself or as one
time in another. And if it is generated as itself in
itself, it will be a thing which has come to exist before
it has come to exist ; which is absurd. For since that 208
in which a thing becomes must exist before that
which is generated in it, time also, as generated in
itself, must have come into existence before itself ;
just as a statue is wrought in a workshop, but the
workshop existed before the statue, and a ship is con-

[a] With §§ 206-211 cf. P.H. iii. 149-150.

ἐργαστήριον, καὶ ἐν τόπῳ τινὶ συνίσταται ναῦς,
ἀλλὰ καὶ προϋφέστηκε τῆς νεὼς ὁ τόπος. τοίνυν εἰ
καὶ ὁ χρόνος ἐν ἑαυτῷ γίνεται, προϋπάρξει ἑαυτοῦ·
καὶ οὕτως ᾗ[1] μὲν γίνεται, οὔπω ἔσται, ἐπεὶ πᾶν
τὸ γινόμενον, ὅτε γίνεται, οὔπω ἔστιν, ᾗ[1] δὲ ἐν
209 ἑαυτῷ γίνεται, ὀφείλει προϋπάρχειν. ἔσται οὖν ἅμα
χρόνος καὶ οὐκ ἔσται. ᾗ μὲν γίνεται, οὐκ ἔσται,
ᾗ δὲ ἐν ἑαυτῷ γίνεται, ἔσται. ἄτοπον δὲ τὸ αὐτὸ
κατὰ τὴν αὐτὴν ἐπιβολὴν εἶναί τε καὶ μὴ εἶναι·
ἄτοπον ἄρα καὶ τὸ ἐν αὐτῷ λέγειν γίνεσθαι τὸν
210 χρόνον. καὶ μὴν οὐδὲ ἕτερος ἐν ἑτέρῳ γίνεται
χρόνος, οἷον ὁ μέλλων ἐν τῷ ἐνεστῶτι καὶ ὁ ἐνεστὼς
ἐν τῷ παρῳχημένῳ. εἰ γὰρ ἕτερος ἐν ἑτέρῳ γίνεται χρόνος, ἐξ ἀνάγκης ἕκαστος τῶν χρόνων
ἀπολείπων τὴν ἰδίαν θέσιν τὴν ἑτέρου ἐπιλήψεται
τάξιν. οἷον εἰ[2] ὁ μέλλων χρόνος γίνεται ἐν τῷ
ἐνεστῶτι χρόνῳ, ὁ μέλλων κατὰ τὸν ἐνεστῶτα
γινόμενος ἔσται ἐνεστὼς ἀλλ' οὐ μέλλων· καὶ εἰ ὁ
ἐνεστὼς ἐν τῷ παρῳχημένῳ γίνεται, πάντως κατὰ
τὸν παρῳχημένον γινόμενος οὐκ ἔσται ἐνεστὼς
211 ἀλλὰ παρῳχημένος. ὁ δ' αὐτὸς λόγος κἂν ἀνα-
στρέψωμεν, τὸν μὲν παρῳχημένον ποιοῦντες ἐν τῷ
ἐνεστῶτι γινόμενον, τὸν δὲ ἐνεστῶτα ἐν τῷ μέλ-
λοντι· αἱ γὰρ αὐταὶ πάλιν ἀκολουθοῦσιν ἀπορίαι.
    εἰ οὖν οὔτε ἐν αὐτῷ γίνεται χρόνος οὔθ' ὡς
ἕτερος ἐν ἑτέρῳ, οὐκ ἔστι γενητὸς ὁ χρόνος. εἰ δὲ
μήτε ἀγένητός ἐστι μήτε γενητός, παρὰ δὲ ταῦτα
τρίτον ἐπινοεῖν ἀμήχανον, λεκτέον μηδὲν ὑπάρχειν
212 τὸν χρόνον. ὅτι γὰρ καὶ ἀγένητος οὐ δύναται
εἶναι, σφόδρα εὐπαραμύθητον. εἰ γὰρ ἀγένητός

---

[1] ᾗ Heintz: ἡ N: εἰ cet., Bekk.
[2] εἰ Heintz: ἐπεὶ mss., Bekk.

structed in a certain place, but the place was existing before the ship. So, then, if time too becomes in itself, it will exist before itself; and thus, inasmuch as it becomes, it will not yet exist, since everything which becomes, while it is becoming, does not exist as yet; but inasmuch as it becomes in itself, it must exist beforehand. Time, then, will be at once both 209 existent and non-existent. Inasmuch as it becomes it will not exist, but inasmuch as it becomes in itself it will exist. But it is absurd that the same thing at the same instant should both exist and not exist; therefore it is also absurd to say that time becomes in itself.—Nor yet does it become as one time in 210 another,—the future, for instance, in the present, and the present in the past. For if one time becomes in another, each of the times will necessarily quit its own position and occupy the post of the other. If, for example, the future time becomes in the present time, the future as becoming during the present will be present and not future; and if the present becomes in the past, as becoming during the past it will certainly not be present but past. And the same 211 argument applies if we reverse their order, making the past becoming in the present and the present in the future; for here again the same difficulties follow.—If, then, time does not become either in itself or as one time in another, time is not generable. But if it is neither ingenerable nor generable, and besides these one can conceive no third possibility, one must declare that time is nothing.—Now the fact 212 that it cannot be ingenerable is extremely easy to demonstrate. For if it is ingenerable and neither has

SEXTUS EMPIRICUS

ἐστι καὶ οὔτε γέγονεν οὔτε γενήσεται, εἶς ἔσται
μόνος ὁ ἐνεστὼς χρόνος, καὶ οὔτε ὁ μέλλων ἔτι
μέλλων, οὐδὲ τὰ ἐν αὐτῷ πράγματα, οὔτε ὁ παρ-
ῳχηκὼς ἔτι παρῳχηκώς, οὐδὲ τὰ ἐν αὐτῷ πρατ-
τόμενα. οὐχὶ δέ γε τοῦτο· τοίνυν οὐδὲ ἀγένητός
213 ἐστιν ὁ χρόνος.   καὶ μὴν οὐδὲ τὶς μὲν γενητὸς
τὶς δὲ ἀγένητος, ἐπεὶ ἐπισυντεθήσονται αἱ ἀπορίαι.
ὅ τε γὰρ γενητὸς ἢ ἐν ἑαυτῷ γίνεσθαι ὀφείλει ἢ ἐν
ἑτέρῳ· ἀλλ' ἐὰν μὲν ἐν ἑαυτῷ γένηται, προϋπάρξει
ἑαυτοῦ, ἐὰν δὲ ἐν ἑτέρῳ, οὐκέτι ἐκεῖνος ὁ χρόνος
ἔσται, ἀλλὰ καθ' ὃν γίνεται ἀπολείπων τὴν ἰδίαν
214 τάξιν. ὁ δ' αὐτὸς λόγος καὶ ἐπὶ τοῦ ἀγενήτου·
εἰ γὰρ ἀγένητός ἐστιν, οὔτε ὁ μέλλων ποτὲ ἔσται
χρόνος οὔτε ὁ παρῳχηκώς, ἀλλ' εἶς μόνος ὁ ἐν-
εστηκώς. ἄτοπα δὲ ταῦτα. λείπεται ἄρα λέγειν,
μήτε γενητοῦ ὄντος τοῦ χρόνου μήτε ἀγενήτου μήτε
τινὸς μὲν γενητοῦ τινὸς δὲ ἀγενήτου, μὴ εἶναι
χρόνον.
215 Ἐνέσται δὲ τοῦτο ἀπορεῖν καὶ ἀπὸ τῆς οὐσίας,
ὡς καὶ ἀπὸ τῆς ἐννοίας προηπόρηται. αὐτίκα γὰρ
τῶν δογματικῶν φιλοσόφων φασὶν οἱ μὲν σῶμα
εἶναι τὸν χρόνον οἱ δὲ ἀσώματον, καὶ τῶν ἀσώματον
φαμένων οἱ μὲν ὡς καθ' αὑτό τι νοούμενον πρᾶγμα
216 οἱ δ' ὡς συμβεβηκὸς ἑτέρῳ. σῶμα μὲν οὖν ἔλεξεν
εἶναι τὸν χρόνον Αἰνησίδημος κατὰ τὸν Ἡρά-
κλειτον· μὴ διαφέρειν γὰρ αὐτὸν τοῦ ὄντος καὶ τοῦ
πρώτου σώματος. ὅθεν καὶ διὰ τῆς πρώτης εἰσ-
αγωγῆς κατὰ ἐξ πραγμάτων τετάχθαι λέγων τὰς
ἁπλᾶς λέξεις, αἵτινες μέρη τοῦ λόγου τυγχάνουσι,
τὴν μὲν χρόνος προσηγορίαν καὶ τὴν μονάς ἐπὶ τῆς

316

become nor will become, one time alone, the present, will exist, and neither will the future, and the things therein, be any longer future, nor will the past, and the things done therein, be any longer past. But this is not so ; nor, consequently, is time ingenerable.— Nor yet is it partly generable and partly ingenerable, 213 since, if so, the difficulties will be combined. For the generable must become either in itself or in another ; but if it becomes in itself it will exist before itself, and if in another it will no longer be that time but, quitting its own post, it will be the time during which it becomes. And the same argument applies also to 214 the ingenerable ; for if it is ingenerable, neither will the future time ever exist nor the past, but one time only, the present. But these results are absurd. It only remains, then, to say that as time is neither generable nor ingenerable, nor partly generable and partly ingenerable, time does not exist.

And it will be possible to doubt about this matter 215 in respect of its substance, just as we have previously shown its doubtfulness in regard to its conception. Thus, for instance, some of the Dogmatic philosophers assert that time is a body, others that it is incorporeal; and of those who assert it to be incorporeal some regard it as a thing conceived as self-existent, others as a property of something else. Thus Aenesidemus 216 " according to Heracleitus "[a] stated that time is a body ; for it does not differ from the existent and the first body. Hence, too, when he mentions in his *First Introduction* that the simple appellations, which are the parts of speech, apply to six things, he asserts that the names " time " and " unit " are

------

[a] *Cf. P.H.* iii. 138; *Adv. Phys.* i. 337. By "the existent and the first body " is meant " air "; see §§ 232 f. *infra.*

217 οὐσίας τετάχθαι φησίν, ἥτις ἐστὶ σωματική, τὰ δὲ
μεγέθη τῶν χρόνων καὶ τὰ κεφάλαια τῶν ἀριθμῶν
ἐπὶ πολλαπλασιασμοῦ μάλιστα ἐκφέρεσθαι. τὸ μὲν
γὰρ νῦν, ὃ δὴ χρόνου μήνυμά ἐστιν, ἔτι δὲ τὴν
μονάδα οὐκ ἄλλο τι εἶναι ἢ τὴν οὐσίαν, τὴν δὲ
ἡμέραν καὶ τὸν μῆνα καὶ τὸν ἐνιαυτὸν πολλαπλα-
σιασμὸν ὑπάρχειν τοῦ νῦν, φημὶ δὲ τοῦ χρόνου, τὰ
δὲ δύο καὶ τρία καὶ δέκα καὶ ἑκατὸν πολυπλα-
σιασμὸν εἶναι τῆς μονάδος. ὥσθ' οὗτοι μὲν σῶμα
218 ποιοῦσι τὸν χρόνον, οἱ δὲ ἀπὸ τῆς στοᾶς φιλόσοφοι
ἀσώματον αὐτὸν ᾠήθησαν ὑπάρχειν· τῶν γὰρ τινῶν
φασι τὰ μὲν εἶναι σώματα τὰ δὲ ἀσώματα, τῶν δὲ
ἀσωμάτων τέσσαρα εἴδη καταριθμοῦνται ὡς λεκτὸν
καὶ κενὸν καὶ τόπον καὶ χρόνον. ἐξ οὗ δῆλον
γίνεται ὅτι πρὸς τῷ ἀσώματον ὑπολαμβάνειν τὸν
χρόνον, ἔτι καὶ καθ' αὑτό τι νοούμενον πρᾶγμα
δοξάζουσι τοῦτον.

219 Ἐπίκουρος δέ, ὡς αὐτὸν Δημήτριος ὁ Λάκων
ἐξηγεῖται, τὸν χρόνον σύμπτωμα συμπτωμάτων
εἶναι λέγει, παρεπόμενον ἡμέραις τε καὶ νυξὶ καὶ
ὥραις καὶ πάθεσι καὶ ἀπαθείαις καὶ κινήσεσι καὶ
μοναῖς. πάντα γὰρ ταῦτα συμπτώματά ἐστι
τισὶ συμβεβηκότα, καὶ ὁ χρόνος πᾶσι τούτοις
συμπαρεπόμενος εἰκότως ἂν λεχθείη σύμπτωμα
220 συμπτωμάτων. καθόλου γάρ, ἵνα μικρὸν ἄνωθεν
προλάβωμεν εἰς τὴν τοῦ λεγομένου παρακολού-
θησιν, τῶν ὄντων τὰ μέν τινα καθ' ἑαυτὰ ὑφέστηκεν,
τὰ δὲ περὶ τοῖς καθ' ἑαυτὰ ὑφεστῶσι θεωρεῖται.
καὶ καθ' ἑαυτὰ μὲν ὑφέστηκε πράγματα οἷον αἱ
οὐσίαι, ὡς τὸ σῶμα καὶ κενόν, περὶ δὲ τοῖς καθ'

applied to the substance, which is corporeal, whereas 217
the extents of the times and the sums of the numbers
are chiefly expressed by multiples of these. For
" now," which is an indication of time, and also
" unit " are nothing else than the substance ; while
" day " and " month " and " year " are multiples of
" now " (I mean, of time), and " two " and " three "
and " ten " and " a hundred " are multiples of
" unit." So that these people make time a body ;
but the Stoic philosophers supposed it to be incor- 218
poreal ; for they assert that of the " Somethings " [a]
some are bodies, others incorporeal, and they enumerate four kinds of the incorporeals, namely, " expression " and void and place and time. And from this
it is evident that, in addition to supposing time to be
incorporeal, they also regard it as a thing conceived
as self-existent.

Epicurus, as Demetrius the Laconian interprets 219
him, declares that time is " a symptom of symptoms,[b]
accompanying days and nights and hours and affections and non-affections and motions and rests." For
all these are symptoms attached to things, and as
accompanying all these time may naturally be called
" a symptom of symptoms." For in general—to go 220
back a little, for the readier following of our exposition—some existent things are self-existent, while
others are viewed as attached to such as are self-
existent. And such things as substances (like body
and void) are self-existent ; and such as are viewed

[a] In the Stoic logic " Something " (τό τι) was the highest
universal (*summum genus*) ; see Introd. Vol. I. p. xxvi. For
" expression " (*i.e.* " meaning " of a term, or the subjective
idea which it excites) *cf. P.H.* ii. 81, *Adv. Log.* ii. 12.

[b] *Cf.* § 81 *supra* ; *P.H.* iii. 137. " Symptom " (or " concurrence ") nearly=" attribute " or " property ", *cf.* § 221.

ἑαυτὰ ὑφεστῶσι θεωρεῖται τὰ καλούμενα παρ'
221 αὐτοῖς συμβεβηκότα. τούτων δὲ τῶν συμβεβηκότων τὰ μέν ἐστιν ἀχώριστα τῶν οἷς συμβέβηκεν,
τὰ δὲ χωρίζεσθαι τούτων πέφυκεν. ἀχώριστα μὲν
οὖν ἐστὶ τῶν οἷς συμβέβηκεν ὥσπερ ἡ ἀντιτυπία
222 μὲν τοῦ σώματος, εἶξις δὲ τοῦ κενοῦ· οὔτε γὰρ
σῶμα δυνατόν ἐστί ποτε νοῆσαι χωρὶς τῆς ἀντιτυπίας οὔτε τὸ κενὸν χωρὶς εἴξεως, ἀλλ' ἀίδιον
ἑκατέρου συμβεβηκὸς τοῦ μὲν τὸ ἀντιτυπεῖν τοῦ δὲ
τὸ εἴκειν. οὐκ ἀχώριστα δέ ἐστι τῶν οἷς συμβέβηκε
223 καθάπερ ἡ κίνησις καὶ ἡ μονή. τὰ γὰρ συγκριτικὰ
τῶν σωμάτων οὔτε κινεῖται διὰ παντὸς ἀνηρεμήτως
οὔτ' ἀκινητίζει διὰ παντός, ἀλλὰ ποτὲ μὲν συμ-
βεβηκυῖαν ἔχει τὴν κίνησιν ποτὲ δὲ τὴν μονήν,
καίπερ τῆς ἀτόμου, ὅτε καθ' ἑαυτήν ἐστιν, ἀεικινή-
του καθεστώσης. ἢ γὰρ κενῷ πελάζειν ὀφείλει ἢ
σώματι· εἴτε δὲ κενῷ πελάζοι, διὰ τὴν εἶξιν φέρεται
δι' αὐτοῦ, εἴτε σώματι, διὰ τὴν ἀντιτυπίαν ἀποπαλτικῶς ποιεῖται τὴν ἀπ' αὐτοῦ κίνησιν.
224 συμπτώματα οὖν ταῦτ' ἔστιν οἷς χρόνος παρέπεται,
φημὶ δὲ τήν τε ἡμέραν καὶ νύκτα καὶ ὥραν καὶ τὰ
πάθη καὶ τὰς ἀπαθείας κινήσεις τε καὶ μονάς. ἤ
τε γὰρ ἡμέρα καὶ νὺξ τοῦ περιέχοντος ἀέρος εἰσὶ
συμπτώματα, ὧν ἡ μὲν ἡμέρα κατὰ τὸν ἐξ ἡλίου
φωτισμὸν συμβαίνει, ἡ δὲ νὺξ κατὰ φωτισμοῦ
225 στέρησιν τοῦ ἐξ ἡλίου ἐπιγίνεται. ἡ δὲ ὥρα ἤτοι
τῆς ἡμέρας ἢ τῆς νυκτὸς μέρος καθεστηκυῖα πάλιν
σύμπτωμα γίνεται τοῦ ἀέρος, ὥσπερ καὶ ἡ ἡμέρα
καὶ ἡ νύξ. ἀντιπαρεκτείνεται δὲ πάσῃ ἡμέρᾳ καὶ
πάσῃ νυκτὶ καὶ ὥρᾳ ὁ χρόνος· παρ' ἣν αἰτίαν μακρά
τις ἢ βραχεῖα λέγεται ἡμέρα καὶ νύξ, φερομένων

as attached to the self-existents are what they call
" properties." And of these properties some are 221
inseparable from the objects whereto they belong,
while others are naturally separated from them.[a]
Inseparable, for instance, from the things whereto
they belong are the resistance [b] of body and the non-
resistance of void ; for body can never be conceived 222
as without resistance, or void without non-resistance ;
but each has a property that is eternal, the one
resistance, the other non-resistance. But not inseparable from the things whereto they belong are
such properties as motion and rest. For such bodies 223
as are composite are neither in restless motion continually nor continually motionless, but have at one
time the property of motion, at another that of rest,
although the atom, when it is by itself, is in perpetual
motion. For it must collide either with a void or
with a body ; and if it collides with a void, it passes
through this because of its non-resistance ; but if
with a body, it moves back from this by way of rebound, because of its resistance.—Thus these things 224
are " symptoms " which time accompanies—I mean
day and night and hour and affections and non-affections and motions and rests. For day and night are
symptoms of the surrounding air, of which day is a
property due to the illumination from the sun, while
night results from the privation of the illumination
from the sun. And hour again, being a part either 225
of day or of night, is a symptom of the air, like day
and night. And time extends parallel to every day
and every night and hour ; and for this reason a day
or a night is called long or short, as we pass over the

---

[a] Such " properties " are (in logical phrase) " accidents."
[b] Or " solidity," cf. § 239 ; P.H. iii. 39.

SEXTUS EMPIRICUS

ἡμῶν ἐπὶ τὸν ταύτῃ συμβεβηκότα χρόνον. τά τε
πάθη καὶ αἱ ἀπάθειαι ἤτοι ἀλγηδόνες ἢ ἡδοναὶ
ἐτύγχανον, διὰ δὲ τοῦτο οὐκ οὐσίαι τινὲς καθειστή-
κεισαν ἀλλὰ συμπτώματα τῶν πασχόντων ἤτοι
ἡστικῶς ἢ ἀλγεινῶς, καὶ συμπτώματα οὐκ ἄχρονα.
226 πρὸς τούτοις καὶ ἡ κίνησις, ἔτι δὲ ἡ μονή, ὡς ἤδη
παρεστήσαμεν, τῶν σωμάτων ἐστὶ συμπτώματα
καὶ οὐ χωρὶς χρόνου· τὴν γοῦν ὀξύτητα καὶ βρα-
δυτῆτα τῆς κινήσεως, ἔτι δὲ τὴν πλείονα καὶ
227 ἐλάττονα μονὴν χρόνῳ καταμετροῦμεν. ἀλλὰ γὰρ
ἐκ τούτων φανερὸν ὅτι ὁ Ἐπίκουρος ἀσώματον
οἴεται τὸν χρόνον ὑπάρχειν, οὐ παραπλησίως δὲ
τοῖς στωικοῖς· ἐκεῖνοι μὲν γάρ, ὡς λέλεκται,
ἀσώματόν τι καθ' αὑτὸ νοούμενον ὑπεστήσαντο
τὸν χρόνον, Ἐπίκουρος δὲ συμβεβηκός τισιν.
228 Ὧδε μὲν οὗτοι, Πλάτων δὲ ἔλεγεν, ὡς δέ τινες
Ἀριστοτέλης, χρόνον εἶναι ἀριθμὸν τοῦ ἐν κινήσει
προτέρου καὶ ὑστέρου, Στράτων δὲ ὁ φυσικός, ὡς
δ' ἄλλοι Ἀριστοτέλης, μέτρον κινήσεως καὶ μονῆς.
229 Ὅθεν τοιαύτης οὔσης καὶ περὶ τῆς κατὰ τὸν
χρόνον οὐσίας διαστάσεως, πάρεστι μὲν ἤδη συμβαλεῖν ἐκ τῶν προηπορημένων ὅτι οὐδ' ἐκ ταύτης
οἷόν τέ ἐστι βεβαίως τι μαθεῖν, ὅμως δὲ καὶ τὰ νῦν
λεκτέον πρὸς μὲν Πλάτωνα καὶ Ἀριστοτέλην καὶ
Στράτωνα τὸν φυσικὸν τὰ ἐν ἀρχαῖς ἀντειρημένα,
ὅτε ἐκ τῆς ἐννοίας τοῦ χρόνου συνήγομεν τὸ μηδὲν
230 εἶναι τὸν χρόνον, πρὸς δὲ τοὺς σωματικὴν ἀξιοῦντας
εἶναι τὴν οὐσίαν τοῦ χρόνου, φημὶ δὲ τοὺς Ἡρακλειτείους, ἐκεῖνο τὸ[1] προχειρότατον ὅτι εἰ χρόνος
σῶμά ἐστι, πᾶν δὲ σῶμα ἢ μένον ἢ κινούμενον

[1] ἐκεῖνο τό cj. Bekk.: κινοῖτο mss., Bekk.

322

time which is a property thereof. The affections, too, and non-affections are either pains or pleasures, and on this account are not substances but symptoms of those who are affected either pleasurably or painfully, and not timeless symptoms. And besides these, 226 motion and also rest are, as we have already established,[a] symptoms of bodies and not without time ; for certainly we measure by time the quickness and slowness of motion, and the greater or less amount of rest. Well then, from this it is plain that Epicurus 227 thinks that time is incorporeal, but not in the same sort of way as do the Stoics ; for whereas they, as has been said, supposed that time is an incorporeal thing conceived as self-existent, Epicurus supposed it to be a property of certain things.

Such were the views of these men ; but Plato— 228 and, as some say, Aristotle [b]—declared that " time is the number of the prior and posterior in motion " ; and Strato the physicist—and, as others say, Aristotle —that it is " the measure of motion and rest."

Hence, as there also exists such a divergence of 229 opinion regarding the substance of time, one can already infer from the difficulties stated above that from it too it is impossible to learn anything for certain ; but still we ought now to bring against Plato and Aristotle and Strato the physicist the objections we made at the beginning [c] when we deduced from the conception of time that time is nothing, and against 230 those who maintain that the substance of time is corporeal—I mean the Heracleiteans [d]—we should bring the argument most ready to hand that if time is a body, and every body is conceived as either at rest

[a] Cf. §§ 176-177.
[b] Cf. § 176 ; P.H. iii. 137.　　　[c] See §§ 170 ff.
[d] Cf. § 216.

νοεῖται, τὸ δὲ μένον ἢ κινούμενον ἐν χρόνῳ μένον ἢ
κινούμενον νοεῖται, ⟨ἐν σώματι τὸ σῶμα μένον ἢ
κινούμενον νοεῖται,⟩[1] οὐχὶ δέ γε ἐν σώματι τὸ σῶμα
μένον ἢ κινούμενον νοεῖται, οὐκ ἄρα σῶμά ἐστιν ὁ
231 χρόνος.   τό τε ὂν κατὰ τοὺς Ἡρακλειτείους, ὃ
δὴ σῶμά ἐστιν, ἐν χρόνῳ ἐστίν· οὐχὶ δέ γε ὁ χρόνος
ἐν χρόνῳ ἐστίν· οὐκ ἄρα τὸ ὂν καὶ τὸ σῶμα χρόνος
ἐστίν. τό τε ζῷον ἐν χρόνῳ ζῇ, ὡς καὶ τὸ τεθνηκὸς
ἐν χρόνῳ τέθνηκεν· διὸ οὐκ ἔστι ζῷον ἢ σῶμα ὁ
232 χρόνος.   καὶ μὴν οἱ λέγοντες μὴ ὑπάρχειν τὸ
πρῶτον σῶμα κατὰ τὸν Ἡράκλειτον οὐ κωλύονται
χρόνον νοεῖν· εἰ δέ γε χρόνος ἦν τὸ πρῶτον κατὰ
τὸν Ἡράκλειτον σῶμα, κἂν ἐκωλύοντο τὸν χρόνον
νοεῖν· οὐκ ἄρα τὸ ὂν κατὰ τὸν Ἡράκλειτον ἐστὶ
233 χρόνος.   τό τε ὂν κατὰ τὸν Ἡράκλειτον ἀήρ ἐστιν,
ὡς φησὶν ὁ Αἰνησίδημος, μακρῷ δὲ ἀέρος διέφερεν
ὁ χρόνος, καὶ ᾧ λόγῳ οὐθεὶς τὸ πῦρ ἢ τὸ ὕδωρ ἢ
τὴν γῆν χρόνον λέγει εἶναι, τῷ αὐτῷ οὐδὲ τὸν ἀέρα
φήσει· οὐ τοίνυν τὸ ὄν ἐστι χρόνος.

234   Ταῦτα μὲν οὖν ὡς ἐν συντόμοις πρὸς ταύτην
εἰρήσθω τὴν στάσιν, βραχὺς δ' ἐστὶ καὶ πρὸς τοὺς
ἀπὸ τῆς στοᾶς λόγος, φάσκοντας τῶν τινῶν τὰ μὲν
εἶναι σώματα τὰ δὲ ἀσώματα, καὶ τῶν ἀσωμάτων
εἶδός τι καθ' αὑτὸ νοούμενον οἰομένους τὸν χρόνον.
τὸ γὰρ τὶ γενικώτατον τῷ μήτε σῶμά τι δύνασθαι
εἶναι μήτε ἀσώματον μήτε σῶμα ἅμα καὶ ἀσώματον
235 οὐκ ἂν εἴη. εἰ γὰρ σῶμά ἐστι, δεήσει πάντα αὐτοῦ
τὰ εἴδη σώματα τυγχάνειν καὶ μηδὲν ἀσώματον·
καὶ ὃν τρόπον πάντα τὰ τοῦ ζῴου εἴδη ζῷά ἐστι καὶ
οὐδὲν ἄψυχον καὶ τὰ τοῦ φυτοῦ φυτὰ καὶ οὐδὲν

---

[1] ⟨ἐν . . . νοεῖται⟩ add. Heintz (lac. in N).

[a] Cf. § 218.   With §§ 234-236 cf. P.H. ii. 223-225.

or in motion, and what is at rest or in motion is conceived as at rest or in motion in time, ⟨then the body
is conceived as being at rest or in motion in a body⟩ ;
but the body is not conceived as at rest or in motion
in a body ; therefore time is not a body.—Also, 231
according to the Heracleiteans, " the existent," which
is body, is in time ; but time is not in time ; therefore
the existent and body is not time. Also, the living
creature lives in time, as also the dead is dead in
time ; wherefore time is not a living creature or a
body.—Moreover, those who assert that " the first 232
body " of Heracleitus does not exist are not precluded
from conceiving time ; but if time had been the first
body of Heracleitus, they would have been precluded ;
therefore " the existent " of Heracleitus is not time.
Also, the existent of Heracleitus, as Aenesidemus says, 233
is air ; but time is vastly different from air, and just
as nobody says that fire or water or earth is time, so
for the same reason nobody will say that air is time ;
so, then, the existent is not time.

Let this, then, serve as a concise statement of the 234
objections to this view ; and brief, too, is our argument against the Stoics, who declare that of the
" Somethings " some are bodies, others incorporeals,[a]
and suppose that time is a particular species of the
incorporeals which is conceived as self-existent. For
the " Something," the highest genus, will not exist
owing to its being unable to be either a body or an incorporeal or at once both body and incorporeal. For 235
if it is a body, all its particulars will have to be bodies
and none incorporeal ; and just as all the particulars
of Animal are animals and none inanimate, and those

ἔμψυχον, οὕτως ἀκολουθήσει καὶ τὰ τοῦ τινὸς εἴδη
σώματος ὄντος σώματα τυγχάνειν καὶ μηδὲν αὐτῶν
ἀσώματον. εἰ δὲ ἀσώματόν ἐστιν, ἔσται πάντα
236 αὐτοῦ τὰ εἴδη ἀσώματα καὶ οὐδὲν σῶμα. ὡσαύτως
δὲ κἂν σῶμα ἅμα καὶ ἀσώματον ὑπάρχῃ, πάντα τὰ
ἐπὶ μέρους ἔσται σώματα ἅμα καὶ ἀσώματα, καὶ
οὐδὲν κατ᾿ ἰδίαν ἢ σῶμα μόνον ἢ ἀσώματον. ὥστε
εἰ μὴ σῶμά ἐστι τὸ τὶ μηδὲ ἀσώματον ἢ σῶμα ἅμα
καὶ ἀσώματον, οὐδέν ἐστι τὸ τί. τούτου δ᾿ ἀναιρουμένου συναναιρεῖται καὶ τὰ ἐπ᾿ εἴδους πάντα·
237 ὅπερ ἐστὶν ἄτοπον.   καὶ μὴν καὶ ἕκαστον τῶν
συναποδοθέντων τῷ χρόνῳ ἀσωμάτων ἠπόρηται
τοῖς ἀπὸ τῆς σκέψεως, οἷον τὸ λεκτὸν καὶ τὸ κενὸν
καὶ ὁ τόπος· ἑκάστου δὲ τούτων ἠπορημένου καὶ ὁ
χρόνος οὐ συγχωρηθήσεται ἐκ τοῦ αὐτοῦ γένους
εἶναι τούτοις.

238 Πρὸς δὲ τὸν Ἐπίκουρον σύμπτωμα συμπτωμάτων ἀξιοῦντα τυγχάνειν τὸν χρόνον, πολλῶν καὶ
ἄλλων λέγεσθαι δυναμένων, ἐκεῖνο πρὸς τὸ παρὸν
ἀπαρκέσει λέγειν, ὅτι αἱ μέν πως ἔχουσαι οὐσίαι
τάχα θεωροῦνται καὶ εἰσὶ τῶν ὑποκειμένων πραγμάτων, τὰ δὲ λεγόμενα συμβεβηκέναι ταῖς οὐσίαις,
οὐχ ἕτερα ὄντα τῶν οὐσιῶν, ἀνυπόστατά ἐστιν·
239 οὔτε γὰρ ἀντιτυπία τις ἔστι παρὰ τὸ ἀντίτυπον
σῶμα οὔτε εἶξις ὑπόκειται παρὰ τὸ εἶκον καὶ κενόν,
οὐ κίνησις παρὰ τὸ κινούμενον σῶμα, οὐ μονὴ παρὰ
τὸ ἠρεμοῦν, ἀλλ᾿ ὡς οὐδέν ἐστι στρατηγία παρὰ
τὸν στρατηγοῦντα οὐδὲ γυμνασιαρχία παρὰ τὸν
γυμνασιαρχοῦντα, οὕτως οὐδὲ ἕκαστον τούτων τῶν
240 συμβεβηκότων ἔστι παρὰ τὸ ᾧ συμβέβηκεν. ὅθεν

ᵃ Cf. § 218.   ᵇ Cf. §§ 219, 227.
  ᶜ Or " solidity," a property of " body," cf. § 12.

326

of Vegetable vegetables and none animate, so too it will follow that, as "Something" is a body, its particulars are bodies and none of them incorporeal. But if it is incorporeal, its particulars will all be incorporeal and none will be a body. And in the 236 same way, if it is at once both body and incorporeal all its particulars will be at once both bodies and incorporeals and none will be by itself either a body only or an incorporeal. So that if the "Something" is not a body nor incorporeal, nor at once both body and incorporeal, the "Something" is nothing. And if this is destroyed, there are also destroyed along with it all its particulars ; which is absurd.—Further- 237 more, each of the incorporeals assumed together with time [a]—such as "expression" and void and place—have been doubted by the Sceptics ; and as each of these has been doubted, it will not be granted that time is of the same genus as they.

And as against Epicurus, who maintains that time 238 is a "symptom of symptoms," [b] although many other arguments can be brought, it will suffice for the present to state this one—that whereas substances in a certain condition are perhaps observed and belong to the class of things really existent, what are called the properties of substances, being not other than the substances, are non-existent ; for there exists no 239 "resistance" [c] apart from the resistant body, nor does any non-resistance subsist apart from the non-resistant and void, nor motion apart from the moving body, nor rest apart from the stationary ; but just as generalship is nothing apart from the acting general, nor headship of a training-school apart from the acting head, so too each of these properties is non-existent apart from that whereof it is a property.

SEXTUS EMPIRICUS

καὶ ἐπειδὰν λέγῃ ὁ Ἐπίκουρος τὸ σῶμα νοεῖν κατ'
ἐπισύνθεσιν μεγέθους καὶ σχήματος καὶ ἀντιτυπίας
καὶ βάρους, ἐκ μὴ ὄντων [σωμάτων]¹ βιάζεται τὸ
ὂν σῶμα νοεῖν· εἰ γὰρ μήτε μέγεθός τι ὑπόκειται
παρὰ τὸ μεμεγεθωμένον μήτε σχῆμα παρὰ τὸ ἐσχη-
ματισμένον μήτε ἀντιτυπία παρὰ τὸ ἀντιτυποῦν,
πῶς ἐκ τῶν μὴ ὑποκειμένων οἷόν τε τὸ ὑποκείμενον
241 νοεῖν σῶμα; ὥσθ' ἵνα ᾖ χρόνος, συμπτώματα
εἶναι δεῖ, ἵνα δὲ τὰ συμπτώματα ὑπάρχῃ, συμβεβηκός τι ὑποκείμενον· οὐδὲν δέ ἐστι συμβεβηκὸς
ὑποκείμενον· τοίνυν οὐδὲ χρόνος δύναται ὑπάρχειν.
242   ἐῶ λέγειν ὅτι καὶ τὰ οἷς λέγεται συμβεβηκέναι ὁ χρόνος, καὶ τὰ ὧν λέγεται σύμπτωμα
τυγχάνειν, ἀνεύρετά ἐστιν, οἷον ἡ ἡμέρα ἡ νύξ, ὥρα,
κίνησις μονή, πάθος ἀπάθεια. ἡ γοῦν ἡμέρα
δωδεκάωρος λεγομένη εἶναι, καθὼς πρότερον ὑπ-
εδείξαμεν, οὐχ ὑφέστηκε κατὰ τὰς δώδεκα ὥρας
ἀλλὰ κατὰ μίαν μόνην τὴν ἐνεστῶσαν, ἥτις οὐκ
243 ἔστιν ἡμέρα. ὁ δ' αὐτὸς λόγος καὶ ἐπὶ τῆς νυκτός.
ἥ τε ὥρα ἐν πλάτει νοουμένη καὶ οἷον τριμερὴς
πάλιν σκεψαμένοις ἡμῖν ἀνυπόστατος φαίνεται.
οὔτε γὰρ ὅτε τὸ πρῶτον αὐτῆς μέρος ἔστιν ὑφέστηκεν, οὔπω γὰρ τὰ λοιπὰ ἔστιν, οὔτε ὅτε τὸ δεύ-
τερον· τότε γὰρ τὸ μὲν πρῶτον οὐκέτι ἔστιν τὸ δὲ
244 τρίτον οὔπω ἔστιν. τῶν δὲ πλειόνων αὐτῆς μερῶν
κατὰ τοῦτον τὸν τρόπον μὴ ὑπαρχόντων οὐδ' αὐτὴ
δύναται ὑπάρχειν. ἀλλ' ἔστω γε ἡμέραν εἶναι καὶ
νύκτα ὑπάρχειν καὶ ὥρας. οὐκοῦν ἐπεὶ ταῦτά ἐστι
χρόνος, ὁ δὲ Ἐπίκουρος σύμπτωμά φησιν αὐτῶν
εἶναι τὸν χρόνον, ἔσται κατὰ τὸν Ἐπίκουρον ὁ

¹ [σωμάτων] secl. Heintz.

Hence when Epicurus asserts that we conceive body 240
by means of a combination of size and shape and
resistance and weight, he is forcing us to form a
conception of existent body out of non-existents;
for if no size exists apart from that which is endowed
with size, nor shape apart from what is shaped, nor
resistance apart from what resists, how is it possible
from things non-existent to form a conception of an
existent body? So that, in order that time may 241
exist, symptoms must exist, and in order that symptoms may exist there must be a really existent property; but there is no really existent property; so
then, time cannot exist.—I pass over the argument 242
that the things of which time is said to be a property
and also the things of which it is said to be a symptom
are indiscoverable,—such as day, night, hour, motion,
rest, affection, non-affection. Thus " day," which is
said to be of twelve hours—as we pointed out above [a]
—does not exist during the twelve hours but during only
one, the present, which is not a day. And the same 243
account holds good of " night." And " hour " again,
being conceived as extended and, as it were, tripartite,[a]
appears to us when we examine it to be non-existent.
For neither does it exist when the first part of it
exists (for the other parts do not as yet exist), nor
when the second; for then the first part exists no
longer and the third does not as yet exist. But since, 244
in this way, most of its parts are non-existent, it cannot
exist itself. But let it be granted that day exists and
that night and hours exist; then, since these are
time, and Epicurus asserts that time is a symptom
of them, time itself, according to Epicurus, will be a

---

[a] See § 182 *supra.* " Hour " may be regarded as " tripartite " as being divisible into past, present, and future.

245 χρόνος αὐτὸς ἑαυτοῦ σύμπτωμα.   καὶ μὴν καὶ
ὁ περὶ τῆς κινήσεως λόγος ποικίλως ἄπορος δέδεικται διὰ τὸ μήτε ἐν ᾧ τι ἔστι τόπῳ δύνασθαι
κινεῖσθαι μήτε ἐν ᾧ μὴ ἔστι. συνανήρηται δὲ καὶ
τὸ περὶ τῆς μονῆς· κινήσεως γὰρ μὴ οὔσης οὐδὲ
μονὴ γένοιτ᾽ ἄν. κατὰ γὰρ ἀντιπαραβολὴν τοῦ
κινουμένου νοεῖται τὸ ἀκίνητον καὶ τοῦ ἀκινητίζοντος τὸ κινούμενον· ὅθεν ὡς δεξιοῦ μὴ ὄντος οὐδὲ
ἀριστερὸν ἔστιν, οὕτως τοῦ ἑτέρου τούτων μὴ ὑπ-
246 άρχοντος οὐδὲ τὸ λοιπὸν δύναται νοεῖσθαι.   καὶ
ἄλλως, φασὶν οἱ ἀπορητικοί, τὸ μένον ὑπό τινος
αἰτίας ἀναγκάζεται μένειν, τὸ δὲ ἀναγκαζόμενον
πάσχει, τὸ δὲ πάσχον κινεῖται· τὸ ἄρα μένον κινεῖται.
ἀλλ᾽ εἰ περὶ τὰ συμπτώματά φησιν εἶναι τὸν χρόνον
ὁ Ἐπίκουρος, δέδεικται δὲ ἠπορημένα, δεήσει ὁμολογεῖν καὶ τὸν συμβεβηκότα τούτοις χρόνον ἠπορῆ-
247 σθαι.   πρὸς τούτοις ἀσώματόν τι[1] ἐστιν ἡ
κίνησις καὶ τὸ πάθος καὶ ἕκαστον τῶν κατηγορη-
μένων, ἀσώματον δὲ καὶ ὁ χρόνος. ἐπεὶ οὖν οὐ
πιθανὸν τοῖς ἀσωμάτοις ἀσώματα συμβεβηκέναι,
λέγωμεν μηδὲ τὸν χρόνον σύμπτωμα εἶναι τῶν
ἐκκειμένων συμπτωμάτων.

Ἀλλὰ γὰρ καὶ ἀπὸ τῆς οὐσίας τὸν χρόνον ἀπορή-
σαντες τὸ μετὰ τοῦτο ζητῶμεν καὶ περὶ ἀριθμοῦ.

Δ΄. ΠΕΡΙ ΑΡΙΘΜΟΥ

248   Ἐπεὶ ἔτι τῶν συζυγούντων τῷ χρόνῳ πραγμάτων ἐστὶ καὶ ὁ ἀριθμὸς διὰ τὸ μὴ χωρὶς ἐξαρι-
θμήσεως τὴν τοῦ χρόνου γίνεσθαι καταμέτρησιν,
καθάπερ ὡρῶν καὶ ἡμερῶν καὶ μηνῶν ἔτι δὲ

---

[1] ἀσώματόν τι NLE: ἀσώματός cet., Bekk.

symptom of itself.—Furthermore, the account given 245
of motion [a] has been shown to be in many respects
dubious owing to the impossibility of a thing moving
either in the place where it is or in that where it is
not. And along with this the doctrine of rest is also
destroyed ; for if motion does not exist, neither will
rest exist. For it is by contrast with the moving
object that the motionless is conceived, and by contrast with the motionless the moving ; hence as left
does not exist if right is non-existent, so if either of
these does not exist, the other cannot be conceived.
And besides, say the Doubters, that which is at rest 246
is compelled to be at rest by some cause [b] ; but that
which is compelled is affected, and what is affected
moves ; therefore that which is at rest moves. But
if Epicurus asserts that time is related to the symptoms, and they have been shown to be doubtful, he
will have to confess that their property, time, is also
doubtful.—And further : motion is an incorporeal, 247
and also affection, and each of the things mentioned,[c]
and time too is an incorporeal. Since, then, it is not
probable that incorporeals are properties of incorporeals, let us declare that time is not a symptom of
the symptoms mentioned.

So now that we have shown the difficulties about
time in respect of its substance, let us inquire next
about number.

CHAPTER IV.—CONCERNING NUMBER

Since number also is one of the things linked closely 248
with time—seeing that the measurement of time (as,
for instance, of hours and days and months, and years

---

[a] See §§ 87 ff.

[b] With § 246 cf. P.H. iii. 116.   [c] Cf. § 242.

ἐνιαυτῶν, καλῶς ἔχειν ἡγούμεθα μετὰ τὴν προ-
ανυσθεῖσαν ἡμῖν περὶ ἐκείνου ζήτησιν καὶ τὸν περὶ
τούτου διαθέσθαι λόγον, καὶ μάλισθ' ὅτι οἱ ἐπιστη-
μονέστατοι τῶν φυσικῶν οὕτω μεγάλην δύναμιν
τοῖς ἀριθμοῖς ἀπένειμαν ὥστε ἀρχὰς καὶ στοιχεῖα
τῶν ὅλων τούτους νομίζειν. οὗτοι δέ εἰσιν οἱ περὶ
249 τὸν Σάμιον Πυθαγόραν. ἐοικέναι γὰρ λέγουσι τοὺς
φιλοσοφοῦντας γνησίως τοῖς περὶ λόγον πονου-
μένοις. ὡς γὰρ οὗτοι πρῶτον τὰς λέξεις ἐξετά-
ζουσιν (ἐκ λέξεων γὰρ ὁ λόγος), καὶ ἐπεὶ ἐκ
συλλαβῶν αἱ λέξεις, πρῶτον σκέπτονται τὰς συλ-
λαβάς· τῶν δὲ συλλαβῶν ⟨εἰς⟩¹ τὰ στοιχεῖα τῆς
ἐγγραμμάτου φωνῆς ἀναλυομένων, περὶ ἐκείνων
250 πρῶτον ἐρευνῶσιν· οὕτω δεῖν φασὶν οἱ περὶ Πυθαγόραν τοὺς ὄντως φυσικούς, τὰ περὶ τοῦ παντὸς
ἐρευνῶντας, ἐν πρώτοις ἐξετάζειν εἰς τίνα τὸ πᾶν
λαμβάνει τὴν ἀνάλυσιν. τὸ μὲν οὖν φαινομένην
εἶναι λέγειν τὴν τῶν ὅλων ἀρχὴν ἀφύσικόν πως
ἐστίν· πᾶν γὰρ τὸ φαινόμενον ἐξ ἀφανῶν ὀφείλει
συνίστασθαι, τὸ δ' ἔκ τινων συνεστὼς οὐκ ἔστιν
251 ἀρχή, ἀλλὰ τὸ ἐκείνου αὐτοῦ συστατικόν. ὅθεν καὶ
τὰ φαινόμενα οὐ ῥητέον ἀρχὰς εἶναι τῶν ὅλων, ἀλλὰ
τὰ συστατικὰ τῶν φαινομένων, ἅπερ οὐκέτι ἦν
φαινόμενα.   τοίνυν ἀδήλους καὶ ἀφανεῖς ὑπ-
252 έθεντο τὰς τῶν ὄντων ἀρχάς, καὶ οὐ κοινῶς. οἱ γὰρ
ἀτόμους εἰπόντες ἢ ὁμοιομερείας ἢ ὄγκους ἢ κοινῶς
νοητὰ σώματα πάντων τῶν ὄντων ἄρχειν πῇ μὲν

---

¹ τῶν δὲ σ. ⟨εἰς⟩] καὶ ἐπεὶ ἐκ σ. N Mutsch.: ἐκ γὰρ σ. cet.,
Bekk. (" cumque syllabae resolvantur ex litteris " Herv.).

as well) does not take place without numeration,—
after the investigation of the latter which we have
now completed we consider that it is well for us to give
an orderly discussion of the former ; and that the
more so because the most learned of the Physicists [a]
have attributed so great a potency to numbers as to
deem them the principles and elements of all things.
These men are Pythagoras of Samos and his school.
For they say that those who are genuinely philo- 249
sophizing are like those who work at language. Now
the latter first examine the words (for language is
composed of words) ; and since words are formed
from the syllables, they scrutinize the syllables first ;
and as syllables are resolved into the elements of
written speech, they investigate these first ; so like- 250
wise the true physicists, as the Pythagoreans say,
when investigating the Universe, ought in the first
place to inquire what are the elements into which
the Universe can be resolved.—Now to assert that
the principle of all things is apparent is contrary to
physical science ; for every apparent thing must be
composed of non-apparents, and what is composed of
things is not a principle, but rather the component
of that compound ⟨is a principle⟩. Hence one ought 251
not to say that the apparent things are principles
of all things, but the components of the apparent
things, and these are no longer apparent.—Thus they
assumed the principles of existing things to be non-
evident and non-apparent, yet they did not do so
with one consent. For those who declared that 252
atoms or homoeomeries or molecules [b] or, in general,
intelligible bodies are the principles of all existing

[a] *i.e.* the Pythagoreans ; *cf. P.H.* iii. 152.
[b] *Cf. Adv. Phys.* i. 363.

κατώρθωσαν πῇ δὲ διέπεσον. ᾗ μὲν γὰρ ἀδήλους
νομίζουσιν εἶναι τὰς ἀρχάς, δεόντως ἀναστρέφονται,
ᾗ δὲ σωματικὰς ὑποτίθενται ταύτας, διαπίπτουσιν.
253 ὡς γὰρ τῶν αἰσθητῶν σωμάτων προηγεῖται τὰ
νοητὰ καὶ ἄδηλα σώματα, οὕτω καὶ τῶν νοητῶν
σωμάτων ἄρχειν δεῖ τὰ ἀσώματα. καὶ κατὰ λόγον·
ὡς γὰρ τὰ τῆς λέξεως στοιχεῖα οὐκ εἰσὶ λέξεις,
οὕτω καὶ τὰ τῶν σωμάτων στοιχεῖα οὐκ ἔστι
σώματα· ἤτοι δὲ σώματα ὀφείλει τυγχάνειν ἢ
254 ἀσώματα· διὸ πάντως ἐστὶν ἀσώματα.   καὶ μὴν
οὐδὲ ἔνεστι φάναι ὅτι αἰωνίους συμβέβηκεν εἶναι
τὰς ἀτόμους, καὶ διὰ τοῦτο δύνασθαι σωματικὰς
οὔσας τῶν ὅλων ἄρχειν. πρῶτον μὲν γὰρ καὶ οἱ
τὰς ὁμοιομερείας καὶ οἱ τοὺς ὄγκους καὶ οἱ τὰ
ἐλάχιστα καὶ ἀμερῆ λέγοντες εἶναι στοιχεῖα αἰώνιον
ἀπολείπουσι τούτων τὴν ὑπόστασιν, ὥστε μὴ μᾶλ-
255 λον τὰς ἀτόμους ἢ ταῦτ’ εἶναι στοιχεῖα. εἶτα καὶ
δεδόσθω ταῖς ἀληθείαις αἰωνίους εἶναι τὰς ἀτόμους·
ἀλλ’ ὃν τρόπον οἱ ἀγένητον καὶ αἰώνιον ἀπολεί-
ποντες τὸν κόσμον οὐδὲν ἧττον πρὸς ἐπίνοιαν
ζητοῦσι τὰς πρῶτον συστησαμένας αὐτὸν ἀρχάς,
οὕτω καὶ ἡμεῖς, φασὶν οἱ Πυθαγορικοὶ τῶν φυσικῶν
φιλοσόφων, κατ’ ἐπίνοιαν σκεπτόμεθα τὸ ἐκ τίνων
τὰ αἰώνια ταῦτα καὶ λόγῳ θεωρητὰ συνέστηκε
256 σώματα. ἤτοι οὖν σώματά ἐστι τὰ συστατικὰ
αὐτῶν ἢ ἀσώματα. καὶ σώματα μὲν οὐκ ἂν εἴπαιμεν, ἐπεὶ δεήσει κἀκείνων σώματα λέγειν εἶναι
συστατικὰ καὶ οὕτως εἰς ἄπειρον προβαινούσης τῆς
257 ἐπινοίας ἄναρχον γίνεσθαι τὸ πᾶν. λείπεται ἄρα
λέγειν ἐξ ἀσωμάτων εἶναι τὴν σύστασιν τῶν νοητῶν
σωμάτων· ὅπερ καὶ Ἐπίκουρος ὡμολόγησε, φήσας

_____
[a] Cf. § 240.

things proved partly right, but partly went wrong.
For in so far as they consider the principles to be
non-evident, their procedure is correct, but in so far
as they assume them to be corporeal they go wrong.
For just as the intelligible and non-evident bodies 253
precede the sensible bodies, so the incorporeals ought
to be the principles of the intelligible bodies. And
logically so : for just as the elements of a word are
not words, so also the elements of bodies are not
bodies ; but they must be either bodies or incorporeals ; certainly, then, they are incorporeals.—
Moreover, it is not admissible to say that it is a 254
property of atoms to be eternal, and that on this
account they can be the principles of all things
although they are corporeal. For, in the first place,
those who assert that homoeomeries or molecules
or minimals and indivisibles are elements assign to
them an eternal existence, so that the atoms are no
more elements than they. Next, let it be granted 255
that the atoms are in very truth eternal ; yet, just
as those who allow that the Universe is ingenerable
and eternal seek none the less, in theory, for the
principles which first composed it, so also we—as
those Physical philosophers, the Pythagoreans, say—
examine theoretically the problem as to what are
the components of these eternal bodies perceptible
by the reason. Their components, then, are either 256
bodies or incorporeals. And we will not say that they
are bodies, since then we should have to say that
the components of these also are bodies, and, as the
conception thus proceeds *ad infinitum*, that the Whole
is without beginning. It only remains, therefore, to 257
declare that the intelligible bodies are composed of
incorporeals ; and this, too, Epicurus [a] acknowledged,

κατὰ ἀθροισμὸν σχήματός τε καὶ μεγέθους καὶ
ἀντιτυπίας καὶ βάρους τὸ σῶμα νενοῆσθαι.

Ἀλλ' ὅτι ἀσωμάτους εἶναι δεῖ τὰς ἀρχὰς τῶν
λόγῳ θεωρητῶν σωμάτων, ἐκ τῶν εἰρημένων
258 συμφανές. ἤδη δὲ οὐκ εἴ τινα προϋφέστηκε τῶν
σωμάτων ἀσώματα, ταῦτ' ἐξ ἀνάγκης στοιχεῖά
ἐστι τῶν ὄντων καὶ πρῶταί τινες ἀρχαί. ἰδοὺ γὰρ
καὶ αἱ ἰδέαι ἀσώματοι οὖσαι κατὰ τὸν Πλάτωνα
προϋφεστᾶσι τῶν σωμάτων, καὶ ἕκαστον τῶν γινομένων πρὸς αὐτὰς γίνεται· ἀλλ' οὐκ εἰσὶ τῶν ὄντων
ἀρχαί, ἐπείπερ ἑκάστη ἰδέα κατ' ἰδίαν μὲν λαμ-
βανομένη ἓν εἶναι λέγεται, κατὰ σύλληψιν δὲ ἑτέρας
ἢ ἄλλων δύο καὶ τρεῖς καὶ τέσσαρες, ὥστε εἶναί τι
ἐπαναβεβηκὸς αὐτῶν τῆς ὑποστάσεως, τὸν ἀριθμόν,
οὗ κατὰ μετοχὴν τὸ ἓν ἢ τὰ δύο ἢ τὰ τρία ἢ τὰ
259 τούτων ἔτι πλείονα ἐπικατηγορεῖται αὐτῶν. καὶ
τὰ στερεὰ σχήματα προεπινοεῖται τῶν σωμάτων,
ἀσώματον ἔχοντα τὴν φύσιν· ἀλλ' ἀνάπαλιν οὐκ
ἄρχει τῶν πάντων· προάγει γὰρ καὶ τούτων κατὰ
τὴν ἐπίνοιαν τὰ ἐπίπεδα σχήματα διὰ τὸ ἐξ ἐκείνων
260 τὰ στερεὰ συνίστασθαι. ἀλλὰ μὴν οὐδὲ τὰ ἐπίπεδα
σχήματα θείη τις ἂν τῶν ὄντων στοιχεῖα· ἕκαστον
γὰρ αὐτῶν πάλιν ἐκ προαγόντων συντίθεται, τῶν
γραμμῶν, καὶ αἱ γραμμαὶ προεπινοουμένους ἔχουσι
τοὺς ἀριθμούς, παρόσον τὸ μὲν ἐκ τριῶν γραμμῶν
τρίγωνον καλεῖται καὶ τὸ ἐκ τεσσάρων τετράγωνον.
καὶ ἐπεὶ ἡ ἁπλῆ γραμμὴ οὐ χωρὶς ἀριθμοῦ νενόηται,
ἀλλ' ἀπὸ σημείου ἐπὶ σημεῖον ἀγομένη ἔχεται τῶν
δυοῖν, οἵ τε ἀριθμοὶ πάντες καὶ αὐτοὶ ὑπὸ τὸ ἓν
πεπτώκασιν (καὶ γὰρ ἡ δυὰς μία τις ἐστὶ δυάς, καὶ

ᵃ Cf. Adv. Phys. i. 364.

when he said that " body is conceived by means of a combination of form and magnitude and resistance and weight."

Well then, it is plain from what has been said that the principles of the bodies perceptible by reason must be incorporeal. But if certain incorporeals 258 exist before the bodies, these are not already of necessity elements of existing things and primary principles. For see how the Ideas, which are incorporeal,[a] exist before the bodies, according to Plato, and everything which becomes becomes because of its relation to them ; yet they are not principles of existing things since each Idea taken separately is said to be a unit, but two or three or four when taken in conjunction with one or more others, so that there is something which transcends their substance, namely number, by participation in which the terms one or two or three or a still higher number than these is predicated of them. The solid 259 forms also, which are of an incorporeal nature, are conceived before bodies ; but they, again, are not principles of all things, for the plane forms precede them in conception, since out of these the solid are composed. Yet, indeed, one should not 260 posit the plane forms either as elements of existing things, for each of these likewise is composed of prior things—namely lines—and lines have numbers already pre-conceived, inasmuch as the compound of three lines is called a triangle and that of four a quadrangle. And since the simple line is not conceived apart from number but, as drawn from a point to a point, involves the number two, and all the numbers themselves fall under the One (for the two is a single two, and the three is one particular thing,

ἡ τριὰς ἕν τι ἐστί, τριάς, καὶ ἡ δεκὰς ἓν ἀριθμοῦ
261 κεφάλαιον), ἔνθεν κινηθεὶς ὁ Πυθαγόρας ἀρχὴν
ἔφησεν εἶναι τῶν ὄντων τὴν μονάδα, ἧς κατὰ
μετοχὴν ἕκαστον τῶν ὄντων ἓν λέγεται· καὶ ταύτην κατ᾽ αὐτότητα μὲν ἑαυτῆς νοουμένην μονάδα
νοεῖσθαι, ἐπισυντεθεῖσαν δ᾽ ἑαυτῇ καθ᾽ ἑτερότητα
ἀποτελεῖν τὴν καλουμένην ἀόριστον δυάδα διὰ τὸ
μηδεμίαν τῶν ἀριθμητῶν καὶ ὡρισμένων δυάδων
εἶναι [τὴν]¹ αὐτήν, πάσας δὲ κατὰ μετοχὴν αὐτῆς
δυάδας νενοῆσθαι, καθὼς καὶ ἐπὶ τῆς μονάδος
262 ἐλέγχουσιν. δύο οὖν τῶν ὄντων αἱ ἀρχαί, ἥ τε
πρώτη μονάς, ἧς κατὰ μετοχὴν πᾶσαι αἱ ἀριθμηταὶ
μονάδες νοοῦνται μονάδες, καὶ ἡ ἀόριστος δυάς, ἧς
κατὰ μετοχὴν αἱ ὡρισμέναι δυάδες εἰσὶ δυάδες.

Καὶ ὅτι ταῖς ἀληθείαις αὗταί εἰσι τῶν ὅλων
263 ἀρχαί, ποικίλως οἱ Πυθαγορικοὶ διδάσκουσιν. τῶν
γὰρ ὄντων, φασί, τὰ μὲν κατὰ διαφορὰν νοεῖται,
τὰ δὲ κατ᾽ ἐναντίωσιν, τὰ δὲ πρός τι. κατὰ διαφορὰν μὲν οὖν εἶναι τὰ καθ᾽ ἑαυτὰ καὶ κατ᾽ ἰδίαν
περιγραφὴν ὑποκείμενα, οἷον ἄνθρωπος ἵππος
φυτὸν γῆ ὕδωρ ἀὴρ πῦρ· τούτων γὰρ ἕκαστον
ἀπολύτως θεωρεῖται καὶ οὐχ ὡς κατὰ τὴν πρὸς
264 ἕτερον σχέσιν· κατ᾽ ἐναντίωσιν δὲ ὑπάρχειν ὅσα
ἐξ ἐναντιώσεως ἑτέρου πρὸς ἕτερον θεωρεῖται, οἷον
ἀγαθὸν καὶ κακόν, δίκαιον ἄδικον, συμφέρον
ἀσύμφορον, ὅσιον ἀνόσιον, εὐσεβὲς ἀσεβές, κινούμενον ἠρεμοῦν, τὰ ἄλλα ὅσα τούτοις ἐμφερῆ.
265 πρός τι δὲ τυγχάνειν τὰ κατὰ τὴν ὡς πρὸς ἕτερον

¹ [τὴν] secl. Heintz.

ᵃ The Pythagoreans regarded " the ten " (Decad) as the
" perfect " number as being the sum of the first four numbers

a three, and the ten is one sum of number [a]), Pyth- 261
agoras, moved by these considerations, declared that
the One is the principle of existing things, by participation in which each of the existing things is termed
one ; and this when conceived in its self-identity is
conceived as One, but when, in its otherness, it is
added to itself it creates the " Indefinite Dyad," [b]
so-called because it is not itself any one of the
numbered and definite dyads but they all are conceived as dyads through their participation in it, even
as they try to prove in the case of the monad.   There 262
are, then, two principles of existing things, the First
One, by participation in which all the numbered ones
are conceived as ones, and also the Indefinite Dyad,
by participation in which the definite dyads are dyads.

And that these are in very truth the principles of
all things the Pythagoreans teach in a variety of
ways. [c] Of existing things some, they say, are con- 263
ceived absolutely, some by way of contrariety, some
relatively.   Absolute, then, are those which subsist
of themselves and in complete independence, such
as man, horse, plant, earth, water, air, fire ; for each
of these is regarded absolutely and not in respect of
its relation to something else.   And contraries are all 264
those which are regarded in respect of their contrariety one to another, such as good and evil, just and
unjust, advantageous and disadvantageous, holy and
unholy, pious and impious, in motion and at rest,
and all other things similar to these.   And relatives 265
are the things conceived as standing in a relation to

$(1 + 2 + 3 + 4 = 10)$; cf. Aristot. *Metaph.* i. 5, 986 [a] 8 τέλειον ἡ
δεκὰς εἶναι δοκεῖ καὶ πᾶσαν περιειληφέναι τὴν τῶν ἀριθμῶν φύσιν.

[b] Cf. *P.H.* iii. 155. The "Indefinite Dyad" is the generic
Two, or principle of Duality.

[c] With §§ 263-265 cf. *Adv. Log.* ii. 161-162 ; *P.H.* i. 137.

σχέσιν νοούμενα, οἷον δεξιὸν ἀριστερόν, ἄνω κάτω,
διπλάσιον ἥμισυ· τό τε γὰρ δεξιὸν νοεῖται κατὰ
τὴν ὡς πρὸς τὸ ἀριστερὸν σχέσιν καὶ τὸ ἀριστερὸν
κατὰ τὴν ὡς πρὸς τὸ δεξιόν, τό τε κάτω κατὰ τὴν
ὡς πρὸς τὸ ἄνω καὶ τὸ ἄνω κατὰ τὴν ὡς πρὸς τὸ
κάτω· καὶ ἐπὶ τῶν ἄλλων τὸ παραπλήσιον.

266 διαφέρειν δέ φασι τὰ κατὰ ἐναντίωσιν νοούμενα
τῶν πρός τι. ἐπὶ μὲν γὰρ τῶν ἐναντίων ἡ τοῦ
ἑτέρου φθορὰ γένεσίς ἐστι τοῦ ἑτέρου, οἷον ἐπὶ
ὑγιείας καὶ νόσου κινήσεώς τε καὶ ἠρεμίας· νόσου
τε γὰρ γένεσις ἆρσίς ἐστιν ὑγιείας, ὑγιείας τε
γένεσις ἆρσίς ἐστι νόσου, καὶ κινήσεως μὲν ὑπόστασις φθορὰ στάσεως, γένεσις δὲ στάσεως ἆρσις
κινήσεως. ὁ δ' αὐτὸς λόγος καὶ ἐπὶ λύπης καὶ
ἀλυπίας ἀγαθοῦ τε καὶ κακοῦ καὶ κοινῶς τῶν
267 ἐναντίαν φύσιν ἐχόντων. τὰ δὲ πρός τι συνύπαρξίν
τε καὶ συναναίρεσιν ἀλλήλων περιεῖχεν· οὐδὲν γὰρ
δεξιόν ἐστιν, ἐὰν μὴ καὶ ἀριστερὸν ὑπάρχῃ, οὐδὲ
διπλάσιον, ἐὰν μὴ καὶ τὸ ἥμισυ προϋποκέηται οὗ
268 διπλάσιον ἐστίν. πρὸς τούτοις ἐπὶ μὲν τῶν
ἐναντίων ὡς ἐπίπαν οὐδὲν θεωρεῖται μέσον,
καθάπερ εὐθέως ἐπὶ ὑγιείας καὶ νόσου ζωῆς τε
καὶ θανάτου κινήσεώς τε καὶ μονῆς· μεταξὺ γὰρ
τοῦ ὑγιαίνειν καὶ νοσεῖν οὐδέν ἐστι, καὶ μεταξὺ
τοῦ ζῆν καὶ τεθνάναι καὶ ἔτι τοῦ κινεῖσθαι καὶ
μένειν. ἐπὶ δὲ τῶν πρός τί πως ἐχόντων ἔστι
τι μέσον· τοῦ γὰρ μείζονος, εἰ τύχοι, καὶ τοῦ
μικροτέρου τῶν πρός τί πως καθεστώτων μεταξὺ
γένοιτ' ἂν τὸ ἴσον, ὡσαύτως δὲ καὶ τοῦ πλείονος
καὶ ἥττονος τὸ ἱκανόν, ὀξέος τε καὶ βαρέος τὸ
269 σύμφωνον. ἀλλὰ γὰρ τῶν τριῶν ὄντων γενῶν,
τῶν τε καθ' ἑαυτὰ ὑφεστώτων καὶ τῶν κατ'

something else, such as right and left, above and below, double and half; for right is conceived as standing in relation to left, and left also as standing in relation to right, and below as related to above, and above as related to below; and similarly in the other cases.—And they say that things conceived as 266 contraries differ from relatives. For in the case of contraries the destruction of the one is the generation of the other, as in the case of health and disease, of motion and rest; for the generation of disease is the removal of health and the generation of health is the removal of disease, and the existence of motion is the destruction of rest and the generation of rest the removal of motion. And the same account holds good also in the case of pain and painlessness, of good and evil, and in general of all things that are of opposite natures. But relatives have the property 267 both of co-existence and of co-destruction one with the other; for there is no right unless a left also exists, nor a double unless the half also, whereof it is the double, pre-exists.—Furthermore, in the case of 268 opposites, as a universal rule, no intermediate state is conceived, as for instance in the cases of health and disease, life and death, motion and rest; for there is nothing between healthiness and illness, and between living and being dead, or again between moving and resting. But in the case of relatives there is a middle state; for the equal (let us say) will be between the greater and the smaller, these being relatives; and so likewise the adequate between the more and the less, and the harmonious between the high and the deep.—So then, as there are these three classes—the 269 self-existent things, those conceived as in opposition,

ἐναντιότητα καὶ ἔτι τῶν πρός τι νοουμένων,
ὀφείλει κατ' ἀνάγκην καὶ τούτων αὐτῶν ἐπάνω
τι γένος τετάχθαι, καὶ πρῶτον ὑπάρχειν διὰ τὸ
καὶ πᾶν γένος προϋπάρχειν τῶν ὑφ' αὐτὸ τεταγμένων εἰδῶν. ἀναιρουμένου γοῦν αὐτοῦ πάντα τὰ
εἴδη συναναιρεῖται, τοῦ δὲ εἴδους ἀναιρεθέντος
οὐκέτ' ἀνασκευάζεται τὸ γένος· ἤρτηται γὰρ ἐξ
270 ἐκείνου τοῦτο, καὶ οὐκ ἀνάπαλιν.   καὶ δὴ
τῶν μὲν καθ' αὑτὰ νοουμένων γένος ὑπεστήσαντο
Πυθαγορικῶν παῖδες, ὡς ἐπαναβεβηκός, τὸ ἕν·
καθὰ γὰρ τοῦτο καθ' αὑτὸ ἔστιν, οὕτω καὶ ἕκαστον
τῶν κατὰ διαφορὰν ἕν τέ ἐστι καὶ καθ' ἑαυτὸ
271 θεωρεῖται. τῶν δὲ κατ' ἐναντίωσιν ἔλεξαν ἄρχειν,
γένους τάξιν ἐπέχον, τὸ ἴσον καὶ τὸ ἄνισον· ἐν
τούτοις γὰρ ἡ πάντων τῶν ἐναντιουμένων θεωρεῖται
φύσις, οἷον μονῆς μὲν ἐν ἰσότητι, οὐ γὰρ ἐπιδέχεται
τὸ μᾶλλον καὶ τὸ ἧσσον, κινήσεως δὲ ἐν ἀνισότητι,
272 ἐπιδέχεται γὰρ τὸ μᾶλλον καὶ τὸ ἧσσον. ὡσαύτως
δὲ τὸ μὲν κατὰ φύσιν ἐν ἰσότητι, ἀκρότης γὰρ ἦν
ἀνεπίτατος, τὸ δὲ παρὰ φύσιν ἐν ἀνισότητι, ἐπ-
εδέχετο γὰρ τὸ μᾶλλον καὶ ἧσσον. ὁ δ' αὐτὸς
λόγος καὶ ἐπὶ ὑγιείας καὶ νόσου εὐθύτητός τε καὶ
273 στρεβλότητος. τὰ μέντοι γε πρός τι ὑφέστηκε
γένει τῇ τε ὑπεροχῇ καὶ τῇ ἐλλείψει· μέγα μὲν
γὰρ καὶ μεῖζον πολύ τε καὶ πλεῖον ὑψηλόν τε καὶ
ὑψηλότερον καθ' ὑπεροχὴν νοεῖται, μικρὸν δὲ καὶ
μικρότερον ὀλίγον τε καὶ ὀλιγώτερον ταπεινόν τε
274 καὶ ταπεινότερον κατ' ἔλλειψιν.   ἀλλ' ἐπεὶ τὰ
καθ' αὑτὰ καὶ τὰ κατ' ἐναντίωσιν καὶ τὰ πρός τι,
γένη ὄντα, εὕρηται ἄλλοις γένεσιν ὑποταττόμενα,
καθάπερ τῷ τε ἑνὶ καὶ τῇ ἰσότητι καὶ ἀνισότητι
ὑπεροχῇ τε καὶ ἐλλείψει, σκοπῶμεν εἰ καὶ ταῦτα

and also those conceived as relatives,—above all these
there must stand of necessity a certain genus, and it
must exist first for the reason that every genus must
exist before the particulars classed under it. When
it, then, is abolished all the particulars are abolished
along with it, but when the particular is abolished the
genus is not also done away with ; for the former
depends on the latter, and not conversely.—Thus the 270
disciples of the Pythagoreans postulated the One as
the supreme genus of the things conceived as self-
existent. For even as this is self-existent, so also
each of the absolute things is one and is conceived by
itself. But of the opposites the equal and the un- 271
equal are, they said, the principles and hold the rank
of genus ; for in them is seen the nature of all the
opposites,—that of rest, for instance, in equality (for
it does not admit of the more and the less), and that
of motion in inequality (for it does admit of the more
and the less). So too the natural in equality (for it 272
is an inextensible extreme),[a] but the unnatural in
inequality (for it admits of the more and less). The
same account holds good also in the case of health
and disease, and of straightness and crookedness.
The relatives, however, are classed under the genus of 273
excess and defect ; thus great and greater, much and
more, high and higher are conceived by way of excess ;
but small and smaller, few and fewer, low and lower
by way of defect.—But since self-existents and oppo- 274
sites and relatives, which are genera, are found to be
subordinate to other genera—namely, the One, and
equality and inequality, and excess and defect,—let

---

[a] *i.e.* a fixed (and best) state which is " extreme " and
" inextensible " as incapable of alteration for the better.

τὰ γένη δύναται ἐπ' ἄλλα λαμβάνειν τὴν ἀναπομπήν.
275 οὐκοῦν ἡ μὲν ἰσότης τῷ ἑνὶ ὑπάγεται, τὸ γὰρ ἓν
πρώτως αὐτὸ ἑαυτῷ ἐστὶν ἴσον, ἡ δὲ ἀνισότης
ἐν ὑπεροχῇ τε καὶ ἐλλείψει βλέπεται· ἄνισα γάρ
ἐστιν ὧν τὸ μὲν ὑπερέχει τὸ δὲ ὑπερέχεται. ἀλλὰ
καὶ ἡ ὑπεροχὴ καὶ ἡ ἔλλειψις κατὰ τὸν τῆς ἀορίστου δυάδος λόγον τέτακται, ἐπειδήπερ ἡ πρώτη
ὑπεροχὴ καὶ ἡ ἔλλειψις ἐν δυσίν ἐστι, τῷ τε
276 ὑπερέχοντι καὶ τῷ ὑπερεχομένῳ. ἀνέκυψαν ἄρα
ἀρχαὶ πάντων κατὰ τὸ ἀνωτάτω ἥ τε πρώτη μονὰς
καὶ ἡ ἀόριστος δυάς· ἐξ ὧν γίνεσθαί φασι τό τ'
ἐν τοῖς ἀριθμοῖς ἓν καὶ τὴν ἐπὶ τούτοις πάλιν
δυάδα, ἀπὸ μὲν τῆς πρώτης μονάδος τὸ ἕν, ἀπὸ
δὲ τῆς μονάδος καὶ τῆς ἀορίστου δυάδος τὰ δύο.
δὶς γὰρ τὸ ἓν δύο, καὶ μήπω ὑποκειμένου ἐν
τοῖς ἀριθμοῖς τοῦ δύο οὐδὲ τὸ δὶς ἦν ἐν τούτοις,
ἀλλ' ἐλήφθη ἐκ τῆς ἀορίστου δυάδος, καὶ οὕτως
ἐκ ταύτης τε καὶ τῆς μονάδος ἐγένετο ἡ ἐν τοῖς
277 ἀριθμοῖς δυάς. κατὰ ταῦτα δὲ καὶ οἱ λοιποὶ
ἀριθμοὶ ἐκ τούτων ἀπετελέσθησαν, τοῦ μὲν ἑνὸς
ἀεὶ περατοῦντος,[1] τῆς δὲ ἀορίστου δυάδος δύο
γεννώσης καὶ εἰς ἄπειρον πλῆθος τοὺς ἀριθμοὺς
ἐκτεινούσης.   ὅθεν φασὶν ἐν ταῖς ἀρχαῖς ταύταις
τὸν μὲν τοῦ δρῶντος αἰτίου λόγον ἐπέχειν τὴν
μονάδα, τὸν δὲ τῆς πασχούσης ὕλης τὴν δυάδα.
καὶ ὃν τρόπον τοὺς ἐξ αὐτῶν ὑποστάντας ἀριθμοὺς
ἀπετέλεσαν, οὕτω καὶ τὸν κόσμον καὶ πάντα τὰ
278 ἐν τῷ κόσμῳ συνεστήσαντο. εὐθέως γὰρ τὸ
σημεῖον κατὰ τὸν τῆς μονάδος λόγον τετάχθαι·
ὡς γὰρ ἡ μονὰς ἀδιαίρετόν τι ἐστίν, οὕτω καὶ τὸ
σημεῖον, καὶ ὃν τρόπον ἡ μονὰς ἀρχή τίς ἐστιν ἐν
ἀριθμοῖς, οὕτως καὶ τὸ σημεῖον ἀρχή τίς ἐστιν
344

us consider whether these genera also can be referred back to others. Equality, then, is brought under the 275 One (for the One first of all is equal to itself), but inequality is seen in excess and defect ; for things of which the one exceeds and the other is exceeded are unequal. But both excess and defect are ranked under the head of the Indefinite Dyad, since in fact the primary excess and defect is in two things, that which exceeds and that which is exceeded. Thus as 276 the highest principles of all things there have emerged the primary One and the Indefinite Dyad ; and from these, they say, spring both the numerical one and the numerical two,—the one from the primary One, and the two from the One and the Indefinite Dyad. For the two is twice the one, and when the two did not as yet exist among the numbers neither did the twice exist amongst them, but it was taken from the Indefinite Dyad, and in this way the numerical two sprang from it and the One. And in the same way 277 the rest of the numbers were constructed from these, the One always limiting and the Indefinite Dyad generating two and extending the numbers to an infinite amount.—Hence they say that, of these principles, the One holds the position of the efficient cause and the Dyad that of the passive matter ; and just as they have constructed the numbers composed of these, so also they have built up the Universe and all things in the Universe. Thus the point, for ex- 278 ample, is ranked under the head of the One ; for as the One is an indivisible thing, so also is the point ; and just as the One is a principle in numbers, so too

---

[1] περατοῦντος NLE : περιπατοῦντος cet., Bekk.

ἐν γραμμαῖς. ὥστε τὸ μὲν σημεῖον τὸν τῆς
μονάδος εἶχε λόγον, ἡ δὲ γραμμὴ κατὰ τὴν τῆς
δυάδος ἰδέαν ἐθεωρεῖτο· κατὰ μετάβασιν γὰρ καὶ
279 ἡ δυὰς καὶ ἡ γραμμὴ νοεῖται.   καὶ ἄλλως, τὸ
μεταξὺ δυοῖν σημείων νοούμενον ἀπλατὲς μῆκος
ἔστι γραμμή. τοίνυν ἔσται κατὰ τὴν δυάδα ἡ
γραμμή, τὸ δὲ ἐπίπεδον κατὰ τὴν τριάδα, ὃ μὴ
μόνον μῆκος αὐτὸ θεωρεῖται καθὸ ἦν ἡ δυάς, ἀλλὰ
καὶ τρίτην προσείληφε διάστασιν τὸ πλάτος.
280 τιθεμένων δὲ τριῶν σημείων, δυοῖν μὲν ἐξ ἐναντίου
διαστήματος, τρίτου δὲ κατὰ μέσον τῆς ἐκ τῶν
δυοῖν ἀποτελεσθείσης γραμμῆς, πάλιν ἐξ ἄλλου
διαστήματος, ἐπίπεδον ἀποτελεῖται. τὸ δὲ στερεὸν
σχῆμα καὶ τὸ σῶμα, καθάπερ τὸ πυραμοειδές, κατὰ
τὴν τετράδα τάττεται. τοῖς γὰρ τρισὶ σημείοις,
ὡς προεῖπον, κειμένοις ἐπιτεθέντος ἄλλου τινὸς
ἄνωθεν σημείου πυραμοειδὲς ἀποτελεῖται σχῆμα
στερεοῦ σώματος· ἔχει γὰρ ἤδη τὰς τρεῖς δια-
281 στάσεις, μῆκος πλάτος βάθος.   τινὲς δ' ἀπὸ
ἑνὸς σημείου τὸ σῶμά φασι συνίστασθαι· τουτὶ
γὰρ τὸ σημεῖον ῥυὲν γραμμὴν ἀποτελεῖν, τὴν δὲ
γραμμὴν ῥυεῖσαν ἐπίπεδον ποιεῖν, τοῦτο δὲ εἰς
βάθος κινηθὲν τὸ σῶμα γεννᾶν τριχῆ διαστατόν.
282 διαφέρει δὲ ἡ τοιαύτη τῶν Πυθαγορικῶν στάσις
τῆς τῶν προτέρων. ἐκεῖνοι μὲν γὰρ ἐκ δυοῖν ἀρχῶν,
τῆς τε μονάδος καὶ τῆς ἀορίστου δυάδος, ἐποίουν
τοὺς ἀριθμούς, εἶτ' ἐκ τῶν ἀριθμῶν τὰ σημεῖα
καὶ τὰς γραμμὰς τά τε ἐπίπεδα σχήματα καὶ τὰ
στερεά· οὗτοι δὲ ἀπὸ ἑνὸς σημείου τὰ πάντα τεκται-

the point is a principle in lines. So that the point comes under the head of the One, but the line is regarded as belonging to the class of the Dyad; for both the Dyad and the line are conceived by way of transition.—And again: the length without breadth 279 conceived as lying between two points is a line. So then, the line will belong to the Dyad class, but the plane to the Triad since it is not merely regarded as length, as was the Dyad, but has also taken to itself a third dimension, breadth. Also when three points 280 are set down, two at an interval opposite to each other, and a third midway in the line formed from the two, but at a different interval,[a] a plane is constructed. And the solid form and the body, as also the pyramid, are classed under the Tetrad. For when the three points are placed, as I said before, and another point is placed upon them from above,[b] there is constructed the pyramidal form of the solid body; for it now possesses the three dimensions length, breadth, and depth.—But some assert that the body is constructed 281 from one point; for this point when it has flowed produces the line, and the line when it has flowed makes the plane, and this when it has moved towards depth generates the body which has three dimensions. But this view of the ⟨later⟩ Pythagoreans 282 differs from that of the earlier ones. For these latter formed the numbers from two principles, the One and the Indefinite Dyad, and then, from the numbers, the points and the lines and both the plane and the solid forms; but the former build up all of them from a

[a] Any triangle ABC will illustrate this.
[b] Here the plane triangle ABC is assumed to be horizontal, and relatively to it the 4th point is in a vertical line (" from above "), thus forming a " pyramid," having " depth."

νουσιν. ἐξ αὐτοῦ μὲν ⟨γὰρ⟩[1] γραμμὴ γίνεται, ἀπὸ
γραμμῆς δὲ ἐπιφάνεια, ἀπὸ δὲ ταύτης σῶμα.

283 Πλὴν οὕτω μὲν ἀποτελεῖται τὰ στερεὰ σχήματα[2]
ἡγουμένων τῶν ἀριθμῶν· ἀφ' ὧν λοιπὸν καὶ τὰ
αἰσθητὰ[3] συνίσταται, γῆ τε καὶ ὕδωρ καὶ ἀὴρ καὶ
πῦρ, καὶ καθόλου ὁ κόσμος, ὅν φασι καθ' ἁρμονίαν
διοικεῖσθαι πάλιν ἐχόμενοι τῶν ἀριθμῶν, ἐν οἷς οἱ
λόγοι εἰσὶ τῶν συστατικῶν τῆς τελείου ἁρμονίας
συμφωνιῶν, τῆς τε διὰ τεσσάρων καὶ τῆς διὰ πέντε
καὶ τῆς διὰ πασῶν, ὧν ἡ μὲν ἐν ἐπιτρίτῳ ἔκειτο
284 λόγῳ, ἡ δὲ ἐν ἡμιολίῳ, ἡ δὲ ἐν διπλασίονι. εἴρηται
δὲ περὶ τούτων ἀκριβέστερν κἂν τῇ περὶ κριτηρίου
σκέψει κἂν τοῖς περὶ ψυχῆς.

Νῦν δὲ ὑποδειχθέντος ὅτι μεγάλην δύναμιν
ἀπονέμουσι τοῖς ἀριθμοῖς οἱ ἀπὸ τῆς Ἰταλίας
φυσικοὶ μετελθόντες καὶ τὰς ἀκολούθους τῷ τόπῳ
285 κομίζωμεν ἀπορίας. ὅταν οὖν λέγωσι τῶν ἀριθμητῶν, οἷον τῶν αἰσθητῶν καὶ ὑποπιπτόντων,
μηδὲν εἶναι ἕν, μετοχῇ δὲ τοῦ ἑνὸς τοῦ ὡσανεὶ
πρώτου καὶ στοιχείου ἕν τι καλεῖσθαι, εἰ οὖν τὸ
δεικνύμενον [καὶ τὸ μένον][4] ζῷον ἓν εἴη, τὸ μὴ
δεικνύμενον φυτὸν οὐκ ἔσται ἕν. οὐ γὰρ δεῖ
πολλὰ ⟨ἓν⟩[5] εἶναι, μετοχῇ δὲ τοῦ ἑνὸς ἕκαστον
286 νοεῖσθαι ἕν, οἷον ζῷον ξύλον φυτόν. εἰ γὰρ τὸ

---

[1] ⟨γὰρ⟩ add. E, cj. Bekk.
[2] σχήματα] σώματα mss., Bekk. (νοητὰ σώμ. Heintz).
[3] αἰσθητὰ NE : στερεὰ cet., Bekk.
[4] [καὶ τὸ μένον] secl. Kayser.
[5] ⟨ἓν⟩ add. ego.

---

[a] *Cf. P.H.* iii. 155; *Adv. Log.* i. 96. The terms are
those of the Pythagorean musical theory and denote the
" intervals " (" fourth " " fifth," and " octave ") between the
notes. With διὰ τεσσάρων—πέντε—πασῶν sc. χορδῶν.

single point. For from this the line is produced, and from the line the plane, and from this the body.

This, however, is the way in which the solid forms 283 are constructed, with the numbers leading ; and, finally, from these ⟨solids⟩ the sensibles are composed, earth and water and air and fire, and the Universe at large ; and it, they declare (holding fast once more to the numbers), is ordered according to harmony,[a] since it is in numbers that the ratios reside of those symphonies which make up the perfect harmony,— namely, the " By-Fours " and the " By-Fives " and the " By-alls," of which the first lies in the ratio 4 : 3, the second in the ratio 3 : 2, the third in that of 2 : 1. But this subject has been discussed more exactly in 284 our inquiry regarding the criterion [b] and in our treatise *On the Soul*.

And now that it has been shown that the Italian Physicists ascribe a great potency to numbers, let us pass on and bring forward the difficulties consequent on this position.[c] Thus when they assert [d] that none 285 of the numerables—such as things sensible and perceived—is one, but is called one through its participation in the One which is, as it were, primary and elemental, then if the animal pointed out is one, the plant which is not pointed out will not be one. For many things must not really be one, but each of them —such as an animal, a stick, a plant—must be conceived as one through participation in the One. For 286

---

[b] *i.e. Adv. Log.* i. 96 ff. The treatise *On the Soul* is not extant.

[c] With §§ 285-287 *cf. P.H.* iii. 156. The text here (from μετοχῇ . . . ἔσται ἕν §§ 285-286) is probably corrupt (a conflation of two versions).

[d] From here to the end of § 287 we are given the Pythagorean doctrine ; the criticism follows in §§ 288 ff.

349

δεικνύμενον ζῷον ἕν ἐστι, τὸ μὴ ὂν ζῷον, οἷον τὸ
φυτόν, οὐκ ἔσται ἕν· καὶ εἰ τὸ φυτὸν ἕν ἐστι, τὸ
μὴ ὂν φυτόν, οἷον τὸ ζῷον, οὐκ ἔσται ἕν. ἀλλὰ
λέγεταί γε τὸ μὴ ὂν ζῷον ἕν, καθάπερ τὸ φυτόν,
καὶ τὸ μὴ ὂν φυτὸν πάλιν ἕν, ὡς τὸ ζῷον. οὐκ
ἄρα ἕκαστον τῶν ἀριθμητῶν ἕν ἐστιν. τὸ δὲ οὗ
ἕκαστον μετοχῇ νενόηται ἕν, ἐκεῖνο ἕν τέ ἐστι καὶ
πολλά, ἓν μὲν καθ᾽ ἑαυτό, πολλὰ δὲ κατὰ περί-
287 ληψιν. ὅπερ πλῆθος πάλιν οὐκ ἔστιν ἐν τοῖς
ἀριθμητοῖς δεικνύμενον. εἰ γὰρ τὸ τῶν ζῴων
πλῆθος ⟨πλῆθός⟩[1] ἐστιν, τὸ τῶν φυτῶν οὐκ ἔσται
πλῆθος, καὶ εἰ τὸ τούτων, ἀνάπαλιν οὐκ ἔσται τὸ
τῶν ζῴων. λέγεται δέ γε καὶ ἐπὶ φυτῶν καὶ ἐπὶ
ζῴων καὶ ἐπ᾽ ἄλλων ἱκανῶν πλῆθος· οὐκ ἄρα τὸ
ἐν τοῖς ἀριθμητοῖς δεικνύμενον πλῆθος τῷ ὄντι
πλῆθός ἐστιν, ἀλλὰ ἐκεῖνο τὸ οὗ μετοχῇ νενόηται
288 τοῦτο πλῆθος.   ὅταν δὴ τὰ τοιαῦτα λέγωσιν
οἱ Πυθαγορικοὶ τῶν φιλοσόφων, ὅμοιόν τι λέγουσι
τῷ μηδένα τῶν ἐπὶ μέρους ἀνθρώπων ἄνθρωπον
εἶναι, ἀλλὰ τὸν οὗ μετοχῇ ἕκαστος εἷς τε ἄνθρωπος
νενόηται καὶ πολλοὶ ἄνθρωποι καλοῦνται. νοεῖται
γὰρ ὁ ἄνθρωπος ζῷον λογικὸν θνητόν, καὶ διὰ
τοῦτο οὔτε Σωκράτης ἄνθρωπός ἐστιν οὔτε
289 Πλάτων, οὐκ ἄλλος τις τῶν ἐπ᾽ εἴδους. εἰ γὰρ
Σωκράτης, καθὸ Σωκράτης ἐστίν, ἄνθρωπος καθέστηκεν, ὁ Πλάτων οὐκ ἔσται ἄνθρωπος, οὐδὲ Δίων
ἢ Θέων· καὶ εἰ Πλάτων ἐστὶν ἄνθρωπος, ὁ Σωκράτης οὐκ ἔσται. λέγεται δέ γε καὶ Σωκράτης
ἄνθρωπος καὶ Πλάτων καὶ ἕκαστος τῶν ἄλλων·

[1] ⟨πλῆθος⟩ add. Heintz.

[a] The otiose repetitions in this passage make the text
doubtful.

if the animal pointed out is one, that which is not an animal,—a plant, for instance,—will not be one[a]; and if the plant is one, that which is not a plant— for instance, an animal—will not be one. But, in fact, that which is not an animal—for instance, a plant—is termed one ; and, again, that which is not a plant—for instance, an animal—is termed one. It is not true, therefore, that each of the numerables is one. But that by participation in which each thing is conceived as one is both one and many, one in respect of itself but many in respect of its comprehension. And this plurality, again, is not exhibited 287 in the case of the numerables. For if the plurality of animals is a plurality, that of plants will not be a plurality ; and if that of the latter is a plurality, that of animals, conversely, will not be a plurality. But in fact plurality is predicated both of plants and of animals, and of many other things ; therefore it is not the plurality exhibited in the case of numerables which is really plurality, but rather that plurality by participation in which this plurality was conceived. —Now when the Pythagorean philosophers make 288 such statements, what they say resembles the assertion that no particular man is Man, but only He[b] by participation in whom each single person is conceived as a man and many are termed men. For Man is conceived as " a rational mortal animal," and because of this neither Socrates is Man nor Plato nor any other particular man. And if Socrates, as Socrates, 289 is Man, Plato will not be Man, nor will Dion or Theon ; and if Plato is Man, Socrates will not be Man. But in fact Socrates is termed man and Plato too and each of

---

[b] *i.e.* the " generic Man," or " Man " as a universal concept.

οὐκ ἄρα τῶν ἐπὶ μέρους ἀνθρώπων ἕκαστός ἐστιν
ἄνθρωπος, οὗ δὲ μετοχῇ ἕκαστος αὐτῶν νενόηται
290 ἄνθρωπος, ὃς οὐκ ἔστιν εἷς ἐξ αὐτῶν. ὁ δ' αὐτὸς
λόγος καὶ ἐπὶ φυτοῦ καὶ πάντων τῶν λοιπῶν.
ἄτοπον δέ γέ ἐστι μηδένα τῶν ἐπὶ μέρους ἀνθρώπων
λέγειν ἄνθρωπον εἶναι, μηδὲ τῶν φυτῶν φυτόν·
ἄτοπον ἄρα καὶ τὸ ἕκαστον τῶν ἀριθμητῶν κατὰ
291 τὸν ἴδιον λόγον μὴ λέγειν ἕν.   ἄλλως τε καὶ
ἡ κομιζομένη κατὰ τοῦ γένους ἀπορία φθάνειν
ἔοικε καὶ ἐπὶ τὴν τοιαύτην τῶν Πυθαγορικῶν
δόξαν. ὡς γὰρ ὁ γενικὸς ἄνθρωπος οὔτε μετὰ τῶν
ἐπ' εἴδους ἀνθρώπων θεωρεῖται, ἐπεὶ καὶ αὐτὸς
ἔσται εἰδικός, οὔτε κατ' ἰδίαν ὑφέστηκεν, ἐπεὶ οὐ
γενήσονται οἱ κατὰ μέρος ἄνθρωποι μετοχῇ αὐτοῦ
ἄνθρωποι, οὔτ' ἐν αὐτοῖς τούτοις περιέχεται
292 (ἀδιανόητον γὰρ τούτου μετοχὴν ἀπείροις[1] εἶναι
καὶ τοῦτο μὲν τεθνηκόσι τοῦτο δὲ ζῶσι περιέχεσθαι),—ὡς οὖν οὗτος ὁ λόγος ἄπορος, οὕτω
καὶ ὁ περὶ τοῦ ἑνὸς τούτου μᾶλλόν ἐστιν ἀπορώ-
τερος τῷ μήτε σὺν τοῖς κατὰ μέρος ἀριθμητοῖς[2]
αὐτὸ θεωρεῖσθαι, μήτε κατὰ παντὸς αὐτὸ δύνασθαι
τετάχθαι, μήτε μετοχὴν αὐτοῦ τοῖς ἀπείροις ὑπ-
293 άρχειν.   ἥ γε μὴν τοῦ ἑνὸς ἰδέα, ἧς κατὰ
μετοχὴν ἕκαστον νοεῖται ἕν, ἤτοι μία ἐστὶν ἰδέα
τοῦ ἑνὸς ἢ πλείους ἰδέαι τοῦ ἑνός. καὶ εἰ μὲν μία,
ἤτοι ὅλης μετέχει ἕκαστον τῶν ἀριθμητῶν ἢ
μέρους τινὸς αὐτῆς. καὶ εἰ μὲν ὅλης μετέσχηκεν,
οὐκ ἔστι μία· εἰ γὰρ ὅλην ἔχει τὴν τοῦ ἑνὸς ἰδέαν
λόγου χάριν τὸ Α, ἐξ ἀνάγκης τὸ Β, μὴ ἔχον οὗ

---

[1] μετοχὴν ἀπείροις Heintz: μετοχῇ ἀπείρους mss., Bekk.
[2] ἀριθμητοῖς Heintz: ἀριθμοῖς mss., Bekk.

the others ; therefore it is not each of the particular
men which is Man, but he by participation in whom
each of them is conceived as a man, and he is not one
of themselves. And the same argument applies also 290
in the case of plants and all the rest. But it is absurd
to say that none of the particular men is a man, nor of
the plants a plant ; therefore it is also absurd to deny
that each of the numerables, in respect of its own
definition, is one.—And again, the difficulty brought 291
against genus [a] seems to tell beforehand against this
theory of the Pythagoreans. For as generic Man
neither is perceived along with particular men (since
then it will itself also be particular), nor subsists
separately (since then the particular men will not
become men by participation in it), nor is included
amongst these men themselves (for it is inconceiv- 292
able that an infinite number of them should have participation in it and that it should be included partly
amongst the dead and partly amongst the living) ;—
as then this account is doubtful, so also the account
given of this One is still more doubtful, owing to the
fact that it is neither perceived along with the particular numerables, nor is capable of being ranked as
a universal, and that the infinite ⟨particulars⟩ do not
participate in it.—Moreover, the Idea of the One, by 293
participation in which each thing is conceived as one,
is either one Idea of the One or several Ideas of the
One.[b] And if it is one, each of the numerables partakes either of the whole of it or of a part of it. And
if it partakes of the whole, the Idea is not one ; for if
A (so to call it) has the whole of the Idea of the One,
B, as it has nothing whereof to partake, will of neces-

[a] Cf. P.H. ii. 219 ff.
[b] With §§ 293-298 cf. P.H. iii. 158-162.

294 μετάσχῃ, οὐκ ἔσται ἕν· ὅπερ ἄτοπον. εἰ δὲ
πολυμερής ἐστιν ἡ τοῦ ἑνὸς ἰδέα καὶ ἕκαστον τῶν
ἀριθμητῶν [ἑκάστου]¹ μέρους αὐτῆς μετείληφεν,
πρῶτον μὲν ἕκαστον τῶν ὄντων οὐ τῆς τοῦ ἑνὸς
ἰδέας ἔσται μετειληφὸς ἀλλὰ μέρους αὐτῆς, καὶ
διὰ τοῦτο οὐκέτι γενήσεται ἕν· ὡς γὰρ τὸ μέρος
ἀνθρώπου οὐκ ἔστιν ἄνθρωπος καὶ τὸ μέρος τῆς
λέξεως οὐκ ἔστι λέξις, οὕτω τὸ μέρος τῆς τοῦ ἑνὸς
ἰδέας οὐκ ἔσται ἡ τοῦ ἑνὸς ἰδέα, ἵνα καὶ τὸ μετ-
295 εσχηκὸς αὐτῆς γένηται ἕν. εἶτα ἡ τοῦ ἑνὸς ἰδέα
οὐκέτι γίνεται ἑνὸς ἰδέα, οὐδὲ μία ἀλλὰ πλείους.
τὸ γὰρ ἕν, ᾗ ἕν ἐστιν, ἀδιαίρετον καθέστηκεν, καὶ
ἡ μονάς, ᾗ μονάς ἐστιν, οὐ διχάζεται· ἢ εἴπερ εἰς
πολλὰ διαιρεῖται, ἀθροισμὸς πλειόνων μονάδων
296 γενήσεται καὶ οὐκέτι μονάς. εἰ δὲ πλείους εἶεν
ἰδέαι τοῦ ἑνός, ὡς ἕκαστον τῶν ἀριθμητῶν ἰδίας
τινὸς μετέχειν ἰδέας καθ᾽ ἣν ἓν νοεῖται, ἤτοι ἡ τοῦ
Α ἰδέα καὶ ἡ τοῦ Β μετέχουσιν ἑνός τινος ἰδέας,
καθ᾽ ἣν ἑκάτερον αὐτῶν προσαγορεύεται ἕν, ἢ οὐ
297 μετέχουσιν. καὶ εἰ μὲν οὐ μετέχουσιν, ὃν τρόπον
αὗται δύνανται τῆς τοῦ ἑνὸς ἐπικατηγορίας
ἀξιοῦσθαι μὴ μετέχουσαί τινος ἐπαναβεβηκυίας
τοῦ ἑνὸς ἰδέας, οὕτω δύναται καὶ πᾶν τὸ ὁπωσοῦν
λεγόμενον ἓν μὴ κατὰ μετοχὴν τῆς τοῦ ἑνὸς ἰδέας
298 προσαγορεύεσθαι ἕν. εἰ δὲ μετέχουσιν, ἡ ἀρχῆθεν
μένει ἀπορία· πῶς γὰρ αἱ δύο ἰδέαι τῆς μιᾶς
μετέχουσιν ἰδέας; ὅλης ἑκατέρα, ἢ μέρους αὐτῆς;
ὁπότερον γὰρ ἂν λέγωσιν, ἐπαχθήσονται αἱ μικρῷ
πρόσθεν ἀποδοθεῖσαι πρὸς ἡμῶν ἀπορίαι.
299 Σὺν τούτοις ἐπεὶ πᾶν τὸ λαμβανόμενον ἀνθρώπῳ

¹ [ἑκάστου] secl. ego: ἑτέρου cj. Heintz (? ἑνός του).

sity not be one ; which is absurd.   But if the Idea of 294
One is multipartite and each of the numerables
participates in some one part of it, then, in the first
place, each of the existents will be participating not
in the Idea of the One but in a part of it, and for this
reason will no longer become one ; for just as the part
of a man is not a man and the part of a word is not a
word, so the part of the Idea of the One will not be
the Idea of the One so that what partakes thereof may
also become one.   And secondly, the Idea of the One 295
becomes no longer an Idea of one, nor itself one but
several.   For the One, in so far as it is one, is indivisible,
and the monad, in so far as it is a monad, is not dissected ;
or if it is divided into many parts, it will become an
aggregation of several monads and no longer a monad.
And if there are several Ideas of the One, then, since 296
each of the numerables partakes of a separate Idea
owing to which it is conceived as one, either the
Idea of A and the Idea of B participate in some one
Idea, owing to which each of them is termed one,
or they do not participate.   And if they do not par- 297
ticipate, then, just as these can have the title " one "
assigned to them although they do not participate
in any supreme Idea of the One, so also everything
which is in any way called one can be designated
" one " without participation in the Idea of the One.
But if they do participate, the original difficulty 298
remains ; for how can the two Ideas partake of the
one Idea ?   Will each partake of the whole or of a
part of it ?   For whichever answer they give, those
difficulties which we mentioned a short while ago [a]
will be brought up against them.

   And besides ; since everything perceived by man 299

* See § 293.

ἤτοι αἰσθήσει λαμβάνεται καὶ κατὰ ψιλὴν ἐγκύρησιν
ἢ διανοίᾳ, πάντως καὶ ὁ ἀριθμός,[1] εἴπερ ἀνθρώπῳ
ληπτός ἐστιν, ἤτοι αἰσθήσει ἢ διανοίᾳ κατα-
300 ληφθήσεται. ἀλλὰ αἰσθήσει μὲν καὶ ἁπλῇ ἐμφάσει
οὐκ ἂν ληφθείη· πλανᾷ γὰρ ἐνίους ἡ τῶν ἀριθμητῶν
ὑπόστασις, ἐπείπερ βλέποντες ταῦτα λευκὰ ἢ
μέλανα ἢ κοινῶς αἰσθητὰ ὑπονοοῦσιν ὅτι καὶ ὁ
ἀριθμὸς αἰσθητόν τί ἐστι καὶ φαινόμενον πρᾶγμα,
μὴ ἐχούσης οὕτω τῆς ἀληθείας. τὸ μὲν γὰρ λευκὸν
καὶ μέλαν καί, εἰ οὕτω τύχοι, τὸ φυτὸν καὶ ὁ
λίθος καὶ τὸ ξύλον καὶ τῶν ἀριθμητῶν ἕκαστον
φαίνεται καὶ αἰσθήσει ληπτόν ἐστιν, ὁ δ᾽ ἀριθμὸς
ὡς ἀριθμὸς οὐκ ἔστιν ἡμῖν αἰσθητὸς οὐδὲ φαίνεται.
301 σκοπῶμεν δὲ τὸν τρόπον τοῦτον. τὰ αἰσθητὰ
ὡς αἰσθητὰ ἀδιδάκτως ἡμῖν λαμβάνεται· οὐθεὶς
γὰρ τὸ λευκὸν ἢ τὸ μέλαν ὁρᾶν διδάσκεται, οὐδὲ
τραχέος ἢ λείου ἀντιλαμβάνεσθαι. ὁ δὲ ἀριθμὸς
ὡς ἀριθμὸς οὐκ ἀδιδάκτως ἡμῖν λαμβάνεται· ὅτι
γὰρ τὰ δὶς δύο τέσσαρά ἐστι καὶ τὰ τρὶς δύο ἕξ
ἐστι καὶ τὰ δεκάκις δέκα ἑκατόν, ἐκ μαθήσεως
ἔγνωμεν. οὐκ ἄρα αἰσθητόν τί ἐστιν ὁ ἀριθμός.
302 εἰ δὲ μνήμῃ κατ᾽ ἐπισύνθεσίν τινων ἔγνωσται,
ἀπορήσει τις τῶν αἰσθητῶν ἀποστάς, καθὼς καὶ
ὁ Πλάτων ἠπόρει ἐν τῷ περὶ ψυχῆς πῶς τὰ δύο
κατ᾽ ἰδίαν μὲν ὄντα οὐ νοεῖται δύο, συνελθόντα δὲ
303 εἰς ταὐτὸ γίνεται δύο. εἰ γὰρ τοιαῦτά ἐστι μετὰ
τὴν σύνοδον ὁποῖα ἦν πρὶν τῆς συνόδου, ἢν δ᾽
ἑκάτερον αὐτῶν πρὶν τῆς συνόδου ἕν, ἔσται καὶ

---

[1] ἀριθμός Heintz : ἀθροισμός mss., Bekk.

---

[a] i.e. as a sense-impression, cf. Adv. Log. i. 85.
[b] See Plato, Phaedo 96 E ff. ; § 306 infra ; Adv. Log.
ii. 91.

is perceived either by sense and through mere occurrence [a] or by intellect, number also, if it is perceptible by man, will certainly be apprehended either by sense or by intellect. But it will not be 300 perceived by sense and simple impression ; for the nature of the numerables leads some people astray, since, when they see these to be white or black, or, in general, objects of sense, they suppose that number too is an object of sense and an apparent thing, whereas the truth is otherwise. For the white thing and the black, and (shall we say ?) the plant and the stone and the stick and each of the numerables is apparent and is perceptible by sense, but number, as number, is not an object of sense for us nor is it apparent.—But 301 let us consider it in this way :—The sensibles, as sensibles, are perceived by us without teaching ; for no one is taught to see the white or the black, or to perceive the rough or the smooth. But number, as number, is not perceived by us without teaching ; for it is by learning that we get to know that twice two is four, and that three times two is six, and ten times ten a hundred. Therefore number is not an object of sense.—And if number becomes known by 302 memory through the combination of certain things, when one has left the sensibles one will be perplexed, even as Plato was perplexed in his book *On the Soul*,[b] as to how the two when existing separately are not conceived as two but become two when they are combined together. For if they are of the same 303 sort after the combination as they were before the combination, and before the combination each of them was one, then each of them will also be one

357

SEXTUS EMPIRICUS

μετὰ τὴν σύνοδον ἑκάτερον ἕν, ἐπεὶ ἂν δῶμεν
προσγίνεσθαί τι αὐτοῖς περισσότερον μετὰ τὴν
σύνοδον παρ' ὃ ἦν, οἷον τὴν δυάδα, ἔσται ἡ τῶν
304 δυοῖν συνέλευσις τετράς. εἰ γὰρ τῷ συνελθόντι
ἑνὶ καὶ ἑνὶ πλεῖόν τι προσγίνεται ἡ δυάς, ἐπεὶ ἐν
ταύτῃ μονὰς καὶ μονὰς νοεῖται, κατὰ τὴν τοῦ ἑνὸς
καὶ ἑνὸς συνέλευσιν τετρὰς γενήσεται, δυοῖν μὲν
νοουμένων τῶν συνιόντων, διττῆς δὲ κατὰ τὴν
φύσιν οὔσης τῆς προσγινομένης αὐτοῖς δυάδος.

κὰι πάλιν εἰ τοῖς κατὰ σύνοδον ποιοῦσι τὴν
δεκάδα πλεῖόν τι προσγίνεται ἡ δεκάς, ἐπεὶ ἐν τῇ
δεκάδι νοεῖται τὰ ἐννέα καὶ τὰ ὀκτὼ καὶ τὰ ἑπτὰ καὶ
καθ' ὑπόβασιν οἱ λοιποὶ ἀριθμοί, ἀπειράκις ἀπείρων
ἔσται πλῆθος τὰ δέκα, ὡς ἀνώτερον δεδείχαμεν.

305 Ὁ δὲ Πλάτων καὶ ἄλλως ἐπιχειρεῖν βούλεται.
εἴπερ γὰρ τὸ ἕν, φησίν, ὅτε διαιρεῖται καὶ χωρίζεται,
δύο νοεῖται, πάντως καὶ ἡ ἑκατέρου τῶν ἀνὰ ἕν
εἰς ταὐτὸ σύνοδος οὐ νοηθήσεται δύο· ἐναντίον γάρ
ἐστι τῷ πρώτῳ αἰτίῳ τὸ δεύτερον αἴτιον, καὶ εἰ
τὰ ἐκ τοῦ αὐτοῦ χωριζόμενα δύο ἐστί, τὰ εἰς ταὐτὸ
συναγόμενα καὶ ἀλλήλοις παρατεθειμένα οὐκ ἂν
εἴη δύο. ἔχει δὲ καὶ τὸ ῥητὸν παρ' αὐτῷ τὸν
306 τρόπον τοῦτον· '' θαυμάζω γὰρ εἰ ὅτε μὲν ἑκάτερον
αὐτῶν ἦν χωρὶς ἀλλήλων, ἓν ἦν ἑκάτερον καὶ οὐκ
ἤστην τότε δύο, πλησιάσαντα δ' ἀλλήλοις, αὕτη
ἄρα αὐτῶν αἰτία ἐγένετο δυοῖν γενέσθαι, σύνοδος
τοῦ πλησίον ἀλλήλων τεθῆναι. οὐδέ γε ὡς ἐάν
τις ἓν διασχίσῃ, δύναμαι ἔτι πεισθῆναι ὅτι ὡσαύτως
αἰτία γέγονεν ἡ σχίσις τοῦ δύο γεγονέναι. ἐναντία
γὰρ γέγονεν ἢ[1] τότε αἰτία τοῦ δύο γενέσθαι· τότε

---

[1] ἢ Mutsch. (sec. Platonis text.): ἡ mss., Bekk.

[a] See *Adv. Phys.* i. 303 ff.　　[b] See Plato, *Phaedo* 97 A.

358

after the combination ; since if we admit that after the combination some further new attribute was bestowed on them, such as duality, the combination of the two will make four. For if to the one and one which 304 were combined the Dyad is attached as something further, then, since a monad and a monad are conceived as existing therein, a four will be formed by the combination of the one and the one,—the things combined being conceived as two, and the Dyad attached to them being of its own nature twofold.— And again, if to the numbers which by combination make up the Decad the Decad is attached in addition, since the nine is conceived as included in the Decad, and the eight and the seven and the rest of the numbers in descending order, the ten will be infinity times infinity in number, as we have previously pointed out.[a]

And Plato attempts also to argue in another way. 305 If the one, he says, when it is divided and separated is conceived as two, the combination of each of these single ones taken together will certainly not be conceived as two ; for the second cause is opposed to the first, and if the separated parts of the same thing are two, those which are brought together and set side by side will not be two. His statement [b] is put in this form : " For I am surprised that, whereas 306 when each of them was apart from the other each of them was one and they were not then two, yet when they came close to each other this coming together in mutual juxtaposition actually proved the cause of their becoming two. Nor can I yet come to believe that if a man bisects a one the act of bisection likewise is the cause of its having become two ; for this cause of its becoming two is the opposite of the former

μὲν ὅτι συνήγετο πλησίον ἀλλήλων καὶ προσετίθετο
ἕτερον ἑτέρῳ, νῦν δ᾽ ὅτι ἀπάγεται καὶ χωρίζεται
307 ἕτερον ἀφ᾽ ἑτέρου.'' ῥητῶς γὰρ διὰ τούτων φησὶν
ὡς εἴπερ ἡ ψιλὴ σύνοδος τοῦ ἑνὸς καὶ ἑνὸς καὶ ἡ
αὐτὸ μόνον παράθεσις αἴτιόν ἐστι τοῦ δύο γενέσθαι
τὰ πρότερον μὴ ὄντα δύο, πῶς ἔτι πεισθῆναι
δύναμαι ὅτι τὸ ἕν, ὅτε χωρίζεται καὶ διασπᾶται,
δύο γίνεται; ἐναντία γὰρ τῇ συνόδῳ ἡ σχίσις
ἐστὶ καὶ ὁ χωρισμός.
308 Τοιοῦτος μὲν καὶ ὁ Πλάτων· ἔνεστι δὲ καὶ ὧδε
συνερωτᾶν. εἰ ἔστι τι ἀριθμός, ὅτε παρατίθεταί
τι ἑτέρῳ, οἷον τῇ μονάδι ἡ μονάς, τότε ἢ προσγίνεταί τι ταῖς συνελθούσαις μονάσιν ἢ ἀπογίνεται
τῶν συνελθουσῶν ἢ οὔτε προσγίνεταί τι αὐταῖς
οὔτε ἀπογίνεται. ἀλλ᾽ εἰ μήτε προσγίνεταί τι
αὐταῖς μήτε ἀπογίνεται αὐτῶν, οὐκ ἔσται δυὰς
κατὰ τὴν παράθεσιν τῆς ἑτέρας τῇ ἑτέρᾳ, ὡς οὐδὲ
309 πρὶν τῆς συνόδου ἐτύγχανεν. εἰ δὲ ἀπογίνεταί τι
κατὰ τὴν παράθεσιν αὐτῶν, ἐλάσσωσις ἔσται τῆς
μιᾶς μονάδος καὶ οὐκέτι δυὰς γενήσεται. εἰ δὲ
προσγίνεταί τι αὐταῖς, οἷον ἡ δυάς, τὰ ὀφείλοντα
δύο εἶναι τέσσαρα γενήσονται. δυὰς γὰρ ἡ ἐπι-
γενομένη μονὰς ἦν καὶ μονάς· προσελθοῦσα οὖν
μονάδι καὶ μονάδι, ταῖς συνερχομέναις, τὸν
τέσσαρα ποιήσει ἀριθμόν· ὅπερ ἐστὶν ἄτοπον.
τοίνυν οὐκ ἔστι τι ἀριθμός.

Ε΄.—ΠΕΡΙ ΓΕΝΕΣΕΩΣ ΚΑΙ ΦΘΟΡΑΣ

310 Ἡ περὶ γενέσεως καὶ φθορᾶς ζήτησις συνίσταται
τοῖς σκεπτικοῖς πρὸς τοὺς φυσικοὺς σχεδόν τι περὶ

cause ; for then it was because the ones were brought close to each other and added to each other, but now it is because they are taken apart and separated the one from the other." In these words he says 307 expressly that if the mere combination of one and one and their simple juxtaposition is the cause of those which formerly were not two becoming two, how can I still believe that the one when it is separated and pulled apart becomes two ? For bisection and separation is the opposite of combination.

Such, then, is Plato's view. But it is also possible 308 to argue thus [a] : " If number is anything, when something is set beside another, say the monad beside the monad, then either something is added to the combined monads or subtracted from them, or nothing is either added to them or subtracted. But if nothing is either added to them or subtracted from them, there will not be a dyad because of the setting of the one beside the other, just as none existed before the combination. And if something is subtracted 309 because of their being set side by side, there will be a decrease of one monad and no longer will a dyad come into existence. And if something is added to them, say the dyad, those which ought to be two will become four [b] ; for the added dyad was a monad *plus* a monad ; when, then, this is added to the monad and monad which are being combined, it will make the number four ; which is absurd. So then, number is nothing.

Chapter V.—Concerning Becoming and Perishing

The inquiry concerning becoming and perishing, 310 as undertaken by the Sceptics against the Physicists,

[a] With §§ 308-309 *cf. P.H.* iii. 164-165.
[b] *Cf.* §§ 303, 304.

τῶν ὅλων, εἴγε τῶν σκεψαμένων περὶ τῆς τοῦ
παντὸς συστάσεως οἱ μὲν ἐξ ἑνὸς ἐγέννησαν τὰ
πάντα οἱ δ᾽ ἐκ πλειόνων, καὶ τῶν ἐξ ἑνὸς οἱ μὲν
311 ἐξ ἀποίου οἱ δὲ ἐκ ποιοῦ, καὶ τῶν ἐκ ποιοῦ οἱ μὲν
ἐξ ἀέρος οἱ δ᾽ ἐξ ὕδατος οἱ δ᾽ ἐκ πυρός, ἄλλοι ἐκ
γῆς, καὶ τῶν ἐκ πλειόνων οἱ μὲν ἐξ ἀριθμητῶν οἱ
δ᾽ ἐξ ἀπείρων, καὶ τῶν ἐξ ἀριθμητῶν οἱ μὲν ἐκ δύο
οἱ δ᾽ ἐκ τεσσάρων οἱ δ᾽ ἐκ πέντε οἱ δ᾽ ἐξ ἕξ, καὶ
τῶν ἐξ ἀπείρων οἱ μὲν ἐξ ὁμοίων τοῖς γεννωμένοις
οἱ δὲ ἐξ ἀνομοίων, καὶ τούτων οἱ μὲν ἐξ ἀπαθῶν
312 οἱ δ᾽ ἐκ παθητῶν. ἐξ ἀποίου μὲν οὖν καὶ ἑνὸς
σώματος τὴν τῶν ὅλων ὑπεστήσαντο γένεσιν οἱ
στωικοί· ἀρχὴ γὰρ τῶν ὄντων κατ᾽ αὐτούς ἐστιν
ἡ ἄποιος ὕλη καὶ δι᾽ ὅλων τρεπτή, μεταβαλλούσης
τε ταύτης γίνεται τὰ τέσσαρα στοιχεῖα, πῦρ καὶ
313 ἀήρ, ὕδωρ καὶ γῆ. ἐξ ἑνὸς δὲ καὶ ποιοῦ γεγενῆσθαι
τὰ πάντα θέλουσιν οἵ τε περὶ τὸν Ἵππασον καὶ
Ἀναξιμένη καὶ Θαλῆ, ὧν Ἵππασος μὲν καὶ κατά
τινας Ἡράκλειτος ὁ Ἐφέσιος ἐκ πυρὸς ἀπέλιπον
τὴν γένεσιν, Ἀναξιμένης δὲ ἐξ ἀέρος, Θαλῆς δὲ
ἐξ ὕδατος, Ξενοφάνης δὲ κατ᾽ ἐνίους ἐκ γῆς·

ἐκ γαίης γὰρ πάντα, καὶ εἰς γῆν πάντα τελευτᾷ.

314 ἐκ πλειόνων δὲ καὶ ἀριθμητῶν, δυοῖν μὲν, γῆς τε
καὶ ὕδατος, ὁ ποιητὴς Ὅμηρος, ὁτὲ μὲν λέγων

ᵃ Cf. P.H. iii. 30 ; Adv. Phys. i. 379 ff.
ᵇ Homer, Il. xiv. 201.

is practically concerned with the Whole of things, seeing that of those who have investigated the structure of the Universe some have generated all things from one, others from several things [a]; and of those who have generated them from one, some have done so from an unqualified and others from a qualified thing; and of those who have done so from 311 a qualified thing, some make this air, others water, others fire, others earth; and of those who have generated all from several things, some have done so from numerable things, others from things infinite in number; and of those who adopt numerables, some make them two, others four, others five, others six; and of those who adopt things infinite in number, some make these like to the things generated, others unlike; and some of these last make them impassive, others passive things. Thus the Stoics supposed 312 the becoming of all things to be derived from one unqualified body; for the principle of existing things, according to them, is the unqualified and wholly convertible matter, and by its changes the four elements come into being,—fire and air, water and earth. But Hippasus and Anaximenes and 313 Thales hold that all things have become from one thing which is qualified; and of these Hippasus—and, according to some, Heracleitus of Ephesus—derived the becoming from fire, but Anaximenes from air, and Thales from water, and Xenophanes (according to some) from earth,—

All things spring from the earth, and all in the earth have their ending.

And of those who derive all from things several and 314 numerable, the poet Homer makes them two, earth and water, as he says in one place [b]—

Ὠκεανόν τε θεῶν γένεσιν καὶ μητέρα Τηθύν,
ὁτὲ δὲ

ἀλλ' ὑμεῖς μὲν πάντες ὕδωρ καὶ γαῖα γένοισθε.

συμφέρεσθαι δ' αὐτῷ δοκεῖ κατ' ἐνίους καὶ ὁ
Κολοφώνιος Ξενοφάνης· φησὶ γὰρ

πάντες γὰρ γαίης τε καὶ ὕδατος ἐκγενόμεσθα.

315 ἐκ γῆς δὲ καὶ αἰθέρος Εὐριπίδης, ὡς πάρεστιν
ἐκδέξασθαι ἐκ τοῦ λέγειν αὐτὸν

αἰθέρα καὶ γαῖαν πάντων γενέτειραν ἀείδω.

ἐκ τεσσάρων δὲ ὁ Ἐμπεδοκλῆς·

τέσσαρα γὰρ πάντων ῥιζώματα πρῶτον ἄκουε·
Ζεὺς ἀργὴς Ἥρη τε φερέσβιος ἠδ' Ἀιδωνεὺς
Νῆστίς θ', ἣ δακρύοις τέγγει κρούνωμα βρότειον.

316 ἐκ πέντε δὲ Ὄκελλος ὁ Λευκανὸς καὶ Ἀριστοτέλης·
συμπαρέλαβον γὰρ τοῖς τέσσαρσι στοιχείοις τὸ
πέμπτον καὶ κυκλοφορητικὸν σῶμα, ἐξ οὗ λέγουσιν
317 εἶναι τὰ οὐράνια. ἐκ δὲ τῶν ἓξ τὴν πάντων ὑπέθεντο γένεσιν οἱ περὶ τὸν Ἐμπεδοκλέα. ἐν οἷς
μὲν γὰρ λέγει τέσσαρα τῶν πάντων ῥιζώματα, ἐκ
τεσσάρων ποιεῖ τὴν γένεσιν· ὅταν δὲ προσθῇ

νεῖκός τ' οὐλόμενον δίχα τῶν, ἀτάλαντον ἀπάντῃ,
καὶ φιλίη μετὰ τοῖσιν, ἴση μῆκός τε πλάτος τε,

ἐξ παραδίδωσι τὰς τῶν ὄντων ἀρχάς, τέσσαρας μὲν
τὰς ὑλικάς, γῆν ὕδωρ ἀέρα πῦρ, δύο δὲ τὰς δραστη-

---

[a] Homer, *Il.* vii. 99.
[b] Eurip. *Frag.* 1023 (Nauck).
[c] *Cf. Adv. Phys.* i. 362, with note *ad loc.*
[d] *i.e.* the aether, *cf. P.H.* iii. 31.

Ocean, sire of the gods, and Tethys the mother that bare
them ;

and again,[a]

Nay, but I would that ye all might be turnèd to earth and
to water.

And with him Xenophanes of Colophon is thought by
some to agree ; for he says—

All we men from earth and from water have our beginning.

And Euripides ⟨derives all things⟩ from earth and 315
aether, as one may gather from his saying [b]—

Aether I hymn and Earth, the goddess-mother of all things.

And Empedocles from four things [c]—

Four are the roots of all things, and list thou first to their
titles :—
Shining Zeus, and Herê the life-bringer, and Aïdoneus,
Nestis too, who wetteth with tears the fountain of mortals.

And from five things Ocellus the Lucanian and Aris- 316
totle ; for along with the four elements they also
adopted the fifth body which revolves in a circle,[d] and
from which they say that the celestial objects are
derived.   And Empedocles assumed that the genera- 317
tion of all things is from the six.   For in the verses
where he speaks of " the four roots " of all things he
makes their generation to be from four ; but when
he adds [e]—

Strife pernicious, divided from these and evenly balanc'd,
Love, together with these, in length and breadth perfectly
equal,—

he is handing down six as the principles of existing
things, four material (earth, water, air, fire), and

[e] Cf. Adv. Phys. i. 10 ; and with § 318 cf. P.H. iii. 32 ;
Adv. Phys. i. 363.

318 ρίους, φιλίαν καὶ νεῖκος. ἐξ ἀπείρων δ᾿ ἐδόξασαν
τὴν τῶν πραγμάτων γένεσιν οἱ περὶ Ἀναξαγόραν
τὸν Κλαζομένιον καὶ Δημόκριτον καὶ Ἐπίκουρον
καὶ ἄλλοι παμπληθεῖς, ἀλλ᾿ ὁ μὲν Ἀναξαγόρας ἐξ ὁμοίων τοῖς γεννωμένοις, οἱ δὲ περὶ τὸν
Δημόκριτον καὶ Ἐπίκουρον ἐξ ἀνομοίων τε καὶ
ἀπαθῶν, τουτέστι τῶν ἀτόμων, οἱ δὲ περὶ τὸν
Ποντικὸν Ἡρακλείδην καὶ Ἀσκληπιάδην ἐξ ἀνομοίων μὲν παθητῶν δέ, καθάπερ τῶν ἀνάρμων
ὄγκων.

319 Προειληφότες οὖν ὅτι πᾶσι τούτοις ἄπορος
δείκνυται ὁ τῆς φυσιολογίας τρόπος ἀναιρεθείσης
τῆς γενέσεως καὶ τῆς φθορᾶς, προθυμότερον
ἁπτώμεθα τῶν λόγων. καίτοι γε ἐὰν ἐξετάζωμεν,
διὰ τῶν ἔμπροσθεν αὐτάρκως ἤδη συμβεβίβασται
320 τὸ κεφάλαιον. τὸ γὰρ γινόμενον καὶ φθειρόμενον
ἐν χρόνῳ γίνεται καὶ φθείρεται, χρόνος δὲ οὐκ
ἔστιν, ὡς ἀνώτερον παρεστήσαμεν, ὥστε οὐδὲ τὸ
321 γινόμενον καὶ φθειρόμενον ἔσται.   πᾶσά τε
γένεσις καὶ φθορὰ μεταβλητικαί τινές εἰσι κινήσεις,
οὐδὲν δ᾿ ἐστὶ κίνησις, ὡς προκατεστησάμεθα·
322 τοίνυν οὐδὲ γένεσις καὶ φθορὰ γενήσεται. καὶ πᾶν
τὸ γεννώμενον ἢ φθειρόμενον οὐ χωρὶς τοῦ δρῶντος
καὶ πάσχοντος γεννᾶται ἢ φθείρεται, οὔτε δὲ δρᾷ
τι οὔτε πάσχει, ὥστ᾿ οὐδὲ γεννᾶταί τι οὐδὲ
323 φθείρεται.   καὶ μὴν εἰ γίνεταί τι καὶ φθείρεται,
ὀφείλει τί τινι προστίθεσθαι καὶ τί τινος ἀφαιρεῖσθαι
ἤ τι ἔκ τινος μεταβάλλειν· γένεσις γὰρ καὶ φθορὰ
κατά τινα τῶν τριῶν τούτων τρόπων ὀφείλει
συνίστασθαι, οἷον ἐπὶ τῆς δεκάδος κατ᾿ ἀφαίρεσιν

366

two efficient (Love and Strife). But Anaxagoras of 318
Clazomenae and Democritus and Epicurus and a host
of others held that the generation of things is from
innumerables ; yet whereas Anaxagoras said that
these are like to the things generated, Democritus
and Epicurus said that they are unlike and impassive
(namely, the atoms), while Heracleides of Pontus and
Asclepiades said that they are unlike but passive
(namely, the irregular molecules).

Having, then, first grasped the fact that the physical 319
theory of all these men is shown to be hopeless if
becoming and perishing are abolished, let us deal
with their arguments all the more confidently. Yet,
if we examine them, the main point has been
sufficiently established already by our previous arguments. For what becomes and perishes becomes and 320
perishes in time ; but, as we showed above,[a] time
does not exist, so that what becomes and perishes
will not exist either.—Also, becoming and perishing 321
are always change-causing motions ; but, as we have
previously shown,[b] motion is nothing ; neither, then,
will becoming and perishing exist. Nothing, too, 322
which is generated or perishes is generated or perishes
without an agent and a patient,[c] but nothing is agent
or patient, so that nothing is generated or perishes.—
Moreover, if anything becomes and perishes, some- 323
thing must be added to something and something
be subtracted from something or something changed
from something. For becoming and perishing must
come about in some one of these three ways,[d]—as,
for instance, in the case of the ten, the nine becomes

----

[a] See §§ 170 ff.   [b] See §§ 37 ff.
[c] Cf. Adv. Phys. i. 195 ff.
[d] Cf. P.H. iii. 109 ; Adv. Phys. i. 277 ff.

τῆς μονάδος γίνεται μὲν ἡ ἐννεὰς φθείρεται δὲ ἡ
δεκάς, καὶ πάλιν ἐπὶ τῆς ἐννεάδος κατὰ πρόσθεσιν
μονάδος γίνεται μὲν ἡ δεκὰς φθείρεται δὲ ἡ ἐννεάς.
καὶ ἐπὶ τῶν κατὰ τροπὴν φθειρομένων ἢ γεννωμένων ὁ αὐτὸς λόγος· οὕτω γὰρ φθείρεται μὲν ὁ
324 οἶνος γίνεται δὲ ὄξος. εἰ δὴ τοίνυν πᾶν τὸ γεννώμενον καὶ φθειρόμενον ἤτοι κατὰ πρόσθεσιν ἢ
κατ᾽ ἀφαίρεσιν ἢ κατὰ μεταβολὴν γίνεται καὶ
φθείρεται, ἐπεὶ παρεστήσαμεν μήτε πρόσθεσιν
οὖσαν μήτε ἀφαίρεσιν μήτε μεταβολήν, δυνάμει
προκατεστησάμεθα τὸ μηδὲ γένεσιν ἢ φθορὰν
325 ὑπάρχειν.   πρὸς τούτοις τὸ γεννώμενον ἢ
φθειρόμενον ψαύειν ὀφείλει ἐκείνου τοῦ ἐξ οὗ
φθείρεται καὶ τοῦ εἰς ὃ μεταβάλλει, οὐδὲν δὲ
ψαῦσίς ἐστιν, ὡς παρέσταται· τοίνυν οὐδὲ γένεσις
ἢ φθορὰ συστῆναι δύναται.

326 Πάρεστι δὲ καὶ προηγουμένως ἀποροῦντας
λέγειν ὡς εἴπερ τι γίνεται, ἤτοι τὸ ὂν γίνεται ἢ
τὸ μὴ ὄν. οὔτε δὲ τὸ μὴ ὂν γίνεται· τῷ γὰρ μὴ
ὄντι οὐδὲν συμβέβηκεν, ᾧ δὲ μηδὲν συμβέβηκεν,
327 οὐδὲ τὸ γίνεσθαι συμβέβηκεν. καὶ ἄλλως, τὸ
γινόμενον πάσχει, τὸ δὲ μὴ ὂν οὐδὲν δύναται
πάσχειν· ὄντος γὰρ τὸ πάσχειν· οὐκ ἄρα τὸ μὴ ὂν
γίνεται. καὶ μὴν οὐδὲ τὸ ὄν· ἔστι γὰρ ἤδη τὸ ὄν,
καὶ οὐκ ἔχει χρείαν γενέσεως· οὐκ ἄρα οὐδὲ τὸ
ὂν γεννᾶται. ἀλλ᾽ εἰ μήτε τὸ ὂν μήτε τὸ μὴ ὂν
γίνεται, παρὰ ταῦτα δ᾽ οὐδέν ἐστι τρίτον ἐπινοεῖν,
328 οὐδὲν γεννᾶται.   ἄλλως τε, ἐν τοῖς φαινομένοις

---

[a] Cf. *Adv. Phys.* i. 277 ff. ; *P.H.* iii. 85, 102 ; *Adv. Log.*
i. 378 ff.

through the subtraction of the one but the ten perishes ; and again, in the case of the nine, through the addition of the one the ten becomes but the nine perishes. And the same account holds of the things which perish or are generated through conversion ; for in this way wine perishes and vinegar becomes. If, then, everything which is becoming and perishing 324 becomes and perishes either through addition or through subtraction or through change, then, since we have established [a] that neither addition exists nor subtraction nor change, we have already virtually established that neither does becoming or perishing exist.—And further, that which is being generated or 325 is perishing must be touching that wherefrom it perishes and that whereinto it changes ; but, as has been shown,[b] touch is nothing ; so then, becoming or perishing cannot subsist either.

It is also possible for us, as doubters, to argue 326 directly that if a thing becomes, either the existent becomes or the non-existent.[c] But the non-existent does not become ; for the non-existent has no property, and of that which has no property neither is becoming a property. And again : what becomes 327 is affected, but the non-existent cannot be affected at all ; for affection belongs to the existent ; therefore the non-existent does not become. Nor yet does the existent ; for the existent exists already and has no need of becoming ; neither, therefore, is the existent generated. But if neither the existent becomes nor the non-existent, and besides these no third thing can be conceived, nothing is generated.—And again, 328

[b] *Cf. Adv. Phys.* i. 258 ff. ; *P.H.* iii. 45 ff.
[c] With §§ 326-327 *cf. P.H.* iii. 112.

θεωρεῖται τὰ μὲν ἐξ ἑνὸς γεννώμενα κατὰ μετα-
329 βολήν, τὰ δ' ἐκ πλειόνων κατὰ σύνθεσιν· καὶ ἐξ
ἑνὸς μὲν κατὰ μεταβολὴν ὁπόσα τῆς αὐτῆς οὐσίας
μενούσης ἑτέραν ἐξ ἑτέρας μεταλαμβάνει ποιότητα,
οἷον ὅταν τοῦ αὐτοῦ ὑγροῦ μένοντος ἐν τῷ αὐτῷ
πλήθει τὸ μὲν γλεῦκος ἀφανισθῇ οἶνος δὲ γένηται,
ἢ ὁ οἶνος μὲν ἀφανισθῇ ὄξος δὲ ὑποστῇ, ἢ τοῦ
κηροῦ μένοντος ἡ μὲν σκληρότης ἀφανίζηται ἡ δὲ
330 μαλακότης γένηται, ἢ ἀνάπαλιν· ἐκ πλειόνων δὲ
κατ' ἐπισύνθεσιν ὡς ἅλυσις μὲν κατ' ἐπισύνδεσιν
κρίκων, οἰκία δὲ κατὰ σύνοδον λίθων, ἐσθὴς δὲ
331 κατὰ κρόκης καὶ στημόνων συμπλοκήν.   εἰ δὲ
κἂν τοῖς νοητοῖς γίνεταί τι, ἤτοι ἐξ ὄντος γίνεταί
τι ἢ ἐκ μὴ ὄντος. καὶ ἐκ μὲν τοῦ μὴ ὄντος οὐδὲν
δύναται γίνεσθαι· δεῖ γὰρ τὸ γεννητικόν τινος
οὐσίαν ἔχειν καὶ ποιὰν ἀναδέχεσθαι κίνησιν, ὥστ'
οὐκ ἂν εἴη τι ἐκ τοῦ μὴ ὄντος γεννώμενον. καὶ
332 μὴν οὐδ' ἐκ τοῦ ὄντος. εἰ γὰρ ἐκ τοῦ ὄντος
γίνεταί τι, ἤτοι ἐξ ἑνὸς γίνεται ἢ ἐκ πλειόνων.
καὶ ἐξ ἑνὸς μὲν οὐκ ἂν εἴη γεννώμενον. εἰ γὰρ ἐξ
ἑνὸς γίνεται, ἤτοι αὐξανομένου ἢ μειουμένου ἢ
333 ἐν τῷ αὐτῷ μένοντος γίνεται. ἀλλ' αὐξάνεσθαι
μὲν καὶ μειοῦσθαι οὐχ οἷόν τε ταὐτό, καὶ οὐκ ἂν
δυνηθείη ἑαυτοῦ τι μεῖζον ἢ ἑαυτοῦ τι ἔλαττον
ἀποτελεῖσθαι ταὐτόν. ἐάν τε γὰρ αὐτοῦ πλεῖον
γένοιτο, ἐπεὶ οὐδὲν ἔχει πλεῖον παρ' ἑαυτό, ἐξ οὐκ
ὄντος ἕξει τὴν πρόσθεσιν· ἐάν τε ἔλαττον ἑαυτοῦ,
πάλιν, ἐπεὶ οὐδὲν ἔχει παρ' ἑαυτό⟨, τὸ⟩¹ ἀπολλύμενον
αὐτοῦ εἰς τὸ μὴ ὂν ἀπολεῖται. οὐδὲν ἄρα δύναται

¹ ⟨, τὸ⟩ add. Rüstow.

amongst things apparent some are observed to be generated from one thing through change, others from several things by combination ; and from one thing through 329 change come all those which take on one quality in place of another while the same substance remains, —as for example when, while the same fluid remains in the same quantity, the must disappears and wine becomes, or the wine disappears and vinegar is formed; or, while the wax remains, its hardness disappears and softness becomes, or the converse. But ⟨others are 330 formed⟩ from several things by combination, such as the chain formed by the joining together of the links and the house by the combination of stones, and the robe by the weaving together of woof and warp.—And 331 if amongst the intelligibles also something becomes, something becomes either from an existent thing or from a non-existent. But from the non-existent nothing can become ; for that which is generative of anything must possess existence and admit of qualified motion, so that nothing will be generated from the non-existent. Nor yet from the existent. For if 332 anything becomes from the existent, it becomes either from one thing or from several. And it will not be generated from one. For if it becomes from one, it becomes through this being increased or decreased or remaining in the same state. But it is not possible 333 for the same thing to increase and decrease, and the same thing will not be able to be made into something greater than itself or less than itself. For if it should become more than itself, it will get the addition from a non-existent, since it has nothing more beyond itself ; and again, if it becomes less than itself, what vanishes from it will vanish into the non-existent, since it has nothing except itself. Nothing, there-

SEXTUS EMPIRICUS

334 ἐκ τοῦ αὐξομένου ἢ μειουμένου γίνεσθαι. καὶ μὴν
οὐδ' ἐκ τοῦ ἐν τῷ αὐτῷ μένοντος ἔσται τὸ γεννώμενον. εἰ γὰρ τοῦτο, ἤτοι ἀτρέπτου καὶ ἀμετα-
βλήτου μένοντος αὐτοῦ γεννᾶταί τι ἐξ αὐτοῦ, ἢ ἐκ
τρεπομένου καὶ μεταβάλλοντος. ἀλλ' ἐξ ἀτρέπτου
μὲν καὶ ἀεὶ ὡσαύτως μένοντος οὐκ ἂν γεννηθείη
335 τι· ἑτεροίωσις γάρ τίς ἐστιν ἡ γένεσις. εἰ δὲ ἐκ
τρεπομένου καὶ μεταβάλλοντος, ἤτοι εἰς ἑαυτὸ
μεταβάλλοντος γίνεται τὸ γεννώμενον ἢ εἰς ἕτερον.
καὶ εἰ μὲν εἰς ἑαυτὸ μεταβάλοι τὸ γεννητικόν τινος,
πάλιν μένει τὸ αὐτό, καὶ μένον τὸ αὐτὸ οὐδενὸς
ἔσται περισσοτέρου γεννητικόν. εἰ δὲ εἰς ἕτερον
τρέποιτο, ἤτοι ἐκβαίνει τῆς ἰδίας ὑποστάσεως ὅτε
τρέπεται καὶ γεννᾶται, ἢ μένει μὲν ἐν τῇ οἰκείᾳ
ὑποστάσει, ἄλλο δὲ εἶδος ἀντ' ἄλλου εἴδους μετα-
λαμβάνον γεννᾶται, ὡς ὁ μετασχηματιζόμενος
κηρὸς καὶ ἄλλοτε ἄλλην μορφὴν ἀναδεχόμενος.
336 ἀλλ' ἐκβαῖνον μὲν τῆς ἰδίας ὑποστάσεως εἰς τὸ μὴ
ὂν φθαρήσεται, καὶ εἰς τὸ μὴ ὂν φθειρόμενον
γεννήσει οὐδέν. εἰ δὲ μένον ἐν τῇ ἰδίᾳ ὑποστάσει
καὶ ἄλλην ἀντ' ἄλλης ποιότητα ἀναδεχόμενον
337 γεννᾶται, κρατεῖται τῇ αὐτῇ ἀπορίᾳ. ἤτοι γὰρ
μένοντος τοῦ πρώτου εἴδους καὶ τῆς προτέρας
ποιότητος περὶ αὐτῷ γίνεται τὸ δεύτερον εἶδος
καὶ ἡ δευτέρα ποιότης, ἢ μὴ μένοντος. οὔτε δὲ
μένοντος τοῦ πρώτου εἴδους γίνεται τὸ δεύτερον
οὔτε μὴ μένοντος, ὡς ἔμπροσθεν παρεστήσαμεν,
ὅτε περὶ τοῦ πάσχοντος ἐσκεπτόμεθα. τοίνυν οὐδ'

* Cf. P.H. iii. 112 ff.
b Cf. Adv. Phys. ii. 266 ff. "The patient" means "what

fore, can become from what increases or decreases. Nor yet will that which is generated be from that 334 which remains in the same state. For if so, something is generated from it either while it remains unconverted and unchanged or while it is being converted and changed.[a] But while it is unconverted and remaining constantly as it was nothing will be generated from it ; for becoming is a form of alteration. And 335 if it is being converted and changed, that which is being generated from it becomes while it is changing either into itself or into another. And if that which is generative of something changes into itself, it remains again the same, and remaining the same it will not be generative of anything further. And if it is converted into another thing, either it passes out from its own substance when it is converted and generated, or it remains in its proper substance and is generated by assuming one form instead of another, just like the wax which changes its shape and receives various forms at various times. But if it passes out from 336 its own substance it will perish into the non-existent, and perishing into the non-existent it will generate nothing. And if it is generated while remaining in its own substance and assuming one quality in place of another, it is defeated by the same difficulty. For the 337 second form and the second quality become either while the first form and the first quality remain in it or while they do not remain. But, as we showed before [b] when we were investigating " the patient," the second form does not become either while the first form remains or while it does not remain. So then, what is generated does not become from one

is affected," or " acted upon," as opposed to " the agent " (or " efficient cause ").

338 ἐξ ἑνὸς γίνεται τὸ γεννώμενον.   καὶ μὴν οὐδ᾽
ἐκ πλειόνων. δυοῖν γὰρ συνελθόντων τρίτον οὐκ
ἂν γένοιτο, μενόντων τῶν δυοῖν, καὶ πάλιν τριῶν
ὄντων τέταρτον οὐκ ἂν γένοιτο, μενόντων τῶν
τριῶν. εἴρηται δὲ περὶ τούτων ἀκριβέστερον, ὅτε
περὶ τῆς τοῦ ἀνθρώπου ὑποστάσεως ἐζητοῦμεν,
παριστάντες ὅτι οὔτε σῶμά ἐστιν ὁ ἄνθρωπος οὔτε
339 ψυχὴ οὔτε τὸ σύνθετον. διόπερ εἰ μήτε ἐξ ἑνός
ἐστι τὸ γεννώμενον μήτε ἐκ πλειόνων, παρὰ δὲ
ταῦτα οὐδὲν ἔστιν, ἐξ ἀνάγκης οὐδὲν τῶν ὄντων
γεννᾶται.

340   Ταῦτα μὲν οἱ ἀπορητικοὶ περὶ γενέσεως διεξ-
ίασιν· οἱ δὲ δογματικοὶ μὴ πρὸς νοῦν ἀπαντῶντες
πάλιν ἐπὶ τὰ ἐξ ἐναργείας ὑποδείγματα συμφεύ-
γουσιν. τὸ γὰρ ὕδωρ θερμὸν ὄν, μὴ ὂν δὲ ψυχρόν,
γίνεται ψυχρόν· καὶ ὁ ὑπάρχων χαλκός, μὴ ὢν
ἀνδριάς, γίνεται ἀνδριάς· καὶ τὸ ᾠὸν κατὰ δύναμιν
μέν ἐστι νεοσσός, κατ᾽ ἐντελέχειαν δὲ οὐκ ἔστιν,
[ἀλλὰ λέγεται κατὰ δύναμιν εἶναι νεοσσὸς εἰς τὸ
κατ᾽ ἐντελέχειαν ὑπάρχειν].[1] καὶ τὸ ὂν τοίνυν
δύναται γίνεσθαι καὶ τὸ μὴ ὄν. εἶτα καὶ ὁρῶμεν
βρέφος μὲν γεννώμενον ἐξ ἀνθρώπου, χυλὸν δ᾽ ἐκ
πόας. ὥστε πάντα τὸν τῶν ἀπορητικῶν[2] λόγον
341 παρὰ τὴν ἐνάργειαν χωρεῖν.   πλανῶνται δ᾽ οἱ
ταῦτα λέγοντες, καὶ οὐ πρὸς τὸ προκείμενον
ὑπαντῶσιν. τὸ γὰρ θερμὸν ⟨ὂν⟩[3] ὕδωρ καὶ οὐκ ὂν
ψυχρὸν οὔτε θερμὸν γίνεται τῷ εἶναι οὔτε ψυχρὸν
τῷ μὴ εἶναι· παρὰ δὲ τὸ εἶναι καὶ μὴ εἶναι οὐδὲν
ἔστιν· οὐκ ἄρα οὐδ᾽ ἐπὶ τοῦ ὕδατος ἔστι τις γένεσις.

---

[1] [ἀλλὰ . . . ὑπάρχειν] secl. ego (? ἀλλ᾽ ἄγεται ⟨ἐκ τοῦ⟩ κ. δ.).
[2] ἀπορητικῶν Heintz : δογματικῶν mss., Bekk.
[3] ⟨ὂν⟩ addo.

thing.—Nor yet does it become from several things. **338**
For when two things are combined a third will not
become while the two remain ; and again, if there are
three, a fourth will not become while the three remain.   But we made a more precise statement about
these matters when we were investigating the substance of Man [a] and showed that Man is neither body
nor soul nor the compound of both.   Wherefore, if the **339**
thing generated is neither from one thing nor from
several, and besides these there is no further possibility, then of necessity no existent thing is generated.

Such are the arguments concerning Becoming **340**
which the Doubters rehearse in detail ; but the
Dogmatists, without resorting to reason, take refuge
once more in examples drawn from the evidence
of sense.   Thus water being warm, and not being
cold, becomes cold ; and the bronze, which is not a
statue, becomes a statue ; and the egg is potentially
a chick but is not so actually [but is said to be a chick
potentially until it is one actually].[b]   Both the
existent, then, and the non-existent can become.
Moreover, we also see a baby generated from a
human being, and juice from grass.   So that all the
argumentation of the Sceptics runs contrary to the
evidence of sense.—But those who say this are in **341**
error, and are not facing the problem before them.
For the water which is hot and is not cold neither
becomes hot by being so nor cold by not being so ;
but besides being and not being nothing exists ; not
even, therefore, in the case of water is there any

[a] *Cf. Adv. Log.* i. 263 ff., 288 ff.
[b] As this clause seems futile, one may suspect (with
Heintz) that the text is incomplete, the original being to the
effect that " it is said <to become a chick in that it changes
from being> a chick potentially to being one actually."

καὶ πάλιν, οὔτε ὁ χαλκὸς γίνεται τῷ εἶναι χαλκὸς
342 οὔτε [ὁ]¹ ἀνδριὰς τῷ μὴ εἶναι. καὶ ἐπὶ τῶν
κατὰ δύναμιν καὶ ἐντελέχειαν ὁ αὐτός ἐστι λόγος.
ἄλλως τε ἤτοι πλεῖόν τί ἐστιν ἐν τῷ κατ᾽
ἐντελέχειαν παρὰ τὸ ἐν δυνάμει ἢ οὐκ ἔστιν· καὶ
εἰ μὲν οὐδὲν πλεῖόν ἐστιν, αὐτόθεν οὐδὲν γίνεται
τῷ κατὰ δύναμιν εἶναι, εἰ δὲ ἔστι τι πλέον, ἐκ τοῦ
343 μὴ ὄντος τοῦτο γίνεται, ὅπερ ἄτοπον. ναί, ἀλλὰ
καὶ βρέφος ἐκ τῆς ἐγκύμονος γεννᾶται καὶ χυλὸς
ἐκ τῆς πόας συνίσταται. καὶ τοῦτο τί πρὸς τὸ
ζητούμενον; ἐροῦμεν. οὔτε γὰρ τὸ βρέφος γίνεται
τικτόμενον, εἰς τοὐμφανὲς δὲ ἐκ τοῦ ἀφανοῦς
ἄγεται, οὔτε ὁ χυλός· καὶ γὰρ ἐν τῇ πόᾳ προϋπ-
ῆρχεν, καὶ ἐκτὸς τῆς πόας γινόμενος τόπον μόνον
ἤλλαξεν. ὥσπερ οὖν τὸν ἐκ τοῦ ζόφου εἰς τὸ φῶς
προελθόντα οὐ λέγομεν γίνεσθαι, τόπον δ᾽ ἐκ τόπου
μεταβεβηκέναι, κατὰ τὸν αὐτὸν τρόπον οὐδὲ τὸ
βρέφος ἐροῦμεν γίνεσθαι ἀλλ᾽ ἐξ ἑτέρου τινὸς
τόπου εἰς ἕτερον μεταβαίνειν τόπον. οὐδὲν οὖν
γεννᾶται.

344 Κατὰ ταὐτὰ δὲ·οὐδὲ φθείρεται. εἰ γὰρ φθείρεταί
τι, ἤτοι τὸ ὂν φθείρεται ἢ τὸ μὴ ὄν. οὔτε δὲ τὸ
μὴ ὂν φθείρεται· τὸ γὰρ φθειρόμενον εἰς τὸ μὴ
εἶναι χωρεῖ, τὸ δὲ μὴ ὂν [τι] ἤδη ἐν τῷ μὴ εἶναι
ὂν οὐ δεῖται τῆς εἰς τοῦτο μεταβάσεως. τοίνυν
345 οὐ φθείρεται τὸ μὴ ὄν. καὶ μὴν οὐδὲ τὸ ὄν. ἤτοι
γὰρ μένον ἐν τῷ εἶναι φθείρεται ἢ μὴ μένον. καὶ
εἰ μὲν μένον, ἔσται ἅμα καὶ οὐκ ἔσται, ἐφθαρμένον

¹ [ὁ] secl. Heintz.

ᵃ With §§ 344-345 cf. *P.H.* iii. 113-114.

becoming. And again : neither does the bronze become bronze by being so nor a statue by not being so. And the same may be said of the cases of potentiality 342 and actuality.—And further, there either is or is not something more in the actual than in the potential ; and if there is nothing more, it follows that nothing becomes by existing potentially ; but if there is something more, this becomes from the non-existent, which is absurd. Yes, ⟨they reply,⟩ but the babe is 343 generated from the mother, and juice is formed from the grass. And how, we shall ask, does this affect the question ? For neither does the babe become by being born (being merely brought from obscurity into sight), nor does the juice become (for it was pre-existing in the grass, and in becoming outside the grass it has merely changed its place). As, then, we do not say that the man who has advanced out of the darkness into the light is becoming, but that he has passed on from place to place, so in the same way we shall not say that the babe becomes, but that it passes on from one place to another place. Nothing, then, is generated.

Nor, for the same reasons, does anything perish.[a] 344 For if anything perishes, either the existent perishes or the non-existent. But the non-existent does not perish ; for what perishes passes into a state of non-existence, but the non-existent, as it is already in the state of non-existence, does not require transference into this state. So then, the non-existent does not perish. Nor yet does the existent. For 345 it perishes either while remaining in existence or while not remaining. And if it does so while remaining, it will be at once existent and non-existent, perished and not perished ; but if it does so while not

καὶ μὴ ἐφθαρμένον· εἰ δὲ μὴ μένον, ἀπόλλυται,
καὶ οὐκέτι τὸ ὂν ἀλλὰ τὸ μὴ ὂν φθείρεται. ὥστε
346 εἰ μήτε τὸ ὂν μήτε τὸ μὴ ὂν φθείρεται, παρὰ δὲ
ταῦτα οὐδὲν ἔστιν, οὐδὲν φθείρεται.

Τινὲς δὲ καὶ τῶν χρόνων ἐχόμενοι τῆς τε
γενέσεως καὶ φθορᾶς οὕτω συνερωτῶσιν. εἰ
ἀπέθανε Σωκράτης, ἤτοι ὅτε ἔζη ἀπέθανεν ἢ ὅτε
ἐτελεύτα. καὶ ζῶν μὲν οὐκ ἀπέθανεν· ἔζη γὰρ
347 δήπουθεν καὶ ζῶν οὐκ ἐτεθνήκει. οὔτε δ' ὅτε
ἀπέθανεν· δὶς γὰρ ἔσται τεθνηκώς. οὐκ ἄρα
ἀπέθανε Σωκράτης. ἀπὸ δὲ τῆς αὐτῆς δυνάμεως, ἐπὶ διαφέροντος δὲ ὑποδείγματος, λόγον
συνηρώτηκε καὶ ὁ Κρόνος τοιοῦτον. εἰ φθείρεται
τὸ τειχίον, ἤτοι ὅτε ἅπτονται ἀλλήλων οἱ λίθοι
καὶ εἰσὶν ἡρμοσμένοι φθείρεται τὸ τειχίον, ἢ
ὅτε διεστᾶσιν· οὔτε δὲ ὅτε ἅπτονται ἀλλήλων
348 καὶ εἰσὶν ἡρμοσμένοι φθείρεται τὸ τειχίον, οὔτε
ὅτε διεστᾶσιν ἀπ' ἀλλήλων· οὐκ ἄρα φθείρεται τὸ
τειχίον. καὶ ὁ μὲν λόγος τοιοῦτος, ἡ δὲ δύναμις
αὐτοῦ προφανής. δύο γάρ εἰσι χρόνοι κατ' ἐπίνοιαν, ἐν ᾧ ἅπτονται ἀλλήλων οἱ λίθοι καὶ εἰσὶν
ἡρμοσμένοι, καὶ ἐν ᾧ διεστᾶσιν· παρὰ δὲ τούτους
349 οὐδ' ἐπινοηθῆναι τρίτος τις δύναται χρόνος. εἰ
οὖν φθείρεται τὸ τειχίον, ἐν τῷ ἑτέρῳ τούτων
ὀφείλει φθείρεσθαι. ἀλλ' ἐν μὲν ᾧ ἅπτονται ἀλλήλων οἱ λίθοι καὶ εἰσὶν ἡρμοσμένοι, οὐ δύναται
φθείρεσθαι· ἔστι γὰρ ἔτι τειχίον, καὶ εἰ ἔστιν, οὐ
φθείρεται. οὔτε δὲ ἐν ᾧ διεστᾶσιν ἀπ' ἀλλήλων·
οὐκέτι γὰρ ἔστι τειχίον, τὸ δὲ μὴ ὂν οὐ δύναται
350 φθείρεσθαι. εἰ οὖν μήτε ὅτε ἅπτονται ἀλλήλων
οἱ λίθοι φθείρεται τὸ τειχίον, μήτε ὅτε διεστᾶσιν

remaining, it is destroyed, and it is no longer the existent but the non-existent which perishes. So that if neither the existent nor the non-existent perishes, and besides these there is nothing, nothing perishes.

Some also, fastening on the times of becoming and 346 perishing, argue thus : If Socrates died, he died either when he was living or when he was dead.[a] But he did not die while living ; for assuredly he was living, and as living he had not died. Nor when he died ; for then he would be twice dead. Therefore Socrates did not die.—And to the same effect, 347 although using a different example, Cronos [b] propounded an argument of this kind : If the wall perishes, the wall perishes either while the stones are touching one another and are fitted together or when they are disparted. But neither when they touch one another and are fitted together nor when they are disparted does the wall perish ; therefore the wall does not perish. Such is the argument, and the force 348 of it is quite plain. There are two times conceived, that in which the stones touch one another and are fitted together and that in which they are disparted ; and besides these no third time can be conceived. If, then, the wall perishes, it must perish in one or other of these times. But it cannot perish in the time when 349 the stones are touching one another and are fitted together ; for it still exists as a wall, and if it exists it does not perish. Nor in the time when they are disparted from one another; for then it no longer exists as a wall, and the non-existent cannot perish. If, then, the wall does not perish either when the stones are touching one another or when they are disparted

* Cf. Adv. Phys. i. 269 ; P.H. iii. 111.
  [b] i.e. Diodorus Cronos (cf. § 85).

350 ἀπ' ἀλλήλων, οὐ φθείρεται τὸ τειχίον.   καὶ
οὕτω δὲ δυνατὸν συνερωτᾶν. εἰ γίνεταί τι καὶ
φθείρεται, ἤτοι ἐν ᾧ ἔστι χρόνῳ γίνεται καὶ
φθείρεται, ἢ ἐν ᾧ μὴ ἔστιν. καὶ ἐν ᾧ μὲν ἔστιν,
οὔτε γίνεται οὔτε φθείρεται· ἐφ' ὅσον γὰρ ἔστι
τοῦτο, οὔτε γίνεται οὔτε φθείρεται. καὶ μὴν οὐδὲ
ἐν ᾧ μὴ ἔστι πάθοι ἄν τι τούτων· ἐν ᾧ γάρ τι μὴ
ἔστιν, οὔτε παθεῖν τι οὔτε ποιεῖν δύναται. εἰ δὲ
τοῦτο, οὐδὲν οὔτε γίνεται οὔτε φθείρεται.

351 Ταῦτα μὲν οὖν πρὸς τοὺς φυσικοὺς τῶν φιλοσόφων εἰρήσθω· καιρὸς δ' ἂν εἴη μετελθεῖν καὶ ἐπὶ
τοὺς τὸ ἠθικὸν μέρος τῆς φιλοσοφίας ἀσπασα-
μένους.

from one another, the wall does not perish.—And 350
it is also possible to argue thus : If a thing both
becomes and perishes, it becomes and perishes either
in the time in which it exists or in that in which it does
not exist.   But in that in which it exists it neither becomes nor perishes ; for inasmuch as it exists as this
thing it neither becomes nor perishes.   Nor yet will
it undergo any of these affections in the time in which
it does not exist ; for in the time in which a thing does
not exist it can neither affect nor be affected at all.
And if so, nothing either becomes or perishes.

Let these, then, be our answers to those of the 351
philosophers who are Physicists ; but now it will be
time for us to pass on to those who have embraced
the Ethical division of philosophy.

AGAINST THE ETHICISTS

ΠΡΟΣ ΗΘΙΚΟΥΣ

1 Τὰς μὲν κομιζομένας ὑπὸ τῶν σκεπτικῶν ἀπορίας
εἴς τε τὸ λογικὸν καὶ φυσικὸν τῆς φιλοσοφίας
μέρος πρότερον ἐπεληλύθαμεν, ὑπόλοιπον δέ ἐστι
καὶ τὰς εἰς τὸ ἠθικὸν φέρεσθαι δυναμένας προσ-
υποτάττειν· οὕτω γὰρ ἕκαστος ἡμῶν τὴν τελείαν καὶ
σκεπτικὴν ἀπολαβὼν διάθεσιν κατὰ τὸν Τίμωνα
βιώσεται

ῥῇστα μεθ' ἡσυχίης
αἰεὶ ἀφροντίστως καὶ ἀκινήτως κατὰ ταὐτά,
μὴ προσέχων αἴνοις[1] ἡδυλόγου σοφίης.

2 ἀλλ' ἐπεὶ τὴν ἠθικὴν θεωρίαν συμφώνως σχεδὸν
ἅπαντες ὑπειλήφασι περὶ τὴν τῶν ἀγαθῶν τε καὶ
κακῶν διάκρισιν γίνεσθαι, καθὸ καὶ ὁ πρῶτος αὐτὴν δόξας κεκινηκέναι Σωκράτης παρήγγειλεν ὡς
ἀναγκαιότατον ζητεῖν

ὅττι τοι ἐν μεγάροισι κακόν τ' ἀγαθόν τε τέτυ-
κται,

δεήσει καὶ ἡμᾶς ἐν ἀρχαῖς εὐθὺς περὶ τῆς ἐν τούτοις
διαφορᾶς σκοπεῖν.

---

[1] αἴνοις: δειλοῖς mss., Bekk.: δίνοις Nauck (λήροις cj.
Bekk.).

AGAINST THE ETHICISTS

WE have already discussed the difficulties brought 1
forward by the Sceptics with regard to the Logical
and Physical divisions of philosophy, and now it
remains for us to subjoin further those which can be
brought against the Ethical division ; for in this way,
by acquiring the perfect and sceptical frame of mind,
each of us will (in the words of Timon [a]) pass his
life—

> In great comfort and calm,
> Ever devoid of care, uniformly free from distraction,
> Quite regardless of all Sweet-voiced Science's tales.

But since almost all have with one accord supposed 2
that the study of Ethics is concerned with the distinction between things good and evil,[b]—even as
Socrates, who is thought to be the first who introduced it, proclaimed as the most necessary subject of
inquiry—

> Whatso of evil and good within these homes is enacted,[c]

we too shall have to begin at once by considering
the difference which exists between them.

---

[a] Cf. Vol. I. Introd. p. xxxi.
[b] With §§ 2, 3 cf. P.H. iii. 168.
[c] Homer,*Odyss.* iv. 392 ; cf. *Adv. Log.* i. 21.

Α΄.—ΤΙΣ ΕΣΤΙΝ Η ΟΛΟΣΧΕΡΗΣ ΤΩΝ ΚΑΤΑ ΤΟΝ ΒΙΟΝ
ΠΡΑΓΜΑΤΩΝ ΔΙΑΦΟΡΑ

3 Πάντες μὲν οἱ κατὰ [τὸν] τρόπον στοιχειοῦν
δοκοῦντες τῶν φιλοσόφων, καὶ ἐπιφανέστατα παρὰ
πάντας οἵ τε ἀπὸ τῆς ἀρχαίας Ἀκαδημίας καὶ οἱ
ἀπὸ τοῦ περιπάτου ἔτι δὲ τῆς στοᾶς, εἰώθασι
διαιρούμενοι λέγειν τῶν ὄντων τὰ μὲν εἶναι ἀγαθὰ
τὰ δὲ κακὰ τὰ δὲ μεταξὺ τούτων, ἅπερ καὶ ἀδιά-
4 φορα λέγουσιν· ἰδιαίτερον δὲ παρὰ τοὺς ἄλλους ὁ
Ξενοκράτης καὶ ταῖς ἑνικαῖς πτώσεσι χρώμενος
ἔφασκε " πᾶν τὸ ὂν ἢ ἀγαθόν ἐστιν ἢ κακόν ἐστιν
5 ἢ οὔτε ἀγαθόν ἐστιν οὔτε κακόν ἐστιν." καὶ τῶν
λοιπῶν φιλοσόφων χωρὶς ἀποδείξεως τὴν τοιαύτην
διαίρεσιν προσιεμένων αὐτὸς ἐδόκει καὶ ἀπόδειξιν
συμπαραλαμβάνειν. εἰ γὰρ ἔστι τι κεχωρισμένον
πρᾶγμα τῶν ἀγαθῶν καὶ κακῶν καὶ τῶν μήτε
ἀγαθῶν μήτε κακῶν, ἐκεῖνο ἤτοι ἀγαθόν ἐστιν ἢ
οὐκ ἔστιν ἀγαθόν. καὶ εἰ μὲν ἀγαθόν ἐστιν, ἐν τῶν
τριῶν γενήσεται· εἰ δ' οὐκ ἔστιν ἀγαθόν, ἤτοι κακόν
ἐστιν ἢ οὔτε κακόν ἐστιν οὔτε ἀγαθόν ἐστιν· εἴτε
δὲ κακόν ἐστιν, ἐν τῶν τριῶν ὑπάρξει, εἴτε οὔτε
ἀγαθόν ἐστιν οὔτε κακόν ἐστι, πάλιν ἐν τῶν τριῶν
καταστήσεται. πᾶν ἄρα τὸ ὂν ἤτοι ἀγαθόν ἐστιν ἢ
κακόν ἐστιν ἢ οὔτε ἀγαθόν ἐστιν οὔτε κακόν ἐστιν.
6 δυνάμει δὲ καὶ οὗτος χωρὶς ἀποδείξεως προσήκατο
τὴν διαίρεσιν, ἐπείπερ ὁ εἰς κατασκευὴν αὐτῆς
παραληφθεὶς λόγος οὐχ ἕτερός ἐστιν αὐτῆς· ὅθεν εἰ
ἐν ἑαυτῇ περιέσχηκε τὴν πίστιν ἡ ἀπόδειξις, ἔσται
καὶ ἡ διαίρεσις ἐξ ἑαυτῆς πιστὴ μὴ διαφέρουσα τῆς
ἀποδείξεως.
7 Ἀλλ' ὅμως, καίπερ συμφώνου δοκοῦντος ὑπάρχειν κατὰ πάντας τοῦ ὅτι τρισσή ἐστιν ἡ τῶν ὄντων

Chapter I.—What is the main Difference in the Things which concern Life?

All the philosophers who seem to teach systematic- 3
ally the principles ⟨of Ethics⟩, and, most notably of
all, those of the Old Academy and the Peripatetics,
and the Stoics also, are accustomed to make a distinction by saying that " of existing things some are
good, some evil, some between these two," and these
last they term " indifferent " ; but Xenocrates,[a] in 4
phrases peculiar to himself and using the singular
case, declared that " Everything which exists either
is good or is evil or neither is good nor is evil."   And 5
whereas the rest of the philosophers adopted this
division without a proof, he thought it right to
introduce a proof as well.   " If," he argued, " anything exists which is apart from things good and evil
and things neither good nor evil, that thing either is
good or is not good.   And if it is good, it will be one
of the three ; but if it is not good, it is either evil or
neither evil nor good ; and if it is evil, it will be one
of the three, and if it is neither evil nor good, again
it will be one of the three.   Therefore everything
which exists either is good or is evil or neither is good
nor is evil."   But he, too, virtually accepted the 6
division without proof, since the argument adopted to
establish it is nothing else than the division itself ;
hence, if the proof contains in itself the confirmation,
the division, too, will be its own confirmation as it
does not differ from the proof.

But yet, although it seems to be agreed by all that 7
the distinction between existing things is threefold,

a Head of the Platonic " Academy," 339–314 B.C.

διαφορά, τινὲς οὐδὲν ἧττον εὑρεσιλογοῦσιν, ὁμο
λογοῦντες μὲν τὴν ἐν τοῖς οὖσι διαφορὰν ὅτι τοιαύτη
τίς ἐστι, σοφιστικῶς δὲ προσειλούμενοι τῇ ἐκτε
θείσῃ διαιρέσει. καὶ τοῦτο εἰσόμεθα μικρὸν ἄνωθεν
προλαβόντες.

8 Τὸν γὰρ ὅρον φασὶν οἱ τεχνογράφοι ψιλῇ τῇ
συντάξει διαφέρειν τοῦ καθολικοῦ, δυνάμει τὸν
αὐτὸν ὄντα. καὶ εἰκότως· ὁ γὰρ εἰπὼν " ἄνθρωπός
ἐστι ζῷον λογικὸν θνητόν " τῷ εἰπόντι " εἴ τί ἐστιν
ἄνθρωπος, ἐκεῖνο ζῷόν ἐστι λογικὸν θνητόν " τῇ
μὲν δυνάμει τὸ αὐτὸ λέγει τῇ δὲ φωνῇ διάφορον.
9 καὶ ὅτι τοῦτο, συμφανὲς ἐκ τοῦ μὴ μόνον τὸ καθ
ολικὸν τῶν ἐπὶ μέρους εἶναι περιληπτικόν, ἀλλὰ καὶ
τὸν ὅρον ἐπὶ πάντα τὰ εἴδη τοῦ ἀποδιδομένου
πράγματος διήκειν, οἷον τὸν μὲν τοῦ ἀνθρώπου ἐπὶ
πάντας τοὺς κατ᾽ εἶδος ἀνθρώπους, τὸν δὲ τοῦ
ἵππου ἐπὶ πάντας τοὺς ἵππους. ἑνός τε ὑποταχ
θέντος ψεύδους ἑκάτερον γίνεται μοχθηρόν, τό τε
10 καθολικὸν καὶ ὁ ὅρος. ἀλλὰ γὰρ ὡς ταῦτα φωναῖς
ἐξηλλαγμένα κατὰ δύναμίν ἐστι τὰ αὐτά, ὧδε καὶ
ἡ τέλειός φασι διαίρεσις, δύναμιν ἔχουσα καθολικήν,
συντάξει τοῦ καθολικοῦ διενήνοχεν. ὁ γὰρ τρόπῳ
τῷδε διαιρούμενος " τῶν ἀνθρώπων οἱ μέν εἰσιν
Ἕλληνες οἱ δὲ βάρβαροι " ἴσον τι λέγει τῷ " εἴ
τινές εἰσιν ἄνθρωποι, ἐκεῖνοι ἢ Ἕλληνές εἰσιν ἢ
βάρβαροι." ἐὰν γάρ τις ἄνθρωπος εὑρίσκηται μήτε
Ἕλλην μήτε βάρβαρος, ἀνάγκη μοχθηρὰν μὲν εἶναι
τὴν διαίρεσιν, ψεῦδος δὲ γίνεσθαι τὸ καθολικόν.
11 διόπερ καὶ τὸ οὕτω λεγόμενον " τῶν ὄντων τὰ μέν

ᵃ In a " perfect division " the two *species* into which the
genus is divided are contradictories (*e.g.* Men = Greeks + non-

none the less some people invent captious objections, and while allowing that the distinction between things is of this kind, yet attack the division as set forth in sophistical fashion. And this we shall learn when we have first gone back a little.

The professional Logicians assert that the definition 8 differs merely in its verbal construction from the universal, being identical in meaning. And rightly ; for he who says " Man is a rational, mortal animal " says what is identical in meaning, though different in wording from him who says " Whatever thing is man, that thing is a rational, mortal animal." And that this is 9 so is plain from the fact that not only is the universal inclusive of the particulars but the definition also extends to all the particular instances of the thing in question,—that of Man, for example, to all the particular men, and that of Horse to all the horses. Also, if one false instance is classed under it each of them is vitiated, both the universal and the definition. Well 10 then, just as these, which vary in wording, are identical in meaning, so also, they declare, the perfect division, which has a universal meaning, differs from the universal in verbal construction.[a] For he who divides in this fashion—" Of men some are Greeks, others barbarians "—says what is equivalent to " Whosoever are men, they are either Greeks or barbarians." For if any man is found who is neither a Greek nor a barbarian, the division must necessarily be vicious and the universal false. Hence, too, a 11 statement in the form " Of existing things some are

Greeks); as thus inclusive of all possible instances (*i.e.* " exhaustive ") it is " universal in meaning " and differs only in form from a regular " universal proposition " (*e.g.* " All men are either Greeks or non-Greeks ").

SEXTUS EMPIRICUS

ἐστιν ἀγαθὰ τὰ δὲ κακὰ τὰ δὲ τούτων μεταξύ"
δυνάμει κατὰ τὸν Χρύσιππον τοιοῦτόν ἐστι καθολικόν " εἴ τινά ἐστιν ὄντα, ἐκεῖνα ἤτοι ἀγαθά ἐστιν
ἢ κακά ἐστιν ἢ ἀδιάφορα." τὸ μέντοι γε τοιοῦτον
καθολικὸν ψεῦδός ἐστιν ὑποτασσομένου τινὸς αὐτῷ
12 ψεύδους. δυοῖν γάρ φασιν ὑποκειμένων πραγμάτων, τοῦ μὲν ἀγαθοῦ τοῦ δὲ κακοῦ, ἢ τοῦ μὲν
ἀγαθοῦ τοῦ δὲ ἀδιαφόρου, ἢ κακοῦ καὶ ἀδιαφόρου,
τὸ μὲν " τοῦτ' ἔστι τῶν ὄντων ἀγαθόν " ἀληθές
ἐστι, τὸ δὲ " ταῦτ' ἔστιν ἀγαθά " ψεῦδος· οὐ γάρ
ἐστιν ἀγαθά, ἀλλὰ τὸ μὲν ἀγαθὸν τὸ δὲ κακόν.
13 καὶ τὸ " ταῦτ' ἔστι κακά " πάλιν ψεῦδος· οὐ γάρ
ἐστι κακά, ἀλλὰ τὸ ἕτερον αὐτῶν. ὡσαύτως δὲ καὶ
ἐπὶ τῶν ἀδιαφόρων· ψεῦδος γὰρ τὸ " ταῦτ' ἔστιν
ἀδιάφορα," ὥσπερ καὶ τὸ " ταῦτ' ἔστιν ἀγαθὰ ἢ
κακά." ἡ μὲν οὖν ἔνστασις τοιαύτη πως καθέστη-
14 κεν, φαίνεται δὲ μὴ καθάπτεσθαι τοῦ Ξενοκράτους
διὰ τὸ μὴ ταῖς πληθυντικαῖς πτώσεσι κεχρῆσθαι,
ὥστ' ἐπὶ τῆς τῶν ἑτερογενῶν δείξεως ψευδοποιη-
θῆναι τὴν διαίρεσιν.
15 Ἄλλοι δὲ κἀκείνως ἐνέστησαν. πᾶσα γάρ,
φασίν, ὑγιὴς διαίρεσις γένους ἐστὶ τομὴ εἰς τὰ
προσεχῆ εἴδη, καὶ διὰ τοῦτο μοχθηρὰ καθέστηκεν ἡ
τοιαύτη διαίρεσις " τῶν ἀνθρώπων οἱ μέν εἰσιν
Ἕλληνες οἱ δὲ Αἰγύπτιοι οἱ δὲ Πέρσαι οἱ δὲ Ἰνδοί."
τῷ γὰρ ἑτέρῳ τῶν προσεχῶν εἰδῶν οὐ τὸ συζυγοῦν
καὶ προσεχὲς εἶδος ἀντιδιέζευκται, ἀλλὰ τὰ τούτου
εἴδη, δέον οὕτως εἰπεῖν " τῶν ἀνθρώπων οἱ μέν
εἰσιν Ἕλληνες οἱ δὲ βάρβαροι," καὶ καθ' ὑποδι-
αίρεσιν λοιπὸν " τῶν βαρβάρων οἱ μέν εἰσιν Αἰγύ-
16 πτιοι οἱ δὲ Πέρσαι οἱ δὲ Ἰνδοί." ὅπερ καὶ ἐπὶ τῆς
τῶν ὄντων διαιρέσεως, ἐπεὶ ὅσα μέν ἐστιν ἀγαθὰ

390

good, others evil, others between these two," is
virtually, according to Chrysippus, a universal such
as this—" Whatsoever things are existent, they either
are good or are evil or indifferent." Such a universal,
however, is false if a false instance is classed under it.
For, they say, when two things subsist, the one good 12
and the other evil, or the one good and the other
indifferent, or an evil and an indifferent, the statement " This one of existing things is good " is true,
but " These things are good " false ; for they are not
⟨both⟩ good, but the one is good and the other evil.
And again the statement " These things are evil " is 13
false ; for they are not ⟨both⟩ evil but only the one
of them. And so likewise in the case of the things
indifferent ; for " These things are indifferent " is
false, just as is " These things are good, or evil."
Something like this, then, is the objection, but it 14
appears not to affect Xenocrates because he does not
employ plural cases, which would result in the
falsification of his division when things of different
kinds are to be indicated.

And others have raised the following objection : 15
Every sound division, they say, is the cutting up of a
genus into its proximate species, and for this reason
a division such as this is unsound—" Of men some
are Greeks, others Egyptians, others Persians, others
Indians." For the first proximate species has
matched against it not its correlative proximate
species but the sub-species of this, the correct statement being, " Of men some are Greeks, others
barbarians," and next, by subdivision, " And of
barbarians some are Egyptians, others Persians,
others Indians." And this applies also to the 16
division of existing things, since all such as are good

καὶ κακά, διαφέροντά ἐστιν ἡμῖν, ὅσα δὲ μεταξὺ
τῶν τε ἀγαθῶν καὶ κακῶν, ταῦτ' ἔστιν ἡμῖν ἀδιάφορα. ἐχρῆν οὖν μὴ οὕτως ἔχειν τὴν διαίρεσιν ὡς
ἔχει, μᾶλλον δ' ἐκείνως " τῶν ὄντων ἃ μέν ἐστιν
ἀδιάφορα ἃ δὲ διαφέροντα, τῶν δὲ διαφερόντων ἃ
17 μὲν ἀγαθὰ ἃ δὲ κακά." ἐῴκει γὰρ ἡ μὲν τοιαύτη
διαίρεσις τῇ λεγούσῃ " τῶν ἀνθρώπων οἱ μέν εἰσιν
Ἕλληνες οἱ δὲ βάρβαροι, τῶν δὲ βαρβάρων οἱ μὲν
Αἰγύπτιοι οἱ δὲ Πέρσαι οἱ δὲ Ἰνδοί"· ἡ δὲ ἐκκει-
μένη ᾠμοίωτο τῇ τοιουτοτρόπῳ " τῶν ἀνθρώπων
οἱ μέν εἰσιν Ἕλληνες οἱ δὲ Αἰγύπτιοι οἱ δὲ Πέρσαι
οἱ δὲ Ἰνδοί."

Ἀλλὰ περὶ μὲν τούτων τῶν ἐνστάσεων οὐκ
18 ἀνάγκη νῦν μηκύνειν, ἐκεῖνο δ' ἴσως ἁρμόσει
προδιαρθρῶσαι ὅτι τὸ ἔστι δύο σημαίνει, καὶ ἓν μὲν
τὸ οἷον ὑπάρχει, καθὸ φαμὲν ἐπὶ τοῦ παρόντος τὸ
ὅτι ἡμέρα ἔστιν ἀντὶ τοῦ ἡμέρα ὑπάρχει, ἕτερον δὲ
τὸ οἷον φαίνεται, καθὸ τινες τῶν μαθηματικῶν
εἰώθασι λέγειν πολλάκις ὅτι τὸ μεταξὺ δυοῖν τινῶν
ἀστέρων διάστημα πηχυαῖόν ἐστιν, ἐν ἴσῳ λέγοντες
τῷ φαίνεται καὶ οὐ πάντως ὑπάρχει· τάχα γὰρ
ὑπάρχει μὲν σταδίων ἑκατόν, φαίνεται δὲ πηχυαῖον
παρὰ τὸ ὕψος καὶ παρὰ τὴν τῆς ὄψεως ἀπόστασιν.
19 διττοῦ δὴ τυγχάνοντος τοῦ ἔστι μορίου, ὅταν
λέγωμεν σκεπτικῶς " τῶν ὄντων τὰ μέν ἐστιν
ἀγαθὰ τὰ δὲ κακὰ τὰ δὲ μεταξὺ τούτων," τὸ ἔστι
ἐντάττομεν οὐχ ὡς ὑπάρξεως ἀλλ' ὡς τοῦ φαίνεσθαι δηλωτικόν. περὶ μὲν γὰρ τῆς πρὸς τὴν φύσιν
ὑποστάσεως τῶν τε ἀγαθῶν καὶ κακῶν καὶ οὐδετέρων ἱκανοί πώς εἰσιν ἡμῖν ἀγῶνες πρὸς τοὺς

2

and evil are "different"[a] to us, but all that lie
between the good things and the evil are "indifferent" to us. The division, then, ought not to have been
stated in its present form but rather in this form—
"Of existing things some are indifferent, others
different; and of the different some are good, others
evil." For this form of division resembles that which 17
runs—"Of men some are Greeks, others barbarians;
and of the barbarians some are Egyptians, others
Persians, others Indians"; but the division put
forward resembled one of this type—"Of men some
are Greeks, others Egyptians, others Persians, others
Indians."

However, there is no necessity now to speak at
length about these objections; but it will, perhaps, 18
be fitting to explain first that the word "is" has
two meanings, one of these being "really exists" (as,
at the present moment, we say "it is day"
for "day really exists"); and the other "appears"[b]
(as some of the mathematicians are frequently in the
habit of saying that the distance between two stars
"is" a cubit's length, this being equivalent to
"appears to be but is not really"; for perhaps it
is really "one hundred stades" but appears to be a
cubit owing to its height and owing to the distance
from the eye). When, then, as Sceptics, we say that 19
"Of existing things some are good, others evil, others
between these two," as the element "are" is twofold
in meaning, we insert the "are" as indicative not of
real existence but of appearance. For concerning
the real and substantial existence of things good and
evil and neither we have contests enough with the

[a] i.e. such as to "make a difference" to us, important.
[b] Cf. P.H. i. 135, 198.

20 δογματικούς· κατὰ δὲ τὸ φαινόμενον τούτων ἕκαστον ἔχομεν ἔθος ἀγαθὸν ἢ κακὸν ἢ ἀδιάφορον
προσαγορεύειν, καθάπερ καὶ ὁ Τίμων ἐν τοῖς
ἰνδαλμοῖς ἔοικε δηλοῦν, ὅταν φῇ

ἢ γὰρ ἐγὼν ἐρέω ὥς μοι καταφαίνεται εἶναι,
μῦθον ἀληθείης ὀρθὸν ἔχων κανόνα,
ὡς ζῇ[1] τοῦ θείου τε φύσις καὶ τἀγαθοῦ αἰεί,
ἐξ ὧν ἰσότατος γίνεται ἀνδρὶ βίος.

Κειμένης οὖν κατὰ τὸν ὑποδεδειγμένον τρόπον
τῆς προειρημένης διαιρέσεως, ἴδωμεν ἃ χρὴ φρονεῖν
περὶ τῶν ἐν αὐτῇ, τὴν ἀρχὴν τῶν λόγων ἀπὸ τῆς
ἐννοίας ποιησάμενοι.

Β'.—ΤΙ ΕΣΤΙ ΤΟ ΑΓΑΘΟΝ ΚΑΙ ΚΑΚΟΝ ΚΑΙ ΑΔΙΑΦΟΡΟΝ

21 Τῆς κατὰ τὸν τόπον χειριζομένης ἡμῖν πρὸς τοὺς
δογματικοὺς ἀντιρρήσεως τὸ κυριώτατον μέρος
ἐχούσης ἐν τῇ διαγνώσει τῶν τε ἀγαθῶν καὶ κακῶν,
πρὸ παντὸς ἁρμόσει τὴν ἐπίνοιαν τούτων στῆσαι·
κατὰ γὰρ τὸν σοφὸν Ἐπίκουρον οὔτε ζητεῖν ἔστιν
22 οὔτε ἀπορεῖν ἄνευ προλήψεως. οἱ μὲν οὖν στωικοὶ
τῶν κοινῶν ὡς εἰπεῖν ἐννοιῶν ἐχόμενοι ὁρίζονται
τἀγαθὸν τρόπῳ τῷδε '' ἀγαθόν ἐστι ὠφέλεια ἢ οὐχ
ἕτερον ὠφελείας,'' ὠφέλειαν μὲν λέγοντες τὴν
ἀρετὴν καὶ τὴν σπουδαίαν πρᾶξιν, οὐχ ἕτερον δὲ
ὠφελείας τὸν σπουδαῖον ἄνθρωπον καὶ τὸν φίλον.
23 ἡ μὲν γὰρ ἀρετή πως ἔχον ἡγεμονικὸν καθεστηκυῖα,
καὶ ἡ σπουδαία πρᾶξις ἐνέργειά τις οὖσα κατ'
ἀρετήν, ἀντικρύς ἐστιν ὠφέλεια· ὁ δὲ σπουδαῖος
ἄνθρωπος καὶ ὁ φίλος, πάλιν τῶν ἀγαθῶν ὄντες καὶ

---

[1] ζῇ: ἡ mss., Bekk.

Dogmatists ; but as regards the appearance of each 20
of these things we are in the habit of designating it
good or evil or indifferent, even as Timon seems to
make plain in his " Images," when he says—

> Verily I will relate each fact as to me it appeareth,
> Standard exact of truth having in this my speech,
> How that the nature of God and of Goodness abideth for
> ever,
> Whence proceedeth for man Life that is equal and just.

So then, the division mentioned above having been
laid down in the form described, let us see what view
we should take of the terms contained in it, beginning
our discussion with the conception ⟨implied by those
terms⟩.

CHAPTER II.—THE ESSENCE OF GOOD AND EVIL AND INDIFFERENT

Since the controversy which we wage on this 21
subject with the Dogmatists has for its most important
point the differentiation of things good and evil, it
will be fitting first of all to formulate a conception of
these ; for, according to the sapient Epicurus, " It
is not possible either to seek or to doubt without a
preconception." Now the Stoics, holding fast to the 22
common notions (so to call them), define the good in
this way [a]—" Good is utility or not other than
utility," meaning by " utility " virtue and right
action, and by " not other than utility " the good
man and the friend. For virtue, being a certain state 23
of the regent part, and right action, being an activity
in accordance with virtue, are exactly utility ; and
the good man, again, and the friend, belonging also
themselves to the class of " good things," cannot be

[a] With §§ 22-27 cf. P.H. iii. 169-171.

αὐτοί, οὔτε ὠφέλεια λεχθεῖεν ἂν ὑπάρχειν οὔθ᾽
24 ἕτεροι ὠφελείας δι᾽ αἰτίαν τοιαύτην. τὰ γὰρ μέρη,
στωικῶν φασὶ παῖδες, οὔτε τὰ αὐτὰ τοῖς ὅλοις ἐστὶν
οὔτε ἑτεροῖα τῶν ὅλων, οἷον ἡ χεὶρ οὔτε ἡ αὐτή
ἐστιν ὅλῳ ἀνθρώπῳ, οὐ γὰρ ὅλος ἄνθρωπός ἐστιν
ἡ χείρ, οὔτε ἑτέρα τοῦ ὅλου, σὺν γὰρ τῇ [ὅλῃ]¹
χειρὶ ὅλος ὁ ἄνθρωπος νοεῖται ἄνθρωπος. ἐπεὶ οὖν
καὶ τοῦ σπουδαίου ἀνθρώπου καὶ τοῦ φίλου μέρος
ἐστὶν ἡ ἀρετή, τὰ δὲ μέρη οὔτε ταὐτὰ τοῖς ὅλοις
ἐστὶν οὔτε ἕτερα τῶν ὅλων, εἴρηται ὁ σπουδαῖος
ἄνθρωπος καὶ ὁ φίλος οὐχ ἕτερος ὠφελείας. ὥστε
πᾶν ἀγαθὸν τῷ ὅρῳ ἐμπεριειλῆφθαι, ἐάν τε ἐξ
εὐθείας ὠφέλεια τυγχάνῃ ἐάν τε μὴ ᾖ ἕτερον ὠφε-
25 λείας. ἔνθεν καὶ κατὰ ἀκολουθίαν τριχῶς εἰπόντες
ἀγαθὸν προσαγορεύεσθαι, ἕκαστον τῶν σημαινομένων κατ᾽ ἰδίαν πάλιν ἐπιβολὴν ὑπογράφουσιν.
λέγεται γὰρ ἀγαθόν, φασί, καθ᾽ ἕνα μὲν τρόπον τὸ
ὑφ᾽ οὗ ἢ ἀφ᾽ οὗ ἔστιν ὠφελεῖσθαι, ὃ δὴ ἀρχικώτατον ὑπῆρχε καὶ ἀρετή· ἀπὸ γὰρ ταύτης ὥσπερ
26 τινὸς πηγῆς πᾶσα πέφυκεν ἀνίσχειν ὠφέλεια. καθ᾽
ἕτερον δὲ τὸ καθ᾽ ὃ συμβαίνει ὠφελεῖσθαι· οὕτως οὐ
μόνον αἱ ἀρεταὶ λεχθήσονται ἀγαθὰ ἀλλὰ καὶ αἱ
κατ᾽ αὐτὰς πράξεις, εἴπερ καὶ κατὰ ταύτας συμ-
27 βαίνει ὠφελεῖσθαι. κατὰ δὲ τὸν τρίτον καὶ τελευταῖον τρόπον λέγεται ἀγαθὸν τὸ οἷόν τε ὠφελεῖν,
ἐμπεριλαμβανούσης τῆς ἀποδόσεως ταύτης τάς τε
ἀρετὰς καὶ τὰς ἐναρέτους πράξεις καὶ τοὺς φίλους
καὶ τοὺς σπουδαίους ἀνθρώπους, θεούς τε καὶ
28 σπουδαίους δαίμονας. παρ᾽ ἣν αἰτίαν οὐκ ἐν
ἴσῳ λέγεται παρά τε τοῖς περὶ τὸν Πλάτωνα καὶ
Ξενοκράτη πολλαχῶς ὀνομάζεσθαι τἀγαθὸν καὶ
παρὰ τοῖς στωικοῖς. ἐκεῖνοι μὲν γὰρ ὅταν φῶσιν

said either to be utility or to be other than utility, for
the following reason : The parts, say the sons of the 24
Stoics, are neither the same as their wholes nor of a
different kind from their wholes, even as the hand
(for instance) is neither the same as the whole man
(for the hand is not the whole man), nor other than
the whole (for the whole man is conceived as man
when including the hand). Since, then, virtue is a
part both of the good man and of the friend, and the
parts are neither the same as their wholes nor other
than their wholes, the good man and the friend are
called " not other than utility." So that every good
thing is comprehended in the definition, whether it
be directly " utility " or whether it be " not other
than utility." Next, and by way of corollary, they 25
state that " good " has three senses, and in each of its
significations, again, they portray it by a separate
description. In one sense " good," they say, means
that by which or from which " utility " may be
gained, this being the most principal good and virtue ;
for from virtue, as from a fountain, all utility naturally
springs. And in another sense, good is that of which 26
utility is an accidental result ; thus not only will the
virtues be called " good," but also the actions in
accordance therewith, inasmuch as utility results also
from them. And in the third and last sense, " that 27
which is capable of being useful " is termed " good,"
this description comprehending the virtues and the
virtuous actions and the friends and the good men,
and both gods and good daemons.—And because of 28
this Plato and Xenocrates do not mean the same as
the Stoics when they say that " good " has several
senses. For when the former declare that the Idea

---

¹ [ὅλῃ] secl. Arnim.

ἑτέρως λέγεσθαι ἀγαθὸν τὴν ἰδέαν καὶ ἑτέρως τὸ
μετέχον τῆς ἰδέας, σημαινόμενα ἐκτίθενται καὶ κατὰ
πολὺ ἀλλήλων διεστῶτα καὶ μηδεμίαν ἔχοντα
κοινωνίαν, οἷόν τι καὶ ἐπὶ τῆς κύων φωνῆς θεω-
29 ροῦμεν. ὡς γὰρ ἐκ ταύτης σημαίνεται μὲν πτῶσις
ὑφ' ἣν τὸ ὑλακτικὸν πέπτωκε ζῷον, καὶ ἔτι ὑφ' ἣν
τὸ ἔνυγρον, καὶ πρὸς τούτοις ὑφ' ἣν ὁ φιλόσοφος,
οὐ μὴν ἀλλὰ καὶ ὑφ' ἣν τὸ ἄστρον, οὐδὲν δὲ κοινὸν
ἔχουσιν αἱ τοιαῦται πτώσεις, οὐδ' ἐμπεριέχεται τῇ
δευτέρᾳ ἡ πρώτη καὶ τῇ τρίτῃ ἡ δευτέρα, οὕτω κἂν
τῷ φάναι ἀγαθὸν τὴν ἰδέαν καὶ τὸ μετέχον τῆς
ἰδέας ἔκθεσις μέν ἐστι σημαινομένων, κεχωρισμένων δὲ καὶ οὐδεμίαν περίληψιν ἐμφαινόντων.
30 ἀλλ' οἱ μὲν ἀρχαιότεροι, ὡς προεῖπον, τοιοῦτοί τινες
ἦσαν· οἱ δ' ἀπὸ τῆς στοᾶς θέλουσιν ἐπὶ τῆς τοῦ
ἀγαθοῦ προσηγορίας τὸ δεύτερον σημαινόμενον
ἐμπεριληπτικὸν εἶναι τοῦ πρώτου καὶ τὸ τρίτον
περιληπτικὸν τῶν δυοῖν. ἦσαν δὲ οἱ φάσκοντες
ἀγαθὸν ὑπάρχειν τὸ δι' αὐτὸ αἱρετόν. οἱ δ' οὕτως
" ἀγαθόν ἐστι τὸ συλλαμβανόμενον πρὸς εὐδαιμονίαν," τινὲς δὲ " τὸ συμπληρωτικὸν εὐδαιμονίας."
εὐδαιμονία δέ ἐστιν, ὡς οἵ τε περὶ τὸν Ζήνωνα καὶ
Κλεάνθην καὶ Χρύσιππον ἀπέδοσαν, εὔροια βίου.

Πλὴν τὸ μὲν γένος τῆς τοῦ ἀγαθοῦ ἀποδόσεώς
31 ἐστι τοιοῦτον· εἰώθασι δ' ἔνιοι, τριχῶς λεγομένου
τἀγαθοῦ, πρὸς τὸν τοῦ πρώτου σημαινομένου ὅρον
εὐθὺς ἐπιζητεῖν, [καθὸ λέγει " τὸ ἀγαθόν ἐστι τὸ
ὑφ' οὗ ἢ ἀφ' οὗ ἔστιν ὠφελεῖσθαι,"][1] ὡς εἰ ταῖς

_____
[1] [καθὸ . . . ὠφελεῖσθαι] secl. Heintz (? λέγεται pro λέγει).

is termed " good " in one sense and that which
partakes of the Idea in another sense, they propose
significations which differ greatly from one another
and have no connexion, as we see in the case of the
word " dog." For just as by this is signified a 29
meaning [a] under which falls the barking animal, and
also the marine animal, and besides them the philosopher, and moreover the star as well ; but these
meanings have nothing in common, and the first is
not included in the second nor the second in the
third,—so also in the statement that the Idea is good,
and also that which partakes of the Idea, we have a
declaration of significations, but of such as are separate
and display no mutual connexion. Such then, as I 30
said before, were the views of the earlier thinkers ;
but the Stoics hold that, in the case of the term
" good," the second signification should be inclusive
of the first and the third inclusive of the other two.
And there have been some who have asserted that
" good " is " that which is desirable for its own
sake." [b] And others put it thus : " Good is that
which contributes to happiness " ; and some—" that
which helps to fulfil happiness." And happiness, as
Zeno and Cleanthes and Chrysippus have defined it,
is " an equable flow of life." [c]

Such, in fine, is the general form of the definition of
" the good." But as " the good " is used in three 31
senses,[d] with regard to the definition of the first
signification [which says " The good is that by which
or from which utility can result "] some are wont to

[a] Literally, " case " (falling), as a grammatical term
" Dog " is variously applied to " dogs," " dog-fish," " Dog-
men " (Cynics), " Dog-star."
[b] Cf. P.H. iii. 172 ; Aristot. Eth. Nic. i. 1.
[c] Cf. § 110 infra.   [d] See § 25 supra.

SEXTUS EMPIRICUS

ἀληθείαις ἀγαθόν ἐστι τὸ ἀφ' οὗ ἔστιν ὠφελεῖσθαι,
μόνην ῥητέον τὴν γενικὴν ἀρετὴν ἀγαθὸν ὑπάρχειν
(ἀπὸ μόνης γὰρ ταύτης συμβαίνει τὸ ὠφελεῖσθαι),
ἐκπίπτειν δὲ τοῦ ὅρου ἑκάστην τῶν εἰδικῶν, οἷον
τὴν φρόνησιν καὶ τὴν σωφροσύνην καὶ τὰς λοιπάς.
32 ἀπ' οὐδεμιᾶς γὰρ αὐτῶν συμβαίνει [τὸ]¹ αὐτὸ τοῦτο
ὠφελεῖν, ἀλλ' ἀπὸ μὲν τῆς φρονήσεως τὸ φρονεῖν
καὶ οὐ κοινότερον τὸ ὠφελεῖν (εἰ γὰρ αὐτὸ τοῦτο
συμβαίνοι, τὸ ὠφελεῖν, οὐκ ἔσται ὡρισμένως φρόνησις, γενικὴ δ' ἀρετή), καὶ ἀπὸ τῆς σωφροσύνης
τὸ κατ' αὐτὴν κατηγόρημα, σωφρονεῖν, οὐ τὸ κοινόν,
33 ὠφελεῖν, καὶ ἐπὶ τῶν λοιπῶν τὸ ἀνάλογον.   οἱ
δ' ἀντικαθιστάμενοι πρὸς τοῦτο τὸ ἔγκλημα τοῦτό
φασιν· ὅταν λέγωμεν "ἀγαθόν ἐστιν ἀφ' οὗ συμβαίνει τὸ ὠφελεῖσθαι," ἐν ἴσῳ τοῦτο λέγομεν τῷ
"ἀγαθόν ἐστιν ἀφ' οὗ συμβαίνει τι τῶν ἐν τῷ βίῳ
ὠφελεῖσθαι." οὕτω γὰρ καὶ ἑκάστη τῶν ἐπ' εἴδους
ἀρετῶν ἀγαθὸν γενήσεται, κοινῶς μὲν τὸ ὠφελεῖν
μὴ ἐπιφέρουσα, τὶ δὲ τῶν ἐν τῷ βίῳ ὠφελεῖσθαι
παρεχομένη, οἷον ἡ μὲν φρονεῖν, καθάπερ ἡ φρό-
34 νησις, ἡ δὲ [τὸ] σωφρονεῖν, ὡς ἡ σωφροσύνη.   θελήσαντες δὲ οὗτοι ὡς ἀπολογούμενοι τὸ πρότερον
ἔγκλημα φυγεῖν, εἰς ἕτερον ἀπεκυλίσθησαι . εἰ γὰρ
ἔστι τὸ λεγόμενον τοιοῦτο "ἀγαθόν ἐστιν ἀφ' οὗ
συμβαίνει τι τῶν ἐν τῷ βίῳ ὠφελεῖσθαι," ἡ γενικὴ
ἀρετὴ ἀγαθὸν οὖσα οὐχ ὑποπεσεῖται τῷ ὅρῳ· οὐ γὰρ
ἀπ' αὐτῆς συμβαίνει τι τῶν ἐν τῷ βίῳ ὠφελεῖσθαι,
ἐπεὶ μία τῶν ἐπ' εἴδους γενήσεται, ἀλλ' ἁπλῶς τὸ
ὠφελεῖσθαι.
35   Καὶ ἕτερα δὲ εἴωθε λέγεσθαι πρὸς τοὺς τοιούτους
ὅρους, δογματικῆς ἐχόμενα περιεργίας. ἡμῖν δὲ

¹ [τὸ] secl. Mutsch.

400

argue further that if in very truth good is " that from which utility can result," we must declare that generic virtue alone is good (for it is from this alone that utility results), and that each of the particulars—such as wisdom, temperance, and the rest—fall outside the definition. For the precise fact of being useful does 32 not result from any of these, but from wisdom " being wise " results and not " being useful " more generally, (for if just this—namely, being useful—were its result it would not be wisdom in particular but generic virtue), and from temperance results what is named after it (namely, " being temperate ") and not the general result (namely, " being useful "), and similarly with the rest.—But those who resist this 33 indictment say this : When we state that " good is that from which utility results," this is equivalent to saying " good is that from which results one of the things useful in life." For thus each of the particular virtues also will be a good, not as procuring utility in general but as providing some one of the things useful in life—one of them (namely, wisdom) providing the state of being wise, and another (namely, temperance) the temperate state. But these men, in attempting 34 by this defence to escape the previous charge, have involved themselves in another one. For if the statement is this—" Good is that from which results one of the things useful in life," then generic virtue, which is a good, will not fall under the definition ; for none of the things useful in life results from it (since otherwise it will become one of the particulars), but simply utility.

[a]And other objections, which partake of Dogmatic 35 over-subtlety, are customarily made against these

---

[a] With §§ 35-39 *cf. P.H.* iii. 173-174.

ἀπόχρη ἀποδεῖξαι ὅτι ὁ λέγων ἀγαθὸν τὸ ὠφελοῦν
ἢ τὸ δι' αὐτὸ αἱρετὸν ἢ τὸ συνεργὸν πρὸς εὐδαιμονίαν, ἢ οὕτω πως ἀποδιδούς, οὐχ ὃ ἔστιν ἀγαθὸν
διδάσκει, ἀλλὰ τὸ συμβεβηκὸς αὐτῷ παρίστησιν.
ὁ δὲ τὸ συμβεβηκὸς τἀγαθῷ παριστὰς οὐκ αὐτὸ
δείκνυσι τἀγαθόν. εὐθέως γοῦν τὸ μὲν ὅτι ὠφελεῖ
τἀγαθὸν καὶ τὸ ὅτι αἱρετόν ἐστι, παρὸ ἀγαθὸν
εἴρηται τὸ οἷον ἀγαστόν, ὅτι τε εὐδαιμονίας ἐστὶ
36 ποιητικόν, πάντες συγχωροῦσιν· ἀλλ' ἐὰν προσ-
εξετάζηται τί ποτε ἔστι τοῦτο τὸ ὠφελοῦν καὶ δι'
αὐτὸ αἱρετὸν καὶ εὐδαιμονίας ποιητικόν, οὐκέτι
ὁμοφρονήσουσι, καίπερ συμφώνως πρότερον αὐτὸ
λέγοντες τὸ ὠφελοῦν καὶ τὸ αἱρετόν, ἀλλ' εἰς
ἄσπειστον ἐξενεχθήσονται πόλεμον, τοῦ μὲν ἀρετὴν
λέγοντος τοῦ δ' ἡδονὴν τοῦ δ' ἀλυπίαν τοῦ δ' ἄλλο
37 τι τῶν διαφερόντων. εἰ δέ γε ἐκ τῶν προειρημένων ὅρων ἐδείκνυτο ὃ ἔστι τὸ ἀγαθόν, οὐκ ἂν
ἐπεστασίαζον ὡς ἀγνοουμένης τῆς τἀγαθοῦ φύσεως.
τοίνυν οὐχ ὃ ἔστι τὸ ἀγαθὸν οἱ ἐκκείμενοι ὅροι
διδάσκουσιν, ἀλλὰ τὸ συμβεβηκὸς τἀγαθῷ. διόπερ
οὐδὲ κατὰ τοῦτο μόνον εἰσὶ μοχθηροί, ἀλλὰ καὶ
38 καθόσον ἀδυνάτου τινὸς ἐφίενται πράγματος· ὁ γὰρ
ἀγνοῶν τι τῶν ὄντων, οὗτος οὐδὲ τὸ συμβεβηκὸς
ἐκείνῳ γινώσκειν δύναται. οἷον ὁ πρὸς τὸν ἀγ-
νοοῦντα τί ἐστιν ἵππος λέγων '' ἵππος ἐστὶ ζῷον
χρεμετιστικόν '' οὐ διδάσκει ὃ ἔστιν ἵππος· τῷ γὰρ
μὴ γινώσκοντι τὸν ἵππον καὶ τὸ χρεμετίζειν ἀγ-
νοεῖται, ὅπερ ἦν τοῦ ἵππου συμβεβηκός. καὶ ὁ
πρὸς τὸν μὴ κατειληφότα τί ἐστι βοῦς προφερό-

---

definitions. But for us it is sufficient to show that
he who asserts that the good is " the useful," or
" what is choiceworthy for its own sake," or " that
which contributes to happiness," or gives some such
description of it, does not teach us what good is
but states its accidental property. But he who
states the property of the good does not show us
the good itself. For certainly all agree that the
good is useful and that it is choiceworthy (and for
this reason it is called " good " as being " delightful " [a]), and that it is productive of happiness ; but 36
if one inquires further what this thing is which is
useful and choiceworthy for its own sake and productive of happiness, they will no longer be of one
mind, although they previously agreed in calling it
the useful and the choiceworthy, but will be swept
away into a truceless war, one man calling it virtue,
another pleasure, another painlessness, another something else quite different. But if it had in fact been 37
shown by the definitions mentioned above what the
good is, they would not have been at strife as though
the real nature of the good were unknown. So then,
the definitions set forth do not teach us what the good
is but the accidental property of the good. Consequently, they are unsound not only in this respect but
also inasmuch as they aim at something which is impossible ; for he who is ignorant of an existing object 38
cannot get to know the property of that object either.
For example, the man who says to one who is ignorant
of what a horse is, " A horse is an animal capable of
neighing," does not teach him what a horse is ; for
" neighing," too, is unknown to the person who does
not know the horse, as it is a property of the horse.
And he who to the man who has not grasped

μενος '' βοῦς ἐστὶ ζῷον μυκητικόν '' οὐ παρίστησι
τὸν βοῦν· τῷ γὰρ μὴ γινώσκοντι τοῦτον συνακα-
ταληπτεῖται καὶ τὸ μυκᾶσθαι, συμβεβηκὸς ὑπάρχον
39 τοῦ βοός. οὐκοῦν καὶ πρὸς τὸν ἀνεννόητον ὄντα
τἀγαθοῦ μάτην καὶ ἀνωφελῶς λέγεται ὅτι ἀγαθόν
ἐστι τὸ αἱρετὸν ἢ τὸ ὠφελοῦν. πρῶτον γὰρ δεῖ
μαθεῖν τὴν αὐτοῦ τοῦ ἀγαθοῦ φύσιν, εἶτα τότε
συνιέναι ὅτι ὠφελεῖ καὶ ὅτι αἱρετόν ἐστι καὶ εὐδαιμονίας ποιητικόν. ἐπ' ἀγνοουμένῃ δὲ ταύτῃ καὶ οἱ
τοιοῦτοι τῶν ὅρων οὐ διδάσκουσι τὸ ζητούμενον.
40 Δείγματος μὲν οὖν χάριν ἀπαρκέσει ταῦτ' εἰρῆ-
σθαι περὶ τῆς τἀγαθοῦ νοήσεως. ἐξ ὧν, ὡς οἶμαι,
σαφῆ τυγχάνει καὶ τὰ περὶ τοῦ κακοῦ τεχνολογούμενα παρὰ τοῖς ἑτεροδόξοις. κακὸν γάρ ἐστι τὸ
ἐναντίον τῷ ἀγαθῷ· ὅπερ βλάβη ἐστὶν ἢ οὐχ ἕτερον
βλάβης, καὶ βλάβη μὲν ὥσπερ κακία καὶ ἡ φαύλη
πρᾶξις, οὐχ ἕτερον δὲ βλάβης καθάπερ ὁ φαῦλος
41 ἄνθρωπος καὶ ὁ ἐχθρός. μεταξὺ δὲ τούτων, φημὶ
δὲ τοῦ τε ἀγαθοῦ καὶ κακοῦ, ὅπερ καὶ ἀδιάφορον
ὠνομάζετο, ἔστι τὸ οὐδετέρως ἔχον. τίς δ' ἦν ἡ
τῶν ὅρων τούτων δύναμις καὶ τίνα ῥητέον πρὸς τοὺς
ὅρους, ἐκ τῶν περὶ τἀγαθοῦ λεγομένων πάρεστι
μαθεῖν. νῦν δ' ἐπὶ προκατασταθεῖσι τούτοις μετελθόντες σκεψώμεθα εἰ ὥσπερ ἐπινοεῖταί τι ἀγαθὸν
καὶ κακόν, οὕτω καὶ πρὸς τὴν φύσιν ὑπαρκτόν
ἐστιν.

Γ'.—ΕΙ ΕΣΤΙ ΦΥΣΕΙ ΑΓΑΘΟΝ ΚΑΙ ΚΑΚΟΝ

42 Ὅτι μὲν οὖν οὐ κεκρατημένως ὑπέγραψαν οἱ
δογματικοὶ τὴν ἐπίνοιαν τοῦ τε ἀγαθοῦ καὶ κακοῦ,

---

what an ox is propounds the definition, "An ox is an animal capable of bellowing," does not explain the ox, for " bellowing " too is equally uncomprehended by the man who does not know the ox, it being a property of the ox. Therefore also it is vain and 39 useless to say to the man who is devoid of a conception of the good that the good is the choiceworthy or the useful. For one ought first to learn the real nature of the good itself, and then, in the next place, perceive that it is useful and that it is choiceworthy and productive of happiness. But if this is unknown such definitions as these do not inform us of what we seek.

It will be enough, then, to have said thus much, by 40 way of illustration, regarding the conception of the Good. And from this the logical subtleties which the Dogmatists devise regarding Evil will also be plain.[a] For the evil is the contrary of the good ; and it is harm or not other than harm ; and it is " harm " as in the case of badness and wicked action, but " not other than ' harm ' " as in the case of the wicked man and the enemy. And between these (I mean, between 41 the good and the evil, and termed the " indifferent ") is that which is in neither state. And what the significance of these definitions is, and what is to be said against the definitions, one may learn from our discussion of the good.[b] But now, on the assumption that these are already established, let us pass on and consider whether good and evil are really existent in the way in which they are conceived.

CHAPTER III.—DO GOOD AND EVIL REALLY EXIST?

Now that the Dogmatists have not described the 42 conception of Good and Evil convincingly we have

πρότερον ἐπελογισάμεθα· πρὸς δὲ τὸ εὐχερέστερον
συμπεριφέρεσθαι τοῖς περὶ τῆς ὑπάρξεως αὐτοῦ
λόγοις αὔταρκές ἐστιν εἰπεῖν ὡς ἄρα πάντες ἄνθρωποι, καθάπερ ἔλεγε καὶ ὁ Αἰνησίδημος, ἀγαθὸν
ἡγούμενοι τὸ αἱροῦν αὐτούς, ὁποῖον ἄν ποτ' ᾖ,
μαχομένας ἔχουσι τὰς ἐν εἴδει περὶ αὐτοῦ κρίσεις.
43 καὶ ὃν τρόπον συμφωνοῦντες, εἰ τύχοι, περὶ τοῦ
εἶναί τινα σωματικὴν εὐμορφίαν περὶ τῆς εὐμόρφου
καὶ καλῆς γυναικὸς στασιάζουσιν, τοῦ μὲν Αἰθίο-
πος τὴν σιμοτάτην καὶ μελαντάτην προκρίνοντος,
τοῦ δὲ Πέρσου τὴν γρυποτάτην καὶ λευκοτάτην
ἀποδεχομένου, ἄλλου δὲ τὴν μέσην κατά τε τὸν
χαρακτῆρα καὶ κατὰ τὴν χρόαν πασῶν καλλίονα
44 λέγοντος, τὸν αὐτὸν τρόπον καὶ κατὰ κοινὴν πρόληψιν δοξάζοντες εἶναί τι ἀγαθὸν καὶ κακὸν οἵ τε
ἰδιῶται καὶ οἱ φιλόσοφοι, ἀγαθὸν μὲν τὸ αἱροῦν
αὐτοὺς καὶ ὠφελοῦν, κακὸν δὲ τὸ ἐναντίως ἔχον,
κατ' εἶδος πρὸς ἀλλήλους πολεμοῦσιν·

ἄλλος γάρ τ' ἄλλοισιν ἀνὴρ ἐπιτέρπεται ἔργοις,

καὶ κατ' Ἀρχίλοχον

ἄλλος ἄλλῳ ἐπ' ἔργῳ καρδίην ἰαίνεται,

εἴγε ὁ μὲν δόξαν ἀσπάζεται ὁ δὲ πλοῦτον, ἄλλος
εὐεξίαν, τὶς δὲ ἡδονήν. καὶ ἐπὶ τῶν φιλοσόφων ὁ
45 αὐτὸς λόγος. οἱ μὲν γὰρ ἀπὸ τῆς Ἀκαδημίας καὶ
τοῦ περιπάτου τρία γένη φασὶν εἶναι τῶν ἀγαθῶν,
καὶ ἃ μὲν περὶ ψυχὴν ὑπάρχειν ἃ δὲ περὶ σῶμα ἃ δὲ
ἐκτὸς ψυχῆς τε καὶ σώματος, περὶ μὲν οὖν ψυχὴν
τὰς ἀρετάς, περὶ δὲ τὸ σῶμα ὑγίειαν καὶ εὐεξίαν

---

a With §§ 42-44 cf. P.H. iii. 175.
b Homer, Odyss. xiv. 228 ; cf. P.H. i. 86.

already argued [a]; but in order to become more easily
familiar with the arguments about its existence it is
quite sufficient to say that, after all (as Aenesidemus
used to assert), whereas all men consider that the good
is what attracts them, whatever that may be, the
particular views they hold about it are conflicting.
And just as, although men agree (shall we say ?) 43
that comeliness of body exists yet they are at variance
about the comely and beautiful woman,—the Ethio-
pian preferring the blackest and most snub-nosed,
and the Persian approving the whitest and most
hook-nosed, and someone else declaring that she
who is intermediate both in feature and in colouring
is the most beautiful of all,—so in the same way both 44
laymen and philosophers share the same pre-concep-
tion and believe that good and evil exist,—good being
that which attracts them and is useful, and evil that
which is of the opposite nature,—but as to particular
instances they are at war with one another :—

One thing is pleasing to one man, another thing to another.[b]

and, in the words of Archilochus,[c]—

Men differ as to what things cheer their hearts,

seeing that this man welcomes glory, that man wealth,
another well-being, and another pleasure. And the
same account applies to the philosophers. [d] For the 45
Academics and the Peripatetics [e] assert that there are
three classes of goods, and that some belong to the
soul, some to the body, and others are external to
both soul and body,—the virtues belonging to the
soul, and to the body health and well-being and keen-

---

[c] *Frag.* 36 (Bergk).
[d] With §§ 45-47 *cf. P.H.* iii. 180-181.
[e] *Cf.* Aristot. *Eth. Nic.* i. 8.

SEXTUS EMPIRICUS

καὶ εὐαισθησίαν καὶ κάλλος καὶ πᾶν ὃ τῆς ὁμοίας
ἐστὶν ἰδέας, ἐκτὸς δὲ ψυχῆς καὶ σώματος πλοῦτον
46 πατρίδα γονεῖς τέκνα φίλους, τὰ παραπλήσια. οἱ
δὲ ἀπὸ τῆς στοᾶς τρία μὲν γένη τῶν ἀγαθῶν καὶ
αὐτοὶ τυγχάνειν ἔλεξαν, οὐχ ὡσαύτως δέ· τούτων
γὰρ τὰ μὲν περὶ ψυχὴν τὰ δ' ἐκτὸς τὰ δὲ οὔτε περὶ
ψυχὴν οὔτε ἐκτός, ἐξαιροῦντες τὸ γένος τῶν περὶ τὸ
σῶμα ἀγαθῶν ὡς μὴ ἀγαθῶν. καὶ δὴ περὶ μὲν
ψυχὴν εἶναί φασι τὰς ἀρετὰς καὶ τὰς σπουδαίας
πράξεις, ἐκτὸς δὲ εἶναι τόν τε φίλον καὶ τὸν σπουδαῖον ἄνθρωπον καὶ τὰ σπουδαῖα τέκνα καὶ γονεῖς
καὶ τὰ ὅμοια, οὔτε δὲ περὶ ψυχὴν οὔτε ἐκτὸς αὐτὸν
τὸν σπουδαῖον ἄνθρωπον ὡς πρὸς ἑαυτόν. οὔτε γὰρ
ἐκτὸς ἑαυτοῦ δυνατὸν εἶναι αὐτὸν οὔτε περὶ ψυχήν·
47 ἐκ γὰρ ψυχῆς καὶ σώματος συνέστηκεν. εἰσὶ δὲ οἱ
τοσοῦτον ἀπέχοντες τοῦ ἐξαιρεῖν τὸ γένος τῶν περὶ
σώματι ἀγαθῶν ὡς καὶ ἐν αὐτοῖς τὸ ἀρχικώτατον
ἀπολιπεῖν ἀγαθόν· ὁποῖοί εἰσιν οἱ τὴν κατὰ σάρκα
ἡδονὴν ἀσπαζόμενοι. καὶ ἵνα μὴ δοκῶμεν νῦν ἐπὶ
πλεῖον ἐκτείνειν τὸν λόγον, παριστάντες ὅτι ἀσύμ-
φωνός ἐστι καὶ μαχομένη ἡ περὶ ἀγαθοῦ τε καὶ
κακοῦ τῶν ἀνθρώπων κρίσις, ἐπὶ ἑνὸς ὑποδείγματος[1]
ποιησόμεθα τὴν ὑφήγησιν, καθάπερ τῆς ὑγείας,
ἐπεὶ καὶ συνηθέστερός ἐστιν ἡμῖν ὁ περὶ αὐτῆς
λόγος.

48 Οὐκοῦν τὴν ὑγείαν οἱ μὲν νομίζουσιν ἀγαθὸν εἶναι
οἱ δ' οὐκ ἀγαθόν, καὶ τῶν ἀγαθὸν ὑπολαμβανόντων
οἱ μὲν μέγιστον ἀγαθὸν ταύτην ἔλεξαν οἱ δ' οὐ
μέγιστον, καὶ τῶν οὐκ ἀγαθὸν εἰπόντων οἱ μὲν
ἀδιάφορον προηγούμενον, οἱ δὲ ἀδιάφορον μέν, οὐ

---

[1] ὑποδείγματος Heintz : ὑποδειγματικῶς mss., Bekk.

ness of sense and beauty and everything which is of a similar character, and external to soul and body being wealth, country, parents, children, friends, and the like. But the Stoics, though they too declared that 46 there are three classes of good things, yet classed them differently, saying that some of them belong to the soul, that some are external, and that some are neither psychical nor external, and eliminating the class of bodily goods as not being goods. Thus those belonging to the soul are, they say, the virtues and right actions ; and external are the friend and the good man and good children and parents and the like ; and neither psychical nor external is the good man in his relation to himself, for it is impossible for him to be either external to himself or psychical ; for he is composed of soul and body. And there are some who 47 are so far from eliminating the class of bodily goods that they even assign to them the most principal good ; and of this sort are they who approve of carnal pleasure. But lest we may seem now to be unduly prolonging our argument in showing that the judgement of men regarding Good and Evil is discordant and conflicting, we shall base our exposition on one example only—namely health, since the discussion of this is specially familiar to us.[a]

Health, then, is by some considered to be a good, by 48 others not a good ; and of those who suppose it to be a good some have declared it to be the greatest good, others not the greatest ; and of those who have said that it is not a good, some have counted it "a preferred indifferent," others an indifferent but not

---

[a] Since Sextus himself was a physician.

49 προηγούμενον δέ. ἀγαθὸν μὲν οὖν, καὶ τοῦτο
πρῶτον, εἰρήκασι τὴν ὑγείαν οὐκ ὀλίγοι τῶν τε
ποιητῶν καὶ τῶν συγγραφέων καὶ καθόλου πάντες
οἱ ἀπὸ τοῦ βίου. Σιμωνίδης μὲν γὰρ ὁ μελοποιὸς
φησι μηδὲ καλᾶς σοφίας εἶναι χάριν, εἰ μή τις ἔχοι
σεμνὴν ὑγείαν· Λικύμνιος δὲ προειπὼν ταῦτα

λιπαρόμματε, μᾶτερ ὑψίστα,[1] θρόνων
σεμνῶν Ἀπόλλωνος βασίλεια ποθεινά,
πραΰγελως ὑγεία,

ποῖον ὑψηλὸν ἐπιφέρει·

τίς γὰρ πλούτου χάρις ἢ τοκήων
ἢ τᾶς ἰσοδαίμονος ἀνθρώπου βασιληῒδος ἀρχᾶς;
σέθεν δὲ χωρὶς οὔ τις εὐδαίμων ἔφυ.

50 Ἡρόφιλος δὲ ἐν τῷ διαιτητικῷ καὶ σοφίαν φησὶν
ἀνεπίδεικτον καὶ τέχνην ἄδηλον καὶ ἰσχὺν ἀν-
αγώνιστον καὶ πλοῦτον ἀχρεῖον καὶ λόγον ἀδύνατον
51 ὑγείας ἀπούσης.   ἀλλ' οὗτοι μὲν οὕτως· ἀγαθὸν
δ' εἶπαν αὐτὴν ὑπάρχειν, οὐ μὴν καὶ πρῶτον, οἵ τε
ἀπὸ τῆς Ἀκαδημίας καὶ οἱ ἀπὸ τοῦ περιπάτου.
δεῖν γὰρ ὑπέλαβον ἑκάστῳ τῶν ἀγαθῶν τὴν οἰκείαν
τάξιν τε καὶ ἀξίαν ἀπονέμειν. ἔνθεν καὶ ὁ Κράντωρ
εἰς ἔμφασιν τοῦ λεγομένου βουλόμενος ἡμᾶς ἄγειν
52 πάνυ χαρίεντι συνεχρήσατο παραδείγματι. εἰ γὰρ
νοήσαιμεν, φησί, κοινόν τι τῶν Πανελλήνων θέα-
τρον, εἰς τοῦτό τε ἕκαστον τῶν ἀγαθῶν παριὸν καὶ
τῶν πρωτείων ἀντιποιούμενον ἥκειν, εὐθὺς καὶ εἰς
ἔννοιαν ἀναχθησόμεθα τῆς ἐν τοῖς ἀγαθοῖς δια-

[1] ὑψίστα Wilamowitz: ὑψίστων mss., Bekk.

---

[a] For the two subdivisions of the " indifferent "—" preferred " and " rejected "—cf. §§ 59 ff. infra; P.H. iii. 191 f.;
Vol. I. Introd. p. xxvii.

" preferred." [a] Now that health is a good, and the 49
prime good, has been asserted by not a few of the
poets and writers and generally by all ordinary folk.
Thus Simonides the lyric poet declares [b] that " Even
fair Wisdom lacks grace unless a man possesses
august Health."   And Licymnius, after first uttering
this prelude [c]—

> Mother sublime, with eyes bright-shining,
> Lov'd queen of the holy throne of Apollo,
> Gently-smiling Lady of Health—

adds this lofty strain—

> Where is the joy of wealth or of kindred,
> Or of kingly dominion that maketh man god-like ?
> Nay, parted from thee can no one be blessed.

And Herophilus [d] in his *Dietetics* affirms that wisdom 50
cannot display itself and art is non-evident and
strength unexerted and wealth useless and speech
powerless in the absence of health.—Such then are 51
the views of these men. But the Academics and
Peripatetics [e] said that health is indeed a good, but
not the prime good. For they held that one ought
to assign to each of the goods its own proper rank
and value. Hence Crantor,[f] wishing to bring us to
have a clear image of the object under discussion,
made use of a very delightful illustration. If we were 52
to imagine, he says, a general theatre, common to all
the Greeks, and that each of the goods were to come
and present itself in this and challenge for the first
prize, we should be brought at once to a realization of
the difference between the goods. For in the first 53

[b] *Frag.* 70 (Bergk).   [c] *Frag.* 4 (Bergk).
 [d] A physician of Cos, *circa* 300 B.C. ; *cf. P.H.* ii. 245.
          [e] *Cf.* § 77 *infra.*
 [f] An Academic, disciple of Xenocrates, *circa* 300 B.C.

53 φορᾶς. πρῶτον μὲν γὰρ ὁ πλοῦτος παραπηδήσας
ἐρεῖ '' ἐγώ, ὦ ἄνδρες Πανέλληνες, κόσμον παρέχων
πᾶσιν ἀνθρώποις καὶ τὰς ἐσθῆτας καὶ τὰς ὑποδέσεις
καὶ τὴν ἄλλην ἀπόλαυσιν χρειώδης εἰμὶ νοσοῦσι καὶ
ὑγιαίνουσι, καὶ ἐν μὲν εἰρήνῃ παρέχω τὰ τερπνά,
54 ἐν δὲ πολέμοις νεῦρα τῶν πράξεων γίνομαι.'' τούτων γὰρ δὴ τῶν λόγων ἀκούσαντες οἱ Πανέλληνες
ὁμοθυμαδὸν κελεύσουσιν ἀποδοῦναι τὰ πρωτεῖα τῷ
πλούτῳ. ἀλλ' ἐὰν τούτου ἤδη ἀνακηρυττομένου
ἐπιστᾶσα ἡ ἡδονή,

τῇ ἔνι μὲν φιλότης, ἔνι δ' ἵμερος, ἐν δ' ὀαριστύς,
πάρφασις, ἥ τ' ἔκλεψε νόον πύκα περ φρονεόντων,

55 λέγῃ δὲ εἰς μέσον καταστᾶσα ὅτι αὐτὴν δίκαιόν
ἐστιν ἀναγορεύειν

(ὁ γὰρ ὄλβος οὐ βέβαιος, ἀλλ' ἐφήμερος
ἐξίπτατ' οἴκων, μικρὸν ἀνθήσας χρόνον,

διώκεταί τε πρὸς τῶν ἀνθρώπων οὐ δι' ἑαυτὸν ἀλλὰ
τὴν ἐξ αὐτοῦ περιγινομένην ἀπόλαυσιν καὶ ἡδονήν),
πάντως οἱ Πανέλληνες, οὐκ ἄλλως ἔχειν τὸ πρᾶγμα
ἢ οὕτως ὑπολαβόντες, κεκράξονται δεῖν τὴν ἡδονὴν
56 στεφανοῦν. ἀλλὰ καὶ ταύτης τὸ βραβεῖον φέρεσθαι
μελλούσης, ἐπὴν εἰσβάλλῃ ἡ ὑγεία μετὰ τῶν συν-
έδρων αὐτῇ θεῶν, καὶ διδάσκῃ ὡς οὔτε ἡδονῆς οὔτε
πλούτου ὄφελός τί ἐστιν ἀπούσης αὐτῆς

(τί γάρ με πλοῦτος ὠφελεῖ νοσοῦντά γε[1];
μίκρ' ἂν θέλοιμι καὶ καθ' ἡμέραν ἔχων
ἄλυπον οἰκεῖν βίοτον ἢ πλουτῶν νοσεῖν),

57 ἀκούσαντες πάλιν οἱ Πανέλληνες καὶ καταλαβόντες

---

[1] νοσοῦντά γε Fabr., Bekk.: νόσον mss. (? μεστὸν ὠφελεῖ
νόσων).

place Wealth, springing to the front, will say—" I,
O all ye Greeks, by providing adornment to all men
and garments and shoes and all other comforts am
indispensable both to the sick and to the whole, and
while I furnish delights in peace, in war I become the
sinews of action." Then all the Greeks, on hearing 54
these words, will with one consent give orders that
the first prize be bestowed on Wealth. But if,
whilst he is already being proclaimed the victor,
Pleasure should present herself—

> In whom love doth abide and longing and amorous converse,
> Speech seductive which stealeth the wits, yea e'en of the
> wisest,[a]—

and taking her stand in the middle should declare 55
that it is right to proclaim her victor—

> For unsure is Wealth : it lasteth but a day,
> Then, after briefest flow'ring, takes to flight,[b]

also it is pursued by men not for its own sake but
for the enjoyment and pleasure which accrue because
of it,—then certainly all the Greeks, conceiving that
this is in fact the case, will cry aloud that they must
crown Pleasure. But when she, too, is about to carry 56
off the palm, as soon as Health makes her entry in
company with her fellow-deities,[c] and explains that
in her absence there is no profit either in pleasure or
in wealth—

> What doth wealth profit me when I am sick ?
> Better a little portion day by day
> With painless life than riches with disease [d]—

then, once again, when they have heard her and have 57

---

[a] Homer, *Il.* xiv. 216.
[b] *Cf.* Eurip. *Phoen.* 558, *Electra* 944.
[c] Such as Asclepios, Panacea, Athenê (an altar to Athenê
Hygieia was set up in Athens by Pericles).
[d] From Eurip. *Telephus* (*Frag.* 714 Nauck).

ὡς οὐκ ἔνεστι κλινοπετῆ καὶ νοσοῦσαν ὑποστῆναι
τὴν εὐδαιμονίαν, φήσουσι νικᾶν τὴν ὑγείαν. ἀλλὰ
καὶ τῆς ὑγείας ἤδη νικώσης, ἐπὰν εἰσέλθῃ ἡ ἀνδρία
πολὺ στῖφος ἀριστέων καὶ ἡρώων ἔχουσα περὶ
58 ἑαυτήν, καταστᾶσά τε λέγῃ '' ἐμοῦ μὴ παρούσης,
ὦ ἄνδρες Ἕλληνες, ἀλλοτρία γίνεται ἡ κτῆσις τῶν
παρ' ὑμῖν ἀγαθῶν, εὔξαιντό τ' ἂν οἱ πολέμιοι
περιουσιάζειν ὑμᾶς πᾶσι τοῖς ἀγαθοῖς ὡς μελλή-
σοντες ὑμῶν κρατεῖν,'' καὶ τούτων οὖν ἀκούσαντες
οἱ Ἕλληνες τὰ μὲν πρωτεῖα τῇ ἀρετῇ ἀποδώσουσι,
τὰ δὲ δευτερεῖα τῇ ὑγείᾳ, τὰ δὲ τρίτα τῇ ἡδονῇ,
τελευταῖον δὲ τάξουσι τὸν πλοῦτον.

59 Καὶ δὴ ὁ μὲν Κράντωρ τὴν ὑγείαν ἐν δευτέρᾳ
μοίρᾳ ἐτίθετο, στοιχῶν τοῖς προειρημένοις φιλο-
σόφοις· οὐκ ἀγαθὸν δ' οἱ ἀπὸ τῆς στοᾶς ἔλεξαν
αὐτὴν ἀλλ' ἀδιάφορον. τὸ ἀδιάφορον δ' οἴονται
λέγεσθαι τριχῶς, καθ' ἕνα μὲν τρόπον πρὸς ὃ μήτε
ὁρμὴ μήτε ἀφορμὴ γίνεται, οἷόν ἐστι τὸ περιττοὺς
ἢ ἀρτίους εἶναι τοὺς ἀστέρας ἢ τὰς ἐπὶ τῇ κεφαλῇ
60 τρίχας, καθ' ἕτερον δὲ πρὸς ὃ ὁρμὴ μὲν καὶ ἀφορμὴ
γίνεται, οὐ μᾶλλον δὲ πρὸς τόδε ἢ τόδε, οἷον ἐπὶ
δυοῖν δραχμῶν ἀπαραλλάκτων τῷ τε χαρακτῆρι καὶ
τῇ λαμπρότητι, ὅταν δέῃ τὸ ἕτερον αὐτῶν αἱρεῖ-
σθαι· ὁρμὴ μὲν γὰρ γίνεται πρὸς τὸ ἕτερον αὐτῶν
61 [αἱρεῖσθαι], οὐ μᾶλλον δὲ πρὸς τόδε ἢ τόδε. κατὰ
δὲ τρίτον καὶ τελευταῖον τρόπον φασὶν ἀδιάφορον
τὸ μήτε πρὸς εὐδαιμονίαν μήτε πρὸς κακοδαιμονίαν
συλλαμβανόμενον, καθ' ὃ σημαινόμενόν φασι τήν τε
ὑγείαν καὶ νόσον καὶ πάντα τὰ σωματικὰ καὶ τὰ
πλεῖστα τῶν ἐκτὸς ἀδιάφορα τυγχάνειν διὰ τὸ μήτε

come to realize that happiness cannot exist when bed-ridden and diseased, all the Greeks will declare that Health is the victor. But even while Health is already claiming the victory, as soon as Courage enters, surrounded by a great press of nobles and heroes, and taking her stand speaks thus—" If I am 58 not present, O ye Greeks, the ownership of your goods falls into other hands, and your enemies would pray that you might abound in all things good since they intend to conquer you " ; then, on hearing this, the Greeks will assign the first prize to valour, and the second to health, and the third to pleasure, and they will rank wealth last.

Thus Crantor put health in the second place, 59 adopting the order of the philosophers previously mentioned ; but the Stoics affirmed that it is not a " good " but an " indifferent." [a] They suppose that the term " indifferent " has three senses : in one sense it is applied to that for which there exists neither inclination nor disinclination,—such as the fact that the stars or the hairs of the head are odd in number or even ; in another sense it applies to that 60 for which there exists inclination and disinclination but not more for this thing than for that—as in the case of two drachmae indistinguishable both in markings and in brightness, when one is required to choose one of them, for there exists an inclination for one of them but no more for this one than for that. And in the third and last sense the indifferent, they 61 say, is that which contributes neither to happiness nor to unhappiness ; and indifferent in this signification, they say, are health and disease and all things of the body and most external things because they

---

[a] With §§ 59–61 cf. P.H. iii. 177.

πρὸς εὐδαιμονίαν μήτε πρὸς κακοδαιμονίαν συν-
τείνειν. ᾧ γὰρ ἔστιν εὖ καὶ κακῶς χρῆσθαι, τοῦτ᾽
ἂν εἴη ἀδιάφορον· διὰ παντὸς δ᾽ ἀρετῇ μὲν καλῶς,
κακίᾳ δὲ κακῶς, ὑγείᾳ δὲ καὶ τοῖς περὶ σώματι
ποτὲ μὲν εὖ ποτὲ δὲ κακῶς ἔστι χρῆσθαι, διὸ ταῦτ᾽
62 ἂν εἴη ἀδιάφορα.   ἤδη δὲ τῶν ἀδιαφόρων φασὶ
τὰ μὲν εἶναι προηγμένα τὰ δ᾽ ἀποπροηγμένα τὰ
δὲ μήτε προηγμένα μήτε ἀποπροηγμένα, καὶ προηγμένα μὲν εἶναι τὰ ἱκανὴν ἀξίαν ἔχοντα, ἀποπροηγμένα δὲ τὰ ἱκανὴν ἀπαξίαν ἔχοντα, μήτε δὲ
προῆχθαι μήτε ἀποπροῆχθαι οἷον τὸ ἐκτεῖναι ἢ
συγκάμψαι τὸν δάκτυλον καὶ πᾶν ὃ τούτῳ παρα-
63 πλήσιόν ἐστιν. τάττεσθαι δ᾽ ἐν μὲν τοῖς προηγ-
μένοις τήν τε ὑγείαν καὶ τὴν ἰσχὺν καὶ τὸ κάλλος
πλοῦτόν τε καὶ δόξαν καὶ τὰ ἐοικότα, ἐν δὲ τοῖς
ἀποπροηγμένοις νόσον καὶ πενίαν καὶ ἀλγηδόνα καὶ
τὰ ἀνάλογα.   ὧδε μὲν καὶ οἱ ἀπὸ τῆς στοᾶς·
64 μὴ εἶναι δὲ προηγμένον ἀδιάφορον τὴν ὑγείαν καὶ
πᾶν τὸ κατ᾽ αὐτὴν παραπλήσιον ἔφησεν Ἀρίστων ὁ
Χῖος. ἴσον γάρ ἐστι τὸ προηγμένον αὐτὴν λέγειν
ἀδιάφορον τῷ ἀγαθὸν ἀξιοῦν, καὶ σχεδὸν ὀνόματι
65 μόνον διαφέρον. καθόλου γὰρ τὰ μεταξὺ ἀρετῆς
καὶ κακίας ἀδιάφορα μὴ ἔχειν μηδεμίαν παρ-
αλλαγήν, μηδὲ τινὰ μὲν εἶναι φύσει προηγμένα τινὰ
δὲ ἀποπροηγμένα, ἀλλὰ παρὰ τὰς διαφόρους τῶν
καιρῶν περιστάσεις, ⟨ὡς⟩[1] μήτε τὰ λεγόμενα προῆχθαι πάντως γίνεσθαι προηγμένα μήτε τὰ λεγόμενα
ἀποπροῆχθαι κατ᾽ ἀνάγκην ὑπάρχειν ἀποπροηγ-
66 μένα. ἐὰν γοῦν δέῃ τοὺς μὲν ὑγιαίνοντας ὑπηρετεῖν
τῷ τυράννῳ καὶ διὰ τοῦτο ἀναιρεῖσθαι, τοὺς δὲ

_____

[1] ⟨ὡς⟩ add. cj. Heintz.

tend neither towards happiness nor towards unhappiness. For that which it is possible to use either well or ill will be indifferent; and whereas one always uses virtue well and vice ill, one can use health and the things of the body at one time well and at another ill, and consequently they will be indifferent.—And they say too that of things 62 indifferent some are "preferred," others "rejected," others neither preferred nor rejected,[a] and that the preferred are those which have considerable "worth," and the rejected those which have considerable "unworthiness," and that extending the finger, for example, or contracting it, and everything like that, is neither preferred nor rejected. And 63 amongst the things preferred are ranked health and strength and beauty, wealth and glory and the like; but amongst the things rejected, sickness and poverty and pain and suchlike.—So say the Stoics; but 64 Ariston of Chios [b] affirmed that health, and everything of a similar kind, is not a "preferred indifferent"; for to call it a "preferred indifferent" is equivalent to claiming it to be a "good," and practically differs only in name. For, without exception, amongst the 65 indifferent things which lie between virtue and vice there is no distinction; nor are some of them preferred, others rejected naturally, but owing to the different circumstances of the various occasions; ⟨so that⟩ neither are those said to be preferred inevitably preferred, nor those said to be rejected necessarily rejected. Were it, for instance, obligatory that men 66 in sound health should serve under the tyrant and on this account be destroyed, but that the sick should

---

[a] *Cf.* § 48 *supra.* With §§ 62-66 *cf. P.H.* iii. 191-192.
[b] A Stoic, with Cynic tendencies, *circa* 260 B.C.

νοσοῦντας ἀπολυομένους τῆς ὑπηρεσίας συναπο-
λύεσθαι καὶ τῆς ἀναιρέσεως, ἕλοιτ' ἂν μᾶλλον ὁ
σοφὸς τὸ νοσεῖν κατὰ τοῦτον τὸν καιρὸν ἢ [ὅτι]¹ τὸ
ὑγιαίνειν. καὶ ταύτῃ οὔτε ἡ ὑγεία προηγμένον ἐστὶ
67 πάντως οὔτε ἡ νόσος ἀποπροηγμένον. ὥσπερ οὖν
ἐν ταῖς ὀνοματογραφίαις ἄλλοτ' ἄλλα προτάττομεν
στοιχεῖα, πρὸς τὰς διαφόρους περιστάσεις ἀρτιζό-
μενοι, καὶ τὸ μὲν δέλτα ὅτε τὸ τοῦ Δίωνος ὄνομα
γράφομεν, τὸ δὲ ἰῶτα ὅτε τὸ τοῦ Ἴωνος, τὸ δὲ ὦ
ὅτε τὸ τοῦ Ὠρίωνος, οὐ τῇ φύσει ἑτέρων παρὰ τὰ
ἕτερα γράμματα προκρινομένων, τῶν δὲ καιρῶν
τοῦτο ποιεῖν ἀναγκαζόντων, οὕτω κἂν τοῖς μεταξὺ
ἀρετῆς καὶ κακίας πράγμασιν οὐ φυσική τις γίνεται
ἑτέρων παρ' ἕτερα πρόκρισις, κατὰ περίστασιν δὲ
μᾶλλον.

68   Ἀλλὰ γὰρ ἐκ τούτων ἀσυμφώνου δειχθείσης καὶ
ὑποδειγματικώτερον τῆς περὶ τῶν ἀγαθῶν τε καὶ
κακῶν ἔτι δὲ ἀδιαφόρων προλήψεως, δεήσει λοιπὸν
καὶ τῶν παρὰ τοῖς σκεπτικοῖς εἰς τὸ προκείμενον
69 λεγομένων ἐφάπτεσθαι. εἰ τοίνυν ἔστι τι φύσει
ἀγαθὸν καὶ ἔστι τι φύσει κακόν, τοῦτο ὀφείλει
κοινὸν εἶναι πάντων καὶ πᾶσιν ὑπάρχειν ἀγαθὸν ἢ
κακόν. ὥσπερ γὰρ τὸ πῦρ φύσει ἀλεαντικὸν καθεστὼς πάντας ἀλεαίνει καὶ οὐχ οὓς μὲν ἀλεαίνει
οὓς δὲ ψύχει, καὶ ὃν τρόπον ἡ χιὼν ⟨φύσει⟩² ψύ-
χουσα οὐχὶ τοὺς μὲν ψύχει τοὺς δὲ ἀλεαίνει, πάντας
δ' ὁμοίως ψύχει, οὕτω τὸ φύσει ἀγαθὸν πᾶσιν
ὀφείλει τυγχάνειν ἀγαθὸν καὶ οὐχὶ τοῖς μὲν ἀγαθὸν
70 τοῖς δ' οὐκ ἀγαθόν. παρὸ καὶ ὁ Πλάτων συνιστὰς
ὅτι φύσει ἀγαθόν ἐστιν ὁ θεός, ἀπὸ τῶν ὁμοίων
ἐπικεχείρηκεν. ὡς γὰρ θερμοῦ, φησίν, ἴδιόν ἐστι

_____

¹ [ὅτι] secl. Arnim (? οὕτως).   ² ⟨φύσει⟩ add. cj. Mutsch.

be set free from that service and freed likewise from destruction, on such an occasion the wise man would choose sickness rather than health. And thus neither is health inevitably preferred nor sickness rejected. As, then, in the writing of names we place different 67 letters first at different times, adapting them to the varying circumstances,—Delta when we are writing the name of Dion, Iota when it is Ion, Omega when it is Orion,—no one letter being preferable to the others by nature, but the occasions compelling us to act thus,—so also in the things which lie between virtue and vice there exists no natural precedence of some before others, but rather a precedence due to circumstance.

But now that we have thus shown, mainly by means 68 of examples, that there is no agreement about the preconception regarding things good and evil, and the indifferent as well, it will be our next task to deal with the arguments of the Sceptics about the problem before us. If, then, there exists anything good by 69 nature or anything evil by nature, this thing ought to be common to all men and be good or evil for all.[a] For just as fire which is warmth-giving by nature warms all men, and does not warm some but chill others,—and like as snow which chills ⟨by nature⟩ does not chill some and warm others, but chills all alike,—so what is good by nature ought to be good for all, and not good for some but not good for others. Wherefore also Plato,[b] in establishing that God is 70 good by nature, argued on similar lines. For, he says, as it is the special property of heat to make hot

---

[a] With § 69 *cf. P.H.* iii. 179.
[b] *Cf.* Plato. *Rep.* ii. 379 A ff., and 335 D.

τὸ θερμαίνειν καὶ ψυχροῦ ἴδιόν ἐστι τὸ ψύχειν,
οὕτω καὶ ἀγαθοῦ ἴδιόν ἐστι τὸ ἀγαθοποιεῖν· τὰ-
γαθὸν δέ γε ὁ θεός· ἴδιον ἄρα ἐστὶ θεοῦ τὸ ἀγαθο-
71 ποιεῖν. ὥστε εἰ ἔστι τι φύσει ἀγαθόν, τοῦτο πρὸς
ἅπαντάς ἐστιν ἀγαθόν, καὶ εἰ ἔστι τι φύσει κακόν,
τοῦτο πρὸς ἅπαντάς ἐστι κακόν. οὐδὲν δὲ κοινὸν
πάντων ἐστὶν ἀγαθὸν ἢ κακόν, ὡς παραστήσομεν·
72 οὐκ ἄρα ἔστι τι φύσει ἀγαθὸν ἢ κακόν. ἤτοι γὰρ
πᾶν τὸ ὑπό τινος δοξαζόμενον ἀγαθὸν ῥητέον ταῖς
ἀληθείαις ἀγαθόν, ἢ οὐ πᾶν. καὶ πᾶν μὲν οὐ ῥη-
τέον· εἰ γὰρ πᾶν τὸ ὑπό τινος δοξαζόμενον ἀγαθὸν
λέγοιμεν ἀγαθόν, ἐπεὶ ταὐτὸν ὑπὸ ἑτέρου δοξάζεται
κακὸν καὶ ὑπὸ ἄλλου ἀγαθὸν καὶ ὑπὸ διαφέροντος
[δοξάζεται] ἀδιάφορον, δώσομεν τὸ αὐτὸ ἅμα καὶ
73 κακὸν καὶ ἀγαθὸν καὶ ἀδιάφορον ὑπάρχειν. οἷον
τὴν ἡδονὴν ὁ μὲν Ἐπίκουρος ἀγαθὸν εἶναί φησιν,
ὁ δὲ εἰπὼν " μανείην μᾶλλον ἢ ἡσθείην " κακόν, οἱ
δὲ ἀπὸ τῆς στοᾶς ἀδιάφορον καὶ οὐ προηγμένον,
ἀλλὰ Κλεάνθης μὲν μήτε κατὰ φύσιν αὐτὴν εἶναι
μήτε ἀξίαν ἔχειν [αὐτὴν] ἐν τῷ βίῳ, καθάπερ δὲ τὸ
κάλλυντρον κατὰ φύσιν μὴ εἶναι, ὁ δὲ Ἀρχέδημος
κατὰ φύσιν μὲν εἶναι ὡς τὰς ἐν μασχάλῃ τρίχας,
οὐχὶ δὲ καὶ ἀξίαν ἔχειν, Παναίτιος δὲ τινὰ μὲν
74 κατὰ φύσιν ὑπάρχειν τινὰ δὲ παρὰ φύσιν.   εἰ δὴ
τοίνυν πᾶν τό τινι φαινόμενον ἀγαθόν, τοῦτο πάντως
ἔστιν ἀγαθόν, ἐπεὶ ἡ ἡδονὴ τῷ μὲν Ἐπικούρῳ
φαίνεται ἀγαθὸν τινὶ δὲ τῶν κυνικῶν κακὸν τῷ δ'
ἀπὸ τῆς στοᾶς ἀδιάφορον, ἔσται ἡ ἡδονὴ ἀγαθὸν

and the property of cold to chill, so also it is the special
property of good to do good ; but the Good is God ;
therefore it is the property of God to do good. So 71
that if there exists anything good by nature, this is
good in relation to all men, and if there exists anything
evil by nature, that is evil in relation to all. But
there is nothing good or evil which is common to all,
as we shall establish ; therefore there does not exist
anything good or evil by nature. For we must 72
declare either that everything which is supposed
by anyone to be good is in very truth good, or not
everything. But we must not declare that everything is so ; for if we should call good everything
which is supposed by anyone to be good, then, since
the same thing is supposed by one man to be evil,
and by another good, and by yet another [is held
to be] indifferent, we shall be granting that the same
thing is at once both evil and good and indifferent.
Epicurus, for example, asserts that pleasure is a good, 73
but he who said " I would rather be mad than enjoy
pleasure " [a] counted it an evil, while the Stoics say it
is indifferent and not preferred ; but Cleanthes says
that neither is it natural nor does it possess value for
life, but, like a cosmetic, has no natural existence,
whereas Archedemus [b] says that it has a natural
existence, like the hairs in the armpit, but possesses
no value, and Panaetius that it exists partly by nature
and partly contrary to nature.—If, then, everything 74
that seems good to anyone is altogether good, then,
since pleasure seems good to Epicurus, and evil
to one of the Cynics, and indifferent to the Stoic,

[a] Antisthenes, the Cynic : with this § 73 cf. P.H. iii.
180-181.
[b] A Stoic, like Cleanthes and Panaetius.

ἅμα καὶ κακὸν καὶ ἀδιάφορον. οὐχὶ δέ γε δύναται
τῇ φύσει τὸ αὐτὸ τὰ ἐναντία τυγχάνειν, ἀγαθὸν ἅμα
καὶ κακὸν καὶ ἀδιάφορον· οὐκ ἄρα πᾶν τό τινι
φαινόμενον ἀγαθὸν ἢ κακόν, τοῦτο ῥητέον εἶναι
75 ἀγαθὸν ἢ κακόν. εἰ δὲ ⟨οὐ πᾶν⟩[1] τό τινι
φαινόμενον ἀγαθὸν καὶ πάντῃ ἔστιν ἀγαθόν, ὀφείλομεν καταληπτικοὶ εἶναι καὶ διακρίνειν δύνασθαι
τὴν ἐν τοῖς δοξαζομένοις ἀγαθοῖς διαφοράν, ὥστε
λέγειν τὸ μὲν τῷδε δοξαζόμενον ἀγαθὸν ταῖς ἀληθείαις εἶναι ἀγαθόν, τὸ δὲ τῷδε δοξαζόμενον μὲν
76 ἀγαθόν, οὐκέτι δὲ τῇ φύσει ἀγαθόν. ἤτοι οὖν δι᾽
ἐναργείας ταύτην τὴν διαφορὰν λαμβάνεσθαι συμβέβηκεν ἢ διὰ λόγου τινός. ἀλλὰ δι᾽ ἐναργείας
ἀμήχανον. πᾶν γὰρ τὸ δι᾽ ἐναργείας προσπῖπτον
κοινῶς τε καὶ συμφώνως λαμβάνεσθαι πέφυκεν ὑπὸ
τῶν ἀπαραποδίστους ἐχόντων τὰς ἀντιλήψεις, ὡς
παρὸν ἰδεῖν ἐπὶ πάντων σχεδὸν τῶν φαινομένων.
οὐχὶ δέ γε συμφώνως τὸ αὐτὸ πᾶσιν ἀγαθὸν εἶναι
λέγεται, ἀλλὰ τοῖς μὲν ἀρετὴ καὶ τὸ μετέχον ἀρετῆς,
τοῖς δὲ ἡδονή, τοῖς δὲ ἀλυπία, τισὶ δ᾽ ἄλλο τι. οὐκ
ἄρα ἐναργῶς προσπίπτει πᾶσι τὸ ὄντως ἀγαθόν.
77 εἰ δὲ λόγῳ λαμβάνεται, ἐπεὶ ἕκαστος πάντων
τῶν κατὰ διαφόρους αἱρέσεις κοσμουμένων ἴδιον
ἔχει λόγον, καὶ ἄλλον μὲν Ζήνων, δι᾽ οὗ τὴν ἀρετὴν
ἀγαθὸν εἶναι δεδόξακεν, ἄλλον δ᾽ Ἐπίκουρος, δι᾽
οὗ τὴν ἡδονήν, οὐ τὸν αὐτὸν δὲ Ἀριστοτέλης, δι᾽
οὗ τὴν ὑγείαν, ἴδιον πάλιν ἕκαστος εἰσηγήσεται
ἀγαθόν, ὅπερ οὐκ ἦν τῇ φύσει ἀγαθόν, οὐδὲ κοινὸν
78 πάντων. τοίνυν οὐδέν ἐστι φύσει ἀγαθόν. εἰ γὰρ
τὸ μὲν ἴδιον ἑκάστου οὐκ ἔστιν ἀγαθὸν πάντων οὐδὲ

[1] ⟨οὐ πᾶν⟩ add. Heintz.

[a] Cf. § 36 supra.

pleasure will be at once good and evil and indifferent ;
but it is impossible for the same thing to be by nature
opposite things,—at once good and evil and indifferent
therefore we must not declare that everything which
seems good or evil to anyone is good or evil.—But 75
if what seems good to anyone is not in all cases altogether good, we ought to be gifted with discernment
and able to distinguish the difference between the supposed goods so as to declare that this thing which is
supposed by this man to be good is in very truth good,
whereas that thing which is supposed by that man to
be good is not also good by nature. This difference, 76
then, comes to be perceived either through sensible
evidence or through a process of reasoning.—But it
cannot be through sensible evidence. For everything
which causes an impression through sensible experience is of such a nature as to be perceived with one
accord by all in common who have their perceptions
undistorted, as one may see in the case of nearly all
appearances. But the same thing is not accounted
good by all with one accord, but by some virtue and
what partakes of virtue, by others pleasure, by others
painlessness,[a] by others something else. Therefore
the really good does not impress all men through
sense-evidence.—And if it is perceived by reasoning, 77
then, since each of those persons who are held in
honour in the different sects has his own peculiar
reason—Zeno one by which he opined that virtue is
the good, Epicurus another by which he chose
pleasure, Aristotle a different one by which he chose
health,—each of them likewise will introduce his own
peculiar good, which is not a good by nature nor
common to all. So then nothing is good by nature. 78
For if the private good of each is not the good of all

φύσει, παρὰ δὲ τὸ ἴδιον ἑκάστου ἀγαθὸν οὐδέν ἐστι
συμφώνως ἀγαθόν, οὐδὲν ἔστιν ἀγαθόν.

79 Καὶ μὴν εἰ ἔστι τι ἀγαθόν, τοῦτο κατὰ τὸν ἴδιον
λόγον αἱρετὸν ὀφείλει τυγχάνειν, ἐπεὶ πᾶς ἄνθρωπος
αἱρεῖται τούτου τυγχάνειν ὥσπερ καὶ τὸ κακὸν
φυγεῖν. οὐδὲν δέ γε αἱρετόν ἐστι κατὰ τὸν ἴδιον
λόγον [ὡς αἱρετόν],¹ καθάπερ δείξομεν· οὐκ ἄρα
80 τι ἔστιν ἀγαθόν. εἰ γάρ ἐστί τι κατὰ τὸν ἴδιον
λόγον αἱρετόν, ἤτοι αὐτὸ τὸ αἱρεῖσθαι αἱρετόν
ἐστιν ἢ ἕτερόν τι παρὰ τοῦτο, οἷον ἤτοι τὸ αἱρεῖσθαι τὸν πλοῦτον αἱρετόν ἐστιν ἢ αὐτὸς ὁ πλοῦτος
81 αἱρετός ἐστιν. καὶ αὐτὸ μὲν τὸ αἱρεῖσθαι οὐκ ἂν
εἴη αἱρετόν. εἰ γὰρ αἱρετόν ἐστι κατὰ τὸν ἴδιον
λόγον τὸ αἱρεῖσθαι, οὐκ ὀφείλομεν σπουδάζειν
τυχεῖν οὗπερ αἱρούμεθα, ἵνα μὴ ἐκπέσωμεν τοῦ
ἔτι αἱρεῖσθαι. ὥσπερ γὰρ ⟨φευκτέον⟩² τὸ πίνειν
ἢ ἐσθίειν, ἵνα μὴ πιόντες ἢ φαγόντες ἐκπέσωμεν
τοῦ ἔτι θέλειν τὸ πίνειν ἢ ἐσθίειν, οὕτως εἰ τὸ
αἱρεῖσθαι πλοῦτον ἢ ὑγείαν αἱρετόν ἐστιν, οὐκ
ἐχρῆν ἡμᾶς διώκειν τὸν πλοῦτον ἢ τὴν ὑγείαν, ἵνα
μὴ τυχόντες αὐτῶν ἐκπέσωμεν τοῦ ἔτι αἱρεῖσθαι.
82 διώκομεν δέ γε τὴν τεῦξιν αὐτῶν· οὐκ ἄρα αἱρετόν
ἐστι τὸ αἱρεῖσθαι, φευκτὸν δὲ μᾶλλον. καὶ ὃν
τρόπον ὁ ἐρῶν σπεύδει τυχεῖν τῆς ἐρωμένης, ἵνα
φύγῃ τὴν ἐν τῷ ἐρᾶν ὄχλησιν, καὶ ὡς ὁ διψῶν
ἐπείγεται πιεῖν, ἵνα φύγῃ τὴν ἐν τῷ διψῆν βάσανον,
ὧδε καὶ ὁ ἐν τῷ αἱρεῖσθαι πλοῦτον ὀχλούμενος
[κατὰ τὸ αἱρεῖσθαι]³ ἐπείγεται τυχεῖν πλούτου, ἵνα
83 ἀπαλλαγῇ τοῦ ἔτι αἱρεῖσθαι. εἰ δ' ἕτερόν τί

---

¹ [ὡς αἱρετόν] secl. Heintz.
² ⟨φευκτέον⟩ addo: ⟨ἐμβραδύνομεν τῷ⟩ cj. Bekk.
³ [κατὰ τὸ αἱρεῖσθαι] secl. Heintz.

nor by nature, and besides the private good of each there exists no good upon which all are agreed, no good exists.

Moreover, if good exists, it ought to be desirable 79 on its own account, since every man desires to obtain it even as he desires to escape evil.[a] But, as we shall show, nothing is desirable on its own account ; therefore there does not exist any good. For if there is 80 anything desirable on its own account, either the desire itself is desirable or something other than this,—for example, either the desire for wealth is desirable or wealth itself is desirable. But the desire 81 itself will not be desirable. For if the desire is desirable on its own account, we ought not to be eager to obtain that which we desire lest we should cease from desiring any longer. For just as ⟨we ought to avoid⟩ [b] drinking or eating lest by having eaten or drunk we should cease to wish any longer to drink or eat, so, if the desire for wealth or health is desirable, we ought not to pursue after wealth or health, lest by acquiring them we cease to desire them any longer. But we 82 do desire the acquisition of them ; therefore the desire is not desirable but rather to be avoided. And just as the lover is eager to obtain his beloved that he may escape from the distress which love entails, and as the thirsty man hurries to drink that he may escape the torment of thirst, so also he who is distressed through his desire for wealth hurries to obtain wealth that he may be relieved from further desire.—

[a] With §§ 79–84 cf. P.H. iii. 183–184.
[b] Probably more words have been lost from the Greek, as we should rather expect " we ought to have avoided drinking or eating if the desire for them is desirable," or the like.

SEXTUS EMPIRICUS

ἐστι τὸ αἱρετὸν παρ' αὐτὸ τὸ αἱρεῖσθαι, ἤτοι τῶν
κεχωρισμένων ἐστὶν ἡμῶν ἢ τῶν περὶ ἡμᾶς. καὶ
εἰ μὲν κεχώρισται ἡμῶν καὶ ἐκτός ἐστιν, ἤτοι
συμβαίνει τι περὶ ἡμᾶς ἐξ αὐτοῦ ἢ οὐδὲν συμβαίνει·
οἷον ἀπὸ τοῦ φίλου ἢ τοῦ σπουδαίου ἀνθρώπου ἢ
τέκνου ἢ ἄλλου τινὸς τῶν ἐκτὸς εἶναι λεγομένων
ἀγαθῶν ἢ συμβαίνει τι περὶ ἡμᾶς ἐξ αὐτοῦ ἀστεῖον
κίνημα καὶ ἀποδεκτὸν κατάστημα καὶ ἀγαστὸν
πάθος, ἢ οὐδὲν συμβαίνει τοιοῦτον οὐδέ ἐσμεν ἐν
διαφόρῳ κινήματι, ὅτε αἱρετὸν ἡγούμεθα τὸν φίλον
84 ἢ τὸ τέκνον. καὶ εἰ μὲν οὐδὲν ἁπλαξαπλῶς γίνεταί
τι τοιοῦτον περὶ ἡμᾶς, οὐδ' ὅλως ἔσται τὸ ἐκτὸς
αἱρετὸν ἡμῖν. πῶς γὰρ πρὸς ὃ ἀκινήτως διακείμεθα,
85 τούτου οἷόν τε αἵρεσιν ποιεῖσθαι ἡμᾶς; καὶ γὰρ
ἄλλως, εἴπερ τὸ μὲν χαρτὸν νενόηται ἐκ τοῦ
χαίρειν ἡμᾶς ἀπ' αὐτοῦ, τὸ δὲ λυπηρὸν ἐκ τοῦ
λυπεῖσθαι, τὸ δὲ ἀγαθὸν ἐκ τοῦ ἄγασθαι, ἀκολουθήσει, ἐξ οὗ μήτε χαρά τις ἡμῖν ἐγγίνεται μήτε
ἀγαστὴ διάθεσις μήτε ἀσμενιστόν τι κίνημα, ἐκ
86 τούτου μηδὲ αἵρεσίν τινα ἐμφύεσθαι. εἰ δὲ γίνεταί τι περὶ ἡμᾶς ἀπὸ τοῦ ἐκτός, οἷον τοῦ φίλου ἢ
τοῦ τέκνου, προσηνὲς κατάστημα καὶ ἀσμενιστὸν
πάθος, ἔσται οὐ δι' αὐτὸν αἱρετὸς ὁ φίλος ἢ τὸ
τέκνον, διὰ δὲ τὸ προσηνὲς τοῦτο κατάστημα καὶ
ἀσμενιστὸν πάθος. ἀλλ' ἦν γε τὸ τοιοῦτο κατάστημα οὐκ ἐκτὸς ἀλλὰ περὶ ἡμᾶς. οὐδὲν ἄρα τῶν
87 ἐκτὸς δι' αὐτὸ αἱρετόν ἐστιν ἢ ἀγαθόν.   καὶ
μὴν οὐδὲ τῶν περὶ ἡμᾶς ἐστι τὸ αἱρετὸν καὶ
ἀγαθόν. ἤτοι γὰρ σωματικόν ἐστι τοῦτο μόνον
ἢ ψυχικόν. ἀλλὰ σωματικὸν μὲν μόνον οὐκ ἂν
εἴη· εἰ γὰρ σωματικὸν μόνον ὑποκέοιτο, οὐκέτι

426

But if the desirable is something other than the desire 83
itself, it is either a thing separate from ourselves or a
thing belonging to ourselves.   And if it is separate
from us and external, either some effect is produced
in us by means of it, or no effect ; as, for instance, by
the friend or the good man or the child, or any other
of the so-called external goods, either there is produced in us a pleasing motion and a welcome state
and a delightful affection, or no such result occurs
and we do not experience any different motion when
we regard the friend or the child as desirable.   And 84
if absolutely no such effect is produced in us, no
external thing at all will be desirable in our eyes.
For how can we possibly have a desire for a thing in
regard to which we feel no emotion ?   And besides, 85
if the enjoyable is so conceived because we get joy
from it, and the painful because we get pain, and
the good because we get delight,[a] it will follow that
no desire is implanted by that which produces in us
no joy nor delightful feeling nor agreeable emotion.
But if there is produced in us by an external object, 86
such as the friend or the child, a welcome state and an
agreeable affection, the friend or the child will not be
desirable for his own sake but for the sake of this
welcome state and agreeable affection.   But such a
state is not an external thing but is personal to ourselves.   Therefore none of the external things is
desirable for its own sake or good.—Nor yet is the 87
desirable and good one of the things personal to ourselves.[b]   For it is either solely corporeal or psychical.
But it will not be solely corporeal ; for if it really were
solely corporeal, and no longer a psychical affection,

---

[a] For the derivation of ἀγαθόν from ἄγασθαι cf. § 35 supra.
[b] With §§ 87-89 cf. P.H. iii. 185-186.

δὲ καὶ ψυχικὸν πάθος, ἐκφεύξεται τὴν γνῶσιν
ἡμῶν (ψυχῆς γάρ ἐστι πᾶσα γνῶσις) καὶ ἴσον ἔσται
τοῖς ἐκτὸς ὑποκειμένοις καὶ μηδεμίαν ἔχουσι πρὸς
88 ἡμᾶς συμπάθειαν. εἰ δὲ διατείνουσαν ἔχει τὴν
εὐαρέστησιν εἰς ψυχήν, ἔσται κατ' αὐτὴν αἱρετὸν
καὶ ἀγαθόν, ἀλλ' οὐ καθὸ ψιλῶς σωματικόν ἐστι
κίνημα. πᾶν γὰρ αἱρετὸν κατὰ αἴσθησιν ἢ νόησιν
κρίνεται, οὐ κατ' ἄλογον σῶμα. ἀλλ' ἥγε τὸ
αἱρετὸν λαμβάνουσα αἴσθησις ἢ διάνοια ψυχῆς
ἐστι [κατὰ τὸν ἴδιον λόγον]¹· οὐδὲν ἄρα τῶν περὶ
σῶμα συμβαινόντων δι' αὐτὸ αἱρετόν ἐστι καὶ
89 ἀγαθόν, ἀλλ' εἰ ἄρα, τῶν περὶ ψυχήν, ὃ πάλιν εἰς
τὴν ἀρχῆθεν κυλίεται ἀπορίαν. τῆς γὰρ ἑκάστου
διανοίας ἀσυμφώνους ἐχούσης τὰς κρίσεις πρὸς τὴν
τοῦ πέλας, ἀνάγκη ἕκαστον τὸ φαινόμενον αὐτῷ
ἀγαθὸν ἡγεῖσθαι. οὐκ ἦν δὲ τὸ ἑκάστῳ φαινόμενον
ἀγαθὸν φύσει ἀγαθόν. οὐδὲ ταύτῃ τοίνυν τί ἐστιν
ἀγαθόν.
90 Ὁ δ' αὐτὸς λόγος καὶ περὶ κακοῦ. δυνάμει γὰρ
συναποδέδοται² τῇ περὶ τοῦ ἀγαθοῦ ζητήσει,
πρῶτον μὲν ὅτι [ἐπεὶ]³ τοῦ ἑτέρου ἀναιρουμένου
συναναιρεῖται καὶ τὸ ἕτερον, ἑκάτερον γὰρ κατὰ
τὴν ὡς πρὸς τὸ ἕτερον σχέσιν νενόηται· εἶτα
ἐπεὶ καὶ προηγουμένως ἔνεστι τὸ τοιοῦτον ⟨ἡμῖν
παριστᾶν, πειρασόμεθα⟩⁴ πάλιν ἐπὶ ἑνὸς ὑποδείγματος καταστήσασθαι τὸν λόγον, καθάπερ τῆς
ἀφροσύνης, ἣν μόνην φασὶν εἶναι κακὸν οἱ ἀπὸ
91 τῆς στοᾶς. εἰ γὰρ φύσει κακόν ἐστιν ἡ ἀφροσύνη, δεήσει, ὃν τρόπον τὸ θερμὸν γνωρίζεται ὅτι

¹ [κατὰ . . . λόγον] secl. Heintz.
² συναποδέδοται Mutsch.: ἀποδέδοται mss., Bekk.

428

it would elude our perception (for all perception is a property of the soul) and it would be on a par with the things which exist externally and have no fellow-feeling with us. But if the pleasure it contains 88 extends to the soul, it will be desirable and good on account of this but not on account of its being a merely corporeal motion. For every desirable thing is judged to be so by means of a sensation or perception and not by means of an irrational body. But the sense or intelligence which apprehends the desirable is of the soul; therefore none of the things which happen to the body is desirable for its own sake and good, but, if any, those which happen to the soul; 89 and this involves us once again in the original difficulty.[a] For since the intelligence of each man disagrees with that of his neighbour in respect of its judgements, each must necessarily regard as good that which appears so to himself. But what appears good to each man is not good by nature. So in this way, too, nothing is good.

And the same argument applies also to evil. For 90 it virtually results from our investigation of the good that, in the first place, when one of these is abolished the other also is abolished along with it (for each of them is conceived in its relation to the other); and next, since it is possible ⟨for us to establish⟩ this directly, ⟨we shall attempt⟩ once more to base our argument upon a single example, namely folly, which alone, say the Stoics, is evil. For if folly is evil by nature, then, 91 just as the hot is known to be hot by nature from

_____

[a] See § 77 _supra._

_____

³ [ἐπεὶ] secl. Mutsch.
⁴ ⟨ἡμῖν . . . πειρασόμεθα⟩ addo (sec. Mutsch.).

θερμόν ἐστι φύσει ἐκ τοῦ τοὺς προσπελάσαντας
αὐτῷ θερμαίνεσθαι, καὶ τὸ ψυχρὸν ἐκ τοῦ ψύχεσθαι, οὕτω καὶ τὴν ἀφροσύνην φύσει κακὸν ὑπ-
άρχουσαν γνωρίζεσθαι ἐκ τοῦ κακοῦσθαι. ἤτοι οὖν
οἱ λεγόμενοι ἄφρονες κακοῦνται ὑπὸ τῆς ἀφρο-
92 σύνης ἢ οἱ φρόνιμοι. ἀλλ᾽ οἱ μὲν φρόνιμοι οὐ
κακοῦνται· ἐκτὸς γάρ εἰσι τῆς ἀφροσύνης, ὑπὸ δὲ
τοῦ μὴ παρόντος αὐτοῖς κακοῦ ἀλλὰ κεχωρισμένου
οὐκ ἂν κακωθεῖεν. εἰ δὲ τοὺς ἄφρονας κακοῖ ἡ
ἀφροσύνη, ἤτοι πρόδηλος αὐτοῖς οὖσα κακοῖ αὐτοὺς
93 ἢ ἄδηλος. καὶ ἄδηλος μὲν οὐδαμῶς· εἰ γὰρ ἄδηλός
ἐστιν αὐτοῖς, οὐδὲ κακὸν οὐδὲ φευκτόν ἐστιν αὐτοῖς,
ἀλλ᾽ ὡς τὴν μὴ φαινομένην λύπην καὶ ἀνεπαίσθητον
ἀλγηδόνα οὔτε φεύγει τις οὔτε ταράσσεται, ὧδε
καὶ τὴν ἀνυπόπτωτον ἀφροσύνην καὶ τὴν ἀδηλου-
94 μένην οὐδεὶς ὡς κακὸν περιστήσεται. εἰ δὲ προδήλως αὐτοῖς γινώσκεται καὶ ἔστι φύσει κακόν,
ὤφειλον οἱ ἄφρονες φεύγειν αὐτὴν ὡς φύσει κακόν.
οὐχὶ δέ γε οἱ ἄφρονες τὸ λεγόμενον ὑπὸ τῶν
ἐκτὸς ἀφραίνειν ὡς πρόδηλον κακὸν φεύγουσιν,
ἀλλ᾽ ἕκαστος τὴν μὲν ἰδίαν κρίσιν ἀποδέχεται
τὴν δὲ τοῦ τὸ ἐναντίον δοξάζοντος κακίζει.
95 ὥστ᾽ οὐδὲ πρόδηλός ἐστι τοῖς ἄφροσιν ὡς φύσει
κακὸν ἡ ἀφροσύνη. ὅθεν εἴπερ οὔτε οἱ φρόνιμοι
κακοῦνταί τι πρὸς τῆς ἀφροσύνης οὔτε τοῖς ἄφροσι
φευκτόν ἐστιν ἡ ἀφροσύνη, ῥητέον μὴ εἶναι φύσει
κακὸν τὴν ἀφροσύνην. εἰ δὲ μὴ ταύτην, οὐδ᾽ ἄλλο
τι τῶν λεγομένων κακῶν.
96 Ἀλλ᾽ εἰώθασί τινες τῶν ἀπὸ τῆς Ἐπικούρου
αἱρέσεως, πρὸς τὰς τοιαύτας ἀπορίας ὑπαντῶντες,
λέγειν ὅτι φυσικῶς καὶ ἀδιδάκτως τὸ ζῷον φεύγει

the fact that those who approach it are made hot,[a] and the cold from their being made cold, so also it will be necessary for folly to be known as being evil by nature from the fact that people are made evil. Either, then, it is those who are called fools that are made evil by folly, or the wise. But the wise are not 92 made evil ; for they are outside of folly, and they will not be made evil by an evil which is not present with them but separated. And if folly makes evil the fools, it makes them evil either when evident to them or when non-evident. But certainly not when non- 93 evident ; for if it is non-evident to them it is neither evil for them nor to be avoided, but just as a man neither avoids nor is perturbed by a non-apparent pain and a non-perceptible pang, so also no one will account as evil the folly which is unsuspected and non-evident. But if it is quite plainly perceived by 94 them and is evil by nature, the fools ought to have avoided it as evil by nature. But the fools do not avoid as an evident evil that which is called by out-siders " foolishness," but each one accepts his own judgement and reckons that of the man who holds an opposite opinion to be evil. So that it is not evident 95 to the fools that folly is evil by nature. Hence, if neither are the wise made evil at all by folly nor is folly a thing avoided by the fools, we must declare that folly is not a thing evil by nature. And if it is not, neither is any other of the so-called evils.

But some of those who belong to the sect of Epicurus, 96 in answer to these objections, are wont to argue that the animal avoids pain and pursues pleasure naturally

----

[a] *Cf.* § 69 *supra.*

μὲν τὴν ἀλγηδόνα διώκει δὲ τὴν ἡδονήν· γεννηθὲν
γοῦν καὶ μηδέπω τοῖς κατὰ δόξαν δουλεῦον ἅμα
τῷ ῥαπισθῆναι ἀσυνήθει ἀέρος ψύξει ἔκλαυσέ τε
καὶ ἐκώκυσεν. εἰ δὲ φυσικῶς ὁρμᾷ μὲν πρὸς
ἡδονὴν ἐκκλίνει δὲ τὸν πόνον, φύσει φευκτόν τέ
97 ἐστιν αὐτῷ ὁ πόνος καὶ αἱρετὸν ἡ ἡδονή. οὐ
συνεῖδον δὲ οἱ ταῦτα λέγοντες τὸ μὲν πρῶτον ὅτι
καὶ τοῖς ἀτιμοτάτοις ζῴοις μεταδιδόασι τἀγαθοῦ,
πολλὴ γὰρ μετουσία κἀκείνοις ἐστὶν ἡδονῆς, εἶθ᾽
ὅτι οὐδὲ τὸ καθάπαξ φευκτόν ἐστιν ὁ πόνος· καὶ
γὰρ πόνῳ πραΰνεται πόνος, καὶ ὑγεία, ἔτι δὲ
ῥῶσις καὶ θρέψις, γίνεται σωμάτων διὰ πόνων,
τέχνας τε καὶ ἐπιστήμας τὰς ἀκριβεστάτας
ἀναλαμβάνουσιν ἄνδρες οὐ χωρὶς πόνου, ὥστ᾽ οὐ
98 πάντως φύσει φευκτὸν ὁ πόνος. καὶ μὴν οὐδὲ τὸ
δοκοῦν ἡδὺ φύσει πάντως αἱρετόν· πολλάκις γοῦν
τὰ κατὰ τὴν πρώτην ἐμπέλασιν ἡστικῶς ἡμᾶς
διατιθέντα, ταῦτα ἐκ δευτέρου, καίπερ ὄντα τὰ
αὐτά, ἀηδῆ νομίζεται ὡς ἂν τοῦ ἡδέος οὐ φύσει
ὄντος τοιούτου, ἀλλὰ παρὰ τὰς διαφόρους περιστάσεις ὁτὲ μὲν οὕτως ὁτὲ δ᾽ ἐκείνως κινοῦντος
ἡμᾶς.

99 Ναί, ἀλλὰ καὶ οἱ μόνον τὸ καλὸν ἀγαθὸν δοξάζοντες δείκνυσθαι νομίζουσιν ὅτι φύσει τοῦτο αἱρετόν
ἐστι καὶ ἀπὸ τῶν ἀλόγων ζῴων. ὁρῶμεν γάρ,
φασίν, ὥς τινα γενναῖα ζῷα, καθάπερ ταῦροι καὶ
ἀλεκτρυόνες, καίπερ[1] μηδεμιᾶς αὐτοῖς ὑποκειμένης
τέρψεως καὶ ἡδονῆς διαγωνίζεται μέχρι θανάτου.
100 καὶ τῶν ἀνθρώπων δὲ οἱ ὑπὲρ πατρίδος ἢ γονέων
ἢ τέκνων εἰς ἀναίρεσιν ἑαυτοὺς ἐπιδιδόντες οὐκ
ἂν ποτε τοῦτ᾽ ἐποίουν, μηδεμιᾶς αὐτοῖς ἐλπι-

---

[1] καίπερ Apelt: ἅπερ mss., Bekk.

and without teaching ; thus when it is born, and is
not as yet a slave to opinions, it cries and screams as
soon as it is smitten by the air's unwonted chill. But
if it naturally has an inclination for pleasure and a
disinclination for toil, toil is a thing naturally avoided
by it and pleasure a thing desirable. But they who **97**
argue thus have failed to notice, in the first place,
that they are giving a share in the good even to the
basest animals (for they too have a large share in
pleasure) ; and, next, that toil is not a thing to be
absolutely avoided ; for, in fact, pain is alleviated
by toil, and health of body, as well as strength and
growth, comes by means of toils, and men do not
acquire the most exact arts and sciences without
toil, so that toil is not a thing naturally to be avoided
altogether. Moreover, what seems to be pleasant **98**
is not in all cases naturally desirable ; thus it often
happens that things which on their first occurrence
affect us pleasurably, on the second occasion, although
they are the same, are deemed unpleasant, just as
though the pleasant were not so by nature, but affected
us now this way and now that according to the differing circumstances.

Yes, but even those who hold that only the fair is **99**
good think that it is proved by the irrational animals
that this is desirable by nature.[a] For we see, they
say, how certain noble animals, such as bulls and
cocks, contend unto the death even when they have
no feeling of delight and pleasure. And those men **100**
who have given themselves over to destruction for the
sake of country or parents or children would never
have done so, when they had no hope of pleasure after

[a] With §§ 99–100 *cf. P.H.* iii. 193.

ζομένης μετὰ θάνατον ἡδονῆς, εἰ μὴ φυσικῶς τὸ
καλὸν καὶ ἀγαθὸν τούτους τε καὶ πᾶν τὸ γενναῖον
ἀεὶ ζῷον ἐπεσπᾶτο πρὸς τὴν αὐτοῦ αἵρεσιν.
101 λέληθε δὲ καὶ τούτους ὅτι τελέως ἐστὶν εὔηθες τὸ
νομίζειν τὰ προειρημένα τῶν ζῴων ἐννοίᾳ τἀγαθοῦ
μέχρι τῆς ὑστάτης ἀναπνοῆς διαγωνίζεσθαι. αὐτῶν
γὰρ πάρεστιν ἀκούειν λεγόντων ὅτι ἡ φρονίμη
διάθεσις μόνη βλέπει τὸ καλόν τε καὶ ἀγαθόν,
ἡ δὲ ἀφροσύνη τυφλώττει περὶ τὴν τούτου διά-
γνωσιν, ὅθεν καὶ ὁ ἀλεκτρυὼν καὶ ὁ ταῦρος μὴ
μετέχοντα τῆς φρονίμης διαθέσεως οὐκ ἂν βλέποι
102 τὸ καλόν τε καὶ ἀγαθόν. ἄλλως τε, εἰ ἔστι τι περὶ
οὗ διαγωνίζεται ταῦτα τὰ ζῷα μέχρι θανάτου,
τοῦτο οὐκ ἄλλο τί ἐστιν ἢ τὸ νικᾶν καὶ τὸ ἡγεῖσθαι.
ἔσθ' ὅτε δὲ τὸ νικᾶσθαι καὶ τὸ ὑποτάσσεσθαι
κάλλιόν ἐστιν, ὅπου γε ἑκάτερόν ἐστιν ἀδιάφορον.
οὐ τοίνυν φύσει ἀγαθόν ἐστιν ἀλλ' ἀδιάφορον τὸ
103 νικᾶν καὶ τὸ ἡγεῖσθαι. ἄλλως τε[1] εἰ φαῖεν καὶ
τὸν ἀλεκτρυόνα ἢ ταῦρον ἢ ἄλλο τι τῶν ἀλκίμων
ζῴων τοῦ καλοῦ ἐφίεσθαι, πόθεν ὅτι καὶ ὁ ἄνθρωπος
τοῦ αὐτοῦ στοχάζεται; οὐ γὰρ ἐν τῷ ἐκεῖνα δεῖξαι
τούτου προνοούμενα καὶ ὁ ἄνθρωπος τοιοῦτος ὢν
104 δέδεικται, ἐπεί τοι εἰ ὅτι τινὰ τῶν ζῴων ἄλκιμά
ἐστι καὶ καταφρονητικὰ μὲν τοῦ ἡδέος κατεξ-
αναστατικὰ δὲ τῶν ἀλγηδόνων, λέγεται καὶ ὁ
ἄνθρωπος προνοεῖσθαι τοῦ καλοῦ, ἐπεὶ τὰ πολλὰ
λίχνα ἐστὶ καὶ γαστρὸς ἥττονα, τοὔμπαλιν ἐροῦμεν
καὶ τὸν ἄνθρωπον τοῦ ἡδέος μᾶλλον ἀντιποιεῖσθαι.
105 εἰ δὲ λέγοιεν εἶναι μέν τινα ζῷα φιλήδονα, τὸν
δ' ἄνθρωπον μὴ πάντως τοιοῦτον ὑπάρχειν, ἀνα-
στρέψαντες καὶ ἡμεῖς ἐροῦμεν, οὐκ εἴ τινα τῶν

[1] ἄλλως τε Apelt: ὥστε mss., Bekk.

death, unless the fair and good had naturally drawn
them, and every noble animal, to desire it.   But these 101
people, too, fail to notice that it is perfectly silly to
suppose that the animals just mentioned contend to
their last breath owing to a conception of the good.
For one may hear them declaring themselves that it
is only the wise state of mind which beholds the fair
and good, while folly blinds men for discerning it ;
and hence the cock and the bull, as they have no
share in the wise state of mind, will not behold the
fair and good.   And besides, if there is anything 102
about which these animals contend unto the death,
it is nothing else than victory and leadership.   But
sometimes it is a fairer thing to be vanquished and
subdued, at least where either result is indifferent.ᵃ
Therefore victory and leadership is not good by nature
but indifferent.   And besides, if they should assert 103
that the cock or the bull or any other of the valiant
animals strives after the fair, whence comes it that
man also aims at the same thing ?   For in proving
that those animals have a preconception of this, it is
not proved that man is of a like kind, since, to be sure, 104
if man too is said to have a preconception of the fair
because some animals are valiant and contemptuous
of pleasure and capable of resisting pains, then, since
most of them are greedy and the slaves of their bellies,
we shall declare also, conversely, that man is still
more eager for pleasure. And if they should argue that, 105
though some animals are pleasure-loving, man is not
wholly so, we too shall turn round and say that it does

ᵃ *i.e.* when neither victory nor defeat is (strictly speaking)
either " good " or " evil " the latter may be " fairer " (*i.e.*
more " good ") than the former.

ζώων κατὰ φυσικὸν λόγον μεταδιώκει τὸ καλόν,
εὐθέως καὶ ὁ ἄνθρωπος τοῦ αὐτοῦ στοχάζεται
106 τέλους.   ἄλλος δέ τις φήσει περιμάχητον εἶναι
τὸ νικᾶν καὶ τὸ ἡγεῖσθαι τοῖς ζώοις [δι' αὐτό,
ἀνθρώπῳ δ']¹ οὐ δι' αὐτό, διὰ δὲ τὴν ἐπακολου-
θοῦσαν αὐτῷ κατὰ ψυχὴν τέρψιν καὶ γῆθος, προσ-
ηνές τι τυγχάνον κατάστημα. καὶ μᾶλλόν γε
τοῦτο ἐπ' ἀνθρώπων ἔστιν ὑπολαβεῖν, ἐφ' ὧν καὶ
τιμὴ καὶ ἔπαινος καὶ δωρεαὶ καὶ δόξαι ἱκανά ἐστιν
ἥδειν καὶ διαχεῖν τὴν διάνοιαν καὶ παρ' αὐτὸ τοῦτο
κατεξαναστατικὴν αὐτὴν τῶν ὀχληρῶν παρέχειν.
107 ὅθεν καὶ οἱ μέχρι τελευτῆς ἀριστεύοντες καὶ ὑπὲρ
πατρίδος εἰς ἀναίρεσιν αὑτοὺς ἐπιδιδόντες διὰ
ταύτην ἴσως τὴν αἰτίαν ἐπάνδρως ἀγωνίζονται
καὶ θνήσκουσιν· καὶ γὰρ εἰ τελευτῶσι καὶ τοῦ ζῆν
μεθίστανται, ἀλλά τοί γε ὅτε ζῶσιν ἥδονται καὶ
108 γήθονται πρὸς τοὺς ἐπαίνους.   εἰκὸς δ' ἔστιν
ἐνίους αὐτῶν καὶ προσδοξάζοντας ὅτι μετὰ
τελευτὴν ὅμοιος αὐτοὺς ἔπαινος περιμένει, προὔπ-
τον αἱρεῖσθαι θάνατον. οὐκ ἀπίθανον δ' ἄλλους
τοῦτο πάσχειν βλέποντας ὅτι δυσυπομένητα μᾶλλον
αὐτοῖς ἔσται τὰ κατὰ τὴν ζωήν, θεασαμένοις

υἷάς τ' ὀλλυμένους ἑλκυσθείσας τε θύγατρας
καὶ θαλάμους κεραϊζομένους καὶ νήπια τέκνα
βαλλόμενα ποτὶ γαίῃ ἐν αἰνῇ δηιοτῆτι.

109 διὰ πολλοὺς οὖν τρόπους τὸν μετ' εὐκλείας τινὲς
αἱροῦνται θάνατον, καὶ οὐ διὰ τὸ περισπούδαστον
ἡγεῖσθαι τὸ παρά τισι τῶν δογματικῶν θρυλού-
μενον καλόν. ἀλλὰ τὰ μὲν περὶ τούτων ἐπὶ
τοσοῦτον ἠπορήσθω.

¹ [δι' . . . δ'] secl. Heintz.

not at once follow that, if some animals for a natural reason pursue after the fair, man also aims at the same goal.—But some other man will assert that 106 victory and leadership is a thing highly prized by the animals not for its own sake but for the sake of the delight and joy of soul which follow upon it, this being an agreeable state. And one may suppose that this is even more true of men, with whom reputation and praise and gifts and honours are sufficient to please and thrill the mind and because of this to render it capable of resisting hardships. Whence, too, it is 107 probably owing to this cause that those who prove valiant to the end and devote themselves to destruction for their country's sake struggle manfully and die. For even if they die and depart from life, yet to be sure while they are alive they take pleasure and joy in the praise. And it is likely also that some of them 108 believe further that similar praise awaits them after death, and thus they desire a conspicuous death. And it is not improbable that others endure death through seeing that the woes of life will be still harder for them to endure, when they behold—

> Death overtaking their sons and ravishers seizing their
>   daughters,
> Plunderers wrecking their chambers, and even their infant
>   children
> Brutally dashed to the ground in the fearful fury of
>   fighting.[a]

It is for many reasons, then, that some desire death 109 with glory, and not because they regard " the fair " (so harped upon by certain of the Dogmatists) as a thing to be greatly sought after. But let this serve to conclude our discussion of these problems.

* Homer, *Il.* xxii. 62 ff.

SEXTUS EMPIRICUS

110 Περὶ μὲν οὖν τοῦ μηδὲν εἶναι φύσει ἀγαθόν τε
καὶ κακὸν αὐτάρκως ἐσκεψάμεθα· νυνὶ δὲ ζητῶμεν
καὶ εἰ συγχωρηθέντων αὐτῶν δυνατόν ἐστιν εὐρόως
ἅμα καὶ εὐδαιμόνως βιοῦν. οἱ μὲν οὖν δογματικοὶ
τῶν φιλοσόφων οὐδ᾽ ἄλλως φασὶν ἢ οὕτως ἔχειν·
ὁ γὰρ τυχὼν τοῦ ἀγαθοῦ κατ᾽ αὐτοὺς καὶ ἐκκλίνων
τὸ κακόν, οὗτός ἐστιν εὐδαίμων· παρὸ καὶ ἐπιστήμην τινὰ περὶ τὸν βίον εἶναι λέγουσι τὴν
φρόνησιν, διακριτικὴν μὲν οὖσαν τῶν τε ἀγαθῶν
111 καὶ κακῶν, περιποιητικὴν δὲ τῆς εὐδαιμονίας. οἱ
δ᾽ ἀπὸ τῆς σκέψεως μηδὲν εἰκῇ τιθέντες ἢ ἀναιροῦντες, ἅπανθ᾽ ὑπὸ τὴν σκέψιν εἰσάγοντες,
διδάσκουσιν ὡς τοῖς μὲν φύσει ἀγαθὸν καὶ κακὸν
ὑποστησαμένοις ἀκολουθεῖ τὸ κακοδαιμόνως βιοῦν,
τοῖς δ᾽ ἀοριστοῦσι καὶ ἐπέχουσι

  ῥήϊστη βιοτὴ πέλει ἀνθρώποισιν.[a]

112 καὶ τοῦτο μάθοιμεν ἂν μικρὸν ἄνωθεν προλαβόντες.
  Πᾶσα τοίνυν κακοδαιμονία γίνεται διά τινα
ταραχήν. ἀλλὰ καὶ πᾶσα ταραχὴ παρέπεται τοῖς
ἀνθρώποις ἤτοι διὰ τὸ συντόνως τινὰ διώκειν
113 ἢ καὶ διὰ τὸ συντόνως τινὰ φεύγειν. διώκουσι
δέ γε συντόνως πάντες ἄνθρωποι τὸ δοξαζόμενον
αὐτοῖς ἀγαθὸν καὶ φεύγουσι τὸ ὑποσταθὲν κακόν.
πᾶσα ἄρα κακοδαιμονία γίνεται παρὰ τὸ τἀγαθὰ
μὲν διώκειν ὡς ἀγαθὰ τὰ δὲ κακὰ φεύγειν ὡς
κακά. ἐπεὶ οὖν ὁ δογματικὸς πεπίστευκεν ὅτι

---

[a] Alluding to the Stoic definition of happiness as the
" equable flow of life " ; cf. § 31 supra.

CHAPTER IV.—ASSUMING THAT THINGS GOOD AND EVIL
EXIST BY NATURE, IS IT POSSIBLE TO LIVE HAPPILY?

We have, then, sufficiently considered the question 110
of the non-existence of any thing good or evil by
nature ; and now let us inquire whether, if ⟨the
existence of⟩ these be conceded, it is possible to live at
once equally *a* and happily. Now the dogmatic philosophers assert that this, and nothing else, is actually
the case ; for according to them the man who acquires
the good and avoids the evil is happy. Wherefore
also they allege that wisdom is a science of life, it
being capable of distinguishing things good and evil *b*
and of securing happiness. But the Sceptics, 111
neither affirming nor denying anything rashly but
subjecting all things to criticism, maintain that
those who assume the existence of good and evil
by nature have in consequence an unhappy life,
whereas for those who refuse to define and suspend
judgement—

> Freest from care is the life they lead.*e*

And this we may learn if we first go back a little. 112
Now every unhappy state occurs because of some
perturbation. But every perturbation in men is a
consequence due either to an eager pursuit of certain
things or to an eager avoidance of certain things.
And all men eagerly pursue what is believed by them 113
to be good and avoid what is supposed to be evil.
Therefore every case of unhappiness occurs owing to
the pursuit of the good things as good, and the avoidance of the evil things as evil. Since, then, the Dog-

b Cf. *P.H.* iii. 240.
e Homer, *Odyss.* iv. 565.

τόδε ἐστὶ φύσει ἀγαθὸν καὶ τόδε ἐστὶ φύσει κακόν,
ἀεὶ τὸ μὲν διώκων τὸ δὲ φεύγων, καὶ διὰ τοῦτο
114 ταραττόμενος, οὐδέποτε εὐδαιμονήσει. ἤτοι γὰρ
πᾶν ὃ διώκει τις, τοῦτ' εὐθὺς καὶ τῇ φύσει ἀγαθόν
ἐστι, καὶ πᾶν ὃ φεύγει τις ὡς φευκτόν, τοῦτο τῷ
ὄντι τοιοῦτόν ἐστιν· ἢ τὶ τῶν διωκομένων ἐστὶν
αἱρετόν, καὶ οὐ πᾶν, καὶ τὶ τῶν φευγομένων
φευκτόν· ἢ ἐν τῷ πρός τί πως ἔχειν ἐστὶ ταῦτα,
καὶ ὡς μὲν πρὸς τόνδε τόδ' ἐστὶν αἱρετὸν ἢ φευκτόν,
ὡς δὲ πρὸς τὴν φύσιν τὴν τῶν πραγμάτων οὔτε
αἱρετόν ἐστιν οὔτε φευκτόν, ἀλλὰ νυνὶ μὲν αἱρετὸν
115 νυνὶ δὲ φευκτόν.   εἰ μὲν οὖν πᾶν τὸ ὁπωσοῦν
ὑπό τινος διωκόμενον ὑπόθοιτό τις φύσει ἀγαθὸν
καὶ τὸ φευγόμενον φύσει φευκτόν, ἀβίωτον ἕξει
τὸν βίον, ἀναγκαζόμενος τὸ αὐτὸ διώκειν ἅμα καὶ
φεύγειν, καὶ διώκειν μὲν ᾗ πρός τινων αἱρετὸν
ὑπείληπται, φεύγειν δὲ παρόσον ἑτέροις φευκτὸν
116 δεδόξασται.   εἰ δὲ πᾶν μὲν τὸ διωκόμενον ἢ
φευγόμενον μὴ λέγοι αἱρετὸν καὶ φευκτόν, τὶ δὲ
αὐτῶν αἱρετὸν καὶ τὶ φευκτόν, βιώσεται μέν, οὐ
χωρὶς δὲ ταραχῆς βιώσεται· διὰ παντὸς γὰρ τὸ
δοξασθὲν αὐτῷ φύσει τυγχάνειν ἀγαθὸν διώκων
καὶ τὸ ὑποληφθὲν κακὸν περιστάμενος οὐδέποτε
ἀπαλλαγήσεται ταραχῆς, ἀλλὰ καὶ μήπω δραξά-
μενος τἀγαθοῦ διὰ τὴν τοῦ τυχεῖν ἐπιθυμίαν
σφοδρῶς ταραχθήσεται, καὶ τυχὼν διὰ τὴν ὑπερ-

matist firmly believes that this thing is good by nature
and that thing is evil by nature, as he is always
pursuing the one and avoiding the other and being,
consequently, perturbed, he will never be happy.
For either everything which anyone pursues is at 114
once and by nature good and everything which anyone avoids as a thing to be avoided is such in reality ;
or else some one of the things pursued is desirable,
but not every one, and some one of the things avoided
is to be avoided ; or else these things belong to the
relative class, and in relation to this man this thing is
desirable or to be avoided, whereas in relation to the
real nature of the things it is neither desirable nor
to be avoided, but at one time desirable, at another
to be avoided.—If, then, a man should assume that 115
everything which is in any way pursued by anyone is
good by nature and that everything which is avoided
is by nature to be avoided, he will have a life that is
unlivable, through being compelled both to pursue
and to avoid at the same time the same thing,—to
pursue it, inasmuch as it is conceived by some to be
desirable, but to avoid it, in so far as it is deemed by
others a thing to be avoided.—But if he were to say 116
not that everything which is pursued or avoided is
desirable and to be avoided, but that some one of
them is desirable and some one to be avoided, he
will have a life indeed, but not a life free from perturbation ; for through continually pursuing what
he believes to be good by nature and shunning what
he supposes to be evil he will never be clear of
perturbation, but both when he has failed as yet
to grasp the good he will be extremely perturbed
because of his desire to gain it, and when he has
gained it he will never be at rest owing to the excess

βολὴν τῆς χαρᾶς ἢ διὰ τὴν φρουρὰν τοῦ κτηθέντος
117 οὐδέποτε ἠρεμήσει. ὁ δ' αὐτὸς λόγος καὶ περὶ
κακοῦ· οὔτε γὰρ ὁ ἐκτὸς ὢν αὐτοῦ ἀμέριμνός ἐστιν,
ἱκανῶς ποινηλατούσης αὐτὸν τῆς τε κατὰ τὸ
φεύγειν καὶ τῆς κατὰ τὸ προφυλάττεσθαι ταραχῆς,
οὔτε ὁ ἐν αὐτῷ καθεστὼς παῦλαν ἔχει τῶν βασάνων,
σκεπτόμενος " πῶς ἂν φύγοι αἰπὺν ὄλεθρον."
118 Εἰ δὲ μὴ μᾶλλόν τις λέγοι τι φύσει αἱρετὸν ἢ
φευκτὸν μηδὲ μᾶλλον φευκτὸν ἢ αἱρετόν, ἑκάστου
τῶν ὑποπιπτόντων πρός τί πως ἔχοντος καὶ κατὰ
διαφέροντας καιροὺς καὶ περιστάσεις νυνὶ μὲν
αἱρετοῦ καθεστῶτος νυνὶ δὲ φευκτοῦ, βιώσεται μὲν
εὐδαιμόνως καὶ ἀταράχως, μήτε ἐπ' ἀγαθῷ ὡς
ἀγαθῷ ἐπαιρόμενος μήτε ἐπὶ κακῷ ταπεινούμενος,
τὸ μὲν κατ' ἀνάγκην συμβαῖνον γεννικῶς δεχόμενος,
τοῦ δὲ κατὰ δόξαν ὀχληροῦ, καθ' ἣν κακόν τι παρ-
εῖναι ἢ ἀγαθὸν δοξάζεται, ἐλευθερούμενος. τοῦτο
μὴν αὐτῷ παρέσται ἐκ τοῦ μηδὲν φύσει ἀγαθὸν
ἢ κακὸν δοξάζειν. οὐκ ἄρα ἔνεστιν εὐδαιμόνως
βιοῦν φύσει ἀγαθά τινα ἢ κακὰ ὑποστησάμενον.
119 Καὶ μὴν τό τινος κακοῦ ποιητικόν, τοῦτο πάντως
ἐστὶ φευκτὸν ὡς καὶ ⟨τὸ⟩¹ κακόν. οἷον εἰ ἡ
ἀλγηδών ἐστι κακόν, πάντως καὶ τὸ ποιητικὸν τῆς
ἀλγηδόνος ἐπισυστήσεται τῇ ἀλγηδόνι φευκτὸν ὄν·
καὶ εἰ ὁ θάνατος τῶν κακῶν ἐστιν, ἔσται καὶ τὸ
θανατοῦν τῶν κακῶν ἅμα καὶ φευκτῶν. τοίνυν καὶ
κοινῶς, εἰ τὸ κακὸν φευκτόν ἐστιν, ἐξ ἀνάγκης καὶ
τὸ ποιητικὸν τοῦ κακοῦ φευκτὸν ἔσται καὶ κακόν.
120 τὰ δὲ λεγόμενά τισι φύσει ἀγαθὰ καὶ κακῶν
ἐστι ποιητικά, ὡς διδάξομεν. δυνάμει ἄρα κακά

¹ ⟨τὸ⟩ add. cj. Bekk.

of his joy or on account of keeping watch over his acquisition. And the same argument applies also to 117 evil ; for neither he who is without it is care-free, as he is no little tormented by the perturbation caused both by avoiding it and by taking precautions ; nor does he who is in an evil state have any cessation of his torments, through taking thought—

How to escape from the steep of destruction.[a]

But if a man should declare that nothing is by 118 nature an object of desire any more than of avoidance, nor of avoidance more than of desire, each thing which occurs being relative, and, owing to differences of times and circumstances, being at one time desirable, at another to be avoided, he will live happily and unperturbed, being neither exalted at good, as good, nor depressed at evil, manfully accepting what befalls him of necessity, and being liberated from the distress due to the belief that something evil or good is present. This, in fact, will accrue to him from his belief that nothing is good by nature or evil. Therefore it is not possible to live happily if one posits any things good or evil by nature.

Moreover, that which is productive of any evil is 119 certainly to be avoided, just as is the evil. For instance, if pain is an evil, certainly also what is productive of the pain will take rank with the pain as a thing to be avoided ; and if death is one of the evils, what causes death will also be at once both evil and a thing to be avoided. So then in general, if evil is to be avoided, what is productive of evil will of necessity be a thing to be avoided and an evil. But, as we shall 120 show, things which are said by some to be good are also productive of evils. Therefore the things which

[a] Homer, *Il.* xiv. 507.

ἐστι τὰ ὑπό τινων λεγόμενα ἀγαθά, καὶ διὰ τοῦτο
κακοδαιμονίας τυγχάνει αἴτια. διὰ γὰρ δὴ τὰ τοιαῦτα ἀγαθὰ πάντα ἐστὶ τὰ κακά, φιλαργυρία τε
καὶ φιλοδοξία καὶ φιλονεικία καὶ φιληδονία καὶ
121 τἆλλα ὁπόσα τούτοις ἐμφερῆ ἐστίν. ἕκαστος γὰρ
τῶν ἀνθρώπων τὸ δοξασθὲν ὑπὸ αὐτοῦ ἀγαθόν
τε καὶ αἱρετὸν συντόνως διώκων καὶ μετὰ σφοδροῦ
πείσματος λεληθότως εἰς τὴν ἀγχίθυρον κακίαν
ἐμπίπτει.   οἷον (ἔσται γὰρ τὸ λεγόμενον σαφὲς
122 τῶν οἰκείων ἡμῖν τεθέντων ὑποδειγμάτων) ὁ μὲν
τὸν πλοῦτον ἀγαθὸν εἶναι προειληφὼς ὀφείλει
πάντα ἐσπευσμένως ποιεῖν εἰς τὸ τυχεῖν τοῦ
πλούτου, καὶ ἑκάστοτε πρὸς ἑαυτὸν τὸ κωμικὸν
ἀναμελετᾶν παράγγελμα,

κέρδαιν᾿ ἑταῖρε καὶ θέρους καὶ χειμῶνος,

καὶ τὸ τραγικὸν ἀποδέχεσθαι,

ὦ χρυσὲ, δεξίωμα κάλλιστον βροτοῖς.

τὸ δέ γε πάντα ποιεῖν εἰς τὸ πλούτου τυχεῖν οὐκ
ἄλλο τί ἐστιν ἢ φιλαργυρεῖν. ὁ ἄρα τὸν πλοῦτον
μέγιστον ἀγαθὸν ἰνδαλλόμενος ἐν τῷ σπεύδειν ἐπὶ
123 τοῦτον γίνεται φιλάργυρος. πάλιν ὁ τὴν δόξαν
αἱρετὴν ὑποτιθέμενος συντόνως ἐφίεται τῆς δόξης,
τὸ δὲ συντόνως ἐφίεσθαι τῆς δόξης ἐστὶ φιλοδοξεῖν·
τὸ ἄρα τὴν δόξαν αἱρετὸν καὶ φύσει ἀγαθὸν ὑπο-
τίθεσθαι μεγάλου κακοῦ τινὸς γεννητικόν ἐστι,
124 τῆς φιλοδοξίας. καὶ ἐπὶ τῆς ἡδονῆς δὲ ταὐτὸν
εὑρήσομεν· τοῖς γὰρ ἐπὶ τὴν τεῦξιν αὐτῆς σπεύ-
δουσιν ἀνάγκη ⟨ἕξιν⟩[1] τινὰ μοχθηρὰν[2] συνεξακο-
λουθεῖν, τὴν φιληδονίαν. ὥστε εἰ τὸ ποιητικὸν

---

[1] ⟨ἕξιν⟩ addo: ⟨ταραχήν⟩ cj. Bekk.
[2] μοχθηρὰν cj. Bekk.: μοχθηρὰ mss.

are said by some to be good are potentially evil, and on account of this are causes of unhappiness. For, in fact, it is owing to such goods that all these evils exist,—love of money and love of fame and love of strife and love of pleasure and all the other things which resemble these. For it is by pursuing earnestly 121 and with extreme persistence what he himself believes to be good and desirable that each man unwittingly falls into the evil lying next-door.[a] Thus for instance (for our meaning will be clear if we take examples familiar to us), the man who has already assumed that 122 wealth is a good must make every effort for the obtaining of wealth, and keep always rehearsing to himself the injunction of the Comedy [b]—

> Winter and summer get thee gain, good sir;

and he must accept what the Tragedy says [c]—

> Thou fairest of all boons to mortals, Gold!

But to make every effort for the gaining of wealth is nothing else than to be a money-lover. Therefore he who imagines wealth to be the greatest good, in his zeal for this, becomes a money-lover. Again, the 123 man who supposes fame to be desirable earnestly strives for fame, and the earnest striving for fame is love of fame; therefore the supposition that fame is desirable and good by nature serves to generate a great evil, love of fame. And in the case of pleasure 124 we shall find the same thing; for to those who are eager for its acquisition there results necessarily a certain depraved condition, love of pleasure. So that, if what is productive of evils is evil, and it has

---

[a] *Cf.* Genesis iv. 7 " Sin lieth at the door."
[b] *Frag. Com. adesp.* 1255 (Kock).
[c] Eurip. *Frag.* 324 (Nauck).

τῶν κακῶν κακόν ἐστι, δέδεικται δὲ τὰ δοξασθέντα
τισὶ τῶν φιλοσόφων ἀγαθὰ πάντων τῶν κακῶν
ποιητικά, ῥητέον τά τισι δοξασθέντα ἀγαθὰ τῇ
δυνάμει τυγχάνειν κακά.

125 Καὶ μὴν οὐδὲ ἔνεστι λέγειν τοῖς ἐξ ἐναντίας ὡς
κατὰ μὲν τὴν δίωξιν αὐτῶν καὶ τὴν ἐπ' αὐτὰ
ὁρμὴν πάρεστί τι τοῖς ὁρμῶσι καὶ διώκουσι κακόν,
οἷον τῷ μὲν τὸν πλοῦτον μετιόντι ἡ φιλαργυρία,
τῷ δὲ τὴν δόξαν ἡ φιλοδοξία, τῷ δ' ἄλλο τι ἀλλοία
τις ταραχή, κατὰ δὲ τὴν τεῦξιν αὐτῶν ἀπαλλαγὴ
γίνεται τῶν ταραχῶν καὶ ἀνάπαυλα τῆς πρότερον
126 ὀχλήσεως· ὁ γὰρ τυχὼν τοῦ πλούτου οὐκέτι
συντόνως ἐπιζητεῖ τὸν πλοῦτον, καὶ ὁ λαβόμενος
τῆς ἡδονῆς λύσει τὸ σύντονον τῆς περὶ αὐτὴν
σπουδῆς. καθάπερ οὖν τὰ κρημνοβατοῦντα τῶν
ζώων ὑπὲρ τοῦ πιεῖν δι' ἀλγηδόνος ἵεται ἐπὶ τὴν
ἡδονὴν καὶ ἅμα τῷ κορεσθῆναι παύεται τῶν πρὶν
μόχθων, οὕτω καὶ ὁ ἄνθρωπος ἐν μὲν τῷ ἐπείγεσθαι
πρὸς τὸ ἀγαθὸν ἐξ ἀνάγκης ὀχλεῖται, τυχὼν δὲ οὗ
127 ἐπόθει καὶ τῆς ὀχλήσεως ἀπαλλάττεται.   οὐ
δὴ δυνατὸν εἶναί φαμεν ταῦτα λέγειν, οὐδ' οὕτως
ἔχειν τὸ πρᾶγμα. κἂν γὰρ τύχωσι τῶν νομιζομένων αὐτοῖς ἀγαθῶν, συνέχονται καὶ ἐπι-
λυποῦνται μᾶλλον, ὅτι οὐ μόνοι ταῦτα ἔχουσιν·
σὺν τούτῳ γὰρ τἀγαθὰ τίμια καὶ περιμάχητα
νομίζουσι, σὺν τῷ μόνοι ταῦτα κεκτῆσθαι, διὸ
καὶ ζῆλος αὐτοῖς ἐμφύεται πρὸς τοὺς πέλας καὶ
βασκανία καὶ φθόνος. ὥστε καὶ τὴν δίωξιν τῶν
λεγομένων ὑπάρχειν ἀγαθῶν οὐκ ἀταλαίπωρον
446

been shown that the things which are believed by some philosophers to be good are productive of all the evils, one must declare that the things believed by some to be good are potentially evil.

Moreover, it is not possible for our opponents to 125 argue that although, through their pursuit of them and their impulse towards them, there accrues some evil to the subjects of the impulse and the pursuit (love of money, for example, to the man who goes after wealth, and love of fame to him who goes after fame, and some other kind of perturbation to him who is after something else), yet as a result of their acquisition there comes about a relief from the perturbations and a cessation of the previous distress ; for he who has acquired the wealth no longer seeks 126 earnestly after wealth, and he who has got the pleasure will relax the intensity of his zeal for it. For just as the animals which haunt the crags are driven for the sake of drinking through pain to pleasure and as soon as they are satisfied cease from their previous distress, so also man is necessarily distressed during his efforts after the good, but when he has gained what he yearned for he is also relieved from his distress.—But we assert that it is not possible to 127 argue thus, nor is this the truth of the matter. For even if men obtain what they regard as goods, they are still more oppressed and vexed that they are not alone in possessing them ; for it is when accompanied with this—with their being alone in possessing them—that they regard the goods as precious and highly to be prized, and hence they are infected with jealousy towards their neighbours and ill-will and envy. So that while the pursuit of the things said to be goods is not devoid of misery, the

εἶναι, καὶ τὴν περίκτησιν πλειόνων κακῶν ὑπάρχειν
128 ἐπισύστασιν.   πάλιν τε καὶ περὶ αὐτῶν τῶν
κακῶν ὁ αὐτός ἐστι λόγος. προειληφὼς γάρ τις
εἶναί τινα φύσει κακά, καθάπερ ἀδοξίαν πενίαν
πήρωσιν ἀλγηδόνα νόσον, κοινῶς ἀφροσύνην, οὐ
μόνοις ὀχλεῖται τούτοις ἀλλὰ καὶ παμπληθέσιν
129 ἄλλοις τοῖς δι’ αὐτὰ κακοῖς. παρόντων μὲν γὰρ
αὐτῶν χειμάζεται οὐχ ὑπ’ αὐτῶν μόνον ἀλλὰ καὶ
τῆς περὶ αὐτῶν δόξης, καθ’ ἣν πεπίστευκεν ὅτι
κακὸν αὐτῷ πάρεστιν, καὶ ὡς ὑπὸ μείζονος κακοῦ
πορθεῖται τῆς τοιαύτης προλήψεως. μὴ παρόντων
δὲ ὁμοίως οὐκ ἀναπαύεται, ἀλλ’ ἤτοι προφυλατ-
τόμενος τὸ μέλλον ἢ δεδιὼς σύνοικον ἔχει τὴν
130 μέριμναν. λόγου δὲ παραστήσαντος ὅτι οὐδὲν
τούτων φύσει ἐστὶν ἀγαθὸν ἢ φύσει κακόν, λύσις
ἔσται τῆς ταραχῆς καὶ εἰρηναῖος ἡμᾶς ἐκδέξεται
βίος.

Ἀλλὰ γὰρ ὅτι μὲν διὰ τὰ δοξαζόμενά τισιν
ἀγαθὰ πλῆθος ἐπισυμβαίνει κακῶν καὶ διὰ τὰ κακὰ
ἕτερα γίνεται κακά, ὡς χάριν αὐτῶν ἀνέφικτον
γίνεσθαι τὴν εὐδαιμονίαν, ἐκ τῶν εἰρημένων
131 συμφανές· ἀκολούθως δὲ ὑποδεικτέον ὅτι οὐδὲ
βοηθείας ἐνδέχεται τυχεῖν διὰ τῆς δογματικῆς
πορευομένους φιλοσοφίας. ὑποκειμένου γάρ τινος
φύσει ἀγαθοῦ ἢ φύσει κακοῦ, ὁ παραμυθούμενος
τὸν ταρασσόμενον ἐπὶ τῷ συντόνως διώκειν
τἀγαθὸν ὡς ἀγαθὸν ἢ σφοδρῶς φεύγειν τὸ κακὸν
ὡς κακὸν καταστέλλει τὴν ταραχὴν ἤτοι τοῦτο
λέγων, ὅτι καθῆκόν ἐστι μήτε τἀγαθὸν διώκειν
132 μήτε τὸ κακὸν φεύγειν, ἢ τοῦτο παριστὰς ὅτι τόδε
μὲν τὸ διωκόμενον ὑπ’ αὐτοῦ ἐλαχίστην ἔχει
ἀξίαν, καὶ οὐκ ἔστιν οἰκεῖον αὐτὸ διώκειν, τόδε δὲ

acquisition of them is the heaping up of more numerous evils.—And again, the same account holds 128 good also of the evils themselves. For when a man has a preconception that certain things are by nature evil (such as ill-repute, poverty, lameness, pain, disease, folly in general), he is not distressed by these alone but also by hosts of other evils due to them. For when they are present he is tempest-tost not only 129 by them but also by his belief about them, through which he is convinced that evil is present with him ; and by such a preconception he is devastated as by a greater evil. And he is equally devoid of rest when they are not present, and, either through taking precautions against the future or through fear, he has anxiety as his house-mate. But when reasoning has 130 established that none of these things is good by nature or evil by nature, we shall have a release from perturbation and there will await us a peaceful life.

Well then, it is plain from what has been said that a multitude of evils occur as the result of the things believed by some to be goods, and as a result of the evils other evils come about, so that owing to these happiness becomes unattainable. And, in the next 131 place, we must show that we cannot gain assistance either by taking the road of the dogmatic philosophy. For if anything good by nature or evil by nature is assumed to exist, he who is consoling the man who is perturbed owing to his strenuous pursuit of the good as good, or his excessive avoidance of the evil as evil, checks the perturbation either by declaring that it is a duty neither to pursue the good nor to avoid the evil, or by showing that the object which the man 132 pursues possesses very little value and that it is not proper to pursue it, whereas this other object has

μείζονα, καὶ ἁρμόζει αὐτὸ μετέρχεσθαι, οἷον ἐλάττονα μὲν ἔχει ἀξίαν ὁ πλοῦτος μείζονα δὲ ἡ ἀρετή,
καὶ οὐκ ἐκεῖνον ἀλλὰ ταύτην διωκτέον, ἢ ὅτι
τοῦτο μὲν ὀλιγωφελὲς ὂν πολλὰς ἔχει τὰς ὀχλήσεις,
τοῦτο δὲ πολυωφελὲς καθεστὼς ὀλίγας ἔχει τὰς
133 ὀχλήσεις. ἀλλὰ τὸ μὲν λέγειν ὅτι οὔτε τἀγαθὸν
οἰκεῖόν ἐστι συντόνως διώκειν οὔτε τὸ κακὸν
φεύγειν, παρὰ τὴν τῶν δογματικῶν ἀξίωσίν ἐστιν,
ἀεί ποτε τὴν ἐκλογὴν καὶ ἀπεκλογὴν τούτων τάς
134 τε αἱρέσεις καὶ φυγὰς θρυλούντων. τὸ δὲ φάναι
τόδε μὲν μὴ δεῖν διώκειν ὡς ταπεινόν, ἐπὶ τόδε δ'
ἐπείγεσθαι ὡς λαμπρότερον, ἀνδρῶν ἦν οὐκ ἀπο-
λυόντων τὴν ταραχὴν ἀλλὰ μεταγωγὴν ταύτης
ποιουμένων· ὡς γὰρ τὸ πρῶτον διώκων τις
ὠχλεῖτο, οὕτω καὶ τὸ δεύτερον διώκων τις ὀχλη-
135 θήσεται, ὥστε νόσον ἀντὶ νόσου ποιεῖν τὸν τοῦ
φιλοσόφου λόγον, ἐπείπερ τὸν ἐπὶ πλοῦτον ἢ δόξαν
ἢ ὑγείαν ὡς ἀγαθὸν ὁρμῶντα ἀποστρέφων εἰς τὸ
μὴ ταῦτα διώκειν ἀλλὰ τὸ καλόν, εἰ τύχοι, καὶ τὴν
ἀρετήν, οὐκ ἐλευθεροῖ τῆς διώξεως ἀλλ' ἐφ' ἑτέραν
136 μετατίθησι δίωξιν. ὡς οὖν ὁ ἰατρὸς ἀναιρῶν
μὲν πλευρῖτιν ποιῶν δὲ περιπνευμονίαν, ἢ ἀνα-
σκευάζων μὲν φρενῖτιν ἀντεισάγων δὲ λήθαργον,
οὐκ ἀπαλλάττει τὸν κίνδυνον ἀλλ' ἐναλλάττει,
οὕτω καὶ ὁ φιλόσοφος ἑτέραν ταραχὴν ἀνθ' ἑτέρας
137 εἰσηγούμενος οὐ βοηθεῖ τῷ ταραττομένῳ. οὐ γὰρ
ἔνεστι λέγειν ὅτι ἡ μὲν ἀντεισαγομένη ταραχὴ
μέτριός ἐστιν ἡ δὲ ἀναιρουμένη σφοδροτέρα. οἵαν
γὰρ εἶχε δόξαν ὁ ταραττόμενος περὶ τοῦ πρότερον
450

greater value and to follow after it is a fitting thing
(wealth, for example, possesses less and virtue more
value, and one ought not to pursue the former but
the latter) ; or ⟨by showing⟩ that this object is of
little use and entails many annoyances, whereas that
object is of great use and entails few annoyances.
But to declare that it is not proper either to pursue 133
the good or to avoid the evil strenuously is contrary
to the view of the Dogmatists, who are always harp-
ing on the selection or rejection of these things and
on desires and avoidances. And to say that one 134
ought not to pursue this object as being base, but to
strive after that object as being more noble, is the
action of men who are not getting rid of the perturbation but effecting a change in its position ; for
just as the man who pursued the first object was
distressed, so also he who pursues the second will be
distressed, so that the philosopher's discourse creates 135
a new disease in place of the old, since, by turning
away the man who strives after wealth or fame or
health, as being a good, towards the pursuit not of
these things but of " the fair " (shall we say) and of
virtue, he does not set him free from the pursuit
but makes him change over to another pursuit.—As, 136
then, the physician, if he does away with a pleurisy
but creates inflammation of the lungs, or removes
brain-fever but in its place introduces lethargy, does
not get rid of the danger but shifts it over, so also
the philosopher, who introduces one perturbation
in place of another, gives no succour to the person
perturbed. For it is not possible to argue that the 137
perturbation introduced is a moderate one, whereas
the one removed was more violent. For the perturbed person has the same sort of belief about the

διωκομένου, τοιαύτην ἔχει καὶ περὶ τοῦ δευτέρου·
ἐδόξαζε δὲ τό γε πρῶτον ὡς ἀγαθόν, καὶ διὰ
138 τοῦτο ἔσπευδεν ἐπ᾽ αὐτό· τοίνυν καὶ τὸ δεύτερον
ἀγαθὸν εἶναι δοξάζων καὶ ἐπ᾽ ἴσης ἐπ᾽ αὐτὸ σπεύ-
δων τὴν ἴσην ἕξει ταραχήν, τάχα δὲ καὶ σφοδρο-
τέραν, ὅσῳ μεταπέπεισται εἰς τὸ μείζονος ἀξίας
εἶναι τὸ νῦν ὑπ᾽ αὐτοῦ διωκόμενον. οὐκοῦν εἰ
ἕτερον ἀνθ᾽ ἑτέρου ὁ φιλόσοφος παρασκευάζοι τὸν
ὀχλούμενον διώκειν, οὐκ ἀπολύσει τῆς ὀχλήσεως.
139 εἰ δ᾽ ἁπλῶς διδάσκει ὅτι τουτὶ μὲν ὀλιγωφελές
ἐστι, πλείονας δ᾽ ἔχει τὰς ὀχλήσεις, ⟨τουτὶ δὲ
πολυωφελὲς καθεστὼς ὀλίγας ἔχει τὰς ὀχλήσεις,⟩[1]
σύγκρισιν ἔσται ποιῶν αἱρέσεως καὶ φυγῆς πρὸς
ἑτέραν αἵρεσιν καὶ φυγήν, καὶ οὐκ ἀναίρεσιν τῆς
ταραχῆς. ὅπερ ἄτοπον· ὁ γὰρ ὀχλούμενος οὐ
βούλεται μαθεῖν τί μᾶλλον ὀχλεῖ καὶ τί ἧττον,
140 ἀλλ᾽ ἀπαλλαγῆναι τῆς ὀχλήσεως πεπόθηκεν. μόνως
οὖν ἔσται φυγεῖν ταύτην, εἰ ὑποδείξαιμεν τῷ
ταραττομένῳ κατὰ τὴν τοῦ κακοῦ φυγὴν ἢ κατὰ
τὴν τοῦ ἀγαθοῦ δίωξιν ὅτι οὔτε ἀγαθόν τι ἔστι
φύσει οὔτε κακόν,

ἀλλὰ πρὸς ἀνθρώπων ταῦτα νόῳ κέκριται

κατὰ τὸν Τίμωνα. τὸ δέ γε διδάσκειν τὸ τοιοῦτον
ἴδιον τῆς σκέψεως. ταύτης ἄρα ἦν τὸ εὐδαίμονα
βίον περιποιεῖν.

---

[1] ⟨τουτὶ . . . ὀχλήσεις⟩ add. cj. Bekk.

second object of pursuit as he had about the previous
one ; but he believed that the first object was good
and because of this he went after it eagerly ; so, as 138
he also believes that the second is good and goes after
it with equal eagerness, he will be equally perturbed,
or perhaps even more violently in so far as he has
been converted to the belief that his present object of
pursuit is of greater value.   If, then, the philosopher
should cause the distressed person to pursue one
object in place of another, he will not rid him of his
distress. And if he simply teaches that this object is 139
of little use but entails many annoyances, ⟨while that
object is of great use and entails few annoyances,⟩ he
will be making a comparison between one desire and
avoidance and another desire and avoidance, and
will not be removing the perturbation.   But this is
absurd ; for the person in distress does not wish to
learn which thing is more distressing and which less,
but yearns to be rid of his distress.   It will only be 140
possible, then, to avoid this by making it evident to
the person who is in distress, owing to his avoidance
of evil or his pursuit of good, that there does not exist
anything which is either good or evil by nature,—

> But by the judgement of men Sentence upon them is
> pass'd,

as Timon says.   And to teach this is, in fact, the
peculiar task of Scepticism ; therefore it belongs to
it to secure a happy life.

SEXTUS EMPIRICUS

Ε΄.—ΕΙ Ο ΠΕΡΙ ΤΗΣ ΤΩΝ ΑΓΑΘΩΝ ΚΑΙ ΚΑΚΩΝ ΦΥΣΕΩΣ
ΕΠΕΧΩΝ ΚΑΤΑ ΠΑΝΤΑ ΕΣΤΙΝ ΕΥΔΑΙΜΩΝ

141 Εὐδαίμων μὲν ἐστιν ὁ ἀταράχως διεξάγων καὶ
ὡς ἔλεγεν ὁ Τίμων, ἐν ἡσυχίᾳ καὶ γαληνότητι
καθεστώς·

πάντῃ γὰρ ἐπεῖχε γαλήνη

καὶ

τὸν δ᾽ ὡς οὖν ἐνόησ᾽ ἐν νηνεμίῃσι γαλήνης.

τῶν δὲ λεγομένων ὑπάρχειν ἀγαθῶν τε καὶ κακῶν
τὰ μὲν κατὰ δόξαν εἰσῆκται τὰ δὲ κατ᾽ ἀνάγκην.
142 ἀλλὰ κατὰ μὲν [λογικὴν]¹ δόξαν εἰσῆκται ὅσα κατὰ
κρίσιν διώκουσιν ἄνθρωποι ἢ φεύγουσιν, οἷον ἐν
μὲν τοῖς ἐκτὸς αἱρετὰ λέγεται καὶ ἀγαθὰ πλοῦτος
καὶ δόξα καὶ εὐγένεια καὶ φιλία καὶ πᾶν τὸ ἐοικός,
ἐν δὲ τοῖς περὶ σῶμα κάλλος ἰσχὺς εὐεξία, ἐν
δὲ τοῖς περὶ ψυχὴν ἀνδρία δικαιοσύνη φρόνησις,
κοινῶς ἀρετή, καὶ φευκτὰ τὰ ἐναντία τούτοις.
143 κατ᾽ ἀνάγκην δὲ παρῆλθεν ὁπόσα κατ᾽ ἄλογον
αἰσθήσεως πάθος συνίσταται περὶ ἡμᾶς, καὶ ὅσα
φυσική τις ἀνάγκη παρέχει, "ἑκὼν δ᾽ οὐκ ἄν τις
144 ἕλοιτο" ἢ φύγοι, ὡς ἀλγηδὼν καὶ ἡδονή. διόπερ
τοιαύτης οὔσης ἐν τοῖς πράγμασι διαφορᾶς, περὶ
μὲν τοῦ μόνον ἀταράχως διεξάγειν ἐν τοῖς κατὰ
δόξαν ἀγαθοῖς καὶ κακοῖς τὸν περὶ πάντων ἐπ-
έχοντα ἤδη παρεστήσαμεν καὶ πρότερον, ὅτε περὶ
τοῦ σκεπτικοῦ τέλους διελεγόμεθα, καὶ ἐπὶ τοῦ
παρόντος, ὅτε ἐδείκνυμεν ὅτι οὐκ ἔστιν εὐδαιμονεῖν

¹ [λογικὴν] secl. Heintz.

ᵃ From Homer, *Il.* iii. 66.
ᵇ *Cf. P.H.* i. 25 ff.   ᶜ *Cf.* §§ 110 ff. *supra.*

CHAPTER V.—IS HE WHO SUSPENDS JUDGEMENT RE-
GARDING THE NATURE OF THINGS GOOD AND EVIL
IN ALL RESPECTS HAPPY?

He, then, is happy who lives to the end without 141
perturbation and, as Timon said, existing in a state
of quietness and calm—

> For on all sides calm was prevailing,

and—

> Him when thus I descried in a calm with no winds to disquiet.

And of the goods and evils which are said to exist
some are introduced by belief, others by necessity.
Thus by [rational] belief are introduced all those 142
which men pursue or avoid of their own judgement,—
as, for example, amongst things external, wealth and
fame and noble birth and friendship, and everything
of the kind, are called desirable and good; and,
amongst qualities of the body, beauty and strength
and sound condition; and, amongst qualities of the
soul, courage and justice and wisdom and virtue in
general; and the opposites of these are regarded as
things to be avoided. But by necessity are brought 143
about all such things as befall us because of an
irrational affection of sense, and all that some natural
necessity brings about, " but no one would willingly
choose them," *a* or avoid them,—such as pain and
pleasure. Hence, since there exists such a difference 144
as this in these things, the fact that it is only the man
who suspends judgement about all things who lives
to the end an unperturbed life in respect of the goods
and evils due to belief we have already established,
both in our previous discussion of the Sceptic " end," *b*
and also on the present occasion *c* when we showed
that it is not possible to be happy if one assumes the

145 φύσει ἀγαθόν τι καὶ κακὸν ὑποστησάμενον. ὁ μὲν
γὰρ τοῦτο ποιῶν ἀνηνύτοις συμπεριεφέρετο τara-
χαῖς, τὰ μὲν φεύγων τὰ δὲ διώκων, καὶ πολλὰ μὲν
αὑτῷ ἐπισπώμενος κακὰ διὰ τἀγαθά, ἐν πολλα-
πλασίοσι δὲ τριβόμενος κακοῖς διὰ τὴν περὶ τῶν
146 κακῶν δόξαν.   οἷον ὁ λέγων, εἰ τύχοι, ἀγαθὸν
μὲν τὸν πλοῦτον κακὸν δὲ τὴν πενίαν, μὴ ἔχων μὲν
τὸν πλοῦτον διχῶς ταράττεται, καὶ ὅτι οὐκ ἔχει
τὸ ἀγαθὸν καὶ ὅτι πραγματεύεται τὴν περίκτησιν
αὑτοῦ, κτησάμενος δ' αὐτὸν κατὰ τρεῖς τιμωρεῖται
τρόπους, καὶ ὅτι πέραν τοῦ μετρίου γέγηθε, καὶ
ὅτι πραγματεύεται εἰς τὸ παραμένειν αὑτῷ τὸν
πλοῦτον, καὶ ὅτι ἀγωνιᾷ καὶ δέδιεν αὐτοῦ τὴν
147 ἀποβολήν. ὁ δὲ μήτε ἐν τοῖς φύσει ἀγαθοῖς
τάττων τὸν πλοῦτον μήτε ἐν τοῖς φύσει κακοῖς,
τὴν δὲ " οὐ μᾶλλον " προφερόμενος φωνήν, οὔτε
ἐπὶ τῇ ἀπουσίᾳ τούτου ταράττεται οὔτε ἐπὶ τῇ
παρουσίᾳ γέγηθεν, μένει δὲ καθ' ἑκάτερον ἀτάραχος.
ὥστ' ἐν μὲν τοῖς κατὰ δόξαν νομιζομένοις ἀγαθοῖς
τε καὶ κακοῖς καὶ ἐν ταῖς τούτων αἱρέσεσι καὶ
148 φυγαῖς τελέως ἐστὶν εὐδαίμων, ἐν δὲ τοῖς κατ'
αἴσθησιν καὶ ἀλόγοις κινήμασι μετριάζει.[1] τὰ
γὰρ μὴ παρὰ τὴν τοῦ λόγου διαστροφὴν συμβαίνοντα καὶ τὴν φαύλην δόξαν, ἀλλὰ κατὰ ἀκούσιον
τῆς αἰσθήσεως πάθος, ἀμήχανόν ἐστιν ὑπὸ τοῦ
149 κατὰ τὴν σκέψιν λόγου ἀπαλλάττεσθαι· τῷ γὰρ
διὰ λιμὸν ἢ δίψος ὀχλουμένῳ οὐ δυνατὸν ἐμποιεῖν
πεῖσμα διὰ τοῦ κατὰ τὴν σκέψιν λόγου ὅτι οὐκ
ὀχλεῖται, καὶ τῷ ἐν ταῖς τούτων παρηγορίαις

[1] μετριάζει cj. Bekk.: εἰκάζει mss. (? ἀναχάζει).

existence of anything good and evil by nature. For 145
he who does this is tossed about with endless perturbations, through avoiding these things and pursuing those, and drawing upon himself many evils
because of the goods, and being afflicted by many
times more evils because of his belief about evils.—
Thus the man who declares that wealth (shall we say ?) 146
is a good and poverty an evil is perturbed in two ways
if he has not wealth,—both because he has not the
good and because he is toiling for the acquisition of
it,—and when he has acquired it he is punished in
three ways,—because he is immoderately overjoyed,
and because he toils to ensure that his wealth stays with
him, and because he is painfully anxious and dreads the
loss of it. But he who ranks wealth neither amongst 147
the natural goods nor amongst the natural evils, but
utters the formula " Not more," [a] is neither perturbed
at its absence nor overjoyed at its presence, but in
either case remains unperturbed. So that in respect
of the things held, as a matter of belief, to be good
and bad, and in respect of the desires and avoidances
thereof, he is perfectly happy, while in respect of the 148
sensible and irrational affections he preserves a due
mean. For the things which occur, not because of
a distortion of the reason and foolish belief but,
owing to an involuntary affection of the sense it is
impossible to get rid of by means of the Sceptical
argument [b] ; for in a man who is distressed because 149
of hunger or thirst, it is not feasible to implant, by
means of the Sceptical argument, the conviction that
he is not in distress, and in the man who is overjoyed

[a] For this Sceptic formula (denoting suspense of judgement) see *P.H.* i. 187 ff.
[b] *Cf. P.H.* i. 30, iii. 237.

διαχεομένῳ οὐκ ἐνδέχεται πειθὼ ἐμποιεῖν περὶ
150 τοῦ ὅτι οὐ διαχεῖται.   τί οὖν, φασίν, ὄφελος
ὑμῖν, οἱ δογματικοί, πρὸς εὐδαιμονίαν ἐκ τῆς
ἐποχῆς, εἰ ταράττεσθαι πάντως δεῖ καὶ ταραττο-
μένους κακοδαιμονεῖν; μέγα, φήσομεν, ὄφελος.
καὶ γὰρ εἰ ταράττεται ὁ περὶ πάντων ἐπέχων κατὰ
τὴν τοῦ ἀλγύνοντος παρουσίαν, ἀλλ᾽ εὐφορώτερον
παρὰ τὸν ἀπὸ τῶν δογμάτων φέρει τὴν ὄχλησιν,
151 πρῶτον μὲν ὅτι οὐκ ἔστιν ἴσον ἄπειρα τῷ πλήθει
τἀγαθὰ διώκοντα καὶ περιστάμενον τὰ κακὰ ὡς
ὑπὸ Ἐρινύων ἐλαύνεσθαι τῶν κατὰ τὰς διώξεις
καὶ φυγὰς ταραχῶν, ἢ τοῦτο μὲν μὴ πάσχειν, ἓν
δὲ μόνον ἐξ ἁπάντων ἀποτεμνόμενον κακὸν τούτου
152 τὴν ἔκκλισιν καὶ φυλακὴν πραγματεύεσθαι.   δεύτερον δὲ καὶ τοῦτο ὅπερ φεύγουσιν οἱ ἐφεκτικοὶ ὡς
κακόν, οὐκ ἄγαν ἐστὶ ταρακτικόν. ἢ γὰρ μικρός
τις ὁ πόνος ἐστί, καθάπερ ὁ καθ᾽ ἑκάστην ἡμέραν
ἐγγινόμενος ἡμῖν λιμὸς ἢ δίψος ἢ ψῦχος ἢ θάλπος
153 ἤ τι τῶν παραπλησίων, ἢ τοὐναντίον σφοδρότατος
καὶ ἀκρότατος, ὡς ἐπὶ τῶν ἀνηκέστοις συνεχο-
μένων βασάνοις, δι᾽ ὧν πολλάκις οἱ ἰατροὶ ἀν-
ωδύνους πορίζουσι δυνάμεις πρὸς τὸ βραχεῖάν τινα
λαβεῖν ἀναστροφὴν εἰς βοήθειαν, ἢ μέσος καὶ
154 παρατείνων, καθάπερ ὁ ἔν τισι νόσοις. τούτων
δὲ ὁ μὲν καθ᾽ ἑκάστην ἡμέραν συναντῶν εὐπορί-
στους ἔχων τὰς παρηγορίας, τροφὴν καὶ πόμα καὶ
σκέπην, πρὸς ἐλάχιστον ταράττει· ὁ δὲ ἀκρότατος
καὶ εἰς τὰ μάλιστα ταρακτικώτατος, ἀλλά τοί
γε πρὸς ἀκαρὲς ἀστραπῆς τρόπον δειματώσας ἢ
155 ἀναιρεῖ ἢ ἀναιρεῖται. ὁ δὲ μέσος καὶ παρατείνων
οὔτε παρ᾽ ὅλον ἐστὶ τὸν βίον οὔτε συνεχὴς τὴν

at getting relief from these sufferings it is not in its
power to implant the belief that he is not overjoyed.
—What help, then, towards happiness (ask the Dogma- 150
tists) do we get from suspension of judgement if one
has to be perturbed in any case and unhappy because
perturbed? Great help, we shall reply. For even
though he who suspends judgement about all things is
perturbed owing to the presence of what causes pain,
yet as compared with the Dogmatist he bears the
distress more lightly, because, firstly, to pursue goods 151
and to shun evils which are endless in number and thus
to be harassed by the perturbations due to these pur-
suits and avoidances as by Furies is much worse than
not to suffer thus but merely to be engaged in avoiding
and guarding against only one isolated form of evil.
And, secondly, even the thing which the Ephectics [a] 152
avoid as evil, is not excessively perturbing. For the
suffering is either small, such as that which befalls us
every day,—hunger or thirst or cold or heat or something similar ;—or, on the contrary, it is very violent 153
and intense, as in the case of those afflicted with
incurable torments, during which the doctors often
provide powerful anodynes to assist the patient in
obtaining some relief ; or else it is moderate and
protracted, as in some diseases. And of these, that 154
which faces us every day perturbs us least as the
remedies for it (food and drink and shelter) are easy
to provide ; and that which is most intense and in the
highest degree perturbing terrifies us, after all, but
for a moment, like a lightning-flash, and then either
destroys us or is destroyed. And the moderate and 155
protracted kind neither remains all through life nor

[a] *i.e.* the Sceptics (as " suspenders " of judgement), *cf.*
P.H. i. 7, 196.

φύσιν ἀλλὰ πολλὰς διαναπαύσεις ἔχων καὶ ῥαστώ-
νας· διηνεκὴς γὰρ ὢν οὐκ ἂν παρέτεινεν.
μέτριος οὖν ἐστὶ καὶ οὐχ οὕτω φοβερὰ ἡ περὶ τὸν
156 σκεπτικὸν συμβαίνουσα ταραχή. οὐ μὴν ἀλλὰ κἂν
μεγίστη τις ᾖ, οὐχ ἡμᾶς αἰτιᾶσθαι δεῖ τοὺς
ἀκουσίως καὶ κατ' ἀνάγκην πάσχοντας, ἀλλὰ τὴν
φύσιν,

ᾗ νόμων οὐδὲν μέλει,

καὶ τὸν δοξαστικῶς καὶ κατὰ κρίσιν ἐπισπώμενον
ἑαυτῷ τὸ κακόν. ὥσπερ γὰρ τὸν πυρέττοντα οὐκ
αἰτιατέον ὅτι πυρέττει, ἀκουσίως γὰρ πυρέττει,
τὸν δὲ μὴ ἀπεχόμενον τῶν ἀσυμφόρων αἰτιατέον,
ἐπ' αὐτῷ γὰρ ἔκειτο τὸ ἀπέχεσθαι τῶν ἀσυμφόρων,
οὕτω τὸν μὲν ταραττόμενον ἐπὶ παροῦσι τοῖς
157 ἀλγεινοῖς οὐκ αἰτιατέον· οὐ γὰρ παρ' αὐτὸν γίνεται
ἡ διὰ τὸν πόνον ταραχὴ ἀλλ', ἐάν τε θέλῃ ἐάν τε
καὶ μή, γίνεσθαι κατ' ἀνάγκην ὀφείλει· τὸν δὲ παρὰ
τὰς ἰδίας ὑπολήψεις ἀναπλάττοντα αὑτῷ αἱρετῶν
τε καὶ φευκτῶν πραγμάτων πλῆθος αἰτιατέον·
ἑαυτῷ γὰρ ἐγείρει κακῶν πλήμμυραν. καὶ
ταὐτὸ[1] πάρεστιν ἰδεῖν ἐπ' αὐτῶν τῶν λεγομένων
158 κακῶν. ὁ μὲν γὰρ μηδὲν προσδοξάζων περὶ τοῦ
κακὸν εἶναι τὸν πόνον ἔχεται τῷ κατηναγκασμένῳ
τοῦ πόνου κινήματι· ὁ δέ γε προσαναπλάσσων ὅτι
μόνον ἀνοίκειόν ἐστιν ὁ πόνος, ὅτι μόνον κακόν,
διπλασιάζει τῇ δόξῃ ταύτῃ τὸ κατὰ παρουσίαν
159 αὐτοῦ συμβαῖνον ὄχλημα. ἢ γὰρ οὐ θεωροῦμεν
ὡς καὶ ἐπὶ τῶν τεμνομένων πολλάκις αὐτὸς μὲν
ὁ πάσχων καὶ τεμνόμενος ἀνδρικῶς ὑπομένει τὴν
ἐκ τῆς τομῆς βάσανον, μήτε

[1] ταὐτὸ Heintz : τοῦτο mss., Bekk.

460

is continuous in its nature but has many intervals of
rest and periods of relief; for were it unceasing it
would not have been protracted.—The perturbation,
then, which befalls the Sceptic is moderate and not
so very alarming. Notwithstanding, even if it be 156
very great, we ought not to blame those who suffer
involuntarily and of necessity but Nature,

Who recks not aught of custom,[a]

and the man who through his beliefs and owing to his
own judgement draws upon himself the evil. For just
as the man with a fever is not to be blamed because
he has a fever (for he has the fever involuntarily), but
the man who does not abstain from things inexpedient
is to be blamed (for it lay in his own power to abstain
from things inexpedient),—so the man who is perturbed at the presence of painful things is not to be
blamed; for the perturbation caused by the pain is 157
not due to himself but is bound to occur of necessity
whether he wishes it or not; but he who through his
own imaginations invents for himself a host of things
desirable and to be avoided is deserving of blame; for
he stirs up for himself a flood of evils.[b]—And one may
see the same thing in the case of the so-called " evils "
themselves. For he who has no additional belief 158
about pain being an evil is merely affected by the
necessitated motion of the pain; but he who imagines
in addition that the pain is objectionable only, that
it is evil only, doubles by this belief the distress which
results from its presence. For do we not observe 159
frequently how, in the case of those who are being
cut, the patient who is being cut manfully endures
the torture of the cutting—

[a] Eurip. *Frag.* 920 (Nauck).
[b] *Cf.* Hamlet's " Take arms against a sea of troubles."

SEXTUS EMPIRICUS

ὠχρήσας χρόα κάλλιμον μήτε παρειῶν
δάκρυ᾽ ὀμορξάμενος,

διὰ τὸ μόνῳ τῷ κατὰ τὴν τομὴν ὑποπίπτειν
κινήματι· ὁ δὲ παρεστὼς αὐτῷ, σύναμα τῷ βρα-
χεῖαν ἰδεῖν αἵματος ῥύσιν, ὠχριᾷ τρέμει περιδροῖ
ἐκλύεται, τὸ τελευταῖον ἄφωνος καταπίπτει, οὐ
διὰ τὸν πόνον, οὐδὲ γὰρ πάρεστιν αὐτῷ, διὰ δὲ
160 τὴν περὶ τοῦ κακὸν εἶναι τὸν πόνον δόξαν; οὕτω
μείζων ἐστὶν ἐνίοτε ἡ διὰ τὴν περί τινος κακοῦ ὡς
κακοῦ δόξαν ταραχὴ τῆς δι᾽ αὐτὸ τὸ λεγόμενον
εἶναι κακὸν συμβαινούσης.   οὐκοῦν ὁ περὶ
πάντων [μὲν] ἐπέχων τῶν κατὰ δόξαν τελειοτάτην
161 καρποῦται τὴν εὐδαιμονίαν, ἐν δὲ τοῖς ἀκουσίοις
καὶ ἀλόγοις κινήμασι ταράττεται μέν

(οὐ γὰρ ἀπὸ δρυός ἐστι παλαιφάτου, οὐδ᾽ ἀπὸ
πέτρης,
ἀλλ᾽ ἀνδρῶν γένος ἦεν),

162 μετριοπαθῶς δὲ διατίθεται. ὅθεν καὶ καταφρονεῖν
ἀναγκαῖον τῶν εἰς ἀνενεργησίαν αὐτὸν περι-
163 κλείεσθαι νομιζόντων ἢ εἰς ἀπέμφασιν, καὶ εἰς
ἀνενεργησίαν μὲν ὅτι τοῦ βίου παντὸς ἐν αἱρέσεσι
καὶ φυγαῖς ὄντος ὁ μήτε αἱρούμενός τι μήτε
φεύγων δυνάμει τὸν βίον ἀρνεῖται καί τινος φυτοῦ
164 τρόπον ἐπεῖχεν, εἰς ἀπέμφασιν δὲ ὅτι ὑπὸ τυράννῳ
ποτὲ γενόμενος καὶ τῶν ἀρρήτων τι ποιεῖν ἀναγκαζόμενος ἢ οὐχ ὑπομενεῖ τὸ προσταττόμενον ἀλλ᾽
ἑκούσιον ἑλεῖται θάνατον, ἢ φεύγων τὰς βασάνους
ποιήσει τὸ κελευόμενον, οὕτω τε οὐκέτι " ἀφυγὴς
καὶ ἀναίρετος ἔσται " κατὰ τὸν Τίμωνα, ἀλλὰ τὸ
μὲν ἑλεῖται τοῦ δ᾽ ἀποστήσεται, ὅπερ ἦν τῶν μετὰ

> His fair hue paling not, nor from his cheeks
> Wiping the tears away,[a]

because he is affected only by the motion due to the
cutting ; whereas the man who stands beside him, as
soon as he sees a small flow of blood, at once grows
pale, trembles, gets in a great sweat, feels faint, and
finally falls down speechless, not because of the pain
(for it is not present with him), but because of the
belief he has about pain being an evil ? Thus the 160
perturbation due to the belief about an evil as evil is
sometimes greater than that which results from the
so-called evil itself.—He, then, who suspends judgement about all things which depend on belief wins
happiness most fully, and during involuntary and 161
irrational affections although he is perturbed—

> Yea, for he is not sprung from a rock or an oak primeval
> But of the race of men was he,[b]

yet his state of feeling is moderate. Hence, too, one 162
must scorn those who fancy that he is confined to a
state of inactivity or of inconsistency,—to inactivity, 163
because, as all life consists in desires and avoidances,
he that neither desires nor avoids anything is virtually
rejecting life and remaining like a vegetable ; and to 164
inconsistency because, should he ever be subject to a
tyrant and compelled to do something unspeakable,
either he will not submit to the order given him but
will choose a voluntary death, or else to avoid torture
he will do what is commanded, and thus he will no
longer be (in Timon's phrase) " unmov'd by choice
and avoidance," but will choose the one and refuse
the other, which is the action of those who confidently

---

[a] Homer, *Odyss.* xi. 529 f.
[b] The first line is from Homer, *Odyss.* xix. 163 ; the half-
line is S.'s addition.

SEXTUS EMPIRICUS

πείσματος κατειληφότων τὸ φευκτόν τι εἶναι καὶ
165 αἱρετόν.   ταῦτα δὴ λέγοντες οὐ συνιᾶσιν ὅτι
κατὰ μὲν τὸν φιλόσοφον λόγον οὐ βιοῖ ὁ σκεπτικός
(ἀνενέργητος γάρ ἐστιν ὅσον ἐπὶ τούτῳ), κατὰ δὲ
τὴν ἀφιλόσοφον τήρησιν δύναται τὰ μὲν αἱρεῖσθαι
166 τὰ δὲ φεύγειν. ἀναγκαζόμενός τε ὑπὸ τυράννου
τι τῶν ἀπηγορευμένων πράττειν, τῇ κατὰ τοὺς
πατρίους νόμους καὶ τὰ ἔθη προλήψει τυχὸν τὸ
μὲν ἑλεῖται τὸ δὲ φεύξεται· καὶ ῥᾷόν γε οἴσει τὸ
σκληρὸν παρὰ τὸν ἀπὸ τῶν δογμάτων, ὅτι οὐδὲν
ἔξωθεν τούτῳ προσδοξάζει καθάπερ ἐκεῖνος.
167 εἴρηται δὲ περὶ τούτων ἀκριβέστερον ἐν τοῖς περὶ
τοῦ σκεπτικοῦ τέλους σχολασθεῖσι, καὶ οὐκ ἀναγκαῖον

αὖθις ἀριζήλως εἰρημένα μυθολογεύειν.

Ὅθεν περὶ ἀγαθῶν καὶ κακῶν ἀποδόντες, ἀφ' ὧν
αἱ ἀπορίαι ἐπὶ πάντα σχεδὸν τὸν ἠθικὸν διατείνουσι
τόπον, φέρε τὸ μετὰ τοῦτο σκοπῶμεν εἰ ἔστι τις
περὶ τὸν βίον τέχνη.

ʹ.—ΕΙ ΕΣΤΙ ΤΙΣ ΠΕΡΙ ΤΟΝ ΒΙΟΝ ΤΕΧΝΗ

168 Ὅτι μέν ἐστι δυνατὸν κατὰ τρόπον βιοῦν αἱρου-
μένους τὴν περὶ πάντων ἐποχήν, ἀποχρώντως ἡμῖν
δέδεικται· οὐδὲν δὲ κωλύει ἐκ παραλλήλου δοκιμά-
ζειν καὶ τὴν τῶν δογματικῶν στάσιν, καίπερ ἀπὸ
μέρους ἤδη δοκιμασθεῖσαν. ἐπαγγέλλονται γάρ
169 τέχνην τινὰ περὶ τὸν βίον παραδώσειν, καὶ διὰ
τοῦτο Ἐπίκουρος μὲν ἔλεγε τὴν φιλοσοφίαν ἐνέρ-

---

[a] Cf. *P.H.* i. 23.   [b] See *P.H.* i. 25-30.
[c] Homer, *Odyss.* xii. 453.

464

hold that something to be avoided and desirable
exists.—Now in arguing thus they do not comprehend 165
that the Sceptic does not conduct his life according to
philosophical theory (for so far as regards this he is
inactive), but as regards the non-philosophic regula-
tion of life [a] he is capable of desiring some things and
avoiding others. And when compelled by a tyrant to 166
commit any forbidden act he will perchance choose
the one course and avoid the other owing to the preconception due to his ancestral laws and customs ;
and as compared with the Dogmatist he will certainly
endure hardship more easily because he has not, like
the other, any additional beliefs beyond the actual
suffering.—But we have discussed these matters more 167
exactly in our discourse " On the Sceptic End,"[b]
and there is no necessity

Once again to repeat an account most plainly deliver'd.[c]

Hence, as we have completed our account of things
good and evil, the difficulties raised by which extend
over almost the whole sphere of Ethics, come and let
us consider next whether there exists any art of
life.[d]

Chapter VI.—Does there exist any Art of Life?

We have proved sufficiently that it is possible to 168
live a satisfactory life by adopting suspension of
judgement about all things ; but nothing hinders us
from examining also in a similar fashion the view
of the Dogmatists, although it has been partially
examined already. For they promise to present us
with an " art of life," and because of this Epicurus 169
declared that " philosophy is an activity which

[d] For the " art of living " *cf. P.H.* iii. 239 ff.

γειαν εἶναι λόγοις καὶ διαλογισμοῖς τὸν εὐδαίμονα
170 βίον περιποιοῦσαν, οἱ δὲ στωικοὶ καὶ ἄντικρύς φασι
τὴν φρόνησιν, ἐπιστήμην οὖσαν ἀγαθῶν καὶ κακῶν
καὶ οὐδετέρων, τέχνην ὑπάρχειν περὶ τὸν βίον, ἣν
οἱ προσλαβόντες μόνοι γίνονται καλοί, μόνοι πλού-
σιοι, σοφοὶ μόνοι. ὁ γὰρ πολλοῦ ἄξια κεκτημένος
πλούσιός ἐστιν, ἡ δὲ ἀρετὴ πολλοῦ ἐστιν ἀξία, καὶ
μόνος ταύτην ὁ σοφὸς κέκτηται· μόνος ἄρα ὁ σοφός
ἐστι πλούσιος. καὶ ὁ ἀξιέραστός ἐστι καλός, μόνος
δὲ ὁ σοφὸς ἀξιέραστος· μόνος ἄρα ὁ σοφός ἐστι
171 καλός. αἱ δὴ τοιαῦται ὑποσχέσεις θηρεύουσι μὲν
τοὺς νέους ἐλπίσι ψυχραῖς, οὐκέτι δέ εἰσιν ἀληθεῖς.
παρὸ καὶ ὁ Τίμων ὁτὲ μὲν τοὺς ἐπαγγελλομένους
τὴν παράδοσιν αὐτῶν ἐπισκώπτει, λέγων

πολλῶν λακεδόνων λυμάντορες αἰπυδολωταί,[1]

172 ὁτὲ δὲ τοὺς προσέχοντας αὐτοῖς μεταμελομένους ἐφ'
οἷς μάτην ἐμόχθησαν παρεισάγει διὰ τούτων·

φῇ δέ τις αἰάζων, οἷα βροτοὶ αἰάζουσιν,
οἴμοι ἐγὼ τί πάθω; τί νυ μοι σοφὸν ἔνθα
γένηται;
πτωχὸς μὲν φρένας εἰμί, νόου δέ μοι οὐκ ἔνι
κόκκος.
ἦ με μάτην φεύξεσθαι οἴομαι αἰπὺν ὄλεθρον.
τρὶς μάκαρες μέντοι καὶ τετράκις οἱ μὴ ἔχοντες

---

[1] αἰπυδολωταί Fabr., Bekk.: ἐπιδολωταί (or -οταί) MSS.:
ἐλπιδοδῶται Usener (? ἀρχιδολωταί).

---

[a] For the Stoic " Wise Man," or " Sage," see Vol. I.
Introd. p. xxviii. "Fair" (καλός), here, means "noble" or

466

secures the happy life by arguments and discussions ";
while the Stoics assert outright that " wisdom, which 170
is the science of things good and evil and neither, is
an art of life, and only those who attain this become
fair, only they rich, as only they are wise. For he
who possesses things of great value is rich, and virtue
is of great value, and it only the Wise man [a] possesses ;
therefore the wise man only is rich. And the lover
of the valuable is fair, but the wise man only is a lover
of the valuable ; therefore the wise man only is fair."
Now promises such as these capture the young with 171
fruitless expectations, but they are not also true.
Wherefore also Timon in one place scoffs at those
who promise us to provide us with these things, calling
them—

> Spoilers of many a doctrine and masters of knavish im-
> posture [b] ;

and in another place he brings in the people who have 172
paid attention to them, repenting of the vain labours
they have undergone, in these words—

One, then, lamenting did cry, as men are wont when lament-
ing,
"Oh, what is to befall me ! Where now shall I gain any
wisdom ?
Beggar'd in soul I am, and of sense not a grain is within me.
Vainly methinks shall I try to escape from sheerest destruc-
tion.
Thrice, yea four times, blessed are those devoid of possessions,

" honourable " (*honestus*),—gifted with " the beauty of
holiness."

[b] For λακεδόνων (" doctrines "), which can scarcely be
right, I suggest βλακεδόνων (" wastrels "), which accords
better with the next quotation (Hervetus has *juvenum*) ; then
λυμάντορες βλ. will mean "those who bring wastrels (or
idlers) to ruin."

μήτε κατατρώξαντες ἐνὶ σχολῇ ὅσσ᾽ ἐπέπαντο.
νῦν δέ με λευγαλέαις ἔρισιν εἵμαρτο δαμῆναι
καὶ πενίῃ καὶ ὅσ᾽ ἄλλα βροτοὺς κηφῆνας ἐλαστρεῖ.

173 διότι δὲ ταῦθ᾽ οὕτως ἔχει, μάθοιμεν ἂν ἐντεῦθεν ἐπι-
στήσαντες. ἡ γὰρ ἀξιουμένη περὶ τὸν βίον εἶναι
τέχνη, καὶ καθ᾽ ἣν εὐδαιμονεῖν ὑπειλήφασιν, οὐ μία
τίς ἐστιν ἀλλὰ πολλαὶ καὶ διάφωνοι, οἷον ἡ μὲν
κατὰ τὸν Ἐπίκουρον, ἡ δὲ κατὰ τοὺς στωικούς, τὶς
δὲ τῶν ἀπὸ τοῦ περιπάτου. ἤτοι οὖν πάσαις ὁμοίως
174 ἀκολουθητέον ἢ μιᾷ μόνῃ ἢ οὐδεμιᾷ. καὶ πάσαις
μὲν ἀκολουθεῖν τῶν ἀμηχάνων διὰ τὴν μάχην· ὃ γὰρ
ἥδε προστάσσει ὡς αἱρετόν, τοῦτο ἥδε ἀπαγορεύει
ὡς φευκτόν, οὐκ ἐνδέχεται δὲ τὸ αὐτὸ ἅμα καὶ
175 διώκειν καὶ φεύγειν. εἰ δὲ μιᾷ κατακολουθητέον
ἐστίν, ἤτοι τῇ ὁποιαδήποτε οὖν, ὅπερ ἀδύνατον.
⟨τὸ μιᾷ⟩ ἀκολουθεῖν[1] γὰρ ἴσον τῷ[2] πάσαις θέλειν
ἕπεσθαι· εἰ γὰρ τῇδε προσεκτέον, τί μᾶλλον τῇδε ἢ
τῇδε· καὶ ἀναστρόφως. λείπεται ἄρα τῇ προκρι-
176 θείσῃ λέγειν δεῖν ἕπεσθαι. ἤτοι οὖν τῇ ὑπ᾽ ἄλλης
προκριθείσῃ κατακολουθήσομεν ἢ τῇ ὑφ᾽ ἑαυτῆς.
καὶ εἰ μὲν τῇ ὑφ᾽ ἑαυτῆς, ἄπιστος ἔσται, ἢ δεήσει
πάσας ἡγεῖσθαι πιστάς· εἰ γὰρ ἥδε καθόσον ὑφ᾽
ἑαυτῆς κέκριται ἔστι πιστή, καὶ αἱ λοιπαὶ γενήσονται πισταί· ἑκάστη γὰρ αὐτῶν ὑφ᾽ ἑαυτῆς
177 κέκριται. εἰ δὲ ὑπ᾽ ἄλλης, δεήσει πάλιν καὶ οὕτως
αὐτὴν ἀπιστεῖσθαι· ὡς γὰρ αὐτὴ παρόσον διαφωνεῖ
ταῖς ἄλλαις ἐδεῖτο κρίσεως, οὕτω καὶ ἡ κρίνουσα
αὐτήν, ᾗ διαφωνεῖ ταῖς λοιπαῖς ἀγωγαῖς, δεήσεται

---

[1] ⟨τὸ μιᾷ⟩ ἀκολουθεῖν] ἀκολουθεῖ mss., Bekk.: ⟨τὸ ταύτῃ⟩
ἀκολουθεῖν Heintz.
[2] τῷ N, Heintz: τὸ mss., Bekk. (ἴσως cj. Bekk.).

---

^a With §§ 173–177 cf. P.H. iii. 239.

Those who never have wasted their goods in idle existence.
But my fate it is now to be stricken by grievous contentions,
Penury, too, and what else doth harry the drones amongst
    mortals."

And the reason why this is so we may learn if we 173
attend to the following point.[a] The art of life which,
it is claimed, exists and owing to which they suppose
that men are happy, is not one art but many and
dissimilar—that, for instance, of Epicurus, and that
of the Stoics, and another of the Peripatetics. Either,
then, one must follow all alike or one only or none.
But to follow them all is impracticable because of 174
their conflicting character ; for what this one enjoins
as desirable that one forbids as a thing to be avoided,
and it is not feasible both to pursue and avoid simultaneously the same object. And if one ought closely 175
to follow one art, either this is anyone whatsoever,
which is impossible ; for then, to follow one is equivalent to being willing to follow them all ; for if we
should give heed to this one, why to this one rather
than that other ? and conversely. It only remains,
then, to say that we ought to follow that one art
which has been judged best. Either, then, we shall 176
follow that which is judged best by another art or
that which is judged best by itself. And if it is that
judged best by itself, it will be distrusted or else we
shall have to count them all trustworthy ; for if this
one is trustworthy inasmuch as it is judged by itself,
the rest also will be trustworthy ; for each of them
is judged by itself. But if it is judged by another art, 177
even in this case, again, it will have to be distrusted ;
for just as it, in so far as it differs from the rest,
needed judgement, so also the art which judges it,
in that it differs from the other doctrines, will need

SEXTUS EMPIRICUS

τῆς κρινούσης καὶ παρ' αὐτὸ τοῦτο οὐκ ἔσται
πιστὸν ἐκείνης κριτήριον. εἰ οὖν μήτε πάσαις
ἐνδέχεται ταῖς περὶ τὸν βίον τέχναις ἀκολουθεῖν
178 μήτε μιᾷ, λείπεται μηδεμιᾷ ἔπεσθαι.   καὶ
ἄλλως, ὡς προεῖπον, πολλῶν οὐσῶν περὶ τὸν βίον
τεχνῶν κατ' ἀνάγκην δεῖ τὸν μιᾷ τούτων προσ-
αναπαυσάμενον κακοδαιμονεῖν, οὐ μόνον διὰ τὰς
προειρημένας αἰτίας ἀλλὰ καὶ διὰ τὴν τοῦ λόγου
προϊόντος λεχθησομένην. ἕκαστος γὰρ τῶν ἀνθρώπων ἔχεται πάθει τινί· ἢ γὰρ φιλόπλουτός ἐστιν
ἢ φιλήδονος ἢ φιλόδοξος. τοιοῦτος δὲ ὢν ὑπ'
οὐδεμιᾶς τῶν δογματικῶν ἀγωγῶν δύναται κατα-
179 στέλλεσθαι, ἀλλ' ὁ μὲν φιλόπλουτος ἢ φιλόδοξος
ἐκπυρσεύεται μᾶλλον τὴν ἐπιθυμίαν ὑπὸ τῆς περι-
πατητικῆς φιλοσοφίας, καθ' ἣν ὁ πλοῦτος καὶ ἡ
δόξα τῶν ἀγαθῶν ἐστίν, ὁ δὲ φιλήδονος προσ-
εκκαίεται ὑπὸ τῆς κατὰ Ἐπίκουρον ἀγωγῆς (τέλος
γὰρ εὐδαιμονίας ἡ ἡδονὴ ἀποδείκνυται κατ' αὐτόν),
ὁ δὲ φιλόδοξος προσεκτραχηλίζεται εἰς αὐτὸ τὸ
πάθος πρὸς τῶν στωικῶν λόγων, καθ' οὓς ἡ ἀρετὴ
μόνον ἐστὶν ἀγαθόν, καὶ τὸ ἀπ' ἀρετῆς γινόμενον.
180 πᾶσα οὖν ἡ λεγομένη περὶ τὸν βίον ἐπιστήμη τοῖς
δογματικοῖς φιλοσόφοις ἐπιτείχισμά ἐστι τῶν
ἀνθρωπίνων κακῶν ἀλλ' οὐ βοήθεια.

Κἂν μίαν δὲ δῶμεν εἶναι τέχνην περὶ τὸν βίον,
καὶ ταύτην σύμφωνον, οἷον τὴν στωικήν, οὐδ'
οὕτως προσησόμεθα διὰ τὸ πολλὰς καὶ ποικίλας
181 αὐτῇ συνεισάγεσθαι κῆρας. εἰ γὰρ ἡ μὲν περὶ τὸν
βίον τέχνη φρόνησις οὖσα ἔστιν ἀρετή, τὴν δὲ
ἀρετὴν μόνος εἶχεν ὁ σοφός, οἱ στωικοὶ μὴ ὄντες
σοφοὶ οὐχ ἕξουσι φρόνησιν οὐδὲ τέχνην τινὰ περὶ

ᵃ See § 173 supra.   ᵇ Cf. §§ 110 ff. supra.

470

one to judge it, and owing to this fact it will not be a trustworthy criterion of the other. If, then, it is not feasible to follow either all the arts of life or one, it only remains to follow none.—And again : since, as I 178 said above,[a] there are many arts of life, he who abides by one of them must necessarily be unhappy, not only for the reasons previously stated [b] but also for that which shall be stated as our argument proceeds. For each individual man is subject to a certain affection ; for either he is a lover of wealth [c] or a lover of pleasure or a lover of fame ; and being such, he cannot be calmed down by any of the dogmatic doctrines ; nay, the lover of wealth or the lover of 179 fame is further enkindled in his desire by the Peripatetic philosophy, according to which wealth and fame are among the goods [d] ; and the lover of pleasure is further inflamed by the doctrine of Epicurus (for on his showing pleasure is proved to be the perfection of happiness) ; and the lover of fame is also plunged headlong into this very affection by the Stoic arguments, according to which virtue alone is good and that which results from virtue. In every case, 180 then, what is called by the Dogmatic philosophers " the science of life " is a bulwark in defence of the evils of mankind rather than an aid against them.

And even if we grant that there is one art of life,[e] and this an agreed one,—for instance, the Stoic,—not even so shall we accept it, since along with itself it brings many and diverse calamities. For if the art of 181 life, as consisting in wisdom, is a virtue, and only the Sage possesses virtue, the Stoics not being sages will not possess wisdom nor any art of life, and not possessing

[a] Cf. § 120 supra.   [d] Cf. §§ 51, 77 supra.
   [e] With §§ 180-183 cf. P.H. iii. 240-242.

τὸν βίον, μὴ ἔχοντες δὲ ταύτην οὐδὲ ἄλλους διδά-
ξουσιν.   εἴπερ τε κατ' αὐτοὺς οὐδεμία δύναται
συστῆναι τέχνη, οὐδ' ἡ περὶ τὸν βίον συστήσεται·
182 ἀλλὰ μὴν τὸ πρῶτον· τὸ ἄρα δεύτερον. τέχνη γάρ
ἐστι σύστημα ἐκ καταλήψεων, καὶ κατάληψίς ἐστι
καταληπτικῆς φαντασίας συγκατάθεσις. οὐδεμία δ'
ἦν καταληπτικὴ φαντασία διὰ τὸ μήτε πᾶσαν ὑπάρχειν φαντασίαν καταληπτικήν, μάχονται γάρ,
μήτε τινὰ διὰ τὴν ἀνεπικρισίαν. μὴ οὔσης δὲ
καταληπτικῆς φαντασίας οὐδὲ συγκατάθεσίς τις
αὐτῆς γενήσεται, οὑτωσὶ δὲ οὐδὲ κατάληψις. μὴ
οὔσης δὲ καταλήψεως οὐδὲ σύστημα ἐκ καταλήψεων γενήσεται, τουτέστι τέχνη. ᾧ ἀκολουθεῖ
183 τὸ μηδὲ περὶ τὸν βίον εἶναί τινα τέχνην.   πρὸς
τούτοις ἡ καταληπτικὴ φαντασία κρίνεται κατὰ
τοὺς στωικούς, ὅτι καταληπτική ἐστι, τῷ ἀπὸ
ὑπάρχοντος γενέσθαι καὶ κατ' αὐτὸ τὸ ὑπάρχον
ἐναπομεμαγμένως καὶ ἐναπεσφραγισμένως· τό θ'
ὑπάρχον δοκιμάζεται, ὅτι ὑπάρχον ἐστίν, ἐκ τοῦ
καταληπτικὴν κινεῖν φαντασίαν. εἰ δὲ ἵνα μὲν ἡ
καταληπτικὴ κρίνηται φαντασία, τὸ ὑπάρχον δεῖ
ἐπεγνῶσθαι, ἵνα δὲ τοῦτο καταληφθῇ, τὴν καταληπτικὴν φαντασίαν βέβαιον εἶναι, ἑκάτερον δὲ διὰ
θάτερόν ἐστιν ἄπιστον, ἀγνωρίστου οὔσης τῆς
καταληπτικῆς φαντασίας ἀναιρεῖται καὶ ἡ τέχνη,
σύστημα οὖσα ἐκ καταλήψεων.
184   Εἴπερ τε ἡ περὶ τὸν βίον ἐπιστήμη, τουτέστιν ἡ
φρόνησις, θεωρητικὴ τῶν τε ἀγαθῶν καὶ κακῶν καὶ
οὐδετέρων ἐστίν, ἤτοι ἑτέρα καθέστηκε τῶν ἀγαθῶν

ᵃ Cf. Adv. Log. i. 388 ff.
ᵇ Cf. Adv. Log. i. 248, 402, ii. 86.

this neither will they teach it to others.—Also, if, on their showing, no art can be constructed, neither will the art of life be constructed ; but in fact the first ⟨is true⟩ ; therefore the second ⟨is true⟩. For an art is 182 " a system constructed of apprehensions," and apprehension is " assent to an apprehensive presentation." But no apprehensive presentation exists [a] because neither is every presentation apprehensive (owing to their conflicting character), nor yet any one of them (owing to their being unjudged). And if an apprehensive presentation does not exist, neither will there be any assent to it, and thus there will not be any apprehension either. And if there is no apprehension, neither will there be a system of apprehensions, that is to say, an art. Wherefrom it follows that there is no art of life either.—Further- 183 more, according to the Stoics the apprehensive presentation is judged to be apprehensive by the fact that it proceeds from an existing object and in such a way as to bear the impress and stamp of that existing object [b] ; and the existing object is approved as existent because of its exciting an apprehensive presentation. But if the existent must be ascertained in order that the apprehensive presentation may be judged, and if the apprehensive presentation must be established in order that the existent may be apprehended, and each of these is untrustworthy because of the other,—then, as the apprehensive presentation is unknowable, art also is abolished, it being a system of apprehensions.

Also, if the science of life,—that is, wisdom,—is 184 cognisant of things good and evil and neither,[c] either it is other than the goods whereof it is said to be the

* Cf. § 170 *supra.*

ὧν λέγεται ἐπιστήμη τυγχάνειν, ἢ αὐτή ἐστι τὸ
ἀγαθόν, καθὸ καὶ ὁριζόμενοί τινες ἐξ αὐτῶν φασὶν
185 " ἀγαθόν ἐστιν ἀρετὴ ἢ τὸ μετέχον ἀρετῆς." καὶ
εἰ μὲν ἑτέρα ἐστὶ παρὰ τἀγαθὰ ὧν λέγεται ἐπιστήμη, οὐδ' ὅλως ἔσται ἐπιστήμη· πᾶσα γὰρ
ἐπιστήμη ὑπαρκτῶν τινῶν ἐστὶ γνῶσις, τὰ δὲ
ἀγαθὰ καὶ κακὰ πρότερον ἐδείξαμεν ἀνύπαρκτα,
ὥστ' οὐδ' ἐπιστήμη τις ἔσται ἀγαθῶν καὶ κακῶν.
186 εἰ δ' αὐτή ἐστιν ἀγαθὸν καὶ ἀξιοῦται τῶν ἀγαθῶν
εἶναι ἐπιστήμη, ἑαυτῆς ἔσται ἐπιστήμη. ὃ πάλιν
ἄτοπον. τὰ γὰρ ὧν ἔστιν ἐπιστήμη, ταῦτα προεπινοεῖται τῆς ἐπιστήμης. οἷον ἰατρικὴ λέγεται
ἐπιστήμη ὑγιεινῶν καὶ νοσερῶν καὶ οὐθετέρων·
ἀλλὰ προϋφέστηκε τῆς ἰατρικῆς καὶ προηγεῖται τὰ
ὑγιεινὰ καὶ νοσερά. πάλιν τε ἡ μουσικὴ ἐμμελῶν
ἐστι καὶ ἐκμελῶν ἐνρύθμων τε καὶ ἐκρύθμων ἐπι-
187 στήμη· ἀλλ' οὐ πρὶν τούτων ἔστιν ἡ μουσική. καὶ
αὐτοὶ δὲ τὴν διαλεκτικὴν ἔφασαν ἐπιστήμην ἀληθῶν τε καὶ ψευδῶν καὶ οὐθετέρων· οὐκοῦν προϋφέστηκε τῆς διαλεκτικῆς τἀληθῆ καὶ ψευδῆ καὶ
οὐθέτερα. εἰ δὴ ἑαυτῆς ἐστιν ἐπιστήμη ἡ φρόνησις,
ὀφείλει προϋφεστάναι ἑαυτῆς· οὐδὲν δὲ δύναται
ἑαυτοῦ προϋφεστηκέναι· οὐδὲ ταύτῃ τοίνυν ῥητέον
εἶναί τινα περὶ τὸν βίον ἐπιστήμην.
188 Πᾶσά τε ὑπαρκτὴ τέχνη καὶ ἐπιστήμη ἐκ τῶν
ἀποδιδομένων ὑπὸ αὐτῆς τεχνικῶν τε καὶ ἐπιστη-
μονικῶν ἔργων καταλαμβάνεται, οἷον ἰατρικὴ μὲν
ἐκ τῶν ἰατρικῶς γινομένων, κιθαριστικὴ δὲ ἐκ τῶν
κιθαριστικῶς καὶ ἤδη ζωγραφία καὶ ἀνδριαντοπλα-
στικὴ καὶ πᾶσαι αἱ ἐμφερεῖς. ἡ δέ γε περὶ τὸν βίον

---

[a] Cf. § 22 supra. [b] Cf. §§ 42-10

science, or it is itself the good, even as some of them assert in their definition—" Good is virtue or what partakes of virtue." [a]   And if it is other than the 185 goods whereof it is said to be the science, it will not be a science at all ; for every science is the knowledge of certain existing things, but we have previously shown [b] that goods and evils are non-existent, so that neither will there exist any science of goods and evils.   But if it is itself the good and claims to be the 186 science of the goods, it will be the science of itself ; and this again is absurd.   For the things which form the object of a science are conceived before the science.   Thus medicine is said to be the science of things healthy and morbid and neither ; but the healthy and morbid things are in existence before medicine and precede it.   And again : Music is the science of things in tune and out of tune, rhythmical and unrhythmical ; but previous to these Music does not exist.   The Stoics, too, have said that Dialectic [c] 187 is " the science of things true and false and neither " ; so, then, before Dialectic the true and false and neither pre-existed.   If, then, wisdom is the science of itself, it must have existed before itself ; but nothing can have existed before itself ; so that neither in this way can it be asserted that any art of life exists.

Also, every existing art and science is apprehended 188 by means of the artistic and scientific effects which it produces,[d]—medicine, for instance, by its medical results, and harp-playing by those of the harper, and painting and sculpture as well, and all arts of a like kind.   But the art which is supposed to be conversant

---

[c] *Cf. P.H.* ii. 94, 247.
[d] With §§ 188-189 *cf. P.H.* iii. 243.

ἀξιουμένη στρέφεσθαι τέχνη οὐδὲν ἔχει συμβεβηκὸς
ἐνέργημα, ὡς παραστήσομεν· οὐκ ἄρα ἔστι τις περὶ
189 τὸν βίον τέχνη. οἷον πολλῶν λεγομένων παρὰ τοῖς
στωικοῖς περί τε τῆς τῶν παίδων ἀγωγῆς καὶ περὶ
τῆς πρὸς τοὺς γονεῖς τιμῆς καὶ ἔτι τῆς πρὸς τοὺς
κατοιχομένους ὁσιότητος, ὀλίγα ἐξ ἑκάστου εἴδους
ἐπιλεξάμενοι δείγματος χάριν προοισόμεθα εἰς τὴν
τῆς ἐπιχειρήσεως κατασκευήν.

190 Καὶ μὴν περὶ μὲν παίδων ἀγωγῆς ἐν ταῖς δια-
τριβαῖς ὁ αἱρεσιάρχης Ζήνων τοιαῦτά τινα διέξεισιν.
" διαμηρίζειν δὲ μηδὲν μᾶλλον μηδὲ ἧσσον παιδικὰ
ἢ μὴ παιδικά, μηδὲ θήλεα ἢ ἄρρενα· οὐ γὰρ ἄλλα
παιδικοῖς ἢ μὴ παιδικοῖς, οὐδὲ θηλείαις ἢ ἄρρεσιν,
ἀλλὰ τὰ αὐτὰ πρέπει τε καὶ πρέποντα ἐστίν." καὶ
πάλιν " διαμεμήρικας τὸν ἐρώμενον; οὐκ ἔγωγε.
πότερον οὐκ ἐπεθύμησας αὐτὸν διαμηρίσαι; καὶ
μάλα. ἀλλὰ ἐπιθυμήσας[1] παρασχεῖν σοι αὐτὸν [ἢ][2]
ἐφοβήθης κελεῦσαι; μὰ Δί'. ἀλλ' ἐκέλευσας; καὶ
μάλα. εἶθ' οὐχ ὑπηρέτησέ σοι; οὐ γάρ."
191 περὶ δὲ τῆς εἰς τοὺς γονεῖς τιμῆς παράθοιτο ἄν τις
τὰ τῆς μητρομιξίας ὑπ' αὐτῶν θρυλούμενα. καί γε
ὁ μὲν Ζήνων τὰ περὶ τῆς Ἰοκάστης καὶ Οἰδίποδος
θεὶς ἱστορούμενα φησὶν ὅτι οὐκ ἦν δεινὸν τρῖψαι τὴν
μητέρα. " καὶ εἰ μὲν ἀσθενοῦσαν τὸ σῶμα ταῖς
χερσὶ τρίψας ὠφέλει, οὐδὲν αἰσχρόν· εἰ δ' ἑτέρῳ
μέρει τρίψας, εὔφραινεν[3] ὀδυνωμένην παύσας, καὶ
παῖδας ἐκ τῆς μητρὸς γενναίους ποιήσας, τί ἦν
192 αἰσχρόν;" ὁ δὲ Χρύσιππος ἐν τῇ πολιτείᾳ κατὰ

---

[1] ἐπιθυμήσας cj. Bekk.: ἐπεθύμησας mss., Bekk.
[2] [ἢ] secl. Arnim (εἶτ' cj. Bekk.).
[3] εὔφραινεν Arnim: ἐφ' ᾧ εὗρεν mss., Bekk.

with life has no resultant effect, as we shall establish ; therefore, no art of life exists. Thus, since much is said 189 by the Stoics both about the education of children and about the honouring of parents, and also about piety towards the departed, we shall select a few points under each of these heads by way of illustration and bring them forward in support of our criticism.

Well then, as regards the education of children, 190 Zeno, the founder of the School, gives the following exposition in his discourses [a] : " Have carnal knowledge no less and no more of a favourite than of a non-favourite child, nor of a female than of a male ; favourite or non-favourite, males or females, no different conduct, but the same, befits and is befitting in respect of all alike." And again,—" Have you had intercourse with your beloved one ? I have not. Did you not desire to have intercourse with him ? Certainly. But, though desiring to win him for yourself, were you afraid of inviting him ? Not at all. But you invited him ? Certainly. Then he did not yield to you ? He did not."—And with regard 191 to honouring one's parents one might adduce the cases of incest which they harp upon. Thus Zeno, after stating the facts about Jocasta and Oedipus, asserts that there was nothing dreadful in his rubbing his mother. " If she had been ailing and he had done her good by rubbing her body with his hands, it had not been shameful ; what shame was it, then, if he stopped her grief and gave her joy by rubbing her with another member, and begat noble children by his mother ? " And Chrysippus, in his *State* says 192

---

[a] With §§ 190-196 *cf. P.H.* iii. 245-249. The Stoics seem to have derived these ugly tenets from the Cynics; *cf. P.H.* 200 n.

λέξιν φησὶν οὕτως· '' δοκεῖ μοι καὶ ταῦτα οὕτως διεξάγειν[1] καθάπερ καὶ νῦν οὐ κακῶς παρὰ πολλοῖς εἴθισται, ὥστε καὶ ⟨τὴν μητέρα ἐκ τοῦ υἱοῦ τεκνο- ποιεῖσθαι καὶ⟩[2] τὸν πατέρα ἐκ τῆς θυγατρὸς καὶ τὸν ὁμομήτριον ἐκ τῆς ὁμομητρίας.''   δεῖγμα δὲ τῆς πρὸς τοὺς κατοιχομένους αὐτῶν ὁσιότητος γένοιτ' ἂν καὶ τὰ περὶ τῆς ἀνθρωποφαγίας παραγ- γελλόμενα· οὐ γὰρ μόνον ἀξιοῦσι τοὺς τετελευτη- κότας ἐσθίειν, ἀλλὰ καὶ τὰς αὑτῶν σάρκας, εἴ ποτε

193 τύχοι τι μέρος τοῦ σώματος ἀποκοπέν.   λέγεται δ' ἐν τῷ περὶ δικαιοσύνης ὑπὸ Χρυσίππου ταυτί· '' καὶ ἂν τῶν μελῶν ἀποκοπῇ τι μέρος πρὸς τὴν τροφὴν χρήσιμον, μήτε κατορύττειν αὐτὸ μήτε ἄλλως ῥίπ- τειν, ἀναλίσκειν δὲ αὐτό, ὅπως ⟨ἐκ⟩[3] τῶν ἡμετέρων

194 ἕτερον μέρος γένηται.''   ἐν δὲ τῷ περὶ τοῦ καθ- ήκοντος περὶ τῆς τῶν γονέων ταφῆς διεξερχόμενος ῥητῶς φησιν '' ἀπογενομένων δὲ τῶν γονέων ταφαῖς χρηστέον ταῖς ἁπλουστάταις, ὡς ἂν τοῦ σώματος καθάπερ ὄνυχος ἢ τριχῶν οὐδὲν ὄντος πρὸς ἡμᾶς, οὐδ' ἐπιστροφῆς καὶ πολυωρίας προσδεομένων ἡμῶν τοιαύτης τινός.   διὸ καὶ χρησίμων μὲν ὄντων τῶν κρεῶν τροφῇ χρήσονται αὐτοῖς, καθάπερ καὶ τῶν ἰδίων μερῶν, οἷον ποδὸς ἀποκοπέντος ἐπέβαλλε χρῆσθαι αὐτῷ, καὶ τοῖς παραπλησίοις· ἀχρείων δὲ ὄντων αὐτῶν ἢ κατορύξαντες τὸ μνῆμα ἐποίσουσιν, ἢ κατακαύσαντες τὴν τέφραν ἀφήσουσιν, ἢ μακρό- τερον ῥίψαντες οὐδεμίαν ἐπιστροφὴν αὐτῶν ποιή- σονται καθάπερ ὄνυχος ἢ τριχῶν.''

195   Ὧδε μὲν οἱ ἀπὸ τῆς στοᾶς, ἐπακτέον δ' αὐτοῖς τὸ

---

[1] διεξάγειν Fabr.: ἐξαγαγεῖν mss., Bekk.
[2] ⟨τὴν . . . καὶ⟩ add. Fabr.
[3] ⟨ἐκ⟩ add. Mutsch.

expressly : " I approve of carrying out those practices—which, quite rightly, are customary even nowadays amongst many peoples—according to which ⟨the mother has children by her son, and⟩ the father by his daughter, and the brother by his full sister."— And their recommendations concerning cannibalism may serve as an example of their piety towards the departed ; for they deem it right to eat not only the dead but even their own flesh, if ever any part of their body should happen to be cut off. This is what is stated by Chrysippus in his treatise *On Justice* :— " And if any part of the limbs be cut off that is good **193** for food, we should neither bury it nor otherwise get rid of it, but consume it, so that from our parts a new part may arise." And in his book *On Duty*, when **194** discoursing about the burial of parents, he says expressly : " When our parents decease we should use the simplest forms of burial, as though the body— like nails or hair—were nothing to us, and we need bestow on it no care or attention of that kind. Hence, also, when their flesh is good for food, men shall make use of it, just as also of their own parts, —when, for instance, a foot is cut off it is proper for them to use it, and things like it ; but when the flesh is not good, either they shall bury it and lay the mound upon it, or burn it up and scatter the ashes, or cast it far away and pay no more regard to it than to nails or hair."

Such is the Stoics' doctrine ; but against them we **195**

ἀκόλουθον τῆς ἐπιχειρήσεως. ἤτοι γὰρ οὕτω παρ-
αγγέλλουσι ταῦτα ποιεῖν ὡς μελλόντων αὐτοῖς
χρῆσθαι τῶν νέων ἢ ὡς μὴ χρησομένων. καὶ ὡς
χρησομένων μὲν οὐδαμῶς· οἱ γὰρ νόμοι κωλύουσιν,
εἰ μή τι παρὰ Λαιστρυγόσι καὶ Κύκλωψι δεήσει
βιοῦν, παρ' οἷς θεμιτόν ἐστιν

ἀνδρόμεα κρέ' ἔδειν καὶ ἐπ' ἄκρητον γάλα πίνειν.

196 εἰ δ' ὡς μὴ χρησομένων, παρέλκουσα γίνεται ἡ περὶ
τὸν βίον τέχνη, ἧς ἡ χρῆσίς ἐστιν ἀδύνατος· ὡς γὰρ
ἐν τυφλῶν δήμῳ ἄχρηστός ἐστι ζωγραφία, βλε-
πόντων γὰρ ἡ τέχνη, καὶ ὃν τρόπον ἐν πόλει κωφῶν
ἀνόνητός ἐστι κιθαριστική, ἀκούοντας γὰρ τέρπει,
οὕτω καὶ ἡ περὶ τὸν βίον τέχνη πρὸς μηδέν ἐστι
τοῖς μὴ δυναμένοις αὐτῇ χρῆσθαι.

197 Καὶ μὴν πᾶσα τέχνη, ἐάν τε θεωρητικὴ καθ-
εστήκῃ ὡς γεωμετρία καὶ ἀστρολογική, ἐάν τε
πρακτικὴ ὡς ὁπλομαχητική, ἐάν τε ἀποτελεσμα-
τικὴ ὡς ζωγραφία καὶ ἀνδριαντοπλαστική, ἴδιον
ἔχει ἔργον ᾧ διαφέρει τῶν ἄλλων διαθέσεων, ⟨τῆς
δὲ φρονήσεως οὐκ ἔστιν ἴδιον ἔργον,⟩[1] ὡς παρα-
στήσω· οὐκ ἄρα τέχνη τίς ἐστι περὶ τὸν βίον ἡ
198 φρόνησις. ὡς γὰρ τὸ κοινὸν μουσικοῦ καὶ ἀμούσου,
τοῦτ' οὐκ ἔστι μουσικόν, καὶ τὸ κοινὸν γραμματικοῦ
καὶ ἀγραμμάτου, τοῦτ' οὐκ ἔστι γραμματικόν, οὕτω
καὶ συλλήβδην τὸ κοινὸν τοῦ τεχνίτου καὶ ἀτέχνου,
τοῦτ' οὐκ ἔστι τεχνικόν. διόπερ καὶ τὸ τοῦ φρονίμου καὶ ἄφρονος κοινὸν οὐκ ἂν εἴη τῆς φρονήσεως
199 ἴδιον ἔργον. πᾶν δέ γε τὸ ὑπὸ τοῦ φρονίμου γίνε-

---

[1] ⟨τῆς . . . ἔργον⟩ add. N.

must bring the next point in our criticism. Either they enjoin these actions with the idea that young people will perform them or with the idea that they will not perform them. But certainly not with the idea that they will perform them ; for the laws forbid them, unless it shall be their lot to live amongst the Laestrygones and Cyclopes, where it is permissible—

Human flesh to devour, and pure milk swallow thereafter.[a]

And if they enjoin them with the idea that they will 196 not perform them, the art of life becomes redundant, as the practice of it is impossible. For just as painting is useless in a country of the blind (for this art is for men who have sight), and just as harp-playing is valueless in a city of the deaf (for it is those who have hearing that it delights), so also the art of life is of no benefit to those who are unable to make use of it.

Moreover, every art,[b] whether it be theoretical, 197 like geometry and astronomy, or practical, like the military art, or creative, like painting and sculpture, possesses a special work of its own whereby it differs from the other states of mind, ⟨whereas there is no special work which belongs to wisdom,⟩ as I shall establish ; therefore wisdom is not an art of life. For just as the work common to the musical 198 man and the unmusical is not music, and the work common to the literary and the non-literary is not literature, so too, in general, the work common to the artistic and the non-artistic is not artistry. Hence also the work common to the wise man and the unwise will not be the special work of wisdom. But in fact every work which seems to be done by 199

a Homer, *Odyss.* ix. 297.
b With §§ 197-199 *cf. P.H.* iii. 243.

σθαι δοκοῦν ἔργον, τοῦτο κοινὸν εὑρίσκεται καὶ τοῦ
μὴ φρονίμου ἔργον· οἷον ἐάν τε τιμᾶν γονεῖς θώμεθα
τοῦ φρονίμου ἔργον, ἐάν τε τὸ παρακαταθήκην ἀπο-
διδόναι τοῖς πιστεύσασιν, ἐάν τ' ἄλλο τι τῶν τοιούτων, καὶ τοὺς μὴ σπουδαίους εὑρήσομεν τούτων
τι ποιοῦντας. ὥστε μηδὲν ἴδιον εἶναι τοῦ σοφοῦ
ἔργον, ᾧ διοίσει τῶν μὴ σοφῶν. εἰ δὲ τοῦτο, οὐδὲ
φρόνησις ἔσται τέχνη τις περὶ τὸν βίον, ἧς ἴδιον
οὐδὲν τεχνικόν ἐστιν ἔργον.

200 Ἀλλὰ πρὸς τοῦθ' ὑπαντῶντές φασι πάντα μὲν
κοινὰ εἶναι καὶ πάντων τὰ ἔργα, διορίζεσθαι δὲ τῷ
ἀπὸ τεχνικῆς διαθέσεως ἢ ἀπὸ ἀτέχνου γίνεσθαι.
οὐ γὰρ τὸ ἐπιμελεῖσθαι γονέων καὶ ἄλλως τιμᾶν
γονεῖς τοῦ σπουδαίου ἐστὶν ἔργον, ἀλλὰ σπουδαίου
201 τὸ ἀπὸ φρονήσεως τοῦτο ποιεῖν· καὶ ὡς τὸ μὲν
ὑγιάζειν κοινόν ἐστι τοῦ τε ἰατροῦ καὶ ἰδιώτου, τὸ
δὲ ἰατρικῶς ὑγιάζειν τοῦ τεχνίτου ἴδιον, ὧδε καὶ τὸ
μὲν τιμᾶν τοὺς γονεῖς κοινὸν τοῦ τε σπουδαίου καὶ
μὴ σπουδαίου, τὸ δὲ ἀπὸ φρονήσεως τιμᾶν τοὺς
γονεῖς ἴδιον τοῦ σοφοῦ, ὥστε καὶ τέχνην αὐτὸν ἔχειν
περὶ τὸν βίον, ἧς ἴδιόν ἐστιν ἔργον τὸ ἕκαστον τῶν
πραττομένων ἀπὸ ἀρίστης διαθέσεως πράττειν.

202 ἐοίκασι δ' οἱ ταύτῃ χρώμενοι τῇ ὑπαντήσει
ἐθελοκωφεῖν καὶ πάντα μᾶλλον ἢ πρὸς τὸ ἐπιζητού-
μενόν τι λέγειν. ἡμῶν γὰρ ἄντικρυς δεικνύντων ὅτι
οὐδὲν ἴδιόν ἐστι τοῦ φρονοῦντος ἔργον, ᾧ διαφέρει
τῶν μὴ φρονίμων, ἀλλὰ πᾶν τὸ γινόμενον ὑπὸ αὐτοῦ, τοῦτο καὶ ὑπὸ τῶν μὴ σπουδαίων γίνεσθαι,
αὐτοὶ τοῦτο μὲν οὐκ ἴσχυσαν ἀνελεῖν, ἔξωθεν δέ
φασιν ὅτι τὸ κοινὸν ἔργον ὁτὲ μὲν ἀπὸ φρονίμης

the wise man is found to be a work common also to the unwise ; if, for example, we count honouring parents as a work of the wise man, or rendering back a deposit to those who have entrusted it, or any other thing of the kind, we shall also find men who are not virtuous doing any one of these things. So that there is no work peculiar to the wise man whereby he shall differ from the not wise. And if this is so, neither will wisdom be an art of life, as it has no artistic work peculiar to itself.

But in reply to this they say that although all the works are common to all men, yet they are distinguished by their proceeding either from an artistic or from a non-artistic disposition. For the work of the virtuous man is not that of caring for his parents and generally honouring his parents, but doing this because of wisdom is the act of the virtuous ; and just as procuring health is common both to the medical man and to the layman, but to procure health medically is peculiar to the man of art, so also honouring one's parents is common both to the virtuous man and the non-virtuous, but the honouring of his parents because of wisdom is peculiar to the wise man, so that he possesses also an art of life, of which the special work is the performance of each of his actions from the best disposition.—But those who make this reply would seem to be wilfully deaf, and doing anything rather than answer the question before them. For when we were definitely proving that there is no work peculiar to the wise man whereby he differs from the not wise, but everything which is done by him is done also by those who are not virtuous, the Stoics were unable to disprove this ; but they assert irrelevantly that the work common to both proceeds in

203 γίνεται διαθέσεως ότὲ δὲ ἀπὸ φαύλης. ὅπερ ἀπόδειξις μὲν τοῦ μὴ εἶναι κοινὸν ἔργον τῶν τε φρονίμων καὶ τῶν μὴ τοιούτων οὐκ ἔστιν, δεῖται δὲ
⟨αὐτὸ⟩¹ ἀποδείξεως, ζητήσαντος ἄν τινος πόθεν γε
διαγνωσόμεθα πότε γίνεται ταῦτα ἀπὸ φρονίμης
διαθέσεως καὶ πότε οὐ γίνεται· αὐτὰ γὰρ τὰ κοινὰ
ἔργα τοῦτ' οὐκ ἐμφαίνει, παρόσον ἐστὶ κοινά.
204 ἔνθεν καὶ τὸ ἀπὸ ἰατρικῆς κομισθὲν ὑπόδειγμα
κατ' αὐτῶν μᾶλλον εὑρίσκεται. ὅταν γὰρ φῶσι
τὸ ὑγιάζειν κοινὸν ἰατροῦ τε καὶ οὐκ ἰατροῦ καθ-
εστηκὸς ἐξαίρετον γίνεσθαι τοῦ τεχνίτου, ἐπειδὰν
ἰατρικῶς ἀποτελεσθῇ, τότε ἤτοι ἴσασί τι διαφόρως
γινόμενον ὑπὸ τοῦ ἰατροῦ παρὰ τὸν ἰδιώτην, οἷον
τὸ συντόμως καὶ ἀπόνως καὶ μετὰ τάξεως καὶ
ποιότητος, ἢ οὐκ ἴσασιν ἀλλὰ καὶ ταῦτα πάντα
205 κοινὰ τῶν ἰδιωτῶν ὑπειλήφασιν. καὶ εἰ μὲν ἴσασιν,
αὐτόθεν ἴδιόν τι τοῦ ἰατροῦ φαινόμενον ἔργον
ὡμολογήκασιν ὑπάρχειν, καὶ ἀκόλουθον ἦν αὐτοῖς
ἀπὸ τούτου μετελθοῦσι διδάσκειν καὶ τοῦ σοφοῦ τι
ἴδιον ἔργον, ᾧ διοίσει τοῦ μὴ σοφοῦ. εἰ δὲ οὐκ
ἴσασιν ἀλλὰ πᾶν τὸ ὑπὸ τοῦ ἰατροῦ γινόμενον, τοῦτ'
ἐροῦσι καὶ ὑπὸ τοῦ ἰδιώτου γίνεσθαι, ἀφελοῦνται
τοῦ ἰατροῦ τὸ ἴδιον ἔργον καὶ ἀπαραλλαξίας οὔσης
κατὰ τὸ φαινόμενον ἐν τοῖς γινομένοις ἔργοις οὐ
διαγνώσονται τόν τε τεχνίτην καὶ τὸν ἄτεχνον, οὐδὲ
τὸ ἀπὸ τεχνικῆς διαθέσεως ἐνεργούμενον οὐδὲ τὸ
ἀπὸ ἀτέχνου, διὰ τὸ μηδὲ τὴν καθ' ἕκαστον [ἀφανῆ]²
διάθεσιν ἐξ ἑαυτῆς δύνασθαι γνωρίζεσθαι οὖσαν

¹ ⟨αὐτὸ⟩ addo.
² [ἀφανῆ] secl. Heintz.

ª Cf. § 201 supra.

the one case from a wise disposition and in the other from a foolish. But this is not a proof that there is no 203 work common both to those who are wise and those who are not so, but itself needs proof, since one might inquire how we are to discern when these works proceed, and when they do not proceed, from a wise disposition ; for the common works themselves do not make this clear, inasmuch as they are common.— Hence, too, the example brought forward from the 204 art of medicine [a] is found to tell rather against them. For when they assert that procuring health, which is a thing common both to the medical and the non-medical man, belongs specially to the man of art when it is effected medically, then either they know that there is some difference in what is done by the doctor as compared with the layman,—the work being, for instance, rapid and painless and done systematically and on a definite plan,—or else they do not know this, but conceive that all these things are also common to laymen. And if they know it, they are directly 205 confessing that there is an apparent work which is peculiar to the doctor, and their next task is to pass on from this and to show that there is also a work peculiar to the wise man, wherein he will differ from the not wise. But if they do not know it, but shall declare that everything which is done by the doctor is also done by the layman, they will be robbing the doctor of his own peculiar work, and, —since there exists, apparently, exact similarity in the works executed,—they will not distinguish between the expert and the non-expert, nor between what is performed by an artistic disposition and by a non-artistic, because the disposition of the individual cannot be discerned of itself, as it is non-apparent.

206 ἀφανῆ. τοίνυν οὐδὲν ὠφελεῖ αὐτοὺς τὸ ὁμολογεῖν
μὲν κοινὰ εἶναι τὰ ὑπό τε τοῦ σοφοῦ γινόμενα
ἔργα καὶ τὰ μὴ ὑπὸ τοῦ σοφοῦ, διαφέρειν δ᾽ αὐτὰ
⟨φάναι⟩¹ τῷ νυνὶ μὲν ἀπὸ φρονίμης γίνεσθαι διαθέσεως νυνὶ δὲ ἀπὸ ἄφρονος.

Ἄλλοι δέ εἰσιν οἱ τῷ διομαλισμῷ καὶ τάξει ταῦτα
207 διορίζεσθαι νομίζοντες. καθὰ γὰρ ἐπὶ τῶν μέσων
τεχνῶν ἴδιόν ἐστι τοῦ τεχνίτου τό τε τεταγμένως
τι ποιεῖν καὶ τὸ ἐν τοῖς ἀποτελέσμασι διομαλίζειν
(ποιῆσαι γὰρ ἄν ποτε καὶ ἰδιώτης τὸ τεχνικὸν
ἔργον, ἀλλὰ σπανίως καὶ οὐ πάντοτε, οὐδὲ κατὰ τὸ
αὐτὸ καὶ ὡσαύτως), ὧδε καὶ τοῦ μὲν φρονίμου
φασὶν ἔργον εἶναι τὸ ἐν τοῖς κατορθώμασι διομαλί-
208 ζειν, τοῦ δὲ ἄφρονος τοὐναντίον. φαίνονται δὲ καὶ
οὗτοι οὐ κατὰ τὴν τῶν πραγμάτων φύσιν περὶ τῆς
ἐν χερσὶ ζητήσεως διαταττόμενοι. τὸ γὰρ εἶναί τινα
βίου τάξιν κατὰ τεχνικὸν λόγον ὡρισμένως εἰρημένην εὐχῇ μᾶλλον ἔοικεν. πᾶς γὰρ ἄνθρωπος πρὸς
τὰς τῶν ὑποπιπτόντων πραγμάτων διαφορὰς καὶ
ποικιλίας ἀρτιζόμενος οὐδέποτε δύναται τὴν αὐτὴν
τάξιν φυλάττειν, καὶ μάλιστα ὁ ἔμφρων τό τε
ἄστατον τῆς τύχης καὶ τὸ ἀβέβαιον τῶν πραγμάτων
209 ἐννοούμενος. ἄλλως τε, εἴπερ μίαν καὶ ὡρισμένην
εἶχε βίου τάξιν ὁ φρόνιμος, κἂν ἐκ ταύτης ἐναργῶς
κατείληπτο τοῖς μὴ φρονίμοις· οὐχὶ δέ γε καταλαμβάνεται τούτοις· τοίνυν οὐδ᾽ ἐκ τῆς τάξεως τῶν
ἔργων ληπτός ἐστιν ὁ φρόνιμος. ὅθεν εἰ πᾶσα μὲν
τέχνη ἐκ τῶν ἰδίων ἔργων φαίνεται, τῆς δὲ φρονή-

¹ ⟨φάναι⟩ add. cj. Heintz.

So then, it does not profit them at all to agree that the **206** works performed by the wise man and by the not wise are common to both, while alleging that they differ by being done in the one case from a wise disposition, in the other from an unwise.

But there are others who think that these works are distinguished by ⟨the presence or absence of⟩ unvarying quality and order. For just as in the **207** case of the intermediate arts [a] it is the peculiarity of the artist to produce a thing in an orderly way and to be unvarying in his products (for the layman, too, may at times produce an artistic work, but rarely and not at all times, nor consistently and in the same way),—so also they say that the work of the wise man is to be unvarying in his right actions, and that of the unwise the opposite. But these men, **208** too, are evidently not dealing with the question in hand according to the real state of the facts. For that there exists some order of life definitely formulated by the artistic reason seems rather like an illusory hope. For no man, in preparing himself to meet the different and varied occurrences, is ever able to preserve the same order,[b] and, least of all, the wise man who is aware both of the instability of fortune and the insecurity of events. And besides, if the **209** wise man had a single definite order of life, he would also have been plainly recognized through this by the not wise ; but in fact he is not recognized by them ; so then, the wise man cannot be discerned through the order of his works. Hence, if every art is apparent through its own special works, whereas

---

[a] With §§ 207-209 *cf. P.H.* iii. 243-244. By " intermediate " is meant " common " or " vulgar " arts (*cf. ἐς μέσον*, "in public").

[b] *i.e.* rule of life, programme of conduct.

σεως οὐδέν ἐστιν ἴδιον ἔργον ἐξ οὗ φαίνεται, οὐκ ἂν
εἴη τις τέχνη περὶ τὸν βίον ἡ φρόνησις.

210 Καὶ μὴν εἰ τέχνη τίς ἐστι περὶ τὸν βίον ἡ φρόνησις, οὐκ ἄλλον ἄν τινα μᾶλλον ὠφέλησεν ἢ τὸν
κεκτημένον αὐτὴν σοφόν, ἐγκράτειαν αὐτῷ παρα-
σχομένη ἐν ταῖς πρὸς τὸ κακὸν[1] ὁρμαῖς καὶ ἐν ταῖς
ἀπὸ τοῦ ἀγαθοῦ[1] ἀφορμαῖς. οὐχὶ δέ γε τὸν σοφὸν
ὠφελεῖ ἡ φρόνησις, ὡς παραστήσομεν· οὐκ ἄρα
211 τέχνη τίς ἐστι περὶ τὸν βίον. ὁ γὰρ λεγόμενος
ἐγκρατὴς σοφὸς ἤτοι κατὰ τοῦτο λέγεται ἐγκρατής,
καθόσον ἐν οὐδεμιᾷ γίνεται ὁρμῇ τῇ πρὸς τὸ κακὸν
καὶ ἀφορμῇ τῇ ἀπὸ τοῦ ἀγαθοῦ, ἢ καθόσον ἔχει μὲν
φαύλας ὁρμὰς περικρατεῖ δὲ τούτων τῷ λόγῳ. καὶ
κατὰ μὲν τὸ μὴ γίνεσθαι ἐν φαύλαις κρίσεσιν οὐκ
ἂν λεχθείη ἐγκρατὴς εἶναι· οὐ γὰρ κρατήσει οὗ οὐκ
212 ἔχει. καὶ ᾧ τρόπῳ οὐκ ἂν εἴποι τις τὸν εὐνοῦχον
ἐγκρατῆ πρὸς ἀφροδισίων μῖξιν καὶ τὸν κακοστο-
μαχοῦντα πρὸς ἐδεσμάτων ἀπόλαυσιν (οὐδ᾽ ὅλως
γὰρ ἐν αὐτοῖς ἐπιζήτησίς τις γίνεται τούτων, ἵνα
καὶ ἐγκρατῶς κατεξαναστῶσι τῆς ἐπιζητήσεως), τῷ
αὐτῷ τρόπῳ οὐδὲ τὸν σοφὸν ἐγκρατῆ ῥητέον διὰ τὸ
213 μὴ φύεσθαι ἐν αὐτῷ τὸ οὗ ἔσται ἐγκρατής. εἰ δὲ
κατὰ τοῦτο ἀξιώσουσιν αὐτὸν ὑπάρχειν ἐγκρατῆ,
καθόσον γίνεται μὲν ἐν φαύλαις κρίσεσι περιγίνεται
δ᾽ αὐτῶν τῷ λόγῳ, πρῶτον μὲν δώσουσι τὸ ὅτι
οὐδὲν ὠφέλησεν αὐτὸν ἡ φρόνησις ἀκμὴν ἐν ταρα-
χαῖς ὄντα καὶ βοηθείας δεόμενον, εἶτα καὶ κακοδαι-
214 μονέστερον τῶν φαύλων εὑρίσκεσθαι. ᾗ μὲν γὰρ
ὁρμᾷ ἐπί τι, πάντως ταράσσεται, ᾗ δὲ περικρατεῖ

---

[1] κακὸν . . . ἀγαθοῦ Heintz : ἀγαθὸν . . . κακοῦ mss., Bekk.

of wisdom there is no special work through which it is apparent, then wisdom will not be an art of life.

Moreover, if wisdom is an art of life,[a] it would have 210 benefited no one more than the wise man who possesses it, by furnishing him with self-control in his inclinations towards evil and in his disinclinations towards good. But wisdom does not in fact benefit the wise man, as we shall establish ; therefore it is not an art of life. For the wise man who is termed 211 " self-controlled " is termed self-controlled either in respect of the fact that he has no inclination towards evil or disinclination towards good, or in respect of the fact that he has foolish inclinations but keeps them in control by his reason. But in respect of his not forming foolish judgements he will not be called self-controlled ; for he will not control what he has not got. And just as one would not call the eunuch self- 212 controlled as regards sexual intercourse, nor the man with a bad stomach as regards the enjoyment of food (for they do not possess any appetite at all for these things, so that through self-control they might rise superior to the appetite),—in the same way one ought not to call the wise man self-controlled because the thing which he is to keep in control does not arise in him. And if they shall maintain that he is self- 213 controlled in respect of the fact that he forms foolish judgements but keeps them in control by his reason, they will be granting, firstly, that his wisdom has not benefited him at all, as he is still beset by perturbations and needing succour, and, secondly, that he is found to be even more unhappy than the foolish. For in that he has an inclination for something he 214 is certainly perturbed, and in that he controls it by

a With §§ 210-215 cf. P.H. iii. 273-277.

τῷ λόγῳ, συνέχει ἐν ἑαυτῷ τὸ κακόν, καὶ διὰ τοῦτο
μᾶλλον ταράττεται τοῦ φαύλου μηκέτι τοῦτο πά-
σχοντος· ᾗ μὲν γὰρ ὁρμᾷ, ταράττεται, ᾗ δὲ τυγχάνει τῶν ἐπιθυμουμένων, ὑπεκλυομένην ἴσχει τὴν
215 ταραχήν. οὐ τοίνυν ἐγκρατὴς γίνεται ὅσον ἐπὶ
τῇ φρονήσει ὁ σοφός· ἢ εἴπερ γίνεται, πάντων
ἀνθρώπων κακοδαιμονέστερος γίνεται. ἀλλ' εἰ
ἑκάστη τέχνη τὸν κεκτημένον αὐτὴν ὠφελεῖ μᾶλλον,
δέδεικται δὲ ἡ περὶ τὸν βίον ἀξιουμένη τυγχάνειν
τέχνη μηδὲ τὸν κεκτημένον ὠφελοῦσα, ῥητέον μὴ
εἶναί τινα περὶ τὸν βίον τέχνην.

Ζ΄.—ΕΙ ΔΙΔΑΚΤΗ ΕΣΤΙΝ Η ΠΕΡΙ ΤΟΝ ΒΙΟΝ ΤΕΧΝΗ

216 Δυνάμει μὲν οὖν συναποδέδεικται τῷ μὴ εἶναι
τινα περὶ τὸν βίον τέχνην τὸ μηδὲ διδακτὴν αὐτὴν
καθεστάναι· τῶν γὰρ μὴ ὄντων οὐ γίνεται μάθησις·
ὅμως δ' ἐκ περιττοῦ συγχωρήσαντες αὐτῆς τὴν
217 ὕπαρξιν διδάσκωμεν ὡς ἔστιν ἀδίδακτος. πολὺς
μὲν οὖν καὶ ποικίλος ἐστὶ παρὰ τοῖς φιλοσόφοις ὁ
περὶ τῆς μαθήσεως λόγος· ἀλλ' ἡμεῖς γε τὰ κυριώτατα ἐπιλεξάμενοι θήσομεν, ὧν τὰ μὲν κοινότερον
ἐπιχειρεῖται παρὰ τοῖς σκεπτικοῖς εἰς τὸ μηδὲν
εἶναι μάθησιν, τὰ δὲ καὶ ἰδιαίτερον λέγεται περὶ
αὐτῆς τῆς φρονήσεως. τάξει δὲ πρώτας σκοπῶμεν
τὰς κοινοτέρας ἐπιχειρήσεις.

218 Ἐπὶ πάσης τοίνυν μαθήσεως ὁμολογεῖσθαι δεῖ τό
τε διδασκόμενον πρᾶγμα καὶ τὸν διδάσκοντα καὶ
τὸν μανθάνοντα καὶ τὸν τρόπον τῆς μαθήσεως.
οὐδὲν δὲ τούτων ἐστὶν ὁμόλογον, ὡς δείξομεν· οὐκ
ἄρα ἔστι τις μάθησις. καὶ ἐπεὶ πρῶτον ἐμνήσθημεν
τοῦ διδασκομένου πράγματος, περὶ αὐτοῦ πρῶτον
219 ἀπορητέον. εἰ γὰρ διδάσκεταί τι πρᾶγμα, ἤτοι τὸ
490

his reason he retains the evil within himself and is, on this account, more perturbed than the fool who is no longer affected in this way ; for the latter is perturbed in that he feels inclination, but in that he obtains the things desired he has his perturbation gradually diminished. So then the wise man is not 215 self-controlled in virtue of his wisdom ; or if he is so, he is of all men the most unhappy. But if every art especially benefits him who possesses it, and it has been shown that that which is, as they maintain, the art of life does not even benefit its possessor, one must declare that there does not exist any art of life.

Chapter VII.—Can the Art of Life be taught?

Now in the proof that no art of life exists there is 216 virtually involved the proof that it is incapable of being taught ; for there is no learning of non-existent things. However, let us concede, gratuitously, that it exists, and let us teach that it cannot be taught. Now amongst the philosophers the arguments about 217 learning are many and varied ; but we, for our part, shall select and state the most important points, of which some are the more general criticisms of the Sceptics which go to show that learning is nothing, and others the more special discussions of wisdom itself. And first in order let us consider the more general criticisms.

In every instance, then, of learning there ought to 218 be agreement regarding the subject taught and the teacher and the learner and the mode of learning ; but, as we shall show, none of these things is agreed ; therefore no learning exists. And since we have mentioned first the subject taught, we must raise questions about it first. Now if any subject is taught, 219

ὂν διδάσκεται ἢ τὸ μὴ ὄν· οὔτε δὲ τὸ ὂν διδάσκεται,
ὡς δείξομεν, οὔτε τὸ μὴ ὄν, ὡς παραμυθησόμεθα·
οὐκ ἄρα διδάσκεταί τι πρᾶγμα. καὶ δὴ τὸ μὲν μὴ
ὂν οὐ διδάσκεται· οὐδὲν γὰρ αὐτῷ συμβέβηκεν, ὥστ᾽
220 οὐδὲ τὸ διδάσκεσθαι. καὶ ἄλλως, εἰ τὸ μὴ ὂν
διδάσκεται, ἀληθὲς ἔσται τὸ μὴ ὄν· τῶν γὰρ ἀληθῶν
ἐστιν ἡ μάθησις. εἰ δὲ ἀληθὲς ἔσται τὸ μὴ ὄν,
εὐθὺς καὶ ὑπαρκτὸν γενήσεται· ἀληθὲς γοῦν φασιν
οἱ στωικοὶ ὃ ὑπάρχει τε καὶ ἀντίκειταί τινι. ἄτοπον
δέ γε τὸ μὴ ὂν ὑπάρχειν· οὐκ ἄρα τὸ μὴ ὂν διδάσκεται.   τό γε μὴν διδασκόμενον κινοῦν φαντασίαν διδάσκεται, τὸ δὲ μὴ ὂν οὐ δύναται κινεῖν
221 φαντασίαν· οὐκ ἄρα διδακτόν ἐστι τὸ μὴ ὄν. πρὸς
τούτοις, εἰ τὸ μὴ ὂν διδάσκεται, οὐδὲν ἀληθὲς
διδάσκεται· τῶν γὰρ ὄντων καὶ ὑπαρχόντων ἐστὶ
τἀληθές. εἰ δὲ μηδὲν ἀληθὲς διδάσκεται, πᾶν τὸ
διδασκόμενόν ἐστι ψεῦδος. ἄτοπον δέ γε πᾶν τὸ
διδασκόμενον εἶναι ψεῦδος· οὐ τοίνυν τὸ μὴ ὂν
διδάσκεται. ἐπεί τοι εἴπερ τὸ μὴ ὂν διδάσκεται,
ἤτοι καθὸ μὴ ὄν ἐστι διδάσκεται, ἢ κατ᾽ ἄλλο τι.
καθὰ μὲν οὖν μὴ ὄν ἐστιν, οὐ διδάσκεται· εἰ γὰρ τὸ
μὴ ὂν καθὸ μὴ ὄν ἐστι διδάσκεται, οὐδὲν ὂν διδα-
χθήσεται, ὅπερ ἄτοπον. καὶ μὴν οὐδὲ κατ᾽ ἄλλο τι·
τὸ γὰρ ἄλλο τι ἔστι, τὸ δὲ μὴ ὂν οὐκ ἔστιν, ὥστ᾽
222 οὐκ ἂν διδαχθείη τὸ μὴ ὄν.   λείπεται οὖν
λέγειν τὸ ὂν διδάσκεσθαι· ὃ καὶ αὐτὸ τῶν ἀδυνάτων
δείξομεν. εἰ γὰρ τὸ ὂν διδάσκεται, ἤτοι καθὸ ὂν

ᵃ With §§ 219-223 cf. *P.H.* iii. 256-258.
ᵇ Cf. *Adv. Log.* ii. 10.

either the existent is taught or the non-existent.[a] But neither is the existent taught, as we shall show, nor the non-existent, as we shall argue ; therefore no subject is taught. Now the non-existent is not taught ; for it has no property, so that it has not that of being taught. And besides, if the non-existent is 220 taught, the non-existent will be true ; for learning is of things true. And if the non-existent shall be true, it will straightway be real as well : for certainly the Stoics say that " the true is that which is real and is opposed to something." [b] But it is absurd that the non-existent should be real. Therefore the non-existent is not taught. And, certainly, what is taught excites an impression when being taught, but the non-existent cannot excite an impression ; therefore the non-existent is not capable of being taught. Furthermore, if the non-existent is taught, nothing 221 true is taught ; for the true belongs to the class of things existent and real. And if nothing true is taught, everything which is taught is false. But it is, in fact, absurd that everything which is taught should be false ; so then the non-existent is not taught. For, of course, if the non-existent is taught, it is taught either in virtue of its non-existence or in virtue of something else. Now it is not taught in virtue of its non-existence ; for if the non-existent is taught in virtue of its non-existence, nothing existent will be taught ; which is absurd. Nor yet in virtue of something else ; for that " something else " exists, but the non-existent does not exist. So that the non-existent will not be taught.—It remains then to say that the existent is 222 taught ; and this too we shall prove to be a thing impossible. For if the existent is taught, it is either

SEXTUS EMPIRICUS

ἐστιν ἢ κατ' ἄλλο τι. καὶ εἰ μὲν καθὸ ὄν ἐστι
διδάσκεται, οὐδὲν ἔσται ἀδίδακτον· εἰ δὲ τῶν ὄντων
οὐδέν ἐστιν ἀδίδακτον, οὐδέ γε ἔσται τὸ διδασκό-
μενον· δεῖ γὰρ ἀδίδακτόν τι εἶναι, ἵνα ἐκ τούτου
μάθησις γένηται. ὥστε καθὸ μὲν ὄν ἐστιν, οὐκ ἂν
223 διδαχθείη τὸ ὄν. καὶ μὴν οὐδὲ κατ' ἄλλο τι⟨· τὸ
γὰρ ὄν οὐκ ἔχει ἄλλο τι⟩¹ συμβεβηκὸς αὐτῷ, ὅπερ
μὴ ὄν ἐστιν, ἀλλὰ πᾶν τὸ συμβεβηκὸς αὐτῷ ὄν
ἐστιν. ὥστ' εἰ τὸ ὄν καθὸ ὄν ἐστιν οὐ διδάσκεται,
οὐδὲ κατ' ἄλλο τι διδαχθήσεται· ἐκεῖνο γὰρ ὁτιποτέ
ἐστιν ἄλλο συμβεβηκὸς αὐτῷ, ὄν ἐστιν. εἰ οὖν μήτε
τὸ ὄν διδάσκεται μήτε τὸ μὴ ὄν, παρὰ δὲ ταῦτα
οὐδὲν ἔστιν, οὐδὲν τῶν ὄντων διδάσκεται.

224 Καὶ ἄλλως, ἐπεὶ τῶν τινῶν τὰ μέν ἐστι σώματα
τὰ δὲ ἀσώματα, εἰ διδάσκεταί τι, ἤτοι τὸ σῶμα
διδάσκεται ἢ τὸ ἀσώματον· οὔτε δὲ τὸ σῶμα
διδάσκεται οὔτε τὸ ἀσώματον· οὐκ ἄρα διδάσκεταί
τι. τὸ μὲν οὖν σῶμα οὐ διδάσκεται, καὶ μάλιστα
κατὰ τοὺς ἀπὸ τῆς στοᾶς λεκτὰ γάρ ἐστι τὰ
225 διδασκόμενα, σῶμα δ' οὐκ ἔστι τὰ λεκτά. καὶ
ἄλλως, εἰ τὸ σῶμα μήτε αἰσθητόν ἐστι μήτε νοητόν
ἐστιν, οὐ διδάσκεται τὸ σῶμα. δεῖ γὰρ τὸ διδασκόμενον ἢ αἰσθητὸν εἶναι ἢ νοητόν, μηθέτερον δὲ ὄν
οὐ διδάσκεται. τὸ δ' ὅτι οὔτε αἰσθητόν ἐστιν οὔτε
νοητόν ἐστι τὸ σῶμα, παρεστάκαμεν ἐν τοῖς πρὸς
226 τοὺς φυσικούς. ἐάν τε γὰρ ἀθροισμός τις ᾖ τὸ
σῶμα, ὡς φησὶν ὁ Ἐπίκουρος, μεγέθους καὶ σχή-

¹ ⟨· τὸ . . . τι⟩ add. Heintz.

ᵃ With §§ 224-231 cf. P.H. iii. 255. " Something " was
the highest category of the Stoics, cf. Vol. I. Introd. p. xxvi.
494

in virtue of its existence or in virtue of something else. But if it is taught in virtue of its existence, nothing will be untaught ; and if of existing things none is untaught, neither will there exist anything taught ; for something untaught must exist in order that from it learning may come about. So that the existent will not be taught in virtue of its existence. Nor yet in virtue of something else ; ⟨for the existent 223 has no other⟩ property belonging to it which is non-existent, but every property which belongs to it is existent. So that if the existent is not taught in virtue of its existence, neither will it be taught in virtue of something else ; for that other property, whatsoever it be, which belongs to it is existent. If, then, neither the existent is taught nor the non-existent, and besides these there is no other alternative, no existing thing is taught.

And again [a] : since of the " Somethings " some are 224 bodies, others incorporeal, if something is taught either it is a body that is taught or an incorporeal ; but neither is the body taught nor the incorporeal ; therefore nothing is taught. Now the body is not taught, according to the Stoics especially ; for the things taught are " expressions," and expressions are not bodies.[b] And besides, if the body is neither 225 sensible nor intelligible, the body is not taught. For what is taught must be either sensible or intelligible, and if it is neither it is not taught. And the fact that body is neither sensible nor intelligible we have established in our treatise *Against the Physicists*.[c] For whether body is, as Epicurus asserts, a combina- 226

---

[b] For the incorporeality of " expressions " (λεκτά) *cf. Adv. Log.* ii. 12 ; *P.H.* ii. 81.

[c] See *Adv. Phys.* i. 437-439, 361 ff. ; *cf. P.H.* ii. 47 ff.

ματος καὶ ἀντιτυπίας, ἐάν τε τὸ τὰς τρεῖς ἔχον
διαστάσεις μετὰ ἀντιτυπίας, ἐπεὶ πᾶν τὸ κατὰ
σύνοδον πλειόνων λαμβανόμενον οὐκ ἔστι τῆς
ἀλόγου αἰσθήσεως λαβεῖν ἀλλὰ λογικῆς τινος δυνά-
227 μεως, οὐκ ἔσται τῶν αἰσθητῶν τὸ σῶμα. καὶ εἰ
αἰσθητὸν δὲ ὑπάρχοι, πάλιν ἀδίδακτον γενήσεται·
τῶν γὰρ αἰσθητῶν οὐδὲν διδάσκεται, οἷον οὐδεὶς
λευκὸν ὁρᾶν μανθάνει, οὐδὲ γλυκέος γεύεσθαι, οὐχ
ὑπό τινος εὐωδίζεσθαι ψύχεσθαι ἀλεαίνεσθαι, ἀλλ᾽
ἀδίδακτός ἐστιν ἡ πάντων τούτων ἀντίληψις. οὔτε
τοίνυν αἰσθητόν ἐστι τὸ σῶμα, οὔτ᾽ εἰ αἰσθητὸν
228 ὑπάρχει, κατὰ τοῦτ᾽ ἔσται διδακτόν.   καὶ μὴν
οὐδ᾽ ὡς νοητὸν δύναται διδάσκεσθαι. εἰ γὰρ μήτε
τὸ μῆκος κατ᾽ ἰδίαν ἐστὶ σῶμα μήτε τὸ πλάτος
μήτε τὸ βάθος, τὸ δὲ ἐξ ἁπάντων τούτων σύνθετον,
δεήσει πάντων ἀσωμάτων ὄντων καὶ τὸ ἐξ αὐτῶν
ἄθροισμα ἐννοεῖν ἀσώματον καὶ οὐ σῶμα· διὰ δὲ
229 τοῦτο καὶ ἀδίδακτον εἶναι τὸ σῶμα. τῶν τε σωμάτων τὰ μέν ἐστιν αἰσθητὰ τὰ δὲ νοητά. διόπερ
εἰ διδάσκεται τὸ σῶμα, ἤτοι τὸ αἰσθητὸν διδάσκεται
ἢ τὸ νοητόν. οὔτε δὲ τὸ αἰσθητὸν διδάσκεται διὰ
τὸ φαίνεσθαι καὶ ἐξ αὐτοῦ πᾶσι πρόδηλον ὑπάρχειν,
οὔτε τὸ νοητὸν διὰ τὴν ἀδηλότητα καὶ τὴν ἀνεπί-
κριτον μέχρι τοῦ νῦν περὶ αὐτοῦ διαφωνίαν, τῶν μὲν
ἄτομον αὐτὸ λεγόντων τῶν δὲ τμητόν, καὶ τῶν μὲν
ἀμερὲς καὶ ἐλάχιστον, τῶν δὲ μεριστὸν καὶ εἰς
ἄπειρον τέμνεσθαι δυνάμενον. οὐκ ἄρα διδακτόν
230 ἐστι τὸ σῶμα.   ἀλλὰ μὴν οὐδὲ τὸ ἀσώματον.
ἢ γὰρ ἰδέα τίς ἐστι Πλατωνικὴ ἢ τὸ παρὰ τοῖς

---

[a] With §§ 227-228 cf. *P.H.* iii. 254.
[b] This last is the Stoic view, whereas the Epicureans believed in indivisibles (" atoms ").
496

tion of size and form and solidity, or whether it is that which has the three dimensions plus solidity, since it is not the part of the irrational sense but of some rational faculty to perceive everything which is perceived owing to the concourse of several elements, body will not be an object of sense. And even if it should be 227 sensible, it will, once again, be incapable of being taught.[a] For no sensible thing is taught,—as, for instance, no one learns to see the white, or to taste the sweet, to derive a sweet smell from something, to feel cold or heat, but the perception of all these things is untaught. So, then, neither is body sensible nor, should it be sensible, will it on that account be capable of being taught.—Moreover, even supposing 228 it to be intelligible it cannot be taught. For if neither length by itself is body, nor breadth nor depth, but the compound of them all, as they are all incorporeal we shall have to conceive of the combination of them as being incorporeal and not body ; and because of this body is also incapable of being taught. Also, some bodies are sensible, others intelligible. 229 Hence, if body is taught, either the sensible is taught or the intelligible. But neither is the sensible taught (because it appears and is of itself quite evident to all), nor the intelligible (because of its obscurity and the hitherto undecided controversy about it, some saying that it is indivisible, others divisible, and some that it is without parts and minimal, others that it has parts and can be divided *ad infinitum*[b]). Body, therefore, is not capable of being taught.—Nor, indeed, is the incorporeal. For 230 it is either a Platonic Idea, or the " expression " of

SEXTUS EMPIRICUS

στωικοῖς λεκτὸν ἢ κενὸν ἢ τόπος ἢ χρόνος ἢ ἄλλο
τι τῶν τοιούτων. ὅ τι δ᾽ ἂν ᾖ τούτων, ἔτι ζητου-
μένην καὶ ἀνεπικρίτως διαφωνουμένην ἔχει τὴν
231 ὑπόστασιν· τὸ δὲ τὰ ἔτι ἀμφισβητούμενα ὡς ἀν-
αμφίλεκτα λέγειν διδάσκεσθαι τελέως ἐστὶν ἄτοπον.
ἀλλ᾽ εἰ τῶν ὄντων τὰ μέν ἐστι σώματα τὰ δὲ
ἀσώματα, δέδεικται δὲ μηθὲν τούτων διδασκόμενον,
οὐθέν ἐστι τὸ διδασκόμενον.
232 Καὶ ἄλλως, εἰ διδάσκεταί τι, ἤτοι ἀληθές ἐστιν ἢ
ψεῦδος. καὶ ψεῦδος μὲν οὐκ ἔστιν, ὡς αὐτόθεν
φαίνεται· ἀληθὲς δ᾽ εἴπερ ἐστίν, ἄπορόν ἐστιν, ὡς
ἐν τοῖς περὶ κριτηρίου ἐδείξαμεν, καὶ περὶ ἀπόρων
οὐκ ἔστι μάθησις· οὐκ ἄρα ἔστι τὸ διδασκόμενον.
233   πρὸς τούτοις τὸ διδασκόμενον ἢ τεχνικόν
ἐστιν ἢ ἄτεχνον. ἀλλ᾽ ἄτεχνον μὲν οὐκ ἔστιν, ἐπεὶ
οὐδὲ δεήσεται μαθήσεως. εἰ δὲ τεχνικόν ἐστιν, ἤτοι
αὐτόθεν φαίνεται ἢ ἄδηλόν ἐστιν. καὶ εἰ μὲν αὐτόθεν φαίνεται, καὶ ἄτεχνόν ἐστι καὶ ἀδίδακτον· εἰ δὲ
ἄδηλόν ἐστιν, οὐ γίνεται δι᾽ αὐτὸ τὸ ἀδηλεῖσθαι
διδακτόν.
234 Ἐκ τούτων μὲν οὖν ἄπορον παρίσταται τὸ διδασκόμενον πρᾶγμα· συναναιρεῖται δ᾽ αὐτῷ ὅ τε
διδάσκων διὰ τὸ μὴ ἔχειν ὃ διδάξει, ὅ τε μανθάνων
διὰ τὸ μὴ ἔχειν ὃ μάθῃ. οὐθὲν δ᾽ ἧττον ἔσται καὶ
235 ἐπ᾽ αὐτῶν τούτων τὰς ὁμοίας κινεῖν ἀπορίας. εἰ
γάρ ἔστι τις ὁ διδάσκων καὶ ἔστι τις ὁ μανθάνων,
ἤτοι τεχνίτης τὸν τεχνίτην διδάξει ἢ ἄτεχνος τὸν
ἄτεχνον ἢ ἐναλλὰξ ὁ τεχνίτης τὸν ἄτεχνον ἢ ἄτεχνος
τὸν τεχνίτην. οὔτε δὲ ὁ ἄτεχνος τὸν ἄτεχνον

---

* Cf. Adv. Phys. ii. 258 ; Adv. Log. ii. 12.
b With §§ 232-233 cf. P.H. iii. 253.

the Stoics, or void or place or time or something else of the kind.[a] But whichsoever of these it be, its real existence is still a matter of doubt and of unsettled controversy. But to say that things still in dispute 231 are taught as though they were uncontroverted is perfectly absurd. But if of things existent some are bodies, others incorporeal, and it has been shown that none of these is taught, then what is taught is nothing.

Yet again : if anything is taught, it is either true 232 or false.[b] But it is not false, as is apparent at once ; and if it is true it is doubtful, as we have shown in our chapter " On the Criterion," and concerning things doubtful no learning exists. Therefore what is taught does not exist.—Furthermore, what is 233 taught is either technical or non-technical. But it is not non-technical, since then it would not require learning. And if it is technical, either it is apparent of itself or it is non-evident. But if it is apparent of itself, it is both non-technical and incapable of being taught ; while if it is non-evident, because of the very fact of its being non-evident it is not capable of being taught.

By these arguments it is established that the thing 234 taught is open to doubt [c] ; and along with it both the teacher is abolished, because he will have nothing to teach, and the learner, because he will have nothing to learn. None the less, in their case also it will be possible to raise similar difficulties. For if a teacher 235 exists and a learner exists, either the expert will teach the expert, or the non-expert the non-expert, or conversely the expert the non-expert, or the non-expert the expert. But neither can the non-expert

---

[c] With §§ 234-238 *cf.* *P.H.* iii. 259-260.

διδάσκειν δύναται, ὡς οὐδὲ ὁ τυφλὸς τὸν τυφλὸν
ὁδηγεῖν, οὔθ' ὁ τεχνίτης τὸν τεχνίτην· οὐ γὰρ
ἔχει πάντως ὃ διδάξει. οὔτε μὴν ὁ ἄτεχνος τὸν
τεχνίτην, ὡς οὐδὲ ὁ τυφλὸς ὁδηγεῖν ποτὲ δύναται
τὸν βλέποντα· πεπήρωται γὰρ ὁ ἰδιώτης εἰς τὰ τῆς
τέχνης θεωρήματα, καὶ διὰ τοῦτ' ἀνεπιτήδειος πρὸς
236 τὸ διδάσκειν.   ἀπολείπεται οὖν λέγειν ὅτι ὁ
τεχνίτης τὸν ἰδιώτην διδάσκει, ὃ πάλιν τῶν ἀμη-
χάνων· καὶ γὰρ ὁ τεχνίτης συνηπόρηται ἡμῖν τοῖς
237 τῆς τέχνης θεωρήμασιν, καὶ ὁ ἄτεχνος εἰ διδάσκεται
καὶ γίνεται τεχνίτης, ἤτοι ὅτε ἄτεχνός ἐστι γίνεται
τεχνίτης ἢ ὅτε τεχνίτης ἐστίν, οὔτε δὲ ὅτε ἄτεχνός
ἐστι δύναται γίνεσθαι τεχνίτης, οὔτε ὅτε τεχνίτης
238 ἐστὶν ἔτι γίνεται τεχνίτης, ἀλλ' ἔστιν. καὶ κατὰ
λόγον· ὁ μὲν γὰρ ἄτεχνος ἔοικε τῷ ἐκ γενετῆς
τυφλῷ ἢ κωφῷ, καὶ ὃν τρόπον οὔτε ὁ ἐκ γενετῆς
τυφλὸς εἰς ἔννοιαν ἔρχεται χρωμάτων οὔτε ὁ ἐκ
γενετῆς κωφὸς εἰς ἔννοιαν ἔρχεται φωνῶν, οὕτω καὶ
ὁ ἄτεχνος, ἐφ' ὅσον ἐστὶν ἄτεχνος, πεπηρωμένος
πρὸς τὴν τῶν τεχνικῶν θεωρημάτων ἀντίληψιν οὐ
δύναται τούτων αὐτῶν ἔχειν τὴν γνῶσιν. ὁ δὲ
τεχνίτης οὐκέτι διδάσκεται ἀλλὰ δεδίδακται.
239 Καὶ μὴν ὡς ταῦτ' ἔστιν ἄπορα, οὕτω καὶ ὁ
τρόπος τῆς μαθήσεώς ἐστιν ἄπορος. ἢ γὰρ ἐναργείᾳ γίνεται ἢ λόγῳ· οὔτε δὲ ἐναργείᾳ οὔτε λόγῳ
γίνεται, ὡς παραστήσομεν, ὥστε οὐδὲ ὁ τρόπος τῆς
240 μαθήσεώς ἐστιν εὔπορος. ἐναργείᾳ μὲν οὖν οὐ
γίνεται μάθησις, ἐπείπερ τῶν δεικνυμένων ἐστὶν ἡ
ἐνάργεια, τὸ δὲ δεικτόν ἐστι φαινόμενον· τὸ δὲ

---

[a] Cf. Adv. Log. i. 55.
[b] Cf. P.H. iii. 264.
• With §§ 239-242 cf. P.H. iii. 266-268.

teach the non-expert (just as the blind cannot lead the blind [a]) nor the expert the expert, for certainly he has nothing to teach him.   Nor yet the non-expert the expert, just as the blind man can never lead the man who sees ; for the layman is incapacitated for grasping the theorems of the art, and on this account is unfitted for teaching.—It remains, then, to say that the **236** expert teaches the layman, which again is a thing impracticable ; for together with the theorems of the art the expert was doubted by us; and the non-expert **237** too, if he is taught and becomes an expert, becomes an expert either when he is non-expert or when he is expert ; but he cannot become an expert when he is non-expert, and when he is expert he no longer becomes an expert but is one.   And reasonably so ; **238** for the non-expert resembles the man who is blind or deaf from birth, and just as he who is blind from birth [b] does not attain to a conception of colours, nor does he who is deaf from birth attain to a conception of sounds, so also the non-expert, in so far as he is non-expert, seeing that he is incapacitated for grasping the technical theorems cannot possess knowledge of them.   And the expert is no longer being taught but has been taught.

Moreover, just as these things are doubtful, so also **239** is the method of learning doubtful.[c]   For learning takes place either by the evidence of the senses or by speech.   But, as we shall establish, it takes place neither by evidence nor by speech, so that the method of learning is not free from doubt either.   Now **240** learning is not by means of evidence, since evidence is of things pointed out.   But what can be pointed out is apparent ; and the apparent, in so far as it is

φαινόμενον, ᾗ φαίνεται, κοινῶς πᾶσι ληπτόν ἐστι,
τὸ δὲ κοινῶς πᾶσι ληπτὸν ἀδίδακτον. οὐκ ἄρα τὸ
241 ἐναργείᾳ δεικτὸν διδακτόν ἐστιν. καὶ μὴν οὐδὲ
λόγῳ τι διδάσκεται. ἢ γὰρ σημαίνει τι ὁ λόγος ἢ
οὐδὲ ἓν σημαίνει. ἀλλὰ μηδὲ ἓν σημαίνων οὐδ᾽
ἔσται τινὸς διδάσκαλος. εἰ δὲ σημαίνει τι, ἤτοι
φύσει σημαίνει ἢ θέσει. καὶ φύσει μὲν οὐ σημαίνει
διὰ τὸ μὴ πάντας πάντων ἀκούειν, ⟨οἷον⟩[1] Ἕλληνας
242 βαρβάρων καὶ βαρβάρους Ἑλλήνων, θέσει δ᾽ εἴπερ
σημαίνει, δῆλον ὡς οἱ μὲν προκατειληφότες καθ᾽
ὧν αἱ λέξεις εἰσὶ τεταγμέναι ἀντιλήψονται τούτων,
οὐκ ἐξ αὐτῶν διδασκόμενοι ἅπερ ἠγνόουν, ἀλλ᾽
ἀναμιμνησκόμενοι καὶ ἀνανεούμενοι ταῦθ᾽ ἅπερ
ᾔδεσαν, οἱ δὲ χρῄζοντες τῆς τῶν ἀγνοουμένων
μαθήσεως, καὶ ἀγνοοῦντες καθ᾽ ὧν εἰσὶ τεταγμέναι
243 αἱ λέξεις, οὐδενὸς ἀντίληψιν ἕξουσιν. διόπερ εἰ
μήτε τὸ διδασκόμενον ἔστι πρᾶγμα μήτε ὁ διδάσκων μήτε ὁ μανθάνων μήτε ὁ τρόπος τῆς μαθήσεως, οὐδέν ἐστι μάθησις.

Κοινότερον μὲν οὖν οὕτως ἐπιχειρεῖται τοῖς
σκεπτικοῖς[a] εἰς τὸ μὴ εἶναι μάθησιν· ἐνέσται δὲ
μεταφέρειν τὰς ἀπορίας καὶ ἐπὶ τὴν λεγομένην περὶ
244 τὸν βίον τέχνην. ἤτοι γὰρ ὁ φρόνιμος τὸν φρόνιμον
ταύτην διδάξει ἢ ὁ ἄφρων τὸν ἄφρονα ἢ ὁ ἄφρων
τὸν φρόνιμον ἢ ὁ φρόνιμος τὸν ἄφρονα. οὔτε δὲ ὁ
φρόνιμος τὸν φρόνιμον λέγοιτ᾽ ἂν ταύτην διδάσκειν,
ἀμφότεροι γὰρ τέλειοι κατ᾽ ἀρετήν εἰσι καὶ οὐθέτερος αὐτῶν δεῖται μαθήσεως, οὔτε ὁ ἄφρων τὸν
ἄφρονα, ἀμφότεροι γὰρ χρείαν ἔχουσι μαθήσεως

[1] ⟨οἷον⟩ add. cj. Heintz.

[a] Cf. P.H. ii. 214.

apparent, is perceptible by all alike, and what is perceptible by all alike is incapable of being taught. Therefore what is pointed out by evidence is not capable of being taught. Nor yet is anything taught by speech. For either the speech signifies something 241 or it signifies nothing. But if it signifies nothing it will not be a teacher of anything. And if it signifies something, it signifies either by nature or by convention. But it does not signify by nature,[a] because all men do not hear all men,—Greeks, for instance, barbarians and barbarians Greeks. And if it signifies by convention, evidently those who have apprehended 242 beforehand the objects to which the terms are assigned will comprehend those terms, not because they are taught by them things of which they were ignorant but by recalling and being reminded of the things which they knew ; while those who need to learn the unknown things, and are in ignorance of the things to which the terms are assigned, will have no comprehension of anything. Wherefore, if neither the thing taught exists nor the teacher nor the learner 243 nor the method of learning, learning is nothing.

These, then, are the objections of a more general character brought forward by the Sceptics to show the non-existence of learning[b] ; and it will be possible also to apply these difficulties in turn to the so-called art of life. For either the wise man will teach this to the wise, or the unwise to the unwise, or the unwise 244 to the wise, or the wise to the unwise. But neither would the wise man be said to teach it to the wise (for both are perfect in virtue and neither of them needs to learn), nor the unwise to the unwise (for both of them have need of learning and neither of

[b] With §§ 243-246 cf. P.H. iii. 270-272.

SEXTUS EMPIRICUS

καὶ οὐθέτερος αὐτῶν φρόνιμός ⟨ἐστιν⟩,[1] ἵνα τὸν
245 ἕτερον διδάξῃ. καὶ μὴν οὐδ' ὁ ἄφρων διδάξει τὸν
φρόνιμον· οὐδὲ γὰρ ὁ τυφλὸς μηνυτικὸς γίνεται τῷ
βλέποντι χρωμάτων. λείπεται ἄρα τὸν φρόνιμον
διδακτικὸν εἶναι τοῦ ἄφρονος· ὃ καὶ αὐτὸ τῶν
246 ἀπόρων. εἰ γὰρ ἡ φρόνησίς ἐστιν ἐπιστήμη ἀγαθῶν καὶ κακῶν καὶ οὐθετέρων, ὁ ἄφρων μὴ ἔχων
τινὰ φρόνησιν, ἄγνοιαν δὲ ἔχων τούτων πάντων,
διδάσκοντος τοῦ φρονίμου τὰ ἀγαθὰ καὶ κακὰ καὶ
οὐθέτερα ἀκούσεται μόνον τῶν λεγομένων, οὐ
γνώσεται δ' αὐτά. εἰ γὰρ ἀντιλαμβάνοιτο αὐτῶν
ἐν ἀφροσύνῃ καθεστώς, ἔσται ἡ ἀφροσύνη τῶν τε
ἀγαθῶν καὶ κακῶν καὶ οὐθετέρων γνωριστική. οὐχὶ
δέ γε τούτων κατ' αὐτούς ἐστιν ἡ ἀφροσύνη θεω-
ρητική· ὁ ἄρα ἄφρων οὐκ ἀντιλήψεται τῶν ὑπὸ
τοῦ φρονίμου λεγομένων ἢ πραττομένων κατὰ τὸν
247 τῆς φρονήσεως λόγον. καὶ ὃν τρόπον ὁ ἐκ γενετῆς
πηρός, μέχρις οὗ πηρός ἐστιν, οὐκ ἔχει ἔννοιαν
χρωμάτων, καὶ ὁ ἐκ γενετῆς κωφός, μέχρις οὗ
κωφός ἐστιν, οὐκ ἀντιλαμβάνεται φωνῶν, οὕτω καὶ
ὁ ἄφρων, ἐφ' ὅσον ἄφρων ἐστίν, οὐκ ἀντιλαμβάνεται
τῶν φρονίμως λεγομένων καὶ πραττομένων. οὐδ'
ὁ φρόνιμος ἄρα δύναται τοῦ ἄφρονος ἐν τῇ περὶ τὸν
248 βίον τέχνῃ καθηγεῖσθαι.   καὶ μὴν εἰ ὁ φρόνιμος
διδάσκει τὸν ἄφρονα, θεωρητικὴ ὀφείλει εἶναι ἡ
φρόνησις τῆς ἀφροσύνης ὥσπερ καὶ ἡ τέχνη τῆς
ἀτεχνίας· οὐχὶ δέ γε ἡ φρόνησις δύναται εἶναι
θεωρητικὴ τῆς ἀφροσύνης· οὐκ ἄρα ὁ φρόνιμος τοῦ
ἄφρονός ἐστι διδακτικός. ὁ γὰρ γενόμενος φρόνιμος ἔκ τινος συνασκήσεως καὶ τριβῆς (φύσει γὰρ

[1] ⟨ἐστιν⟩ addo (post αὐτῶν add. Mutsch.).

504

them is wise so as to teach the other).   Nor yet will 245
the unwise teach the wise ; for neither is the blind
man capable of instructing the man who sees about
colours.   It only remains, therefore, that the wise
man is capable of teaching the unwise ; and this too
is a matter of doubt.   For if wisdom is " the science 246
of things good and evil and neither," [a] the unwise
man, when the wise man is teaching him the things
good and evil and neither, will merely hear the things
spoken and will not know the things themselves,[b]
since he does not possess any wisdom but is in ignorance of all these things.   For if he should comprehend
them while he is in a state of unwisdom, unwisdom
will be capable of knowing things good and evil and
neither.   But, according to them, unwisdom is not
capable of perceiving these things ; therefore the
unwise man will not comprehend the things said or
done by the wise man in pursuance of the rule of his
wisdom.   And just as he who is blind from birth,[c] so 247
long as he is blind, has no conception of colours, and
he who is deaf from birth, so long as he is deaf, does
not apprehend sounds, so also the unwise man, in so
far as he is unwise, does not comprehend things
wisely said and done.   Neither, therefore, can the
wise man guide the unwise in the art of life.—
Moreover, if the wise man teaches the unwise, wisdom 248
must be cognisant of unwisdom, even as art is of lack
of art ; but wisdom cannot be cognisant of unwisdom ;
therefore the wise man is not capable of teaching the
unwise.   For he who has become wise owing to some
joint exercise [d] and practice (for no one is such by

---

[a] Cf. § 170 supra.   [b] Cf. §§ 238, 242 supra.
[c] Cf. Adv. Phys. ii. 175.   With § 247 cf. P.H. iii. 264.
[d] i.e. simultaneous training of several parts or faculties:
cf. Adv. Log. i. 146.

οὐδείς ἐστι τοιοῦτος) ἤτοι ὑποκειμένης ἐν αὐτῷ
τῆς ἀφροσύνης προσεκτήσατο τὴν φρόνησιν, ἢ κατὰ
τὴν ἐκείνης ἀποβολὴν καὶ τὴν ταύτης κτῆσιν γέγονε
249 φρόνιμος. καὶ εἰ μὲν ὑποκειμένης ἐν αὐτῷ τῆς
ἀφροσύνης προσεκτήσατο τὴν φρόνησιν, ἔσται ὁ
αὐτὸς φρόνιμος ἅμα καὶ ἄφρων· ὅ ἐστιν ἀδύνατον.
εἰ δ' ἀποβολῇ ἐκείνης ἐκτήσατο ταύτην, οὐ δυνήσεται διὰ τῆς ὑστερογενοῦς διαθέσεως τὴν προ-
οῦσαν διάθεσιν, νῦν δὲ μὴ παροῦσαν γνωρίζειν.
250 καὶ εἰκότως. παντὸς γοῦν πράγματος αἰσθητοῦ
ἢ νοητοῦ γίνεται κατάληψις ἤτοι κατὰ ἐνάργειαν
περιπτωτικῶς ἢ κατὰ τὴν ἀπὸ τῶν περιπτωτικῶς
πεφηνότων ἀναλογιστικὴν μετάβασιν, καὶ ταύτην
251 ἤτοι ὁμοιωτικήν, ὡς ὅταν ἀπὸ τῆς Σωκράτους
εἰκόνος γνωρίζηται ὁ μὴ παρὼν Σωκράτης, ἢ
συνθετικήν, ὡς ὅταν ἀπ' ἀνθρώπου καὶ ἵππου κατ'
ἐπισύνθεσιν νοῶμεν τὸν ἀνύπαρκτον ἱπποκένταυρον,
ἢ κατὰ ἀναλογίαν, ὡς ὅταν ἀπὸ τοῦ κοινοῦ ἀνθρώπου παραυξητικῶς μὲν λαμβάνηται ὁ Κύκλωψ, ὃς
οὐκ ἐῴκει

ἀνδρί γε σιτοφάγῳ ἀλλὰ ῥίῳ ὑλήεντι,

252 μειωτικῶς δὲ ὁ πυγμαῖος ἄνθρωπος. ὅθεν εἰ καὶ
τῇ φρονήσει λαμβάνεται ἡ ἀφροσύνη καὶ τῷ φρο-
νίμῳ ὁ ἄφρων, ἤτοι κατὰ περίπτωσιν θεωρεῖται ἢ
κατὰ τὴν ἀπὸ τῆς περιπτώσεως μετάβασιν. οὔτε
δὲ κατὰ περίπτωσιν θεωρεῖται (οὐδεὶς γὰρ ὡς
λευκὸν καὶ μέλαν καὶ γλυκὺ καὶ πικρὸν κατὰ
περίπτωσιν ἔγνω, οὕτω καὶ ἀφροσύνην) οὔτε κατὰ

ª With §§ 250-251 cf. Adv. Log. ii. 58-60 ; Adv. Phys.
i. 393-395.

nature) either has acquired wisdom in addition while his unwisdom still subsists within him, or else has become wise through getting rid of the latter and acquiring the former.   But if he has acquired wisdom 249 in addition while his unwisdom still subsists within him, the same man will be at once both wise and unwise, which is impossible.   And if he has acquired the former by getting rid of the latter, he will not be able to know his pre-existing condition, which is not now present, by means of a condition of later origin. And 250 naturally so[a] ; for certainly the apprehension of every object, whether sensible or intelligible, comes about either empirically by way of sense-evidence or by way of analogical inference from things which have appeared empirically, this latter being either through resemblance (as when Socrates, not being present, is recognized from the likeness of Socrates), 251 or through composition (as when from a man and a horse we form by compounding them the conception of the non-existent hippocentaur), or by way of analogy (as when from the ordinary man there is conceived by magnification the Cyclops who was

> Less like a corn-eating man than a forest-clad peak of the mountains,[b]

and by diminution the pygmy).   Hence, if unwisdom 252 is perceived by wisdom and also the unwise man by the wise, the perception takes place either by experience or by inference from experience.   But the perception does not take place by experience (for no one gets to know wisdom in the same way as white and black and sweet and bitter), nor by inference from

[b] Homer, *Odyss.* ix. 191 ; *cf. Adv. Phys.* i. 45.

τὴν ἀπὸ τῆς περιπτώσεως μετάβασιν· οὐδὲν γὰρ
τῶν ὄντων ἐστὶν ἐοικὸς ἀφροσύνῃ [εἰ δ' ἀπὸ τούτου ποιεῖται τὴν μετάβασιν ὁ φρόνιμος, ἤτοι ὁμοιωτικὴν ἢ συνθετικὴν ἢ ἀναλογιστικήν,]¹ ὥστε οὐ
253 λήψεταί ποτε τὴν ἀφροσύνην ἡ φρόνησις.   ναί,
ἀλλ' ἴσως τις ἐρεῖ ὅτι ὁ φρόνιμος τῇ ἐν αὐτῷ
φρονήσει τὴν περὶ ἄλλον ἀφροσύνην δύναται κατα-
νοεῖν· ὅπερ ἐστὶν εὔηθες. ἡ γὰρ ἀφροσύνη διάθεσίς
254 ἐστιν ἔργων τινῶν ἀποδοτική. εἰ οὖν αὐτὴν ἐν
ἄλλῳ θεωρεῖ καὶ καταλαμβάνεται ὁ φρόνιμος, ἤτοι
αὐτὴν ἐξ ἑαυτῆς καταλήψεται τὴν διάθεσιν, ἢ τοῖς
ἔργοις αὐτῆς ἐπιβάλλων ἀπὸ τούτων καὶ αὐτὴν
255 γνωριεῖ, καθάπερ τὴν μὲν ἰατρικὴν διάθεσιν ἀπὸ
τῶν ἰατρικῶς γινομένων ἔργων, τὴν δὲ ζωγραφικὴν
ἀπὸ τῶν ζωγραφικῶς γινομένων. οὔτε δὲ αὐτὴν ἐξ
αὑτῆς δύναται τὴν διάθεσιν λαβεῖν· ἀφανὴς γάρ ἐστι
καὶ ἀθεώρητος, καὶ οὐχ οἷόν τέ ἐστιν αὐτὴν διὰ τῆς
τοῦ σώματος μορφῆς περιαθρῆσαι· οὔτε ἐκ τῶν ὑπὸ
αὐτῆς ἀποδιδομένων ἔργων· πάντα γὰρ τὰ φαινόμενα ἔργα, καθάπερ καὶ πρότερον ἐδείκνυμεν, κοινὰ
256 φρονήσεως καὶ ἀφροσύνης ἐστίν. ἀλλ' εἴπερ, ἵνα ὁ
φρόνιμος τὸν ἄφρονα διδάξῃ τὴν περὶ τὸν βίον τέχνην,
δεῖ θεωρητικὸν αὐτὸν εἶναι τῆς ἀφροσύνης καθάπερ
καὶ τὸν τεχνίτην τῆς ἀτεχνίας, δέδεικται δ' ἄληπτος
αὐτῷ ἡ ἀφροσύνη, οὐκ ἂν δύναιτο ὁ φρόνιμος τὸν
ἄφρονα τὴν περὶ τὸν βίον τέχνην διδάσκειν.
257   Καὶ δὴ τὰ συνεκτικώτατα τῶν κατὰ τὸν ἠθικὸν
τόπον ζητουμένων ἠπορηκότες, ἐν τοσούτοις τὴν
σύμπασαν τῆς σκεπτικῆς ἀγωγῆς διέξοδον ἀπ-
αρτίζομεν.

¹ [εἰ δ' . . . ἀναλογιστικήν] secl. ego (ἀλλ' L, ἵν' E, οὐδ' R,
εἰ δ' cet., Bekk.: ? ἵν' . . . ποιῆται κτλ.).
508

experience (for no existing thing resembles unwisdom) [But if the wise man makes the inference from this, it is either through resemblance or through composition or through analogy] ; so that wisdom will never perceive unwisdom.—Yes, but possibly someone will 253 say that the wise man can discern the unwisdom of another by the wisdom within himself ; but this is puerile. For unwisdom is a condition productive of certain works. If, then, the wise man sees and 254 apprehends this in another, either he will apprehend the condition directly by means of itself, or by attention to its works he will also get to know the condition itself, just as one knows the condition of the medical 255 man from works in accordance with the art of medicine, and that of the painter from works in accordance with the art of painting. But he cannot perceive the condition by means of itself ; for it is obscure and invisible, and it is not possible to view it closely through the shape of the body ; nor by means of the works which result from it ; for all the apparent works are, as we showed above,[a] common to wisdom and unwisdom alike. But if it is necessary 256 that the wise man, in order that he may teach the art of life to the unwise, should himself be capable of perceiving unwisdom—even as the artist lack of art,— and it has been shown that unwisdom is to him imperceptible, then the wise man will not be able to teach the unwise the art of life.

So now that we have critically discussed the most 257 essential of the problems which belong to the department of Ethics, we herewith bring to a close the whole of our exposition of the Sceptic Way.[b]

[a] See §§ 197-209 *supra*.
[b] For this expression *cf. P.H.* i. 4 n.

EDITOR'S NOTE

THIS volume contains the two books " Against the Physicists " (commonly cited as *Adversus Dogmaticos* iii., iv., or *Adversus Mathematicos* ix., x.) and the single book " Against the Ethicists " (cited as *Adv. Dogm.* v., or *Adv. Math.* xi.). The authorities for the text are the same as those for " Against the Logicians," viz. the manuscripts L, E, and N (see Vol. I. Introd. p. xliii, and Vol. II. Prefatory Note).

The Glossary is designed to include Greek words, phrases, and usages which are technical or rare or otherwise noteworthy.

In this, as in the previous volumes, the text is based on that of Bekker, the chief deviations being indicated in the footnotes.

GLOSSARY

[In the Glossary and Indexes the following abbreviations are used:
  I. = Introduction (in Vol. I.);
  P. = "Outlines of Pyrrhonism" (in Vol. I.);
  L. = "Against the Logicians" (in Vol. II.);
  Ph. = "Against the Physicists" (in Vol. III.);
  E. = "Against the Ethicists" (in Vol. III.).]

ἀγωγή, (doctrinal) procedure, method : ἡ σκεπτικὴ ἀγ., " the Sceptic Way," P. i. 4, 7, etc.

ἀδιάκριτος, indistinguishable, P. ii. 152, 155 f.

ἀδιάπτωτος (φαντασία), unerring, infallible, L. i. 110, etc.

ἀδιάστροφος, unperverted, acting instinctively, P. iii. 194.

ἀδιάφορα, "indifferents," i.e. (in Stoic ethics) things which lie midway between " good " and " evil "; see P. iii. 177, Vol. I. Introd. p. xxvii.

ἀδοξάστως (oppd. to δογματικῶς), undogmatically, P. i. 15.

ἀθετεῖν, set aside, reject, L. i. 260 ; so ἀθέτησις, L. ii. 142 ; ἄθετος πρός (τι), unfitted for, L. i. 183.

ἀθιγής, intangible, Ph. i. 281, etc.

αἱρεσιάρχης, leader or Head of a School or sect, P. iii. 245.

αἵρεσις, choice, approval, preference, P. i. 230 ; " doctrinal rule," P. i. 16 ; sect, School, L. i. 27, etc.

αἱρετά, preferred, choiceworthy (oppd. to φευκτά), P. i. 55, etc.

ἀκαθεκτούμενον (oppd. to κατεχόμενον), unoccupied (space), P. iii. 124, Ph. ii. 3.

ἀκαρές : πρὸς ἀκ., for a moment, suddenly, E. 154.

ἀκαριαῖος, minute, momentary, P. i. 132, iii. 142 : κατὰ τὸ ἀκ., to the smallest extent, a hair's breadth, P. iii. 79.

ἀκαταληπτεῖν, be non-apprehensive, fail to grasp, P. i. 201 ; so ἀκατάληπτος, P. ii. 22 : ἀκαταληψία, P. i. 1.

ἀκμήν (adv. accus.), still, just (while), P. ii. 11, iii. 276, L. ii. 257, E. 213.

ἀκολουθία, (logical) sequence, coherence, P. i. 16, ii. 114 ; pursued method, practice, P. i. 237.

ἀκύλιστος (Timon), lacking in versatility or energy, Ph. i. 57.

511

GLOSSARY

ἀμενθήριστος (c. genit., Timon), untroubled by, heedless of, P. i. 224.

ἀμφιβολία, verbal ambiguity, P. ii. 256 (cf. Diog. L. vii. 62).

ἀναιρεῖν, abolish (logically), deny (oppd. to τιθέναι, posit, affirm), P. i. 19, iii. 119, etc.

ἀναλογία, proportion, L. i. 106.

ἀναλογισμός, (reasoning from) analogy, P. i. 147 ; so ἀναλογιστικός, E. 250.

ἀνάλυσις (συλλογισμῶν), analysis, resolution, L. ii. 231.

ἀναμφίλεκτος (oppd. to ἀμφισβητούμενος), undisputed, E. 231.

ἀναντίτυπος (oppd. to ἀντίτυπος), non-resistent, yielding, Ph. i. 411.

ἀναπόδεικτοι(λόγοι), indemonstrable (of syllogisms or principles assumed, as not requiring demonstration), P. i. 69 n., ii. 156 ff. ; so ἀναποδείκτως, without demonstration, P. i. 60, etc.

ἀνασκευαστικός, (logically) destructive, contradictory (oppd. to κατασκευαστικός), L. ii. 196.

ἀναστροφή : κατὰ ἀν., reversely, vice versa, L. i. 430 ; so ἀναστρόφως, L. i. 302, etc.

ἀνεπίκριτος (διαφωνία), incapable of decision, unsettled, P. i. 98, 112, etc. ; so ἀνεπικρισία, E. 182.

ἀνεπινόητος, inconceivable, P. ii. 22, etc. ; so -ήτως, imperceptibly, P. iii. 145.

ἀνεπίτατος, inextensible, Ph. ii. 272 (cf. ἐπίτασις).

ἀνετεροίωτος, immutable, unaltered, L. ii. 455.

ἀνέφικτος, unattainable, E. 130.

ἀνηρεμήτως, unrestingly, Ph. ii. 223.

ἀνθυποφέρειν, object, retort, L. i. 440.

ἀνοχλητικῶς, by heaving up, Ph. ii. 83 f.

ἀντακολουθεῖν, mutually follow, involve, be interdependent, P. i. 68 (cf. Diog. L. vii. 125).

ἀντίληψις, perception, apprehension, P. i. 44, etc. ; so ἀντιληπτικός, P. i. 70.

ἀντιπαρεκτείνεσθαι, be stretched out side by side with, be extended so as to equal, Ph. i. 262, etc.

ἀντιπαρεξαγωγή : κατὰ ἀντ., by way of attacking, as a counter-blast, L. i. 150.

ἀντιπαρήκειν, stretch parallel to, be co-extensive with, L. i. 361, etc.

ἀντιπεριέλκειν, draw round to the other side, convert to an opposite belief, L. i. 189.

512

GLOSSARY

ἀντιπίπτειν, conflict, tell against, refute, P. i. 179, etc.:
(c. dat.) L. i. 333.

ἀντιποίησις, seeking possession of, pursuit of, P. iii. 183.

ἀντιστηρίζειν (Democr.), press against, resist, L. i. 136.

ἀντίστροφος, corresponding, equivalent, L. i. 6.

ἀντιτυπία, resistance, solidity, P. iii. 39, etc.

ἀνυπαρξία (oppd. to ὕπαρξις), unreality, non-existence, P. i.
21, etc.; so ἀνύπαρκτος, P. i. 104, etc.

ἀνυπόστατος, non-substantial, unreal, P. ii. 80.

ἀνυτικώτατος (λόγος), most effective, Ph. i. 182.

ἀνωτάτω (as adj.), most generic (or inclusive), main types of,
P. i. 4, iii. 65; so κατὰ τὸ ἀν., Ph. ii. 38, 45.

ἀξίωμα, (logical) judgement, proposition, assertion, P. i. 189,
ii. 81, etc.

ἀοριστία, (Sceptic) indetermination, refusal to define, P. i.
198; so ἀοριστεῖν, P. i. 28.

ἀόριστος (δυάς, Pythagorean), indefinite (Dyad, i.e. the "two"
as principle of plurality), P. iii. 154.

ἀοχλησία (Epicur. and Sceptic), unperturbedness, serenity,
P. i. 10; so ἀόχλητος, P. i. 29.

ἀπαξία (oppd. to ἀξία, Stoic ethics), worthlessness, E. 62.

ἀπαράλλακτος, indistinguishable, P. iii. 177, etc.; so ἀπαρ-
αλλαξία, L. i. 108, 403, etc.

ἀπαραπόδιστος, unimpeded, clear, L. ii. 187, E. 76.

ἀπαρέμφατον, infinitive (mood), P. i. 204.

ἀπαρτίζειν, complete, express fully, P. ii. 176, E. 257.

ἀπειρομεγέθης, infinitely large, P. iii. 44.

ἄπειρον: εἰς ἄπ., (regress) ad infinitum, P. ii. 78, etc.; so
μέχρις ἀπείρου, P. i. 122, etc.

ἀπεκλογή (oppd. to ἐκλογή, Stoic), rejection, E. 133.

ἀπεμφαίνειν, be incongruous, absurd, P. i. 112, ii. 188, etc.;
so ἀπέμφασις, P. iii. 61 (="improbable presentation,"
Carneades), L. i. 169.

ἀπέραντος (λόγος), indefinite, inconclusive, L. ii. 429.

ἀπεριέργως, simply, not positively or dogmatically, P.
240.

ἀπερίσπαστος (φαντασία), irreversible, indubitable, P. i. 227,
L. i. 166.

ἀπλανής, unerring, infallible, L. i. 138, 146, etc.; so ἀπλανησία,
L. i. 394.

ἀπλατές (μῆκος), (length) without breadth (def. of γραμμή),
P. iii. 39, Ph. ii. 279, etc.

513

GLOSSARY

ἀπλοπαθεῖς (αἰσθήσεις), simply-passive, *i.e.* receptive of only one kind of impression, P. iii. 47, 108.

ἀπό : οἱ ἀπό (τῆς Στοᾶς), members of (the Stoic School), P. iii. 181 etc.

ἀποβρασμός, frothy emission (of a fluid), Ph. i. 103.

ἀπόδοσις, account rendered, description, E. 30.

ἀποδοτικός (c. genit.), productive of, E. 253.

ἄποιος (ὕλη), devoid of quality, P. iii. 33, Ph. ii. 310, etc.

ἀποκληρωτικός, acting at random, capricious, P. iii. 79.

ἀπολείπειν (oppd. to ἀναιρεῖν), admit, allow (the existence or truth of a thing), P. ii. 43, 219, etc.

ἀπόλυτα (oppd. to πρός τι), absolute, existing in their own right, L. ii. 273 ; so ἀπολύτως, P. i. 135, etc., and ἀπολελυμένως, L. ii. 162.

ἀποπάλλειν, hurl away, Ph. ii. 73 : ἀποπαλτικῶς, by way of rebound, Ph. ii. 223.

ἀποπροηγμένα (oppd. to προηγμένα), unpreferred, rejected, P. iii. 191, E. 62.

ἀπορητικός, doubting, sceptical : οἱ ἀπ., Sceptics ; ἡ ἀπ., Scepticism ; P. i. 7, 221, etc. ; so ἀπορητικῶς, L. i. 30, etc.

ἀποροποίητον (σῶμα), made without pores, impermeable, L. ii. 309.

ἀποσυμβεβηκότα (oppd. to συμβεβηκότα), non-attributes, not properties, L. i. 281.

ἀποσυνεργεῖν, thwart, counteract, P. i. 212.

ἀποτέλεσμα, completed result, product, P. iii. 11, 14, etc. ; so ἀποτελεσματική, E. 197, ἀποτελεστικόν, P. iii. 27.

ἀποτομή : κατ᾽ ἀπ., separately, independently, L. i. 446.

ἀπόφασις, declaration, formula, P. i. 5 ; affirmation (καταληπτικὴ ἀπ.), P. ii. 123 ; so ἀποφαντόν, declaratory, P. ii. 104, ἀποφαντικόν, L. ii. 71.

ἀπόφασις, negation, P. i. 192 : ἀποφατικόν, negating, negative, P. i. 192, ii. 161, etc.

ἀποφορά, effluvia, scent, P. i. 101 ; so ἀποφόρησις, P. i. 126.

ἀπτερέως (Xenophanes), without wavering, firmly, L. i. 111.

ἀπτώτως, firmly, securely, L. ii. 187.

ἀραιώματα (νοητά), interstices, pores, L. ii. 220.

ἀρρεψία (Sceptic), state of even balance, equipoise, mental neutrality, P. i. 190, L. ii. 159, etc.

ἆρσις (oppd. to θέσις), removal, abolition, denial, P. i. 70, 192, iii. 86, etc.

GLOSSARY

ἀρχικώτατον (αἴτιον), most principal, original, supreme, Ph. i. 5, etc.

ἄσημοι (φωναί), non-significant, without distinct meaning, P. ii. 130.

ἀστεία (κίνησις), soothing, kindly, P. iii. 184, L. i. 42, 45.

ἀσυγκαταθετεῖν, withhold assent (= ἐπέχειν), L. i. 157.

ἀσύνακτος (λόγος), inconclusive (oppd. to συνακτικός), P. ii. 137, etc.

ἀσυνάρτητα (λήμματα), inconsistent, without logical coherence, P. ii. 153 (cf. διάρτησις).

ἀσυνύπαρκτος, incapable of co-existence, P. ii. 202.

ἀσύστατος (ἐπίνοια), without cohesion, impossible to construct, P. ii. 27.

ἀταραξία (Sceptic), unperturbedness, quietude (of mind), P. i. 8, 25, etc.; so ἀταρακτεῖν, P. i. 12, etc., and ἀταράχως, E. 118, etc.

αὐτόθεν, of itself, at once, ipso facto, P. ii. 164, passim.

αὐτοτελής, self-complete, P. ii. 104 ; so αὐτοτελῶς, wholly of itself, independently, Ph. i. 237, etc.

αὐτότης : κατ᾽ αὐτότητα ἑαυτῆς, in its self-identity, Ph. ii. 261.

ἀφαίρεσις (oppd. to πρόσθεσις), subtraction, P. iii. 84, (distingd. fr. ἆρσις) P. iii. 86, (fr. ἀναίρεσις) Ph. i. 298.

ἀφάνταστος (φύσις), devoid of apprehension, non-perceptive (oppd. to νοερά), Ph. i. 114.

ἀφασία (oppd. to φάσις), non-assertion, (Sceptic) refusal to say " Yes " or " No " about anything, P. i. 192, ii. 211.

ἀφορμή (oppd. to ὁρμή), disinclination, aversion (Stoic), P. iii. 177, 273-274, E. 210-211.

βίος, life, ordinary belief or conduct, P. i. 237 ; hence ὁ βίος and οἱ ἀπὸ τοῦ β., ordinary folk (oppd. to philosophers), P. i. 165, etc., E. 49 ; so βιωτικός, P. i. 23 ; βιωτικὰ (κριτήρια), ordinary, taken from common life, P. ii. 15.

γενικώταται (αἱρέσεις), most comprehensive, leading (Schools), L. i. 27.

γῆθος, joy, delight, E. 106.

γλυκαντικῶς (κινεῖσθαι), (be affected by, or taste) sweetness, L. i. 344.

γνησίη (oppd. to σκοτίη), genuine, true (γνῶσις Democr.), L. i. 138-139.

515

GLOSSARY

γυμναστικοί (λόγοι), exercitatory, providing mental exercise (of the Socratic dialogues of Plato), P. i. 221.

δεδολιευμένος (λόγος), cunningly framed (sophism), P. ii. 229.
δεῖγμα, indication, example, proof, P. i. 85 ; so δείγματος χάριν, by way of example, as specimens, E. 40.
δεῖξις, pointing out, indicating, P. ii. 25, etc. ; so δεικτικῶς, L. i. 267.
διαγνωστική, capable of distinguishing, P. ii. 229 ; so διάγνωσις, ascertaining distinctly, discerning, L. i. 24.
διάθεσις, condition, disposition, state (of mind or body), P. iii. 243, etc.
διαθήκη (Democr.)= διάθεσις, L. i. 136.
διαίρεσις, division (4 kinds of), P. ii. 213 ff.; τέλειος δ., E. 10 ; so διαιρετική, P. ii. 213.
διάκενος (ἑλκυσμός), vacuous (attraction), of a purely subjective impression, L. i. 241, ii. 67.
διαλεκτική, dialectic, logic (Stoic def., " Science of things false and true and neither "), P. ii. 94, 213, etc. ; so οἱ διαλεκτικοί, the Logicians, P. ii. 146, etc.
διάλληλος (τρόπος), circular mode (of reasoning), arguing in a circle, P. i. 117, 164, etc. ; so ὁ δι' ἀλλήλων τρόπος, P. ii. 202, L. i. 426, etc.
διὰ πασῶν (συμφωνία), the octave-scale (ratio of 2 : 1), P. iii. 155, L. i. 95 ; so διὰ τεσσάρων (= 4 : 3), and διὰ πέντε (= 3 : 2), loc. cit. (all terms of Pythagorean musical theory).
διαπίπτειν, collapse, fail, go wrong, P. i. 185, (oppd. to κατορθοῦν) Ph. ii. 252.
διάρτησις, inconsistency, lack of congruity (in the premisses of an argument), P. ii. 146, 152, L. ii. 429.
διάστασις, dissension, dispute, L. ii. 11, 118, 177 ; (Spatial) dimension, P. iii. 44, 125, etc. ; so (τριχῇ) διαστατόν, P. ii. 30, etc.
διαφορά : τὰ κατὰ δ. (oppd. to τὰ πρός τι), things which have a distinct existence of their own, self-existent (= ἀπόλυτα, absolutes), P. i. 137, L. ii. 37, 161, Ph. ii. 263.
διαφορούμενον (ἀξίωμα), duplicated, P. ii. 112, L. ii. 108, etc. (cf. Diog. L. vii. 69 : ? διφορ., as Prantl).
διεξωδευμένη (φαντασία), thoroughly scrutinized, tested, P. i. 227, L. i. 181, 438 (cf. περιωδευμένη).
διήκειν (Methodic School), pervade, P. i. 240 n. ; Ph. i. 40.
διολκή, dissension, dispute, L. ii. 322.

GLOSSARY

διομαλισμός, evenness, uniform quality, P. iii. 244, E. 206;
    so διομαλίζειν, not vary, E. 207.
διοριστικός, capable of distinguishing, L. i. 64; serving to
    divide, marking off, Ph. ii. 128.
διπλασίων (λόγος), duplicate (ratio), double, L. i. 97.
διχάζειν, cut in two, divide, Ph. i. 292; so διχοτόμησις,
    bisection, Ph. i. 284.
δογματολογίαι, expositions of dogmas, L. ii. 367.
δοκιμαστικός, capable of scrutinizing, testing, L. i. 27, etc.
δόκος (= δόξα, Xenophanes), opinion, P. ii. 18.
δόκωσις, laying beams, raftering, P. iii. 99, Ph. i. 343.
δοξαστής, one who opines, conjecturer, L. i. 157; so δοξα-
    στικῶς, E. 156.
δόξις (= δόξα, Democr.), opinion, L. i. 137.
δραστήριος (ἀρχή), active, efficient, L. i. 115, etc.; so δραστική,
    P. iii. 1, δραστικώτατον (αἴτιον), P. iii. 2.
δύναμις, ability, potency, P. i. 8, etc.; δυνάμει (oppd. to
    ἐνεργείᾳ), potentially, virtually, implicitly, P. i. 11, ii.
    225-226; ἰατρικαὶ δυνάμεις=medicines, P. i. 133, E. 153.

ἐγγράμματος (φωνή), written (speech), Ph. ii. 249.
ἐγκεκαλυμμένος (λόγος), "the Veiled" (classed, with the
    "Sorites," among the "insoluble" (ἄποροι) arguments
    by the Stoics, see Diog. L. vii. 82), L. i. 410.
ἐθελοκωφεῖν, affect deafness, be wilfully obtuse, E. 202.
εἴδησις, cognition, awareness, L. i. 163.
εἶδος (oppd. to ὕλη), form, Ph. ii. 26; (distingd. fr. γένος)
    species, particular, L. ii. 41; so οἱ (τὰ) ἐπ' εἴδους (or κατ'
    εἶδος), particulars, individual cases, L. i. 20, E. 9, etc.
εἰδωλοποιήσεις, image-formations, imaginary objects, P. ii. 222.
εἰλικρίνεια, purity, Ph. i. 73; ἡ κατ' εἰλ. κίνησις, absolute (or
    complete) motion, Ph. ii. 113; so εἰλικρινὴς κριτής, im-
    partial (perfect) judge, P. i. 113; εἰλικρινῶς, clearly,
    absolutely, P. i. 207, ii. 25, etc.
εἶξις (oppd. to ἀντιτυπία), yielding, non-resistance, Ph. ii.
    221 ff.
εἰσοχή (oppd. to ἐξοχή), concavity, depression, P. i. 92, ii.
    70, etc.
ἐκβάλλειν, throw over, reject, P. i. 177, etc.; ἐκβ. εἰς ἄπειρον,
    make regress ad infinitum, P. i. 164.
ἐκκαλυπτικός, serving to reveal, disclosing, P. ii. 101, 116,
    etc.; so ἐκκαλυπτικῶς, by way of disclosure, P. ii. 141.

517

GLOSSARY

ἐκπεριοδεύειν, (go right round,) inspect closely, scrutinize, L. i. 188 (cf. διεξοδεύειν).

ἐκπίπτειν (c. genit.), be ousted from, lose, L. i. 268, etc.; ἔκπ. εἰς (ἄπειρον), be forced off into, be lost (wrecked) in, P. i. 186, ii. 253, etc. ; so ἔκπτωσις, P. ii. 207, etc.

ἐλαστρεῖν (= ἐλαύνειν, Timon), drive, worry, E. 172.

ἑλκυσμός (διάκενος), (vacuous) attraction, or compulsion (of wholly subjective impressions), L. i. 241.

ἐμμέθοδος (λόγος), orderly, systematic, P. ii. 21, 48.

ἐμπειρία, practice, experience, P. ii. 256; (medical) empiricism, P. i. 236, L. ii. 191 ; so ἐμπειρικῶς (ἰατρεύειν), L. ii. 204.

ἐμπέλασις, approach, impact, Ph. i. 393; so ἐμπελάζειν (Democr.), Ph. i. 19.

ἔμφασις (reflection), probable subjective appearance (Carneades), L. i. 169 ; implication, P. ii. 112 ; indication, allusion, P. iii. 199.

ἐναλλαγή (στοιχείων), interchange (of letters), Ph. i. 278.

ἐναλλάξ, alternately, in turn, alternando, P. i. 9, 186, etc.

ἐναπειροκαλεῖν, (deal tastelessly,) fool with, P. ii. 245.

ἐναπεσφραγισμένη (φαντασία), stamped (or imprinted) on (the mind), P. ii. 4 ; so ἐναπεσφραγισμένως, E. 183.

ἐναπόθεσις (καταλήψεων), storing within, deposit, P. iii. 188.

ἐναπομεμαγμένη (φαντασία), impressed upon (the mind), P. ii. 4 (cf. E. 183).

ἐνάργεια (oppd. to λόγος), sensible evidence, P. iii. 266; sense-impression (= φαντασία, Epicur.), L. i. 203.

ἔναρθροι (φωναί), articulate, L. ii. 275.

ἐνδεικτικὸν (σημεῖον), indicative (sign), P. ii. 99 ff., L. i. 161.

ἔνδειξις, indication (techn. term of the Methodic School of Medicine), P. i. 240.

ἐνδιάθετος (oppd. to προφορικός) λόγος, internal reason, mental discourse, P. i. 65, L. ii. 275.

ἐνδιήκουσαι (κοινότητες), pervading (of a class qualifying all its particulars), L. ii. 41.

ἔννοια (Peripatetic), comprehension, concept, L. i. 223 f.; κοιναὶ ἔννοιαι, common conceptions, general opinion, Ph. i. 178, 199.

ἐννομολέσχης (Timon), prating about (discussing) laws or customs, moralizer, L. i. 8.

ἔνστασις, objection, (logical) hindrance, L. i. 256 ; lodgement (of bodies, so as to block a passage,—medical term), L. ii. 220.

GLOSSARY

ἔνστημα, objection, contradictory fact, L. i. 256.
ἔντασις (κώνου), tension (of coniform light, or visual stream),
  P. iii. 51.
ἐντελέχεια (oppd. to δύναμις), actuality, Ph. ii. 340.
ἐξαλλαγή, variety, differing nature, P. i. 36.
ἐξαπλοῦν, unfold, explain, P. i. 217 ; so κατὰ ἐξάπλωσιν,
  when stated simply, L. i. 51.
ἕξις, state, condition, faculty (oppd. to στέρησις), P. iii. 49, 50 ;
  cohesion (distingd. from φύσις and ψυχή, as ground of
  inorganic unity), Ph. i. 81 (cf. Vol. I. Introd. p. xxv).
ἐξοχή (oppd. to εἰσοχή), convexity, prominence, P. i. 92, 120 ;
  κατ᾽ ἐξ., P. ii. 70, L. i. 372.
ἐπαγωγή, induction (arguing from parts to whole), P. ii. 204 ;
  so ἐπαγωγικὸς (τρόπος), P. ii. 196 ; ἐπαγωγικῶς, P. ii. 195, 197.
ἐπακολούθημα : κατ᾽ ἐπ. (oppd. to προηγουμένως), as a sequel,
  secondarily, L. i. 34.
ἐπαναβεβηκώς, super-ordinate, (logically) higher or more comprehensive, P. i. 38, 174, iii. 160, etc.
ἐπεισκρίνεσθαι, enter in separately, P. iii. 82.
ἐπεισκυκλεῖν, roll in on, surround with, P. ii. 210.
ἐπέχειν, come to a halt, withhold judgement, P. i. 26, 29, etc.
  (cf. ἐποχή).
ἐπιβάλλειν (c. dat.), approach, perceive, attend to, deal with,
  P. i. 69, ii. 72, etc. ; (c. infin.) undertake, proceed to,
  P. ii. 16, (mid.) L. i. 37.
ἐπιβολή, objection, criticism, P. iii. 67, L. i. 65 ; aspect,
  occurrence, instant, L. i. 222, Ph. ii. 209, E. 25.
ἐπιθεωρεῖν, theorize about, imagine, assume in addition,
  L. i. 22, P. iii. 162, 164.
ἐπικράτεια, predominance, P. i. 80 ; so ἡ κατ᾽ ἐπ. κίνησις
  (oppd. to κατ᾽ εἰλικρίνειαν), majority-motion (when most
  parts move, but a few are at rest), Ph. ii. 113 f.
ἐπικρίνειν, judge, distinguish, P. i. 26, etc. ; decide, settle (a
  controversy), P. ii. 19, 113, etc.
ἐπίκρισις, judging, deciding, P. i. 12 ; ἐπ. εἰδώλων (oppd. to
  ἀποκρίσεις), immissions, P. iii. 51.
ἐπιλογισμός, reckoning, reasoning, P. ii. 123, L. i. 352.
ἐπιμαρτύρησις, confirmatory evidence, P. i. 181, L. i. 212.
ἐπίμετρον : ἐξ ἐπιμέτρου, by way of excess, into the bargain,
  P. ii. 47, 194, L. ii. 2.
ἐπιμιξία, admixture, intermixture, P. i. 36, 126, 128 ; so
  ἐπιμιγή, P. i. 124 ; ἐπίμικτος, P. i. 185.

519

GLOSSARY

ἐπίνοια (oppd. to ὕπαρξις), concept, notion, L. ii. 381 ; κατ'
   ἐπ., conceptually, Ph. ii. 348.
ἐπίπεδος (ἡ), plane surface, plane, Ph. i. 387, 420, 428.
ἐπιρυσμίη (δόξις, Democr.), in-flowing, adventitious, L. i. 137.
ἐπισπαστικῶς (oppd. to προωστικῶς), by pulling (after,
   oppd. to pushing), P. iii. 69, Ph. ii. 83.
ἐπίστασις, attention, close observation, L. i. 23, 114 ; so
   ἐπιστατικῶς, attentively, L. i. 182.
ἐπιστατεῖν, have charge of, control, L. i. 43, 124.
ἐπιστημονικός (oppd. to δοξαστὸς λόγος), cognitive, scientific,
   L. i. 111, 114 ; (κατάληψις), L. i. 110 ; (αἴσθησις), L. i. 145 ;
   so ἐπιστημονικῶς, scientifically, Ph. i. 283.
ἐπιστροφή, attention, regard, P. iii. 248, E. 194.
ἐπισύνθεσις, composition, enlargement by addition, P. iii. 153,
   L. ii. 58, 60, Ph. ii. 302.
ἐπίτασις (oppd. to ἄνεσις), intensification, increase, P. ii. 40 ;
   κατ' ἐπ., Ph. i. 403.
ἐπιφορά, conclusion, Ph. i. 135, 206.
ἐπιχείρειν, handle, attempt, argue against, object, P. iii. 13,
   270, Ph. ii. 69, 305.
ἐπιχείρημα, (hostile) argument, critique, P. ii. 188 ; so ἐπιχείρησις, P. ii. 192, 219, E. 217.
ἐποχή, checking, stopping, P. i. 238 ; (Sceptic) suspension of
   judgement, withholding assent, P. i. 5, 8, 11, etc.
ἐρωτᾶν (λόγον), propound (an argument, regarded as in the
   form of question and answer, or " dialectic "), P. i. 20, 33,
   ii. 134, etc.
ἔστω (c. accus. and infin.), let it be granted (that), P. ii. 51,
   L. i. 423, etc.
ἐτεῇ (Democr.), verily, in sooth, P. i. 214, L. i. 135, 137,
   ii. 62.
ἑτερογενῶς (διαφέρειν), by generic distinction, L. i. 361.
ἑτερόδοξος (c. genit.), differing in opinion (from), P. ii. 6,
   118, etc.
ἑτεροίωσις, alteration, modification, P. ii. 70, L. i. 230, 372
   (as def. of φαντασία, Chrysippus) ; so ἑτεροιωτικός, P. ii. 70.
εὐαπόδοτος (λόγος), easy to explain, or state, L. i. 343, ii. 85.
εὐαρεστεῖν, be well-pleased, Ph. i. 141 ; so εὐαρέστησις, E. 88.
εὐδόκησις (Cyrenaic), approval, satisfaction, L. i. 200.
εὐδρομεῖν, run easily, prove satisfactory, Ph. ii. 36 (cf. εὐοδεῖν,
   L. ii. 67).
εὐεπηβολώτερος, more sharp-witted, more shrewd, L. i. 322.

GLOSSARY

εὐεπιλόγιστος, easily inferred, L. i. 75.
εὐθέως, at once, for instance, P. ii. 214, (with οἷον) L. i. 298, Ph. i. 114, E. 35.
εὐθικὴ (κίνησις), in a straight line, rectilinear, Ph. ii. 51.
εὔλογχα (εἴδωλα, Democr.), lucky, propitious, Ph. i. 19.
εὐρεσιλογία, word-play, sophistry, P. ii. 9, 84; so εὐρεσιλογεῖν, P. i. 63, E. 7.
εὔροια (βίου), smooth current, fair course (= εὐδαιμονία, Stoic), P. iii. 172, E. 30; so εὐρόως (βιοῦν), E. 110.
εὔσημος (διδασκαλία), easily intelligible, plain, P. iii. 158, Ph. ii. 167.
εὐχρηστεῖν, be useful, Ph. i. 18.
ἐφεκτικὴ (ἀγωγή), suspensive (= Sceptic), P. i. 7, 209, ii. 9; (masc.) P. ii. 10, E. 152; so ἐφεκτός, P. i. 219, iii. 55; ἐφεκτέον, P. ii. 94, iii. 55, L. ii. 160.
ἐφιστάναι (c. accus.), check, make pause, P. i. 180; (c. dat.) dwell on, attend to, P. ii. 229, iii. 13, 198, L. i. 410; (c. ὅτι) argue, make out, P. iii. 56.
ἐφοδεύειν, inspect, examine, P. i. 200, 209, etc.
ἐφοδευτικῶς (oppd. to ἐκκαλυπτικῶς), by (logical) advance, or progression, P. ii. 141-142, L. ii. 307-308.
ἔφοδος, mode of approach or attack, counter-argument, method, P. i. 183, ii. 222, 258; L. ii. 140, 142.

ζητητικὴ (ἀγωγή), (way) of investigation (*i.e.* Scepticism), P. i. 7.
ζωγραφικῶς, in accordance with the art of painting, artistically, E. 255.
ζωΰφια, animalcules, P. i. 41.

ἡγεμονικόν (Stoic), ruling principle, regent part, P. i. 128, ii. 70; L. i. 233 f., etc. (*cf.* Vol. I. Introd. p. xxv).
ἡγούμενον (oppd. to λῆγον), antecedent (clause), P. ii. 111 f., 148, etc.
ἡμιόλιος (λόγος), ratio of 3 : 2, one and a half times, P. iii. 155.
ἡστικῶς (oppd. to ἀλγεινῶς), pleasurably, agreeably, Ph. ii. 225, E. 98.

θεματίζειν, propose, assume, L. ii. 202; so θέματα, assumptions (distingd. fr. λήμματα), L. ii. 302.
θεοφορεῖν, deify, Ph. i. 32; (pass.) be god-possessed, in a state of ecstasy, P. i. 101.

GLOSSARY

θέσις, (local) position, P. i. 36, 118 ; (oppd. to φύσις) assumption, convention, P. ii. 214, 256.

θετικός : θ. χρῆσις, conventional, agreed use, P. ii. 256 ; so θετικῶς, as laid down, on trust, P. i. 38.

θεωρεῖσθαι, be seen, observed, found as a fact (hence almost= εἶναι), P. ii. 198, 224 ; L. i. 183, 362, etc.

θεώρημα, argument, principle, lesson, P. ii. 3, 70, iii. 261; L. ii. 291.

θίξις, touching, contact, P. iii. 56, Ph. i. 260, 265 (cf. ἀφή).

θλιπτικῶς, by pressure, Ph. ii. 83.

ἰδιάζειν (Heracleit.), be peculiar, act (or think) on one's own, L. i. 133.

ἰδιαζόντως, privately, in a peculiar way, P. i. 182.

ἴδιος : κατ᾽ ἰδίαν, privately, by (one)self, solely, P. iii. 259, L. i. 277 f., 296, etc. ; ἰδιαίτερον, more particularly, specifically, L. ii. 272, 396 ; Ph. ii. 182.

ἰδιοσυγκρισία, peculiar constitution (or temperament), idiosyncrasy, P. i. 79, 89.

ἰδιότης, peculiar nature, individuality, L. ii. 41 f.

ἰδίωμα, peculiar property, characteristic, L. i. 55, ii. 425, Ph. i. 410 f.

ἰδιωτική (ἀπόφασις), crude, common-place, L. i. 265, Ph. i. 63 (cf. ἰδιώτης) (τεχνίτης, L. i. 55).

ἰκτερικοί, jaundiced, P. i. 101, 126, etc. ; so ἰκτεριῶν(τες), P. i. 44, L. i. 192, etc.

ἰσοκρατεῖν, be of equal force, Ph. ii. 81.

ἰσοσθένεια, equality of (logical) force, equipollence, P. i. 8, 190, 196, etc. ; so ἰσοσθενής, P. i. 26, etc.

ἱστάναι (λόγον ἐπί τινος), base (an argument on), P. i. 66, 72, 77, etc. : ἵστασθαι, halt, pause, P. i. 186, ii. 253 : ἔστηκε (ἑστώς), stands still, remains constant, L. ii. 427.

ἱστορία, inquiry, account, L. i. 140, ii. 1, 14 ; so ἱστορικῶς, as a chronicler, in detail, P. i. 4.

καθάπαξ, once for all, wholly, absolutely, P. i. 104, ii. 97, 208, etc.

καθίστασθαι (= γίγνεσθαι), become, L. i. 130 ; so καθεστάναι (= εἶναι), be, L. i. 29, 50, etc. ; καθεστώς (= ὤν, ὄν), being, L. i. 69, 73, etc.

καθολικός, general, universal, P. ii. 196, E. 8 ; so καθολικώτερος, P. ii. 84, iii. 205.

522

GLOSSARY

κανονίζειν, measure (by a rule or standard), judge, L. i. 158, 175, etc. (so κανών, carpenter's rule, P. ii. 15, L. i. 27).
κανονικά (Epicur.), rules (of thought), logic, L. i. 22.
Καταβάλλοντες (οἱ), The Down-Throwers (wrestling term, title of a book of Protagoras, also called Ἀλήθεια), L. i. 60.
κατάκλειστος, shut up, treasured, P. i. 143.
καταλαμβάνειν, grasp, apprehend, perceive, P. i. 26, 99, 182, etc. : καταλαμβάνεσθαι (pass.), P. i. 178, ii. 8, etc. ; (mid.) L. i. 300, 305, 310, ii. 209, etc.
καταλήγειν (εἰς), fall back on, terminate in, P. i. 12, 163, 165, etc. ; so κατάληξις, end, Ph. ii. 61.
καταληπτικός, apprehensive, capable of perceiving, E. 75 : κ. φαντασία (Stoic), P. i. 68, 235, iii. 241 f., etc. (cf. Vol. I. Introd. p. xxv) ; so καταληπτός, apprehensible, P. i. 235, etc.
κατάληψις, apprehension, perception, P. i. 179, L. i. 151 f., etc.
κατασκευάζειν, make out, argue, demonstrate, establish, P. i. 32, 61, 168, etc. ; so κατασκευαστικός, L. ii. 343.
κατασκευή, (physical) construction, constitution, P. i. 48, 54, 217, etc. ; (logical) demonstration, P. i. 169, 173.
κατάστημα, (physical) condition, P. iii. 184.
κατάχρησις (oppd. to ἀκρίβεια), misuse (of words), loose language, L. ii. 129 ; so καταχρηστικὰ (ὀνόματα), L. ii. 129 ; καταχρηστικῶς, P. i. 191, 207 ; καταχρηστικώτερον (oppd. to κυρίως), L. ii. 400.
κατεξαναστατικός (c. genit.), fit to resist, impervious to, E. 104, 106 (cf. κατεξαναστῆναι, P. iii. 275, etc.).
κατηγόρημα, predicate, asserted fact, P. ii. 230, 232, Ph. i. 211, E. 32.
κατηγορικὸς (λόγος), affirmative, categorical (oppd. to hypothetical), P. ii. 163, 166.
κατηναγκασμένος, necessitated, unavoidable, P. i. 13, 29, iii. 235, etc.
κατόρθωμα (Stoic), right action, L. i. 158, Ph. i. 16 (cf. Vol. I. Introd. p. xxvii).
κεκρατημένως, convincingly, E. 42.
κενοπαθεῖν (Stoic), have empty affections (of illusory sensation), P. ii. 49, L. ii. 213 ; so κενοπάθεια (Democr.), L. ii. 184 ; κενοπάθημα, L. ii. 354.
κεφαλαιωδέστερον, rather summarily, Ph. i. 206.
κινεῖν, move, excite, affect, P. i. 193, etc. ; remove, overthrow, dispute, P. ii. 84, iii. 1, L. i. 137, etc. ; arouse, set agoing, L. i. 6.

GLOSSARY

κοινότης (medical term), general (morbid) state, type, P. i. 240.

κοσκινευόμενα (σπέρματα, Democr.), sifted, winnowed, L. i. 117.

κουφοφορεῖν, rise lightly, soar, Ph. i. 71.

κρατύνειν, confirm, establish, P. i. 147, ii. 96.

Κρατυντήρια, *Confirmations* (title of a work by Democr.), L. i. 136.

κριτήριον, standard (of belief or conduct), criterion, P. i. 21 f., P. ii. 13 ff., L. i. 26 ff. (*cf.* Vol. I. Introd. pp. xxv, xxxiii ff.).

κυκλογραφεῖν, describe a circle, Ph. i. 420 ff., 426.

κυκλοφορητικός, moving in a circle, revolving, P. iii. 31, Ph. ii. 51, 316 : -κῶς, Ph. ii. 58.

κυλίεσθαι, be bandied about, be current talk, L. i. 116 ; (εἰς), be brought up against, involved in, L. ii. 169, E. 89.

κύων, dog, P. i. 63, etc. ; Cynic, L. i. 48, ii. 5 ; (various senses of) E. 28 f.

κωβιός, kind of fish, gudgeon, Ph. i. 278.

λακεδών (Timon), cry, utterance, E. 171 (dubious word).

λαμβάνειν, take, accept, admit, P. i. 186, etc.; grasp, discern, diagnose, P. ii. 39, L. i. 179.

λαμπηδών, sparkle, lustre, P. i. 45.

λειποψυχεῖν, lose consciousness, faint, P. iii. 236.

λεκτόν (Stoic), expressible, expression (= meaning of a name, or mental image evoked by it), P. ii. 81, 104, 107 ff., L. ii. 12, 70, Ph. ii. 218, E. 224 (*cf.* note on P. ii. 81).

λέξις, word, part of speech, Ph. ii. 216 ; κατὰ λ., word for word, expressly, Ph. i. 92.

λεπτός : τὰ κατὰ λεπτόν, refinements, subtle points, minutiae, L. ii. 295.

λευκαίνεσθαι, have a sensation of whiteness, sense white colour, L. i. 191, 197, 293.

λευκανθίζοντες (ὀφθαλμοί), flecked with white, albino, P. i. 44.

λευκαντικῶς (διατεθῆναι, etc.), have a feeling, or sense, of whiteness, L. i. 192, 198, 344, ii. 397.

λῆγον (oppd. to ἡγούμενον), (logical) consequent, P. ii. 111 ff., etc.

λήμματα, (logical) premisses, P. ii. 135, etc.

ληπτός, within reach, attainable, L. i. 124.

ματαιάζειν, speak foolishly, talk nonsense, Ph. i. 282.

GLOSSARY

ματαιοπονία, useless labour, P. ii. 206.

μάχεσθαι (c. dat.), conflict with, contradict, P. i. 184, etc.; so μάχιμον, disputed, L. ii. 45.

μεγεθοποιεῖν, make great, enlarge, L. i. 108.

μεγεθοῦν: μεμεγεθωμένον, magnified, enlarged, Ph. ii. 240.

μέθοδος, " Method " (i.e. the doctrinal system of the Methodic School of Medicine), P. i. 236; so μεθοδικός (ἰατρός), P. i. 239 ff.: μεθοδικώτερον, more systematically, in due order, L. ii. 141.

μειωτικῶς (oppd. to παραυξητικῶς), by diminution, E. 251.

μέρος, part, parties to, P. i. 59, 90, etc.: ἀνὰ μ., in turn, Ph. i. 429; ἀπὸ μέρους, in part, L. i. 283; ἐν μέρει, in turn, L. i. 28, ii. 183; (c. genit.) by way of, L. ii. 118; τὰ ἐπὶ μέρους, (logical) particulars (oppd. to "genus," or "universal"), P. ii. 87, L. i. 399, etc.; so (τὰ) κατὰ μέρος, P. ii. 84, 86, 195 f., etc.; παρὰ μέρος, by turns, alternately, L. i. 286, 376, etc.

μεσολαβεῖν, intercept, Ph. i. 265, 386.

μεταβατικὴ (φαντασία), transitive (impression, i.e. passing on so as to combine with others and form knowledge), L. ii. 276, 288; μ. κίνησις, (distingd. from μεταβλητικὴ κ.) Ph. i. 195, ii. 38, 41. So μεταβατικῶς, by transition, P. iii. 97, 129, Ph. ii. 43, 53.

μεταβλητικὴ (δύναμις), capable of changing, P. i. 103; μ. κίνησις, Ph. i. 195, ii. 42, 321.

μετάθεσις, transposition, substitution, Ph. i. 328.

μετακοσμεῖσθαι, be rearranged, transformed, P. i. 217.

μετουσία, sharing, participation, P. iii. 153, Ph. i. 375.

μετριοπάθεια (Sceptic), moderate feeling, P. i. 25, 30; so μετριοπαθεῖν, P. iii. 235 f.; -παθῶς, E. 161.

μέχρις ἐκείνων, so long as they live, during their lifetime, Ph. i. 62.

μηνυτικός, capable of informing, indicative of, P. i. 187, L. i. 85, ii. 165, E. 245.

μνημονικός, capable of remembering, retentive, L. ii. 274; -ικῶς, by way of memory, L. i. 347.

μονολήμματος (λόγος), with one premiss only, P. ii. 167, L. ii. 443.

μονομάχης, fighter in single combat, gladiator, P. i. 156, iii. 212.

μονόποιος, of one quality only, P. i. 94 f.

μουσουργός, music-maker, musician, P. i. 54.

GLOSSARY

μοχθηρός (oppd. to ὑγιής, ἀληθής), unsound, invalid, P. ii. 105, 111, 146, 175, etc.
μυθοποίησις, myth-making, invention of fables, Ph. i. 192.
μυξωτῆρες, nostrils, P. i. 127.
μύουρος (στοά, oppd. to σύμμετρος), running to a point, curtailed, P. i. 118.

ναστόν (σῶμα), solid, impermeable, P. ii. 142, L. ii. 309 ; (plur.) i. 213.
νηκτικός, able to swim, Ph. i. 171.
νοητοί (πόροι), intelligible (i.e. not perceptible by sense), P. ii. 98, 140, L. ii. 146, 220, 306, Ph. i. 256.
νόστιμος : τὸ ν. τῶν καρπῶν, produce, yield, richness, L. i. 17.
νυκτερήσιον (φάντασμα), nocturnal, Ph. ii. 188; so νυκτεροειδὲς φ., Ph. ii. 184: νυκτοειδὲς φ. (Democr., Epicur.), Ph. ii. 181.
νυκτίνομος (ὄρνις), (feeding, or) flying by night, Ph. i. 247.

ξέσματα, filings, slivers, P. i. 129.
ξυνός (= κοινός, Heracleit.), common, universal, L. i. 133.

ὄγκος, mass, material body, molecule, L. i. 287, 290 f., P. iii. 152 ; (ἄναρμοι) P. iii. 32, Ph. i. 363, (νοητοί) L. ii. 220.
ὀδμᾶσθαι (Democr.), smell, L. i. 139.
ὁδός, way, avenue (to), P. i. 210 ff. ; ὁδῷ (ζητεῖν), methodically, L. i. 2 : ὁδοῦ πάρεργον, as a bye-work on the road, in passing, L. ii. 378.
οἴησις, conceit, (idle) fancy, P. ii. 258, iii. 280 f. ; (c. genit.) belief in, opinion about, L. i. 5, Ph. i. 74.
ὀλμίσκος, socket of door-hinge, Ph. ii. 54.
ὀλοσχερής, whole, entire, P. i. 130 ; so ὀλοσχερέστερον (εἰπεῖν, adv.), in general terms, broadly, P. i. 31 : κατὰ ὀλοσχέρειαν (oppd. to κατὰ μέρη), as a whole, totally, Ph. ii. 53.
ὁλότης : κατὰ ὁλότητα (oppd. to κατὰ μέρη), as a whole, completely, P. iii. 46, 64, Ph. ii. 52, 57, 103.
ὁμοιομέρειαι (Anaxagoras), homoeomeries, substances composed of homogeneous parts, P. iii. 32 f., Ph. i. 6, ii. 252, 254.
ὁμοιοπαθεῖν (c. dat.), be similarly affected, share the sensation of, L. i. 301, 363.
ὁμοιωτικός : κατὰ ὁμοιωτικὴν μετάβασιν, by inference based on similarity, E. 250 ; so ὁμοιωτικῶς (νοεῖσθαι), Ph. i. 394.
ὁμόλογος, agreed, granted, L. i. 75, ii. 183, 194.

GLOSSARY

ὀνειροπολεῖν, dream of, imagine (vainly), P. ii. 157, iii. 41,
156 ; (mid.) L. ii. 57 ; (pass.) P. i. 91, etc.

ὀνοματογραφίαι, writing down names, E. 67.

ὀξυηκούστατος, with most acute hearing, Ph. i. 65.

ὀξυωπεῖν, have keen sight, be sharp, L. i. 55, Ph. i. 65 ; so
ὀξυωπέστατος, Ph. i. 65.

ὁρατικῶς (κινεῖσθαι), (affected) by the sensation of sight,
L. i. 355 ; so ὁρατικὸν πάθος, L. i. 355.

ὁρίζεσθαι (mid.= ὁρίζειν), define, P. ii. 101, 207, etc. ; so
ὁριστόν, object of definition, P. ii. 207.

ὁρικῶς, by defining, through a definition, L. i. 426.

ὁρμή, impulse, instinct, P. iii. 70 ; (oppd. to ἀφορμή), inclination, desire, P. iii. 177, 273 f., E. 59 f.

ὅρος, (logical) definition, P. ii. 27, 205 ff., (distingd. fr.
τὸ καθολικόν) E. 8.

οὐριοδρομεῖν, run before the wind, Ph. ii. 56.

οὐσία, being, what exists, P. ii. 5 ; (material) substance
(ἀεὶ ῥεῖ, ῥευστή), P. iii. 82, 115 ; τρεῖς οὐσίαι (Xenocr.),
L. i. 147, Ph. ii. 169.

ὀφθαλμοφανῶς, plainly before their eyes, Ph. i. 39.

ὀχυρωτικός (c. genit.), serving to fortify, L. i. 23.

πάγιος, firm, certain, (oppd. to εἰκός) L. i. 110, ii. 187 ; so
παγίως, L. ii. 186.

παθηματικῶς (ὑποπίπτοντα), (things experienced) by way of
passive affection, P. ii. 10.

παθητός (oppd. to ἀπαθής), subject to affection or change,
passible, Ph. ii. 311.

πάθος, suffering, P. i. 70 ; affection, impression, feeling, P. i.
192, etc.: τὰ πρῶτα π. (Epicur.), L. i. 203.

παλαιστιαῖος, of a palm's breadth (about 3 inches), Ph. i.
300, 321.

παραβάλλειν (c. dat.), compare, set against, object to, Ph. i. 96,
108, 133 ; so παραβολή, analogous contradictory argument,
objection, Ph. i. 97, 109, 134.

παραγγελματικῶς, by way of command, imperatively, P. i. 204.

παραγράψιμος (φαντασία), exceptionable, rejected, L. i. 170.

παραθλίβειν (ὀφθαλμόν), press at the side, P. i. 47.

παρακειμένως, similarly, in the next place, L. i. 77, 182, 227,
Ph. i. 321, etc.

παρακμή (medical), post-crisis stage, abatement (of disease),
P. ii. 237 f., 257.

GLOSSARY

παρακολούθησις, connexion, comprehension, P. ii. 236, Ph. ii.
220.
παράλειψις (logical, = ἔλλειψις), omission, deficiency, P. ii.
150.
παραλογίζεσθαι, be fallacious, reason falsely, P. ii. 250.
παραμυθεῖσθαι (= διδάσκειν), show, argue, establish, L. i. 66,
344, ii. 17, etc.
παραμυθητικός, capable of relieving, P. i. 70, 72.
παραμυθία, proof, confirmatory evidence, L. i. 116, ii. 240,
469, etc.
παραπέμπειν (oppd. to παραλαμβάνειν), dismiss, reject, P. i.
183, L. i. 11, 81.
παραπιέζειν, press on the side, L. i. 192.
παραπλοκὴ (χυμῶν), blending, intermixture, P. i. 102.
παρασπορά, extra sprinkling, P. i. 46.
παραστὰς (βαλανείου), vestibule, P. i. 110, ii. 56.
παράστασις, establishing, proof, L. i. 119.
παραστατικός (= μηνυτικός), able to establish, probative,
L. i. 85, ii. 202, 214, etc.
παράτασις, extension (in time), P. iii. 107 ; (in space) Ph. i.
367, ii. 7.
παρατατικόν (oppd. to συντελεστικόν), imperfect (or present)
time, Ph. ii. 91 f., 97, 101 ; so -ικῶς, Ph. ii. 101.
παρατυπωτικός: π. (φαντασίαι), incorrectly impressed, fallacious, L. ii. 67.
παραύξησις, additional increase, enlargement, P. iii. 80, L. ii.
58 f. ; so παραυξητικῶς, E. 251.
παρεγχειρεῖν, hand on to, transfer to, P. i. 234.
παρέκβασις: κατὰ παρέκβασιν, by way of digression, P. iii. 101.
παρέλκειν, be superfluous, redundant, P. ii. 77, 147, 156,
163, 175, L. i. 334.
παρέμπτωσις, occurrence, L. i. 175.
παρενθήκη, parenthesis, supplement, L. ii. 378.
παρηγορία, relief, assuagement, E. 149, 154.
παριστᾶν (-ιστάναι), set forth, make good, establish, prove,
P. ii. 21 f., 108, etc. ; (pass.) defend, P. ii. 42.
παρολκή, (logical) redundancy, P. ii. 146, 156, 159, 166, 175,
L. ii. 292, 429, etc.
παρόσον (= παρ' ὅσον), in so far as, inasmuch as, L. i. 405,
407, 419, etc.
παρυφίστασθαι (c. dat.), be dependent on, result from, P. i. 205,
L. ii. 12.

GLOSSARY

παχυμέρεια, thickness, density of parts, Ph. i. 86 ; so παχυμερὴς (ἀήρ), P. i. 125.

πεῖσις, feeling, passive affection, P. i. 22, L. i. 237, 239, 384, Ph. i. 209.

πεῖσμα, conviction, assurance, E. 149 ; μετὰ πείσματος, P. i. 18, L. ii. 159, E. 121, 164.

πεποίθησις, confidence, assurance, P. i. 60, 197, iii. 238.

περατοῦν: πεπερατωμένον, limited, (spatially) bounded, Ph. i. 431 ff., ii. 27.

περιαυτολογεῖν, to laud oneself, brag, P. i. 62.

περιγράφειν, conclude, P. ii. 259, iii. 279 ; cancel, annul, P. i. 15, L. i. 268 ; encircle, enclose, Ph. i. 257.

περιγραφή: κατὰ π. (= κατ᾽ ἰδίαν), separately, by itself, solely, L. i. 277, ii. 161 f., 394, Ph. i. 103, 261, ii. 263.

περιεργία, needless labour, over-elaboration, subtlety, P. ii. 246, iii. 151, (plur.) 167.

περίεργος: οὐ κατὰ τὸ π. (= ἀπεριέργως), not in a special, or technical, sense, P. i. 9.

περιέχειν: τὸ περιέχον (Heracleit.), that which encompasses, the environing (atmosphere), L. i. 127, 129, ii. 286, Ph. i. 75, 79.

περίκτησις, acquisition, L. i. 166, E. 127, 146.

περιληπτικός, inclusive, comprehensive, L. i. 143; so περιληπτός, comprehensible, L. i. 141 f.

περινούστατος, most keen-witted, cleverest, L. i. 326.

περίπτωσις, occurrence, P. i. 144 ; actual impression, experience, (κατὰ π.) L. ii. 56 f., E. 252 ; so περιπτωτικῶς, actually, experientially, P. ii. 8, E. 250.

περισπᾶν, draw away, cause to doubt, L. i. 179 (cf. ἀπερίσπαστος).

περίστασις, circumstance, condition, P. i. 30, 100, L. i. 185.

περιτρέπειν, overthrow, confute, P. i. 122, ii. 64, 78, etc. ; (εἰς) change over, convert (to), P. i. 81, ii. 76, L. ii. 295 f. ; so περιτροπή (λόγου), reversal, refutation, P. i. 200, ii. 128, 185, 187.

περιτυποῦν, mould round, enfold, P. iii. 75, 131 ff.

περιφορητικὸς (λόγος), bandied about, familiar, Ph. ii. 87.

περιωδευμέναι (φαντασίαι), scrutinized, fully tested, P. i. 227 ff., L. i. 182, 187, 437 (cf. διεξωδευμέναι).

περιών: ἐκ (τοῦ) περιόντος (lit. from our reserves, or extra resources), over and above, into the bargain, P. i. 63, 78, ii. 96, iii. 273 ; so ἐκ περιουσίας, P. i. 62, 76, ii. 192, L. ii. 183, 262, 296.

GLOSSARY

πιθανότης, credibility, probability, plausibility, P. ii. 79, 229, iii. 281.

πικραντικῶς (διατίθεμαι), am affected by (have a sensation of) bitterness, L. i. 367.

πλασματικός, fictitious, fanciful, P. i. 103 ; so πλασματώδης, L. ii. 367.

πλατύτερον (oppd. to ἐν ὑποτυπώσει, λέγειν), more fully, at length, P. i. 222.

πληκτικός, pungent, overpowering, P. i. 125 ; striking, convincing, P. iii. 71, 240 ; (φαντασία) L. i. 173, 257 f.

ποιότης, quality, P. i. 94 ff., iii. 32, 57.

πολυμιγία, multi-mixture, amalgam, Ph. i. 6.

πολυπλασιασμός, multiplication, Ph. ii. 217.

πολυσχιδεῖς (γνῶμαι), much divided, various, L. i. 349.

πολυωρία (Zeno), attention, regard, P. iii. 248, E. 194.

ποριστικός : π. (τέχνη), capable of providing, P. i. 66, 72.

πόροι (νοητοί, q.v.), (bodily) passages, pores, P. ii. 140, etc. ; (sing.) P. i. 50.

ποροποιεῖν : πεποροποιημένον (σῶμα, oppd. to ναστόν), provided with pores, permeable, L. ii. 309.

πραγματικῶς (ἀντιλέγειν), in a practical way, effectively, P. iii. 13.

πρακτικός (λόγος), systematic, direct, P. i. 62.

πρίν (c. genit.), before, L. i. 162, ii. 445, etc.

προάγειν (c. genit.), precede, Ph. ii. 259 : προηγμένα (Stoic), preferred, P. iii. 191 f., E. 62 ff.

προανυσθέν, accomplished before, already completed, L. ii. 1, Ph. ii. 248.

πρόδηλον, pre-evident, quite obvious, P. i. 91, 210, etc. ; (oppd. to ἄδηλον) P. i. 138, ii. 97 ff. ; so προδηλοτάτη, P. i. 214 : προδήλως, P. i. 226, L. i. 141.

προδιάθεσις, predisposition, antecedent condition, P. i. 100, 110.

προδιακρίνεσθαι, be distinguished first, P. ii. 68 (-διευκρινεῖσθαι cj. Bekk.).

προδιαρθροῦν, enucleate (make clear) beforehand, Ph. i. 338, E. 18.

προδιεξοδεύειν, go through (make sure by scrutiny) beforehand, L. i. 188.

προηγουμένῳ λόγῳ, by direct argument, Ph. ii. 189 ; so προηγουμένως, firstly, principally, directly, P. ii. 16, 247. Ph. i. 390, etc.

GLOSSARY

προθεσμία, appointed day : ὑπὸ μίαν προθεσμίαν, at one and the same moment, L. ii. 165.

προκαθηγούμενον (oppd. to λῆγον, logical), antecedent (proposition), P. ii. 101, 106, 115.

προκαταρκτικά, antecedents, immediate causes, P. iii. 16.

προκαταταχεῖν, get the start of, outspeed, Ph. ii. 145 f., 153.

προκεντήματα, preliminaries, first outgoings, L. i. 107.

προκόπτειν, advance, proceed (of arguments, etc.), P. ii. 240, L. ii. 369, etc. ; (spatially) Ph. ii. 57, 60, etc.

προκρίνειν, prefer, P. i. 60 f., 78, 90, etc. ; so πρόκρισις, preferring, P. ii. 45.

πρόληψις (κοινή), preconception, instinctive judgement, P. i. 211, L. i. 443, ii. 157, 337 ff., etc.

προνοητικῶς, providentially, by design, L. ii. 286.

προπάλεια (ἀγγείων), prominence, swollen state, L. ii. 219.

προπετεία, precipitancy, rashness, P. i. 20, 177, etc. ; so προπετής, P. iii. 79, etc. : προπετῶς, P. i. 212, ii. 17, 37 : προπετεύεσθαι, P. i. 20, 205, 237, etc.

πρός : τὰ πρός τι, things related to something else, (logical) relatives, P. ii. 125, 175, 179, L. ii. 38, etc.

προσαλλοτριοῦσθαι (c. dat.), be averse from, L. i. 140.

προσαναπλάσσειν, invent besides, fancy in addition, E. 158.

προσβολὴ (φαντασίας), impact, application, occurrence, P. ii. 16, L. i. 36 f. ; (μύωπος) stroke, L. ii. 271.

προσδιασαφεῖν, explain further, L. i. 114.

προσδοξάζειν, suppose besides, hold the additional opinion, P. i. 30, iii. 236, etc.

προσειλεῖσθαι (c. dat.), press against, oppose, Ph. i. 3, E. 7.

προσεχῇ (πάθη), persistent, chronic, P. ii. 240 ; (εἴδη) related, appropriate, E. 15.

προσηνὲς (κατάστημα), congenial, agreeable, P. iii. 184, E. 86, 106.

πρόσκλισις (c. dat.), adherence to, dependence on, P. i. 16 ; inclination, assent, P. i. 230.

πρόσληψις (logical), minor premiss, P. ii. 149, 234, L. ii. 333, etc.

προσοικειοῦσθαι (c. dat.), be naturally attached to, find congenial, L. i. 140.

προσπάθεια, tendency towards, inclination, consent, P. i. 230.

προστακτικὰ (λεκτά, Stoic), imperative, L. ii. 71, P. i. 204.

προσφέρεσθαι (mid.), give oneself, consume, P. i. 81, 83, 108, 110 ; (pass.) P. i. 52, 130.

531

GLOSSARY

πρότασις (logical), premiss (esp. major premiss of a syllogism), P. ii. 164 f., 195 ff.

προφέρεσθαι (φωνάς, etc.), utter, emit, P. i. 14, 73, etc.; (pass.) L. ii. 132, 290; so προφορὰ (φωνῶν), utterance, P. i. 15, 203.

προφορικός (λόγος, oppd. to ἐνδιάθετος, Stoic), uttered (reason, i.e. speech), L. ii. 275, 287.

προωστικῶς (oppd. to ἐπισπαστικῶς), by pushing forward, propulsively, P. iii. 69, Ph. ii. 83 f.

πτῶσις (grammatical), inflexion, case, verbal usage (sense), E. 4, 29; so τὸ πτωτικόν, declinable form, noun, L. ii. 84.

πυρακτοῦσθαι, be heated, Ph. ii. 164 f.

πύρωσις (medical), feverish heat, inflammation, P. ii. 239.

πύσμα, interrogation, question, P. i. 189.

ῥεῖν: ῥυεῖσα (στιγμή, etc.), flowing, moving continuously, L. i. 99, Ph. i. 376, 381, 430.

ῥευστὴ (ὕλη), in (constant) flux, P. i. 217, iii. 115.

ῥητός: τὸ ῥητόν, precise statement, Ph. i. 54, (ῥ. λέξεις) Ph. i. 64; so ῥητῶς, literally, expressly (in quoting), P. iii. 248, etc.; ῥητότατα (oppd. to δυνάμει), most explicitly, distinctly, L. i. 16, 134.

ῥύσις (medical), flux, issue (e.g. sweat), P. i. 238; (ὕλης) P. iii. 54, 115; (γραμμῆς) P. iii. 154, Ph. i. 380.

ῥῶσις (σωμάτων), strengthening, E. 97.

σαλεύειν (ἐν), be engaged in, deal with, P. i. 65; be storm-tossed, in distress, P. ii. 229; shake, upset, L. ii. 56, 337, 339, Ph. i. 3; (pass.) P. ii. 204, L. ii. 385, Ph. i. 417.

σαρκοδακὴς (βίος, Orpheus), flesh-eating, Ph. i. 15.

σαρκοτοκεῖσθαι, be flesh-born (i.e. as fleshy lumps), P. i. 42.

σαρκοφανής, fleshy-looking, coated with flesh, P. i. 50.

σεμνολόγημα, proud position, dignity, P. iii. 201.

σημεῖον (ὑπομνηστικόν) (ἐνδεικτικόν): sign, P. ii. 96 ff., 99 ff., L. ii. 140 ff.; (geometr.= στιγμή), point, P. iii. 39, 154, Ph. ii. 278 ff.

σημείωσις, reading signs, interpreting, L. ii. 269; so σημειωτικῶς, by means of signs, by interpretation, L. ii. 158: σημειωτόν, thing signified, P. ii. 100 f., 116 ff., etc.

σίλλοι (title of book by Timon), Satires, lampoons (fr. σίλλος, squint-eyed), P. i. 224.

σκεπτοσύνη (Timon), speculation, scepticism, P. i. 224.

GLOSSARY

σκέψις, the Sceptic way of thought, scepticism, P. i. 185, 209, 213 ff., etc.

σκηνογραφία, scene-painting, illusion, L. i. 88.

σκινδαψός, (a meaningless word) " what d'ye call it," L. ii. 133.

σκολιόπορα (ὦτα), with winding passages, P. i. 126.

σκοτίη (oppd. to γνησίη, γνῶσις, Democr.), bastard, inferior, L. i. 138 f.

σολοικίζοντες (λόγοι), solecistic, ungrammatical, P. ii. 231, 235 ; so σολοικισμός, L. i. 44.

σπᾶν, draw in, derive (λόγον, φαντασίαν, etc.), L. i. 129, 176, 180, 186, etc.

σπουδαῖος (oppd. to φαῦλος), good, virtuous, P. ii. 83, L. i. 410, 418, etc.

σταθμητικὸς (ζυγός), able to weigh, or measure, L. i. 442.

στάλιξ, stake for nets, Ph. i. 3.

στάσις, rest, immobility, Ph. ii. 46, 81 ; (doctrinal) position, opinion, school of thought, L. i. 53, 89, 190, ii. 13, Ph. ii. 45, etc. ; (= διάστασις) dissension, L. ii. 214.

στασιώτης (partisan), stationer, arrester, Ph. ii. 46.

στερέμνιος, substantial, solid, L. i. 207, ii. 63, 65.

στέρησις (logical), privation, negation, Ph. i. 407 ; so στερητικά, negatives, Ph. i. 407.

στιγμή (geometr.), point, L. i. 99, Ph. i. 376.

στοά (porch), the Stoic School, Stoicism, P. i. 235, ii. 5 ; οἱ ἀπὸ τῆς στοᾶς, Stoics, P. iii. 181, etc.

στοιχεῖν (c. dat.), range oneself with, side with, E. 59.

στοιχεῖον, (physical) element, P. ii. 111, iii. 37.

στοιχειοῦν, teach principles (elements), E. 3.

στοιχηδὸν (κείμενα), in a row, side by side, Ph. i. 380, 386, ii. 59, 144.

συγγεγυμνασμέναι (καταλήψεις, Stoic), co-exercised, used in conjunction, P. iii. 188, 251.

συγκατάθεσις (oppd. to ἄρνησις), assent, P. i. 7, 13, 16, 19, 233, etc.

συγκαταλαμβάνειν, apprehend together with, P. ii. 116 f., 119, etc.

συγκουφίζειν, help to make light, P. iii. 15.

σύγκριμα (Democr.), composite substance, compound, P. ii. 24, iii. 56, Ph. i. 97, etc.

συζυγεῖν (Stoic), be ranked together, be correlative, L. i. 151, ii. 11, Ph. ii. 5 f., etc. ; so συζυγία, correlative pair, L. ii. 172, 175.

533

GLOSSARY

συλλογιστικός (λόγος, Stoic), conclusive, demonstrative, P. ii. 149.

συμβεβηκός (logical), attribute, property, P. ii. 27, 228, L. i. 269 ff., Ph. ii. 220 ff., E. 37 f.

συμβιβάζειν, conclude, demonstrate, (συμβεβίβασται) L. i. 283, Ph. ii. 319.

σύμβλησις, comparison, reference, relation ; κατὰ σ., L. i. 375, 395, ii. 34, 459, Ph. ii. 198.

συμμνημόνευσις (Stoic), simultaneous recollection, P. iii. 108, L. i. 279, Ph. i. 353 ff., ii. 64, 176.

συμπάθεια, feeling for, emotional assent, inclination, P. i. 230 ; sympathy, sharing of affections, Ph. i. 79 f.

συμπαρατηρεῖσθαι (c. dat.), be observed together with, P. ii. 100 f., L. ii. 143, 152 ; so συμπαρατήρησις, simultaneous observation, L. ii. 154.

συμπέρασμα (logical), conclusion (cf. ἐπιφορά), P. ii. 113 f., 134, 139 ff., L. ii. 140.

συμπεριγράφειν, cancel (annul) together with, P. i. 14, 206, ii. 47, etc.

συμπλέκειν, intertwine, combine, (λήμματα) L. ii. 416 f. : συμπεπλεγμένον, (logical) combination, complex, P. ii. 137 f., L. ii. 125, 419, 421.

συμπληρωτικός (Epicur.), serving to fill up, complementary, P. iii. 100, 172, L. i. 98, Ph. i. 337, etc. ; so συμπλήρωσις, filling up, completion, Ph. i. 338.

συμπλοκή, (carnal) conjunction, P. i. 41 ; (logical, cf. συμπλέκειν) combination, P. ii. 113, 137 ff., etc. ; connexion (of meaning) L. ii. 430.

σύμπνοια (καὶ συμπλοκή), accordance, consistency, L. ii. 430 ; so συμπνεῖν, be in accord with, side with, Ph. i. 111.

σύμπτωμα (medical), symptom ; (Epicur.) σ. συμπτωμάτων (as def. of Time), concurrence, P. iii. 137, Ph. ii. 219.

συμφυής, of one substance with, P. i. 225 ; so συμφυΐα, L. i. 129, σύμφυσις, L. i. 130, substantial union, essential connexion.

συνάγειν (logical), infer, conclude, P. i. 32, 35, etc. ; so συναγωγή, inference, deduction, P. ii. 143, 170.

συναγωγός (αἰτία), combining, unifying, Ph. i. 7, 10.

συναδηλεῖσθαι, be non-evident therewith, be likewise obscure, L. ii. 2.

συνακαταληπτεῖσθαι, be also uncomprehended, E. 38.

συνακτικός (λόγος), drawing a conclusion, conclusive, P. ii. 137 ff., 151, L. ii. 120, etc.

GLOSSARY

σύναμα (= σὺν ἅμα), together with, E. 159.

συνανασκευή, joint refutation, L. i. 214; so συνανασκευάζεσθαι, L. i. 214.

συναρπάζειν, (τὸ ζητούμενον) beg the question, P. i. 90, ii. 35, etc.; σ. (ὕπαρξιν), assume, P. iii. 121; συναρπασθεὶς (ὑπὸ φαντασίας), being carried away, influenced, L. i. 186.

συνάρτησις (oppd. to διάρτησις, logical), connexion, coherence, P. ii. 111, L. ii. 265, 430.

συνεκτικός, conclusive: σ. αἴτια, direct, primary causes, P. iii. 15: συνεκτικώτατον, most comprehensive, conclusive, L. i. 333, Ph. i. 1, E. 257.

συνεμφαίνειν (Stoic), indicate therewith, imply also, L. i. 233; so συνέμφασις, added implication, L. i. 239.

συνεξέρχεσθαι (= συνεκβάλλεσθαι), pass out with, be rejected along with, L. i. 421.

συνερανίζειν, contribute: τὸ συνηρανισμένον (ἐκ τούτων), the total made up of, L. i. 295.

συνεργὰ (αἴτια), co-operant, accessory, P. iii. 15.

συνεργοπονεῖν (c. dat.), be fellow-workers with, help in the toil of, Ph. i. 41.

συνερωτᾶν, join in asking; σ. λόγον, propound an argument (by means of question and answer), P. ii. 131, 162, etc.; συνερωτητέον, P. ii. 251; so συνερώτησις, P. ii. 160, etc.

συνέχειν, hold together, retain, L. i. 375: σ. πρὸς (τὰ ἠθικά), relate to, be concerned with, P. i. 145.

συνημμένον (λῆμμα, logical), combination (of clauses or propositions), hypothetical major premiss or syllogism, P. ii. 101, 104, 111 f., 157 n., L. ii. 109, 112 f., 247, etc.

συνθρόησις, (mental) commotion, perturbation, Ph. i. 169.

σύνταγμα, treatise, book, P. i. 241, iii. 247, 279.

συντελεστικός (oppd. to παρατατικός), perfect (tense), past (time), Ph. ii. 91 f.; so -ικῶς, Ph. ii. 101.

συνύπαρξις, co-existence, P. ii. 199; so συνυπάρχειν, P. ii. 109, 144, etc.

συνυπόπτωσις, joint occurrence, being sensed together, L. ii. 174; so συνυποπίπτειν, L. ii. 165, 174.

συστατικὰ (μόρια), component, P. iii. 128, L. ii. 84.

συστηματικός, forming an organized whole, composite, L. i. 40 f.

σχέσις, attitude, (active) relation, application, L. i. 35 ff., 168, 243, ii. 162.

σχῆμα (μοχθηρόν) (ὑγιές, logical), form (of statement of a syllogism), P. ii. 146, L. ii. 413, etc.

535

GLOSSARY

σχηματισμός, formation, configuration, L. i. 229 ; so σχηματίζεσθαι, Ph. i. 75.

σχολάζειν (c. dat.), devote oneself to, L. i. 8 : τὰ σχολασθέντα (περί), lectures on, discussion of, E. 167.

σχολικῶς (πλάττεσθαι), after the style of the Schools (*i.e.* with perverse subtlety), L. ii. 13.

σωματικός, corporeal, E. 61 : σωματικώτερον, more solidly, thoroughly, P. i. 7.

σωματότης, corporeality, Ph. i. 371 ff. ; so σωματοῦν (σεσωμάτωται, is corporealized), Ph. ii. 25.

σωρίτης (logical), the Sorites, (the fallacy known as " the Heap "), P. ii. 253, L. i. 416, Ph. i. 190.

σωριτικὴ (ἀπορία), of the Sorites-argument, P. iii. 80 ; so σωριτικῶς, Ph. i. 182.

ταυτολογεῖν, repeat oneself, L. i. 262.

τελαμών, linen wrapper, swathing-band (for a mummy), P. iii. 228.

τέλος (ethical), final purpose, objective, end, P. i. 25, L. i. 199 f.

τεράστιος (φύσις), monstrous, incredible, L. ii. 104.

τερατολογουμένη (τύπωσις), marvellous, mythical, P. ii. 70, (ὕλη) iii. 31, (δόξα) L. ii. 66.

τερματίζειν, bring to an end, terminate, Ph. ii. 102.

τετρακτύς (Pythag.), the Tetractys (*i.e.* Ten, as sum of first 4 numbers), L. i. 94.

τεχνογράφος, writer on the art (of logic), E. 8.

τεχνολογία, systematic treatment, logical theory (or rules), P. ii. 205, 249, 255, L. ii. 87, 257, 406 ; so τεχνολογούμενα, P. ii. 247, E. 40.

τήρησις, observance, rule of conduct, (βιωτική) P. i. 23, ii. 254 ; (κοιναί) ii. 246 ; (ἀφιλόσοφος) E. 165.

τηρητικὴ (ἀκολουθία), observant (sense of consequence or power of inference), L. ii. 288.

τὶς : τὸ τὶ (Stoic), " something " (the highest logical genus), P. ii. 86, 223 f. ; (plur.) Ph. ii. 234, E. 224.

τιμητικῶς ἔχειν, hold in honour, regard as honourable, Ph. i. 136.

τοιουτόσχημον, of such a shape, L. i. 209.

τοιουτώδης, suchlike, of like kind, L. ii. 206, Ph. i. 52.

τρανὴ (φαντασία), clear, vivid, L. i. 258 ; so τρανῶς, L. i. 172,

GLOSSARY

Ph. i. 164 ; τρανότερον, L. ii. 144, Ph. i. 271 ; τρανότατα, L. i. 404.
τρεπόμενος (οἶνος), turning sour, P. i. 41.
τρεπτὴ (οὐσία), to be changed, alterable, L. i. 434.
τριγένεια (ἀγαθῶν), a trinity, threefold class, P. iii. 181.
τροπικόν (Stoic, = συνημμένον), hypothetical premiss, P. ii. 202, L. ii. 438, 440, 442.
τρόπος (= λόγος), "trope," mode (of argument), P. i. 35 ff., 164 ; (λόγων) L. ii. 227, 235, 237, 292.
τυγχάνειν (= εἶναι), to be, P. i. 105, L. i. 38, 40, etc. : εἰ τύχοι, verbi gratia, P. i. 106, ii. 201, 218, etc.

ὑποδιαιρεῖν, subdivide, P. iii. 75 ; -ρεῖσθαι, L. i. 35 ; so ὑποδιαίρεσις, E. 15.
ὑπόθεσις, supposition, assumption : καθ' ὑπ., P. i. 73, 79, etc. ; ἐξ ὑπ., P. i. 168, ii. 20, etc. ; so ὁ ὑποθετικὸς τρόπος, P. i. 164, 173.
ὑποκείμενον (oppd. to φαινόμενον), substantial (or real object, which underlies the sensible appearance), P. i. 19, 22, 46, 59, etc. : ὑπόκειται = ἐστί, L. i. 183, 278, etc.
ὑπομιμνήσκειν, suggest, show, teach, P. ii. 76, 80, 177, etc. ; so ὑπόμνησις, P. ii. 130, L. ii. 327.
ὑπομνηστικόν (oppd. to ἐνδεικτικὸν σημεῖον), suggestive, commemorative, P. ii. 99 f., L. ii. 151 ; so -ικῶς, L. ii. 289.
ὑποπίπτειν, occur, be noticed or perceived (sub sensus cadere), P. i. 35, 40, 94, etc. : ὑποπεσεῖται ἀπορίαις, fall under, be faced by, Ph. i. 365.
ὑπόπτωσις, occurrence, sense-experience, L. i. 85, 161, 215.
ὑπόστασις, substantiality, real existence, P. ii. 94, 176, 199, etc. ; so ὑπόστατος, Ph. ii. 60.
ὑποστέλλειν (c. dat.), yield, be subordinate to, L. ii. 32, Ph. ii. 40 : (c. accus.) cloak oneself in, adopt (as a disguise), Ph. i. 35 (= ὑποδραμεῖν, Ph. i. 36).
ὑπότευξις, rejoinder, reply, L. i. 359, Ph. i. 251 ; so ὑποτυγχάνειν, L. ii. 375, 440, Ph. i. 249.
ὑποτύπωσις, outline, sketch ; (ὡς ἐν ὑ.) P. i. 206, 222, ii. 79, etc. ; so ὑποτυποῦσθαι, P. iii. 3 ; ὑποτυπωτικὸς (τρόπος) P. i. 239 ; -ικῶς, P. i. 4, ii. 1.
ὑφ' ἕν, in one moment, together, simultaneously, L. i. 229, 231, 303, etc.
ὑφήγησις, sketch, exposition, description, P. i. 6 ; guidance, P. i. 23 f., 237.

GLOSSARY

ὑφίστασθαι, lay down, suppose, L. i. 14, ii. 11, Ph. ii. 270, (derive) 312 : ὑποσταθέν= δοξαζόμενον, E. 113.

φαλάγγιον, venomous spider, P. i. 82, 89.
φαντάζεσθαι, appear, P. i. 47 ; have a presentation, P. i. 104.
φαντασία, presentation, sense-impression (as *appearing* to the sentient subject), P. i. 22, 52, etc. ; (Stoic def. of φ.) P. ii. 70, L. i. 228 ff. ; ἁπλῆ φ., L. ii. 276 ; καταληπτικὴ φ., P. ii. 4, iii. 241, etc. ; λογικὴ φ., L. ii. 70 ; αἰσθητικὴ φ., L. i. 424.
φαντασιοῦν, cause a presentation, produce a mental image in, L. ii. 406 f. ; (pass.) receive an image, be impressed, P. ii. 72, L. i. 99, ii. 397, 402, etc.
φάντασμα, image, imaginary concept, L. i. 222, 224, Ph. ii. 181, 184 ff. ; illusory appearance, phantasm, L. i. 256.
φανταστικῶς (πάσχουσα), (affected) as by a presentation, L. i. 373, ii. 410.
φανταστόν, object presented to sense (the cause of sense-impressions), L. i. 203, 344, 357, etc.
φάσις, affirmation, assertion, P. i. 192, ii. 107, 121, 153, etc.
φαῦλος, (oppd. to σοφός, Stoic), foolish, L. i. 153, 432; (συνημμένον) invalid, P. ii. 191.
φιλαύτως, self-conceitedly, L. i. 314.
φιλοποιΐα, making friends, affection, L. i. 239.
φιμοῦσθαι, be muzzled, silenced, without reply, L. ii. 275.
φοινικτικῶς (πάσχειν), (have a sensation) of redness, L. i. 198.
φρενῆρες (τὸ περιέχον, Heracleit.), intelligent, L. i. 127, ii. 286.
φρενιτίζειν, be delirious, rave, P. i. 101, ii. 52, L. i. 247 ; so φρενιτικὸν βλέπεις, look crazy, P. ii. 231.
φυλοκρινεῖν, select with care, scrutinize, L. i. 183.
φυσιογνωμονικὴ (σοφία), physiognomy, art of judging character by features, P. i. 85.
φυσιολογία, study of nature, physical science, P. i. 18, iii. 62, etc. ; so φυσιολογεῖν, P. i. 18.
φωνή, vocal utterance, speech, sound, L. i. 119, ii. 130 ff. ; φωναὶ (σκεπτικαί), formulae, P. i. 14, 187 ff.
φωνομαχεῖν, fight about words or phrases, P. i. 195, 207.
φωρατός, discoverable, detected, explicable, P. i. 183 ; so φωρᾶσθαι, P. iii. 215, L. ii. 167.
φωτοειδὴς (ὄψις), light-like, resembling light, L. i. 93, 119.

χαλαστικὸς (τρόπος, oppd. to πύκνωσις), loosening, laxative, P. ii. 240.

538

GLOSSARY

χαρακτήρ, distinctive nature, form, characteristic, P. i. 191, 209, iii. 37, etc. ; (oppd. to χρόα) shape, features, E. 43 ; so χαρακτηριστικὰ (τοῦ ἀγαθοῦ), distinguishing marks, peculiarities, P. iii. 173.

χαριέντως, aptly, wittily, L. ii. 325 : χαριεντίζεσθαι, say wittily, jest, P. ii. 245.

χαροπός, blue-eyed, L. i. 198.

χαρτόν (oppd. to λυπηρόν), joyful, delightful, E. 85.

χεῖν (= τήκειν), melt, Ph. i. 248 ; (pass.) P. iii. 14.

χειρίζειν (λόγους, ἀπορίας, etc.), handle, apply, use (as instruments), L. i. 443, ii. 14, E. 21.

χηνώδης (oppd. to φρόνιμος), goose-like, silly, L. i. 329.

χιτών (ὀφθαλμοῦ), skin, membrane, P. i. 126.

χνοώδης (oppd. to κριμνώδης), in a fine state, powdery, P. i. 130.

χολερικὰ (πάθη), like cholera, P. i. 131.

χολοποιός, bile-producing, Ph. i. 96.

χρειοῦν (πρός τι), be helpful, suffice, L. i. 436.

χρῆμα (= πρᾶγμα, Protag.), thing, object or event, P. i. 216 ; amount, sum of money, L. i. 107.

χρησιμεύειν (πρός τι), be of use, be needed, P. ii. 94, 150, 205 f., 236, L. ii. 143, etc.

χρώζειν : κεχρωσμένον, tinged, coloured, Ph. i. 335.

χυλοείδης, like juice, flavour-like, L. i. 119.

χύσις, melting, liquefying, P. iii. 14 ; so χυτὸν (τὸ πνεῦμα), fluid, mobile, P. iii. 188.

χωλεύειν, make lame, maim, P. iii. 217.

χώρα, place, space, (Stoic def.) P. iii. 124, 130, Ph. ii. 2 f.

ψαῦσις (Democr.), (sense of) touch, L. i. 139 ; contact, Ph. ii. 102.

ψευδοποιεῖν, give the lie to, falsify, L. ii. 24, Ph. ii. 96, 110, E. 14.

ψηλαφᾶσθαι, be handled, examined, L. ii. 108.

ψηφοπαίκτης, player with pebbles, juggler, P. ii. 250.

ψιλός (φάσις, ἔννοια, etc.), bare, bald, mere (unconfirmed), P. ii. 121, L. i. 182, ii. 179, 459, etc. ; so ψιλῶς, separately, taken by itself, P. i. 144, (= κατ᾿ ἰδίαν) L. i. 277, ii. 15, E. 88.

ψυκτικὸς (χιών), making cold, chilling, P. iii. 179 ; so ψυχοῦσθαι, be made cold, Ph. ii. 164 f.

ὦμον ἐκβαλεῖν, put out (dislocate) the shoulder, P. ii. 245 (so ὦμος ἐκπέπτωκεν P. ii. 245).

GLOSSARY

ὠμοπλάτη, shoulder-blade, shoulder, P. iii. 223.

ᾠοτοκεῖσθαι, be born as eggs (like birds), P. i. 42.

ὥρα (ἡ πρώτη, δευτέρα), hour (of the day), Ph. ii. 182 ff. ; so ὡριαῖον διάστημα, interval of an hour, Ph. ii. 134.

ὡρισμένως, definitely, L. i. 336, ii. 297 ; in the limited sense, E. 32, 208.

ὡς . . . ὧδε, as . . . so, E. 10 : οὐδὲ ὥς, not even so, P. ii. 42.

ὥσπερ (= τουτέστι), that is to say, namely, L. i. 94 : ὡσπεροῦν, even as, as in fact, P. i. 57, ii. 101, Ph. i. 88.

ὤχρα (oppd. to μέλαν), pale, light-coloured (of wine), L. i. 91 ; so ὠχρόν, L. i. 193.

ὠχραίνεσθαι, be made (have a sense of) yellow, or pale colour, L. i. 193 ; so ὠχραντικῶς κινεῖσθαι, be affected by yellow, see (things) as yellow, L. i. 192, 198.

I. INDEX OF NAMES

541

I. INDEX OF NAMES

I. INDEX OF NAMES

I. INDEX OF NAMES

544

I. INDEX OF NAMES

545

I. INDEX OF NAMES

II. INDEX OF SUBJECTS

547

II. INDEX OF SUBJECTS

II. INDEX OF SUBJECTS

II. INDEX OF SUBJECTS

II. INDEX OF SUBJECTS

II. INDEX OF SUBJECTS

II. INDEX OF SUBJECTS

II. INDEX OF SUBJECTS

II. INDEX OF SUBJECTS

II. INDEX OF SUBJECTS